W9-DFN-076

PUTIN'S RUSSIA

Economy, Defence and Foreign Policy

PUTIN'S RUSSIA

Economy, Defence and Foreign Policy

Editor

Steven Rosefielde

University of North Carolina, Chapel Hill, USA

NEW JERSEY · LONDON · SINGAPORE · BEIJING · SHANGHAI · HONG KONG · TAIPEI · CHENNAI · TOKYO

Published by

World Scientific Publishing Co. Pte. Ltd.

5 Toh Tuck Link, Singapore 596224

USA office: 27 Warren Street, Suite 401-402, Hackensack, NJ 07601

UK office: 57 Shelton Street, Covent Garden, London WC2H 9HE

Library of Congress Cataloging-in-Publication Data
Names: Rosefielde, Steven, editor.
Title: Putin's Russia : economy, defence and foreign policy / editor,
    Steven Rosefielde, University of North Carolina, Chapel Hill, USA.
Description: New Jersey : World Scientific, [2020] | Includes index.
Identifiers: LCCN 2020006567 | ISBN 9789811212673 (hardcover) |
    ISBN 9789811212680 (ebook) | ISBN 9789811212697 (ebook other)
Subjects: LCSH: Russia (Federation)--Economic policy--1991– |
    Russia (Federation)--Economic conditions--1991– |
    Russia (Federation)--Military policy | Russia (Federation)--Foreign relations.
Classification: LCC HC340.12 .P89 2020 | DDC 320.60947--dc23
LC record available at https://lccn.loc.gov/2020006567

British Library Cataloguing-in-Publication Data
A catalogue record for this book is available from the British Library.

For any available supplementary material, please visit
https://www.worldscientific.com/worldscibooks/10.1142/11620#t=suppl

Desk Editors: Balasubramanian Shanmugam/Lixi Dong

Typeset by Stallion Press
Email: enquiries@stallionpress.com

Dedicated to David Rosefielde

Preface

The American intelligence and academic communities had a deep understanding of the Soviet Union during the Cold War. Both employed advanced methodologies, including adjusted factor cost national income accounting (pioneered by Abram Bergson, head of the Russian Division of the Office of Strategic Studies), input–output tables (Wassily Leontief), linear programming and econometrics. The Defense Intelligence Agency (DIA) provided satellite photographic reconnaissance (national technical means). Independent analysts had access to unclassified versions of the DIA's and CIA's series in compendia published annually by the Joint Economic Committee of Congress. The published and secret numbers were the same.[1] The CIA hosted conferences for independent experts. It tutored specialists on the Agency's methodologies and assumptions and was open to dialogue with the DIA, State Department, Arms Control and Disarmament Agency (ACDA), the Department of Commerce and foreign institutions. The White House sponsored scientific exchanges under the auspices of the US–USSR Science and Technology Agreement (May 24, 1972). The Defense Department, State Department and ACDA had high-level technical exchanges with the Kremlin political establishment and the Soviet General Staff (genstab). It was not treasonous to collaborate with Soviet authorities and émigrés.

---

[1] Steven Rosefielde, *False Science, Underestimating the Soviet Arms Buildup*, Transaction, 1982 (Expanded Second Edition, 1987).

President Gerald Ford appointed Steven Rosefielde as coordinator of the US–USSR programme on the application of computers to management with the Central Economics and Mathematics Institute (TsEMI Moscow) under the US–USSR Science and Technology agreement in 1975.[2] He worked with Vitaly Shlykov (Co-Chairman of the Russian Defence Council), Valery Makarov (Director of the Central Economics and Mathematics Institute (TsEMI)), Vladimir Bezrukov (Director of Gosplan's main computing centre), academician Yuri Yaremenko (Director of the Institute of Economic Forecasting of the Academy), Emil Ershov (Director of the Audit Division of the State Statistical Agency), George Kleiner (TsEMI), Stanislav Shatalin (author of the 500 Days Transition programme), Igor Birman (Director of Enterprises in the Construction Materials Ministry), Aron Katsenelinboigen (Head of the Department of Complex Systems, Central Economic-Mathematical Institute, U.S.S.R. Academy of Sciences, 1966–1973) and Boris Yeltsin's adjutant Lieutenant-General Viktor Samoilov. On the Western side, he collaborated with Patrick Parker (Assistant Secretary of Defense for Intelligence), Andrew Marshall (Head of the Office of the Secretary of Defense), William van Cleave (Director of the Department of Defense Transition Team between the administrations of President Carter and President Reagan), George W. Bush (Director of the CIA and Vice President), Bobby Ray Inman (Director of the CIA) and Robert Gates (Director of the CIA).

The high-level interactions between the academic community and government policymakers in America, Russia and across the globe gave all concerned a realistic understanding of Soviet achievements and potentials that placed sensible boundaries on public discourse. Journalists and activists could spout whatever nonsense they pleased about Soviet's intentions and capabilities, but their claims had little influence on decision-makers if they were unsupported by data from the CIA and DIA.

The Joint Economic Committee reports on the Soviet Union painted a positive picture of the Kremlin's health, but one constrained by "growth retardation" that seemed to preclude the Kremlin from catching up with

---

[2]Coordinator of the US–USSR Joint Cooperative Research Program on Science and Technology (between the National Science Foundation and the Soviet Academy of Sciences), Topic 1, subtopic 3, "enterprise modelling," 1977–1981.

and overtaking America. Conservatives and progressives both found solace in this judgement. It provided evidence for the claim that markets were superior to plans, without rejecting the possibility that socialism might ultimately prove its metal, and it also suggested that the Soviet military threat was manageable. In the interim, the West needed a strong deterrent until either the numbers changed or arms control and disarmament proved a viable alternative.

Most government and academic human capital accumulated in the West for the rational assessment of Soviet potential and prospects no longer exist. Interest in Russia gradually declined. The CIA ceased being the primary monitor of Russia's economic performance, a role reassigned to the World Bank and International Monetary Fund (IMF), jointly responsible for guiding post-Soviet nations from central planning to democratic free enterprise. The Joint Economic Committee of Congress stopped publishing annual reports on Russia's performance and prospects. The DIA continues to monitor Russian defence activities, but primarily for internal use. This has provided a green light for journalists and politicians to concoct narratives without fear of authoritative rebuke. Russia's performance and potential for them is whatever they want it to be, and the public is largely at their mercy. Progressives today seem mostly concerned with blaming Hillary Clinton's defeat on the Kremlin cyberwar, while conservatives worry about Russian expansionism. Most people seem to believe that steadfast application of economic sanctions will suffice to keep the bear at bay. They cannot fathom the possibility that the Kremlin, powered by its new market economy, has become a formidable authoritarian global rival impervious to slap-on-the-wrist economic sanctions.

This book seeks to fill the vacuum created by the Joint Economic Committee of Congress's decision to cease publishing comprehensive assessments of Russia's performance and potential. It provides readers with authoritative descriptions of Russia's economy, military prowess and international ambitions. This book does not settle controversies, but does provide readers with an objective basis for assessing Russia's prospects without the distortions caused by fake news and disinformation wars.

About the Contributors

Lance Alred is a National Security Education Program Boren Fellow who holds two Master's degrees: one in Russian from the Middlebury College Academic Year in Moscow Program Track studying at the Russian State University for the Humanities and the Higher School of Economics; the other in Global Affairs, Global Issues Concentration from the University of Denver. He also received a B.A. in Global Studies with a Russian Minor from the University of Denver. His education included several study-abroad programs with American Councils for International Education at the KORA Russian Language Center in Vladimir, Russia; the Herzen State Pedagogical University in St. Petersburg, Russia; and the Kazan Federal University in Kazan, Russia. In 2015, Alred worked for American Councils as a Future Leaders Exchange Program (FLEX) recruiter in Ukraine, Kazakhstan and Kyrgyzstan. He is a former Political-Military Analyst Intern at the Center for Political-Military Analysis at the Hudson Institute under the direction of Dr. Richard Weitz.

Alred's areas of expertise are Russian studies, information-psychological and cognitive security, hybrid warfare analysis and security management. Recent publications include (1) *US Foreign Policy Towards Central Asia Under Trump* by Lance Alred, Sean Michael Kelly, Madina Rubly, Yuliya Shokh, Mariam Tsitsishvili, Richard Weitz (*Journal UNISCI* N° 45, October 2017); (2) *The Surviving Generation of Soviet Totalitarianism* by Dr. Yurii Ezepchuk and translated by Lance Alred (CreateSpace, February 2017); (3) *Putin's Syrian Policy: "We need to Fight the Terrorists: There is No Alternative"*, by Dr. Richard Weitz, Research Assistance by Lance

Alred (Second Line of Defense, November 2016); and (4) *The Bioterrorist Attacks on America* by Dr. Yurii Ezepchuk translated by Lance Alred (*Journal of Bioterrorism and Biodefense*, July 2012).

Dr. Pavel K. Baev is a Research Professor at the Peace Research Institute Oslo (PRIO). He is also a Senior Non-Resident fellow at the Brookings Institution (Washington DC) and a Senior Research Associate at the Institut Francais des Relations Internationales (IFRI, Paris). He writes a weekly column for the *Eurasia Daily Monitor* produced by the Jamestown Foundation (Washington DC).

Harley Balzer retired in July 2016 after 33 years in the Department of Government and School of Foreign Service at Georgetown University. He was the Founding Director of the Center for Eurasian, Russian and East European Studies. Prior to coming to Georgetown, he taught at Grinnell College and Boston University and held post-doctoral fellowships at Harvard's Russian Research Center and the MIT Program in Science, Technology and Society. In 1982–1983, he was a Congressional Fellow in the office of Congressman Lee Hamilton. In the early 1990s, he was the Executive Director of the George Soros' International Science Foundation and continues to work with programmes that aid in Russian education.

His publications include *Soviet Science on the Edge of Reform* (1989); *Five Years That Shook the World: Gorbachev's Unfinished Revolution* (1991, which was named a CHOICE outstanding academic book); and *Russia's Missing Middle Class: The Professions in Russian History* (1996).

Torbjörn Becker is the Director of the Stockholm Institute of Transition Economics (SITE) at the Stockholm School of Economics in Sweden since 2006. He is also a board member of the Swedish development cooperation agency (SIDA) and several economics research institutes in Eastern Europe that together with SITE are part of the Forum for Research on Eastern Europe and Emerging Economies (FREE) Network. Prior to this, he worked for 9 years at the International Monetary Fund (IMF), where his work focused on international macroeconomic crises and issues related to the international financial system. He holds a Ph.D. from the Stockholm School of Economics and has published in top academic journals. He has contributed to several books and authored policy reports focusing on Russia and Eastern Europe. He recently co-edited and contributed to *The Russian Economy under Putin* that was published by Routledge.

Stephen Blank is an internationally recognised expert on Russian foreign and defence policies and international relations across the former Soviet Union. He is also a leading expert on European and Asian security, including energy issues. Since 2013, he has been a Senior Fellow at the American Foreign Policy Council in Washington (www.afpc.org). From 1989 to 2013, he was a Professor of Russian National Security Studies at the Strategic Studies Institute of the U.S. Army War College in Pennsylvania. Dr. Blank has been Professor of National Security Affairs at the Strategic Studies Institute since 1989. From 1998 to 2001, he was the Douglas MacArthur Professor of Research at the War College.

Dr. Blank has consulted for the CIA, major think tanks and foundations; chaired major international conferences in the USA and in Florence, Prague and London; and has been a commentator on foreign affairs in the media in the United States and abroad. He has also advised major corporations on investing in Russia and is a consultant for the Gerson Lehrman Group. He has published over 1,300 articles and monographs on Soviet/Russian, US, Asian and European military and foreign policies, including publishing and editing 15 books, and testified frequently before the Congress of Russia, China and Central Asia for business, government and professional think tanks here and abroad on these issues.

Prior to his appointment at the Army War College in 1989, Dr. Blank was Associate Professor for Soviet Studies at the Center for Aerospace Doctrine, Research, and Education of Air University at Maxwell AFB. He also held the position of Assistant Professor of Russian History, University of Texas, San Antonio from 1980 to 1986 and was the Visiting Assistant Professor of Russian history, University of California, Riverside, from 1979 to 1980.

Dr. Blank's M.A. and Ph.D. are in Russian History from the University of Chicago. His B.A is in history from the University of Pennsylvania.

Victor Gorshkov is Dean and Professor at the Department of International Liberal Arts, Faculty of International Liberal Arts, Kaichi International

University (Japan). He received his M.A. in international economics and finance from Khabarovsk State University of Economics and Law (Russia) and Ph.D. in Economics from Kyoto University (Japan). He is a charter member of the Japanese Association for Comparative Economic Studies. He has taught part-time at Kanagawa University (Japan), Keio University (Japan) and Rikkyo University (Japan) and conducted research as a Visiting Associate Professor at the Institute of Economic Research, Kyoto University. His research interests are in the fields of international economics, international economic relations, comparative economic systems and international education.

Petteri Lalu, Doctor of Military Science, Adjunct Professor, Lieutenant colonel (ret.), is a former military professor and the former head of the Finnish National Defence University's Russian Art of War Group. He has served as a commissioned officer in the Finnish Defence Forces 1990–2020. His military experience includes several positions in Ground Based Air Defence, Military Intelligence, Strategic Research and Russian Defence Studies. Lalu's research interests include the Russian Art of War and Russian Military Politics.

Satoshi Mizobata is Professor and Director at the University of Kyoto, Kyoto Institute of Economic Research. His research areas are comparative studies in economic systems, corporate governance and business organisation and the Russian and East European economies, focusing on the enterprises and market structure. He is editor of *The Journal of Comparative Economic Studies* in Japan and member of the Executive Committee of European Association for Comparative Economic Studies. His recent works include the following: S. Mizobata and K. Yagi, *Melting Boundaries: Institutional Transformation in the Wider Europe* (Kyoto University Press, 2008); S. Mizobata, Diverging and harmonising corporate governance in Russia, in J. Pickles (ed.), *State and Society in Post-socialist Economies* (Palgrave Macmillan, 2008); S. Mizobata, S. Rosefielde and M. Kuboniwa, *Two Asias: The Emerging Postcrisis Divide* (World Scientific, 2012); S. Mizobata and M. Yoshii, Restructuring of the higher educational system in Japan, in J. C. Brada, W. Bienkowski and M. Kuboniwa (eds.), *International Perspectives on Financing Higher Education* (Palgrave Macmillan, 2015); and others.

Susanne Oxenstierna holds a Doctorate in Economics and is the Deputy Research Director at the Swedish Defence Research Agency (FOI). She started her research on the Soviet, later Russian, economy in the 1980s and has specialised in comparative economic systems, institutional economics, labour market, public finance and, after she came to FOI in 2009, in defence economics. In the 1990s and 2000s, she worked as a resident advisor to the Russian Ministry of Finance and the Ministry of Economic Development for 7 years and participated in many other technical assistance projects for Russia and Eastern Europe. She has published widely and edited the Routledge volumes *Russian Energy and Security up to 2030* (2014), *The Challenges for Russia's Politicized Economic System* (2015) and *The Russian Economy under Putin* (2019).

Gudrun Persson is Director of the Russian and Eurasia Studies Programme at the Swedish Defence Research Agency, FOI, and Associate Professor at the Department of Slavic Studies, Stockholm University. She focuses on Russian foreign policy and Russian military strategic thought. She delivers lectures regularly at the Stockholm University and Uppsala University and has published widely on Russian affairs, including four monographs. She is a member of the Royal Swedish Academy of War Sciences and holds a Ph.D. in Government from the LSE, London. Her latest publications include the following: G. Persson, Conflicts and contradictions: Military relations in the Post-Soviet Space, in A. Moshes and A. Racz (eds.), *What Has Remained of the USSR — Exploring the Erosion of the Post-Soviet Space* (FIIA, Helsinki 2019); G. Persson (ed.), *Russian Military Capability in a Ten-Year Perspective – 2016* (2016); and G. Persson, *Learning from Foreign Wars: Russian Military Thinking 1859–1873* (2013).

Steven Rosefielde is Professor of Economics at the University of North Carolina, Chapel Hill. He received his Ph.D. in Economics from the Harvard University and is a member of the Russian Academy of Natural Sciences (RAEN). He has taught in Russia, China, Japan and Thailand. His most recent publications include the following: S. Rosefielde, *Democracy and Its Elected Enemies: The West's Paralysis, Crisis and Decline* (Cambridge University Press, 2013); S. Rosefielde and R. W. Pfouts, *Inclusive Economic Theory* (World Scientific Publishers, 2014);

S. Rosefielde and Q. Mills, *Global Economic Turmoil and the Public Good* (World Scientific Publishers, 2015); S. Rosefielde and B. Dallago, *Transformation and Crisis in Central and Eastern Europe: Challenges and Prospects* (Routledge, 2016); S. Rosefielde, *Kremlin Strikes Back: Russia and the West after Crimea's Annexation* (Cambridge University Press, 2017); S. Rosefielde and Q. Mills, *The Trump Phenomenon and Future of US Foreign Policy* (World Scientific Publishers, 2016); S. Rosefielde, *Trump's Populist America* (World Scientific Publishers, 2017); and S. Rosefielde and J. Leightner, *China's Market Communism: Challenges, Dilemmas, Solutions* (Routledge, 2017).

Madina Rubly received her M.A. in Global Affairs from Rice University and received special recognition for her capstone project titled, "Russia's Nuclear Modernization: A Quest for Nonproliferation". This project assessed changes in Russia's foreign policy, nuclear weapons production and implications of a nuclear arms race, compliance with international non-proliferation treaties, overcoming barriers to non-proliferation, competition in both cyber and outer-space, and ultimately examines Russian and American perceptions on strategic challenges in the post-Cold War world.

Rubly has co-authored articles and contributed to several books and policy reports focused on the transformation of the European political landscape, Sino-Russian relations and the security environment in the MENA region and Central Asia. Her areas of expertise include the US–Russia–China relations, energy and geopolitics, nuclear security, cybersecurity, new technologies, counterterrorism, risk management and crisis management. Her most recent article is *Russian Weapons in Turkey: A Trojan Horse?* (Georgetown University Walsh School of Foreign Service, March 2020). Rubly has studied and worked in Almaty and Moscow, St. Petersburg, San Diego, Washington D.C. and Houston. She is a member of the James Baker's Institute for Public Policy and the World Institute for Nuclear Security.

Andrei P. Tsygankov is Professor at the Department of Political Science and International Relations at the San Francisco State University. Tsygankov is a contributor to both Western and Russian academia. In the West, he co-edited collective projects, most recently, *The Routledge Handbook of Russian Foreign Policy* (2018). His published books include

Russia's Foreign Policy (five editions since 2006), *Russophobia* (2009, also published in Russia), *Russia and the West from Alexander to Putin* (2012, also published in China), *The Strong State in Russia* (2014), *The Dark Double* (2019) and *Russia and America* (2019), as well as many journal articles. In Russia, his best known books are *Modern Political Regimes* (1996), *Russian Science of International Relations* (2005, co-edited with Pavel Tsygankov, also published in Germany and China) and *Russian International Theory* (two editions since 2013). Tsygankov is a member of Valdai Club. He has delivered talks at various international forums, consulted various publishers and state agencies and served as Program Chair of the International Studies Association (ISA), 2006–2007. ISA has over 6,000 members in North America and around the world and is the largest scholarly association in this field.

Judy Twigg is a Professor of Political Science at Virginia Commonwealth University, where she teaches courses on global health, international political economy and Russian politics. She is also a Senior Associate (non-resident) with the Russia & Eurasia Program of the Center for Strategic and International Studies in Washington, DC; consultant for the Independent Evaluation Group of the World Bank; consultant for the Office of Verification and Evaluation of the Inter-American Development Bank and Adjunct Professor at the Center for Eurasian, Russian and East European Studies, Walsh School of Foreign Service, Georgetown University. Twigg's works focus on issues of health, human capital and health systems reform in Eurasia as well as evaluations of human development and public sector management development assistance projects globally. She has performed extensive programme evaluations on health sector reforms and HIV/AIDS interventions based on the field work in Russia, the Kyrgyz Republic, Macedonia and Lesotho. She has been a consultant for John Snow, Inc., UNICEF, the Eurasia Foundation and the Social Science Research Council. Her most recent publications have analysed health reforms in post-Maidan Ukraine, with a specific focus on the response to the outbreak of polio in the summer of 2015 and on its recently passed landmark health system reform legislation; Russian "brain drain"; and Russia's attempted emergence as a global health leader. Twigg has testified as an expert witness before the U.S. Congress and has been a member of several congressional and other high-level advisory groups on Russian affairs. She was a 2005 recipient of the State Council on Higher Education in Virginia Outstanding Faculty Award. She holds a B.S. in Physics from Carnegie Mellon University, an M.A. in Political Science and Soviet studies from the University of Pittsburgh and a Ph.D. in Political Science and Security Studies from MIT.

Contents

Part I

Russian Economy

Chapter 1

Putin's Muscovite Economy

Steven Rosefielde

Russia's economy is an imperfectly competitive market system with Muscovite characteristics (Clark, 1940). The demand and supply of factors, finance, production and distribution are significantly, but not completely, governed by competitive market forces. Private individuals and institutions own most of Russia's productive assets on a freehold basis, but the state holds title to the military industrial complex (MIC) and natural resources in the people's name. Large firms (oligopolies) exert market power, supported by state policy and the judiciary. The rule of contract law assists privileged insiders. Rent-seeking (lucrative state contracting with privileged insiders) and rent-granting are endemic. Criminal influences are strong and the "mafia" operates in collusion with the Federal Security Service [Federal'naya sluzhba bezopasnosti Rossiyskoy Federatsii (FSB)]. The state allows loyal insiders to steal public assets (kleptocracy) (Aslund, 2019a, 2019b; Dawisha, 2014). Entrepreneurship is legal; however, it is restrained by predatory political risks.

Russian producers under these conditions cannot competitively maximise profit, and individuals are unable to maximise consumer utility. The distribution of income is inequitable. Workers are underpaid, and powerful individuals accumulate immense unearned wealth. These imperfections are not unique. Most market systems are inefficient; however, Russia's market deficiencies are especially strong, exceeding those endemic in America, the European Union and China (Rosefielde and Leightner, 2017).

Anti-competitiveness impedes economic growth by hampering consumer-driven technological progress and entrepreneurship, while State controls allow Kremlin leaders to maintain huge military forces in accordance with Muscovite precedent (Rosefielde and Mills, 2020). Ivan the Terrible, Grand Prince of Muscovy from 1533 to 1547 and Tsar of All Rus' until his death in 1584, devised an economic system to serve his great power autocratic aspirations. He claimed freehold ownership of the means of production, including the peasantry, allowing the nobles acting as his agent-servitors to run the economy on assets that Ivan "rented" to them in return for a share of the crop, fealty and military and government service. He dispensed with markets, unconcerned about productive efficiency and consumer satisfaction. His patrimonial "rent-granting" economic scheme fostered affluence for himself and his loyal supporters, military might for his conquests, gradual military-intensive economic development and the perpetuation of his political authority (Rosefielde and Hedlund, 2008).

Putin's contemporary Russian economy is more sophisticated than Ivan Grozny's, but similarly patrimonial. Putin is the system's *de facto* sovereign. Everyone else is his agent-servitor or tool. He not only rationally chooses to support and harness markets to enhance Russia's economic might but also uses market controls and market rigging to build personal wealth, buy the loyalty of his supporters, maintain powerful armed forces for diverse purposes, foster economic modernisation and perpetuate his political authority. Western markets promote consumer sovereignty, that is, consumer control of the private sector through the purse and democratic control over the public sector via the ballot. Russia's economy principally serves Putin's autocrat power agenda. This is why Russia is an imperfectly competitive market system with Muscovite characteristics.

Costs of Private Sector Anti-Competitiveness

Putin pays a price for the benefits the Kremlin reaps from Russia's Muscovite market system. The economy is inefficient and underproductive. The autocrat could improve the system's performance by eliminating anti-competitive aspects that do not serve his purposes. He could streamline rent-granting, curb superfluous anti-competitiveness and improve the climate for entrepreneurship and direct foreign investment. This would enhance the efficiency of factor allocation, enabling at least one producer to increase output without incurring diminished production elsewhere, while making factor prices more consonant with competitive marginal factor productivities. Increased competitiveness would also shift production towards an equilibrium more closely attuned to consumer demand, within limits fixed by Putin's priorities, and the productivity of the whole system would increase through improved entrepreneurship, indigenous technological progress, technology transfer and diffusion. These gains in their entirety would be "Pareto" superior; that is, they would make consumers better off, simultaneously advancing one of Putin's political goals, without entailing losses in other aspects of his agenda.

The competitive principles guiding this line of reasoning assume that workers can freely negotiate terms of employment and the quality of the work environment and are able to insure themselves against layoffs, dismissals and medical exigencies. Insofar as Russia violates these assumptions, room exists for improving the risk insurance aspect of worker well-being on a "Pareto" superior basis. Both workers and Putin could enjoy improved economic security without sacrificing any other benefits. These gains would be invisible in national income statistics because implicit insurance transfers are not included in GDP.

Benefits of Public Transfers

The competitive market ideal is horizontal. The people themselves seeking profits and utility run the economy, with no governmental assistance beyond facilitating private activity through what John Locke called the social contract: "rule of law", basic infrastructural support, border protection, defence and elementary education. This ideal mischaracterises modern realities. Contemporary market economies across the globe have become vertical.

Governments provide a vast array of public programmes, including social safety nets. They establish the rules of market conduct and regulate economic behaviour. Some public programmes in Russia, like munitions production in state-owned factories, education in state schools, roads and mass transportation, are included in the GDP. Standard comparisons of

Russia's economic performance fully capture this value-added. Other government sector activities like unemployment, healthcare and retirement insurance-transfer schemes do not generate value-added for the national income accounting purposes and are disregarded in standard comparisons of Russia's economic performance and potential, making GDP an incomplete indicator of the comparative quality of Russian life. The same principle holds for intangibles like democracy, civil liberties, civic harmony, social justice, environmental purity (greenness) and spiritual community (sobornost). Any comprehensive assessment of the comparative merit of Russia's imperfectly competitive market system with Muscovite characteristics must take into account the utility of insurance transfers and intangibles. Russian economic performance on both these scores is poor by Western standards, but is improving.

Macroeconomic Management

Perfectly competitive freehold market economies in theory should perpetually maximise consumer utility. No one should be involuntarily unemployed, price levels should be stable and GDP should grow at the "golden age" rate of technological progress (Solow, 1956, 1957; Acemoglu, 2009). Business activities may fluctuate, but only as required by transitory factors and changes in people's demand for leisure.

Imperfectly competitive market systems necessarily fail to meet these goals. Involuntary unemployment, business cycles, deficient economic growth and inflation may blight economic performance. Along with assistance from the World Bank and the International Monetary Fund, Russia tries to manage these disorders by applying the same macroeconomic tools used in the West. The Kremlin regulates the supply of money and credit with open market operations and uses fiscal policy to affect aggregate demand. It deficit spends (increases government purchases with borrowed money), reduces taxes, increases subsidies and devalues the ruble when business is weak, reversing the field when business is strong.

Russian macroeconomic management is a challenging task. The Kremlin's banking system is weak, hampered further by Western economic sanctions that bar Russia's access to medium and long-term international credit. State revenues are heavily dependent on volatile natural resource prices. Soaring oil prices swell Moscow's coffers, flood the country with foreign direct investment and stimulate aggregate economic activity. Plunging natural resource prices reverse the process causing recessions and depressions. When the sun shines, Russian macroeconomic policymakers should avoid overspending, creating reserves for rainy days. The Kremlin has been prudent in this regard. Russia's debt-to-GDP ratio is only 13.5%, a small fraction of the American figure.[1]

Russia's macroeconomic performance more broadly has been good, given its exposure to natural resource price shocks. Its labour force participation rate is high,[2] and its 4.8% unemployment rate is close to what World Bank economists consider full non-transitory employment,[3] and the inflation rate is 3.4%.[4] GDP growth is dyspeptic at 1.8% per annum, but still faster than the European Union,[5] and real wages including pensions are growing. Russia ran a 35.4 billion dollar current account trade balance surplus in 2017 and holds relatively high levels of international reserves ($461 billion). It has low external debt levels (about 29% of GDP) and a comfortable import cover (15.9 months) that enables the Federation to readily absorb external shocks.[6] The Kremlin's primary foreign trade vulnerability lies in Russian dependence on natural resource exports to pay for the country's imports. Export diversification is limited. Since 2014,

---

[1] See https://tradingeconomics.com/russia/government-debt-to-gdp. The American debt to GDP ratio is 105.4.

[2] The absolute numbers of employed people was 73.2 million in September 2018. World Bank, *Russia's Economy: Preserving Stability, Doubling Growth, Halving Poverty — How?* December 4, 2018: 40th issue of the Russia Economic Report; http://www.worldbank.org/en/country/russia/publication/rer; http://pubdocs.worldbank.org/en/67363 1543924406524/RER-40-English.pdf.

[3] Most of the unemployment is still long term: 30% of the unemployed had been looking for a job for over a year. The number of part-time employees increased slightly in the first half of 2018 but remained far below the levels of the 2009 crisis period. *Ibid.* https://tradingeconomics.com/russia/unemployment-rate.

[4] See https://tradingeconomics.com/russia/inflation-cpi.

[5] See https://tradingeconomics.com/russia/gdp-growth-annual.

[6] World Bank, *Russia's Economy: Preserving Stability, Doubling Growth, Halving Poverty — How?* December 4, 2018: 40th issue of the Russia Economic Report; http://www.worldbank.org/en/country/russia/publication/rer; http://pubdocs.worldbank.org/en/673 631543924406524/RER-40-English.pdf.

Russia's non-energy export volume growth has been outpacing that of energy, contributing to export diversification. Yet, Russia's progress in export diversification is modest. The share of oil/gas exports in 2017 was still high at 59%, accounting for 25% of the fiscal revenue, with diversification mainly driven by established product lines.

There is little doubt that Russian macroeconomic performance in all these regards would be substantially better, especially its GDP growth rate, if the country were more competitive and the West lifted economic sanctions. Nonetheless, Kremlin macroeconomic policymakers have done a credible job, given Putin's flawed Muscovite economic mechanism.

Welfare

Russian per capita income in 2017 was 46.7% of that of America.[7] The society is inegalitarian, but less so than the United States. Russia's Gini coefficient is high at 41.2 and that of America's is at 45.[8] Russia's poverty rate is 13.2%, a figure the Kremlin predicts will halve over the next 6 years driven by rebounding real income growth.[9] America's poverty rate by comparison was 12.3% in 2017 (Fontenot *et al.*, 2018). This is better than that of Russia's for the moment, but is unlikely to remain so if poverty in the Federation plummets as forecasted by authorities. The World Bank estimates that the average annual growth of 1.5% would bring down the poverty rate from 13.2% to only 10.7% by 2024. A 4.4% rate of growth would be necessary to achieve the state's goal of 6.6%, unless the government increases social assistance and transfers. If growth remains

---

[7] See https://www.cia.gov/library/PUBLICATIONS/the-world-factbook/geos/rs.html. Russia's per capita GDP computed in purchasing power parity dollars in 2017 was $27,900. The counterpart American figure was $59,000.

[8] CIA World Factbook. https://www.cia.gov/library/PUBLICATIONS/the-world-factbook/geos/rs.html.

[9] *Ibid.* Other Russian sources indicated a higher figure. The Russian Presidential Academy of the National Economy and Public Administration says 22% of Russians fall into the "poverty zone", meaning they are unable to buy anything beyond basic staples needed for subsistence. See "One-Fifth of Russians Live in Poverty, 36 Percent in 'Risk Zone,' Study Finds", *Radio Free Europe*, November 21, 2018. https://www.rferl.org/a/study-22-percent-of-russians-live-in-poverty-36-percent-in-risk-zone-/29613059.html.

sluggish in the 1.5% range, halving the poverty would require transferring 0.27% of the GDP to the poor annually over the next 6 years.

The Kremlin's poverty reduction programme although broadly welcome has a downside. A portion of the income gain will come from shortened retirements. Russia's new Pension Law 489161-7 enacted on October 3, 2018 increased the retirement age from 55 to 60 years for women and from 60 to 65 years for men. Although life expectancy at birth is now 72.5 years (77.1 for females; 66.5 for males), the figure is lower for those currently approaching retirement age, causing considerable political consternation. The World Bank supports the Putin administration on the issue from the perspectives of both fiscal prudence and inter-generational justice; nonetheless, the new law is unpopular.

Performance, Potential and Prospects

Russia's economic future viewed through the prism of World Bank global statistics is satisfactory in the short term, better during the remainder of Putin's presidential tenure and superior for decades thereafter under a more liberal regime. Its data show that Russia's economic performance in the recent years has lagged that of the EMDEs (Emerging Markets and Developing Economies; that is, low-tiered advanced nations including Brazil, India, China and South Africa) but paced the West despite a severe petroleum price shock and strong economic sanctions imposed by America and the European Union, behaviour that accords with the World Bank's priors. Russia as a low-tier advanced nation (not an EMDE as the BRICS classification suggests) should have grown less rapidly than emerging nations and should only have slightly outperformed higher tier advanced nations due to the "catch up" effect. Figure 1 confirms that this more or less is how Russia's economy behaved.

The World Bank moreover expects better results in the years immediately ahead because of improving trends in Russia's competitiveness (especially with respect to small and medium-sized enterprises),[10]

---

[10]World Bank, *Russia's Economy: Preserving Stability, Doubling Growth, Halving Poverty — How?* December 4, 2018: 40th issue of the Russia Economic Report, pp. 35–36. http://pubdocs.worldbank.org/en/673631543924406524/RER-40-English.pdf.

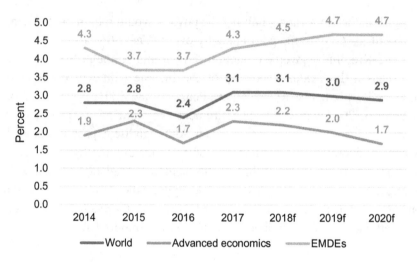

Figure 1:   Global growth is broadly stable (in %).

Source: World Bank.

government administrative efficiency,[11] education[12] and social welfare. Tomorrow, it predicts, should be better than today, and in the fullness of time, the World Bank expects Russia to converge to the global high-economic performance frontier as the Kremlin transitions to democratic free enterprise, contemporary animosities between Washington and Moscow notwithstanding.

Sources of Growth and Macroeconomic Stability

The World Bank's optimism stems from its faith in the power of globalisation, buttressed by the recent statistical trends. Unemployment is declining, wages are recovering and poverty is declining. The employment and labour force participation rates remain at high levels while unemployment is close to minimum (Figure 2).

The labour force participation rate is unchanged at 63.2%. High employment rates, in conjunction with the continued decline in the working-age population, should reduce the unemployment rate further.

---

[11] *Ibid.*, pp. 36–40.

[12] *Ibid.*, pp. 43–44.

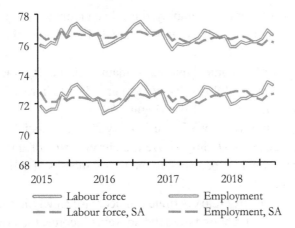

Figure 2:   Labour force and employment (million people).

Source: Rosstat and Haver Analytics.

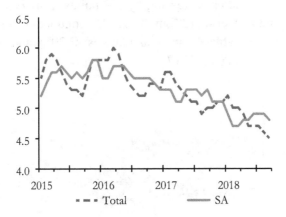

Figure 3:   Unemployment rate (in %).

Source: Rosstat and Haver Analytics.

It decreased to 4.6% in the third quarter of 2018, compared to 5.2% a year earlier (Figure 3).

The employment structure is also steady. The gap between male and female employment remains stable — unemployment for women is usually around 0.3% points lower than that for men. Most of the unemployment is still long term: 30% of the unemployed had been looking for a job for over a year. Regional unemployment is unequal, but echoes the declining national trend.

Real disposable income dynamics remains volatile. Income started to grow at the beginning of 2018. Its average growth rate in real terms in the first 10 months of 2018 was 1.6% (Figure 4).

Labour pensions rose by 3.7% in January 2018 and social pensions by 2.9% in April 2018 — slightly above the current rates of inflation. As a result, the real growth of pensions in the first 9 months of 2018 in Russia was only 1.2%.

The official poverty rate continued to decrease slowly in the first half of 2018. Driven by a rebound in real disposable income, the poverty rates in Russia decreased in the first and second quarters of 2018 (Table 1). The World Bank expects the trend to continue (Table 2).

The share of those who are economically secure in the population was unchanged in 2017, after decreasing by 5% points from 79% in 2014 to 74% in 2015 and further to 72% in 2017. This contraction was driven by a large fall of disposable incomes and wages in 2015 and a continued decline in incomes in 2016–2017.

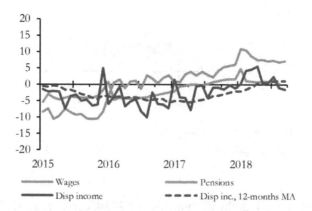

Figure 4:   Real income dynamics (in %, year-on-year).

Note: Pension and disposable income dynamics adjusted for one-time payment in January 2017.

Source: Rosstat and World Bank staff estimates.

Table 1:   Poverty (cumulative).

	2010	2011	2012	2013	2014	2015	2016	Q1 2017	Q2 2017	Q3 2017	Q4 2017	Q1 2018	Q2 2018
Poverty rate (%)	12.5	12.7	10.7	10.8	11.2	13.3	13.3	15.0	14.4	13.8	13.2	14.2	13.6

Source: Rosstat.

Table 2:   The moderate poverty rate is expected to continue to decline in 2018 and throughout 2020.

	2010	2011	2012	2013	2014	2015	2016	2017	2018 f	2019 f	2020 f
Poverty rate (%)	12.5	12.7	10.7	10.8	11.2	13.3	13.3	13.2	12.4	12.0	11.6

Source: Rosstat, World Bank staff calculations.

Consumer price inflation has been rising since July 2018, though it remained below the Central Bank of the Russian Federation's (CBR) annual 4% target (Figure 5).

The increase in inflation since end of 2017 was mostly attributable to two factors. First, higher prices for oil, which affected gasoline prices and transportation costs for producers, and second ruble depreciation (Figure 6), which exerted an upward pressure on inflation through higher prices of imported food and utilities.

Household inflation expectations remain elevated, prompted by a hike in gasoline prices. Domestic inflationary risks stem mainly from VAT rate increase, the closing output gap in 2018, pass-through from the ruble depreciation and elevated inflation expectations. Risks to inflation in the near term tilt towards the upside.

Russia's banking sector remains relatively weak, with less capital buffer (12.2% as of end of September) and higher non-performing loan (NPL) ratio (10.8% as of end of September) than other emerging nations (15.6% and 4.4%, respectively). However, the situation has stabilised, lending activity is recovering and profitability is improving, though the sector remains weighed down by high provisioning charges.

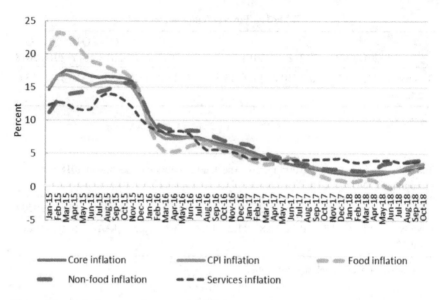

Figure 5:   Inflation rose but remained below the CBR's target (CPI index and its components, in %, year-on-year).

Source: CBR and Haver Analytics.

Figure 6:   Ruble depreciation since the beginning of 2018 (change in oil prices and the nominal exchange rate, logarithmic scale).

Source: CBR.

Lending growth continued in both the retail and corporate segments, though it was much weaker on the corporate side due to weak economic growth. Credit to the corporate sector grew by 9.7%, year-on-year, in the last 10 months. During the same period, loans to households grew by 22.5%, year-on-year. The growth was lead mostly by unsecured loans and mortgage loans, and household debt is at an all-time high. A strong demand for residential mortgages reflects the declining interest rates and anticipated increases in real estate prices due to a change in the funding scheme for the construction companies.

The fiscal balance improved at all levels of the budget system due to higher oil prices, combined with a weaker ruble, a better tax administration and a conservative fiscal policy. To boost growth, the President of Russia issued a "May Decree" in 2018, which introduced a set of goals for 2024. Putin wants Russia to become one of the five largest economies in the world (currently Russia is ranking 6th in terms of PPP); the GDP growth rate to be on par with the world's average; halving the poverty rate; fostering population growth; raising life expectancy to 78 years and paving the way for the digital economy to reach 30% of GDP. These goals have already prompted the government to increase spending on education, health, infrastructure, social policy, digital economy, support of SME and exports starting in 2019. Twelve national projects and the comprehensive plan for modernisation and expansion of infrastructure are included in the federal budget for this purpose.

The World Bank forecasts Russia's growth for 2018–2020 will remain modest at 1.5–1.8% (Figure 7), rates below the EMDE average (4.6%), but exceeding the AE average (1.7%) in 2020. The key factors governing the World Bank's projection are a dyspeptic global environment, a declining labour force and slowing total factor productivity growth (TFP).

The declining trend in TFP is a global phenomenon. Weaker productivity growth has been attributed to slower investment growth, partly because of deleveraging pressures and other crisis legacies, combined with an ageing population and maturing global value chains. In Russia, TFP growth slowed as productivity gains of first-generation reforms wore off. The changing composition of investment from machinery to construction could also have contributed to the lower TFP growth. Globally,

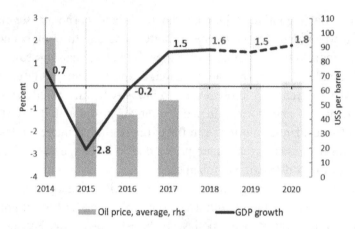

Figure 7:   The growth forecast for Russia suggests benign growth (real GDP growth, %).
Source: Rosstat, World Bank.

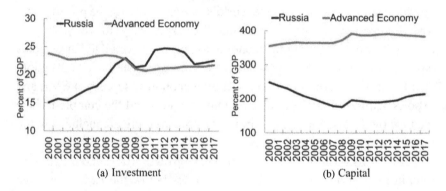

Figure 8:   Russia's investment-to-GDP ratio stopped increasing; capital-to-GDP ratio remains low. (a) Gross fixed capital formation as a percent of GDP for Russia. Capital as a percent of GDP for Russia. (b) Lower line indicates GDP weighted average of 32 advanced economies.

Source: Haver Analytics, Penn World Table, World Bank.

investment growth halved between 2010 and 2016, with the weakness shifting from advanced economies to EMDEs over this period. In Russia, although investment growth slowed from an average growth of 10.4% during the previous decade to 2.8% in 2010–2017, the investment as a share of GDP increased (Figure 8). This helped to accelerate capital growth over the period 2010–2017.

Russian demographic trends are worse than those found in many EMDEs (but not China) as the country's low total fertility rate in the early 1990s accelerated population ageing. Russia's total fertility rate remained low until the mid-2000s. The decline in the total fertility rate began to take a toll on the working-age population after 15 years, with potential labour force growth peaking in 2007 at 0.7% before declining to −0.7% in 2017. This suggests to the World Bank that short of unexpected surges in productivity growth, the outlook for Russian GDP growth is mediocre.

Misleading Benchmark

The World Bank's modest short- and near-term expectations for the Russian economy reflect its outlook for a maturing global economy (perhaps even a climacteric) (Kindleberger, 1974). Its optimistic long-term attitude is a corollary of its faith in globalisation. The World Bank and International Monetary Fund consider most economies "normal" in a comprehensive development scheme that moves backward nations in stages from autarkic illiberal regimes to high-performing liberal members of the global community (Shleifer and Treisman, 2005; Rosefielde, 2005a). Each nation's position in the global development hierarchy and a handful of technical factors including foreign direct investment, technology transfer, state macroeconomic management skills, education and integration into competitive global trade and financial networks determine economic performance everywhere. Moreover, the World Bank believes that political and social progress go hand-in-hand with economic globalisation. It expects Russia to eventually discard its Muscovite characteristics, democratise, liberalise, transition and integrate into a Western-led transnational global order with progressive values.

The World Bank knows that Russia has distinctive Muscovite characteristics, but as it perceives things, this does not change the fundamentals. The immutable laws of globalisation it insists must inevitably govern

Russia's economic, political and social performance. The attitude has some empirical validity. GDP growth does decelerate as emerging nations move up the development ladder. The transfer of macroeconomic management skills does allow less developed nations to cope better with involuntary underemployment, inflation, budgetary deficits, poverty, insurance transfers, education and social safety nets.

However, this is not the whole story. Modernisation does not settle the equally important issues of hegemony, hard power, market power, political power, corruption, inequality, economic justice, social justice, civil rights, environmental purity, other intangibles and well-being. Faster growth, full employment and modest inflation achieved within Russia's imperfectly competitive market system with Muscovite characteristics will bolster the Kremlin's economic power, but this is unlikely to prevent Moscow from continuing to undervalue consumer utility, abuse large segments of society and structurally militarise and browbeat its neighbours.

Tea Leaves and Productivity

The World Bank's approach to economic crystal ball gazing is congruent with Western tradition, especially the important role assigned to globalisation and TFP. The approach is sensible, but too often misses critical turning points (Rosefielde, 2005b, 2017). The Soviet economy grew rapidly under Stalin's autarky during the polarised Cold War era of 1955–1968. TFP calculations suggested smooth sailing ahead, encouraging some observers to conclude that planned economy and communism would triumph, but then the USSR fell prey to "growth retardation" driven by a declining marginal capital productivity. The CIA warned about the danger of Soviet secular stagnation (zero growth) in the 1980s; however, it did not take its own warnings seriously in part because Gorbachev pressed market reforms after 1986 and promoted economic integration with the West (globalization). The CIA was shocked when the wheels came off the cart in 1989.

Later, after Boris Yeltsin privatised business property on a freehold basis, encouraged free enterprise and opened Russia's economy, the catastrophic result took the World Bank entirely by surprise. It expected Russia to recover "up the J-curve" rapidly (Brada and King, 1993), but this never happened. Then, 7 years later when Russia's economy finally began recovering, the World Bank predicted rosier and rosier futures with Russian GDP advancing at 8% per annum until reality hit. GDP fell 8% in 2008 and never rebounded to the fast growth track.

Obviously, neither globalisation nor TFP have proven to be trustworthy indicators of Soviet and Russian economic prospects. This has multiple explanations beyond exogenous economic and political shocks. Statistical fraud and military concealment stand at the top of the list. The Soviets indulged in a practice called "spurious innovation" where they treated established goods as new ones, raised prices and mischaracterised the price increase as value-added instead of inflation. Inflation increased, but it was disguised as real GDP and hence the term "hidden inflation".

Much of the per capita income growth claimed by the Soviets was fake (Rosefielde, 2007). The opposite was true for defence. The Soviets and now the Russians understate military activities, especially weapons procurement in their GDP statistics. The World Bank ignores the issue and the impact of military activities on TFP and macroeconomic stability across arms procurement cycles. Russia's double-digit arms build-up 2010–2015 is invisible in the World Bank's assessment of Russian economic performance and prospects for harmonious globalisation. Caveat emptor.

Merit

The World Bank's data, methods and assessments do not provide inclusive pictures of Russian economic merit (Rosefielde and Pfouts, 2014). They misgauge consumer utility assuming perfect market competition and pay inadequate attention to aspects of well-being omitted from their national income statistics (social externalities and other nonmarket aspects of personal fulfilment). These defects give an unduly favourable impression of Russia's inclusive economic performance. Russian well-being and quality of existence are substantially lower than the World Bank's indicators suggest (Trudolyubov, 2019),[13] while the Kremlin's military and political

---

[13] In the 5 years since 2014, the share of those in Russia who consider themselves middle class has shrunk from 60% to 47%. This is according to a study commissioned by the investment arm of Sberbank, Russia's largest bank, on the "Ivanov index", a measure of

power are higher. Russia is not a typical lower tier advanced economy playing a benign part in the global order. It is a great military power at odds with Western-led globalising that privileges kleptocratic servitors at the expense of ordinary consumers. A system's merit, like beauty, is in the

---

consumer confidence. "Ivanov", a common Russian last name, is used to represent a typical middle-class person in Russia.

If only education and professional status are considered, Russia would have a large middle class of "European" proportions, between 60% and 70% of the population. But to qualify as middle class according to the Institute of Sociology, one must meet all four criteria. And when all four measures are considered, Russia's middle class made up 42% of the population in 2014, the last year for which data are available.

But the decline in incomes and the shrinking middle-income groups are not the whole story. Even members of the Organisation for Economic Cooperation and Development, the group of developed market economies, are experiencing a shrinking middle class, though the decline is less dramatic and slower than that in Russia. The share of the middle class in OECD countries declined from 64% in the 1980s to 61% currently, a recent OECD study found.

In Russia, all income groups, and particularly those associated with the middle class, have become critically dependent on the public sector. Pensions, public transfers and public sector wages account for about half of total incomes in Russia. According to data from the International Labour Organization, public sector employees account for 40% of the total employment in Russia, compared to 13% in Germany, 15% in the United States, 25% in Finland and 31% in Saudi Arabia. It is worth noting that the IMF's estimate of the Russian state's share in formal employment is 50%, higher than the ILO's 40%.

This income dependency has been true for relatively worse-off citizens for a long time. What has changed is that relatively better-off groups of the population have become increasingly dependent on the government budget, World Bank studies show (see especially Figure 39 in that report). The share of income from public wages and pensions for better-off groups has grown, while the share of income coming from entrepreneurial activity or property has declined.

Another important breakdown underlying the political and economic divisions in today's Russia concerns inputs to versus benefits drawn from the system. Those in the bottom 60% of the income distribution are net beneficiaries of Russia's current system if in-kind health and education services are included, the World Bank's Russia Economic Report says. "The top four deciles are net payers to the system, with their tax contributions being greater than the benefits they receive", World Bank economists conclude.

One has to be careful in directly linking Russian society's heavy dependence on public wages and pensions with its political sympathies. It is not that people automatically support those who pay them, though the Kremlin may think so. It is what it is, a dependency. It certainly helps Russia's political managers mobilise support when they need it. But the sincerity of such a support will always remain questionable.

eyes of the beholder. This is a matter of values. Nonetheless, one important aspect of Russia's economic potential should be beyond dispute. Russia can persevere on its current course without foregoing guns, butter, growth and modernisation. It can remain on a Muscovite trajectory as long as the regime holds power by successfully repressing full democratisation.

References

Acemoglu, D. (2009). The Solow Growth Model, in *Introduction to Modern Economic Growth*, Princeton University Press, Princeton, pp. 26–76.

Aslund, A. (2019a, January 29). Money laundering involving Russian individuals and their effect on the EU. Atlantic Council. https://www.atlanticcouncil.org/news/transcripts/money-laundering-involving-russian-individuals-and-their-effect-on-the-eu.

Aslund, A. (2019b). *Russia's Crony Capitalism: The Path from Market Economy to Kleptocracy*, Yale University Press, New Haven.

Brada, J. and King, A. (1993). Is there a J-curve for the economic transition from socialism to capitalism? in *Stabilization and Privatization in Poland*, Poznanski, K. Z. (ed.), Kluwer Academic Publishers, Amsterdam, pp. 251–269.

Clark, J. (1940). Toward a concept of workable competition, *American Economic Review* 30(2), 241–256.

Dawisha, K. (2014). *Putin's Kleptocracy: Who Owns Russia?* Simon & Schuster, New York.

Fontenot, K., Semega, J. and Kollar, M. (2018, September 12). *Income and Poverty in the United States: 2017*, US Census Bureau, Report Number P60-263. https://www.census.gov/library/publications/2018/demo/p60-263.html.

Kindleberger, C. (1974). An American economic climacteric? *Challenge* 16(6), 35–44.

Rosefielde, S. (2005a). Russia: An abnormal country, *European Journal of Comparative Economics* 2(1), 3–16.

Rosefielde, S. (2005b). Tea leaves and productivity: Bergsonian norms for gauging the Soviet future, *Comparative Economic Studies* 47(2), 259–273.

Rosefielde, S. (2007). *Russian Economy from Lenin to Putin*, Wiley, New York.

Rosefielde, S. (2017). *Kremlin Strikes Back: Russia and the West after Crimea's Annexation*, Cambridge University Press, New York.

Rosefielde, S. and Hedlund, S. (2008). *Russia since 1980: Wrestling with Westernization*, Cambridge University Press, New York.

Rosefielde, S. and Leightner, J. (2017). *China's Market Communism: Challenges, Dilemmas, Solutions*, Routledge, London.

Rosefielde, S. and Mills, Q. (2020). *Beleaguered Superpower: America Adrift*, World Scientific Publishers, Singapore.

Rosefielde, S. and Pfouts, R. W. (2014). *Inclusive Economic Theory*, World Scientific Publishers, Singapore.

Shleifer, A. and Treisman, D. (2005). A normal country: Russia after communism, *Journal of Economic Perspectives* 19(1), 151–174.

Solow, R. (1956). A contribution to the theory of economic growth, *Quarterly Journal of Economics* 70(1), 65–94.

Solow, R. (1957). Technical change and the aggregate production function, *Review of Economics and Statistics* 39(3), 312–320.

Trudolyubov, M. (2019, May 9). Who is Mr. Ivanov: Why Russia's middle class today is different. Wilson Center, Available at https://www.wilsoncenter.org/blog-post/who-mr-ivanov-why-russias-middle-class-today-different.

Chapter 2

Russia's Macroeconomy — A Closer Look at Growth, Investment and Uncertainty

Torbjörn Becker

Introduction

Russia is in many ways a special country, which may lead us to believe that regular political and economic analyses are not applicable. This may certainly be true in some regards, but there are still many dimensions that are as relevant in Russia as they are in most other countries. One such dimension is that generating growth and prosperity in a stable macroeconomic environment is something both the leadership and population at large value.[1] However, looking at approval ratings and GDP growth for President Putin does not immediately tell this story.

In the left panel of Figure 1, Putin's approval rating in the Levada Center's surveys is negatively correlated with GDP growth. It is rather unexpected and unusual that a country's leader becomes more popular when growth is lower. A closer look at the data reveals that the negative correlation is generated by three distinct periods; the first year is when Putin was still relatively unknown at the same time as Russia's growth

---

[1]Chappell (1990) shows that both approval ratings and voting depend on growth and inflation in the US.

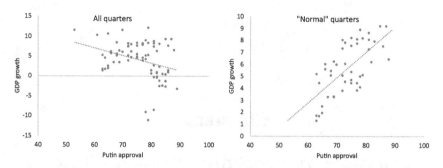

Figure 1:   GDP growth and approval ratings of Putin.

Source: Levada Center and Federal Statistics service.

rates were the highest since the break-up of the Soviet Union due to the rebound after the 1998 crisis; then Russian growth was hit by the global financial crisis in 2008/2009; and then finally, there is the period of Putin's approval getting a significant boost following the annexation of Crimea and period of sanctions and counter-sanctions in a time of very poor growth.

Removing these exceptional periods from the left panel in Figure 1, we get the right panel that shows what we can think of as more "normal" quarters of economic and political developments in Russia. All of a sudden, the approval rating for Putin lines up very well with quarterly growth rates and the correlation between the two variables goes from a negative 0.3 in the left panel to a positive 0.7 in the right panel. In other words, Putin's popularity increases with higher growth like in most other countries. The caveat is of course that when growth turns out to be less than satisfactory, there are other ways for a Russian president to boost his approval ratings.

Again, Russia may be different in the sense that approval ratings and the probability of regime change are less clearly connected than in Western democracies, but it is hard to think that low popularity ratings would not affect the probability of some type of popular or elite movements that challenge the president. Therefore, generating high and sustainable growth is one of the central tools for a president to stay in power in Russia as well. The fundamental question posed in the chapter is whether capital flows and foreign direct investments can help generate more productive domestic investments that in turn lead to higher sustainable growth. In order to analyse the economic–political nexus of growth and popularity ratings, the chapter starts by investigating how Russian growth compares with peer groups and to what extent a regular growth model can be used to understand growth in Russia. The analysis suggests that this is the case and then looks at investments, capital flows and uncertainty to disentangle external factors and domestic policies that have contributed to the developments we have seen in the Russian economy.

What sets this analysis apart from much of the other literature on Russian growth is the focus on uncertainty and the importance of specific policy actions rather than institutions more generally. It also highlights how a serious economic reform programme will contribute to regime stability in the longer run, while external conflicts only have a short-run popularity effect that carries a high price in terms of lost growth opportunities and lower long-term approval ratings.

Growth

Actual growth since the start of transition

Russia's growth since 1991 has gone through several phases as can be seen in Figure 2. These phases are explained by a mix of fundamental growth drivers, external shocks and domestic policies. The problem for Russian voters (and sometimes also for researchers and policymakers) is to disentangle those changes in their income that are due to a capable leader's policies from those that are simply the result of chance or a response to external shocks. The strong positive correlation between approval ratings and growth in the right panel of Figure 1 suggests that voters in more normal times rather indiscriminately reward their leader with higher ratings when growth is higher and vice versa even if much of the variation in growth is due to external factors such as changes in international oil prices. However, the global financial crisis in 2008/2009 is an example of people clearly identifying the shock to be external and where the popularity rating of the president did not fall as would otherwise be expected. The political cost of poor economic performance can also be seen in the first decade of transition from a planned economy to a more market-oriented one. This was not a smooth

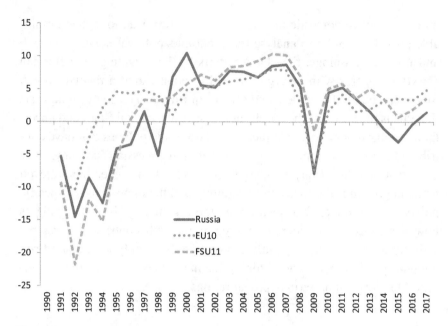

Figure 2:   Real GDP growth.

Source: World Bank.

process, but instead growth was negative for many years and that is still reflected in peoples' views of former leaders such as Gorbachev and Yeltsin.

Russia was not unique among transition countries to experience negative growth in the early years of transition, and both the countries that later joined the EU (EU10 in Figure 2) and the other countries that came out of the Soviet Union (FSU11) had a similar start with declining incomes.[2] However, the rebound to positive growth was significantly faster among the EU10 countries than in Russia and the FSU11 countries.

The differences in growth between Russia and the peer country groups may not look so striking, but when growth differences accumulate over several years, the differences in income levels are significant. In Figure 3, the lines are broken in the first, pre-Putin, phase of transition with income levels set at 100 in 1990. By the end of 1999, Russia had

---

[2]Åslund (2013) discuss the transition process in Russia and other post-communist countries at more length.

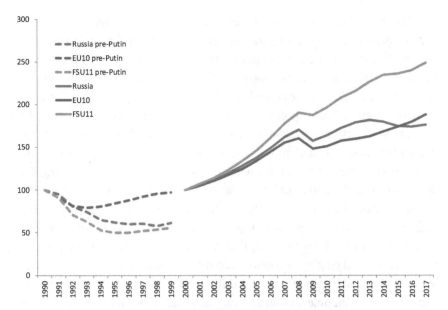

Figure 3: Russia and peers GDP index (1990 = 100 then 2000 = 100).

Source: World Bank and author's calculations.

lost more than 40% of its initial income level, similar to the other FSU countries but far behind the EU10 group of countries that by then had come back to where they started the transition process in terms of income levels.

The second part of Figure 3 restarts the comparison at the time Putin became president for the first time. With 2000 as the starting point, the FSU11 group generated the highest average growth rate, and in 2017, income levels were 2½ times of what they were in 2000. Russia was for a long time ahead of the EU10 countries in terms of growth in this period, but after the very poor growth performance after 2013, Russia was overtaken by the EU10 group as well. Nevertheless, under Putin's watch, income in Russia had increased by 1.7 times in 2017 compared to 2000, in stark contrast to the loss of 40% of income in the first decade of transition. It is not hard to understand that the arrival of a president that coincides with a shift in economic fortunes of this scale generates ample support in the population and that a narrative of Putin creating order from chaos can take hold.

There are many external factors that affect Russia's macroeconomic performance and the volatile and unpredictable world market price of oil is of particular importance. Oil prices have explained around two-thirds of Russian growth and account for a similar share of 1-year ahead forecast errors in the recent decades (Becker, 2017a). Over the years, Russian policymakers have adopted policies to mitigate the volatility of oil prices by first creating different versions of oil fund(s) and then abandoning the fixed exchange rate and moving to inflation targeting. Becker (2017a) shows how these latter policies were important factors in dampening the downturn in 2014 compared with the more severe decline in output that was experienced in the 2008/2009 global financial crisis. Although these measures have been important steps to deal with the shorter run implications of Russia's oil dependence, they cannot change the fact that policies aimed at diversifying the economy are the only solutions to generate stable and sustainable growth at a level that is sufficient to close the income gap with high-income countries and stay ahead of its middle-income emerging market peers (Becker, 2018). In its October 2018 forecast of the world economy, the IMF (2018) projected that Russia will grow by 1.8%, similar to the 2% growth in advanced economies but well behind the 4.7% growth in emerging markets.

Are "normal" growth models relevant for Russia?

If we turn our attention to regular growth models that focus on factors that the literature has identified as fundamental drivers of growth, we may better understand what Russia needs to do to boost growth going forward. Becker and Olofsgård (2018) use a robust empirical growth model to understand differences in growth across 25 transition countries in the first 25 years since the dissolution of the Soviet Union. The model was originally specified and estimated by Levine and Renelt (1992) with a focus on identifying the robust determinants of growth among the long list of variables that have been used in empirical growth models. In the end, the authors show that initial GDP, population growth, human capital measured by secondary schooling and the ratio of investments to GDP are the most robust determinants of growth across a large number of countries and over time. The model was estimated without the transition countries that we study in Becker and Olofsgård (2018). We could therefore use the estimated model to see how well it predicted the growth experience of transition countries to investigate the question if (and when) transition countries can be thought of as "normal" countries from a growth perspective.[3]

Using the same methodology here but with a focus on Russia and the country groups that we used in Figure 1, we can generate predicted growth and compare this with the actual growth for the first decade of transition and then do the same with the 17 years that coincide with Putin being the President and Prime Minister of Russia. For the initial period, the model predicts that Russia would grow at 4.8% per annum, while in fact, income declined by 5% per year on average. Russia thus underperformed the expected growth by almost 10% points per annum. This is similar to the other FSU countries but far behind the EU10 group that "only" underperformed the model by around 5% points.

The picture changes dramatically when we look at the period 2000–2017. Both Russia and the peer groups have growth that comes very close to what the model predicts; the residuals are a few tenths of a percent up or down. In this sense, these countries are in this time period indeed "normal" countries.

The numbers in Table 1 also allow us to discuss the quantitative importance of the different fundamental growth factors in generating the predicted growth rates. The general impression is that human and physical capital as measured by secondary schooling and investments to GDP are of equal importance and of more significance numerically than the other variables. However, the second observation is that there is much less variation in the growth that is generated by human capital than by physical capital. If Russia had the secondary schooling of the average EU10 country, growth would only increase by 0.15% points while if the investment rate was on par with EU10 countries, growth would increase by 1.3% points. In other words, differences in investment to GDP ratios explain almost all of the difference in predicted growth between Russia

---

[3]The notion of Russia being a "normal" country was introduced by Shleifer and Treisman (2005) and then used by the authors to look at a wider set of countries in Shleifer and Treisman (2014).

Table 1: Russia and peers — predicted and actual growth.

	Constant	Initial GDP	Pop growth	Sec school	Inv/ GDP	Predicted	Actual	Residual (a-p)
Variable average 1991–1999								
Russia	1	3.10	–0.08	0.87	0.22	4.80	–5.04	–9.83
FSU11	1	1.68	0.34	0.92	0.14	3.91	–5.95	–9.86
EU10	1	3.24	–0.41	0.94	0.18	4.25	–0.45	–4.71
Impact on predicted growth 1991–1999								
Russia	–0.83	–1.08	0.03	2.77	3.91			
FSU11	–0.83	–0.59	–0.13	2.92	2.53			
EU10	–0.83	–1.14	0.16	2.97	3.10			
Variable average 2000–2017								
Russia	1	1.80	–0.13	0.86	0.16	4.11	3.87	–0.24
FSU11	1	0.88	0.53	0.88	0.15	3.98	3.92	–0.06
EU10	1	2.81	–0.42	0.91	0.23	5.31	5.58	0.27
Impact on predicted growth 2000–2017								
Russia	–0.83	–0.63	0.05	2.72	2.80			
FSU11	–0.83	–0.31	–0.20	2.78	2.54			
EU10	–0.83	–0.98	0.16	2.87	4.09			

Source: Becker and Olofsgård (2018) based on Penn World Data 9.0 and additional calculations.

and the EU10 countries. For the political leaders of Russia, this is an important message. The various proposals to modernise and diversify the economy can have a large impact on expected growth in Russia and with the right incentives to invest in sectors that are less subject to external volatility, this would also make Russia's growth more robust.[4] It is therefore important to understand how investments have evolved over time and how this can be explained. This is the focus in the following sections.

---

[4]The benefits of investments in other sectors than the extractive industries are rather obvious. However, decisions to shift government policies away from extractive industries to the benefit of other sectors would be subject to a political process with strong opposing forces as discussed in Fortescue (2018).

Investments

There are a number of measurement issues related to investments (and other variables) in the national accounts statistics. The data in Table 1 are from the Penn World Table 9.0, where there is an effort to make data comparable between a large number of countries, including Russia. Investments to GDP are measured as the share of gross capital formation at current PPPs and are extremely high in the initial years of transition and much lower later in the sample compared to the official statistics from the Federal Statistics Service. If we use the official data, there are also significant differences in the dynamics of investments between data in current prices or constant prices.

An important factor behind the differences in shares between the current and constant price series is due to the importance of oil exports. The constant price data measure exported quantities, while the current price data measure export values and are therefore subject to changes in both international oil prices (measured in dollars) and changes in the exchange rate (since the accounts are in ruble). Since GDP shares obviously have to add up to 100% (at least when the statistical discrepancy is taken care of), if exports develop very differently for the current and constant price series, so will all the shares, including investments to GDP.

Instead of focusing on how the share of investment in GDP develops, we can look at the growth rate of investment, which is not subject to an adding up constraint. To avoid having inflation that has varied greatly over the years distorting the analysis, growth should be measured in real terms. This implies using either the constant price series or taking the current price series and converting it to dollars with the idea that the exchange rate will move in a direction opposite to that of inflation and provide a measure that is closer to real growth in investments. Since the next step of the analysis involves exploring how capital flows (which are measured in dollars in the balance of payments statistics) are related to investments, the focus will be on how investments measured in dollars have evolved.

The first observation from Figure 4 is that the growth of investments has varied greatly since the start of transition, which is not surprising given the growth charts we have seen. As expected, investment is more volatile than growth but since we are looking at growth in dollar terms,

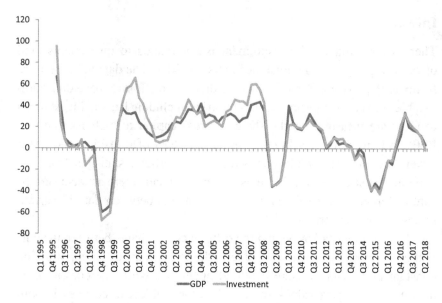

Figure 4:   Investment and GDP growth.

Note: Growth is calculated from the same quarter last year on GDP measured in current terms and converted to USD by using quarterly exchange rates.

Source: Federal Statistics Service and author's calculations.

both series display a very high degree of volatility. Although the initial years of transition were particularly volatile with the initial investment boom followed by the 1998 crash, more recent quarters also display growth rates going from plus to minus 40%, which of course is linked to significant changes in the exchange rate.[5]

What are then the factors that drive changes in investment? In many transition countries, foreign direct investments have been important drivers of investment and growth (see Mileva, 2008). Russia has of course received large foreign investments since 1991, but in many empirical studies of FDI, Russia receives significantly less than what could be expected for an economy the size of Russia.[6] The question here though is whether the FDI

---

[5] In a recent study, Berezinskaya (2017) notes that there has been no growth in investment measured in constant ruble terms in recent years and this is the first prolonged stagnation of investments since Putin became president.

[6] Both Bevan *et al.* (2004) and Frenkel *et al.* (2004) find significant negative Russian dummies in cross-country regressions of FDI determinants.

that comes to Russia has a significant impact on investments in fixed capital at the macro level. In addition to FDI, we can expect that changes in international oil prices will affect investment growth just as they explain overall growth of the economy. Finally, institutional factors that are thought to affect the investment climate could impact investment growth. Table 2 shows the result from running linear regressions on changes in investments on changes in oil prices, changes in foreign direct investments and changes in institutional factors as measured by the EBRD's transition index and a composite index based on the World Governance indicators on rule of law, control of corruption and regulatory quality.

The main result from this is that foreign direct investments do lead to higher investments as do increases in oil prices. The coefficient on FDI is larger than 1, which suggests that there are positive spillovers from FDI to other domestic investments (or crowding in rather than crowding out of domestically financed investments) similar to the finding in Mileva (2008).

At the same time, the amount of FDI is relatively small compared to overall investment and the share has fallen dramatically since the global

Table 2: Correlates of investments.

	Fixed capital investments (USD)	
	(I)	(II)
FDI inflows lagged	1.521	1.586
t-val	*6.51*	*5.97*
Oil price	0.473	0.386
t-val	*3.37*	*2.79*
EBRD index		13.187
t-val		*0.48*
WGI index		−49.998
t-val		*−1.04*
Constant	2.265	3.658
t-val	1.62	*2.65*
Obs	88	74
Adj. R^2	0.37	0.35

Note: All variables are changes in the respective variable.
Source: Author's estimates based on data from Central Bank of Russia, EBRD, World Governance Indicators and US Energy Information Administration.

financial crisis, from a peak of over 20% in 2007 to around 5% in 2018. FDI can also play an important role in modernising and diversifying the economy since foreign investments can be associated with important knowledge transfers in terms of both technology and management practices that can facilitate a structural change of the economy. Therefore, attracting FDI should be high on the list of any policymaker that is serious about generating growth and diversifying the economy. However, the institutional factors fail to generate any significant impact on investments, which is counter to regular arguments on the importance of institutions (see, e.g., Roland, 2000 and Gorodnichenko and Roland, 2016). This can be a result of insufficient variation in the institutional variables over this time period or that the simple analysis here does not account for more complicated causal stories. This may lead to problems with endogeneity with the institutional factors, and this part of the analysis should not be taken too literally for this reason. However, there is clearly an empirical regularity between inflows of foreign direct investments and investments in fixed capital at the macro level that warrants a closer look at capital flows.

Capital Flows

Capital flows are an important link between the domestic economy and global markets in any country. The role of capital flows is not only to finance investments, transfer knowledge and generate growth at home, which is the main focus here, but also to facilitate consumption smoothing and risk management. The latter reasons for international capital flows are likely to have been highly important to understand capital flows between Russia and the rest of the world. The composition and magnitude of flows can provide important signals on how both residents and foreign entities view the growth prospects of a country as well as the functioning of financial markets and the institutions that protect property rights.[7] In emerging markets, sudden reversals of capital flows (sudden stops) have been

---

[7]Fernandez-Arias and Hausmann (2000) discuss the links between institutional quality and the level and composition of capital flows and note that better institutions increase overall flows but that the share of FDI in total flows is negatively correlated with institutional quality.

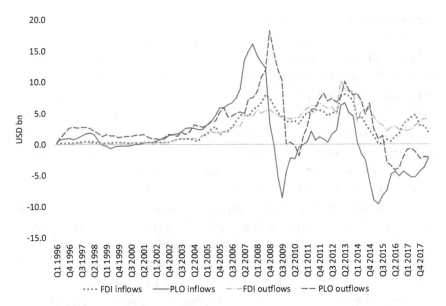

Figure 5:   Private sector capital flows.

Source: Central Bank of Russia.

shown to be the costliest shock that these countries face in terms of loss of income at the macro level (Becker and Mauro, 2006).[8] This suggests that avoiding sudden stops is a key factor for long-term growth and macroeconomic stability.

Figure 5 shows private capital flows in the form of foreign direct investments (FDIs) and portfolio, loans and other flows (PLO).[9] Inflows

---

[8]Calvo (1998) provides a more in-depth analysis of "sudden stops", which apparently come from a banker that said that "it is not the speed that kills, it is the sudden stop".

[9]Capital flows in the balance of payments statistics are divided into foreign direct investments, portfolio flows and "other" flows that include bank loans between domestic and foreign entities. There are also unaccounted flows that fall under the heading "errors and omissions", which capture both statistical errors and unregistered flows that would include capital flight that do not go through the banking system or other official channels. As a country's economic and financial system matures and the statistical agency develops, this component tends to shrink. The balance of payments statistics also makes a distinction between flows in the private sector versus government institutions. This may sound as a relatively straightforward split, but in a country like Russia where many of the large companies have a significant share of government ownership, the distinction is not as clear as

and outflows are shown separately for each category, and note that for the PLO flows, both inflows and outflows can (and do) take on negative values. A number of observations are worth mentioning here. First of all, the PLO flows are both greater in absolute terms and much more volatile than FDI flows. This is very much in line with the discussion about "hot money" flows to emerging markets that say that FDI flows ("good cholesterol") are more stable and beneficial for growth, while portfolio flows and loans ("bad cholesterol") are volatile and associated with the problems of sudden stops discussed earlier (see Fernandez-Arias and Hausmann, 2000). The Russian story seems to be in line with this reasoning, given that large portfolio and loan inflows are in many periods followed by equally large outflows. FDI flows follow a different pattern where inflows and outflows are moving up and down at the same time. This indicates that there are common factors driving both FDI inflows and outflows but no sign that FDI inflows lead to outflows shortly after.

Figure 5 does not provide a very clear picture of how net capital flows have developed over time and what cumulative implications are at the macro level. Figure 6 therefore shows the cumulative net capital flows for FDI, portfolio and loans, and errors and omissions as well as the grand total of private sector capital flows.

Between 1995 and the first quarter of 2018, 700 billion dollars left Russia. This is twice as much as all of the fixed capital investments in 2017 and could obviously have boosted growth significantly if it had been invested in Russia instead. That does not mean that zero flows would have been optimal for the investors making these decisions, but it shows clearly that these flows are extremely important for the macroeconomic development of Russia. Most of the capital left in the form of portfolio flows and loans, but at the end of the sample, all three categories contribute to the outflows. FDI was for a long time the only component that recorded a cumulative net inflow over the period, but after the global financial crisis,

---

it may appear. The share of government ownership in the Russian economy varies over time and across studies, but estimates suggest that the government could account for up to 70% of the economy overall and own 30–50% of asset (see Abramov *et al.*, 2017) and that the share of the government in the economy has increased during Putin's days in office (Djankov, 2015).

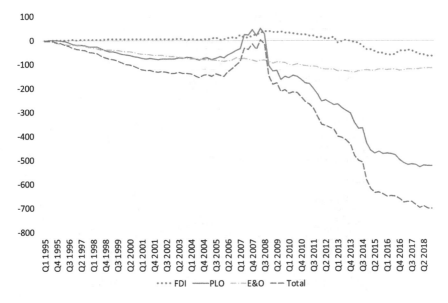

Figure 6: Capital outflows from private sector.

Source: Central Bank of Russia and author's calculations.

there has been a steady outflow in this category as well and these outflows accelerated in 2014. More generally, the global financial crisis represents a very clear shift in capital flows, and outflows then accelerated when sanctions were introduced in 2014 before there was some levelling off in 2018.

The question is then what factors may be behind these capital flows. In principle, we should expect flows to be correlated with the returns and risk on investment in Russia versus the rest of the world. There are different ways of trying to gauge expected returns and risk, but some relatively straightforward measures can be derived from the stock markets in Russia and abroad. Here, we use daily data on the Russian dollar index RTS and the S&P500 index from the US stock market. We also add daily data on oil prices since this is an important determinant of growth in Russia and also a source of foreign capital that can either be invested at home or abroad. From these data, we compute the daily returns and rolling 20- and 60-days standard deviations of our series and take quarterly averages of these measures to generate series with the same frequency that we have

Table 3:   Correlates of private capital flows.

	Net private outflows (USD)	
	(I)	(II)
RTS volatility	34.292	
t-val	*2.98*	
RTS return	0.030	
t-val	*0.00*	
S&P volatility	13.536	
t-val	*0.79*	
S&P return	134.834	
t-val	*2.14*	
Oil price volatility	−10.582	*1.78*
t-val	*−0.94*	*0.18*
Oil price change	−45.067	−28.07
t-val	*−1.63*	*−0.96*
Volatility diff		29.534
t-val		*2.48*
Return diff		6.983
t-val		*0.22*
Constant	−24.525	3.890
t-val	−1.18	*0.19*
Obs	73	73
Adj. R sq.	0.20	0.07

Note: Volatility diff is RTS volatility minus S&P volatility and Return diff is S&P return minus RTS return, so both coefficients are expected to be positive.

for capital flows. This then allows us to run a regression with net capital outflows being explained by the returns and volatility of the Russian and US financial investments as well as oil that are shown in Table 3.

The regression results are quite interesting. The most statistically significant variable is the volatility on the Russian market, which has the expected positive sign that indicates that increased volatility increases net capital outflows. The other statistically significant variable is returns in the US market, but there is no offsetting effect from returns in the Russian market. The oil price variables are also not significant, which is perhaps a bit surprising given their importance for growth and investments. However, it could be the case that high oil prices both generate foreign exchange earnings in Russia that could leave the country as capital flows and encourage inflows into the Russian economy, and this estimate reflects that these two forces cancel each other out.

In principle, the relative volatility and return between the domestic and foreign market should matter for flows, and if the regression is run on these variables instead, the importance of volatility is further enhanced while the return variable becomes statistically insignificant. However, the overall explanatory power of such a regression is greatly reduced and is the reason the more detailed specification discussed earlier is preferred. The exact causal links and mechanisms cannot be investigated fully in this setting since there may be an effect going from capital flows from Russia to volatility in the Russian stock market. In the end, however, it is clear that volatility is an important correlate of capital flows that warrant a closer look.

Determinants of Returns and Volatility

The next item to investigate is how returns and uncertainty in the Russian stock market have developed and to what extent this can be understood by external and domestic factors. Again, the stock market here is viewed as a way to measure returns and uncertainty more broadly that would be correlated with capital flows, investments and likely also consumer confidence (which is not analysed further here but is an important demand side factor for growth). There are several factors that we can expect will affect returns and volatility on the Russian stock market. First, stock markets today are linked globally, and the developments on global markets are captured by the US market's S&P500 index. We also know that many of the companies on the Russian stock market are linked to the energy sector, and therefore, international oil prices should matter for the valuation of the RTS. The S&P500 and Brent oil price are exogenous factors, so we can run a regression explaining variation in the return and volatility of the RTS with these variables as explanatory variables.

Table 4:   Correlates of stock market returns and volatility.

	RTS return		RTS 20 day vol	
	1995–2018	2010–2018	1995–2018	2010–2018
S&P return	0.488	0.643		
t-val	19.16	18.34		
S&P return lag	0.486	0.371		
t-val	19.01	10.55		
Brent return	0.191	0.299		
t-val	14.46	17.36		
Brent return lag	0.064	0.033		
t-val	4.84	1.94		
S&P 20 day vol			0.983	0.764
t-val			41.28	24.92
Brent 20 day vol			0.278	0.272
t-val			16.78	14.97
Constant	0.025	−0.047	0.537	0.513
t-val	0.85	−1.54	15.31	14.37
Obs	6021	2282	2282	6003
Adj. R sq.	0.15	0.32	0.34	0.34

Source: Author's estimate based on market data.

Table 4 confirms that US stock market returns and changes in oil prices have a significant impact on returns in the Russian market. The estimation shows that coefficients are quite robust to estimating the relationship since the start of the RTS index in 1995 or focusing on the years after the global financial crisis.[10] In the case of returns, the lags of US returns and oil price changes are significant, which is somewhat contrary to regular arguments about efficient markets that would immediately include all new information. The reasons for this apparent anomaly could include rather mechanical explanations such that the markets are located

---

[10]Nivorozhkin and Castagneto-Gissey (2016) focus on how relationships between the Russian stock market and international markets have changed significantly after the Ukrainian crisis. This is consistent with the finding here that there are more excessive volatility and negative return days in 2014/2015 than in earlier periods.

in different time zones, to market frictions that would lead to a somewhat delayed response.[11] The coefficients on the lags are slightly smaller in the more recent years, which could be a result of reduced frictions, but the coefficients are still highly significant in both samples.

For volatility in the Russian market, the volatility in the US market and the volatility in oil prices are also highly significant and together explain about a third of the Russian volatility. The coefficients are again stable across the two samples and do not indicate a structural break in the relationship between the earlier and later time period. Note that the full set of explanatory variables that are included in the table were allowed to enter the first set of regressions, but insignificant variables were omitted from the final estimation to generate robust models from which we can compute residuals in the next stage.

The residuals computed from the estimated model mentioned earlier show the returns and volatility in the RTS that are unexplained by the external factors that are included in the model. This would thus include both domestic and foreign policy events that are not captured by changes in the US market or oil prices. Of course, the residuals will also include company-specific factors that influence the expected performance of the Russian stock market that we would not think of as Russian domestic or foreign policy events. For this reason, the residuals are noisy signals of these factors, but we can still use the residuals to look at what happens in the market at times when we know there are important policy events taking place and we have at least filtered out two important external sources of variation in the Russian market.

The residual (or excess) returns and volatility are shown in Figure 7. It is clear that the early years of transition were more volatile in the stock market as well, but at around the new millennium, volatility went down. However, this relative calm was then interrupted with the global financial crisis and then again in 2014. Since this chapter is about macroeconomic developments during the reign of Putin, we will investigate what events have coincided with a large movement in the stock market since 2000.

---

[11]Peresetsky (2011) instead uses the Japanese Nikkei index since this is closer in terms of time, but since the S&P is closer to a global stock market index and this analysis is not about market efficiency, the fact that we have to use a lag of S&P to get a good specification is not an issue.

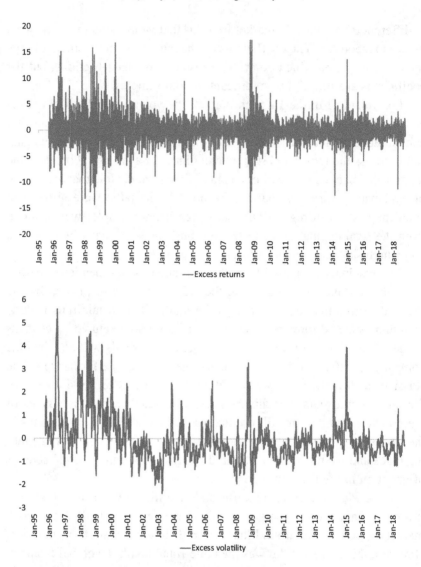

Figure 7:   Excess returns and volatility.

Source: Author's calculations based on data and estimations in Table 4.

In order to select the events to investigate further, we focus on days where the residuals are unusually large and volatility is at extreme levels. In Figure 8, this is defined as negative daily returns of more than 5% and a rolling 20-day daily return volatility of more than 2%. In terms of number of days with negative returns, years 2000 and 2008 stand out. Both years were associated with major events in global financial markets (dot-com crash and global financial crisis), while in 2000, Putin was elected president for the first time and Russia was fighting a war in Chechnya. As for years with high volatility, 2000 and 2008 are again high on the list, but so are 2003 and 2014 (and 2015). In 2003, there was the Yukos affair and trial of its owner Mikhail Khodorkovsky, and in 2014/2015 there was the annexation of Crimea, involvement in Eastern Ukraine and long list of sanctions and counter-sanctions between Russia and the West. For sure, a significant amount of volatility in the Russian market is due to external events, but an even greater amount of volatility is home-made by Russian domestic and foreign policy decisions during Putin's term in office. It is again important to note that volatility plays a key role around the home-made events, so studies that simply focus on the impact on returns and absolute levels of capital flows may miss a significant part of the effect these events will have on investments and future growth.

The observations from Figure 8 can be complemented by a listing of the most negative days on the Russian market and the days with the highest volatility. If we construct a top-20 list of the days with the most negative returns since Putin became president, 2008 stands out with 9 of the 20 days with the stock market falling by 16% on the worst day as Russia was hit by the global financial crisis. The year 2014 accounted for 3 of the 20 worst days with a 1-day drop of 12% being the worst day in 2014. Other years have one or two days of the stock market losing around 10%. When we instead list the 20 days with the highest volatility, 2014 and 2015 account for a stunning 18 of 20 days with the highest volatility, while 2008 only has 1 day on the volatility top-20 list. This again underlines how much uncertainty the annexation of Crimea and subsequent involvement in Eastern Ukraine has generated in the Russian market and most likely in the economy in general.

Since we have seen how volatility reduces capital flows, which in turn lowers investments and growth, this home-made uncertainty carries significant costs both in terms of lost incomes and approval for the president. In the end, these long-run costs have to be weighed against the short-run gains in popularity that the Russian leadership enjoys.

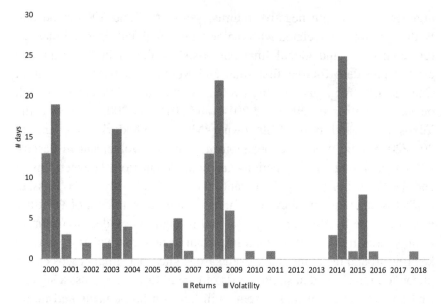

Figure 8:   Days of large negative returns and high volatility.

Source: Author's calculations based on residuals from estimation in Table 4.

Conclusions and Outlook

Growth is a key economic indicator in Russia as elsewhere, with direct effects on the leadership's popularity even if this effect at times is overshadowed by other (often external) events. How to diversify the economy away from oil and boost long-term growth has been the subject of many policy discussion and reform programmes as well as academic studies [see, for example, Kudrin and Gurvich (2015)]. In the academic literature, the focus is often on the role of institutions to create a business environment conducive to sustainable growth and strengthening institutions is an often-heard argument in Russia as well. In particular, improving rule of law, property rights and control of corruption are mentioned.[12]

It is hard to see why this advice would not be true for Russia, given its current rankings in these areas and the importance of these factors in leading

---

[12]See, for example, Knack and Keefer (1995) and Knack (1996) for property rights institutions, Mauro (1995) for corruption and growth and Acemoglu *et al.* (2014) for the importance of democratic institutions for growth.

academic studies of institutions and growth (see, e.g., Rodrik *et al.*, 2004 and Barro, 2015). However, it is hard to show that the institutional changes that have taken place in Russia along a number of dimensions including membership in international organisations, EBRD indicators or business rankings have generated growth, investment or trade within the time frames most often used. This is consistent with the finding in Sutyrin and Trofimenko (2017), where the authors look at the effect of formal institutions on FDI flows to Russia and find very little effect from changing institutions.

One reason for the apparent lack of institutional impact on growth is that so much of growth at the macro level is driven by changes in international oil prices, which is not a domestic policy variable, nor linked to institutional developments in Russia. Furthermore, specific policy actions that are not part of an economic development plan create so much uncertainty that it has a greater effect on growth than regular economic policies. In sum, in the short and medium term, it seems that Russian policy actions speak louder than formal institutions when it comes to capital flows and investments, and thus growth.

What does it mean for the Russian outlook? Table 5 summarises Putin's different terms in office along the dimensions that have been discussed in the previous sections. It is clear that the external factors that facilitate growth in Russia have become increasingly less supportive as we move from the first two terms in office to the third. Instead of the massive increases in oil prices that Putin enjoyed in his two first terms, the third term (and the term as prime minister) saw oil prices falling. This change in fortunes was also reflected in income and investment growth, exchange rates, stock market returns and approval ratings.

The fourth term in office for Putin starts at a time of sanctions and counter-sanctions, volatile oil prices and a general uncertainty in the global economy about trade, financial systems and global growth. As the external environment in general and outlook for oil price increases in particular are less supportive of growth, the priority of the president and his economic team should be on policies and actions that facilitate investments that will generate high growth. This is very much in line with the modernisation and diversification agenda that has been repeated many times in Russia but not been implemented. To make the strategy work this time, the focus should be on a combination of institutional reforms that

Table 5: Putin's record on growth and its correlates.

	Putin I 2000	Putin II 2004 Q2	Medvedev 2008 Q2	Putin III 2012 Q2	Putin IV 2018 Q2
Approval rating (Levada poll)	84	72	83	64	79
GDP (2008 RUB)	45443	61004	81936	85208	88158
% change	*34*	*34*	*4*	*3*	*...*
GDP (USD bn)	209	541	1674	2117	1640
% change	*159*	*209*	*26*	*−23*	*...*
Oil price	25	36	141	95	77
% change	*44*	*292*	*−33*	*−19*	*...*
RUB/USD	25	29	24	33	63
% appreciation	*−14*	*21*	*−27*	*−48*	*...*
Investments (USD bn)	30	100	358	450	348
% GDP	*14.4*	*18.5*	*21.4*	*21.3*	*21.2*
% change	*29*	*16*	*−1*	*0*	*...*
FDI inflows (USD bn)	22	163	183	200	*...*
Private net capital inflows (USD bn)	−54	148	−357	−341	*...*
Stock market index	175	585	2243	1357	1151
% change	*234*	*283*	*−40*	*−15*	*...*
# days with extreme volatility	*35*	*5*	*22*	*33*	*...*

Notes: Approval rating, oil price, exchange rate and stock market index are measured at the start of the period. GDP and investments are the levels at the start of the period computed as the sum of the four most recent quarters. FDI inflows and private net capital inflows are the cumulative flows for the duration of the presidential period, where a negative inflow is a net outflow.

create a stable business environment and offer incentives for innovative foreign companies to make investments in Russia. Reforms on paper will not be enough but have to be followed up with a consistent path of implementation and avoiding short-run fixes that undermine long-run institutional capital. The previous analysis has shown that policy actions in the past have overshadowed the role of formal institutions and this lesson has to be kept in mind when implementing a new growth strategy. It is therefore crucial that the president refrains from external policies that in the short run detract from economic shortcomings but in the process also generate more uncertainty that is detrimental to capital inflows, investments and growth. The economist's choice of generating political support through high growth by reforming institutions and avoiding policies that create uncertainty is obvious, but possibly not the most likely choice of Putin in the current domestic and external environment.

References

Abramov, A., Radygin, A. and Chernova, M. (2017). State-owned enterprises in the Russian market: Ownership structure and their role in the economy, *Russian Journal of Economics*, 3(1), 1–23.

Acemoglu, D., Naidu, S., Restrepo, P. and Robinson, J. A. (2014). Democracy does cause growth. NBER Working Paper No. 20004, NBER, Cambridge, MA. Available at http://www.nber.org/papers/w20004.

Åslund, A. (2013). *How Capitalism Was Built: The Transformation of Central and Eastern Europe, Russia, the Caucasus, and Central Asia*, Cambridge University Press, Cambridge, United Kingdom.

Barro, R. J. (2015). Convergence and modernisation, *The Economic Journal*, 125(585), 911–942.

Becker, T. (2013). Crisis prevention, in Rosefielde, S. (ed.), *Prevention and Crisis Management: Lessons for Asia from the 2008 Crisis*, Chapter 6, Scientific Publishing, Singapore.

Becker, T. (2017a). Russia: Macroeconomic challenges, in Rosefielde, S., Kuboniwa, M., Mizobata, S. and Haba, K. (eds.), *The Unwinding of the Globalist Dream: EU, Russia and China*, Chapter 8, World Scientific, Singapore.

Becker, T. (2017b). Investment relations between Sweden and Russia, in Liutho, K., Sutyrin, S. and Blanchard, J. F. (eds.), *The Russian Economy and Foreign Direct Investment*, Chapter 6, Routledge, London.

Becker, T. (2018). Russia's economy under Putin and its impact on the CIS region, in Becker, T. and Oxenstierna, S. (eds.), *The Russian Economy under Putin*, Chapter 2, Routledge, London.

Becker, T. and Mauro, P. (2006). Output drops and the shocks that matter, IMF Working Paper No. 06/172, IMF, Washington, D.C. Available at: https://www.imf.org/external/pubs/ft/wp/2006/wp06172.pdf.

Becker, T. and A. Olofsgård (2018). From abnormal to normal — Two tales of growth from 25 years of transition, *Economics of Transition*, 26(4), 769–800.

Berezinskaya, O. (2017). Investment drought in the Russian economy: Structural characteristics and turnaround perspectives, *Russian Journal of Economics*, 3(1), 71–82.

Bevan, A., Estrin, S. and Meyer, K. (2004). Foreign investment location and institutional development in transition economies, *International Business Review*, 13(1), 43–64.

Calvo, G. A. (1998). Capital flows and capital-market crises: The simple economics of sudden stops, *Journal of Applied Economics*, 1, 35–54.

Chappell, H. W., Jr. (1990). Economic performance, voting, and political support: A unified approach. *The Review of Economics and Statistics*, 72(2), 313–320.

Djankov, S. (2015). *Russia's Economy under Putin: From Crony Capitalism to State Capitalism*, Policy Brief, PB15-18, Peterson Institute for International Economics, Washington, DC.

Fernandez-Arias, E. and Hausmann, R. (2000, March 26). Foreign direct investment: Good cholesterol? Inter-American Development Bank, Research Department Working Paper No. 417.

Frenkel, M., Funke, K. and Stadtmann, G. (2004). A panel analysis of bilateral FDI flows to emerging economies, *Economic Systems*, 28(3), 281–300.

Fortescue, S. (2018). The political economy of Russia: Is it changing, in Becker, T. and Oxenstierna, S. (eds.), *The Russian Economy under Putin*, Chapter 12, Routledge, London.

Gorodnichenko, Y. and Roland, G. (2016). Culture, institutions and the wealth of nations, *Review of Economics and Statistics*, 99(3), 402–416.

IMF. (2018). *World Economic Outlook*. International Monetary Fund, Washington, DC.

Knack, S. (1996). Institutions and the convergence hypothesis: The cross-national evidence, *Public Choice*, 87(3–4), 207–228.

Knack, S. and Keefer, P. (1995). Institutions and economic performance: Cross-country tests using alternative institutional measures, *Economics and Politics*, 7(3), 207–227.

Kudrin, A. and Gurvich, E. (2015). A new growth model for the Russian economy, *Russian Journal of Economics*, 1, 30–54.

Levine, R. and Renelt, D. (1992). A sensitivity analysis of cross-country growth regressions, *American Economic Review*, 82(4), 942–963.

Mauro, P. (1995). Corruption and growth, *The Quarterly Journal of Economics*, 110(3), 681–712.

Mileva, E. (2008). The impact of capital flows on domestic investment in transition economies. ECB Working Paper No. 871. Available at SSRN: https://ssrn.com/abstract=1090546.

Nivorozhkin, E. and Castagneto-Gissey, G. (2016). Russian stock market in the aftermath of the Ukrainian crisis, *Russian Journal of Economics*, 2(1), 23–40.

Peresetsky, A. A. (2011). What determines the behavior of the Russian stock market. MPRA Paper No. 41508.

Rodrik, D., Subramanian, A. and Trebbi, F. (2004). Institutions rule: The primacy of institutions over geography and integration in economic development. *Journal of Economic Growth*, 9(2), 131–165.

Roland, G. (2000). *Transition and Economics: Politics, Markets, and Firms*, MIT Press, Cambridge, MA.

Shleifer, A. and Treisman, D. (2005). A normal country: Russia after communism, *Journal of Economic Perspectives*, 19(1), 151–174.

Shleifer, A. and Treisman, D. (2014). Normal countries: The East 25 years after communism, *Foreign Affairs*, retrieved February 23, 2018, from https://www.foreignaffairs.com/articles/russia-fsu/2014-10-20/normal-countries.

Sutyrin, S. and Trofimenko, O. (2017). Do formal institutions really matter for foreign direct investments to the Russian federation? The case of FDI flows from the European Union to Russia, in Liutho, K., Sutyrin, S. and Blanchard, J. F. (eds.), *The Russian Economy and Foreign Direct Investment*, Chapter 5, Routledge, London.

Chapter 3

State-Led Innovation and Uneven Adaptation in Russia

Satoshi Mizobata

Russia lost its innovation base inherited from the Soviet period during the 1990s.[1] The Putin regime tried to recover lost ground after 2000 by focusing on a long-term growth strategy. Innovation has become a cornerstone of its economic policy seeking to reduce Russia's heavy dependence on natural resource (oil and gas) exports, diversify, enhance international competitiveness and raise labour productivity in an adverse environment hampered by a decreasing population and an ageing society.

Adverse external conditions exacerbate these problems. On the one hand, Western economic sanctions imposed after 2014 compelled Russia to import substitutes. On the other hand, international competition for technological/scientific hegemony intensified. Innovation became essential because productivity deteriorated in all the developed countries (Knyaginin, 2017, p. 20). The German revolution-dubbed "Industry 4.0" (the Fourth Industrial Revolution) designed to meet this challenge threatens to increase Russia's relative technological backwardness.[2] Japan

---

[1] In the USSR of 1970s, more than 4% of GDP was spent in sciences (Kurbanov, 2019, p. 5).

[2] See Federal Ministry of Education and Research (2006). Germany clarified its lack of competitiveness in terms of cost and sought a new level of competitiveness through innovation. In 2011, based on the negative impact of the Lehman shock of 2008, Germany

emulated Germany with its own "Society 5.0" strategy, and China announced its "Made in China 2025" initiative. All these initiatives seek to accelerate long-term growth. The US–China trade war is also partly a political conflict over innovation policy. Even though the "socio-economic situation in Russia has remained difficult" (Mau, 2019, p. 10), Russia adapted itself to these global trends. It is energetically pursuing its own long-term growth and innovation strategies.

This chapter uses three criteria to evaluate the results of Russia's long-term growth and innovation strategies. It looks at institutional aspects of state-led innovation, the timeliness of Russia's innovations and technological diffusion against the background of global trends.

Evolution of Innovation Policy: Emergence of Long-term Strategy

The Kremlin's Soviet legacy handicaps its innovation policy. Privatisation, property right reforms and market building after 1992 in the wake of a "brain drain" failed to eradicate all the deficiencies of the Soviet command economy (Fonotov, 2013, p. 35). Legal instability weakened the effects of market-oriented measures (Fonotov, 2013, pp. 36–39). A collapse of "innovation industries" made it difficult to implement innovation policy. As a result, fixed assets sharply diminished and equipment obsolesced during the 1990s. Innovation capacity declined due to poor state leadership, inadequate commercialisation, defective implementation and bias towards the defence sector.

Russia's innovation strategy depended on the state sector from the outset of the post-Soviet period because of its backward Soviet era production base, traditional Soviet education/industry–university cooperation and poor linkages with the international division of labour. Russia's overdependence on natural resource exports (Figure 1) and technology imports (including foreign intellectual property) further impaired innovation.

---

started the new controversy on innovation, and in 2013 Recommendations for implementing the strategic initiative Industrie 4.0 (digitalisation), Final report of the Industrie 4.0 Working Group, was adopted. In 2015, Germany expanded the sphere of this initiative to include the service sector.

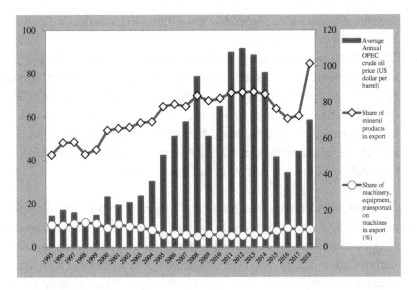

Figure 1: Change of export structure.

Note: Oil price indicated in the right axis, and both shares are indicated in the left axis.

Source: Rosstat, http://www.gks.ru, accessed on 1 May 2019.

Russia tried to overcome these debilities in the 2000s with three long-term strategies:

- The first was "The Russian Federation Socio-Economic Development till 2010" drafted under the Ministry of Economic Development and Trade in 2000, when Vladimir Putin became President. Even though this strategy stressed modernisation, unrealistic assumptions impaired implementation (Dmitriev and Yurtaev, 2010, p. 109).
- The second strategy was "The Russian Federation Long-term Socio-economic Development till 2020" drafted by the National Research University Higher School of Economics and the Russian Presidential Academy of National Economy and Public Administration (Mau and Kuziminov, 2013). It had 6 parts and 25 chapters. The new economic growth model and social policy were at its centre. The government chose not to officially adopt the 2020 strategy and informal implementation was perfunctory for a host of reasons including political machinations, administrative shortcomings, conflicting specialist

views, lobbying and stakeholder opposition (Belanovsky *et al.*, 2016; Polterovich *et al.*, 2017).

- Thereafter, "modernisation" became the dominant theme. Despite the rapid economic growth (recovery) in the first half of the 2000s, Russia failed to reduce its heavy dependence on natural resources. The "resource curse" is difficult to break. "Putin warned of the danger of Russia turning into a third-world country" (Tsygankov, 2014, p. 117) and tried to avert the danger with neoliberal macroeconomic stabilisation and economic recovery, but did not succeed.

In May 2009, the Council for Economic Modernisation was established to promote and oversee breakthroughs in energy efficiency, atomic power, space, telecommunications, medical technologies and strategic information technologies. The Science City, *Skolkovo*, and "national champions" phenomenon exemplify this initiative.[3] Strategy 2020 announced in March 2012 emphasises the need for innovation-driven growth and human capital development. The government adopted a new policy for "Innovative Development Strategy to 2020" (approved on December 8, 2011, No.2227-r, hereafter the "Development Strategy 2020") and the "State Program for Science and Technology Development" (December 20, 2012). The latter programme codifies the tactics for fulfilling "Development Strategy 2020". It stipulates that 3% of the GDP must be dedicated to R&D until 2020 to sustain fundamental sciences and finance priority fields. The approach mimics the mixed model of the Asian development driven by technology transfer from leading countries. The policy includes unrealistic targets like massive high-tech job creation.

Russia wants to move towards a growth strategy compatible with state capitalism. It has become more autarkic, prodded by Western economic and Kremlin counter-import sanctions. The economic sanctions from the West and Russia's own counter-sanctions built barriers against imports and international financing. Shrinking external economic relations brought about cancellations of military technology collaborations, military/civil

---

[3]National champion is a governmental policy through which large organisations not only seek profit but also help "advance the interests of the nation"; the government sets policies favouring these organisations.

technology purchases and joint R&D efforts (Afontsev, 2015, p. 22). The government regarded "the forced import substitution" policy as an anti-crisis measure and drafted numerous counter-initiatives such as state projects, preferential taxes, subsidies, preferential credit, loan guarantees and state orders. It drafted numerous industrial policies to accelerate domestic production. However, forced import substitution did not spur innovation and may have stifling consequences over the long term (Afontsev, 2015, p. 34). The Board of Audit pointed out that import substitution did not satisfy domestic equipment demands (Zagashvili, 2016, p. 146). The lack of domestic import substitutes hindered the substitution process, and high import prices impeded innovation.

The new strategy has become a key force for economic diversification (Mizobata, 2017). On the instructions of the president, the draft of "Strategy for the Science and Technological Development of the RF till 2035" was drawn up by the Center for Strategic Research on May 5, 2016, in parallel with the national security strategy (Ministry of Economic Development, 2016, p. 22). The draft addressed the following issues: the national security threat; global changes in technology; accumulated structural imbalance in the Russian economy; changes in labour markets, social sphere and healthcare; environmental sustainability; food security; the intensification of international competition; and energy efficiency. The main strategic threats to the national economy are poor competitiveness, high dependence on external economic circumstances and technological laggardness. Russia's relatively high technological backwardness and dependence on foreign scientific equipment supplies jeopardise national security.

The updated version of the "Development Strategy 2020", update strategy till 2035, limns three alternative long-term strategies for Russia: (1) a science and technology leader, (2) a leader in specialised sectors and (3) a nation dependent on the imported technology (Table 1). The first scenario is the most attractive because state innovation and industrial policy are indispensable for national security and development (Medvedev, 2016, pp. 6–7).

The presidential decree "Strategy for the Science and Technological Development of the RF" announced in December 2016 elaborated the policy's principles, priorities and guidelines. It stressed the balanced

Table 1:   Basic scenarios of science, technology and innovation development till 2035.

	New economy leader	Leader with tradition	Import dependence
Science and technology policy	Original competent centre, growth of private leader companies	Energy, defence and transportation technology, cooperation with BRICS and the Shanghai Cooperation	Energy, defence and transportation technology, cooperation with BRICS and the Shanghai Cooperation
Institutions	Support of the domestic business	Innovation by big business	Liberalisation and foreign FDI
Technological leader	Local leader	Traditional specialisation	Technology import
Indicators in 2031–2035 by GDP annual growth, labour productivity annual growth, R&D expenditure in GDP, total factor productivity (in turn from the first, %)	4.0, 3.8, 1.73, 1.87	3.4, 3.4, 1.57, 1.12	2.6, 2.9, 1.21, 0.95

Source: The draft of "Strategy for the Science and Technological Development of the RF till 2035", p. 62.

growth of private investments targeted to exceed government funding by 2035. Moreover, the president signed the decree on "National Goals and Strategic Objectives of the RF through to 2024" (May 7, 2018) making population growth and reducing poverty as important priorities. Enhancing the national security ("Russian National Security Strategy" approved in December 2015) was declared an important innovational priority. The concept of national security covers a wide range of state and public security activities, including improving life quality and the economic growth. Science, technology and education are all considered indispensable for realising these purposes. In March 2019, the government adopted the latest national programme on "Science and Technological Development in the RF" from 2019 to 2030. It includes five sub-programmes: development of national intellectual capital; guarantee of global competitiveness of the Russian higher education; fundamental science for long-term development of society/state and competitiveness assurance; a comprehensive science and technology programme and an extensive innovation infrastructure.

State-Led Innovation Policy and Policy Changes

Russia's innovation policy is state led. The government finances innovation and promotes associated legal institutions, industrial policy and infrastructure. This makes Russian innovation strategy state-capitalist. The government influences the innovation activities of private firms, especially vertically integrated state corporations (Uvarov, 2013, p. 94). They are key players in education, R&D, entrepreneurship, venture capital and start-ups. State support is provided by the state development agencies (VEB for long-term financing institution), technology development support (Rosnano and RVC) and government crisis support (*Ekspert*, No. 3, 15–21 January 2018).

The National Innovation System (NIS) guides state-led innovation. Russia was a latecomer in developing an NIS. The NIS creates government research institutions and infrastructure. It mandates education, R&D, service, entrepreneurship and innovation infrastructure sectors as well as scientific cities and their organisation and government enterprises (Akinfeeva and Abramov, 2015, p. 136). Large-scale state corporations and vertically integrated state-owned enterprises play leading roles in innovation.[4] The anti-competitiveness of the approach is rooted in traditional domestic networks (Fonotov, 2015). It is path dependent (Klochikhin, 2012)[5] and a source of inefficiency requiring constant attention (Emel'yanov, 2013, p. 6).

The year 2014 was epochal. On April 15, 2014, the government adopted the state programme "Economic Development and Innovation Economy", which included sub-programmes on improving the business environment, small-medium enterprises support and innovation. It strategically planned basic security and economic development tasks. Funding was channelled through special target programmes. Federal Law of June 28, 2014, No. 172-FZ "On Strategic Planning in the Russian Federation (RF)" became the legal framework for innovation and long-term strategy planning. The April 2014 state programme "Information

---

[4] *Ibid.*
[5] From the geographical angle. Crescenzi and Jaax (2017) emphasises a strong path-dependency.

Society 2011–2020"[6] sought to improve the quality of life with information communication technologies, as did the presidential decree "Development Strategy of Information Society in 2017–2030".

The National Technology Initiative (NTI) implemented this new strategy on December 4, 2014. It heralded the creation of new 100 billion dollar markets which will make Russia a global technology leader by 2035 (https://asi.ru/eng/nti, accessed on 1 May 2019) and establish the Agency for Strategic Initiative (ASI) in 2015. The Russian Venture Company served as an agent for the project office.

NTI differs significantly from prior programmes because it encourages private participation. It is a long-term comprehensive initiative for sustaining Russian enterprise leadership in high-technology markets based on private–public partnership (Idrisov *et al.*, 2018, p. 12).[7] Prominent companies involved in the project include AeroNet (aircrafts and space); MariNet (unmanned maritime transport); NeuroNet (development of Internet and biotechnology markets); EnergyNet (knowledge-intensive energy); AutoNet (unmanned transportation); HealthNet (medicine); SafeNet (personal security system); FinNet (financial systems and currencies); FoodNet (food and water); Digital design; New materials; Big Data and others.

"The Digital Economic Development Programme of Russia till 2035" (No.1632-r), developed in July 2017,[8] makes the digital economy a core element of the innovation programme, following up on President Putin's 2016 address (Bondarenko, 2018). The IT programme aims to make the Kremlin a key global player in the world by diversifying Russia's economic structure with Big Data, e-commerce and smart-grid initiative. Putin envisions the digital economy eventually contributing 19–34% of the aggregate GDP growth.

The Ministry of Information and Communication was renamed the Ministry of Digital Development, Information and Communication in May 2018. It promotes ICT development. The national project predicts that

---

[6]The original programme was drafted by the Ministry of Information in October 2010.

[7]Dmitry Peskov (Director of the Direction "Young Professionals" of the ASI) emphasises that "the NIS cannot be created by bureaucratic methods" (https://asi.ru/eng/nti, accessed on 1 May 2019).

[8]Simultaneously, the government adopted the federal law on "Security of critical information infrastructure in Russia".

domestic expenditures on the digital economy will increase from 1.7% in 2017 to 5.1% of the GDP in 2024. The core funding will come from the federal budget. The digital economy has been given pride of place at the core of innovation and growth strategy, which includes 5G mobile communications[9] and network building between main cities (*Profile*, No. 19, May 21, 2018).

Russia has vigorously pursued its innovation policy after 2014, driven by fears of economic sanctions and petro shock crises. The Russian version of Germany's "Industry 4.0" has become the core for the long-term economic strategy and the policy covers wide-ranging goals such as national security and improvements in the quality of life. It is also a device for vitalising innovation in the private sector.

Results of Innovation Policy as Evidence

The Kremlin's aggressive policymaking has had an impact on Russia's innovation, especially after the year 2009 (Mizobata, 2016). Russia has increased innovation-related investment and the share of the new innovative goods. R&D expenditure in coke and petroleum products, transportation vehicles, and chemical was especially large, with mixed results.

Innovation-related investment increased, and R&D expenditure grew during the 2000s (Figure 2). However, this increase may be overstated because R&D share of the GDP has been puzzlingly stagnant at just 1%. This is only half of the OECD (The Organisation for Economic Co-operation and Development) average and smaller than that of the other emerging countries. Moreover, the contribution of businesses to R&D expenditure was tiny (0.3% of the GDP). The state provides the lion's share of R&D financing (Figure 3). The public–private structure is the reverse of many OECD countries.

The term "service trade balance" refers to international innovation value transfer. Russia recorded a remarkable expansion in imports (Figure 4).[10] Gains were obtained from oil and gas finance technology transfer as well as machinery and equipment imports. Some activities, such as machinery

---

[9]5G is the fifth-generation cellular network technology providing broadband access.

[10]Technology trade also indicates an increasing deficit, and independent of the economic sanction, it exceeds more than 1 billion dollars (2.1 billion in 2017) (Federal State Statistics Office, *Russian Statistical Yearbook*, http://www.gks.ru, accessed on 25 May 2019).

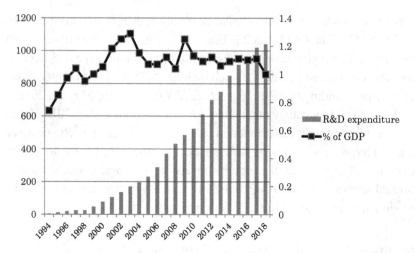

Figure 2:   R&D expenditure trend.

Note: Expenditure indicated in the left axis in billion ruble, and % of GDP in the right axis.

Source: Rosstat, http://www.gks.ru, accessed on 1 May 2019.

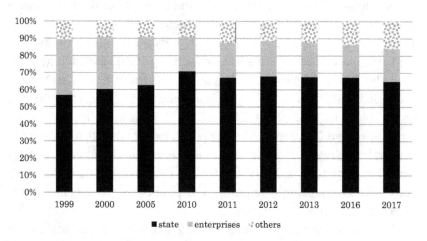

Figure 3:   R&D expenditure by source.

Note: State = budget + non-budget, enterprises = enterprises + foreign capital, others = own funds.

Source: Rosstat, http://www.gks.ru, accessed on 1 October 2018.

design, leasing, and servicing, continue to depend on foreign sources. Dependence on imports has remained, despite import substitution stimulating the effects of economic sanctions.

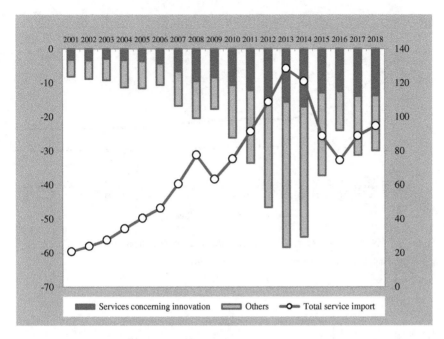

Figure 4:   Service trade deficits (billion dollars).

Note: Total service import indicated in the right axis, and service concerning innovation and others are balance of trade indicated in the left axis.

Source: Central Bank of Russia, http://www.cbr.ru, accessed on 20 May 2019.

The number of R&D staff has declined. Collapse of the Soviet Union destroyed research jobs. The supply of researchers fell sharply during the first half of the 1990s and declined 20.5% more during the period 2000–2017 (Figure 5). The number of assistants plummeted by around 30%, underscoring the magnitude of the brain drain. Such changes distort the age structure of the researchers. Even though the number of young scholars has increased, a sharp reduction in the number of middle-aged staffs engaged in R&D suggests that people with potential to conduct good research have left the country for greener pastures.

As for R&D organisations, after showing a decline in the 2000s, their numbers recently increased. R&D research in state and higher educational institutions rose enough to offset declines in enterprise-based R&D activities, highlighting the state-led character of Russian innovation (Figure 6).

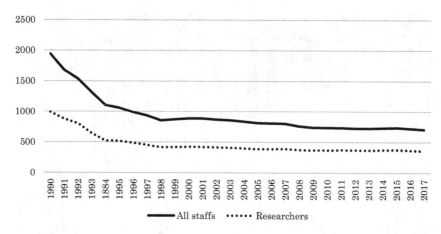

Figure 5:   Number of researchers engaging in R&D in Russia (in thousands).

Source: Rosstat, http://www.gks.ru, accessed on 1 May 2019.

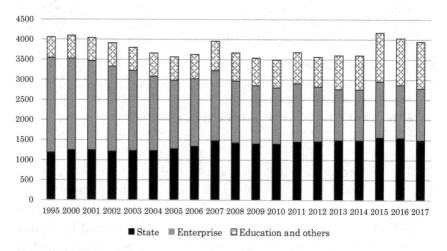

Figure 6:   R&D organisations.

Source: Rosstat, http://www.gks.ru, accessed on 1 May 2019.

Industrial organisations with R&D departments and higher education organisations increased sharply after 2014, reflecting the potential benefits of enterprises and industry–university cooperation.

The statistical data (Gokhberg *et al.*, 2018) show an increase in the shares and services of the total number of shipments after 2010.

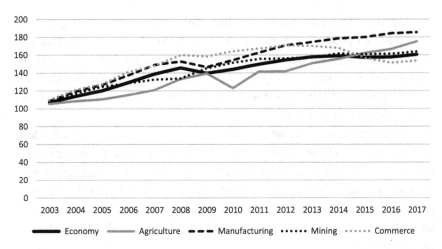

Figure 7: Change of labour productivity by sector (data for the year 2002 in one hundred).

Source: Rosstat, http://www.gks.ru, accessed on 1 May 2019.

The nominal value increased 24.2 times during the period 2000–2016. The share of innovative exports increased 30.3 times during the period 2000–2013 (peak). The largest advances were in transportation machines, coke and oil products, computer and electronics, metalware and chemicals including medicine. The share of innovation goods is high in metallurgy and transportation equipment (by foreign transfer)[11], and in the manufacturing sector, the top three are oil refining, chemicals and machineries (automobile, power plant, and defence). These asymmetries reflect the government's innovation and modernisation priorities. Innovation in the private sector is progressing slowly (World Bank, 2018, pp. 9–10).

Gazprom is making progress on its industrial digital platform (World Bank, 2018, pp. 67–69). The auto company KAMAZ launched a Digitalisation Programme. The UAC, whose main product is the aircraft, created a network of higher education institutions and invested in the Skolkovo Innovation Fund. UAZ invested in digital factories. Promobot produced robots and Conundrum is automating (*Ekspert*, No. 15, 8–14 April 2019).

---

[11]Multinational enterprises facilitate the transmission of global advanced knowledge flows" (Crescenzi and Jaax 2017).

The macroeconomic effect of this innovation has been slight, even though labour productivity improved in the 2000s (Figure 7). Productivity growth in manufacturing after 2009 has been remarkable[12] and agricultural productivity has recently risen. According to the World Bank (2018, pp. 80–85), the digital transformation has targeted agriculture as a top priority for export growth.

Nonetheless, the innovation impact to the economy has been modest. The innovation sphere is limited to priority sectors and the government-led sectors, and high dependence on the state budget has fostered protectionism. In sum, "Russia's technological level is insufficient" (Idrisov *et al.*, 2018, pp. 12–13). The share of mineral resources in export continues to be high and the Russian economy remains vulnerable to volatile oil price (Figure 1).

Unbalanced Technological Diffusion

Diffusion of innovation at the enterprise level is patchy. According to the monitoring survey on the innovation activity of the Russian manufacturing and service sectors by the Higher School of Economics in 2009–2012 (Kuznetsova and Roud, 2013),[13] few enterprises prioritise product innovation and new goods. Their lack of enthusiasm is attributable to the fragile NIS, inefficient and insufficient R&D expenditure, inadequate skills, restricted access to capital markets, a lack of an open innovation culture (World Bank, 2018, p. xxiii) and low resource inputs into research fields. Significant administrative barriers are stultifying (Dezhina, 2016, p. 5). Investors moreover are short-sighted and lack in-house development capabilities, further constraining Russia's domestic innovation potential.[14]

Government statistical data confirm these problems (Figures 8 and 9). Less than 10% of Russian companies actively innovate and have negative

---

[12] However, the level to which robots are used in manufacturing is relatively smaller than that in the developed countries (EBRD, 2018, pp. 36–37).

[13] I use information from the questionnaire surveys provided to top managers in 2005 and 2009 by the High School of Economics (Gonchar, 2014, pp. 195–221).

[14] In the low-technology sectors, enterprises are accustomed to utilising the existing technology, and they do not aim for innovation (Kuznetsova and Roud, 2013, p. 94).

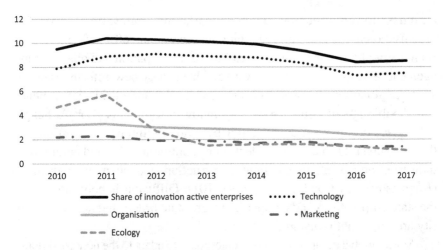

Figure 8: Innovation active enterprises share by type (%).

Source: Rosstat, http://www.gks.ru, accessed on 1 May 2019.

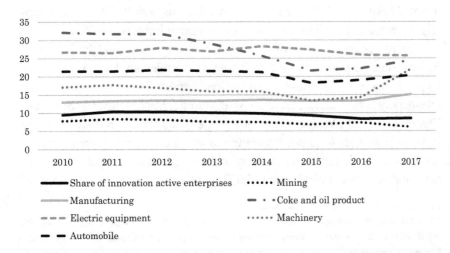

Figure 9: Innovation active enterprises share by type (%).

Source: Rosstat, http://www.gks.ru, accessed on 1 May 2019.

attitudes towards ecological and marketing innovation.[15] As for organisational innovation, even though more than 60% of enterprises implemented reforms to improve employee participation and quality management, enterprises are conservative. They resist new reforms such as strategic alliances, changes in governance, establishing R&D departments and flexible labour hours. Marketing innovation remains poor. Although enterprises do innovate, levels differ by industry. Innovation is strong in the equipment, IT, metallurgy, electronics communication and automobile industries and weak in the light construction and chemical industries (Kuznetsova and Roud, 2013, pp. 91–101). Diffusion is concentrated in the state corporations and companies where state orders and national security are important (Knyaginin, 2017).

Severe global competitions force enterprises to adapt to the new conditions. The people and enterprises/banks/governments must cope with the rapid spread of ICT/digitalisation and the Internet (Figure 10). Search engine and business models using digitalisation have expanded. Taxis, parking, retail and e-transaction, and Internet shopping sites provide illuminating examples (https://www. rbc.ru, 27 April 2018).[16] The share of organisations with ICT technology rapidly increased in the 2000s. Nonetheless, utilisation levels remain low.

Many companies are switching to ICT management models. Successes include state corporations such as Rosnano, Rostelecom, Russia post, military enterprises, Skolkovo innovation centres, software companies (Kaspersky Labs, Yandex, Rambler Media Group, Mail.ru, Rhonda Software, ElcomSoft, ABBYY) and others. Nonetheless, digitalisation is slow. "Many Russian industries have not yet started to adopt emerging technologies, … and companies do not have the ability to develop required digital tools, products, and services" (World Bank, 2018, p. 68). There is no single standard

---

[15]Organisational innovation requires new business procedures, organisation of shops, improvement in external relations, and reductions in management and transaction costs. Marketing innovation means changing the marketing, design and packing, and sales methods and creating a new value strategy. Three and a half percent of Russian enterprises introduced new organisations, and 2.5% of enterprises implemented marketing innovation. Both cases record smaller numbers than total innovation (Kuznetsova and Roud, 2013, p. 98).

[16]Internet in the state order was utilised in 26%, and Internet in Finance in 23%, Website in 43%, and Internet sale in 15% in 2016. IT utilisation rate is low in business and regional gaps are large (*Ekspert,* No. 12, 19–25 March 2018).

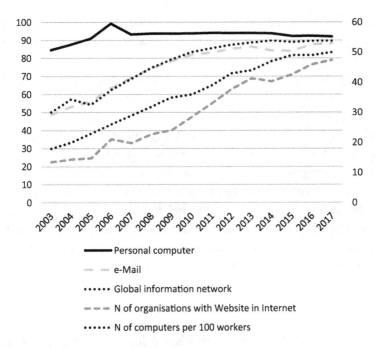

Figure 10:   The spread of ICT (%; number).

Note: Number of organisations and number of computers are indicated in the right axis and others in the left axis (%).

Source: Rosstat, http://www.gks.ru, accessed on 1 May 2019.

for Internet utilisation and enterprises distrust digitalisation. Russia still has a long way to go to achieve a full ICT revolution (Rostelecom, https://www. if24.ru, accessed on 27 April 2018) hindered as it is by economic sanctions and the widening gap between the Russian and foreign companies.

This assessment is confirmed by the pilot survey on the opinions in the manufacturing sector in the second half of 2018 (*Ekonomika i Zhizn,* No. 49, 14 October 2018). While more than 40% of managers consider their digitalisation level high, 35% consider it low. Even though 47% of managers show a positive attitude towards digital technology, 37% do not consider the technology necessary. Positively disposed managers expect digitalisation to increase labour productivity (52%), reduce production costs (44%), increase responsiveness to customers (40%) and spark competitiveness (30%). Barriers to digitalisation persist. Around 60% of managers are concerned about financial stringency and skill shortages. Their cautiousness is attributable to the volatile macroeconomic conditions and sanctions.

Finally, despite the high-technology-led job creation policy, high-tech job growth has been invisible (from 17.49 million in 2013 to 15.98 million in 2016 and 17.11 in 2017), and specialists remain in short supply (Kuvalin *et al.*, 2018, p. 118), despite improvements in higher education. There is a mismatch between education and qualifications. Russia's traditional strengths in human capital and scientific excellence (World Bank, 2018, p. 12) are waning. Educational organisations are conservative (Aleksankov, 2017, pp. 55–56) and Russia's digital education lags the global trend by 6–8 years (Kondakov, 2018). Companies and the public are leery about digitisation and are not yet committed to it. State-led policy is essential in this field.

Conclusion

The distinguishing features of Putin's regime are its energy strategy, administrative discipline and government domination. Even though, the regime has emphasised on "modernization", Russian development is lagging. The economy remains energy dependent and state over-regulation is making it vulnerable to external shocks. The economic crisis, sanctions/ counter-sanctions and global industrial competition have forced Russia to modify its growth strategy. Innovation has become the new cornerstone of Russian economic growth.

The NIS in all countries is path dependent. Russia's state-led innovation policy is aimed for the long term. The state-led National Technology and Digital Economy Initiatives of 2014 marked a turning point in the intensification of state-led development. State corporations and government became the main engines for innovation, with the government introducing fresh initiatives like cluster formations, incubators, academic reforms and state industrial policies.

The results have been mixed. On the one hand, R&D expenditure increased, and some innovation models succeeded. Innovation increased, and the research organisations grew. On the other hand, the share of GDP devoted to innovation has been static, and state control has increased. Even though technology innovation slightly improved, organisational/ marketing/ecological innovation remains immature.

Enterprises' adaptation has been uneven. Information and communication technologies diffused broadly into Russian business/society, but attitudes towards digitalisation have been negative, and the impact of digitalisation on modernisation has been weak. Russia will not be able to keep pace with its competitors economically and militarily unless it does a better job of facilitating innovation.

References

Afontsev, S. (2015). Way out from crisis under the conditions of sanction: Mission impossible? *Voprosy Ekonomiki,* 4, 20–36 (in Russian).

Akinfeeva, E. and Abramov, V. (2015). The role of science cities in the development of national innovation system of Russia, *Problemy Prognozirovaniya,* 1, 129–140 (in Russian).

Aleksankov, A. M. (2017). The fourth industrial revolution and modernization of education: The global experience, *Strategicheskie Prioritety,* 1, 53–69. http://sec.chgik.ru/wp-content/uploads/2017/06/SP-17-1.pdf (in Russian).

Belanovsky, S. A., Dmitriev, M. E., Komarov, V. M., Komin, M. O., Kotyubinsky, V. A. and Nikol'skaya, A. V. (2016). *Analysis of Factors Executing Top-level Strategic Planning Documents,* TsSR, Saint Petersburg (in Russian).

Bondarenko V.M. (2018) Structural modernization under the condition of digital economy formation, *MIR,* 9 (2), 172–191 (in Russian).

Crescenzi R. and Jaax A. (2017) Innovation in Russia: the territorial dimension, *Economic Geography,* 93(1), 66–88, DOI: 10.1080/00130095.2016.1208532.

Dezhina I. (2016) Innovation policy in Russia: development, challenges and prospects, *L'Observatoire,* Centre D'analyse de la CCI France Russie, 12, February 2016, 1–16.

Dmitriev, M. and Yurtaev, A. (2010). Strategy 2010: Results of execution after 10 years, *Ekonomicheskaya Politika,* 3, 107–114 (in Russian).

EBRD (2018) *Transition Report 2018-19 Work in Transition,* EBRD, London, 1–114.

Emel'yanov Yu.S. (2013) *Public-Private Partnership: Innovation and Investment,* URSS, Moscow. (in Russian).

Federal Ministry of Education and Research (2006) *The High-Tech Strategy for Germany,* Public Relations Division, Germany, 1–110.

Fonotov A. (2013) The role of the government science and technology policy in enhancing innovation activity of Russian enterprises, *Problemy Prognozirovaniya*, 3, 35–47 (in Russian).

Fonotov A. (2015) Strategic goals of innovation policy, *Problemy Prognozirovaniya*, 5, 40–51 (in Russian).

Gokhberg, L. M., *et al.*, eds. (2018). *Indicators of Innovation Activity*, Higher School of Economics, Moscow.

Gonchar K. (2014) Innovation behaviour of traditional industrial firms, B. Kuznetsova ed., *Study on Modernization of Russian Industry: Firm Behaviour*, Higher School of Economics, Moscow (in Russian).

Idrisov G.I., Knyaginin V.N., Kudrin A.L., Rozhkova E.S. (2018) New technological revolution: Challenges and opportunities for Russia, *Voprosy Economiki*, 4, 5–25 (in Russian).

Kondakov, A. (2018). *Education in the Period of the Fourth Revolution*, https://vogazeta.ru, accessed on 27 April 2018.

Klochikhin E.A. (2012). Russia's innovation policy: Stubborn path-dependencies and new approaches, *Research Policy*, 41, 9: 1620–1630.

Knyaginin V.N. (Ed.) (2017). *New Technological Revolution: Challenges and Possibilities for Russia*, Centre for Strategy Research, Moscow, 1–134 (in Russian).

Kurbanov, T. (2019). Russia on the way of breakthrough to the new technological structure: Economic and financial aspects, *Ekonomist*, 3, 3–12 (in Russian).

Kuvalin D.B., Moiseev A.K., Lavrinenko P.A. (2018) Russian enterprises at the end of 2017: a lack of significant all economic changes and progresses of machine building, *Problemy Prognozirovaniya*, 3, 105–121 (in Russian).

Kuznetsova T. and Roud V. (2013) Competition, innovation and strategy: empirical evidence from Russian enterprises, *Voprosy Ekonomiki*, 12, 86–108 (in Russian).

Mau V.A. (2019). National goals and model of economic growth: New in the Russian socio-economic policy of 2018–2019, *Voprosy Ekonomiki*, 3, 5–28 (in Russian).

Mau, V. A. and Kuziminov Ya, I. (eds.). (2013). *Strategy 2020: New Growth Model–New Social Policy. Concluding Report on Expert Working Results Concerning Current Problems of Socio-economic Strategy of Russia in the Period by 2020*, Vol. 1, ed. 2, Delo, Moscow (in Russian).

Medvedev, D. (2016). Social and economic development of Russia: Finding new dynamics, *Voprosy Ekonomiki*, 10, 5–30 (in Russian).

Ministry of Economic Development. (2016). *National Report on Innovation in Russia 2016* (in Russian).

Mizobata S. (2016) Innovation policy and market quality in Russia", *Journal of Region and Society,* Osaka University of Commerce, 18, March 2016, 1–27 (in Japanese).

Mizobata, S. (2017). Innovation policy and market quality in Russia, innovation policy and economic actors: State, markets and enterprises (with Olga Bobrova *et al.*), Kyoto Institute of Economic Research, Kyoto University, *Discussion Paper*, 965, January 2017, 1–102.

Polterovich, V. M., Dmitriev, M. E., Yakovlev, A. A., Gurvich, E. T. and Auzan, A. A. (2017). The fate of economic programmes and reforms in Russia, *Voprosy Ekonomiki*, 6, 22–44 (in Russian).

Tsygankov, A. P. (2014). *The Strong State in Russia: Development and Crisis*, Oxford University Press, New York.

Uvarov, V. (2013). *Innovation Development of Russian Companies on the Base of International Integration*, Magistr, Moscow (in Russian).

World Bank. (2018). *Russian Digital Economy Report, September 2018, Competing in the Digital Age: Policy Implications for the Russian Federation*, World Bank, Washington DC.

Zagashvili, V. (2016). Foreign experience of import substitution and possible conclusions for Russia, *Voprosy Ekonomiki*, 8, 137–148 (in Russian).

Chapter 4

Fundamentals and Recent Trends in Russian Banking

Victor Gorshkov

Financial sectors are crucial in establishing sound economic systems, and they play an important role in advancing sustainable economic growth. For many developing and emerging economies, the establishment of sound financial (banking) systems remains a significant challenge. For Russia, in particular, despite being a government priority for years, the development of the financial sector has still failed to facilitate domestic investment and modernisation.

According to the *Global Competitiveness Report* published by *World Economic Forum*, in 2000, Russia ranked 55th in terms of growth competitiveness and 52nd in terms of competitiveness. In 2018, it ranked 43rd out of 140 countries in competitiveness. Progress in building Russia's national competitiveness has been slow. Financial sector development remains the second weakest after health (100th): in 2018, Russia ranked 86th in terms of global competitiveness of its financial system. Soundness of banks (114th), banks' regulatory credit ratio (109th), financing of SMEs (106th) and non-performing loans (97th) remain major "paint points" of the current financial system.

The financial crises of 2008 and 2014–2015 had a negative impact on Russia's economy. Some researchers claim that the banking crisis started in 2008 is still ongoing (Gevorkyan, 2018). Following the imposition of economic and financial sanctions imposed by the West, Russia lost the opportunity to attract cheap financing from international (primarily European) capital markets to provide liquidity to its undercapitalised banking system. Financial sanctions significantly reduced domestic investment and almost eliminated Russian export finance (Åslund, 2019, p. 197). These crises exposed the Bank of Russia's macroprudential deficiencies.

Russia is a bank-based financial system. The banking sector assets-to-GDP ratio significantly exceeds that of insurance companies, non-government pension funds, investment funds, and securities market brokers (Gorshkov, 2018a). This chapter provides an overview of recent trends in Russia's banking sector, focusing on institutional and macroeconomic aspects.

Banking System in Crisis

In recent years, Russia's banking system has been going through a systemic crisis. Some believe it has extremely large "banking holes". In 2013, the Bank of Russia launched a "clearance campaign" revoking the licenses of banks non-compliant with regulatory requirements. The campaign revealed significant discrepancies in the real and book value assets, and capital structure problems attributable to inefficient management practices and highly risky credit policies. In some instances, bank managers provided loans to fictitious one-day paper companies, purchasing assets that had no real value to attract, or off-balance deposits (Katasonov, 2018). The collapse of domestic private banks, particularly the failure of Otkrytie and Binbank in 2017, exposed banking holes of this sort, calling into question the quality of the Bank of Russia's macroprudential control and supervisory function.

In the past 17 years, 2,600 out of almost 3,000 registered banks have lost their licenses due to dubious transactions such as money laundering and tax evasion. Many of these banks were established in the 1990s, and were controlled by industrial capital (including that of oligarchs) that focused on the capital accumulation to finance shareholders' purchases of privatising enterprises rather than providing intermediary functions in the financial market. Some banks that survived the 1990s were hard-hit by the 2008 financial crisis.

Many banks at present are still engaged in illegal transactions and asset-stripping as these activities are far more profitable. Continuous efforts by the Bank of Russia to establish market discipline have led to excessive regulations that make it difficult for many Russian banks to operate legally. In such conditions, many banks issued loans with fake collateral, overstated their assets value, inflated formal capital through structured transactions with affiliated companies and prioritised investing into corporate and sovereign bonds as these investments generate larger profits than investing in the real sector (Movchan, 2018).

The major reasons for the systemic crisis in the banking sector are as follows: (1) rapid expansion through domestic M&A of banks with financial problems; (2) international sanctions; (3) sharp decline in petroleum prices; (4) ruble devaluation and (5) high number of bankruptcies and increased non-performing loans (Guarino, 2017). In particular, a sharp decline in petroleum prices reduced the amount of funds allocated to banks and significantly hurt their cash flows. A depreciating ruble and rising inflation aggravated the liquidity problem of many banks and international sanctions deprived many banks of opportunities to attract cheap financing from traditional international capital markets.

Institutional Developments in the Banking Sector

The present institutional arrangements of Russia's banking sector, namely its high concentration and strong government participation, were to a large extent inherited from the Soviet past, when the *monobank* system was the banking model in socialist economies. The Soviet banking system began with the establishment of *Gosbank* (state bank) in 1923 and liberalised during *perestroika* from 1987 to 1991. Gosbank was responsible for monetary emission and provided domestic credit provision to state-owned enterprises. During late 1980s–early 1990s, five sectoral banks were established to support the most important industries of the Soviet economy. These included Sberbank (savings bank), Promstroibank (Industrial Construction Bank), Vneshekonombank (foreign trade), Agrobank, Agricultural bank and Zhilstroibank (Bank of social and economic public development). These five banks were under the direct supervisory control of Gosbank. Other socialist economies had similar monobank systems (Gevorkyan, 2018, p. 209).

The USSR law "On Cooperatives" established a two-tiered banking system comprised of Gosbank and commercial private banks. It spawned new private banks chartered by individuals, small businesses associations and "mutants" of Soviet era specialised banks. The newly established private banks had mostly been public companies, but fell into private hands through the dilution of state-owned shares, asset-stripping, malicious bankruptcies, and other shady methods, despite their registration as joint stock companies (Vernikov, 2007, p. 8). Oligarchs and industrial groups controlled many of the newly established private banks that had accumulated liabilities to finance shareholder privatisation plans.

Federal law No. 135-1 "On Banks and Banking Activities in Russia" dated December 2, 1990 introduced new basic principles for the development of Russia's banking system during the transition period. The Central Bank of Russia (Bank of Russia) replaced Gosbank. By the end of 1991, Russia had 869 banks and more than a half of them were successors of the specialised banks. The number of banks steadily increased and reached a maximum of 2,439 by the end of 1994.

Bank loans during the 1990s were available to only a small number of borrowers. Banks were reluctant to provide financing due to high inflation rates, plummeting GDP, massive capital outflows and relatively low consumer demand. From 2000 to 2009, due to the gradual adjustment of the key interest rate by the Bank of Russia, bank lending gradually expanded, especially for mortgages and automobile loans. After the financial crisis of 2008–2009, individual household loans grew faster than corporate lending, non-performing household loans surged and credit contracted making it difficult to finance Russia's technological modernisation.

As of February 2019, 479 commercial banks were operating in Russia including state-controlled banks (directly or indirectly controlled by Russia's government or the Bank of Russia); foreign-controlled banks; private banks with capital of more than RUB 1 billion; and private banks with capital of less than RUB 1 billion. The number of banks has been steadily declining due to stricter capitalisation requirements and increased domestic M&A activity by banking holding groups. In recent years, the Bank of Russia has stressed culling weak banks, and enhancing market

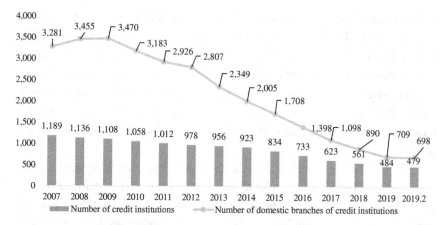

Figure 1: Number of registered credit institutions and their domestic branches in Russia during 2007–2019 (data as on January 1).

Source: Compiled by the author from the Bank of Russia's statistics available at https://www.cbr.ru/Eng/statistics/.

regulation and control. Banks failing to fulfil minimum capitalisation requirements or not complying with the current legislation on banking activities were placed under prudential control. Financial and economic sanctions exacerbated bank insolvencies. The number of banks in Russia almost halved from 2014 to 2018 (Figure 1).

In 2017, the federal law "On Banks and Banking Activities" was amended and banks were divided by the total capital into two categories: banks holding a universal license (minimum total capital requirements of more than RUB 1 billion) and banks with a basic license (minimum total capital requirement — RUB 300 million). The amendments, effective January 1, 2018, had a significant impact on the number of players in Russia's banking industry.

In 2018, 135 banks participated in the banking groups and 47 were bank holding companies. The share of banking groups and bank holding companies in total banking assets was 86.1% and 13.5%, respectively. In December 2018, the top five banks accounted for 60.4% of the banking sector's assets. Concentration of banking services is high. The Herfindahl–Hirschman Indices (HHI) of banks' key performance indicators in 2018 were moderate: assets (0.111), loans and other placed funds provided to resident non-financial institutions (0.158), household deposits (0.227) and capital (0.184). However, HHI for loans, deposits and capital have steadily grown from the years 2016 to 2018, pointing to increasing levels of concentration. This is particularly pronounced in the household deposit market, where the total share of the top five banks is 65.2% with Sberbank alone accounting for 46.1%. The share of state-controlled banks in total banking assets also increased from 59.1% in 2017 to 63.1% in 2018 (Bank of Russia, 2018).

Since 2014, the Bank of Russia has published a list of systematically important banks. This list seeks to facilitate market stabilisation. Russia's government wants to assure banking market participants that there are still reliable banks in the banking system despite continuous license revocations. The selection criteria for banks to be included in the list are stringent. The list included six state-controlled banks (AO "Gazprombank", PAO "Bank VTB", PAO "Sberbank", PAO "Promsvyazbank", PAO Bank "FK Otkrytie", AO "Rosselkhozbank"); three foreign banks (AO "UniCredit Bank" (Italy), AO "Raiffeisenbank" [Austria]), PAO "Rosbank" [Societe Generale, France]); and two private banks (AO "Alfa-Bank" and PAO "Moskovskij Kreditnyj Bank"). These 11 systematically important banks comprise of more than 60% of the total banking assets. Systemically important banks are enormously influential.

Geographical disparities in banking service accessibility are conspicuous. As of December 2018, 56.3% of banks are located in Central federal district (276 banks, including 248 located in Moscow City and Moscow Region), followed by Volga (67 banks, 13.7%); North-West (41 banks, 8.4%); Siberian (28 banks, 5.7%), Southern (27 banks, 5.5%); Ural (23 banks, 4.7%); Far Eastern (16 banks, 3.3%) and North-Caucasian (12 banks, 2.4%) federal districts (Bank of Russia, 2019).

The Role of State in the Banking Sector

The scope of state involvement and control in Russia's banking sector is an enormous echo of the Soviet pattern. The government's participation in the banking sector takes numerous forms. The main ones are as follows: (1) *de jure* state banks (2 banks); (2) state banks with full (100%)

government ownership (5 banks); (3) state banks with partial (51–99% shares) ownership (12 banks); (4) banks with indirect state ownership (2 banks); (5) banks under temporary state prudential control (9 banks). The second (2) and third (3) categories are also referred as state-controlled banks in the Bank of Russia statistics.

De jure state banks are banks established by federal laws. They include the Bank of Russia (federal law No. 86 "On Central Bank of Russian Federation (Bank of Russia)" and Vneshekonombank (federal law No. 82 "On Development Bank"). State banks with full government ownership include AO "Rosselhozbank" (100% shares belong to the Federal Agency for State Property Management [Rosimuschetsvo]); Russian National Commercial Bank (Rosimuschestvo); AKB "Rossijskij Kapital" (AO "Agency for Mortgage Loans"); AO "MSP Bank" (Federal Corporation on Small and Medium Business Development) and AO "Roseksimbank" (Vneshekonombank). State banks with partial ownership are represented by AO "Globeksbank", PAO AKB "Svyaz' Bank", AO "Vserossijskij bank razvitija", Orenburgskij Ipotechyj Kommercheskij Bank "Rus", PAO "VTB", AK "BARS", PAO "Sberbank", AKB "Novikombank", KBER "Bank Kazani", AO "Gazprombank", Khakasskij Municipalnyj Bank and AO "Ruskobank". RNKO "Narat" and PAO "Kraiinvestbank" are the only two banks with indirect state ownership (shares belong to the state-controlled enterprises). Nine banks are under temporary prudential control by institutions like the Bank of Russia or Deposit Insurance Agency: Bank FK "Otkrytie", Genbank, TRAST, Promsvyazbank, Avtovazbank, Rost bank, Aziatsko-Tikhookeanskij Bank, Binbank, Fondervis Bank (*Edinyj bankovskij portal*, 2019).

Federal law No. 86-FZ "On the Central Bank of Russian Federation (Bank of Russia)" established the Bank of Russia, granting it special legal status by Article 75 of the Constitution of the Russian Federation. The goals of the Bank of Russia are managing the ruble and insuring its stability, promoting the development of the Russian banking system, protecting the stability of the national payment system and financial market. The Bank of Russia is an independent special legal institution exclusively authorised to issue currency and regulate its circulation. The Bank of

Russia in collaboration with the government of Russia is responsible for monetary policy and is simultaneously a macroregulator (macroprudential control and supervisory function) of the financial market. In 2000s, the Bank of Russia began decreasing its key policy rate. The rate was 7.75% in March 2019 and the current inflation target is 4%. The Bank of Russia was authorised to resolve problems in the banking system (rehabilitation, bailout of insolvent banks) in June 2017 via the specially established Consolidation Fund of the Banking Sector. It can now acquire shares, bonds, assets and liabilities of insolvent banks and resell them to new investors after financial problems have been resolved. The new resolution mechanism seeks to enhance the Bank of Russia's supervisory control and improves market discipline.

The Bank of Russia is the main shareholder of PAO "Sberbank" (50 + 1% shares), the largest saving state-commercial bank in Russia. Sberbank has a dominant position in Russia's financial market. In 2017, it had 28.9% share in assets, 32.4% in corporate loans, 40.5% in household loans, 20.9% in corporate deposits, 46.1% in individual deposits and 39.3% in capital. The credit portfolio of Sberbank is composed mostly of individual household loans (32.0%), petroleum and gas industry (8.9%), real estate (7.9%), metallurgy (7.5%), commercial trade (7.2%), food and agricultural industry (5.2%) and machine building and telecommunications (4% each). The top 20 affiliated client groups accounted for 26.4% of the credit portfolio in 2017, suggesting there is a bias in favour of large corporate clients (Sberbank, 2019).

Vneshekonombank (VEB) is the largest state-owned development bank in Russia. Its primary objective is to contribute to long-term economic growth. It provides financing for large-scale projects to develop infrastructure, industrial production, the social sphere and strengthen the technological potential in partnerships with commercial banks with the ultimate goal of improving the quality of life. In 2017, the bank loaned RUB 2,695.6 billion, mostly in the form of project financing (56.3%), commercial loans (26.4%), securities purchases (8.6%), and export financing (4.8%). As of December 2017, the top 3 clients accounted for 28.8% of the credit portfolio, and another group of 10 clients accounted for 21.6%. The statistics reveal that Vneshekonombank is financing only a limited number of large-scale projects (Vneshekonombank, 2018).

Overall, the roles of Sberbank and Vneshekonombank (which is not a commercial bank) remain significant. Together with the other directly and indirectly state-controlled banks, they provide the lion's share of financing in Russia.

Foreign Banks

In October 2018, 150 foreign banks operated in Russia, including 63 foreign-controlled banks with 100% foreign share; 17 foreign-controlled banks with foreign shares of 51–99%; and 70 foreign banks with capital participation of less than 50%. The number of foreign banks has steadily declined from 2014 to 2018, suggesting that foreign investors may be reconsidering their investment plans in Russia. Foreign-controlled banks with foreign shares of 51–99% and foreign banks with capital participation of less than 50% decreased by 63% and 54%, respectively. The foreign banks' share in the total charter capital of the Russian banking sector declined from 23% in 2014 to 13.44% in October 2018. It should be noted that about 11% of foreign banks are significantly controlled by Russian residents (Figure 2).

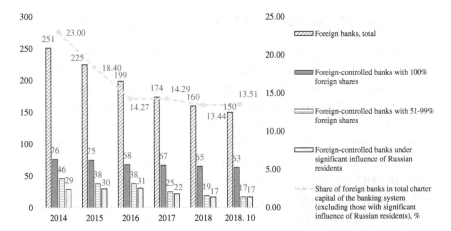

Figure 2: Foreign banks and their share in total charter capital of the banking system (number and percentage).

Source: Compiled by the author from the Bank of Russia (2019) and the Bank of Russia's statistics available at https://www.cbr.ru/Eng/statistics/.

Foreign-controlled banks with 100% capital participation are established by their parent banks in Europe (42.4%), Asia (21.2%), North America (9.1%) and the Middle East (7.6%), while about 7.6% of them are *de facto* controlled by Russian residents round-tripping FDI from offshore territories (Gorshkov, 2018c). The extensive presence of European banks reflects historical and geographical forces. The gravity model of FDI appears to explain the strong presence of European banks such as AO "UniCredit Bank" (Italy) and AO "Raiffeisenbank" (Austria). European banks from Austria, France and Italy have relatively large retail businesses in Russia.

Asian banks, particularly those from Japan, China and South Korea, have recently expanded their presence in Russia, but the scope of their activities remains limited. Most of them support manufacturing FDI from their home countries. This is the standard practice of Japanese banks (Gorshkov, 2017). Other market segments in which Asian foreign banks operate include corporate loans to Russian firms, customers located in Europe and CIS, Russian SMEs, lending activities to Russian banks, retail banking (automobile loans, mortgage, foreign exchange) and investment in Russia's federal bonds (Gorshkov, 2018c).

Macroeconomic Indicators of Russia's Banking Sector

Key macroeconomic indicators of the banking sector in recent years have been significantly affected by the ruble foreign exchange fluctuations, license revocations and reorganisation of credit institutions. Banking sector assets from 2014 to 2018 increased by 72% and amounted to RUB 85 billion rubles (Figure 3). The growth was attributed mainly to the growth in ruble assets rather than assets in foreign currency. The ratio of the banking sector total assets to GDP has declined from a maximum of 99.5% in 2016 to 92.6 in 2018 due to the fast growth of nominal GDP. Banking sector total capital increased by 33% during the years 2014–2018 to RUB 9.4 trillion (10.2% in GDP). The growth of corporate loans (47.3%) outperformed that of loans to individuals (22.3%). Corporate loans reached RUB 30.2 trillion in 2018, while loans to individuals were RUB 12.2 trillion. As for banking sector liabilities, individual household deposits increased by 53.2% (RUB 25.9 trillion) and deposits and funds increased by 47% (RUB 24.8 trillion).

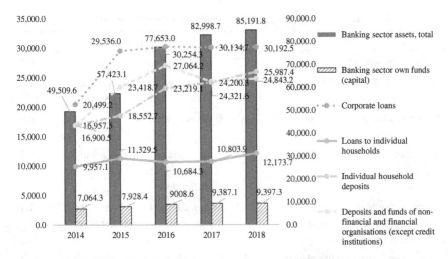

Figure 3: Macroeconomic indicators of the banking sector (billion rubles).

Source: Compiled by the author with data from the Bank of Russia (2019).

The banking sector assets and liabilities structure in 2018 is presented in Table 1. The liabilities structure is balanced and is mainly comprised of household deposits (30.5%), deposits and funds on accounts of non-financial and financial organisations (29.2%), and funds and profits of banks (10.5%). The share of loans, deposits and other funds raised from non-resident banks has shrunk from 3.9% to 1.1% for the years 2014–2018. Russian banks apparently are still facing difficulties in accessing foreign funding sources. The banking sector is attracting financing primarily from domestic sources. The structure of deposits by maturity in 2018 was as follows: long-term deposits (more than 1 year) — 52.0%, short-term deposits — 48% (including, deposits for the period of 181 days–1 year — 25.7%; 91–180 days — 20.6%; 1–90 days — 1.8%). A total of 87.4% of household deposits are in amounts ranging from RUB 100,000 to RUB 1 million. The interest rate on ruble-denominated household deposits for more than one year decreased from 11.7% to 6.4%, 2014–2018.

As for the firm deposits, their structure by maturity has switched from long term (53.1% share in total corporate deposits) to short term (56.5%). Interest rates for both short-term and long-term deposits have declined from 8.0% to 6.6%, respectively. State-controlled banks remain the largest

Table 1:   Banking sector assets and liabilities structure in 2018 (%).

Assets		Liabilities	
Money, precious metals	2.2	Funds and profits of banks	10.5
Accounts with the Bank of Russia	5.6	Funds raised from the Bank of Russia	2.4
Correspondent accounts with credit institutions	1.5	Bank accounts	0.9
Securities	14.5	Loans, deposits and other finds raised from resident credit institutions	9.7
Loans, deposits and other placed funds provided to resident credit institutions	9.5	Loans, deposits and other finds raised from non-resident banks	1.1
Loans, deposits and other placed funds provided to non-resident banks	2.0	Household deposits (residents and non-residents)	30.5
Loans, deposits and other placed funds provided to resident and non-resident households	14.3	Deposits and funds on accounts of non-financial and financial organisations (other than credit institutions)	29.2
Loans and other placed funds provided to resident non-financial institutions	30.5	Bonds, promissory notes and bank acceptances	1.9
Loans and other placed funds provided to non-resident legal entities (other than banks)	5.0	Other liabilities	13.7
Loans and other placed funds provided to financial organisations (other than banks)	5.3		
Fixed assets and intangible assets	1.8		
Other assets	7.9		

Source: Compiled by the author with data from the Bank of Russia (2018). Banking Supervision Report 2017.

providers of total banking sector liabilities with a 66.5% share in household deposits and 62.0% in firm deposits, followed by private banks with capital of more than RUB 1 billion, and foreign-controlled banks (Table 2).

Table 2:   Share of different groups of banks in deposits and loans as of January 1, 2018 (%).

Share in %	Household deposits	Firm deposits	Household loans	Corporate loans	ROA (2017)	ROE (2017)
State-controlled banks	66.5	62.0	67.3	69.7	2.1	16.1
Foreign-controlled banks	6.2	8.6	12.1	5.8	2.4	13.8
Private banks with capital of more than RUB 1 billion	18.5	19.1	15.5	15.5	0.4	10.9
Private banks with capital of less than RUB 1 billion	0.8	0.5	0.5	0.4	0.1	−0.1
Banks under resolution	8.0	8.6	4.6	8.6	—	—
Non-bank credit institutions	0.0	1.1	0.0	0.0	—	—

Note: Firm deposits include deposits and funds on accounts of non-financial and financial organisations (other than credit institutions).
Source: Compiled by author with data from the Bank of Russia (2018). Banking Supervision Report 2017.

The total assets of the banking sector are comprised of loans and other placed funds provided to resident non-financial institutions (30.5%), households (14.3%) and securities (14.5%). Securities are an attractive instrument for many Russian banks and their relatively high share in total banking assets structure is explained by their profitability and relatively low risks, especially considering the fact that about 40% of such instruments are issued by government authorities and 6.5% by the Bank of Russia.

The shares of both corporate and household loans slightly declined during the years 2014–2017. Corporate loans in 2017 were allocated to manufacturing (22.3%), retail estate (17.1%) and wholesale and retail trade (13.9%) (Figure 4). In 2018, the share of manufacturing dropped to 15.1%, while that of wholesale and retail trade increased to 21.9%. Loans to the manufacturing sector were mostly allocated for the production of food and beverages (19.6%) and petroleum products and nuclear materials (18.8%). Thus, the role of banks in providing long-term manufacturing investment crucial for Russia's modernisation remains limited.

State-controlled banks continued providing the majority of loans to both the individual households (67.3%) and the corporate sectors (69.7%). Weighted-average interest rates on ruble loans declined: long-term interest rates now are 9.4% for non-financial organisations and 10.8% for

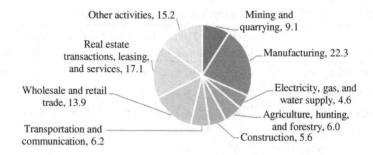

Figure 4:   Banking sector's corporate loans portfolio by sector in 2017 (%).

Source: Compiled by the author with data from the Bank of Russia (2018). Banking Supervision Report 2017.

SMEs, while short-term interest rates are 9.4% and 12.2%, respectively. These interest rates are high particularly for SMEs.

Overall, individual household loans comprise 14.3% of the total banking assets and 13.2% of GDP. The shares of corporate loans are 35.4% and 32.8%, respectively. Generally, banks loans account only for 11.2% of investments into fixed assets, including 5.4% of investments from foreign banks. Pertinent data on the financing of new fixed capital are provided in Table 3. They show that new fixed capital formation is funded mostly by equity financing (51.3%). The share of debt-financing is 48.7%. Bank loans are traditionally the most important source of long-term finance, but were surpassed by federal and municipal budget funds (16.3%). The subsidiary role of banks in providing long-term loans is confirmed by related statistics.

Previous studies have demonstrated that Russia's banking sector does not adequately service the financial needs of the real sector due to its institutional flaws, high domestic interest rates and relatively low national savings (Gorshkov, 2018a, 2018b). According to the World Bank data, in 2017, the national savings — GDP ratio is 29.634%. This is lower than the pre-2008 financial crisis (33.924%) and that of the year 2000 (38.721%).

The present structure of financing is to a great extent explained by Russia's financial market architecture. It is a bank-based financial system, heavily dependent on bank financing instead of stock and insurance markets, non-government pension funds and mutual funds (Gorshkov, 2018b).

Overall, the banking sector's financial resources are too limited to foster vibrant corporate development. In such conditions, foreign banks,

Table 3: Investments into fixed assets by sources of financing (%).

	2014	2015	2016	2017
Investments into fixed capital by sources of financing (total)	100.0	100.0	100.0	100.0
Equity (internal sources of financing including retained profits)	45.7	50.2	51.0	51.3
Debt financing (external (acquired)) sources of financing	54.3	49.8	49.0	48.7
• Bank loans (including foreign bank loans)	10.6	8.1	10.4	11.2
	(2.3)	(1.7)	(2.9)	(5.4)
• Loans and credits from other companies	6.4	6.7	6.0	5.4
• Foreign investments	0.9	1.1	0.8	0.8
• Budget funds (including federal budget funds)	17.0	18.3	16.4	16.3
	(9.0)	(11.3)	(9.3)	(8.5)
• State extra-budgetary funds	0.2	0.3	0.2	0.2
• Investments into construction by firms and individuals	3.5	3.2	3.0	3.3
• Other sources	15.7	12.1	12.2	11.5

Source: Compiled by the author with reference to the Federal State Statistic Service (http://www.gks.ru/wps/wcm/connect/rosstat_main/rosstat/en/main/).

particularly those located in Europe, have seemed to some to be viable supplementary sources of finance. The scope of foreign bank activities in Russia is small and they cannot compete effectively with state giants.

The share of profit-making institutions of the banking sector in January 2018 was 75% (421 banks), while 25% of banks generated significant losses (140 banks). Profits were mostly generated by net interest income (67%), net commission income and premiums (24%) and income from securities trading (7%). Net income from foreign currency and precious metal transactions had significantly declined in the years 2014–2017. The structure of expenses has remained unchanged. They are primarily operational and administrative expenses and net additional provisions (Table 4).

In terms of financial performance, state-controlled and foreign-controlled banks were the most profitable: the return on their assets (ROA) was 2.1% and 2.4%, return on equity (ROE) was 16.1% and 13.8%, respectively. Thus, it can be assumed that state-controlled

Table 4:   Financial performance of the banking sector from 2014 to 2017 (RUB billion).

Profit component	2014	2015	2016	2017
Net interest income	2,534	2,108	2,653	2,593
Net income from securities trading	−155	103	417	258
Net income from foreign currency and precious metals transactions	421	450	25	92
Net commission income and premiums	725	772	893	926
Other net income	484	92	−664	170
Operational and administrative expenses of credit institutions	−1,913	−1,617	−1,731	−1,821
Net additional provisions	−1,505	−1,717	−665	−1,433
Profit before tax	591	193	929	785

Source: Compiled by the author with reference to the Bank of Russia (2016). Banking Supervision Report 2015, Bank of Russia (2017). Banking Supervision Report 2016, Bank of Russia (2018). Banking Supervision Report 2017.

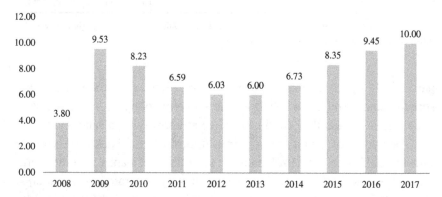

Figure 5:   Bank non-performing loans to gross loans ratio in Russia during 2008–2017 (%).

Source: https://www.statista.com/statistics/460896/non-performing-bank-loans-in-russia/.

commercial banks in Russia operate efficiently. The state development bank, Vneshekonombank is an exception. Its financial results have been negative since 2014. In the years 2016–2017, its uncovered losses doubled, reaching RUB 543.7 billion mostly due to increased impairment provisions (Vneshekonombank, 2018).

The share of non-performing loans in gross loans ratio in 2017 surpassed the peak of 2009 (9.53%) and reached 10.0% (Figure 5).

Non-performing loans remain one of the major concerns for many banks in Russia. In fact, some banks deprived of banking licenses tried to hide the actual level of non-performing loans to improve their asset structures. Non-performing loans for individual households are greater than those of the corporate sector.

Idiosyncratic Features of Russia's Banking Sector

According to Gevorkyan (2018, pp. 208–209), there are similarities in the banking sector development in Central and Eastern Europe (CEE) and the Former Soviet Union (FSU), such as the emergence of strong national central banks; proliferation of private banking activity, mainly driven by foreign banks from Western Europe; and strong growth in private domestic credit. All these features are to some extent applicable to Russia; however, private banks have limited impact in providing banking services and they are subordinates to large directly and indirectly state-controlled banks.

The distinctive features of Russia's banking sector are as follows:

(1) consolidation due to license revocations and intensified domestic M&A;
(2) the primacy of a small number of directly and indirectly state-controlled and private banks;
(3) the small number of foreign banks;
(4) a huge number of minuscule undercapitalised banks;
(5) relatively high concentration of banking assets, liabilities and banking services (lending and deposits) in large state-controlled banks;
(6) low levels of capitalisation;
(7) regional disparities in the distribution of banking services;
(8) chronic problems with long-term financing caused by relatively low level of national savings;
(9) dominance of directly- and indirectly-controlled state banks distorting market competition;
(10) low transparency levels of banks;
(11) offshorization of the banking sector and Russia's economy itself;
(12) increasing state role in the banking sector as a result of bank resolutions.

Recent trends in Russia's banking sector development include the following:

(1) the reshaping of its institutional structure due to increased license revocations and intensified capital consolidation trends;
(2) non-performing loans aggravated by extensive borrowings by individual households and the corporate sector to refinance their debt obligations;
(3) enhanced state support and regulation;
(4) limited access to international capital markets due to international sanctions;
(5) limited role and scope of activities of foreign banks.

Conclusion

The global competitiveness of Russia's economy remains low and its features as a petrostate have intensified in recent years. Russia's banking sector has limited impact on domestic economic activities because it has failed to provide investment to foster long-term economic development and modernisation. The corporate sector finances itself from retained earnings or from international capital markets. Russian banks are active borrowers of these cheap loanable funds, but foreign sanctions now limit their access.

Ruble devaluation, plummeting petroleum prices, rising inflation, geopolitical instability and international sanctions aggravated liquidity problems in the banking sector and destabilised Russia's economy in the years 2014–2018. The problem still persists.

The negative trends of 2014–2018 caused massive bankruptcies, license revocations due to dubious transactions, money laundering, tax evasion and mounting non-performing loans. The Bank of Russia's exposure of asset-stripping activities, overstated asset value and inflated their capital structures highlight institutional flaws of Russia's banking system and underscore the need for radical reform.

First, the Bank of Russia's supervisory role requires fresh attention in light of past failures. The Otkrytie "too big to fail" problem provides a clear case in point. The "clearance campaign" of the Bank of Russia initiated in 2013 is a positive sign, but does not seem sufficient to preclude massive future bank insolvencies.

Second, private banks need to improve their performance as intermediaries, in part by curtailing their investments in corporate and sovereign bonds. The state can mandate private banks to increase their activities as intermediaries, and can reduce interest paid on sovereign debt.

Third, the government should monitor Vneshekonombank's operations more closely to avoid further losses.

The idiosyncratic features of Russia's banking sector such as substantial state participation and strong linkages with industrial groups are likely to persist. The extensive, strong and rigid participation of the state in Russia's banking sector is inherited from the Soviet banking system, together with the strong functions of the Bank of Russia, a successor of Gosbank from the monobank system. Linkages with industrial groups have been transformed into banking holdings and continue serving the interests of the wealthy oligarchs rather than the real sector of the economy. In general, banks' role as intermediaries in the financial market remains limited.

The role of the state in the banking sector need not be detrimental. Russia may be able to achieve satisfactory results if the government prioritises long-term investments essential for further economic development and modernisation. Banks must be compelled to improve their intermediary function as providers of basic finance. However, for the moment it seems that this is not happening. The intensifying state effort to bail-out systematically important banks is impairing competition and discouraging foreign banks from expanding their operations.

References

Åslund, A. (2019). Russia's crony capitalism, in Torbjörn, B. and Oxenstierna, S. (eds.), *The Russian Economy under Putin*, Abingdon, Oxon OX14 4RN: Routledge, pp. 186–201.

Bank of Russia (2018). *Banking Supervision Report 2017*, Moscow: Bank of Russia, p. 105.

Bank of Russia (2019). Review of the Banking Sector of the Russian Federation (Internet version). *Analytical Data*, 195, p. 74.

Gevorkyan, A. (2018). *Transition Economies. Transformation, Development, and Society in Eastern Europe and the Former Soviet Union*, Routledge, p. 272.

Gorshkov, V. (2017). Japanese banks in Russia, *World Economy and International Relations* 61(11), 24–33 (in Russian).

Gorshkov, V. (2018a). Banking outward foreign direct investment: The boundaries of Russia's pivot to Asia, *The Comparative Economic Review* 29(1), 29–58.

Gorshkov, V. (2018b). Finance, in Rosefielde, S., Kuboniwa, M., Mizobata, S., and Haba, K. (eds.), *Unwinding of the Globalist Dream: EU, Russia, China*, Chapter 10, World Scientific, Singapore, pp. 193–212.

Gorshkov, V. (2018c). Asian banks in the Russian market: An overview, UNP-RC Discussion Paper Series, No. 18-E-04, p. 17.

Guarino, A. (2017). 5 reasons Russia's banking system is heading for trouble. 18 December 2017, https://globalriskinsights.com/2017/12/russia-banking-system-risks/ (accessed 4 March 2019).

Katasonov, V. (2018). *Chernye Dyri Bankovskoj Sistemy. Kak Bankiri Miniruut Rossiu* [Black holes of Russia's banking system. How bankers mine Russia], Knizhnij Mir, Moscow, p. 384.

Movchan, A. (2018). How to fix Russia's broken banking system. *Financial Times*, 15 January 2018, https://www.ft.com/content/b90754a8-f7c0-11e7-a4c9-bbdefa4f210b (accessed 4 March 2019).

Sberbank (2019). Konsolidirovannaja financovaja otchetnost' Publishnoe aktsionernoe obschestvo "Sberbank Rossii" i ego dochernie organizatsii za 2018 god s auditorskim zaklucheniem nezavisimogo auditora [Consolidated financial report of public joint-stock company "Sberbank of Russia" for 2018 and the auditing report of an independent auditor]. Available at: https://www.sberbank.com/common/img/uploaded/files/info/ifrs2018/-_sberbank_ifrs-ye2018-rus_.pdf (in Russian).

Systemoobrazuyuschie banki RF: Spisok TsB [Systematically important banks: List of the Bank of Russia], *Edinyj bankovskij portal*, 2019. Available at http://1eb.ru/bank/2543-sistemoobrazuyushhie-banki-rf-spisok-cb.html (accessed 4 March 2019). (in Russian).

Vernikov, A. (2007). Russia's banking sector transition: Where to? BOFIT Discussion Papers, No. 5. p. 30.

Vneshekonombank (2018). Auditorskoe zakluchenie nezavisimogo auditora o konsolidirovannoj financovoj otchetsnosti gosudarstvennoj korporatsii "Bank razvitija I vneshneekonomicheskoj deyatelnosti (Vneshekonombank) i ee dochernih organizatsij za 2017 god" [Financial report and independent audit statement of the state corporation "Bank for development and foreign economic activity (Vneshekonombank) and its subsidiaries" for 2017]. Available at: https://вэб.рф/files/?file=6c30c09e4bcf1956c2c7dd3ec2b2f 6bd.pdf (in Russian).

Chapter 5

Russian Health and Demographic Trends and Prospects

Judyth Twigg

Introduction

Russia's population, after a precipitous drop starting in 1992 that lasted almost 15 years, has rebounded impressively over the last decade (Figure 1). Migration has always been a net positive contributor to Russian population dynamics, but the upswing since 2008 has been predominantly due to an increase in the birth rate and a decrease in mortality. From 2011 through 2016, the significant excesses of deaths over births that characterised the preceding period evened out, with the number of births roughly equal to the number of deaths (Figure 2). Those momentarily positive trend lines have stalled over the last few years, however, and it will be highly challenging to recapture the positive momentum of the early 2010s. Demographic echoes of the low birth rates of the 1990s have virtually locked in a resumption of population decline over the next several decades. Russian policymakers will therefore have to address key issues of *quality* of human capital to compensate for declines in *quantity*: education and well-targeted workforce training, military manpower, ageing and the pension burden, detection and treatment of non-communicable disease, the re-emergent threat of HIV/AIDS, migration and "brain drain" and significant regional variations in circumstances across the country. The failure to capitalise on the resources available to the health sector

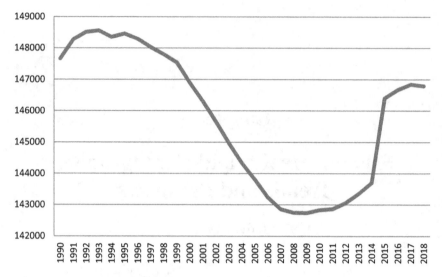

Figure 1:   Population (in thousands) of Russia 1998–2018.

Source: Rosstat (Crimea added in 2015).

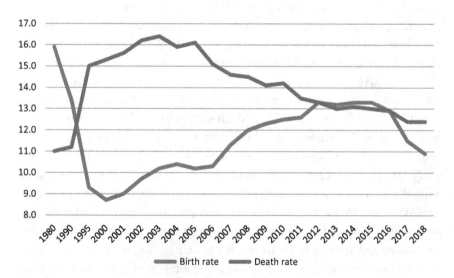

Figure 2:   Birth and death rates, 1980–2018 (Births/deaths per 1,000 population).

Source: Rosstat (2014 forward includes Crimea).

during the flush period of the late 2000s and early 2010s will likely, in the long term, represent a tragic missed opportunity. A resumption of health and demographic progress will require not only a significant investment of increasingly scarce funds but also capacity to invest those resources efficiently — a skill that has never been part of the Russian health sector's playbook.

Population Dynamics

Current Russian demographic trends trace their roots deep into the Soviet period. A significant decline in births during the Great Patriotic War produced generational echoes — smaller numbers of adults of childbearing age, who then had smaller numbers of children — in the late 1960s and again in the 1990s. The chaos of the Soviet collapse drove an even more dramatic decline in family formation. As the Russian economy began to grow during the first two Putin terms, fertility rates increased, a trend that persisted through the mid-2010s.

Recently, however, an important dynamic has begun to emerge: the drop in the number of girls born in the early to mid-1990s has evolved into the cohort of women currently of childbearing age, and there simply will not be enough young adult women in the period 2020–2035 to sustain the increases in numbers of births experienced throughout the 2010s. In other words, the birth rate collapse of the early 1990s will reverberate for decades, virtually locking in an overall population decline at least until 2040.

The magnitude of this decline will largely depend on three factors: migration, total fertility rates (TFR, the number of children born to each woman over her lifetime) and mortality. The state statistics agency Rosstat projects three population scenarios — low, middle and high — each reflecting different assumptions about trends in these areas (Figure 3).

Fertility

The Rosstat "high" variant, which is extremely unlikely, assumes that the TFR will increase steadily through 2035, reaching over two children per

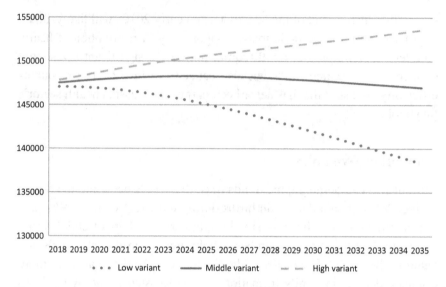

Figure 3: Russian population forecasts, 2018–2035, three variants (population in thousands).

Source: Rosstat.

woman by 2028. The current TFR, however, achieved after a decade of increase — in fact, the highest growth rate of TFR in Europe and the second fastest in the world from 2006 to 2012 — is still only around 1.8, having largely levelled off since 2012 (Figure 4). The Russian government has claimed that this growth rate was spurred by aggressive pro-natalist policy, in the form of "maternity capital" payments of around US$ 12,000 at the birth of the second and each subsequent child, paid at the child's third birthday, and applicable to housing, the child's education or the parents' pension. It is improbable, however, that this policy impacted family formation decisions in most instances, as the amounts of money involved are minor when compared to the overall costs of child-rearing (though there is some evidence that the incentives were meaningful for some rural families or may have accelerated the timing of births of second children, and little doubt that the programme has helped to reduce child poverty, even if it has not much increased the number of children).[1] More persuasive is the

---

[1] See, for example, Valeria Kopeykina, "The Maternity Capital's Impact on Birth Intervals in Russia," Stockholm University, https://su.diva-portal.org/smash/get/diva2:1138660/FULLTEXT03.pdf.

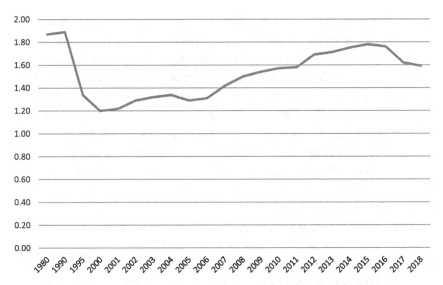

Figure 4: Total fertility rate, 1980–2018 (average number of children per woman).
Source: Rosstat.

straightforward argument that the improved socio-economic situation in the country, beginning in the mid-2000s, provided prospective parents with confidence that they could afford a child and that their home and community environments were, in the longer term, relatively stable and positive in comparison to the previous decade. There was also undoubtedly some "catch-up" childbearing in the 2000s, where women who decided not to have children during the turbulent 1990s had a first or, in many cases, second child later in life.

The more plausible medium-term population scenario for Russia, given the natural fertility trends in advanced industrial societies, is the Rosstat middle or low variant, driven by fertility remaining steady in the best case, immigration remaining either roughly stagnant at current levels (middle variant) or slightly declining (low variant), and the excess of deaths over births evolving as either moderate (middle variant) or severe (low variant). Given the inevitable declining birth trends described above, even the best-case scenario acknowledges that the excess of deaths over births will accelerate to some degree through the early 2030s.

The Russian Orthodox Church, backed by an increasingly aggressive line of Kremlin rhetoric, has framed *abortion* as a demographic issue

(Ferris-Rotman, 2017). The statistics don't bear that out. The number of annual abortions has decreased steadily from around 4.5 million in the late 1980s, when few other means of contraception were available, to fewer than 1 million in 2018. The ratio of abortions to births has completely reversed: there were about twice as many abortions as births in 1980, an equal number in 2006–2007, but 900,000 abortions in 2015 compared to 1.9 million births. As modern forms of contraception have become more widely available, abortion is no longer — as was the case during the late Soviet period — the dominant method of birth control. It may be a convenient political tool in an increasingly conservative society, but it is decreasingly relevant to birth rates.

One stark consequence of the low births rates of the 1990s is the literal halving, between 2003 and 2016, of the number of 18-year-old men available for *conscription* (Figure 5). This cohort will rebound somewhat over the next decade, but demographic factors preclude reliance of the Russian armed forces on sheer numbers of manpower. Russian military planners, of course, have long been aware of these population trends,

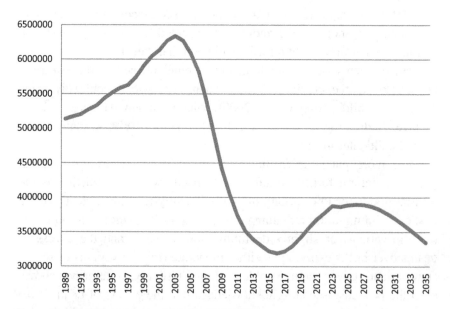

Figure 5:   Russian males, aged 15–19, 1989–2035.

Source: US Census Bureau data and projections.

which have been the primary motivator of years' worth of experimentation with terms of conscription and contract service. This shortage of military manpower — and the extent to which the armed forces will have to compete with higher education and the labour force for the attention of 18-year-old men — will persist through the 2030s.

Indeed, the consequences of the drop in the number of 18-year-olds since the 1990s are also significant for *education and the labour force* over the next several decades. Right now, there are enough spaces in institutions of higher education to accommodate every secondary school graduate. This wastes resources on students whose preparation for university studies is inadequate, and it skews the pursuit of post-secondary education away from fields and skills where need is high. This is the crux of the matter, when it comes to the impact of population decline on the economy: it will not be the *quantity* of people who matter, so much as their *quality* and *skill sets*, and the economic environment in which those skill sets are put to use (Aleksashenko, 2015).[2]

Russian economists are in general agreement that population losses alone will cost Russia 0.4–0.5% of GDP growth annually over the next decade (Goble, 2017a). If Russia's economy remains heavily reliant on natural resource extraction, its need for a large labour force is minimal (as evidenced by ongoing challenges with, for example, underemployment in Saudi Arabia). But if it intends serious diversification and development of a modern post-industrial economy, it will require human capital that is healthy and properly trained. It will require labour productivity increases of the right kind and in the right places. Investments in training must cover at least two bases well. Russia's first and better recognised shortcomings are situated in university-level education in science, engineering and information technology. While plenty of students major in these fields, the training and research base at most Russian universities lags behind world-class standards of scientific method and inquiry (see Harley Balzer's seminal contribution to this book). Equally importantly, however, and less acknowledged, is the extent to which Russia is not producing workers able to maintain the fundamental support services on which industrial and post-industrial economies are based. Because so many students can so

---

[2] See also Harley Balzer's excellent contribution to this book.

easily attend university, fewer have been choosing mid-level vocational career paths.

This leaves the Russian economy with a shrinking, ageing pool of electricians, plumbers, machine tool operators — all the technicians who know how to work with their hands, and how to fix things when they break. As the size of the labour force continues to decline over the next several decades, absent public policy encouraging students to enter these fields, the Russian economy will experience tangible impact from this skills shortage. Russian economist Nikiti Krichevsky summed it up brilliantly: "If you dig a hole not with an excavator but with shovels, then you need to have many workers. But in order to shift from manual labour, one must first produce this excavator and teach people to work it. Those are things that the current Russian government isn't doing."[3]

Mortality

Life expectancy, after plummeting in the early 1990s to an extent never seen before in a society outside wartime and the AIDS crisis in some sub-Saharan African countries, has rebounded considerably over the last decade, now comfortably exceeding pre-crisis levels (Figure 6). Average life expectancy in Russia reached 72.9 years in 2018. (In 2017, U.S. life expectancy was 79.5 and Germany's was 81.1, as points of comparison.) Again, the improving economy is largely responsible for these positive trends, contributing to better healthcare and, more importantly, to decreased levels of harmful personal behaviours.

It is also important, however, to look carefully behind the statistics. Anatoly Vishnevsky, Director of the Moscow Institute of Demography, cautions that the observed increase in life expectancy is due primarily not to decreased mortality among adults, but instead almost entirely to reductions in infant mortality, and that issues of premature death among adult men, especially younger adults in the 35–45 age group, remain high (Vishnevskiy, 2017).

Russia's demographic patterns show significant *geographic and ethnic variation*. Fertility and life expectancy are markedly higher in the

---

[3] Quoted in Goble (2017b).

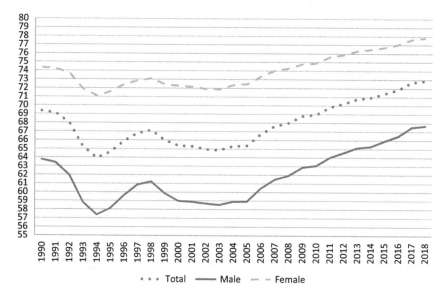

Figure 6: Life expectancy, 1990–2018.

Source: Rosstat.

more traditionally Islamic regions (due to cultural factors around contraception, family formation, social network support and patterns of alcohol consumption), and in the economically advantaged natural resource regions. Mortality is higher in Siberia and the Far East. Though these demographic differentials are not sufficient to support arguments about "Islamization" of the armed forces or the labour force, they do point to the need for more region-specific policy development and investment than is currently the case.

Improved life expectancy coupled with the low birth rates of the 1990s have produced a rapidly *ageing* society. Russia faces significant challenges related to population ageing in the coming decades: how to provide adequate geriatric healthcare; how to provide social support for increases in an already-large number of older women living alone, without the social support structures found in the multi-generational households of the Soviet period; and most importantly, how to deal with a growing *pension* burden (Figure 7) (World Bank, 2015). Several years ago, Russia reached the point where the number of workers, and the amounts they

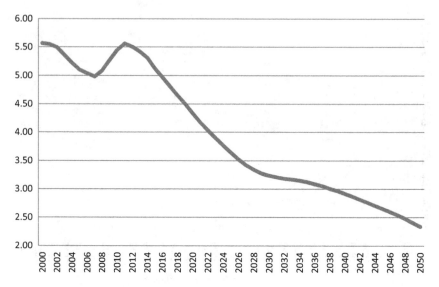

Figure 7: Ratio of working-age to pension-age populations, 2000–2050.

Source: U.S. Census Bureau data and projections.

were paying into the Pension Fund, were simply not adequate to support the payouts due to the current pensioners. Various proposals for pension reform were floated, and some (including a provision for private accounts) partially enacted to little effect, but during the 2000s and most of the 2010s, it was unthinkable to take the political risk of entertaining the response that would bring Russian labour practices in line with international standards: raising the pension age. The long-standing pension ages of 55 for women and 60 for men may have been reasonable in the 1990s, when life expectancy barely reached those thresholds, but by the early 2010s they were clearly no longer affordable. A 2012 International Monetary Fund study found that gradually raising the pension age by just a few years would make the pension burden fiscally sustainable (Figure 8), but for a long time, the Russian government just wasn't ready to alienate pension-age voters in this manner.

That changed after Putin's election to a fourth term. In June of 2018, under cover of Russia's hosting of the World Cup, legislation to raise the pension age was introduced. It proposed a phased increase of the retirement age for men from 60 to 65 (over the period 2019 through 2028), and

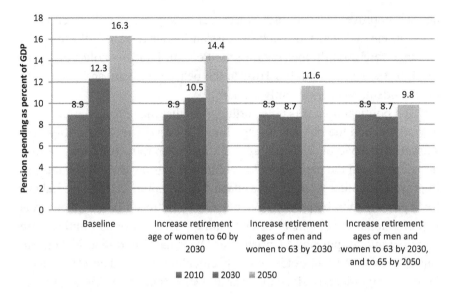

Figure 8: Impact of increasing retirement ages, 2010–2015.

Source: Reproduced from Eich, Gust and Soto (2012, p. 17). IMF staff estimates.

for women from 55 to 63 (2019 through 2034). Public opinion was sharply against this reform (polls showed opposition in the 70–90% range), and Putin's approval and popularity ratings took a hit almost certainly attributable to the policy. Russian Public Opinion Research Center (VCIOM) surveys in December of 2018 confirmed the pension reform as the "main event" of 2018 in the eyes of the Russian public (Afanasyev, 2019). There were large protests, and over 3 million people signed a petition to the President and the Duma stating simply: "Do not raise the retirement age!" Putin, who tried in public statements to shift "blame" for the original proposal to the government, partially caved: the bill that eventually passed in September 2018 dialled back the eligibility increase for women to age 60 and contained several additional provisions to soften the blow for workers reaching the designated ages over the coming decade. Smaller-scale public protests continued through the year nonetheless, and Putin's ruling United Russia party suffered in gubernatorial and legislative elections around the country in September. While there is no question that the solvency of the pension system depended on the long-overdue passage and implementation of this reform, the opposition's main points — that, despite improvements in life expectancy, many men will never reach pension age and that too much of Russian labour remains off the books and therefore doesn't contribute to the Pension Fund — hold sway with much of the Russian public. Trust in the pension system, and perhaps in the President, has permanently eroded.

The political uproar is noteworthy given that many Russians continue to work beyond the old pension age limits anyway. The 2010 census data showed that 25% of Russians aged 55 and over were fully employed a decade ago, and the percentage has continued to grow as health status has improved and older workers have adapted to economic conditions. Labour force participation by pension-age persons could reach even higher levels if professional development or continuing education opportunities were more commonly pursued.[4] Christopher Davis has found that the "human capabilities" of Russia's elderly — specifically those in their 60s — have improved significantly since the year 2000 and that newer waves of older people have higher educational attainment, professional skills and income than previous cohorts. The average circumstances and capability of the "younger elderly" in Russia have converged with those in middle-income European countries (Davis, 2018). Other studies confirm that health problems do not limit the labour force participation potential of those in the age cohorts just above pension eligibility (for example, Bakhtin and Aleksandrova, 2018).

The leading cause of death, and of premature death, in Russia — as is the case in most countries — is *non-communicable disease*, specifically cardiovascular disease (CVD). CVD accounted for 57% of all Russian mortality in 2005, declining to 48% in 2016; in 2016, 59.2% of mortality in men and 46.8% in women were attributable to behavioural risk factors related to CVD, especially alcohol, tobacco and drug use (Global Burden of Disease 2016 Russia Collaborators, 2018). Mortality due to cancer has risen considerably over the last decade (from 12% of all deaths in 2005 to 16% in 2016), in part because of better detection, and in part because

---

[4]Andrey Melnikov, "Ageing Society in Russia: Challenges and Opportunities," blog of the Swiss Education, Research, and Innovation Network, September 27, 2016, https://globalstatement.wordpress.com/2016/09/27/ageing-society-in-russia-challenges-and-opportunities/

people are living longer (and therefore have more older years during which cancer is more commonly diagnosed).

The CVD burden is spurred by a variety of factors, most notably alcohol and tobacco consumption. Russia's per capita *alcohol* consumption is among the highest in the world (Shield and Rehm, 2015; Phillips, 2015). It is not only the sheer amount, however, but the types and patterns of drinking that are of concern. Russia has a high percentage of binge drinkers, a term strictly defined as five or more drinks for men (and four for women) per day, but with specific cultural norms in Russia around intentionally drinking with the intent to lose consciousness over a period of two or several days. This manner of alcohol consumption delivers considerably more damage to human physiology than a comparable amount of drinking that might be spaced over, say, a glass or two of wine with dinner each evening.

VCIOM surveys indicate a significant decline in alcohol consumption over the last decade. Those who report drinking alcohol every day or several times a week decreased from 8% in 2009 to 5% in 2017, and even the prevalence of drinking several times a month went down from 21% to 16%. The percentage of those who claim that they do not drink at all increased from 25% in 2009 to 39% in 2017.[5]

But these numbers should be interpreted with caution. While the health ministry has boasted about a 40% reduction in alcohol purchases since 2005, increased taxes have made store-bought vodka expensive; in terms of work hours required for purchase, Russians pay five to seven times as much for alcohol as their counterparts in Western Europe (Goble, 2018). As much as half the market for alcohol may now be occupied by cheaper surrogates: alcohol not manufactured or packaged for consumption, but purchased in this form when regular alcohol is expensive or unavailable. This list includes cologne, various medications (like cough syrup), industrial lubricants and others. Non-beverage alcohol is responsible for a large percentage of the tens of thousands of cases of deaths classified as direct alcohol poisonings each year. Russia has also always had a creative and vibrant market for the production and sale of self-produced alcohol, or *samogon* (there were sugar shortages

---

[5] "Drinking habits of Russians," VCIOM, Press Release No. 1982, August 16, 2017.

everywhere during Gorbachev's 1985–1987 anti-alcohol campaign). More recently, a significant amount of mass-produced counterfeit alcohol has emerged, much of it sold on the Internet (Neufeld *et al.*, 2017; Kotelnikova, 2017). Russia's consumer safety agency, Rospotrebnadzor, suspended the sale of some surrogate alcohols in 2017 following a number of deaths blamed on drinking a bath lotion with high ethyl alcohol content in Siberia late the previous year. It also ramped up inspection of suppliers and distributors of substances known to serve as inexpensive vodka substitutes. As a result, it claims, the number of deaths due to alcohol poisoning declined by 26% in 2017 compared with the previous year.[6]

Russia is also among the global leaders in the consumption of *tobacco*, resulting in approximately 400,000 premature deaths each year, but smoking rates have been steadily decreasing for over a decade in all age groups, except young women (Stefler *et al.*, 2017).[7] Internationally run surveys indicate that overall smoking rates in Russia declined from 39.4% in 2009 to 30.9% in 2016[8]; internal surveys show a drop of those reporting smoking at least a few cigarettes every day from 37% in 2009 to 29% in 2017.[9]

It is important to give the Russian government credit for a solid set of legislative and regulatory moves that have clearly facilitated these positive trends in smoking and drinking: increased taxation, price increases and minimum price thresholds, and restrictions on points and hours of sale, advertising and consumption (Pogosova and Sokolova, 2017). Russia signed and ratified the 180-country-strong World Health Organization Framework Convention on Tobacco Control in 2008 (a step the United States still has not taken); opened hundreds of Health Centres — in some regions, the only institutions focused on disease prevention — around the country beginning in 2009; passed an Anti-Smoking Concept in 2010 that limited cigarette ads in shops, increased tobacco taxes by over 20%, and

---

[6]Deaths from alcohol fall by 25% in Russia in 2017, *The Moscow Times*, June 3, 2018.

[7]Smoking prevalence and attributable disease burden in 195 countries and territories, 1990–2015: A systematic analysis from the global burden of disease study 2015, *Lancet*, 389, 2017, 1885–1906.

[8]"Russia: Drop in alcohol use and tobacco consumption evident," iogt.org, June 19, 2017.

[9]"Monitoring the smoking situation in Russia," VCIOM, Press Release No. 1958, May 31, 2017.

banned smoking in public places from 2013; hosted the WHO's first Global Ministerial Conference on Healthy Lifestyles and Control of Non-Communicable Disease in 2011, resulting in the internationally regarded Moscow Declaration on NCDs; and declared disease prevention a priority in the 2011 federal law on "Health Care of the Citizens of the Russian Federation" (Pogosova and Sokolova, 2017). In September 2012, the Russian government committed to 10 years' worth of financing the WHO European Office on NCD prevention in Moscow. These policies continue to undergo periodic renewal through new decrees, including a summer 2017 government project "Formation of a Healthy Lifestyle" that aims to increase access to parks and recreation facilities, with the goal of increasing the percentage of Russians "committed to a healthy lifestyle" to 60% by the year 2025 (Starostin, 2018).

Infectious diseases

Estimates vary, but it is generally agreed that the number of Russia's cases of *HIV* passed the 1 million mark in early 2015. That puts HIV prevalence over 1% of the adult population. More importantly, however, Russia (along with Ukraine) has, for several years, been home to the *fastest growing* HIV epidemic in the world, especially in several major Siberian cities. The number of new cases has hovered around 100,000 annually for the last few years, the majority among injectable drug users and their sex partners (although there is certainly a large, undetected number of cases among men who have sex with men). It is impossible to discuss Russia's HIV epidemic outside a recognition of the syndemic with addiction and abuse of injectable drugs — heroin, other opiates and a variety of other home-concocted substances (Heimer, 2018; Girchenko and King, 2017).

The core challenge lies with Russia's approach to illegal drugs: it treats them as a criminal rather than public health matter (Twigg, 2019). Under this conceptualisation, effective support for those who need treatment for addiction disease is scarce. Modern methods, most importantly opioid replacement therapy (methadone or buprenorphine), are illegal in Russia; despite years of attempted persuasion by the international community, there appears to be little chance that this policy will change in the foreseeable future, as high-level political and religious leaders characterise this approach as simply "replacing one drug with another" and fear that the substitutes themselves will emerge as troublesome street drugs. There was a time when non-governmental organisations (NGOs), with funding and technical assistance from international partners, stepped in to offer needle and syringe exchange programmes. These "harm reduction" efforts often included condom distribution and information on reproductive health at the point of exchange, so that addicts would be less likely to pass HIV or any other infection to partners. With the ejection of most international donors/partners at the beginning of Putin's third term, however, the capacity of most Russian HIV/AIDS NGOs has diminished considerably, despite some courageous and valiant efforts by a few existing organisations. The cities of St. Petersburg and Kazan are two relatively bright spots, with St. Petersburg in particular serving as a last remaining hub for international collaborative research on the epidemic and innovative services (including, for example, situating needle exchange points in the outskirts of the neighbourhoods where addicts actually live), and the Andrey Rylkov Foundation for Health and Social Justice continues as a beacon for health and human rights in Moscow.[10]

The Russian government does provide anti-retroviral (ARV) medications for some HIV-positive persons, and it is the case that these ARVs not only prolong life for decades when taken correctly but also suppress viral load to the point that the infected person can no longer pass HIV to someone else. But these medications are available to only a small fraction of those in medical need, and, just as importantly, there are inadequate provisions for monitoring treatment adherence; if patients take these drugs incorrectly or incompletely, there is significant risk of emergence of drug-resistant virus. The bottom line is that, in the absence of effective prevention programmes — not just methadone and needle exchange but pre-exposure prophylaxis (currently uncommon in the country) and a broad range of humane support services and education for addicts, plus effective education and outreach to other risk groups such as sex workers

---

[10]https://en.rylkov-fond.org/.

and men who have sex with men — Russia will fail to "turn off the tap" of new HIV infections (Meylakhs *et al.*, 2017). As a consequence, although HIV is not currently among the leading causes of morbidity and mortality in Russia, it is growing — from the 23rd ranked cause of death in 2007 to 10th in 2017 — and will surely pose an accelerating public health and fiscal burden in the coming years.[11]

The other major infectious disease threat in Russia is *tuberculosis* (TB). Russia remains one of the World Health Organization's "high-burden" TB countries, despite significant progress in control efforts over the last two decades and substantial reductions in incidence and mortality (World Health Organization, 2016). Russia has moved away from older methods of diagnosis (mass X-ray screenings) and treatment (surgery to remove diseased parts of the lung) over the last two decades, largely due to support from the World Bank, the United States Agency for International Development and international NGOs such as Partners in Health. Despite these gains, however, Russia — largely because of incomplete regimens of antibiotic treatment — has become one of the world's leading generators of multi-drug-resistant (MDR) and extra-drug-resistant (XDR) TB.[12] Today, about 40% of the world's cases of drug-resistant TB are found in just four countries: Russia, South Africa, India and the Philippines (Cohen, 2017). In 2016, over a quarter of TB cases in Russia were drug resistant; a recent modelling study predicted that, absent significant policy change/intervention, by 2040 fully one-third of TB cases will be drug resistant and 10% will be XDR.[13] In addition, currently about 20% of all TB patients are found to be co-infected with HIV, and co-infection with hepatitis C is also suspected to be high (Tsui *et al.*, 2016). Moving forward, the TB and HIV/TB co-infection burden will not only strain Russia's fiscal

---

[11] Institute for Health Metrics and Evaluation data, http://www.healthdata.org/russia.

[12] MDR-TB is resistant to two of the four standard first-line drugs used to treat TB infection. XDR-TB is resistant to these drugs and also to any one of the three available second-line injectable treatments. Drug-resistant TB infection is considerably more expensive and difficult to treat, with significantly harsher side effects and a longer treatment period, than drug-susceptible TB.

[13] AVERT, HIV/AIDS in Russia, https://www.avert.org/professionals/hiv-around-world/eastern-europe-central-asia/russia.

and public health resources but also become increasingly troubling to European neighbours concerned about these infections' lack of respect for international borders.

Migration

Since the Soviet Union collapsed, the number of people entering Russia has always exceeded the number of those leaving, and the overwhelming majority of both emigrants and immigrants have been to/from Central Asia and other former Soviet countries (Figure 9). In the absence of this significant in-migration, Russia's population challenges over the last two-and-a-half decades would have been markedly worse. The actual number of immigrants is routinely far above the official statistics, with illegal labour migration accounting for millions of workers in major cities. The political dimension of Russia's migration situation in many ways mirrors that in the US: given relatively low birth rates among the "native"

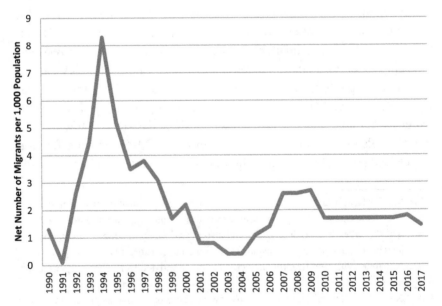

Figure 9:   Net migration, 1990–2017.

Source: Rosstat.

population, both Russia and the US desperately need this workforce to claim the low-skilled jobs that nobody else wants to do, but rising numbers of ethnic minorities also give rise to vicious, sometimes violent, anti-immigrant sentiment and public policies that fall squarely into the category of human rights violations. It is an understatement to label this a culture clash: increasingly, labour immigrants don't speak Russian; they identify not with the common Soviet experience of the past, but instead with the heritage and habits of their own countries; most of them are Muslim. Complicating the situation is the fact that the Central Asian migrant "sending" countries experienced, albeit to a lesser magnitude, the same decline in birth rates as Russia in the early 1990s, meaning that their cohort of young workers available for export to Russia is shrinking. Over the next two decades, the construction and lower level service industries in Russia may suffer labour challenges accordingly.

Migration is another area where the sheer numbers aren't as important as the qualitative dimension. Since the beginning of Putin's third term, Russia has suffered a significant "brain drain" of its so-called "creative class": scientists, journalists, artists, engineers, academics and others, spurred to departure by economic downturn, corruption and/or an increasingly hostile political environment (Twigg, 2016).[14] The exact numbers are impossible to determine, as most of this emigration is not officially registered. Many of these professionals are not formally declaring their departures to the Russian authorities, but they spend most or all of their time living and working in another country (mostly nearby, where they can feel comfortable in Russian-speaking communities, but many also in Western Europe, the US, or East Asia). Based on data from sources like real estate agents and private school enrolments in receiving countries, it is becoming apparent that this "brain drain" includes not just the super-rich but also upper-middle and middle-class Russians who are starting businesses abroad with capital of only a few hundred thousand dollars. These are the very people who should form the backbone of a forward-looking, diversified Russian economy and society. The extent to which many of them have kept one foot in the door, through sustained personal

---

[14]Russia's brain drain worse than previously believed, *The Moscow Times*, October 6, 2016.

or economic ties to home (often sending sizeable remittances back to family, or maintaining apartments or even Internet-based employment in Russia), as well as retaining Russian citizenship, means that this exodus is fairly readily reversible, should conditions in Russia become more hospitable.

One final element worthy of note in the migration discussion centers on the Russian government's repeated claim that Russia's infectious disease burden — particularly HIV and TB — is due in large part to the spread of infection via illegal immigration. Careful research on the subject, however, has found to the contrary: the direction of disease flow is outward, as labour migrants come to Russia, live in crowded conditions and engage in practices (use of sex workers, etc.) that leave them vulnerable to disease, and then take those infections back home.[15]

Healthcare and Public Investment

Healthcare in the Soviet Union was plagued by consistent underfinancing and inefficient resource allocation. The state managed, in the name of socialism, to provide universal access to care — even in the most remote, sparsely populated areas — but the quality of that care was far below what would have been expected for the country's level of overall economic development. That system collapsed in the 1990s. A universal, nationwide mandatory health insurance law has been in place since 1993, containing mechanisms of competition between providers and between insurance companies that, in principle, transition the system towards more provision of primary and preventive care, less resort to costly and unnecessary specialist care and hospitalisation and better focused attention to quality. A refinement of this law, passed in 2010, accelerated the streamlining of the hospital network, but the overall development and implementation of the insurance mechanism have been uneven. The amount of money paid in through social taxation does not cover the actual costs of care, forcing patients into unpredictable out-of-pocket expenditures for

---

[15]Biases, borders, and biohazards: Misconstruing migrants as a public health threat in the Russian federation, *Harriman Institute*, October 28, 2010, http://harriman.columbia. edu/files/harriman/Biases%2C%20Borders%20and%20Biohazards.pdf

medicines and other consumables, and sometimes side payments directly to practitioners. Political economy factors make it very difficult to shut down excess hospital capacity in a rational manner. There are severe shortages of qualified, cost-effective primary care physicians (Sheiman *et al.*, 2018).

Beginning in the mid-2000s, however, when health was one of Prime Minister Dmitry Medvedev's four Priority National Projects (the others were education, housing and agriculture), the Russian health sector has enjoyed substantial additional public investment on top of the insurance system. These resources have significantly and positively impacted the quality of care, from sprucing up basic clinics to constructing dozens of brand-new neonatal and cardiac care centres across the country (Shishkin, 2013; Cook, 2015; Bennetts, 2016; Institute of Modern Russia, 2016). Overall, however, the sector still experiences serious shortcomings in quality and efficiency, mostly held over from norms and incentive structures inherited from the Soviet period (World Bank, 2016).[16] Much of the new infrastructure development has not been accompanied by appropriate training on new equipment — in some instances, leaving that equipment unused and in disrepair — or ongoing investment in consumables (film for X-rays, for example) (Institute of Modern Russia, 2015). Systemically, healthcare providers are still paid in ways that encourage them to waste money and disregard health outcomes. Expensive investments with high political return (and potentially high payoff to corrupt public officials) — think fancy new MRI machines that make good headlines for local politicians — are funded, with insufficient regard for evidence of their medical superiority to cheaper alternatives.

Furthermore, recent attempts to accelerate cost-saving measures have led to the widespread closure of small, underused hospitals, particularly in rural areas, without adequate provision of outpatient primary care and/or availability of transportation to alternative inpatient facilities. During Putin's tenure, the number of hospitals has been cut in half to just over

---

[16]Linda Cook brilliantly summarises the legacies of the Soviet system and post-Soviet reform in "Constraints on Universal Health Care in the Russian Federation: Inequality, Informality, and the Failures of Mandatory Health Insurance Reform," United Nations Research Institute for Social Development, Working Paper 2015–5, February 2015.

5,000, and the number of beds slashed from 1.6 million to 1.2 million. The average length of hospital stay has declined from 14.3 days in 1997 to 9.4 days in 2016.[17] While this may make perfect sense from a health economics perspective, over 15,000 small villages, most of which had at least a midwife with rudimentary training during the Soviet period, now have no medical service at all; most of these are more than 10 miles away from a clinic, and many have no public transportation service. Even larger cities have seen longer lines for treatment. The situation with maternity homes has been a widely publicised example: capacity has been centralised in large facilities in regional capitals, and these centres have been blessed with new equipment and training to deal with complicated cases. That's great news for pregnant women who live in or near those cities. But at the same time, small maternity hospitals in small towns and rural areas were either downsized or eliminated, all in the name of efficiency. From 2005–2010, the total number of maternity beds in the country hovered steadily around 80,000; by 2015, it had dropped to 69,000 — an irony of reduced capacity at the very time the country's birth rate was exploding. Similarly, the number of feldsher–midwife clinics — the traditional nodes of small-town and rural primary care — declined from about 42,000 in 2005 to 34,000 in 2015 (Center for Economic and Political Reforms, 2017). If she can, a pregnant woman living in a rural or remote region now has to travel to a larger city or regional centre a week or so before her due date — and these are precisely the women and families who most frequently do not have the education or resources to take these precautions.

Furthermore, despite some sporadic salary increases, physicians — especially therapists who are supposed to be the first points of contact for primary care — are enormously undercompensated, their pay not far above that of food service or retail workers. The incentives for the "best and brightest" to pursue a career in medicine are definitely not financial. Moderate wage increases, intended to boost physician quality and satisfaction, have been financed at the regional and municipal level through reductions in the number of personnel, leading to staff shortages, longer lines for treatment and physician protests over increased workloads (Holom, 2015; Kramer, 2019). Although it appears that Russia has plenty

---

[17] OECD data, https://data.oecd.org/healthcare/length-of-hospital-stay.htm

of physicians, the structural legacies of the Soviet period — which allocated rewards based on quantity rather than quality in just about every sector — mean that there is an acute shortage of well-trained, qualified doctors (Sheiman and Gerry, 2018). Even worse, there is still an arms-length relationship between science and healthcare; "evidence-based interventions (for example, colon cancer screenings) have not been provided for years, whereas useless interventions, such as homeopathic drugs, are available" (Vlassov, 2017).

Countersanctions in response to Western sanctions in 2014, handily timed to contribute to an aggressive import substitution policy already in place, have reduced the availability of many key *pharmaceutical* products, including components needed for Russian production of key medicines. More than 50% of the patents for drugs currently sold on the Russian market are held by entities outside Russia.[18] Nonsensical state procurement policies also impact pharmaceutical availability.[19] Just one of many results: diabetics sometimes cannot get insulin (the situation appears to be worst in Saratov, where the local NGO that had supported diabetics was declared a foreign agent in 2018 because of support from the Moscow offices of two international drug companies).[20] Palliative care and pain medicines in particular are also in short supply, leading to alarming reports of increases in suicide rates among cancer patients escaping unbearable end-of-life pain.[21]

In 2012, at the beginning of his third term, Putin issued a set of Presidential directives (the "May Decrees") that included major programmes in both demography and health. Ambitious goals were set for

---

[18]Russia prepares for drug shortage in coming years, *The Pharmaletter*, May 13, 2019, https://www.thepharmaletter.com/article/russia-prepares-for-drug-shortage-in-coming-years

[19]Import substitution leads to growth in drug manufacturing, *GMP News*, March 2, 2018, https://gmpnews.net/2018/03/import-substitution-leads-to-growth-of-drug-manufacturing-in-russia/

[20]This isn't a panic, it's a catastrophe, *Meduza*, June 5, 2019, https://meduza.io/en/feature/2019/06/05/this-isn-t-a-panic-it-s-a-catastrophe

[21]Tough painkiller rules push some Russian cancer patients to suicide, *National Public Radio*, July 10, 2015, https://www.npr.org/sections/parallels/2015/07/10/421212545/tough-painkiller-rules-push-some-russian-cancer-patients-to-suicide

increasing the birth rate and life expectancy, decreasing mortality, increasing domestic production of pharmaceuticals and eliminating staff shortages, especially in primary care. The "May Decree" exercise was repeated in 2018, within the framework of a national target to increase life expectancy to 76 by 2024 and 80 in 2030. Demography and health are among the best funded of 2018's 12 new "national projects," behind only road modernisation and ecology (aimed primarily at new waste processing facilities, a sore subject among thousands of protesters around the country in recent years) (see, for example, MacFarquhar (2019)).

The *health project*'s budget, slated at over $33 billion for 2019–2024 (roughly $26.3 billion from the federal budget, $5 billion from regional budgets and the rest from other sources), covers eight distinct federal-level components as follows (Government of Russia, 2019):

- development of primary medical care: $1.2 billion;
- CVD prevention and treatment: $1.4 billion;
- cancer prevention and treatment: $18.6 billion;
- child health, including development of children's medical centres: $4 billion;
- training for medical professionals: $3.2 billion;
- development of national medical research centres and introduction of innovative technologies: $1.2 billion;
- creation of a unified, national-level health information system: $3.4 billion;
- development of export of medical services (medical tourism): $3.8 million.

The goalposts cover the following set of nine targets, all with well-defined baselines, annual benchmarks and reasonably well-defined theories of change explaining what will get them from here to there:

- Reduce working-age mortality, from 484.5/100,000 population in 2018 to 350/100,000 in 2024, to be achieved through introduction of new methods (including clinical practice guidelines) for prevention, diagnosis, treatment and rehabilitation; introduction of new quality control mechanisms at the municipal, regional and federal district levels; and increases in the use of telemedicine for consultation and treatment.

- Reduce mortality due to heart disease, from 587.6/100,000 population in 2018 to 450/100,000 in 2024, to be achieved through rehabilitation and equipping of regional and primary cardiac care centres.
- Reduce mortality due to cancer, from 200.6/100,000 population in 2018 to 185/100,000 in 2024, to be achieved through information and communication campaigns, organisation of centres for ambulatory cancer care in all 85 regions, rehabilitation and equipping of federal and regional medical centres that provide cancer treatment and establishment of new cancer research centres.
- Reduce infant mortality, from 5.6/1,000 births in 2018 to 4.5/1,000 in 2024, to be achieved through training of specialists at regional neonatal centres, rehabilitation and equipping of children's hospitals and clinics and provision of guaranteed medical care to pregnant and postpartum women.
- Eliminate human resource deficits in primary care, including the following.

  o Full staffing of primary care facilities, increased from 79.7% in 2018 to 95% in 2024.
  o Full staffing of primary care facilities with mid-level medical personnel, increased from 88.8% in 2018 to 95% in 2024.
  o Number of specialists involved in continuing medical education of primary care workers (including distance education), increased from 109,000 in 2018 to 1.9 million in 2024.

These targets are to be achieved through development of new interactive training modules/centres and accreditation procedures, through which 1.9 million new primary care specialists will be trained and certified.

- Increase the percentage of Russians receiving full medical check-ups annually, from 39.7% in 2018 to 70% in 2024, with an accelerated timetable for increasing this percentage among those aged 15–17 from 38.7% in 2018 to 80% in 2024.
- Decrease the number of cities with population between 100,000 and 200,000 having residents without adequate access to primary care, from 788 in 2018 to 0 by 2021, to be achieved through development of mobile

medical units and construction of additional helipads at medical centres, replacement of obsolete emergency facilities and building of new primary care/midwife stations.

- Increase the percentage of primary care facilities operating according to a "new model" that decreases wait times and streamlines patient processes for making medical appointments, from 3% in 2018 to 72.3% in 2024.

- Quadruple the dollar volume of services offered to "medical tourists" to Russia, from $250 million in 2018 to $1 billion in 2024, to be achieved through information campaigns, the establishment of a coordinating centre for the export of medical services, and better data collection on medical services offered to foreigners.

All of these activities are to be supported through the development of a country-wide health management information system, connecting administrative and clinical facilities from the federal to municipal levels with an individual patient portal ("My Health"). 90% of medical offices are to be networked with this system by the end of 2021.

The *demography project's* $59.7 billion budget, the majority of it from federal coffers, goes almost entirely ($51.7 billion) to financing the maternity capital programme. Of the rest, $3.2 billion is allocated to child care up to age 3; $2.9 billion to sports and physical fitness initiatives, $1.9 billion to programmes on ageing and $71 million on healthy lifestyles. Its four targets are as follows:

- Increase *healthy* life expectancy to 67 years (no baseline is given). Requires reduction of mortality in people above the working age, from 38.1/1,000 in 2018 to 36.1/1,000 in 2024, to be achieved through increasing medical check-ups, introducing a new system of long-term care for older and disabled people, establishing new regional geriatric/senior centres, and enrolling a half-million pre-pension-age adults in vocational education and training.

- Increase the TFR from 1.62 in 2018 to 1.70 in 2024, to be achieved through continuation of the maternity capital programme; additional monthly payments to families for first-born children and for families with three or more children; subsidised mortgages for families with two or more children; increased availability of in vitro fertilisation, paid by compulsory medical insurance; increased financing for training for women to re-enter the workforce following maternity leave; and construction and staffing of additional day-care and pre-school facilities, including for children with disabilities.

- Increase the share of the population leading a healthy lifestyle. This involves increasing the number of people who consult the healthcare system on questions about healthy lifestyles, from 1.7 million in 2018 to 3 million in 2024, and increasing the number of people for whom health centres recommend individual healthy lifestyle plans ("health passports"), from 4 million in 2018 to 5.5 million in 2024, to be achieved through communication campaigns over mass media and the workplace.

- Increase the share of the population systematically taking part in athletics and sports, from 36.8% in 2018 to 55% in 2024, to be achieved through construction and equipping of new municipal and school-based recreation and sports facilities, with particular focus on hockey, indoor skating and soccer, and employing thousands of additional instructors and trainers.

Target setting can be an important motivator, especially if there are real action plans, money to implement them and accountability for results. It remains unclear whether these prerequisites are currently present in Russia. The economic downturn threatens the medium-term availability of promised resources. Even more importantly, accountability can't work without good information. There has always been uncertainty around Russian health and demographic data, due to both capacity limitations in the reporting system and suspicion of deliberate falsification, but monitoring behaviours around both the 2012 and 2018 decrees have produced another source of doubt. It appears that reports of deaths caused by conditions for which there are specific reduction targets — tuberculosis, cancer and road accidents — are declining, while those from causes in related categories or "unspecified" causes *not* covered by the decrees' targets are on the rise. It seems likely that officials at various levels are fudging the numbers, coding deaths in ways that fall outside national project target areas (Coynash, 2018). This practice calls into question the extent to which evidence is guiding decision-making, breaking the essential link between funded activities and intended outcomes.

Summary

Russia has come a long way from the full-blown demographic and health crisis of the 1990s, but population factors will continue to shape and constrain its development trajectories in important ways for the foreseeable future. It is a cliché, but this really is a blind-men-and-the-elephant situation: the assessment of progress and prospects depends on where you're looking. Russia's recent public health policies — particularly restrictions on tobacco and alcohol sale and consumption — have in general conformed with international best practice, producing tangible results in CVD morbidity and mortality. Birth rates and life expectancy have risen to a degree that virtually nobody would have predicted a decade ago. But serious challenges remain with HIV, tuberculosis and other infectious diseases and with the quality and efficiency of the healthcare provision. In order to maintain and develop human capital of sufficient calibre to compensate for inevitably declining quantity, especially in the face of economic downturn and continued international sanctions, Russia will have to build on its recent track record with geographically targeted, smart investments in healthcare, infectious disease prevention, healthy lifestyles, non-communicable disease management, workforce development, migration policy and other key areas. Most importantly, it will have to do something it has not done well before: do more with less. If not, both access to adequate healthcare and provision of appropriately skilled labour may emerge as ever more important social, economic, and even political challenges in the not-so-distant future.

References

Afanasyev, S. (2019). Pension case: Year of most high-profile reform of 2010s. *Realnoye Vremya*. Available at: https://realnoevremya.com/articles/3597-how-pension-reform-anger-russia-a-year-ago-and-why.

Aleksashenko, S. (2015). The Russian economy in 2050: Heading for labor-based stagnation, The Brookings Institution, https://www.brookings.edu/blog/up-front/2015/04/02/the-russian-economy-in-2050-heading-for-labor-based-stagnation/.

Bakhtin, M. and Aleksandrova, Ye. (2018). Health and labor force participation of elderly Russians, *Applied Econometrics* 49, 5–29.

Bennetts, M. (2016). Russia's bad health care system is getting worse. *Newsweek*, November 21. Available at: http://www.newsweek.com/2016/12/02/dire-russia-health-care-523380.html.

Center for Economic and Political Reforms (2017). What is the result of optimization of Russian maternity homes? Center for Economic and Political Reforms. Available at: http://cepr.su/2017/09/08/оптимизация-российских-роддомов/.

Cohen, J. (2017). Drug-resistant tuberculosis strains gain foothold in Russia, *Science*. Available at: http://www.sciencemag.org/news/2017/05/drug-resistant-tuberculosis-strains-gain-foothold-russia.

Cook, L. (2015). Constraints on universal health care in the Russian Federation, United Nations Research Institute for Social Development Working Paper 2015-5.

Coynash, H. (2018). Dead Souls for Putin: Even Death Statistics Are Fiddles in Russia, Human Rights in Ukraine, Kharkiv Human Rights Protection Group, Kharkiv, Ukraine, http://khpg.org/en/index.php?id=1520943894.

Davis, C. M. (2018). The changing capabilities of cohorts of the elderly in Russia during 1990–2020: Measurement using a quantitative index, *Population Ageing* 11, 153–208.

Ferris-Rotman, A. (2017). Putin's next target is Russia's abortion culture, *Foreign Policy*, October 3.

Girchenko, P. and King, E. J. (2017). Correlates of double risk of HIV acquisition and transmission among women who inject drugs in St. Petersburg, Russia, *AIDS Behavior* 21, 1054–1058.

Global Burden of Disease 2016 Russia Collaborators (2018). The burden of disease from 1980 to 2016: A systematic analysis for the global burden of disease study 2016, *The Lancet* 392, 1138–1146.

Goble, P. (2017a). Russia caught between economic decline and potentially explosive demographic change. Window on Eurasia. Available at: http://windowoneurasia2.blogspot.com/2017/07/russia-caught-between-economic-decline.html.

Goble, P. (2017b). Russian government to blame for looming labor shortage, Moscow experts say, Window on Eurasia. Available at: http://windowoneurasia2.blogspot.com/2017/09/russian-government-to-blame-for-looming.html

Goble, P. (2018). Russians buying less alcohol in stores but compensating with moonshine and surrogates. Window on Eurasia. Available at: http://windowoneurasia2.blogspot.com/2018/04/russians-buying-less-alcohol-in-stores.html

Government of Russia (2019). National projects: indicators and main results. Available at: http://static.government.ru/media/files/p7nn2CS0pVhvQ98O OwAt2dzCIAietQih.pdf.

Heimer, R. (2018). The policy-driven HIV epidemic among opioid users in the Russian Federation, *Current HIV/AIDS Reports* 15(3), 259–265.

Holom, B. (2015). Russian health care protests continue despite Putin's popularity. *Washington Post.* Available at: https://www.washingtonpost.com/news/monkey-cage/wp/2015/01/01/russian-health-care-protests-continue-despite-putins-popularity/?utm_term=.9266c70c5c9e.

Institute of Modern Russia. (2015). *Russia's Health Care System: Current State of Affairs and the Need for Reforms*, Institute of Modern Russia, Moscow.

Kotelnikova, Z. (2017). Explaining counterfeit alcohol purchases in Russia, *Alcoholism: Clinical and Experimental Research* 41(4), 810–819.

Kramer, A. E. (2019). In Russia's provinces, the doctor is in (the streets). *New York Times*, May 25. Available at: https://www.nytimes.com/2019/05/25/world/europe/russia-doctor-protests-navalny.html.

MacFarquhar, N. (2019). Russians, feeling poor and protesting garbage, suffer winter blues. *New York Times*, February 19. Available at: https://www.nytimes.com/2019/02/19/world/europe/russia-putin-landfill.html.

Meylakhs, P. Aasland, A. and Grønningsæter, A. (2017). 'Until people start dying in droves, no actions will be taken': Perception and experience of HIV-preventive measures among people who inject drugs in Northwestern Russia, *Harm Reduction Journal* 14, 33–39.

Neufeld, M., Lachenmeier, D. W., Walch, S. G. and Rehm, J. (2017). The internet trade of counterfeit spirits in Russia: An emerging problem undermining alcohol, public health, and youth protection policies?, *F1000 Research* 6, 520–527.

Phillips, M. (2015). Russia is quite literally drinking itself to death. *Quartz,* May 13. Available at: https://qz.com/403307/russia-is-quite-literally-drinking-itself-to-death/.

Pogosova, N. and Sokolova, O. (2017). Governmental efforts for cardiovascular disease prevention in the Russian Federation, *Cardiovascular Diagnosis and Therapy* 7(Suppl. 1), S48–S54.

Sheiman, I. and Gerry, C. (2018). Too many and too few: The paradoxical case of physicians in the Russian Federation, *International Journal of Health Planning and Management* 33(1), 391–402.

Sheiman, I., Shishkin, S. and Shevsky, V. (2018). The evolving Semashko model of primary health care: The case of the Russian Federation, *Risk Management and Healthcare Policy* 11, 209–220.

Shield, K. D. and Rehm, J. (2015). Russia-specific relative risks and their effects on the estimated alcohol-attributable burden of disease, *Biomed Central Public Health* 15, 482–493.

Shishkin, S. (2013). Russia's health care system: Difficult path of reform, in Alexeev, M. and Weber, S. (eds.), *The Oxford Handbook on the Russian Economy,* Oxford University Press, New York, pp. 748–774.

Starostin, V. P. (2018). Russian state policy towards forming a healthy lifestyle: Major trends over ten years, *International Journal of Applied and Basic Research* 5(part 1), 130–137 (in Russian). Available at: https://applied-research.ru/ru/article/view?id=12230.

Stefler, D., *et al.* (2017). Smoking and mortality in Eastern Europe: Results from the PrivMort Retrospective Cohort Study of 177376 individuals, *Nicotine & Tobacco Research,* 20(6), 749–754.

Tsui, J. I., *et al.* (2016). Insights on the Russian HCV care cascade: Minimal HCV treatment for HIV/HCV co-infected PWID in St. Petersburg, *Hepatology, Medicine, and Policy* 1, 1–14.

Twigg, J. (2016). Russia is losing its best and brightest. *The National Interest,* July 2. Available at: http://nationalinterest.org/feature/russia-losing-its-best-brightest-16572.

Twigg, J. (2019). Russia's avoidable epidemic of HIV/AIDS. PONARS Policy Memo No. 581. Available at: http://www.ponarseurasia.org/memo/russias-avoidable-epidemic-hivaids.

Vishnevskiy, A. (2017). What will happen if only a few major cities remain? *Znak,* August 25. Available at: https://www.znak.com/2017-08-25/demograf_anatoliy_vishnevskiy_o_krizise_rozhdaemosti_roste_smertnosti_i_probleme_migracii.

Vlassov, V. V. (2017). Russian medicine: Trying to catch up on scientific evidence and human values, *The Lancet* 390, 1619–1620.

World Bank (2015). Searching for a new silver age in Russia: The drivers and impacts of population aging. Available at: http://documents.worldbank.org/curated/en/851101467995634363/pdf/99487-WP-P151617-P143250-PUBLIC-Box393203B-silver-aging-web-final.pdf.

World Bank (2016). Russian federation systematic country diagnostic: Pathways to inclusive growth. Available at: http://pubdocs.worldbank.org/en/184311 484167004822/Dec27-SCD-paper-eng.pdf.

World Health Organization (2016). Tuberculosis surveillance and monitoring in Europe: The Russian Federation. Available at: http://www.euro.who.int/__ data/assets/pdf_file/0018/310806/TB-surveillance-report-2016-The-Russian-Federation.pdf.

Chapter 6

Can Russia Catch Up/Keep Up? Russian Science and Education in Putin's Fourth Term

Harley Balzer

As the dissipation of the Soviet Union's hard-won, if deeply uneven, achievements in education and science continues, Vladimir Putin's government persists in making sports facilities and weapons its funding priorities.[1] The fascinating conundrum in this story is how Russia manages to maintain a credible military capacity as its status as a centre of scientific education and research declines. How long this can continue in the face of low economic growth and sanctions and the flight of the creative class has become a crucial question.

The demise of Russia's knowledge economy provides a stark contrast to China's ability to reconfigure Soviet-style education and science-technology (S&T) systems (Balzer and Askonas, 2016; Balzer, 2017, 2010). Russia's decline in human capital capacity is unprecedented in its

---

[1] In his address to the legislature, delivered just before the Presidential election, and his Decrees in May, President Putin (2018a, 2018b) did lay out an ambitious programme for broad economic development. Many of the items on the list repeated promises made in the same fora in 2012.

scale and speed.[2] While it was certainly possible to identify significant weaknesses in Soviet education, science and technology (Gustafson, 1980; Balzer, 1989, 1993), the USSR did manage important achievements in priority areas.

Soviet math and physics, especially in the theoretical realm, were highly regarded. Sputnik created an erroneous but powerful narrative of Soviet leadership in education and science.

The Russian government's failure to adapt the Soviet system to the demands of globalised education systems and increasingly internationalised production processes (Baldwin, 2016) is one of the most important geostrategic phenomena of the 21st century. It will have profound long-term consequences for Russian society, the economy and the balance of military power. Russia's diminished education and science capacity represents a tragic loss to the international scientific community. Russian decline creates opportunities for China to become the leading S&T competitor to the US, assuming the role of an alternative model for developing countries and establishing itself as the rival military power (Ignatius, 2018).[3]

Russia's knowledge economy's decline is the result of inadequate yet wasteful funding, exacerbating problems due to bureaucratic tutelage and competition, ageing personnel who resist change, limited involvement of business in research and development (R&D) and declining ethical standards. Developments following the 2014 Russian annexation of Crimea called attention to the lack of potential partners for Russian technology development, the extent to which military R&D might be a basis for improvement and the impact of Western sanctions.

---

[2]Ancient Greece and the Medieval Arab world were longer processes and are not really comparable with the world after the industrial revolution. Britain experienced *relative* decline in the 19th century, as Germany and the US developed research-based technologies in new disciplines. Both Germany and Japan needed more than a decade to recover from defeat in World War II, but their education systems and some research facilities continued to function at close to pre-war standards.

[3]Ignatius (2018) summarises some of the reports presented at the Aspen Security Conference in 2018 describing Chinese advances in artificial intelligence and new, lower cost weapons systems.

Even the current limited level of funding for education and science may be difficult to maintain. Russian economists have increasingly argued that Russia's economic model based on natural resource, primarily hydrocarbon, exports is no longer sustainable (Kudrin and Gurvich, 2014; Akindinova *et al.*, 2016; Aleksashenko, 2018). Even critics of "liberal dogma" note the problem of an excessive focus on the military (Iaremenko, 2015, p. 9). The problem is not that natural resource/commodity exports inevitably hamper economic growth (Wright and Czleusta, 2007; Lederman and Maloney, 2007; Humphreys *et al.*, 2007) but that so many commodity exporters manage their resources badly (Ascher, 1999; Humphreys *et al.*, 2007; Jones Luong and Weinthal, 2006). Vladimir Putin has created a system based on central control and redistribution of the hydrocarbon rents (Gaddy and Ickes, 2005). This allows him to enrich his family and his cronies; keep government officials, including those in the regions, on a short leash; and deploy Russia's energy resources as a tool of both domestic and foreign policy. The downside is that Russian oil and gas companies remain notoriously inefficient (Baker Institute, 2007; Abdelal and Mitrova, 2013). Relying on hydrocarbon resources as both the major source of government revenue and a tool of geopolitical influence produces contradictory pressures that increase the inefficiencies (Balzer, 2005, 2006; Stulberg, 2015).

If former Finance Minister Aleksei Kudrin and the others who believe that Russia's hydrocarbon-based growth model is exhausted are correct, the ambitious national development agenda Mr. Putin described in his March 1, 2018 address is not affordable (Putin, 2018a). Limited funding for science and education has exacerbated a slew of problems inherited from the Soviet era (Gustafson, 1980; Balzer, 1989, 1993).

Many of the problems are common to both the education system and the R&D establishment, with some nuances. Other difficulties are more specific to one sector.[4]

---

[4] Shortly before this book manuscript went to press, the Russian Accounting Chamber released a scathing report confirming many of the problems discussed in this chapter. Rather than rewriting the entire chapter, the author has added a "Postscript" discussing the most important contributions made by the Accounting Chamber report. It is particularly valuable for descriptions of the poor return on Russia's (relatively modest) investment in R&D. The "Postscript" also provides some recent data, notes the growing impact of the

Beyond the need to more fully revise the Soviet system, problems common to both education and science and technology include the following:

(1) declining quality and international prestige;
(2) inadequate funding, exacerbated by inefficient use of the available funds;
(3) ageing personnel;
(4) continuing brain drain, both internal and external;
(5) a chaotic and ineffective policy environment despite solid analysis by specialists;
(6) resistance to change on the part of epistemic communities;
(7) increasing stratification (general social, education access, across institutions and regional);
(8) contradictory signals regarding internationalisation.

Issues of particular concern in education include the following:

(9) the student pipeline;
(10) persistent weakness in vocational education;
(11) declining standards and pervasive corruption.

Issues of particular concern in S&T include the following:

(12) persisting division between basic and applied research;
(13) lack of business demand for or support of R&D, exacerbating weak innovation;
(14) sanctions;
(15) the advanced weaponry conundrum.

(1) Russian scientists' share of global peer-reviewed scientific publications has diminished, their work is cited less often than that of Western colleagues, Russians apply for and receive a declining share of patents, and there are no Russian brands among global high-technology

---

COVID-19 virus outbreak, and summarises the January 2020 changes in the Russian government that include new Ministers overseeing education and science.

leaders (see Appendices 1–5). Few Russian higher education institutions are among the world's top-ranked universities (see Appendix 6). The situation reflects a failure to adapt the Soviet system to a globally interconnected economy.

The Soviet Union built a system in the second quarter of the 20th century based on higher education institutions (VUZy)[5] engaged primarily in teaching, an Academy of Sciences focused on basic research and industrial research institutes conducting applied research (Korol, 1957; DeWitt, 1961). This system was implemented between the two World Wars, a period when the Great Depression made economic autarky and national science policy reasonable strategies. With the return of internationalisation and globalisation after World War II, systems limiting international collaboration have become less able to compete.

The entire R&D system was funded by the state, either directly or through state enterprises. With the exception of some side payments for tutoring and other educational services, the same was true of the education system. Russia has been one of the less successful former communist countries at diversifying funding.

Some countries where the Soviet system was imposed or copied (Estonia, China) have managed to develop respected and in some cases highly competitive 21st-century knowledge economy capacities.[6] This indicates that Russia's problem is not just in the difficulty of reforming the Soviet system (though this should not be underestimated), but rather a combination of flawed policy decisions, resistance by epistemic communities (professional groups engaged in knowledge-based fields) that continue to favour Soviet practices and a political leadership prioritising control and personal enrichment rather than dynamic if less predictable development.

---

[5]The Soviet system had a limited number of universities. Most higher education was provided by a variety of specialised institutes. All of these institutions were referred to as *Vysshie uchebnye zevedenii*, or VUZy. After the end of communist rule, many of the specialised institutes acquired the formal status of universities to gain additional benefits.
[6]China is now undergoing a "Xi" change that is creating similar problems, turning away from the embrace of international linkages that made high rates of growth possible for three decades (Balzer, 2016).

Not only has Russia's contribution to science been outstripped by China and a number of other industrialising nations but Russia has barely managed to maintain the level of scientific publications and patents it reached in 1990. In 2016, Russia ranked 14th in the world in articles published in journals indexed both by Scopus and Web of Science (*Indikatory nauki*, 2018, pp. 301–302). Russian scholars have increased their share of Scopus and Web of Science publications (*Indikatory nauki*, 2018, p. 214), although several analysts regard this as a product of gaming the system (Moed *et al.*, 2018). Prospects for significant improvement by 2030 are bleak due to economic difficulties, poor management and stagnation-inducing policy conflicts.[7]

Attempts at reform in the 1990s foundered due to massive opposition and economic stringency (Graham and Dezhina, 2008). Near the end of Putin's second term as President, Russia's Academy of Sciences issued a scathing report warning that Russia was falling behind not only developed nations but also "second-tier" countries like China (*Rossiiskaia Akademiia Nauk*, 2008).[8] The authors identified the most serious problems as being in the realm of human capital. Despite providing a long list of shortcomings, the Academy authors insisted the situation could be remedied, claiming that Russia still ranked third in the world in scientific potential. If the government would increase the state budget share for civilian science from 1.1% to 3.5%, Russia could by 2030 rank third globally in the science intensity of GNP. Unfortunately, the Academy's

---

[7]The economic issues are discussed in other chapters. The three crucial points to be noted here are as follows:

(1) The Russian economic model based on hydrocarbon exports is exhausted and increasingly threatened by shifts in global energy markets (Kudrin and Gurvich, 2014; Balzer, 2015).

(2) Analysts who reject the argument that a crisis is imminent instead forecast slow decline (Aleksashenko, 2016, 2018).

(3) Russian regions demonstrate little capacity to develop without being included in major State programmes that are designed to meet Moscow's goals and tend to be both wasteful and riddled with corruption (Balzer, 2008).

[8]That in 2008, the Academy experts viewed China as a "second-tier" performer in science and technology is itself a striking indication of their failure to comprehend changes taking place in the capacities of the two countries.

report appeared just as Russia entered what many have described as a "lost decade" for economic growth and development (Aleksashenko, 2018, p. 8).

Russian officials have consistently suggested that they have ample time to fix the problems. Delay inevitably carries risks. Dezhina (2016) points out that the government finally decided to make innovation a high priority precisely at the time when declining oil prices deprived the state budget of the funds needed to achieve these goals.

Declining Russian performance in most areas of science and technology reflects a combination of unanswered financial and institutional challenges. The Academy of Sciences has withered (McGilvray, 2016). While these problems have been described at length, the shortcomings in education and the failure of Russian universities to expand their role have been particularly serious obstacles.

Given the repressed demand for higher education in the Soviet Union, it was perhaps inevitable that greater freedom after 1991 would result in demands for expanding opportunities for higher education rather than reforming the system. The number of institutions and students increased markedly in the mid-1990s (see Appendices 7–9), at a time when the economy was in difficult circumstances. While the share of high school graduates entering higher education reached levels unmatched in other countries, faculty resources did not increase proportionately (see Appendix 10).

It is often overlooked that one-half of Russian higher education students are enrolled in correspondence programmes rather than full-time study (see Appendix 8). The correspondence programmes are generally described as uneven, with many of questionable quality. Even a majority of full-time students start working by their third year, often to earn money to cover their living expenses rather than as part of their academic programme. A majority do not work in the specialities they study following graduation, a particular problem in medicine.

The declining quality of education in Russia is now widely accepted.

After the *Times* ranking of world universities ceased to include "reputation" as one of the criteria in its rankings, Russian universities vanished from the top 200. One perhaps understandable but dubious response has been to devise new ranking systems designed to prioritise "unique" Russian attributes. While some leading Russian universities have risen rapidly in their own rating system, global rankings indicate that no Russian VUZy rank in the top 100 in 75 of the listed subject areas. No Russian VUZy are listed in rankings in areas including urban studies, transportation, agriculture, medicine, biomedicine and other important fields. This demonstrates a real threat of Russian backwardness in these areas (*Dvenadtsat' Reshenii,* 2018, p. 63).

A recent article noting that Russian universities had achieved a slight improvement in some global rankings admitted that it represented a negligible gain (*Vedomosti,* 2017, p. 1, 6). In a scathing series of articles on the problem of brain drain, Koniukhova (2017a, 2017b) states that Russian higher education is of lower quality than at many institutions in Europe, Asia and North America, yet often costs as much or more. Koniukhova (2017a) asks why any Russian student would pay to study in Russia when for the same price or less they could learn English and earn the right to work in Europe or Asia. This may also help explain why the Russian government has tried to encourage students studying abroad to return, warning them of potential difficulties due to anti-Russian propaganda (Ikonen, 2018).

The most worrisome data for Russia's future pertain not to the number of students, graduate students or scientific workers and engineers but rather to the willingness of the brightest and most creative people to work in their specialities and remain in Russia (see Appendix 12). The talent exodus issues extend beyond education and science and are significant enough to merit more detailed discussion below.

(2) Despite being among global leaders in the numbers of students, scientists and engineers, Russian state funding for both education and science remains well below the average for OECD members and other developed countries. While Russia is one of the world leaders in higher education attainment, it spends far less than other high achievers, just 3.5% of GNP compared to an average of 5.2%. Russia also lags in contributions from the private sector, which constitute just 0.8% of GNP. Compared to OECD member countries, Russia spends 1.7 times less per student in higher education and 2 times less in general education. Experts suggest that education requires an

additional 1–1.5% of GNP to begin to be globally competitive (*Dvenadtsat' Reshenii*, 2018, p. 18). However, due to the country's economic problems, their "base" scenario would increase the current level by just 0.8%. Ideally, the level should rise to 4.8% of GNP (*Dvenadtsat' reshenii*, 2018, p. 89).

Russia's R&D spending is 1.13% of GDP, compared to a world average of 2.23%.

Some 70% of research is funded by the state. Putin's May 2012 Ukaz to increase overall funding was not implemented. The result is that Russia is now actively working in less than 5% of the scientific areas most rapidly developing in the global R&D market (*Dvenadtsat' Reshenii*, 2018, p. 21). Russian spending for R&D at VUZy is eight times less per student than the OECD average (*Dvenadtsat' Reshenii*, 2018, p. 14).

The Academy's insistence that it needs more financial resources would be familiar to most scientific communities. In the Russian case, however, it comes in the context of an astonishing record of poor returns from investments in science. Financial stringency should produce an incentive to make every ruble count, yet in both education and science, funding is not being used effectively. Numerous analyses indicate that Russian spending for science and education is ineffective (Korovkin, 2016; Suvorov *et al.*, 2015, p. 15; Frolov, 2014). Comparative data from BRICS and OECD nations provide compelling evidence of the inefficiencies (Barabash *et al.*, 2017). Russia's Federal budget for civilian R&D increased threefold from 2003 to 2013; yet R&D intensity (the ratio of R&D to value-added within an industry) remained almost flat. It was 1.29 in 2003 and dropped to 1.12 in 2013. The only other countries to experience a decline in R&D intensity were South Africa and the U.K. Turkey nearly doubled its R&D intensity; China increased from 1.13 (about where Russia is now) to 2.02 (Gokhberg and Kuznetsova, 2016, p. 346). As in so many realms, increased funding has not produced visible results. Dezhina (2011) describes a chaotic policy environment that lowers returns. Others emphasise the extent of corruption.[9]

---

[9] See Abramov and Sokolov (2016), Denisova-Schmidt *et al.* (2016), Golunov (2014) and Osipian (2012). The problems are hardly new (Simes, 1982; Popovsky, 1979), but the

At 40% of State VUZY, funding for R&D per faculty member is less than 100,000R (about $1500). Only a small share of regional VUZ faculty and students are involved in research, and they rarely have external partners. The great majority (not less than 70%) of graduate students must work outside their educational institutions to support themselves, limiting their ability to concentrate on their scientific work (*Dvenadtsat' Reshenii,* 2018, p. 22).

The challenges in funding Russia's education system result from a combination of Soviet legacies, expansion during the years of economic difficulty after 1991 and global trends affecting all education systems (Wang, 2000; Bray and Borevskaya, 2001; World Bank, 1993; Scott, 1998; Carnoy *et al.,* 2013).

The Soviet Union created a highly uneven education system. While the USSR achieved universal literacy and developed several outstanding higher education institutions, the system favoured elite students and institutions, performing less well in serving "average" consumers. Discussions of reform under Gorbachev made these difficulties explicit (Kerr, 1994; Liusyi, 2003; Balzer, 1989). Reform programmes in the 1990s focused on expanding opportunities and encouraging diversity, but economic stringency limited what could be accomplished. Since 2000, policy has emphasised modernising Russia's education system, including, at least until 2014, internationalisation (Startsev, 2012).

Since the demise of the USSR, enrolments at the growing number of state higher education institutions have increased while a system of private institutions rapidly developed. There were about 500 higher educational institutions in the Russian Republic (906 in entire USSR) in 1990; by 2004, more than 1500 VUZy were operating in Russia, 40% of them private (see Appendix 7). Enrolments as a proportion of high-school graduates are among the highest in the world. Some 58% of Russians aged 25–34 have a tertiary education; the average for OECD countries is 42% (British Council, 2017). Growth in the education system has been spontaneous and uneven. The vast majority of both state and private institutions

---

Soviet system encouraged both "stealing from the state" and "stealing for the state". Beginning in the Gorbachev era, corruption has shifted to an overwhelming emphasis on personal enrichment. For some recent data, see Åslund (2018).

are starved for resources, a situation that is reaching crisis proportions in a low-growth economy with a declining number of applicants and since 2014 fewer families able to contribute to the cost of education (Mamedli and Sinyakov, 2018).

The inevitable reckoning was first announced in 2012 and began in earnest in 2014. Some one-third of state VUZy were closed, while the cuts in private institutions amount to two-thirds. The total number of state and private institutions, including branch campuses (*filialy*) declined from 2,268 at the beginning of 2014 to 1,171 at the beginning of 2018. In the first quarter of 2018, the total number dropped to 1,097 (Makeeva, 2018; see Appendix 8). This is serious enough that the annual Statistical yearbook (*Statisticheskii ezhegodnik*) ceased publishing the data on the number of state and private VUZy.

Following the demise of the Soviet Union, private money flooded into the state education system, but with little evidence of this involving transparent arrangements or creative partnerships. Now, faced with challenging economic and demographic outlooks, Russia does not need more schools, but requires more effective financial support for existing institutions.

The challenges reflect not merely a lack of funding but serious misallocation of available resources, flawed policy and widespread corruption as well. In an article about the Russian middle classes (Balzer, 2001), I suggested that education and medical care are the two realms where people are likely to utilise all available resources and to draw on families and informal networks. Subsequent research (Gostev *et al.*, 2013) confirms this view. Russians spend more money on education than on medical care. Some 90% of Russians reported making "unofficial" contributions to educational institutions (*Izvestiia*, August 29, 2001, p. 3.) Anecdotal information indicates that admission to a prestigious university may require bribes of as much as $25,000. The ability to extract these rents varies according to the location, quality and size of the institution, the desirability of particular specialties and the economic resources available to students (Popravko and Rykun, 2002).

In 2012, President Putin responded to the need for higher salaries for faculty at all levels by decreeing increases for teachers and university faculty. Resources to fund these pay raises were not forthcoming.

The share of the central government budget devoted to education fell from 4.1% of GDP to 3.6%, one of the lowest in the world (*Dvenadtsat' Reshenii,* 2018, p. 87). The result was to make education one example of a growing number of unfunded mandates for local governments to support if they could. Most could not.

The tradition of state-funded education at all levels, enshrined in constitutions promulgated under Stalin (1935, Article 121), Brezhnev (1977, Article 45) and Yeltsin (1993, Article 43), made it difficult for many educators to accept the idea that people should pay for their education. Yet the reality of for-fee education materialised quite rapidly due to the suppressed demand for higher education. It has been accompanied by a massive flow of "unofficial" payments.

Russia already has surpassed most European countries in *de facto* accepting the model of consumers paying for higher education. The system, however, is neither transparent nor merit based. The massive pool of private money funding the informal system that prepared students for admissions exams at state higher education institutions and now focuses on the Unified State Exam could be put to far better use. Discussion of the need to recapture these resources (variously estimated at between $1 billion and $6 billion) has reached President Putin.

In the 1990s and through the 2000s, Russian families contributed significant funds to compensate for the low state education spending. This is no longer possible due to lower economic growth. Growth at an average of 1% per year does not allow Russian families to begin to compensate for budget cuts or inflation.

Funding issues are particularly difficult in tertiary education, the most expensive and socially regressive level of education spending yet potentially a mechanism of social mobility. At higher education institutions, children from affluent families are more likely to gain admission and to complete their degrees. Some parents, educators and officials view all forms of education as a public good that should be free; for others, free higher education has become a middle-class entitlement guaranteeing a white-collar lifestyle.

In Russia, where the state budget pays for a finite number of students, affluent families have advantages in the competition for budget places (Carnoy *et al.*, 2013).

Russian official data do not include informal payments made by students and their families. This enormous amount of money goes directly into the pockets of faculty and administrators, without benefitting the education system directly.[10]

The financial problems in education were apparent in the 2000s, but became more severe after 2012. The situation is made more complex because the contingent of school-age children will increase by about 12% by 2024 (*Dvenadtsat' Reshenii*, 2018, p. 16), but will decline again after 2030 (Vishnevskii and Shcherbakova, 2018). The Presidential decree on increasing salaries for teachers and professors essentially created an unfunded mandate for local governments that were not able to cover the costs. At the same time, the decline in both budget resources for education and real incomes of the population since 2014 has meant that families are no longer able to compensate for shortfalls as they did in the 1990s and the 7 "fat" years after 2000 (*Dvenadtsat' Reshenii,* 2018, p. 15; Mamedli and Sinyakov, 2018). Any increases in fees for education must include assistance for low-income families to avoid further stratification (*Dvenadtsat' Reshenii,* 2018, p. 17).

Increased funding provided in a way that keeps corruption to a less damaging level would be a good beginning to improving the education system. Yet, the list of other needs is enormous. The most pressing needs include raising the prestige of teaching and increasing faculty salaries at all levels of education; recruiting and retaining young faculty; developing policies to alleviate the growing regional and class stratification in the education system; raising standards; improving vocational education and resolving the contradictions in efforts at internationalisation. Other priorities include curtailing the influence of ideology and corruption in textbook publishing, encouraging the best and brightest to remain in Russia and restoring a sense of caring for young people throughout the education system. Special attention is needed to viewing education as the development of learning skills rather than as preparation for specific narrow

---

[10] Some Russian colleagues have suggested that the side payments permit institutions to control their salary costs. However, the system is not transparent and is not based on merit, and the income individuals derive depends on location and opportunities for predation rather than performance. Significant inequalities are inevitable.

careers that graduates should pursue for their working lives. Russian colleagues note the problem of the state being the monopoly consumer of education resources. It is imperative to foster a much greater degree of competition (*Dvenadtsat' Reshenii,* 2018, p. 102).

Education reforms have had mixed results. Some schools have improved their quality, but often at the cost of decline elsewhere, making stratification a growing problem.

Negative consequences include a grey market in EGE preparation, petty evaluations of teachers, cutting merit pay designed as a stimulus for teachers and raising VUZ faculty salaries by eliminating *sovmestitelstvo* (faculty teaching at more than one institution to increase their income).

(3) Demographic changes,[11] emigration and the impact of reduced funding on salaries have combined to make most university departments and Academy research institutes resemble senior living communities, though with a disproportionate share of males. Low pay, declining status and heavy workloads have made teaching a less desirable profession. At the same time, meagre pensions encourage many teachers and VUZ faculty to continue working long after they reach pension age. At the Academy of Sciences and other research institutes, this phenomenon is even more pronounced. The average age of both VUZ faculty and Academy researchers has remained at around 60 for about two decades.

The ageing is perpetuated in part by low horizontal mobility. Russian university students who go on to do graduate work (*aspirantura*) generally continue their studies at the same institution, and then remain there to teach. The inbreeding helps foster Russia's "scientific schools", but it reduces exposure to alternative points of view that may help stimulate creativity. It is difficult to tell people who have been part of an institution for half a century that they should leave. The exception is the highly talented individuals who find opportunities abroad.

(4) Russia's massive and ongoing brain drain is both external and internal. Many of the best and brightest have left Russia in repeated waves

---

[11]The demographic issues are discussed in the chapter by Judy Twigg. For a good summary by leading Russian demographers, see Vishnevskii and Shcherbakova (2018).

of emigration. An even larger number abandon careers in education and science for more lucrative employment elsewhere. If in the 1990s Russians fled the state sector, now it is the prized employer.

Waves of emigration have been an important feature of Soviet and Russian life for more than a century. Many intellectuals, artists and scientists who survived the Civil War in 1918–1921 departed in the 1920s. A second wave, including many scientists and engineers, left in the mostly Jewish emigration in the Brezhnev era (Balzer, 1989). A "third wave" in the 1990s included a significant portion of Russia's leading mid-career academic personnel. In the 2000s, as the economy recovered, some analysts began to speak of a more normal "brain circulation", with Russian scientists and technical specialists becoming participants in the global talent market. Since 2014, the number of highly qualified personnel leaving the country has again increased, a response to reduced funding and prestige (Kolesova, 2014). Many more have chosen to work in fields other than education and science. The impact has been cumulative.

The departure of many mid-career teachers and researchers in the 1970s, late 1980s and early 1990s contributed to a situation where personnel at universities and research institutes were overwhelmingly either over 60 or new graduates. Departing mid-career specialists increasingly have been joined by young graduates who see their choice as either leaving Russia or changing their speciality due to low salaries, limited job options in many locations and the difficulties they encounter in conducting research (Prikhodchenko, 2013).

Many of the best Russian students seek education abroad or opt to go abroad once they complete their studies (see Appendix 12). Unlike China, where a growing number of those educated abroad now return to China, the proportion of Russians who return is quite small.[12]

(5) *Policy failure*:

Policies for education and science were a battleground in the 1990s, and most of these struggles continued despite a veneer of stability in the Putin era. Dezhina (2011) described policy chaos during

---

[12] See http://russian.news.cn/2017-03/02/c_136096452.htm.

Medvedev's presidency. This was before the 2013 decision to drastically reorganise the Academy of Sciences.

Political considerations and bureaucratic competition have made the problems more acute. Olga Vasil'eva's appointment as Minister of Education and Science in 2016, a choice motivated in part by efforts to encourage teachers to support United Russia in the Duma election that year, created disruptions in education programmes.[13] The 5-100 Program to advance Russian universities in global rankings came under serious threat. The "Megagrant" programme to bring leading international scholars to Russian universities was nearly terminated. Andrei Fursenko, the former Minister who now serves as Putin's Presidential Advisor on Education and Science, had to ask Putin for special funding to preserve these key programmes (personal communications, 2017). The situation continues to remain murky, as institutional interests battle over an increasingly limited pie.

At the same time, a striking disconnect has appeared between Russian experts' discussions of the economy, which have become increasingly pessimistic, and more positive assessments of Russia's science and education potential. Russian analysts consistently churn out reports about the cutting-edge realms of science and technology, ignoring the question of Russia's contributions to these disciplines. The highly critical report by the Higher School of Economics and Center for Strategic Research (*Dvenadtsat' Reshenii,* 2018) includes a long section suggesting that implementing the "digital classroom" could allow Russia to not merely catch up with but also overtake the leading countries in science and education.[14]

---

[13] The appointment of Olga Vasil'eva as Minister of Education and Science on August 19, 2016 — the 25th anniversary of the August 1991 attempted coup against Gorbachev — was inauspicious both in timing and impact. Vasil'eva wrote her dissertation on Stalin and the Russian Orthodox Church during 1941–1948, the years during which he downplayed communist atheism in an effort to enlist Russian history, Tsarist war heroes and Orthodox Christianity to support the war effort. One colleague familiar with the decision claims that Dmitri Medvedev appointed Vasil'eva in response to a demand from Putin to ensure that teachers voted for United Russia in the 2016 Duma election.

[14] The "catch up and overtake" idea will sound familiar to those who studied the Soviet Union. The "digital classroom" is one aspect of the "digital economy" proposed by President Putin in his March 1 address to the State Duma (Putin, 2018a).

The belief in Russia's unique capabilities is attributable in part to the mythology surrounding Sputnik and some real if uneven achievements in education. However, as financial support for science and education remains limited and the creative class increasingly chooses to exit, it has become difficult to identify positive changes.[15]

Changes in portfolios for education and science in the new Government announced in May 2018 suggested new disruptions, at least in the short term. Vasil'eva retained responsibility for elementary and secondary education in the *Ministerstvo Prosveshcheniia* (Ministry of Enlightenment), reverting to the language used in the 19th Century and again in the late Soviet era. A separate Ministry of Science and Higher Education was created, headed by Mikhail Kotiukov.

Responsibility for Secondary Specialised Education remained the province of Vasil'eva's Ministry, shared with Maksim Topilin, the new Minister of Labor and Social Protection. It is not clear that this separation of responsibility for secondary technical and engineering education will address Russia's long-standing difficulties in training technicians (Balzer, 1990, 2010). Technicians' training is discussed in subsequent sections in this chapter.

Following the government's resignation in January 2020, new ministers were appointed to replace both Kostiukov and Vasil'eva. This is discussed in the "Postscript" section.

The broader policy failures will be difficult to surmount. The Academy of Sciences resisted reforms for a long time, prompting the government to drastically curtail its role in administering research institutes. In 2019, the jewel in the Soviet science crown became one of several academies that are honorific rather than conducting research. The research institutes are managed and funded by the Ministry of Science and Higher Education. For the present, the institutes and individual researchers

---

[15] President Putin's March 1 address to the State Duma (Putin, 2018a) included an extensive list of proposals for increased funding for science, education, health and a host of other social programmes. The timing of this somewhat delayed annual speech, coming shortly before the Presidential election, encouraged a slew of promises. Most were repeated proposals made in previous addressees and decrees, few of which were ever fulfilled. Some of the pledges for education spending resulted in unfunded mandates for local governments that lacked the necessary resources.

have been permitted to continue to use the "Academy" designation, which confers some prestige. The Academy itself is engaged in ongoing discussions about a role in oversight, coordination and evaluation. They all face predatory efforts by government officials to garner choice real estate. The painful history of Academy reform has been described at length (Dezhina, 2011, 2014, 2016). A recent assessment by three leading Academy officials concludes that there has been little real reform, with many of the government agents focusing more on allocating valuable real estate than advancing scientific research (Poisk, 2018).

One of the more promising efforts beginning in the late 1990s focused on developing research capacity at institutions of higher education. For a while, the potential seemed genuine.[16] Despite rejecting foreign influences, Putin's May 7, 2018 Decree on tasks for 2024 includes establishing 15 new "Research and Education Centers". However, resistance by faculty and administrators invested in the old system, failure to adjust teaching loads, opposition from the Academy of Sciences and rejection of foreign advice and funding after 2012 and especially after 2014 have made the effort increasingly problematic. Building a high-quality research environment at VUZy is limited almost entirely to a few dozen elite institutions designated as Federal or Research Universities, along with those participating in the 5-100 program adopted in 2012 to raise Russian universities in international rankings.[17] Russian analysts do see some signs that the

---

[16]The author was one of the founders of the Basic Research and Higher Education Program, funded by the MacArthur Foundation and Carnegie Corporation of New York. When I first met with interlocutors at the Ministry of Education about the project in 1997, I was told that they liked the idea, but that we should avoid using the term "Research University", since this was not something that was part of the Russian education experience. In 2006, the Ministry asked for our assistance in developing a programme to select and fund research universities. In one of his pre-election articles during the 2012 Presidential campaign, Vladimir Putin cited the programme as making a valuable contribution to education and something worth adopting at military higher education institutions. In June 2015, former Minister of Education and Science Andrei Fursenko told me that cooperation was at an end and Russians no longer needed to learn anything from foreigners. He stated that this would be the case for at least two decades. In May 2018, Putin again spoke about creating research education centres.

[17]The 5-100 Program initially included 15 VUZy. Because institutions included in the programme were allocated privileged levels of funding, pressure to increase the number of

effort to encourage more publications is paying dividends. Others question the way the effort has been organised. This is discussed in greater detail in the section on internationalisation.

(6) *Resistance to change*:

As David Landes (1998) noted, change is often demonic, disrupting established patterns of behaviour. The Soviet system conferred high prestige and, after Stalin died, allowed a certain amount of leeway for its scientists, a practice sometimes mistaken for autonomy. The Academy of Sciences never deprived Andrei Sakharov of membership, despite pressure from the authorities. It elected its President and new members, occasionally resisting political influence in these processes. Experiencing a decline in prestige and importance has been an unpleasant shock for most Russian scholars, and particularly for Academy personnel.

Many of Russia's epistemic communities have been stubbornly opposed to adopting international standards and work regimes that reject Soviet practices. The most damaging example of rejecting global best practices has been in some fields of medicine, where opposition to needle exchanges and substitution therapy have resulted in Russia being one of the three large countries (the other two are Ukraine and South Africa) where HIV infection rates increased between 2014 and 2017 (*Science*). Insistence on placing tuberculosis patients in sanatoria and failure to monitor patients taking the full course of medication have resulted in Russia becoming a major source of MDRTB infections (multiple drug-resistant TB cannot be cured or arrested by available antibiotics, and its spread is a global health threat).

The overwhelming majority of VUZ faculty have resisted adding research to their job description. Except at a small number of elite institutions (Moscow, Leningrad, Novosibirsk and a few other universities, along with some technical institutes), professors in the USSR devoted their time to teaching, not research. The Soviet system made a clear distinction between the education and Academy of Sciences systems.

---

participants has been constant and the number has fluctuated. As of August 1, 2018, a total of 21 institutions were listed as participating in the programme.

Some Academy researchers did teach, but more commonly graduate students (*aspiranty*) conducted research at Academy institutes and sometimes defended their advanced degrees there. Recent surveys indicate that 80–90% of VUZ faculty do not want to engage in research.

The Academy consistently opposed increased government funding for research at VUZy. Academy researchers cite their far higher productivity, neglecting to mention that with no teaching responsibilities they are able to devote their work time to research and writing. This has changed as salaries have shrunk, and an increasing share of Academy researchers now teach part-time to earn additional income. One of the most serious errors in Russia's reform of higher education was the failure to consider teaching loads when adding research to the responsibilities of VUZ faculty. Professors at US research universities generally spend 6 hours per week in the classroom, with an assumption that another 3–4 hours will be devoted to preparation for each class session. In Russia, 20 classroom hours per week is considered normal, and often, the range of class topics is quite broad. The Russian system offers limited opportunities for research leaves or outside grants, much less buyouts. The institutional damage has been severe for both VUZy and the Academy, impeding efforts to develop a more integrated R&D system.

Limited success in fostering research universities has contributed to Russia's increasing marginalisation in international collaborative programmes. While students from the former Soviet Union, Africa and some Asian countries continue to have an interest in study in Russia, students from more developed areas are less attracted to the country. Those studying Russian language, history and politics are an exception. Students and young researchers in the natural sciences and technology, and in most social science disciplines, infrequently seek to spend time in Russia.

(7) Increasing economic inequality, regional differentiation and *de facto* privatisation of public goods were clearly visible two decades ago (Balzer, 2003). The trends have become more pronounced, with the decline of capacity at all but elite institutions now so severe that some consider the damage irreversible. Some leading Russian specialists view the country as having reached a tipping point in the ability of the system to sustain education at a globally competitive level. Akindinova *et al.* (2016, p. 29) noted that regional budgets now must support a

greater share of education costs, but many regions are seriously in debt. In their view, without major reforms

the negative consequences . . . will be sharp differentiation in the quality of education and medicine available to different social layers of the population.

Families in the upper middle class (15–20 percent of the population, almost entirely living in large cities) will create 'for themselves' private educational and medical services of high quality. Their children will attend the better universities. In other words, the positive results of President Putin's social policy, which form the basis of his social-political support, will be destroyed.

The situation has worsened since this article was written (Gromov *et al.*, 2016). The economic crisis beginning in 2014 reversed the poverty reduction accomplishments of the previous decade, while accentuating the rich–poor disparity. In his March 1, 2018 address, President Putin (2018a) noted that poverty had increased "slightly" from 10% to 20% of the population. Data from the World Wealth Report indicate that during the same years, the number of high net wealth individuals in Russia increased from 154,800 to 189,500 (22.5%).

In a country with a below replacement fertility level and ageing population, the quality of the labour force is crucial. President Putin (2018b) has called for significant improvement in labour productivity to increase economic growth. Yet, rather than facilitating social mobility to promote talent, the specialised secondary education places an increasing burden on social welfare needs. Russian analysts have not begun to explore the potential epigenetic consequences of economic dislocations in the 1990s, again after 2008, and especially since 2015 (*Dean,* 2018; *The Economist,* 2018).[18]

---

[18]Beginning with studies of the famine in the Netherlands following World War II, biologists have explored the significant impact similar events may have not only on the individuals who survive economic and natural disasters but also on their children and potentially subsequent generations as well. For an excellent study of how this research has been received in Russia, see Graham (2016).

In 1999, the Military Medical Administration reported that 300,000 of the young men conscripted into the military were underweight and unfit for military service. The average child in Russia in 1999 was shorter by 5–8 centimetres than children born a decade earlier. Average chest size had decreased by 5–6 centimetres. Conscripts in 1990 were generally capable of doing 50 push-ups, while in 1999 many found it difficult to do 10 (Roberts, 1999).[19] Fewer than one conscript in five was considered "healthy." In 1994, 27% of draft-age Russians were healthy enough to be inducted, but by 2002, the figure had dropped to 11%.[20] At the beginning of 2004, Health Minister Yurii Shevchenko stated that 84% of conscripts were not able to complete a basic test of physical fitness. One Russian colleague in 2002 described the military conscription situation as a case of "fewer but not better". Given the dire demographic situation facing Russia (Aleksashenko, 2018; Vishnevskii and Shcherbakova, 2018), every child born in the country has become more important. Yet, declining living standards since 2014 have had a significant negative impact (Mamedli and Sinyakov, 2018).

Children less physically fit are at a disadvantage in pursuing their studies, and the Russian education system is failing to serve even those who are in good health

> We are talking about hundreds of thousands of children for whom school was not able to provide the necessary support and individual supervision of their education. These children not only are unable to contribute to the economy's development, but themselves will experience a decidedly lower quality of life (*Dvenadtsat' Reshenii,* 2018, p. 43).

Social stratification has been paralleled by institutional stratification. The system of higher education has suffered from three economic crises (1998–1999, 2008–2009 and 2014–2017) with a potentially even more severe crisis developing in early 2020, and has become

---

[19]Roberts' data are based on an article in *Noviye Izvestia*, citing an interview with Aleksandr Baranov, then Chairman of the Russian Union of Pediatricians.
[20]Roundtable discussion transcript is in *Armeiskii Sbornik* (*The Army Collection*, journal of the Russian general staff) January 31, 2004, pp. 11–25.

increasingly differentiated (Abankina *et al.*, 2016a, 2016b). About three dozen elite institutions each now receive on average 1% of the total budget for higher education. The 250 other higher education institutions supported by the Ministry of Higher Education and Science on average receive less than 0.20% of the budget (Abankina *et al.*, 2016b). Few regions are in a position to provide financial support to local universities (Liubimov *et al.*, 2018). The gap between the quality of the elite institutions and the rest is wide and growing (personal communications, June 2017). As a recent report notes, "the price has been an enormous gulf in the quality of professional education between elite institutions and the general group of VUZy" (*Dvenadtsat' Reshenii,* 2018, p. 57).

Special arrangements for federal funding at Moscow and St. Petersburg State universities, the 21 institutions in the 5-100 Program, 10 federal universities and 29 research universities, along with Federal Scientific Centres and the Academy of Sciences, has helped Russia maintain some still-capable centres of science. However, Russian higher education institutions are among the world's leaders in just 25% of subject areas, mostly traditional areas of Russian strength like math and theoretical physics rather than emerging fields in the life sciences and high technology. Improvements will require substantial funding, beginning with expansion of the 5-100 Program (*Dvenadtsat' Reshenii,* 2018, p. 63).

Russia is also experiencing significant geographic stratification (Gromov *et al.*, 2016). Almost all Russian regions are net recipients of the revenue redistributed by the Government, but they differ markedly in their ability to provide additional funds for education. In 29 of Russia's 83 regions, no students achieved a top score on the Unified State Exam (EGE) for admission to higher education in 2017 (*Dvenadtsat' Reshenii,* 2018, p. 57). In the Soviet era, talent scouting and special math and physics olympiads created possibilities for young people from the entire country to compete for places at the best higher education institutions. Now, the cost of living in major cities and the decline of educational quality have severely limited opportunities. In 1990, just 20% of Moscow University students were from Moscow. In 2017, the figure was at least 80%.

Regional universities are particularly weak in R&D. Most are far from the leading edge of technology and have minimal links with business.

Many and often most faculty, including those teaching key classes, are not conducting research and are not involved in practical activity. It is not unusual for someone to teach four or five courses in quite different subject areas (*Dvenadtsat' Reshenii*, 2018, p. 58).

A less noted but equally important form of stratification is the division between full-time and part-time studies in higher education. Many VUZ students, and some 70% of graduate students (*aspiranty*), work while engaged in full-time study. Most of these jobs are unrelated to their educational programmes and limit the time and energy they may devote to academic pursuits.

An entire one-half of VUZ students study in correspondence programmes. This is one realm where Russia truly is the world leader (*Dvenadtsat' Reshenii*, 2018). Correspondence programmes vary widely in quality. The HSE authors endeavoured to portray the situation as positive by suggesting that the correspondence study experience would make students amenable to lifelong learning.[21] While this may be the case for some, available data suggest that many of these students do not acquire serious learning habits, undermining both short-term and lifelong learning goals.

Despite much discussion on the importance of "learning to learn", the Russian system has failed to make sustainable progress in lifelong learning. While many families invested in education for both children and adults in the 1990s, this has changed. This is an important shift that requires more attention. Lifelong education receives limited government funding, and the number participating is declining. The share of adults aged 25–60 enrolled in education programmes is two to three times lower that than in developed nations. Only 17% of Russians are involved in lifelong learning, compared to an average of 40% in EU countries. President Putin's Decree on this topic in May 2012 has not been implemented (Putin, 2012; *Dvenadtsat' Reshenii*, 2018, pp. 13–14, 21).

---

[21] The HSE/CSD report was obviously written as a policy prescription for the new Russian government that was announced in May 2018. It is perhaps unfair to take some of the statements as being more than a way to influence decision-makers.

(8) In the wake of protests following the 2011–2012 election cycle, and more emphatically following annexation of Crimea, Russian leaders have altered their views regarding international partnerships and collaborative efforts in education and science. Vladimir Putin asserts that Michael McFaul was appointed US Ambassador to Russia in order to subvert his regime and replace it with a pro-American government. Internationalisation is still identified as a priority, but policies have become contradictory. Some institutions continue to encourage exchanges and joint projects. Scholars are still evaluated in large part on their publications in international peer-reviewed journals, with an emphasis on Scopus. At the same time, individual foreign colleagues have experienced difficulties and foreign funding is no longer welcome,[22] while the decline in the value of the ruble has seriously limited the ability of Russian institutions to support collaborative work or international travel. The number of Russians who fail to show up at professional meetings has increased markedly, and the funding difficulties have been amplified by longer waits for visas.

Many foreign specialists no longer view Russia as an important destination for education or scientific collaboration. Data on foreign graduate students illustrate the situation. In OECD countries, 27% of graduate students are from abroad. In Russia, the number is 5% (*Dvenadtsat' Reshenii*, 2018, p. 21). The overwhelming majority of students and graduate students from abroad come from the 11 former Soviet Republics that are not EU members. The Americans and Europeans who do come to study in Russia focus overwhelmingly on social sciences and language (Balzer, 2010).

---

[22]The European University at St. Petersburg was forced to cease receiving transfers from the portion of its endowment held in the US to avoid being declared a "foreign agent". Dmitry Zeman's Dynasty Foundation, one of the few independent organisations funding scientific research in Russia, was labelled a foreign agent because Zeman persisted in keeping the Foundation's assets in Germany rather than inside Russia. Zeman's decision allowed the Foundation to preserve its $14.5 million operating budget when the ruble exchange rate declined by 50% after 2015. However, Russian scientists no longer benefit from the funds. The Dynasty Foundation ceased to function in 2015.

Russia's government has responded not only with promises of increased funding but also with a significant effort to alter global rankings in a growing number of areas. This includes developing a new set of criteria for university rankings that include "contributions to society" (Grove, 2017), along with gaming science citation data (Moed *et al.*, 2018) and pressuring the World Bank to change the "Doing Business" rankings (Aleksashenko, 2018, 11; personal communications).

There has been an increase in the number of Russian scientific publications in Scopus journals in the past 2–3 years. One former Academy of Sciences Institute Director in June 2018 told me that everyone now publishes in the international journals. It is certainly the case that the incentive structure has mandated a minimum number of publications each year for Academy and university personnel. However, other conversations in June 2018 provided evidence that in many cases the rise in Scopus publications has resembled the gains in Russia's "Doing Business" and university rankings standings: they reflect gaming the system at least as much as improving quality.

The rise in the number of Russian papers listed in Scopus and Web of Science is attributable in large part to listing more Russia-language journals and volumes of conference proceedings in the two systems. Many of the Russian volumes of conference proceedings are one-off meetings involving almost exclusively Russian participants (Moed *et al.*, 2018).

Although both Scopus and Web of Science have seen significant increases in the number of Russian works listed, there are some important differences between Scopus and Web of Science. Scopus indexes far more Russia journal articles than WoS. Some 75% of Russian-language journals listed in Scopus in 2016 were added after 2012. Russian scholars began to place more of their publications in these journals as they were listed. Most of the papers published in Russian conference proceedings are not read or cited by scholars outside Russia. Some of the increases in Russian researchers' scores on citation indexes are attributable to their citing each other's journal articles and conference papers more often (Kosyakov and Guskov, 2018; Moed *et al.*, 2018).

The major exception to diminishing international cooperation is growing collaboration with China. Presidents Xi and Putin have developed a close relationship, and this rapport at the top has generated many meetings and much discussion. It remains difficult to induce scientists in the two countries to follow-up the top-level initiatives with direct cooperation, but some evidence does suggest that administrative pressure and offers of funding are altering behaviour.

Although some collaborative initiatives are developing, many on both sides remain wary. A 2016 report by Russia's Academy of Sciences warns of the dangers presented by closer collaboration with China (Glinkina *et al.*, 2016). Yet, official Russian sources trumpet the growing coopera-tion. Beginning early in 2017, a marked increase was visible in reports of collaborative projects with China in education and science (Appendix 14; Krivozhikh and Liamtseva, 2017). This may be attributed to the need to demonstrate something concrete in time for the July 2017 Putin–Xi meeting. Yet, the growth in cooperative activity appears to be more than just a public relations campaign. The two countries announced that at two new joint universities the language of instruction would be English rather than Chinese or Russian. This resolved the diplomatic issue of which nation's language to use and likely increases the pool of potential students (Gureeva, 2017). It does not encourage Russian or Chinese students to learn each others' language.

(9) The pipeline of students moving from pre-school to kindergarten, elementary education, secondary school and professional/higher edu-cation functions poorly (Kosaretsky *et al.*, 2016). With the exception of a few, frequently private, elite schools, Russia's general education system has become less effective and less complete in its coverage.

Pre-school opportunities are limited, and good facilities are often private and expensive. Numerous accounts of abuse by staff have been reported.[23] The system of pre-school education fails to deal with emotional, psycho-logical and other problems that may impair cognitive development. One recent study asserts that the failures in pre-school education result in between 5% and 10% of young people having lifelong emotional and

---

[23] At one Moscow kindergarten, parents reported being asked for side payments to guaran-tee that staff would treat their children nicely.

learning difficulties, causing a loss equivalent to 3–7% of GNP each year (*Dvenadtsat' Reshenii,* 2018, p. 27).

A growing share of students in the general education system express no desire to continue their education beyond the 9th year. Those who remain in school choose either specialised secondary education or two additional years of general secondary education designed to prepare students to compete for places in higher education. Between the fifth and ninth classes, one-half of students lose interest in continuing their studies (*Dvenadtsat' Reshenii,* 2018, pp. 22–23). Social mobility is further stifled because secondary technical schools primarily enrol children from less affluent families, and these schools are mostly inferior in quality (*Dvenadtsat' Reshenii,* 2018, p. 40).

In an effort to curb abuses in the higher education admission process, the Russian government established a Unified State Exam (*Edinii gosudarstvennyi examen* or EGE) for admission to higher education. The system remains subject to cases of abuse (some faculty try to rig the system; students who take the exam in the Far East send information to those in time zones where the exam is administered hours later). Some elite institutions have been granted the right to add their own admission requirements in addition to the EGE scores.

Some analysts have suggested that Russia has too many students in the higher education system and overproduces economists, business school graduates and engineers. Yet, recent data indicate while graduates with engineering degrees are more likely to experience downward mobility in their employment and to say that their jobs have little or no connection with their education, those schooled in economics and law fare better on the job market (Varshavskaia, 2016: 859–60).

In the USSR, about half of higher education graduates did not work in the specialities they studied. This is also the case in many countries, where it is viewed as a normal situation. If young people learn how to learn, they may follow their interests and perhaps work in different fields during their lifetime. In the USSR and now in Russia, officials view failure to work in a speciality chosen when a young person applies to enter higher education as a significant problem. Planning for the projected number of personnel in specific (often quite narrow) specialties is more important than individual development. The difficulties in Russia often are exacerbated due to the poor quality of some educational programmes. Engineers in particular are not trained well-enough in their specialities and fail to participate in supplementary education programmes (*Dvenadtsat' Reshenii,* 2018, p. 13).

As one might expect from analysts based at a university and a think tank, the HSE/CSR report recommends prioritising professional, higher and lifelong education. The authors argue that these programmes would have the most immediate impact on the economy (*Dvenadtsat' Reshenii,* 2018, p. 92). This is reminiscent of the Soviet decision in the 1920s to focus on adult education rather than getting young people into the school system. This policy provided opportunities for many individuals, particularly workers, peasants and Party members, but came at the cost of delaying universal literacy for a generation. Emphasizing higher education is always important, but if the pipeline (discussed earlier) is not maintained, the students enrolling in VUZy will not be equipped to perform well. Russia needs skilled labour at least as much as it needs university graduates.

(10) With the possible exception of Germany, everyone complains of inadequate training for skilled workers and technicians. This was a persistent weakness of the Soviet system, where professional technical schools (PTUs) were consistently viewed as the poor sibling in the education system (Balzer, 1990).

Data increasingly show a serious shortage of skilled workers. Russia's perennially weak system of vocational education has atrophied as enrolments in higher education have reached unprecedented levels. Some see the fundamental problem of secondary professional education as failure to teach new technologies, partly due to outdated technical equipment (*Dvenadtsat' Reshenii,* 2018, p. 43). Many analysts agree that the situation has reached crisis proportions (Kuvalin and Moiseev, 2014; Appendix 11). The deficit in skilled workers and technicians reflects the economic returns to higher levels of education. Data from 2016 show that the average higher education graduate earned 67% more than secondary school graduates. Only 3.5% of higher education graduates were unemployed, while the proportion of jobless technical school graduates was 5.7%. Unemployment rose to 8.7% for students completing general secondary school, and more than 17% for those who left school after 9 years of "basic general education." The problems are to be found mainly in the poor quality of secondary technical education and the weak system of lifelong education in Russia. The share of students choosing professional secondary education did increase from 27% to 50% by 2016, but the wage differential for these graduates is not significant, which is a cause for serious concern (*Dvenadtsat' Reshenii*, 2018, pp. 12–14).

(11) Parents and education specialists in most countries criticise the quality of the system. Here again, the Russian situation appears to be at the extreme end of the spectrum. No one is happy with the current situation, but as long as the elite has the option of sending their children to private schools or institutions abroad, demands for change will remain politically weak.

Part of the problem is rampant corruption. It has been described at every level, from kindergarten teachers demanding money to treat children "nicely" to regular side payments for not only admission to higher education but also for passing grades (Golunov, 2014; personal communications).

This is a case where the fish does rot from the head. A Soviet tradition of officials purchasing academic degrees has continued in the Russian Federation. About one-third of Duma deputies in the 2000s had academic credentials. Public discussion of Vladimir Putin's economics dissertation focused overwhelmingly on the 18½ pages plagiarised from an economics textbook by two University of Pittsburgh professors. Less attention was directed to noting that Putin (1997), Sechin (1998) and Zubkov (1999) all defended Kandidat theses at the Mining Institute in St. Petersburg. Institute Rector Litvinenko's estranged daughter has described the thesis racket as well-institutionalised, with a Kandidat degree costing $30,000 and a doctorate costing $120,000. The price includes preparation of the thesis and organisation of the defence, including friendly official "opponents". Rector Litvinenko is reputed to be a billionaire, though his income from the dissertation market pales in comparison to his having been given a major stake in the PhosAgro phosphate-mining company after the Yukos affair (Vochek and Coalson, 2018).

(12) In much of the world, the distinction between science and technology has blurred so completely that it is no longer a major consideration in funding R&D. Russia remains an exception. Even one of the

most comprehensive discussions of weaknesses and potential strengths emphasises "building on Russia's strong base in basic science" (Dezhina, 2018). The impact of continuing cognitive division between basic research and applied technology and lack of clear legal guidelines helps explain the weak links between research institutions and businesses. In the 1990s, Russian scientists endeavoured to sell their ideas to business in a process of technology push, rather than developing connections that might have allowed them to learn what specific businesses needed. This points to a serious problem in what has been called the "Triple Helix": Collaboration among business, universities and government to promote innovation (Balzer and Askonas, 2016; Bychkova *et al.*, 2015).

(13) Aside from a few large corporations, mostly in the resource sector, Russian businesses provide limited demand and little funding for R&D. Until the sanctions imposed following annexation of Crimea, much of the Russian military preferred to purchase key electronic components from abroad rather than rely on domestic production or seek to improve domestic capacity (see Appendix 15).

Between 2007 and 2013, the share of GDP spent on R&D in China increased by 50% (from just under 1% to 1.5%). In Russia, the number remained flat (0.33% in 2007; 0.32% in 2017) (Gokhberg and Kuznetsova, 2016, p. 347). The overwhelming majority of funding (about 70%) is provided by the government (Balzer and Askonas, 2016). At Skolkovo, an innovation complex billed as Russia's "silicon valley" established just outside Moscow, initial plans called for the government share of financing to be no more than half the cost of any project. The government contribution has averaged more than 95% per project (personal communication).

Skolkovo was supposed to be a model of international collaboration. Initially, MIT played a major role. This has changed, as Russians became disenchanted with paying the cost of MIT involvement, and foreign involvement became more problematic following the annexation of Crimea. The shooting down of MH-17, a Malaysian airliner on a flight from Amsterdam to Kuala Lumpur, over Russian-supported Eastern Ukraine on July 17, 2014, resulted in several key Dutch scientists leaving (personal communications).

Russia has never been known for its capacity to innovate (Graham, 2014). Innovation depends on the institutional environment at least as much as on human capital (Graham, 2014; Breznitz, 2007; Balzer and Askonas, 2016). The success achieved by Russian scientists and technology developers outside Russia provides strong evidence that the problems are institutional.

Russians who have left Russia have won Noble prizes (Andre Geim and Konstantin Novoselov in Physics in 2010) and become leaders in emerging technologies (Sergey Brin at Google). The legal and political (and criminal) environments remain major obstacles. Nothing will change Russia's weak innovation system in the short term. This is a realm where significant systemic change is required (*Natsional'nyi doklad ob innovatsiiakh v Rossii*, 2016).

States may encourage an economic environment conducive to innovation in a variety of ways (Breznitz, 2007). But there are few examples of states successfully directing innovation. In an increasingly "unbundled" global economy, the potential to develop high technology without integrating into global supply and production chains has been significantly diminished (Baldwin, 2016).

The state dominates funding for R&D, and the lion's share of that limited funding goes to state-owned enterprises (SOEs) where demand for innovation remains low. Some high-level Russian officials have suggested that innovation comes from large, multinational companies. Most global experience refutes this. State funding inevitably comes with strings attached. Bureaucratic controls limit flexibility in spending, encourage risk avoidance and facilitate corruption. Giant mega-projects like the Sochi Olympics and Kerch Strait Bridge provide huge rents to regime cronies, but the potential economic returns are questionable.

Russia's business landscape is astonishingly weak in the small and medium enterprises (SMEs) that drive innovation, and the number has decreased markedly since 2012 (Krylova, 2018). The overwhelming majority (about 98%) of what are officially listed as small enterprises turn out to be Micro Businesses–individual proprietorships with fewer than three employees and assets of less than $1.7 million (see Appendix 13). Equally telling, small enterprises rarely grow to be successful medium enterprises. Rather than encouraging small businesses as suppliers and sources of new technology, large firms tend to demand control and stifle initiative.

Russia's SME sector is particularly weak in start-up firms. While recent programmes have increased funding to establish start-up companies, there is little support to help them grow. Russia lacks a developed venture capital market or dynamic industrial clusters.[24] The conservatism of large firms, especially SOEs, inhibits cooperation with more dynamic small enterprises.

Even in the realm of IT, where Russia does have a good reputation, innovation is rare. A major exception is the production of malware.[25] The domestic market is weak, and government controls on the Internet stifle innovation. The IT markets in Belarus and Ukraine are more competitive than Russia's. Estonia, a country with a population of 1.5 million that was incorporated into the Soviet Union following the Molotov–Ribbentrop pact, has far more start-ups per capita than Russia and ranks higher in quality and business capacity (StartupBlink, 2017; StartupGenome, 2018).

Russian analysts do see potential for Russia to play a greater role in cybersecurity, the life sciences, robotics and agriculture, but these prospects are limited by a system that still favours top-down "science projects" rather than creating products for the "real" economy.

Commercialisation and marketing remain persistent weaknesses (Graham, 2014).

Failure to address the legal and institutional shortcomings may have produced a genuine tipping point for entrepreneurs. The brain drain discussed in the preceding sections is not limited to education and science. Equally disturbing is the flight of the people who create businesses. Departures have skyrocketed since 2012, and especially since 2014. The exodus has included many involved in start-ups. The protests over dubious Duma elections in 2011 produced a (temporary) excitement among many in the creative class, encouraging some to remain in Russia and help build

---

[24] An instructive exception to the lack of clusters was the automobile industry in Kaluga. Beginning with first one and then several foreign assembly plants, the region became a major centre for related suppliers of parts. Unfortunately, the economic crises of 2008 and 2014–2017 severely undermined this promising development.

[25] One Russian success has been developing a 3-dimensional foot scanner for customers purchasing mail-order shoes.

a different country. After the crackdown on protesters in spring 2012 and especially following the annexation of Crimea and turn against internationalism, the numbers leaving grew rapidly.

In December 2015, President Putin confirmed reports that since 2013 some 350,000 entrepreneurs had moved their families abroad, put their business up for sale and intended to leave. The numbers were far higher. By mid-2017, unofficial estimates provided by colleagues put the number significantly higher. According to official Rosstat data, the number of entrepreneurs registered in Russia declined from 8.3 million in 2008 to 2.8 million in 2015, a drop of two-thirds. The most significant entrepreneur drain came during 2015, when the number shrank from 5.6 million to 2.8 million (Krylova, 2018, p. 2). Extortion exacerbated the effects of the economic crisis. In interviews, many placed the blame on government officials demanding bribes or engaging in outright raiding of businesses. Speakers at a 2015 Moscow economic conference stated that they suffered far more from internal threats than from Crimea-related sanctions (Krylova, 2018). The loss of small and medium businesses, even if a majority were "micro" enterprises employing fewer than three workers, has intensified the Putin-era shift to an economy overwhelmingly based on large enterprises that are either state-owned or heavily dependent on state contracts.

Wealthier Russians — oligarchs and people who are merely rich — have also been departing in significant numbers or simply moving their assets abroad "just in case". The London, New York and Miami property markets are a good barometer of the magnitude of capital flight (Åslund, 2018; Unger, 2018). About 3,000 high net worth (HNW) individuals left Russia in 2017, out of a total HNW population of 190,000, or 1.6%. (For comparison, China with 10 times the population had a net outflow of 10,000, from of a total of 1,120,000 HNW individuals, or a loss of 0.9%.) The main destinations for affluent Russians were the USA, Cyprus, United Kingdom, Portugal and the Caribbean.[26]

The flight of creative people and entrepreneurs undermines the chances for improving employment prospects and the quality of life for those who

---

[26] Data from *World Wealth Report* 2018 and *Asia-Pacific Wealth Report* 2018 (www.world-wealthreport.com/).

remain.[27] Opinion surveys and interviews suggest that only institutional change could induce academics and entrepreneurs to return or convince the next generation to stay. Western sanctions have increased the exodus.

(14) Russia's leaders have used the sanctions imposed following annexation of Crimea to rally patriotic support inside Russia, while simultaneously claiming that the sanctions have had little real impact. The contradiction inherent in this stance does not appear to be receiving much attention. Ironically, the countersanctions imposed by Russia in response to Western measures have likely had a greater negative impact on the general Russian population (Piper, 2014; Kara-Murza, 2018). The American sanctions were designed to affect key regime supporters and specific industries and to have a cumulative impact over time. The intent was to encourage a change in policy before the sanctions resulted in significant deterioration in living standards for ordinary Russians. Regime resistance, countersanctions and several instances of Russian high-risk behaviour have altered the equation.

Despite assertions that the sanctions have been ineffective, some measures have caused serious concern, in some cases bordering on panic, among targeted businessmen with close ties to the Kremlin.[28] Threats to cut off Russian banks' access to the SWIFT funds transfer system in January 2018 prompted Andrey Kostin of VTB to say this would be "an act of war". New sanctions announced on August 9, 2018 produced a response from Prime Minister Medvedev threatening economic war, or worse.[29]

---

[27] One of the best sources on the brain drain is the series of articles in *Komsomol'skaia Pravda* by Koniukhova (2017a, 2017b) under the rubric *Utechka umov*.

In English, see Grady (2017), Maltseva (2016), Appell (2015), Holodny (2014).

[28] Many Russian commentators deny that post-Crimea sanctions have had a significant impact (Ivanter, 2016). While some Russian analysts have reported important successes in import substitution, others have questioned just about every one of these purported achievements (Dmitrievskii *et al.*, 2016; Fal'tsman, 2015a, 2015b; Kokoshin and Bartenev, 2015; Koshovets and Ganichev, 2015).

[29] Medvedev remarked, "it would be necessary, it would be needed to react to this war economically, politically, or, if needed, by other means". www.politico.com/story/2018/08/10/russia-santions-medvedev-ecnomic-war-771294.

British sanctions following the attempted assassination of Skrypal alarmed Russians who make use of the public goods available in Western market democracies, including education, financial services, housing and medical care. Åslund (2018) and Unger (2018) provide accounts of the extent of Russian flight capital laundered in the US and Great Britain, much of it involving real estate.

Less attention has been devoted to the impact of the sanctions on key components for important economic sectors, particularly energy and the defence industry. The Russian energy sector was particularly exposed to dependence on imports. Before 2015, Russian companies imported 56% of the equipment used for horizontal drilling and 93% of equipment used for hydraulic fracturing. An equally heavy reliance on western technology characterised drilling in the Arctic region. A large-scale joint project between Rosneft and ExxonMobil in the Karsk Sea was suspended amid the Ukrainian crisis, and development of Arctic resources was delayed (Kazantsev, 2014). The decline in oil prices during 2014–2017 made the impact more severe. Some have called it a "perfect storm". Lukoil's Leonid Fedun predicted that sanctions would mean a decline of 7% per year in production at Russia's number two oil producer over the next 4–5 years. This may have been a cry for help, given that Lukoil profits were down 50% in the third quarter of 2014 (Kazantsev, 2014).

The problems in the energy sector predate the sanctions, and if the sanctions regime ended tomorrow, it would not significantly improve the situation. The fundamental difficulties are inefficiency and the quality of state management (Kazantsev, 2014). Russian government promises to support firms like Rosneft and Gazprom have not been accompanied by any demands for greater efficiency or less corruption.

In a discussion of the defence and fuel-energy sectors, Fal'tsman (2015a, 2015b) reinforced the descriptions of growing dependence on imported components for crucial Russian production. He noted that much of Russia's innovation capacity is located in the defence industrial sector, while the entire economy relies on the energy sector for financial well-being. The sanctions affect 68% of the imports used in the oil and gas sector. Russia depended on South Korea for 90% of drilling platforms (Fal'tsman, 2015a, p. 118).

Summarising a 2018 report on Russian oil and gas from the Skolkovo School of Management, Mitrova (2018) notes that the sanctions were intended to be cumulative. This helps to explain why Russian analysts are divided between some who expect "catastrophic consequences" due to dependence on foreign technology and financing and those who shrug off the impact. In the short term, Russia can cope. In the longer term, the problems likely will be serious.

The Skolkovo report foresees no serious problems before 2020. However, Russian firms have not added new fracking equipment for 3 years. The lack of technology to increase production from existing fields could result in a 5% reduction in production by 2025, and more serious difficulties by 2030. "Russian companies currently lack native technology and equipment to develop unconventional and offshore reserves. And sanctions limit access to foreign technology" (Mitrova, 2018). If the new sanctions announced in August 2018 are implemented, the impact on financing could be severe. Those with a more positive view cite reports that Novatek has managed to deliver its first shipments of LNG from Arctic fields (Foy, 2018).

The situation in the defence sector is more varied, but in the crucial area of electronics, a persistent Russian bottleneck, it is particularly challenging. Before 2014, 65–79% of the electronics used in Russian missiles and space rockets were imported. Russia produced no drones, and all of the piston motors used in drone aircraft were imported (Kazantsev, 2014).

Even prior to American and European sanctions, the conflict with Ukraine was creating serious problems for the Russian defence sector. The list of components produced in Ukraine included motors for civilian and military helicopters, as well as several types of warships. While some and perhaps many of these components could be produced in Russia, it requires time and money to replace the imports. Fal'tsman (2015a) estimated that replacing the Ukrainian contribution would require a minimum of four years and $20 billion in state expenditures. Other Russian experts, speaking off the record, suggest that the situation will be even more difficult, with enterprises like Yuzmash no longer able to fill Russian orders.

Fal'tsman's data are reinforced by other Russian specialists. Ivanter (2016, pp. 3–4) broadly dismisses the importance of sanctions but does note that they have affected the defence industry. Nearly 100% of Russia's helicopter engines came from "Motor Sich" in Zaporozh'e, Ukraine. A Russian factory is producing about 50 engines per year, but Russia's military needs 300 per year. Mindeli and Chernykh (2016, pp. 116–117) express concern that the shift of funding priority to applied and military science will have a significant negative effect on Russia's overall science capacity. Their article raises what might be called the "advanced weaponry conundrum".

(15) Is it possible for military technology to advance significantly beyond a nation's civilian technological frontier?[30] This was an important topic for specialists on Soviet technology, with occasional exaggerated claims about proton beam weapons, entire underground defence industry facilities and other purported accomplishments. Even Sputnik, a Soviet breakthrough that shocked America, turned out to be less of a technological advance than people assumed at the time.

Does Russia have a large group of scientific and technical specialists secretly working on weapons systems outside the purview of foreign observers? Top scientists having moved to classified work might help explain the decline in Russian scientific publications, but that began well before Vladimir Putin came to power. The Russian government recently announced plans for an elite military R&D complex to be constructed on the Black Sea coast (Bendett, 2018). This suggests that nothing of the sort currently exists and that secrecy is not a priority.

The question of whether a nation's domestic technology frontier limits military technology potential has reappeared since 2008 in the face of serious military reforms in Russia and striking claims by President Putin about new, advanced weapons systems (Putin, 2018a). Russia's president is making these claims (and showing science fiction-style video clips) despite significant limits on what may be obtained from foreign suppliers

---

[30]The editor of this book suggested in a personal communication that the problem could be solved by means of technology transfer. In theory, this is certainly possible. However, in the face of weak domestic demand for innovation and Western sanctions, technology transfer is not easy. Theft is always a possibility, but the Soviet experience demonstrated that stealing the right components is a challenge. China has been able to provide some of the needed technology. Israel may also be helping, either knowingly or through illicit channels.

due to the post-Crimean sanctions. The situation calls for serious analysis (Cooper, 2016). Some of the hardware has been put on display; other new weapons, requiring cutting-edge electronics and guidance systems, have not yet been demonstrated in public.

Elites in the USSR and in the Russian Federation have shared a view that projecting military strength is somehow separate from an economy capable of developing high technology. Soviet generals dismissed Japan's role in the world because the country barely had an army.[31] But it has become increasingly difficult to project military power without the financial resources to support the effort. North Korea illustrates the social costs of such an effort. Russia is unlikely to be able to close off information to the same extent.

An argument may be made that the USSR coped reasonably well with less sophisticated but still adequate (and numerous) conventional weapons. In World War II, Germany consistently sought technology breakthroughs that would confer significant advantage; the Soviet Union stuck to producing a large quantity of their basic artillery (including the highly effective Katyusha rocket launchers), tanks and planes. We know who won. Many of the speakers at the 2018 Aspen Strategy Group meeting noted China's advances in both Artificial Intelligence and new-generation, less costly weaponry. Christian Brose, Staff Director of the Senate Armed Services Committee, stated that "the Pentagon needs a large number of inexpensive, unmanned, expendable, autonomous systems that can survive in the new electronic battlespace and over-whelm any potential adversary" (Ignatius, 2018). Most of what President Putin showed off on March 1 was closer to the existing American arsenal.

Conclusion

The quality of life in hydrocarbon-exporting countries depends far more on the price of oil than on human capital. Resource exporters can thrive as long as they have the money to buy things rather than developing the capacity to make things. Kuwait can probably do reasonably well for a

---

[31] Others overestimated the long-term strength of Japan's economy (Vogel, 1979).

long time, even with lower oil prices. However, for large-population commodity exporters, the equation is more difficult (Karl, 1997). A country the size of Russia is vulnerable to fluctuations in the price of its commodity exports, and all indications are that global energy markets have experienced fundamental long-term changes. Shale oil has become increasingly less costly to produce, with some fields being competitive at prices as low as $30–39 per barrel.

This is still a young technology that may improve. Increased use of LNG makes gas more similar to oil, marketed to meet shifting demand rather than linked to pipelines for delivery. Renewable energy accounts for 10% of the global market and is likely to exceed 20% by 2030.

Vladimir Putin might once again be lucky, with some event causing hydrocarbon prices to increase markedly. Mr. Putin might even find a way to provoke a conflict to achieve this result. Higher prices might allow some growth despite inefficiencies and massive corruption. But, Putin's luck would not necessarily be Russia's luck. The effect of higher hydrocarbon prices would be to depress demand while encouraging greater use of increasingly more competitive alternative energy sources. Landes (1969) described the ways new industrial revolution technologies generated a short-term final flowering of older technologies prior to their obsolescence. Hydrocarbons may now be in that situation.

Unless Russia diversifies its economy, finding ways to improve and benefit more from its human capital, the country faces a protracted period of low economic growth. Given the ambitious programme that President Putin (2018b) announced in his May 7, 2018 decrees, neither he nor the Russian people will be satisfied with this outcome. Diversifying Russia's economy will require major investments, drastic change in the way funds are allocated and spent and a broad array of policy reforms. It will simultaneously require finding ways to participate in global supply and production chains as more than a source of natural resources. Successful change will be impossible without simultaneous top-down and bottom-up efforts to make the education and research systems less corrupt and more competitive, a path to national development that Russia's current leaders continue to reject.

Improving Russia's economy will also require resolving a problem that has bedeviled Russia at least since Peter the Great: crash programs to "catch up" with rivals contradict more sustainable development efforts that require longer time frames but offer the prospect of "keeping up" for the longer term. Peter's vast energy in the first quarter of the 18th Century left Russia exhausted for decades. Stalin's hero projects produced a similar effect. For every adult who learned to read in the Soviet literacy campaign, there was a child growing up unable to read or write. Universal literacy took a generation longer than it might have. Spending large sums in the hope that some elite institutions will catch up in global rankings precludes raising the quality of the entire system to improve economic performance. Would Russia be better off if Moscow University breaks into the top 25 in one of the global university ranking systems, or if several dozen regional institutions make genuine contributions to their local economies? Ideally, both goals should be pursued. Limited resources make this impossible. The global recession of 2020 likely will undermine efforts to accomplish either goal.

Postscript[32]

President Putin dismissed the Russian government on January 20, 2020. The changes in responsibility for education and science in the previous reorganisation in May 2018 are discussed on page 143 above. The changes in 2018 involved delegating responsibility for elementary and general secondary as well as vocational education to a Ministry of Enlightenment (*Prosveshchenoe*) and putting higher education and science in a separate ministry. Vasil'eva remained responsible for elementary and secondary education while Maksim Kotiukhov became Minister for Science and Higher Education. The 2020 government includes a new Prime Minister, Mikhail Mishustin, which by itself augurs significant policy shifts.

---

[32]This chapter was written in December 2018 and finalised in April 2020. Given President Putin's demand for quick results, significant changes in personnel and policy during these 15 months were inevitable. One of the consistent patterns of Putin's administration has been frequent changes in personnel and policy direction. Rather than allowing time for new approaches to work, the failure to foster rapid change produces demand for new policies. In realms like science and education, this often curtails programs that require longer time horizons. The contrast with China in this regard is striking (Balzer and Askonas, 2016).

Vasil'eva has been replaced by Sergei Kravtsov. Kotiukhov's tenure ended after just 19 months, with the Ministry of Science and Higher Education now headed by Valerii Fal'kov.

Kravtsov's major involvement in education policy was in devising and implementing the Unified State Examination (EGE) for admission to higher education. He comes from a Moscow intelligentsia family: his father is an engineer who worked on Russia's Buran Space capsule; his mother was Chief Editor of a journal, *Informatika v shkole* (Informatics for the School). Kravtsov graduated from the Moscow Pedagogical University in 1996 with a degree in math and informatics, and spent the next 2 years teaching math at the high school (Moscow 170) he had attended. In 1997, he moved to the Academy of Education, where he completed his Candidate of Sciences and Doctoral dissertations.

In 2002, Kravtsov became an advisor in the Ministry of Education, and in 2004 moved to the Federal Education Inspectorate. He became head of the Federal Examination Center in 2008, where he assumed responsibility for the EGE. He continued this work as head of the Institute of Education Management, and in 2013 became head of the Federal Education Inspection.[33]

Valerii Fal'kov is from Tiumen in West Siberia. He graduated with a degree in law from the Tiumen State University in 2000 and began teaching. In 2003, he defended a Candidate of Science dissertation on "Improving the Legal Regulation of Election Campaigning in the Russian Federation." Fal'kov held several administrative positions at the University, becoming a Vice Rector in 2011, Acting Rector in 2012, and was elected Rector in 2013. He served in the Tiumen City Duma from 2013 to 2016 and in the Oblast Duma as a United Russia deputy from 2016 to 2020.

Fal'kov was credited with improving Tiumen University and moving it into the status of one of Russia's more competitive institutions.

It generally takes about 6 months for a new Minister to establish clear directions for staffing and policy. One of the first things Fal'kov did was to rescind a much-vilified order Kotiukhov had signed requiring Russian scholars to report every contact they had with foreigners.

---

[33] Borisov, Aleksandr. 2020. Ot uchitel' do ministra (From teacher to Minster), *Sankt-Peterburgskie vedomosti*, No. 22, Feb. 7, p. 4.

While officially abrogating the demand to report all foreign contacts is a positive sign, Fal'kov has continued a trend of "better fewer but better" institutions from the previous Ministers. Faced with inadequate financing and a demand from President Putin to elevate Russian universities into the top levels of global rankings, a sometimes varying number of elite institutions are being targeted for special funding status.

In addition to the 5-100 Program designed to raise five Russian universities into the top 100 in at least one of the international rankings, a program developed in 2019 aims to create world class "research and education centers."[34]

The extent of the challenges Russia's new government faces in science and education is described in detail in a report released in February 2020 by the Russian Government's Accounting Chamber (similar to the U.S. General Accounting Office) on factors impeding Russia's scientific development.[35] The report reinforces and amplifies much of the material presented in this chapter, providing much corroborating data. It received significant attention in the Russian press.

---

[34] The concept of *nauchno-obrazovatel'nye tentry (NOTs)* was introduced as a key element of the Basic Research and Higher Education (BRHE) Program developed by the MacArthur Foundation and Carnegie Corporation in 1997–1998 and co-funded by the Russian Government beginning in 1998. Initially 16 centres were selected through competitions conducted by joint Russian and American committees. Subsequently, the Russian Ministry of Science and Education requested American assistance in selecting an additional four universities to establish centres based on Russian Funding. After American private foundation funding was curtailed, the Russian government adapted and expanded the program. While the initial idea of BRHE was to provide a demonstration project, the Russian government significantly expanded the number of centres. The most recent version of the NOTs concept is another elite program to foster a few globally competitive institutions.

[35] Izotova, G. S. 2020. Rezul'taty Ekspertno-analiticheskogo meropriiatiia 'Opredelenie osnovnykh prichin, sderzhivaiushchih nauchnoe razvitie v Rossiiskoi Federatsii: otsenka nauchnoi infrastruktury, dostatochnost' moitvatsionnykyh mer, obespechenie privlekatel'nosti raboty vedushchikh uchenykh', (Results of the Expert-analytical analysis 'Determining the basic reasons holding back scientific development in the Russian Federation: Evaluation of the scientific infrastructure, adequacy of means of motivating and attracting leading scientists to work'), Schetnaia palata, Moscow.

The most devastating conclusion from Izotova's report is that the Russian government provides a far greater share of the funding for R&D than is the case in other developed countries, yet realises substantially fewer benefits than other countries derive from their investments in R&D (p. 7). Russian state funding is not only inadequate and used ineffectively, it is allocated and monitored in ways causing significant damage to the working environment for Russian education and science.

Over the 2 decades 2000 to 2020 spending has increased significantly (13 times) in nominal terms, but in real terms only doubled, from 77 Billion rubles in 2000 to 153 Billion in the 2020 budget (pp. 3–4). As a share of GNP, spending peaked in 2003. Russia's spending on R&D ranks tenth globally, behind India and Brazil and just ahead of Taiwan, but Russia is not in the top ten in any significant indicators of performance. Russia ranks third after the U. S. and China in total number of researchers, yet has three times the number of scientists per 10,000 population compared with China (pp. 10–11).

In spending per researcher, Russia ranks 20th among the nations listed, at $93,000 compared to India's $177,000 (p. 12).

Russia differs from nearly all other developed and most developing countries in the share of spending provided by the government. China's non-state sector contributes more than 3/4 of R&D funding; in Russia the private sector share is 30% (p. 13). Izotova is explicit regarding the negative consequences of Russia's reliance on direct government financing, calling it "toxic" (p. 18). The requirement to fulfil state orders, particularly those from the military, forces researchers to devote their time to extraneous topics. At many research organisations, especially universities, state demands divert researchers from working on topics that might enable them to garner intellectual property. At the same time, even ordinary state programs, not to mention those for the defence sector, require a massive volume of reporting requirements. This dissuades small and medium enterprises from seeking state funding.[36]

---

[36]My (indirect) personal experience with these problems came in my role in the Governing Council of the BRHE Program and as a member of the Board of Trustees of the European University at St. Petersburg. In BRHE, we found Russian universities competed aggressively for small grants, because these provided funds that were fungible rather than being

The results derived from Russian government spending on education and R&D are quite modest. Russian spending is at the low end for a developed country; its achievements are in the middle range for developing countries. The two major methods used to evaluate performance are bibliometric data on publications and R&D outputs measured by patents. While individual country data on patents are useful, the most significant indicator of global competitiveness is "triadic" patents (awarded by the U.S., European Union and Japan).

Russian scholars have increased their share of publications in journals listed in the main indexes–Web of Science, SCOPUS and ELSEVIER, and are proud of this accomplishment. Section one above included some discussion on the ways the numbers have been raised. Izotova adds data about the quality of the journals where Russian scientists publish (pp. 14–15). Russians have risen to 14th place in the share of both Scopus-listed publications (2.9%) and Web of Science publications (2.8%). However, the Russian articles appear overwhelmingly in journals ranked in the third or fourth quartile. In 2018, just 5% of Russian articles appeared in Scopus journals ranked among the top ten for citations (compared with 22% of American articles, 19% of German articles and 17% of Chinese articles).

Russian scholars are far less likely than their foreign peers to co-author with colleagues at other Russian institutions, much less with those from other countries. Even at Russia's National Research Universities, fewer than half of the publications involve external authors.

An even less impressive return on investment is visible in patenting activity (pp. 16–17). In 2017, Russia ranked tenth in R&D spending and at the top in researchers per capita, yet Americans file 18 times more patent applications and Chinese filed 38 times more.

---

restricted to highly specific purposes. Several years ago, the European University succeeded in winning one of the Ministry of Science and Higher Education "Megagrants." The reporting requirements were so onerous that the University found it imperative to hire an additional accountant whose sole responsibility was to deal with the paperwork for this government grant. The costs of administering Russian state grants may exceed any administrative overhead they provide.

The change over time compared with China is striking, particularly given that China spends less money per capita than Russia on R&D (though Chinese spending represents a larger share of GDP). In 1995 Russians were awarded 63 triadic patents, Chinese just 21. In 2015, Chinese were awarded 3766 triadic patents, Russians in 2016 earned a total of 96.

Despite repeated adoption of plans and programs for scientific and technical development, Russia's institutional infrastructure for R&D has shrunk over the two decades of Vladimir Putin's rule. The ongoing closing of higher education institutions was noted in Appendix 7. Between 2000 and 2018 (p. 20):

— organisations conducting R&D shrank from 2686 to 1574;
— construction Bureaus were reduced from 318 to 254;
— design Bureaus and Pilot Production facilities were cut from 85 to 20.

Izotova notes (p. 23) that the key document for management and funding priorities, the Strategy for Scientific-Technical Development of Russia 2017–2019, required 10 normative laws for implementation. Four of these laws were adopted after the "Strategy" was already being implemented; six were still in preparation when the Report was being written in the second half of 2019.

Failure to provide the legal documents for implementation of strategic development plans and Presidential decrees has been a consistent problem. Programs to support young scientists and the industrial sector of the economy are implemented entirely on the basis of individual decisions by the President and government officials (pp. 25–26).

The ineffectiveness of Russian funding for R&D is a major theme (pp. 30–34). The Academy of Sciences notes that business is reluctant to invest in R&D because state policies are not conducive to innovation. Unstable economic conditions discourage investment, few policies provide incentives for entrepreneurs to invest, and the risks are enormous.[37]

---

[37]The Accounting Chamber report does not mention corruption or administrative pressure on businesses. This is frankly discussed in reports by Russia's business ombudsman (Krylova 2018). In interviews, Russian entrepreneurs operating small businesses have

Russia would need to double the share of GDP it devotes to basic research to reach the level of Japan, the United States and Great Britain. Even this, however, might not accomplish much without significant institutional change. In 2019, nearly half of the budget for R&D went to Federal Executive Agencies *other than* those directly involved in education and science. The Ministry of Science and Higher Education received 41% of the total state funding, the Russian Fund for Basic Research 5%, the Kurchatov Institute 3.5%, and the Academy of Sciences 1%. Accountability for these funds is minimal.

Izotova provides data showing the decline in the number of scientific personnel since 2000. One positive number is a slight increase in the share of researchers age 30–39 since 2010. However, the number of young people who wish to pursue careers in science continues to diminish: less than 1% want to work in science, and of these only 2/3 want to conduct research (p. 39). The number of higher education graduates who became researchers declined from 14,123 in 2001 to 13,725 in 2011 and to just 9,985 in 2017 (p. 36). Izotova is silent regarding the reasons for the drop-off after 2011. Demographics and economics are the most likely reasons. Russia would need to increase salaries by 2.5 times to compete with other developed and developing countries to stem the brain drain. Germany pays researchers more than three times as much as Russia; even the Czech Republic average salary is 1.5 times more (p. 35).

The share of GDP devoted to R&D in Russia in the Putin era peaked in 2003 at 1.29%. It fell to 1.01% in 2011, was at 1.10% to 1.11% during 2015–2017, and fell back to 1.00% in 2018 (p. 27). The number in 2020 is likely to be lower due to the impact of COVID-19.

While it is still early to gauge the global impact of the 2020 Corona Virus crisis, it is clear that China and Russia will be among the major victims. Both countries have been experiencing slowing economic growth since 2011, and both need to revise their economic models. China is experiencing a no-growth first quarter of 2020, and at the time of this writing

---

explained that they endeavour to keep their profits at a modest level and avoid growing too large in order to avoid attracting the attention of criminals or predatory officials. The results from large sums allocated to diverse Executive Branch agencies are difficult to evaluate.

at the end of February recovery appears elusive. Russia will be among the countries most affected by collateral damage.

China has become Russia's most important trading partner, buying growing volumes of oil, gas, timber and other natural resources while supplying more than 1/3 of Russian imports. Russian light industry imports about 2/3 of the inputs it uses, making the Chinese share crucial. The border between China and Russia was closed on January 20, 2020 due to the COVID-19 threat. Even if Russia is spared a major public health crisis, the economic consequences are likely to be enormous. Prices for oil, gas and other commodities have declined, and the impact as economic disruptions spread to more countries will become greater. The cost of pharmaceuticals, medical supplies and other crucial goods that Russia imports will rise given increasing global demand and disrupted supply chains. The still modest level of collaboration between Chinese and Russian scientists will be curtailed for an indefinite period of time.

Economic slowdown in both China and Russia has been creating difficulties for small and medium businesses in both countries since at least 2013. Chinese economic growth fell below double digits after 2011 and has been declining each year since. Growth in 2019 was 6.1%, but in October 2019 the state sector ceased to grow at all. At the start of the COVID-19 outbreak at the end of 2019, 2/3 of Chinese small and medium businesses reported having enough cash on hand to survive for one to two months. Fewer than 10% said they could manage for more than six months.[38]

Decline in the number of Russian businesses reversed temporarily in 2011–2012, but resumed again by 2013. Krylova's (2018) data were noted above. More recent data reported by Eskov[39] show the relative rates of business destruction and creation. In 2017, 510,700 businesses closed in Russia, while 350,400 new businesses opened, or 1.4 times more closures.

---

[38] https://asia.nikkei.com/Business/Industry-in-focus/Virus-hits-China-s-economic-heart-its-small-businesses.

[39] Eskov, Pavel. 2020. "V Rossii v 2019 godu 'umerlo' v 2,3 raza bol'she kompanii, chem bylo sozdano (In 2019 in Russia 2.3 times more companies "died" than were created)," *Finansovaia gazeta*, Feb. 20. https://www.fingazeta.ru/ekonomika/rossiyskaya_ekonomika/460250/

In 2018, 622,200 closed, while 290,200 new businesses began operating, a difference of 2.14 times. In 2019, 2.3 times more businesses closed than opened, with negative figures reported in 78 of the 83 Russian regions. In Moscow closures numbered 124,497. The greatest disruption was in Murmansk, where more than 2,500 businesses closed and just 289 new ones began operations. In these conditions, business demand for innovation is unlikely to grow.

A full analysis of the COVID-19 consequences for Russia and China is beyond the scope of this chapter or this volume. Based on the information available on Leap Day 2020, it appears to be quite serious.

References

Abankina, I. V., Vynaryk, V. A. and Filatova, L. M. (2016a). Gosudarstvennaia politika finansirovaniia sektora vysshego obrazovaniia v usloviiakh biudzhetnykh ogranichenii [State policy for financing the higher education sector in conditions of budgetary limitations], *Zhurnal Novoi Ekonomicheskoi Assotsiatsii*, 3(31), 111–143.

Abankina, I. V., Vynaryk, V. A. and Filatova, L. M. (2016b). Lovushki v finansirovanii i differentsiatsii rossiiskikh vuzov [Snares in financing and differentiation of Russian VUZy], *Actual Problems of Economics and Law* 10(2), 38–58.

Abdelal, R. and Mitrova, T. (2013). U.S.-Russia relations and the hydrocarbon markets of Eurasia, *Working Group Paper 2*, Working Group on the Future of U.S.-Russia Relations, Cambridge, MA.

Abramov, R. A. and Sokolov, M. S. (2016). Theoretical and methodological aspects of the formation of anti-corruption mechanisms in the system of higher education of the Russian Federation. *International Journal of Environmental & Science Education* 11(15), 7431–7440.

Akindinova, N., Kuz'minov, I., and Iasin, E. (2016). Ekonomika Rossii: pered dolgim perekhodom [The Russian economy: Before the long transition], *Voprosy ekonomiki* 6, 5–35.

Aleksashenko, S. (2016). Is Russia's economy doomed to collapse? *The National Interest*, July 2. Available at: http://nationalinterest.org/feature/russias-economy-doomed-collapse-16821?page=show.

Aleksashenko, S. (2018). *The Russian Economy: Short-Term Resilience, Long-Term Stagnation?*, Atlantic Council Eurasia Center, Washington, DC.

Appell, J. (2015). The short life and speedy death of Russia's silicon valley, *Foreignpolicy*, May 6, 2015, http://foreignpolicy.com/2015/05/06/the-short-life-and-speedy-death-of-russias-silicon-valley-medvedev-go-russia-skolkovo/.

Ascher, W. (1999). *Why Governments Waste Natural Resources: Policy Failures in Developing Countries,* Johns Hopkins University Press, Baltimore and London.

Åslund, A. (2018). *How the United States Can Combat Russia's Kleptocracy*, Atlantic Council, Washington, DC. Available at: http://www.atlanticcouncil.org/publications/issue-briefs/how-the-united-states-can-combat-russia-s-kleptocracy.

Baker Institute (2007). The changing role of national oil companies in international energy markets, *Baker Institute Policy Report No. 35*, James A. Baker Institute for Public Policy of Rice University, Houston.

Baldwin, R. (2016). *The Great Convergence: Information Technology and the New Globalization,* Harvard University Press, Cambridge, MA.

Balzer, H. D. (1989). *Soviet Science on the Edge of Reform,* Westview Press, Boulder, CO.

Balzer, H. D. (1990). Secondary technical education in Russia/USSR: The muddled middle level, in: Tortella, G. (ed.), *Education and Economic Development since the Industrial Revolution,* Generalitat Valenciana, Valencia, pp. 289–305.

Balzer, H. D. (1993). Science, technology and education in the former USSR, in U.S. Congress. Joint Economic Committee, *The Former Soviet Union in Transition*, USGPO, Washington, DC, pp. 889–908.

Balzer, H. D. (2001). Russia's self-denying middle class in the global age, in: Segbers, K. (ed.), *Explaining Post-Soviet Patchworks, Vol. I: Actors and Sectors between Accommodation and Resistance to Globalization,* Ashgate Publishing, Aldershot. 37–47.

Balzer, H. D. (2003). Routinization of the new Russians? *Russian Review* 62(1), 11–36.

Balzer, H. D. (2005). The Putin thesis and Russian energy policy, *Post-Soviet Affairs* 21(3), 210–225.

Balzer, H. D. (2006). Vladimir Putin's academic writings and Russian natural resource policy, *Problems of Post-Communism* 53(1), 48–54.

Balzer, H. D. (2008). Russia and China in the global economy, *Demokratizatsiya*, 16(1), 37–47.

Balzer, H. D. (2010). Obuchenie innovatsiiam v Rossii i v Kitae [Learning to Innovate in Russia and China], *Pro et Contra*, May–June, pp. 52–71.

English Version available as Working Paper No. 2011–17, Mortara Center for International Affairs, Georgetown University, and on Research Gate: www.researchgate.net/publication/267411366_Learning_to_Innovate_ Education_and_Knowledge-Based_Economies_in_Russia_and_China.

Balzer, H. D. (2015). Will Russia waste another crisis? The 2014–15 economic downturn and the prospects for Russian economic reform, in *Putin's Third Term: Assessments amid Crisis*, Center on Global Interests, Washington, DC, pp. 29–46.

Balzer, H. D. (2016). What have we learned, and not learned, from a quarter-century of transition?, *ASEEES NewsNet* 56(5), 1–5.

Balzer, H. D. (2017). Russia's knowledge economy decline: Views from inside, in Wimbush, S. E., and Portale, E. M. (eds.), *Russia in Decline*, The Jamestown Foundation, Washington, DC, pp. 113–161. Available online at: https://jamestown.org/program/harley-balzer-russias-knowledge-economy-decline-views-from-inside/.

Balzer, H. D. and Askonas, J. (2016). The triple helix after communism: Russia and China compared, *Triple Helix Journal*, 3(1).

Barabash, N. S., Boskovskii, P. P., and Shamsutdinov, Iu. A. (2017). Vliianie institutsional'noi i infrastructururnoi sred na razvitie innovatsii v sovremen-nom mire [Effect of the institutional infrastructure environment on develop-ment of innovation in the contemporary world], *Problemy Prognozirovaniia* 3, 75–89.

Bendett, S. (2018). Russia wants to build a whole city for developing deadly weapons. Available at: warisboring.com/russia-wants-to-build-a-whole-city-for-developing-weapons/.

Bray, M., and Borevskaya, N. (2001). Financing education in transitional societies: Lessons from Russia and China, *Comparative Education* 37(3), 345–365.

Breznitz, D. (2007). *Innovation and the State: Political Choice and Strategies for Growth in Israel, Taiwan and Ireland*, Yale University Press, New Haven and London.

British Council (2017). 5 facts on the current education market in Russia. Available at: /ei.britishcouncil.org/news.

Bychkova, O., Chernysh, A., and Popova, E. (2015). Dirty dances: Academia-industry relations in Russia, *Triple Helix* 2(13), 1–20.

Carnoy, M., Loyalka, P., Dobryakova, M., Dossani, R., Froumin, I., Kuhns, K., Tilak, J. and Wang, R. (2013). *University Expansion in a Changing Global Economy: Triumph of the BRICS?*, Stanford University Press, Stanford.

Cooper, J. (2016). The military dimension of a more militant Russia, *Russian Journal of Economics* 2(2), 129–145.

Denisova-Schmidt, E., Huber, M. and Leontyeva, E. (2016). On the development of students' attitudes towards corruption and cheating in Russian universities. *European Journal of Higher Education* 6(2), 128–143.

DeWitt, N. (1961). *Education and Professional Employment in the USSR*. National Science Foundation, Washington, DC.

Dezhina, I. (2011). Igra v kukly [Playing with Dolls], Lecture at Polytechnical Museum, Moscow, January 27. Available at: http://polit.ru/article/2011/03/31/dolls/.

Dezhina, I. (2014). *Russia's Academy of Sciences' Reform: Causes and Consequences for Russian Science*, IFRI Russia/NIS Center, Paris, Visions No. 77.

Dezhina, I. (2016). Innovatsionnaia politika v Rossii: Tendentsii, slozhnosti, perspektivy, *Zapiska Analiticheskgo tsentra Observo,* No. 12, February, www.wbsfr.ru.

Dezhina, I. (2018). Science and innovations in Russia in 2017. Available at SSRN: https://ssrn.com/abstract=3211916.

Dmitrievskii, A. N., Komkov, N. I., Krotova, M. V. and Romanov, V. S. (2016). Strategicheskie al'ternativy importozameshcheniia oborudovaniia TEK dlia neftegazovogo kompleksa [Strategic alternatives for import substitution of equipment for the fuel-energy complex for the oil and gas industries], *Problemy Prognozirovaniia* 1, 18–35.

Dvenadtsat' Reshenii dlia novogo obrazovaniia: Doklad Tesntra Strategicheskikh razrabotok i Vysshei Shkoly Ekonomiki. (2018). Higher School of Economics, Moscow.

Fal'tsman, V. (2015a). Importozameschenie v TEK i OPK [Import substitution in the fuel-energy complex and the defense-industrial complex], *Voprosy Ekonomiki* 1, 116–124.

Fal'tsman, V. K. (2015b). Forsirovanie importozameshcheniia v novoi geo-politicheskoi obstanovke [Forcing import-substitution in new geopolitical conditions], *Problemy Prognozirovaniia* 1, 22–32.

Foy, H. (2018). Russia's Novatek shows resilience despite sanctions, *Financial Times.* August 1.

Frolov, A. S. (2014). Problemy planirovaniia nauchno-tekhnologicheskogo razvitiia na gosudarstevnnom urovne [Problems of planning scientific-technical development at the state level], *Problemy Prognozirovaniia* 6, 79–91.

Gaddy, C. G. and Ickes B. W. (2005). Resource rents and the Russian economy, *Eurasian Geography and Economics*, 46(8), 559–583.

Glinkina, S. P., M. O. Turaeva and A. A. Yakovlev. (2016). Kitaiskaia strategiia osvoeniia postsovetskogo prostranstva i sud'ba Evraziiskogo soiuza, Moscow: Instittue of Economics, Russian Academy of Sciences.

Glinkina, S.P, N. V. Kupikova, M. O. Turaeva, A. V. Goilubkin and A. A. Yakovlev. (2018). Kitaiskii faktor v razvitii stran rossiiskogo poiasa sosed-stva: uroki dlia Rossii (The China factor for development of countries in the Russian neighborhood: Lessons for Russia), Moscow: Institute of Economics, Russian Academy of Sciences.

Gokhberg, L. and Kuznetsova, T. (2016). Russian federation, *UNESCO Science Report: Toward 2030*, UNESCO, Paris (published 2015, revised edition 2016).

Golunov, S. (2014). *The Elephant in the Room: Corruption and Cheating in Russian Universities*, Ibidem-Verlag, Stuttgart.

Gostev, A. N., Demchenko, T. S. and Borisova, E. A. (2013). Korruptsiia v sisteme vuzovskogo obrazovaniia: problemy i puti profilaktiki [Corruption in the system of higher education: problems and paths to prevention], *Sotsiologiia Obraovaniia* 7, 82–98.

Grady, J. (2017). Russian military industrial complex struggling to develop new technology, June 20, 2017, https://news.usni.org/2017/06/20/26350.

Graham, L. (2014). *Lonely Ideas: Can Russia Compete?*, MIT Press, Cambridge, MA.

Graham, L. (2016). *Lysenko's Ghost: Epigenetics and Russia*, Harvard University Press, Cambridge, MA.

Graham, L. and Dezhina, I. (2008). *Science in the New Russia: Crisis, Aid, Reform*, Indiana University Press, Bloomington.

Gromov, A. D., Platonova, D. P., Semyonov, D. S. and Pyrova, T. L. (2016). Dostupnost' vysshego obrazovaniia v regionakh Rossii [Access to higher education in Russian regions], *Vysshaia Shkola Ekonomiki. Seriia Sovremennaia Analitika Obrazovaniia* 8, 4–32.

Grove, J. (2017). Russian universities excel in Kremlin-backed rankings. Available at: www.timeshighereducation.com/news/russian-universities.

Gureeva, Y. (2017). Narodnaia dipomatiia: Kak privlech kitaiskikh studentov v rossiiskie vuzy [Public diplomacy: How to attract Chinese students to Russian institutes of higher education], *RT*, January 31, 2017. Available at: https://russian.rt.com/russia/article/354936-kitai-obrazovanie-studenty-rossiya.

Gustafson, T. (1980). Why doesn't soviet science do better than it does?, in Lubrano, L. and Solomon, S. G. (eds.), *The Social Context of Soviet Science*, Westview Press, Boulder, CO, pp. 31–67.

Holodny, E. (2014). Russia's brain drain is astounding, *Business Insider*, December 2, http://www.businessinsider.com/russia-brain-drain-putin-ukraine-crimea-2014-12.

Humphreys, M., Sachs, J. D. and Stigliz, J. E. (eds.) (2007). *Escaping the Resource Curse*, Columbia University Press, New York.

Iaremenko, I. V. (2015). Sovremennaia ekonomika Rossii: analiz i strategiia razvitiia [Russia's economy today: Analysis and strategy for development], *Problemy Prognozirovaniia* 5, 4–10.

Ignatius, D. (2018). The Chinese Threat That an Aircraft Carrier Can't Stop, *Washington Post*, August 7 2018.

Ikonen, C. (2018). 'Get out now' Putin's warning to Russian students living in UK. *Daily Star*, April 19 2018. Available at: www.dailystar.co.uk/news/world-news/697085/ww3-putin-warns-russian-students-uk-return-siberia-salisbury-poisoning-war-syria.

Indikatory Nauki. (2014). *Statisticheskny sbornik* [Statistical yearbook]. Higher School of Economics, National Research University, Moscow, pp. 373–375.

Ivanter, V. V. (2016). Strategiia perekhoda k ekonomicheskomu rostu [Strategy for the transition to economic growth], *Problemy Prognozirovaniia* 1, 3–7.

Jones Luong, P. (2000). The 'use and abuse' of Russia's energy resources: Implications for state-society relations, in Sperling, V. (ed.), *Building the Russian State: Institutional Crisis and the Quest for Democratic Governance*, Westview Press, Boulder, CO, pp. 27–45.

Jones Luong, P. and Weinthal, E. (2006). Rethinking the resource curse: Ownership structure, institutional capacity, and domestic constraints, *Annual Reviews of Political Science* 9, 241–263.

Kara-Murza, V. (2018). Russia sanctions the west — Hurting its own citizens. *Washington Post*, May 25. Available at: /www.washingtonpost.com/news/democracy-post/wp/2018/04/25/russia-sanctions-the-west-hurting-its-own-citizens/.

Karl, T. L. (1997). *The Paradox of Plenty: Oil Booms and Petro-States*. University of California Press, Berkeley and Los Angeles.

Kazantsev, P. (2014). Sanktsii zemedlennogo deistviia, ili Rossiia v neftianoi lovushke [Sanctions are slowly working, or Russia in the oil trap), *Slon.ru*, December 12.

Kerr, S. T. (1994). Diversification in Russian education, in Jones, A. (ed.), *Education and Society in the New Russia*, M.E. Sharpe, Armonk, NY.

Kokoshin, A. A. and Bartenev, V. I. (2015). Problemy vzaimozavisimosti bezopasnosti i razvitiia v strategicheskom planirovanii v Rossiiskoi Federatsii: ot tselepolaganiia k prognozirovaniiu [Problems of interdependence of security and development in Russian Federation strategic planning: from setting goals to forecasting], *Problemy Prognozirovaniia* 6, 6–17.

Kolesova, O. (2014). Chemodan, vokzal … Reforma RAN vyzvala u molodykh zhelanie uekhat [Suitcase, train station … The reform of the Russian Academy of Sciences has encouraged the youth to leave], *Poisk* 4–5.

Koniukhova, K. (2017a). Novaia utechka mozgov: Dazhe v Shveitsarii universitety v chetyre raza deshevle, chem v Moskve [The New brain Drain: Even in Switzerland a University costs four times less than in Moscow], *Komsomol'skaia Pravda* 67, 14.

Koniukhova, K. (2017b). Utechka Mozgov: Pochemu rossiiskie abiturienty vse chashche uezzhaiut uchit'sia v zarubezhnye vuzy? [Brain drain: Why do Russian applicants increasingly often leave to study in foreign higher educational institutions], *Komsomols'kaia Pravda* 73, 22.

Korol, A. (1957). *Soviet Education for Science and Technology*, MIT Press, Cambridge, MA.

Korovkin, V. (2016). Strategy 2030: How to tackle economic challenges in Russia. *Russia Direct*, March 11. Available at: www.russia-direct.org/opinion/strategy-2030-how-tackle-economic-challenges-russia.

Kosaretsky, S., Grunicheva, I. and Goshin, M. (2016). Obrazovatel'naia politika Rossii kontsa 1980- kh–nachala 2000-kh godov: deklaratsii i prakticheskoe vliianie na neravenstvo v obshchem obrazovanii, *Mir Rossii*, 4, 115–135.

Koshovets, O. B. and Ganichev, N. A. (2015). Eksport Rossiiakikh vooruzhenii kak osobyi faktor razvitiia vysokotekhnilogichnoi promyshlennosti Rossii [Export of Russian arms as a special factor in the development of high-technology industry in Russia], *Problemy Prognozirovaniia* 2, 121–134.

Kosyakov, D. and Guskov, A. (2018). Impact of national science policy on academic migration and research productivity in Russia, Paper presented at the 14th International Conference on Current Research Information Systems, Umeå, June 13–16, 2018. Available at: https://dspacecris.eurocris.org/handle/11366/683.

Kotsemir, M. N. (2012). Publication activity of Russian researches [sic] in leading international scientific journals. *Acta Naturae*, 4(2), 14–34.

Krivozhikh, S. and Liamtseva, M. (2017). Obrazovatel'naia ekspansiia kitaia i neispol'zovannye vozmozhnosti rossii [China's educational expansion and

Russia's unexploited opportunities]. Russian Council on International Affairs, January 10. Available at: http://russiancouncil.ru/blogs/digest/3072/.

Krylova, Y. (2018). *Corruption and the Russian Economy: How Administrative Corruption Undermines Entrepreneurship and Economic Opportunities*, Routledge, London and New York.

Kudrin, A. and Gurvich, E. (2014). Novaia model' rosta dlia rossiiskoi ekonomiki [A new Russian economic growth model], *Voprosy Ekonomiki* 12, 4–36.

Kuvalin, D. B. and Moiseev, A. K. (2014). Rossiiskie predpriiatiia vesnoi 2014g: Deiatel'nost' v usloviia zamedlenniia ekonomicheskogo rosta [Russian enterprises in the Spring of 2014: Activity in conditions of slowing economic growth], *Problemy Prognozirovaniia* 6, 99–114.

Landes, D. (1969). *The Unbound Prometheus: Technological Change and Industrial Development in Western Europe from 1750 to the Present*, Cambridge University Press, Cambridge, UK and New York (2nd edition 2003).

Landes, D. (1998). *The Wealth and Poverty of Nations: Why Some Are So Rich and Some Are So Poor*, W. W. Norton, New York and London.

Lederman, D. and Maloney, W. F. (eds.) (2007). *Natural Resources: Neither Curse nor Destiny*, World Bank/Stanford University Press. Palo Alto, CA and Washington, DC.

Liubimov, I. L., Lysiuk, M. V. and Gvozdeva, M. A. (2018). Atlas ekonomicheskoi slozhnosti rossiiskikh regionov [Atlas of economic complexity of Russian regions], *Voprosy Ekonomiki* 6, 71–91.

Liusyi, A. (2003). Kak nam obuchit' Rossiiu? Shkol'noe obrazovanie kak chast' sotsial'noi sistemy, *Novoe vremia* 36(3013), 24–26.

Makeeva, A. (2018). Polovina VUZov Rossii ne sdali zachet [Half of the higher education institutions in Russia did not pass the exam]. *Kommersant*, March 27, 2018.

Maltseva, O. (2016). The problem with Russia's best and brightest, *Stratfor*, June 29, 2016, https://worldview.stratfor.com/article/problem-russias-best-and-brightest.

Mamedli, M. O. and Sinyakov, À. A. (2018). Finansy domokhozaiistv v Rossii: shoki I sglazhivanie potrebleniia [Consumer finance in Russia: Income shocks and consumption smoothing], *Voprosy Ekonomiki* 5, 69–91.

McGilvray, A. (2016). "World's oldest science network faces uneasy future," Nature Index science blog, May 6. https://www.natureindex.com/news-blog/worlds-oldest-science-network-faces-uneasy-future.

Mindeli, L.E. and Chernykh, S. I. (2016). Finansirovanie fundamental'nykh issle-dovanii v Rossii: Sovremennye realii i formirovanie prognoznykh otsenok [Financing basic research in Russia: Contemporary realities and formation of evaluation prognosis], *Problemy Prognozirovaniia* 3, 111–131.

Mitrova, T. (2018). Western sanctions on Russia's oil and gas sector: a damage assessment. Available at: https://carnegie.ru/commendary76906.

Moscow International Ranking IREG Observatory on Academic Ranking and Excellence. (2017). "The Three University Missions,". http://ireg-observatory. org/en/760-moscow-international-ranking-the-three-university-missions-released.

Moed, H. F., Markusova, V. and Akoev, M. (2018). Trends in Russian research output indexed in Scopus and Web of Science, *Scientometrics* 116, 1153. Available at: https://arxiv.org/abs/1805.02434.

Natsional'nyi doklad ob innovatsiiakh v Rossii. (2016). Ministerstvo ekonomi-cheskogo razvitiia Rossiiskoi Federatsii, Moscow.

OECD (2018). Main science and technology indicators (Edition 2018/1). OECD Science, Technology and R&D Statistics (database). https://doi-org.proxy. library.georgetown.edu/10.1787/fe401804-en (accessed 16 August 2018).

Osipian, A. (2012). Education corruption, reform, and growth: case of post-Soviet Russia, *Journal of Eurasian Studies* 3(1), 20–29.

Piper, E. (2014). Crunch time: As sanctions bite, Putin ally gets into apples. Reuters. Available at: www.reuters.com/investigates/special-report/comrade-capitalism-apples/.

Popovsky, M. A. (1979). *Manipulated Science: The Crisis of Science and Scientists in the Soviet Union Today*, Doubleday, New York.

Popravko, N. V. and Rykun, A. Iu. (2002). *Stanovlenie i Razvitie Rynka Dopolnitel'nykh Obrazovatel'nykh Uslug na Territorii Tomskogo Regiona. Analiz Povedeniia Potrebitelei* [Creation and Development of the Market for Supplementary Educational Services in the Tomsk Region. Analysis of Consumer Behavior], Izdatelstvo Tomskogo universiteta, Tomsk.

Prikhodchenko, P. (2013). Zhalko, esli vperedi vybor–professiia ili strana [It is sad if we face a choice between a profession or a country]. *Gazeta.ru*, December 17. Available at: www.gazeta.ru/science.2013/12/17_a_5806413.shstm.

Putin, V. (2018a). Presidential address to the Federal assembly. Available at: http://en.kremlin.ru/events/president/news/56957.

Putin, V. (2018b). Prezident podpisal Ukaz "O natsional'nykh tseliakh i strate-gicheskii zadachakh razvitiia Rossiiskoi Federatsii na period do 2024 goda" [President signed a decree on national goals and strategic tasks for development of the Russian Federation to 2024], May 7, http://kremlin.ru/events/president/news/57425.

Roberts, L. (1999). "A sharp deterioration in the conditions facing Russian youth," World Socialist Web Site, April 24. http://www.wsws.org/ (accessed January 12, 2000).

Rossiiskaia Akademiia Nauk (2008). *Prognoz Nauchno-Tekhnologicheskogo Razvitiia Rossiiskoi Federatsii na Dolgosrochnuiu Perspektivu (do 2030g.)* [Prognosis of the Long-Term Perspective of Scientific-Technical Development of the Russian Federation to 2030.].RAN, Moscow.

Scott, P. (ed.) (1998). *The Globalization of Higher Education*, Open University Press, Buckingham, UK.

Sechin, I. I. (1998). Ekonomicheskaia otsenka investitsionnykh proektov tranzita nefti I nefteproduktov (na primere nefteproduktoprovoda kirishi-batereinaia). Kandidat dissertation, St. Petersburg State Mining Institute.

Shirov, A. A., A. A. Iantovskii and V. V. Potapenko. (2015). "Otsenka potentsial'nogo vliianiia sanktsii na ekonomicheskoe razvitie Rossii i EC (Evaluation of the potential impact of sanctions on the economic development of Russia and the EU)," *Problemy prognozirovaniia*, 4, 3–16.

Simes, K. M. (1982). *USSR: The Corrupt Society. The Secret World of Soviet Capitalism*, Simon and Schuster, New York.

Startsev, B. (2012). *Khroniki Obrazovatel'noi Politki: 1991–2011*, Vysshaia shkola ekonomiki, Moscow.

StartupBlink (2017). Startup ecosystem rankings, October, V. 2. Available at: www.startupblink.com/blog/startup-ecosystem-rankings-startupblink/.

StartupGenome (2018). Global startup ecosystem report 2018. Available at: https://startupgenome.com/all-report-thank-you/?file=2018.

Stulberg, A. (2015). Out of gas? Russia, Ukraine, Europe and the changing geopolitics of natural gas, *Problems of Post-Communism* 62, 112–130.

Suvorov, A. V., Suvorov, N. V., Grebennikov, V. G., Ivanov, V. N. and Boldo, O. N. (2015). Otesenki dinamiki i struktury chelovecheskogo kapitala dlia Rossiiskoi ekonomika 1991–2012 [Evaluation of the dynamics and structure human capital for the Russian economy, 1991–2012], *Problemy Prognozirovaniia* 2, 3–15.

The Economist (2018). How stress echoes down the generations. Available at: www.economist.com/science-and-technology/2018/05/24/how-stress-echoes-down-the-generations.

Unger, C. (2018). *House of Trump; House of Putin: The Untold Story of Donald Trump and the Russian Mafia*, Dutton, New York.

Varshavskaia, E. (2016). "Where Do Highly Educated Russians Work, and What Do They Do for a Living?" *Russian Education & Society*, 58(12), 841–861.

Vedomosti (2017). Pologaia traektoriia [Proposed trajectory], June 29, pp. 1, 6.

Vishnevskii, A. G. and Shcherbakova, E. (2018). Demograficheskie tormoza ekonomiki [Demographic brakes on the economy], *Voprosy Ekonomiki* 6, 48–70.

Vogel, E. F. (1979). *Japan as Number One: Lessons for America*, Harvard University Press, Cambridge, MA.

Volchek, Dmitry and Robert Coalson. (2018). "Cut-And-Paste Job: 'My Father Wrote Putin's Dissertation'," RFERL March 7. https://www.rferl.org/a/russia-litvinenko-olga-says-father-wrote-putins-dissertation/29085343.html

Wang, Y. (ed.) (2000). *Public-Private Partnerships in the Social Sector: Issues and Country Experiences in Asia and the Pacific*, Asian Development Bank Institute, Tokyo. ADBI Policy Papers Series No. 1, www.adbi.org/partnershipsbook.htm.

World Bank (1993). *The East Asian Miracle: Economic Growth and Public Policy*, The World Bank, Washington, DC.

Wright, G. and Czelusta, G. (2007). Resource-based growth past and present, in Lederman, D. and Maloney, W. F. (eds.), *Natural Resources: Neither Curse Nor Destiny*, World Bank/Stanford University Press, pp. 183–211. Palo Alto, CA and Washington, DC.

Zubkov, V. A. (1999). *Nalogooblozhenie v Mineral'no-syr'evom Komplkse Rossii*, St. Petersburg State Mining Institute (University), St. Petersburg.

Appendix 1: Articles published by Russian scholars in Web of Science and essential science indicators in comparison (rank by country, total number, and share in %), 2001 and 2011.

Rank	Country	2001 Number of publications by the country	2001 Share of the country in the total world number of publications (%)	2011 Country	2011 Number of publications by the country	2011 Share of the country in the total world number of publications (%)
1	USA	303,917	31.48	USA	366,507	27.13
2	Japan	86,096	8.92	China	184,029	13.62
3	Great Britain	83,582	8.66	Great Britain	105,411	7.80
4	Germany	77,982	8.08	Germany	97,070	7.19
5	France	55,259	5.72	Japan	79,751	5.90
6	China	44,575	4.62	France	67,990	5.03
7	Canada	38,645	4.00	Canada	58,855	4.36
8	Italy	38,453	3.98	Italy	55,253	4.09
9	Russia	28,667	2.97	Spain	50,256	3.72
10	Spain	26,350	2.73	India	46,172	3.42
11	Australia	25,483	2.64	South Korea	45,971	3.40
12	The Netherlands	21,779	2.26	Australia	44,244	3.28
13	India	19,272	2.00	Brazil	34,122	2.53
14	South Korea	19,194	1.99	The Netherlands	33,523	2.48
15	Sweden	17,422	1.81	Russia	28,577	2.12
16	Switzerland	15,566	1.61	Taiwan	28,553	2.11
17	Brazil	13,324	1.38	Switzerland	24,655	1.83
18	Taiwan	13,018	1.35	Turkey	23,470	1.74
19	Poland	12,824	1.33	Iran	21,768	1.61
20	Belgium	11,964	1.24	Sweden	21,389	1.58

Source: Kotsemir (2012, p.17), based on World of Science data.

Appendix 2: Russian share of total global publications by field, 2001–2005 and 2007–2011.

Field	2001–2005 (%)	2007–2011 (%)
All fields	2.99	2.07
Physics	8.72	7.22
Space science	7.56	6.69
Geosciences	7.51	6.57
Mathematics	5.35	4.61
Chemistry	5.49	4.44
Materials science	4.06	3.03
Engineering	2.97	1.99
Molecular biology and genetics	2.24	1.91
Multidisciplinary	1.29	1.79
Microbiology	2.28	1.69
Biology and biochemistry	1.97	1.60
Environment/ecology	1.04	1.23
Plant and animal science	1.23	1114
Computer science	1.21	0.95
Agricultural science	1.14	0.79
Neuroscience and behaviour	0.74	0.65
Clinical medicine	0.68	0.57
Pharmacology and toxicology	0.32	0.56
Social science	0.80	0.44
Psychiatry and psychology	0.63	0.42
Immunology	0.35	0.41
Economics and business	0.20	0.23

Source: Kotsemir (2012, p. 21).

Appendix 3: BRICs Web of Science publications.

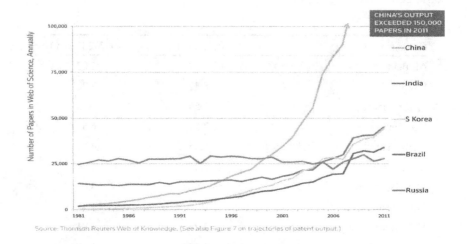

Source: Thomson Reuters Web of Knowledge. (See also Figure 7 on trajectories of patent output.)

Appendix 4: Articles and citations, BRIC and USA, 2008–2012, World of Science.

Country	Number of articles	Citation per article
Russia	135,363	2.56
Brazil	160,443	3.22
India	207,086	3.87
China	699,044	4.01
USA	1,664,136	7.43

Source: Indikatory Nauki (2014, pp. 373–375).

Appendix 5: Nanotechnology patents.

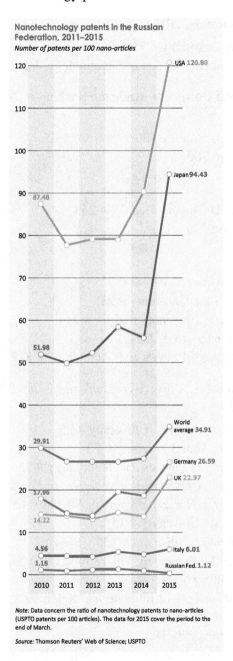

Nanotechnology patents in the Russian Federation, 2011–2015

Number of patents per 100 nano-articles

Note: Data concern the ratio of nanotechnology patents to nano-articles (USPTO patents per 100 articles). The data for 2015 cover the period to the end of March.

Source: Thomson Reuters' Web of Science; USPTO

Source: Gokhberg and Kuznetsova (2016, p. 357).

Appendix 6: Russia in university ranking systems.

Times Higher Education, 2018:

    Moscow State University # 194

    Moscow Institute of Physics and Technology # 251–300

Shanghai Jiao Tong University Academic Ranking of World Universities, 2018

    Moscow State University #86

    No others in top 300

U.S. News, 2018:

    Moscow State University Tied for # 267

    No others in top 300

QS, 2019:

    Moscow State University # 90

    St. Petersburg State University # 235

    Novosibirsk State University tied for # 244

    Tomsk State University # 277

    Moscow Institute of Physics and Technology # 312

Moscow International University Ranking "The Three University Missions", 2017

    Lomonosov Moscow State University # 25

    Saint Petersburg State University # 72

    Moscow Institute of Physics and Technology # 73

    National Research University Higher School of Economics (HSE) # 107

    National Research Nuclear University MEPhI # 131

    Novosibirsk State University # 132

    Tomsk Polytechnic University # 136

    Peter the Great St. Petersburg Polytechnic University # 173

    Tomsk State University # 176

    Moscow State Institute of International Relations # 192

    Kazan Federal University # 194

    Ural Federal University 195

    Russian Presidential Academy of National Economy and Public Administration (RANEPA) # 197

Appendix 7: Number of higher education institutions in Russia.

Year	Total	State (%)	State share of students (%)	Private
1950/1951	516			
1960/1961	430			
1970/1971	457			
1980/1981	494			
1985/1986	502			
1990/1991	514			
1991/1992	519			
1992/1993	535			
1993/1994	**626**	**548 (88%)**		**78**
1994/1995	**710**	**553 (78%)**	**96**	**157**
1995/1996	**762**	**569 (75%)**	**95**	**193**
1996/1997	**817**	**573 (70%)**	**94**	**244**
1997/1998	**880**	**578 (66%)**		**302**
1998/1999	**914**	**580 (64%)**		**334**
1999/2000	939	590 (63%)		349
2000/2001	965	607 (63%)	90	358
2003/2004	1,044	652 (63%)		392
2005/2006	1,068	655 (61%)	85	413
2007/2008	1,108	658 (59%)		450
2009/2010	1,114	662 (59%)		452
2010/2011	1,115	653 (59%)	83	462
2011/2012	**1,080**	634 (59%)	84	446
2012/2013	1,046	609 (58%)	85	437
2013/2014	969	578 (59%)	84	391
2014/2015	950	548 (58%)	85	402
2015/2016	896	530 (59%)	88	366

Note: Does not include branches. The years in bold indicate the two major inflection points since 1991. Expansion in the number of institutions came in 1993--1998, which were the years of the major economic disruption (before COVID); 2011–2012 marks the beginning of the reduction in the number of higher education institutions.

Source: *Rossiiskii statisticheskii ezhegodnik* (2002, p. 227; 2004, 2008, 2011, 2013, 2015, 2016).

Appendix 8: Russian higher education enrolments by type of study.

Year	All students	Full-Time	Evening	Correspondence
1990/1991	2,824,500	1,647,700 (**58%**)	284,500 (03%)	892,300 (32%)
2000/2001	4,741,400	2,625,200 (**53%**)	302,200 (06%)	1,761,800 (37%)
2005/2006	7,064,600	3,508,000 (**50%**)	371,200 (05%)	3,032,000 (43%)
2010/2011	7,049,800	3,073,700 (**44%**)	304,700 (04%)	3,557,200 (51%)
2011/2012	6,490,000	2,847,700 (**44%**)	263,400 (04%)	3,289,700 (51%)
2012/2013	6,079,400	2,724,300 (**45%**)	229,700 (04%)	3,051,400 (50%)
2013/2014	5,646,700	2,618,800 (46%)	189,200 (03%)	2,838,600 (50%)
2014/2015	5,209,000	2,575,000 (49%)	158,500 (03%)	2,475,500 (48%)
2015/2016	4,766,500	2,379,600 (50%)	149,100 (03%)	2,237,800 (47%)
2016/2017	4,399,500	2,403,000 (54.5%)	124,200 (2.8%)	1,872,300 (42.5%)
2017/2018	4,246,000			

Source: Rossiiskii statisticheskii ezhegodnik (2013, p. 215; 2016, p. 201).

Appendix 9: Reduction in the number of higher education institutions, 2014–2018.

Type	January 2014	January 2018
State main	567	484
State branches	908	428
Non-state main	371	178
Non-state branches	422	81
Total	**2,268**	**1,171**

Note: During the first quarter of 2018, the total reduced further to 1097.
Source: Makeeva (2018).

Appendix 10: Higher education faculty resources.

Year	State	Private
1993/1994	239,800	3,800
1995/1996	240,200	13,000
2000/2001	265,200	42,200
2005/2006	322,100	65,200
2007/2008	340,400	78,800
2008/2009	341,100	63,500
2009/2010	342,700	35,100
2010/2011	324,800	32,000
2011/2012	319,000	29,200
2012/2013	312,800	29,200
2013/2014		
2014/2015	299,800	
2015/2016	279,800	
2016/2017	261,000	

Notes: Some data missing due to changes in reporting. Includes *sovmetitelstvo* (faculty teaching at more than one institution). By 2014, student enrolments increased by 165% and faculty appointments grew by 66%.

Source: *Rossiiskie statisticheskii ezhegonik* (various years).

Appendix 11: Where do Russian technical education students enrol?

Year	Higher education	Secondary professional	Elementary professional-technical
1993	22.3%	26.1%	51.3%
1999	36.2%	29.4%	31.1%
2002	42.7%	28.3%	29.1%
2006	49.1%	28.2%	22.5%
2009	54.5%	24.1%	21.4%

Numbers may not total 100% due to rounding
Source: Compiled by the author.

Appendix 12: Emigration from Russia.

<u>PUTIN ERA</u>:

2018	440,831
2017	337,155
2016	313,210
2015	353,233
2014	310,496
2013	186,382
2012	122,751
2011	36,774
2010	33,578
2009	32,458
2008	39,508
2007	47,013
2006	54,061
2005	69,798
2004	79,795
2003	94,018
2002	106,685
2001	121,166
2000	145,720

<u>USSR AND YELTSIN ERA</u>:

1999	237,967
1998	216,691
1997	234,284
1996	288,048
1995	339,600
1994	337,121
1993	483,028
1992	673,143
1991	675,497
1990	729,467
1985	705,090
1980	780,650

Note: These are the official Russian Statistics Committee data. The numbers include those moving to former Soviet republics as well as those going elsewhere. The numbers in the 1990s represent significant movement of people returning to their "home" former Soviet republics that became independent countries at the end of 1991. Other sources put the total number emigrating significantly higher.

[*Source*: Compiled by the author from Rossiiskii statisticheskii exhegodnik, various years.]

Appendix 13: Data on Russian small and medium enterprises, 2010.

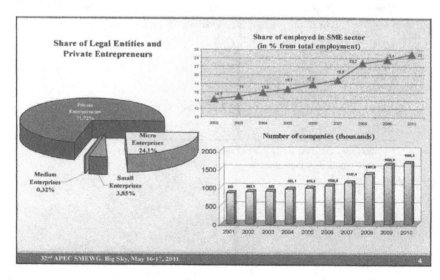

Appendix 14: China–Russia cooperation in education and S&T, 2017.
The following examples of the agreements and projects announced around the 2017 meeting indicate the sort of things that should be monitored:

- *April 6, 2017*: A discussion was conducted to come up with the ways to leverage the active space programmes operated by Russia, China and India to garner a greater share of the $300 billion global space industry.-http://thebricspost.com/brics-to-further-space-science-co-operation/#.WW4gLVGQzrk
- *May 15–16, 2017*: Russian Joint Institute f or Nuclear Research (Dubna) hosted the initial meeting of BRICS Working Group on Research Infrastructure and Mega-Science Projects. The working group was mentioned in the BRICS Jaipur Declaration and authorised at the 4th BRICS Science, Technology and Innovation Ministerial Meeting in October 2016. www.jinr.ru/posts/1st-meeting-of-brics-working-group-on-research-infrastructure-and-mega-science-projects/
- *May 31, 2017*: Regnum carried an item noting that Chinese scientists want to work in Crimea and also discussed the possibility of constructing a tunnel under the Kerch Strait using a new, less costly Chinese technology. https://regnum.ru/news/2282402.html
- *June 13–14, 2017*: Beijing hosted the first Chinese–Russian dialogue on innovations, jointly organised by the Ministry of Science and Technology of China and the Ministry of Economic Development of Russia. The agenda included a broad range of S&T issues. http://russian.china.org.cn/china/txt/2017-06/15/content_41028409.htm
- *June 15, 2017*: At the fourth Russian–Chinese EXPO in Harbin, Alexander Tyurchev, Chairman of Khabarovsk regional organisation "Russian Union of Youth (*Rossiiskii Soiuz Molodezhi*)", announced that the First Russian–Chinese Student Business-Incubator had been created in Kharabovsk. Representatives of businesses from

47 countries, including 23 countries that are part of the Silk Road Economic Belt, participated. Thirteen Russian regions were represented by more than 60 small, medium and large businesses. https://fadm.gov.ru/news/36167

- *June 19, 2017*: Sberbank and Harbin Bank signed an agreement establishing a $50 million investment fund that will focus on technology start-ups. http://amurmedia.ru/news/599399/

- *June 25, 2017*: At the Medical Educational Forum in Harbin, it was announced that since its creation 3 years ago, 106 universities have joined the Association of Sino-Russian Medical Universities. http://russian.china.org.cn/china/txt/2017-06/25/content_41093326.htm

- *June 27, 2017*: Officials announced an agreement on scientific-technical cooperation in agribusiness, including joint research and exchange of information. https://fano.gov.ru/ru/press-center/card/?id_4=38288

- *July 4, 2017*: Among the agreements resulting from the Putin–Xi meeting are several major investment projects, including efforts to support Russian non-resource exports to China. An Innovation Fund of $700 Million will invite Russian start-up firms to solicit financing. The first company will be Dauria Aerospace, a private firm based in Skolkovo. Russia's VEB and the Development Bank of China signed an agreement to spend $850 million on research projects including block chain, digital economics and technologies in the field of quantum physics. At the same time, the two leaders presided over agreements in oil, gas and infrastructure projects valued in billions of dollars. http://www.forbes.ru/biznes-photogallery/347325-nesyrevoy-eksport-v-kitay-smeshariki-kvn-i-kvantovaya-fizika

- *July 5, 2017*: It was announced that the first 200 students, 65 MA and 135 BA, will begin study at the new Chinese–Russian University in Shenzen, a joint project of Peking Polytechnical University and Moscow State University. http://russian.china.org.cn/china/txt/2017-07/05/content_41155807.htm

Appendix 15: Sanctions data.

A. Imported components: increase since 2006 (%).

	2006	2013
Total imported production inputs:	8.5	14.7
Machine building	14.4	36.5
Communications equipment	7	22.3
Pesticides and agricultural chemicals		74
Pharmaceuticals		48.4
Horizontal drilling equipment		56
Hydraulic fracturing equipment		**93**
Drilling platforms		**90**
Electronics for missiles and rockets		**65–79**

Note: The last three are critical for oil/gas or military sectors, HB.

B. Estimated potential for import substitution (%).

Machinery and equipment	31.0
Electrical and optical	34.0
Transport and equipment	22.0
Textiles	89.6
Leather and leather goods	39.0
Metallurgy	29.1
Chemicals	20.2
Rubber and plastic products	42.2

Source: Shirov *et al.* (2015, p. 11).

C. Sources of machine-building imports (%)

	Sanctions countries	China	Other
Laser and ultrasound cutters	25.6	63.3	11.0
Various metal working	50.0	24.7	25.3
Metal cutters	16.6	70.5	12.9
Numeric control metal cutters	44.8	23.1	32.1
Oil rocker pumps	36.4	47.6	16.0

Source: Shirov *et al.* (2015, p. 8).

D. Production and import of machine-building products.

Machine-building product	Production	Import	% Domestic
Mixers (cement)	2,874	518	85
Truck cranes	5,063	646	89
Off-road vehicles	2,457	1,300	65
Bearings, sliding (million)	52.9	15.5	77
Bearings, ball, roller (million)	63.5	81.3	69
Laser and ultrasound cutters	110	9,390	1
Various metal working	1,282	1,120	53
Metal cutters	531	8,531	6
NC metal cutters	133	1,925	6.5
Oil rocker pumps	900	14,238	5.9

Source: Shirov *et al.* (2015, p. 7).

Part II

Russian Defence

Chapter 7

Russian Defence: Economic Constraints and Potential

Steven Rosefielde

I cannot forecast to you the action of Russia. It is a riddle wrapped in a mystery inside an enigma; but perhaps there is a key. That key is Russian national interest. It cannot be in accordance with the interest of the safety of Russia that Germany should plant itself upon the shores of the Black Sea, or that it should overrun the Balkan States and subjugate the Slavonic peoples of south eastern Europe. That would be contrary to the historic life-interests of Russia.

— Winston Churchill, *The Russian Enigma*,
Broadcast October 1, 1939.
http://www.churchill-society-london.org.uk/RusnEnig.html

Eighty years ago, Winston Churchill surmised that even though Russia was a riddle wrapped in a mystery inside an enigma, there was a key: Russian national interest. He intuited that the Soviet Kremlin in the final analysis was guided more by Russian patriotism in national security affairs than communism and deduced that Moscow would do whatever it could to prevent a rival power from planting itself upon the shores of the Black Sea, overrunning the Balkan States and subjugating the people of south-eastern Europe. It is a good bet that Churchill was right about the durability of the Kremlin's Russian mindset, and that his judgement still holds in the post-Soviet era. Whatever Vladimir Putin's external ambitions may be, he is apt to place great stock in maintaining Russia's military defence capability.

Hitler admitted that he got Soviet Russia wrong in June 22, 1941. He underestimated the Kremlin's arsenal, its military industrial strength, its warfighting capability and its tenacity (Steury, 1998; Murphy, 2006; Wegner, 1993).[1] So did American and British intelligence (Kahn, 2012, 2017; Bergson, 1961, 1963; Samuelson, 1996).

This chapter reviews the record of Western assessments of post-war Soviet and Russian military industrial capabilities, economic constraints and performance. It explains why the task of assessing Russian defence activities has been far more difficult than might be supposed, and why politics and conventional wisdom have too often led the intelligence community astray.

Decoding the Enigma: Soviet Era

The Soviet Union was secretive. It published very little information on military industrial production and defence spending. Data on aggregate and sectoral production were copious, but suspect and difficult to interpret

---

[1] "Yet, there can be no doubt that Murphy is correct both in detail and in the sum and substance of his argument: Stalin was well-served by his intelligence departments. The responsibility for ignoring that intelligence was his and his alone".

"In closing, it is worth noting that there was another failure of judgment in BARBAROSSA, that of Adolf Hitler. Hitler, like Stalin, was a victim of his own preconceptions, but, in contrast to Stalin, he was ill-served by his intelligence services. Suffering from what the Japanese, from bitter experience, would call "victory disease", the Germans overestimated their own capabilities, even as they underestimated the Soviet capacity to resist. In July 1942, 1 year after the start of the campaign, Hitler admitted as much to Marshal Carl Gustav Mannerheim, the Finnish military leader, on a visit to Helsinki — Finland then being a cobelligerent with Germany in its war with the Soviet Union. 'We did not ourselves understand — just how strong this state [the USSR] was armed,' Hitler told him, 'If somebody had told me a nation could start with 35,000 tanks, then I'd have said, 'You are crazy!' ... [Yet] ... We have destroyed — right now — more than 34,000 tanks.... It was unbelievable ... I had no idea of it. If I had an idea — then it would have been more difficult for me, but I would have taken the decision to invade anyhow ... .'"

for two reasons: Marxist accounting and falsified data (Rosefielde, 1981). The Kremlin used Marxist accounting and price conventions for valuing national income and falsified data in diverse ways. It "freely invented" statistics, employed fuzzy definitions and left vital information unreported (Treml and Hardt, 1972). This was especially true for the defence sector. For example, in 1989, Mikhail Gorbachev disclosed that the official defence expenditure statistic published annually in *Narodnoe Khoziaistvo SSSR*, which was supposed to be comprehensive, omitted one minor component. It excluded weapons![2] This was shocking because the Central Intelligence Agency (CIA) had assured the Congress and the global intelligence community that weapons were included in the official Soviet budgetary *defence* statistic, while allowing for some modest concealment of defence activities in other budgetary categories.[3] The essential "truthfulness" of the official Soviet defence budgetary figure had been sacrosanct for those who insisted that the USSR's military threat to the West was negligible (Wiles and Efrat, 1985; Holzmam, 1975, 1980; Berkowitz *et al.*, 1993).

Gorbachev's revelation was shocking too because it proved that the Kremlin not only concealed the truth but also used the Soviet's false

---

[2] Soviet Military Budget: $128 Billion Bombshell, *New York Times*, May 31, 1989. http://www.nytimes.com/1989/05/31/world/soviet-military-budget-128-billion-bombshell.html. "Mikhail S. Gorbachev's announcement of what he said was the 'real' Soviet military budget caused an audible stir in the Congress of People's Deputies, but it is likely to produce some consternation among Western analysts of the Soviet military. Mr. Gorbachev said military spending this year would be 77.3 billion rubles, equivalent to $128 billion and nearly four times the nominal defense budget. He said the budget had been frozen since 1987.

'I am announcing this real figure to the congress,' Mr. Gorbachev said".

Becker (1970). The meaning and measure of Soviet military expenditure. In *Soviet Economy in a Time of Change*, Joint Economic Committee of Congress, Vol. 1, pp. 252–268.

[3] Bergson insisted at least since 1953 that the Soviet economic statistics including the military component were reliable. We frequently discussed the issue because Bergson opposed William Lee's estimates of Soviet weapons production based on official machine building data, which implied that the official defence budgetary figures were fake. The position of the CIA and that of Bergson was widely shared in the community and abroad by Peter Wiles and Alec Nove (Lee, 1977, 1995).

defence budgetary statistics to try and trick Washington into halving its annual defence spending.[4] The Soviet ambassador to the United Nations urged America every year to reduce US defence spending to match the USSR's example (Becker, 1977a, 1977b).[5] At least one influential RAND defence expert and advisor to the CIA swallowed the bait and wrote a book urging Washington's compliance under conditions that the Kremlin could have easily exploited (Becker, 1977a).

The Department of Defence and CIA had been at loggerheads over the reliability of the Soviet defence budgetary statistic throughout the Cold War, especially after 1975 when information obtained directly from the books of the Soviet Ministry of Defence seemed to prove that Kremlin defence spending was vastly higher than the budgetary statistic reported.[6] The CIA did not rely solely on the Soviet budgetary statistic, adjusted for

---

[4]The official defence budget statistic in the 1980s was approximately 2.5% of Russian NMP. American defence spending during this period was about 5% of GDP. Washington would have had to cut defence outlays in half to match the Soviet defence spending share of GDP. *Narodnoe Khoziaistvo SSSR za 70 Let*, Finansy i Statistika, Moscow, 1987.

[5]"Traces the history of proposed arms control by reduction of military budgets in the postwar period. The Soviet Union continues frequently to propose moderate-sized reductions by the great powers. Western States never regard these seriously because there has been no provision for comparing budgets or verifying compliance. The author argues that military expenditure limitation poses stringent information requirements and thus is no different than strategic arms limitations or other arms control arrangements. If anything, the information requirements are greater in as much as the information cannot be obtained by 'national technical means'. Regrettably, the Soviet Union remains unmoved by this argument; nor does it show any intent in easing its ban on release of military information. Near-term prospects for agreement by major powers on reductions are not promising, although there is an effort at the United Nations to develop a standardised system of reporting military expenditures".

[6]New information obtained directly from the books of the Soviet Ministry of Defence in 1975 revealed that procurement expenditures alone for 1970 may have been greater than Goskomstat's aggregate defence budgetary entry and thus shattered the Sovietologists' illusion that official statistics were "reliable". Bergson himself swore Goskomstat's defence budget figures were accurate for the period 1928–1958, yet suddenly there was incontrovertible evidence this wasn't so, at least for the years 1969 and 1970. The CIA grudgingly conceded its misassumption, but only on this particular case, and then set about salvaging whatever else it could with an eye, first, to justifying its prior judgement that Soviet defence spending was nonthreatening and second to restoring the prestige of its methodology.

some modest concealment in other budget categories. It had its own independent direct costing method ("building block method"), which yielded results about half the size as the Defense Intelligence Agency's (DIA) (Rosefielde, 2005a; Rowen and Wolf, 1990), but the CIA and DIA had a gentleman's agreement not to publicly battle each other over their conflicting statistics. Each reported its own incompatible indicators on the Soviet military effort separately to the Joint Economic Committee annually, allowing readers to choose the evidence they preferred (Rowen and Wolf, 1990; Lee, 1977, 1990; Rosefielde, 2005a).

Gorbachev's revelation not only made it plain that Soviet statistics were sometimes *unusable*[7] but proved that the Kremlin had deliberately tried to shame Washington policymakers into reducing America's defence spending to faux Soviet levels. The CIA partly recanted some of its erroneous costing estimates in 1998 (Firth and Noren, 1998), but never publicly admitted that lowballing Soviet defence activities had played into the Kremlin's hands.

Deciphering Soviet Economic and Defence Statistics

Western scholars and government authorities paid scant attention to Soviet economic and defence statistics during the 1930s. They did not address problems of Marxist accounting (including state fixed prices) and deception until Germany's invasion of Russia on June 22, 1941 (Operation Barbarossa) and Japan's subsequent attack on Pearl Harbor compelled the Roosevelt administration to prioritise the acquisition of reliable Soviet military and economic statistics. The task of piercing the veil fell to Abram Bergson,[8] who ultimately became chief of the Russian economics

---

[7]Bergson (1953a) made a distinction between "reliable" and "usable" asserting that if Soviet statistics were not 100% reliable, they were good enough to be usable.

[8]Abram Bergson became a Ph.D. candidate in economics in 1933 at the age of 19. Wassily Leontief who arrived at Harvard in 1932 was a mentor. Bergson visited Moscow during the show trials in 1937 to study Soviet wages (Bergson, 1944) and published a pioneering paper on welfare theory in 1938, informally collaborating with Paul Samuelson (Bergson, 1938). Bergson received his Ph.D. from Harvard in 1940 and taught for 2 years at the University of Texas, Austin, before being appointed chief of the Russian economics subsection in the Russian Division of the Office of Strategic Services (OSS). After the war,

subsection in the Russian Division of the Office of Strategic Services (OSS) during World War II, continuing thereafter as the West's doyen of Soviet economics at RAND, Columbia and Harvard and as a consultant to the CIA.

Bergson solved the reliability question to his own satisfaction *a priori* by (1) declaring that Soviet data were not freely invented,[9] (2) conducting internal consistency tests (comparing official aggregate national product with his own aggregation of Soviet sectoral output) and (3) using index number relativity theory to partially rationalise disparities between published and estimated rates of output growth (Bergson, 1950a, 1950b, 1953a, 1953b, 1953c; Bergson and Heymann, 1954; Gerschenkron, 1962a, 1962b; Moorsteen, 1962; Rosefielde, 1975a, 2005c). His arguments convinced two generations of scholars and intelligence analysts that Soviet statistics were "usable" enough to be deemed reliable, but he was wrong. Soviet authorities did sometimes freely invent economic statistics.[10] Internal consistency tests sometimes were misleading, especially in the military machine building residual of Soviet input–output tables (Rosefielde, 1987).[11] Index number relativity glossed over deep problems of padded growth (Rosefielde, 2003).

Bergson continued his research on Soviet national income accounting statistics at Rand, and when the CIA was founded in 1947 under the National Security Act, he served as the authoritative consultant in establishing the Agency's Soviet economic analysis unit. His principal contributions to the field of Soviet national income studies are the following: Bergson (1950a, 1950b, 1951, 1953a, 1953b,1953c, 1954, 1961, 1963, 1968, 1971, 1972a, 1972b, 1972c, 1972d, 1974, 1975, 1978a, 1978b, 1979, 1983, 1987, 1991, 1994, 1995) and Bergson and Levine (1983).

[9]Bergson (1953a) reasoned that Soviet leaders need accurate data to supervise the economy and that he had found no evidence suggesting that the State Statistics Committee used two sets of books: one for internal and the other for external consumption.

[10]Vitaly Shlykov, Co-Chairman of the Russian Defense Council under Yeltsin, told the author that the sole purpose of VPK published statistics is to deceive. Welcome to Smiley's world. Cf. Martin (1980).

[11]Albina Tretyakova worked on the machine building cell of the Soviet input–output table in Moscow and reported after emigrating to America that the Soviet Ministry of Defence provided no information whatsoever on weapons to input–output table builders. She was the wife of Igor Birman, who had been Soviet Minister of the Construction Materials sector.

Soviet fiat value-added was not the close proxy for competitive value-added that Bergson purported it to be.[12]

Vexing problems of Soviet Marxist national income accounting definitions and labour value prices compounded the confusion. Karl Marx distinguished two types of labour: productive and non-productive. He classified factory workers, including white-collar staff, as productive. They produced physical goods for investment, government, defence and consumption. Barbers provided services that did not contribute to investment, government, defence or consumption. Their labour was non-productive. The services of teachers and doctors were productive or non-productive depending on context. The Soviets excluded non-productive services from their net material product (NMP) accounts (Holesovsky, 1961),[13] but Western countries included them in GDP. This impaired the comparability of Soviet and Western national income and product statistics. Bergson successfully resolved the incompatibility by adding non-productive Soviet services to Kremlin NMP data. His "apples-to-apples" standardised GDP findings were interesting, but not momentous from both the national security and consumer welfare perspective. They did not drastically alter assessments of factor productivity and aggregate economic growth.[14]

---

[12] Bergson correctly distinguished consumer sovereignty from consumer choice. Consumer demand in the first case governs product characteristics, production and retail supply. Consumer choice is more limited. It only pertains to retail shopping. However, Bergson downplayed the distinction by suggesting that consumer choice was sufficient to make Soviet and Western value-added data more or less alike.

[13] Marx defines productive labour on pages 476–477 of Capital, vol. 1. He goes into much more detail in Theories of Surplus Value, vol. 1, pages 152–304 and pages 389–413. Supplementary points on circulation capital are included in Chapter 6 of Capital, vol. 2 and chapters 16–19 of Capital, vol. 3 (all page numbers refer to old Lawrence & Wishart editions). https://www.lwbooks.co.uk/MECW-copyright.

[14] There were enormous differences between Bergson's adjusted factor cost GDP and Soviet NMP growth rates 1928–1933 and 1928–1937, even after adjustment for index number relativity, but no attempt was made to identify the source of the discrepancy. The disparities were shrugged off.

Labour value pricing was more challenging (Shaikh, 1998).[15] Soviet prices measured labour time. The State Price Committee administratively set ruble wage rates for different grades of labour. The product price was the average labour time (person hours) to produce a unit of output valued at state fixed wage rates expressed in rubles.[16] The more labour time it took to produce a good, the higher its ruble price regardless of consumer demand.[17] The market value of high fiat priced goods might be nil. The market price of a low fiat priced good might be enormous, but neither dis-correspondence mattered. These dis-correspondences between fiat prices and competitive market values raised the possibility that Soviet NMP and GDP statistics were inscrutable. They did not reflect consumer demand and utility. It was impossible to discern how far published values overstated their competitive market worth.

Bergson accepted this criticism of Soviet national product and value statistics, but counterargued that the deficiency was not fatal by claiming that the Kremlin's NMP statistics had important contingent meaning. He coined the term "production potential" to clarify the nuance (Rosefielde, 1998), which was a supply side distinction. Bergson's solution to the dis-correspondence between Soviet consumer demand (utility) and product supply (unit cost) was the contention that Soviet labour value prices could be adjusted to reflect marginal rates of factor substitution at observed unit levels of production by adding capital charges to Marxist labour cost prices (Bergson, 1961; Moorsteen and Powell, 1966; Becker, 1969; Rosefielde, 1975b; Rosefielde and Lovell, 1977). Adjusted "factor cost" prices were interpreted as quasi-value-added prices on the assumption that they represented the unit

---

[15]Many Marxist economists defended labour value prices, arguing that they were superior.

[16]The Soviet State Price Committee set nationwide wage rates in rubles, differentiated by skill. Enterprise managers paid wages to workers assigned to the production of specific goods. This information was passed along to the State Price Committee, which used it together with counterpart data on production to compute the average unit labour cost of production. These average unit labour product cost statistics were then published in Soviet handbooks as ruble product prices.

[17]Ruble wages were constant. Unit labour production costs, therefore, depended solely on the person hours required to produce an average unit of output.

worth of goods, if product assortments and volumes corresponded with planner preferences. This was tantamount to the claim that a reasonable impression of value-added as central authorities conceived it was computable by adjusting published NMP data with a simple accounting procedure that added hypothetical imputed rents on capital to Soviet fiat ruble unit labour cost prices (Bergson, 1961). Planners, it was implied, planned factor supplies and output assignments for 27.5 million products efficiently enough for the American intelligence community to assess basic national security and consumer welfare with the aid of Bergson's accounting price adjustments to Soviet average unit labour ruble cost statistics.[18]

All these interpretative claims were specious. The Edgeworth–Bowley factor production space makes this plain. Bergson argues that centrally planned production occurred on the contract curve at a system directors preferred point (not the competitive equilibrium) (Rosefielde and Pfouts, 1988), at the double tangency of isoquants and a marginal rate of factor substitution equal to Bergson's estimated wage–rental ratio (see Rosefielde and Pfouts, 2014, Chapter 2). There is no reason to assume that these conditions were satisfied. Soviet central planning in practice was an input rationing scheme completely disconnected from competitive rational choice micro-optimisation (Rosefielde, 2007). Input allocation did not maximise planners or consumers utilities, and wage rates were not uniform across activities as the Pareto ideal requires. Soviet production occurred far from the contract curve at multiple wage–rental ratios. Adjusted factor cost pricing could not capture these inefficiencies in any important way (Rosefielde and Pfouts, 1995; Rosefielde, 2005c). Bergson's alternative Soviet national product and income only provided the

---

[18]Note that prices in competitive economies are determined by the marginal cost, not by average unit cost, except in the case of a specific class of "transcendental" production functions where marginal and average production costs are the same for all activity levels. Cobb–Douglas and CES productions satisfy this requirement. Bergson appreciating this therefore explicitly assumed that Soviet enterprise product-specific production functions were, or nearly were, transcendental. This was acceptable for reflective purposes, but failed to address the further and equally profound issue of the inefficiency of Soviet central planning. Factors were not efficiently allocated across sectors and enterprises, and output assignments were not rationally chosen.

semblance, not the substance of value-added reality needed for sound national security and consumer utility assessments.

No one in the intelligence community understood Bergson's production potential concept, although some of best-known experts on Soviet economy during the Cold War like Abraham Becker, Raymond Powell (Chairman of the Economics Department at Yale) and Richard Moorsteen (RAND) tried (Moorsteen and Powell, 1966; Becker, 1969). Charles Wolf, Jr. (Dean of the RAND Graduate School) admitted it.[19] Even if the CIA, State Department and Arms Control and Disarmament Agency had realised that "production potential" was a conceit, they would not have cared. They needed authoritative independent statistics to support their advocacy of strategic patience; statistics that showed: (1) the Soviet military threat was not imminent (Samuelson, 2000)[20]; (2) living standards although low were adequate, equitable and improving (Schroeder and Severin, 1976; Schroeder and Denton, 1970). Bergson himself probably knew that his "production potential" standard was smoke and mirrors, but never recanted (Bergson, 1991, 1994, 1995; Rosefielde, 1991; Rosefielde and Kleiner, 1998).

Finally, no summary review of the Western Cold War-era Soviet economic and security analysis would be complete without stressing the CIA's role in mudding the waters. The agency's Office of Soviet Analysis (SOVA) using the Soviet Cost Analysis Method, SCAM (yes, this was the acronym) improperly applied a "learning curve" adjustment to its Soviet weapons procurement series that had the effect of reducing real arms growth in 1973–1986 from double-digit rates to zero! (Firth and Noren, 1998; Rosefielde, 1986, 2005a). This intelligence gaff dwarfed Gorbachev's Soviet defence budgetary deception. Some suspect that the misuse of

---

[19] Personal conversation at Airlie House, 1990.

[20] Bergson's statistics supported the narrative that the USSR was building socialism, that the Nazi German menace forced Stalin to slow the construction of socialism and switch to homeland defence and that Soviet weapons procurement then reverted to the pre-1935 pattern (Bergson's notion), which then dovetailed with the CIA's arms procurement series 1960–1987 (zero real weapons growth). The weight of the evidence shows that Stalin's industrialisation drive was about preparing for a Blochian total war long before Hitler came to power and was a primary motive for rapid modernisation.

learning curves was intentional, but the evidence to resolve the issue remains classified (Rosefielde, 1987; Corson *et al.*, 1989).[21]

Decoding the Enigma: Today

A lot has changed, but nothing has changed since 1990 with respect to the enigma of the Kremlin's defence potential and constraints.

The Soviet Union dissolved itself, and Russia has transitioned to a workably competitive market economy with widespread private ownership of the means of production. Central planning, state wage and price fixing and communism are gone. Russia is an open economy with a convertible ruble. Moscow has abandoned Marxist national product and income accounting and embraced Western statistical standards. Its civilian economic statistics are less untrustworthy.

Nonetheless, the Kremlin remains secretive (Donadio, 2007). Russian defence economic statistics are as opaque as ever, and some members of the intelligence community exhibit no qualms in employing Kremlin defence budgetary data as usable and broadly reliable indicators of Russian military activities (Cooper, 2016b, 2017). Official defence data on budgetary spending and the defence burden continue to be low in line with the pre-1989 Soviet series (Christie, 2017). The growth rate of defence outlays 2000–2018 also follows the Soviet pattern, but differs in one important respect. The official series reports a powerful surge in defence spending during 2010–2015 that has no parallel in the Narkhoz series during 1960–1989.

Washington's willingness to rely heavily on Russian economic statistics to support its foreign policies likewise connects the present with the past and the past to the future (Allen, 2003; Nove, 1972).[22] During

---

[21] The authors contend that CIA officer John Paisley did not drown in the Chesapeake Bay as reported in a Congressional hearing. There was informed speculation in the community in 1979 that Paisley fled to Moscow and that the body pulled from the Chesapeake was a ploy to cover his defection. According to the CIA/DIA Soviet defence expert William T. Lee (personal conversation), Paisley had a hand in the SOVA Soviet weapons costing shop that introduced the learning curve adjustment responsible for erasing the growth of the Soviet weapons in the CIA series.

[22] British historians have narrated the Stalin-era Soviet economic experience on the supposition that Soviet data are usable and that they are sufficiently reliable to claim that

the 1990s, when the Clinton administration pressed "transition", the IMF–World Bank group adjusted Russian data to reduce the magnitude of Russia's post-Soviet hyperdepression[23] and to suggest that former Soviet and east European states that established competitive markets outperformed those that retained command economies (Havrylyshyn, 2017; Rosefielde, 2017).

Later, the IMF–World Bank group switched definitions of Russian GDP 2003–2008 so that it could report astonishing rates of growth that validated Washington's triumphalist post-Soviet economic transition claims (Rosefielde, 2017).[24] After the Kremlin annexed Crimea in 2014, IMF–World Bank conventional GDP estimates painted a bleaker picture of Russia's prospects than was justified and exaggerated the Kremlin's vulnerability to Western economic sanctions, while missing Moscow's spectacular rearmament.

These statistical ploys had and may continue to have various political advantages, but they impair dispassionate analysis of the Kremlin's threat that emerged after 2010. Many in the intelligence community, under the sway of IMF–World Bank Group economic indicators, official Russian defence budgetary statistics and VPK's (Voenny-promyshlenny kompleks) [military industrial complex] economic data, unjustifiably discount the importance of counterindicative American Defense Intelligence Agency (DIA) satellite-confirmed statistics on Russia's arsenal and weapon procurement trends.[25] This is a mistake. Official Russian defence

---

the USSR successfully established the foundation for peaceful and prosperous socialism in one country. This makes the Soviet collapse difficult to explain but paves the way for trying to build communism anew on the premise that next time will be even better.

[23]This was done in conjunction with Goskomstat. Initial Goskomstat data showed that the Russian GDP during 1990–1996 fell by nearly 50%. The shoddily revised depression was pared to 37%.

[24]Standard measures of real GDP growth use constant prices of a specified base year without adjustment for windfall gains or losses caused by the appreciation or depreciation of the nation's currency on foreign exchange markets. The IMF–World Bank Group during the sub-period 2003–2008 added the windfall ruble currency gain triggered by 9/11 to conventional GDP, giving the impression that its transition policy recommendations have been astonishingly successful.

[25]The IMF–World Bank Group took no position on Russian military industrial activities, but its fudged statistics allowed intelligence analysts to downplay DIA data.

budgetary statistics and VPK economic data are untrustworthy, and the IMF's numbers can be seriously misleading. When Western leaders desire Russian economic performance cast in a favourable light for geostrategic and political reasons, the IMF–World Bank group complies. When the same leaders want to highlight the Kremlin's vulnerability to economic sanctions, the IMF–World Bank group bends the other way. The remedy is obvious: self-discipline, but this is not enough. Policymakers also need to acquire a better grasp of realities obscured by standard national income statistics to appreciate the full extent to which Russia has become a potent "guns and butter" economic system.

Russian Economic Well-Being: Internalities and Externalities

Economic statistics assist professional economists, the business community, social advocacy groups and the government in quantifying their perceptions of reality and testing hypotheses. National income statistics serve the broad needs of diverse users rather than the narrow requirements of the national security community. Only if the defence components of the GDP series are accurate will they offer limited insight into deterrent and warfighting capabilities, and except in special cases, civilian series only provide fragile insight into prospects for regime change and the potential impact of economic sanctions. Many national security practitioners mislead themselves because they do not adequately appreciate these limitations.

The deficiencies of standard economic indicators of deterrence and warfighting potential are obvious. Aggregate defence spending provides a perception of the cost of military activities. It does not reveal motivations or disclose how money is spent. It does not measure opportunity costs or potentials. It does not illuminate the wisdom or the effectiveness of defence expenditures. These important matters must be inferred.

North Korea offers a sobering example. The CIA lists it as one of the planet's poorest countries, ranked 215th in per capita income just above Togo (CIA, 2018). Its GDP growth rate in recent years is close to zero, and its unemployment rate is 25%. These statistics suggest that Pyongyang's centrally planned communist economy is severely dysfunctional, so much so that it is tottering on the edge of collapse and could not possibility support production of nuclear weapons, ballistic missiles and conventional arms capable of threatening South Korea. Many Western national security pundits relying on this economic evidence persuaded themselves that Kim Jong Un's militarist rhetoric is bombast. Although the facts belie the expectations (Eberstadt, 2018), they have held fast to their premises, insisting that poverty makes North Korea vulnerable to economic sanctions. Perhaps, but this misses the point. DIA satellite photo intelligence should take precedence over fuzzy economic data for North and Russia.

Returning to Russia, per capita GDP data, growth trends, unemployment rates and poverty statistics are fuzzy indicators of vulnerability and regime stability because they only address "internalities". This term means that GDP statistics are supposed to reflect consumer demand (after adjustment for social transfers) driven by the rational desire to maximise utility from current and deferred consumption. It follows that if per capita GDP is high, consumers should enjoy high utility and vice versa. If GDP grows rapidly, it follows that people can look forward to brighter utilitarian tomorrows.

Individual utility however does not depend solely on internalities. People also benefit or suffer from the conditions of labour, opportunities for leisure and the broad cultural and security environment. Job security, job quality, independence, cooperation, congeniality, team spirit, mutual support and solidarity generate positive workplace external utilities. Political, economic, social, religious and personal freedom together with national and income security and psychological and spiritual health provide utility and allow people to enjoy their incomes more fully. Supportive cultures, families, neighbours, communities and compatriots permit richer lives. National income statistics do not capture these non-market utilities and dis-utilities, but they are pertinent to assessing Russia's ability to sustain its arms build-up and its vulnerability to economic sanctions, colour revolutions and regime change.

Internal and external utilities are additive. The sum represents the quality of existence and is computable with a composite well-being function measuring "welltiles":

$$W = u_{A1} + u_{Z1} + u_{A2} + u_{Z2},$$

where the subscripts A1 and Z1 refer to internal utilities and the subscripts A2 and Z2 denote external utilities.

It is plausible to suppose that the economic vulnerability or the stability of Putin's regime is highly correlated with Russian perception of national well-being. Figure 1 shows why Russians in 2018 should have a greater sense of well-being than they had in 1985. The diagram arrays well-being on the ordinate and Russia on the abscissa at different moments in time. The solid vertical bars represent utility derived in consumption. The hatched segments measure utility generated by externalities. Russian per capita consumption indicated by Russia's solid bar 2018 significantly exceeds the Soviet benchmark 1985. The hatched segment is greater too. Russia has sharply increased net positive externalities by introducing elements of democracy; expanding civil liberties; and providing cultural, economic, social and religious freedom while retaining much of the Soviet social safety net. It has significantly curbed domestic political terror, forced labour, excess deaths and other forms of authoritarian oppression. Thus, Russia's well-being is higher today than it was in 1985, assertions to the contrary notwithstanding.

Intelligence analysts know that Russian externalities have improved as Figure 1 indicates, but this seems always forgotten when drawing inferences from fuzzy economic statistics.

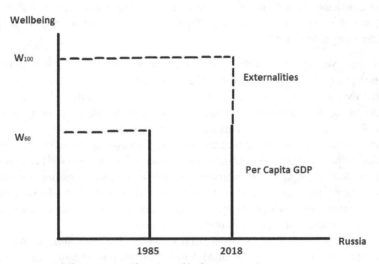

Figure 1: Russian well-being.

Russian Guns and Butter Superpower

The Soviet Union concealed behind Goskomstat's, Bergson's and the CIA's fuzzy economic statistics was an impoverished superpower, just as Rowan and Wolf contended in 1990 (Rowen and Wolf, 1990; Rosefielde, 2005a). The Soviet economy produced a cornucopia of weapons,[26] but few consumer goods to stock people's larders. Negative consumer externalities far outweighed the combined benefits of Soviet full employment and a makeshift social safety net.

The reality behind post-Soviet fuzzy economic statistics is different. The Kremlin today is a "guns and butter" second-tier superpower (Rosefielde and Mills, 2021, Appendix 1). It possesses an immense full-spectrum conventional and nuclear arsenal with mostly fifth-generation technologies.[27] It is a second-tier military superpower because America

---

[26] According to Vitaly Shlykov, Co-Chairman of the Russian Defense Council, the Soviet Union possessed 52,000 nuclear weapons, a figure reduced to approximately 40,000 under President Boris Yeltsin (personal conversation). These numbers from a reliable inside source show that official arms control statistics on nuclear forces are an eyewash, something well understood by insiders.

[27] Fifth-generation technologies refer to modern technologies that are compatible with fifth-generation concepts of warfighting. "Fifth-generation air warfare concepts incorporate four generic elements:

- *Networks*: Network-centric thinking envisions four interconnected and interdependent virtual grids — information, sensing, effects and command — overlaying the operational theatre. The various force elements, from individuals and single platforms to battle groups, are then interacting nodes on the grids. Each node can receive, act on, or pass forward data provided from the various grids as appropriate.
- *Combat Cloud*: In working together, the grids can form a combat cloud that the various nodes can pull data from and add data to as necessary. This brings several tactical benefits including considerably improving situational awareness, making long-range engagements more practical, ensuring no single node is critical to mission success, allowing each node to designate targets to other nodes and ensuring the best use is made of the different diverse capabilities offered by each node.
- *Multi-Domain Battle*: The five operational domains are considered land, sea, air, space and cyber. The key idea animating multi-domain battle is cross-domain synergy, the use of armed force across two or more domains to achieve an operational advantage. Acting in a complementary manner — rather than an additive one — each capability enhances the effectiveness of the whole while lessening the individual vulnerabilities of each

still maintains the technological edge, and the American people enjoy a superior standard of living. The Kremlin government has remained authoritarian and the hopes for Russia rapidly transitioning to a democratic free enterprise have faded into oblivion (Shleifer and Treisman, 2004; Shleifer, 2005; Rosefielde, 2005b).

The intelligence community knows that Russia has changed, but is not yet ready to accept the strategic significance of its "guns and butter" post-Soviet transformation, in part because Russia's liberalisation is incomplete, macroeconomy shaky and the rule of law opaque and insecure (Turley and Luke, 2010). These qualifications are valid, but not decisive. Russia's markets do not have to be perfectly competitive for the Kremlin to sustain its "guns and butter" superpower. The success of Xi Jinping's market communist regime proves the point (Rosefielde and Leightner, 2017). Moscow can give Washington a run for its money merely by establishing a workably competitive market-based consumer sector that provides an adequate and rising living standard,[28] while turbocharging the military industrial complex by introducing for-profit, competitive business principles. Theory clearly teaches that the introduction of workably competitive markets should allow Russia's consumer sector and military industrial complex to outperform their Soviet predecessors (Clark, 1940). The Kremlin is a rising second-tier "guns and butter" superpower capable of sustained competition with the West.[29]

---

platform. Moreover, linking across domains means that the integrated force overall can be self-healing in that destruction of any single node may be able to be compensated for by another node in a different domain.

- *Fusion warfare*: The fusion warfare concept seeks to address command and control concerns arising from the increasing volume and speed of information flows, software incompatibilities and intrinsic vulnerabilities to attack and deception". Peter Layton, "Fifth Generation Warfare: An Evolving Technical Dimension of War", *Over the Horizon*, July 31, 2017. https://overthehorizonmdos.com/2017/07/31/5th-gen-warfare/.

[28] "Russian Economy Returns to Modest Growth in 2017, says World Bank", *World Bank*, November 29, 2017, http://www.worldbank.org/en/news/press-release/2017/11/29/rer-38: "These shoots have allowed consumer demand and consumption to rise, as the business environment improved, and underpin projections that Russia's economy will grow 1.7% in both 2017 and 2018, and 1.8% in 2019."

[29] For a geometrical demonstration, see Rosefielde and Mills (2021, Appendix 1).

Great Arms Modernisation Drive, 2010–2015

Russia's successful arms modernisation drive during 2010–2015[30] and prospects for further improvement support this judgement. The Kremlin's arms modernisation surge was well planned and executed. The founding documents were The Reform and Development of the Defense Industrial Complex Program 2002–2006 signed by Prime Minister Mikhail Kasyanov in October 2001,[31] and the State Armament Programme (Gosudarstvennaia Programma Vooruzhenii) for Russia for the years 2011–2020 signed by President Dmitri Medvedev at the end of 2010.[32] The Russian State Armament Programme 2011–2020 is supported by two

---

[30] Julian Cooper, *Russia's State Armament Programme to 2020: A Quantitative Assessment of Implementation 2011–2015*, FOI, FOI-R-4239-SE, March 2016. "This report provides an overview of the implementation of the Russian state armament programme to 2020 as the end of its first five year approaches. It is an empirical study designed to present data that is not readily accessible to analysts." Cf. Eugene Kogan, *Russian Military Capabilities*, Tiblisi Georgia: Georgian Foundation for Strategic and International Studies, 2016.

Mikhail Barabanov, "Testing a 'New Look', The Ukrainian Conflict and Military Reform in Russia," in Centre for Analysis of Strategies and Technologies (CAST). Bettina Renz, "Russian Military Capabilities after 20 Years of Reform," in *Survival*, vol. 56, no. 3 (June–July 2014), pp. 61–84. Also see Cooper's follow-up paper: Prospects for military spending in Russia in 2017 and beyond, April 2017.

[31] The author possesses a signed copy of the unpublished programme summary. The document reveals that Kremlin intended to move towards reconsolidation of state authority, driven in part by the ageing of the OPK's capital stock, underemployment, low pay and poor enterprise finances. Cf. Vitaly Shlykov, "Russian Defense Industrial Complex after 9-11," paper presented at Russian Security Policy and the War on Terrorism, U.S. Naval Postgraduate School, Monterey, CA, June 4–5, 2002. For a discussion of earlier reforms, see Izyumov *et al.* (2001a, 2001b).

[32] Richard Connolly and Cecilie Sendstad, "Russian rearmament: An assessment of defense-industrial performance", *Problems of Post Communism*, October 2016. "This article addresses two related questions associated with Russia's rearmament program (GPV-2020). First, it examines how the Russian defence industry has performed in the first five years of the rearmament program, by presenting data describing the quantity and quality of new arms procurement in Russia. Second, the article considers which factors explain the nature of Russian defence-industrial performance over the past five years, including the importance of the increase in financial resources allocated to defence procurement, as well as additional structural and institutional factors. It is argued that, although

federal programmes (*federalnye tselevye progammy* — FTsP): FTsP development of the defence-industrial complex, 2011–2020 and the FTsP development, restoration and organisation of the production of strategic scarce and import substituting materials and small-scale chemistry for armaments, military and special technology in 2009–2011 and the period till 2015 (inter-industrial supply). The support programmes underscore the fact that the Russian State Armament Programme is more than a procurement policy. It entails the reform of the VPK and defence inter-industrial supply.

Julian Cooper summarises the programme and its accomplishments through 2015 as follows:

> This was a highly ambitious document setting out plans for the procurement of weapons and other military equipment, plus research and development for the creation of new systems, to a total value of over 20 trillion roubles, or US$680 billion at the exchange rate of the day. The aim of the programme was to increase the share of modern armaments held by the armed forces from 15 per cent in 2010 to 30 percent in 2015 and 70 per cent in 2020. The programme has been implemented through the budget-funded annual state defence order supplemented by state guaranteed credits. By 2014 the military output of the defence industry was growing at an annual rate of over 20 percent, compared with 6 percent three years earlier. The volume of new weapons procured steadily increased, the rate of renewal being particularly strong in the strategic missile forces and the air force, but not as impressive in the navy and ground forces. In 2014 the work of the defence industry began to be affected by the Ukraine crisis, with a breakdown of military-related deliveries from Ukraine and the imposition of sanctions by NATO and European Union member countries. The performance of the economy began to deteriorate, putting pressure on state finances. It was decided to postpone for three years the approval of the successor state armament programme, 2016–2025. Nevertheless, the implementation of the programme to date has secured a meaningful modernisation of the hardware

---

defence-industrial performance between 2011 and 2015 has not been perfect, it can still be considered to have been relatively successful."

of the Russian armed forces for the first time since the final years of the USSR.[33]

Russia has not only succeeded in augmenting the size of its arsenal but also significantly modernised its armed forces.[34] Eugene Kogan, a well-respected defence expert, concurs.[35] The quantitative improvement

---

[33] Rosefielde (2017) and Ellman (2015). But cf. Gustav Gressel, "Russia's quiet military revolution, and what it means for Europe," *European Council on Foreign Relations (ECFR)*, December 31, 2015. http://www.isn.ethz.ch/Digital-Library/Articles/Detail/?id=195415. "The West has underestimated the significance of Russia's military reforms. Western — especially US — analysts have exclusively focused on the third phase of reform: the phasing in of new equipment. Numerous Russian and Western articles have stated that the Russian armed forces were still using legacy equipment from the Soviet Union and that its replacement was occurring more slowly than planned by the Kremlin. [ix] However, this is a misunderstanding of the nature of the reforms. The initial stages were not designed to create a new army in terms of equipment, but to ensure that existing equipment was ready to use, and to make the organisation that uses it more effective and professional. Indeed, to successfully intervene in Russia's neighbourhood, Moscow does not necessarily need the latest cutting-edge defence technology. Rather, such interventions would have to be precisely targeted and quickly executed to pre-empt a proper Western reaction."

[34] Bryan Bender, "The Secret U.S. Army Study that Targets Moscow," *Politico*, April 14, 2016. http://www.politico.com/magazine/story/2016/04/moscow-pentagon-us-secret-study-213811. Lieutenant General H.R. McMaster told the Senate Armed Services committee last week that "in Ukraine, the combination of unmanned aerial systems and offensive cyber and advanced electronic warfare capabilities depict a high degree of technological sophistication."

[35] Eugene Kogan, *Russian Military Capabilities*, Tiblisi Georgia: Georgian Foundation for Strategic and International Studies, 2016. "It can be said that the Russian military has indeed learnt their lessons from the Russia-Georgia war of August 2008. The manner that the military operated in Crimea, and most recently, in Syria demonstrated that military operations combined three most important components: surprise, mobility and swiftness (SMS). Whether or not the same lethal combination would be successfully replicated elsewhere remains to be seen. On the other hand, to state unequivocally that the Russian military is not capable of competing in conventional warfare beyond the post-Soviet space or in confrontation with NATO would be short-sighted and inaccurate. Such an assumption is no longer far-fetched but rather realistic even though experts in the field may disagree with the author. The Western perception of the current Russian military is undergoing a sea of change. It is evident that the agility and the rapidness of the military to perform before other actors intervene took the West at large by surprise. As a result, there is more and more talk about Russian military operations against the Baltic States even though they are NATO members and NATO's famous dictum — an attack on one is an attack on all — appears to no longer be deterring Russia. In other

may be partly attributable to restarting existing weapon production lines with negligible systemic implications (economic recovery), but modernisation is another story. It demonstrates that Russia's post-communist economy, like its Soviet predecessor, is capable of manufacturing large quantities of technologically improved weapons systems.

Russia is rapidly modernising its full-spectrum military capabilities. More than half of the new weapons procured during its arms build-up

---

words, the West at large can no longer take for granted that the Russian military will not seize the opportunity to intervene if they see fit. After all, President Vladimir Putin showed repeatedly his flair for being an opportunist and not being shy of military adventurism. Although the 2008–2012 military reform degraded Russia's combat capabilities in its western regions, Moscow's shift towards operations in limited conflicts [author's italics] riveted more attention to mobile and special operations forces. As a result, not only did the Airborne Forces avoid manpower cuts but they also kept their divisions and amplified their strength. Special Operations Forces (SOFs), too, began their build-up and increased combat readiness. The modernisation of Army Aviation units began swiftly and was accompanied by the procurement of a large number of new helicopters and a substantial number of new combat aircraft. As Barabanov continues, the procurement of a large number of new but not modernised helicopters accentuated mobility. In addition to mobility, large investments in human resources and combat training paid off generously in 2014 with a better army and more skilful personnel, especially officers. Another positive factor is a large number of officers who acquired real combat experience in the Chechen wars, counterterrorism operations in the North Caucasus and various local conflicts in the post-Soviet states. Additionally, numerous exercises have been held at all levels, including regular strategic manoeuvres, introduction of new education and combat training methods and recruitment of more professional soldiers. New arms and hardware supplies since 2007 have considerably improved the army's material status and equipage, primarily in the Air Force and Army Aviation units. A major breakthrough was also made in logistics. After the Georgian campaign, the Russian army has been enhancing its strategic manoeuvre capabilities for years and practicing deployment over great distances, which proved highly instrumental during the Ukrainian crisis. However, the Ukrainian crisis showed once again that the Russian army's weak spot was the dominating number of conscripts, the reduced length of military service (1 year) and the lack of a sufficient number of contract servicemen. Although Russia had declared the goal of creating a permanent readiness army, many military units and formations were not made full use of in 2014 due to both the shortage of personnel in the majority of units and the cyclic nature of conscript training. As a result, "permanent readiness" formations could send no more than two-thirds of their personnel to the operational area, leaving behind untrained soldiers drafted in the fall. Another serious issue is the reserve. No optimal reserve model has so far been worked out for the "new look."

2010–2015 were contemporary fifth-generation systems. The scope of the Kremlin's arms modernisation programme is vast. It includes information

---

Additionally, there are still no clear-cut mechanisms for deploying additional units and formations and replacing lost personnel during wartime. Despite the abovementioned shortcomings, the efficiency with which Russian forces have assumed control over Crimea is hard to reconcile with the image of an inadequate military close to collapse. Despite claims to the contrary, Russia is much closer to having the military it needs that has often been suggested. In other words, the Western perception of the not sufficiently prepared Russian military was deeply mistaken. The 2008–2012 military reform prepared the military for the year 2013. The Kremlin began to set up a pool of rapid deployment forces in 2013 in order to be able to intervene in its neighbourhood. These well-equipped, well-trained, modern forces consist of Airborne Forces (four divisions, five brigades), Marines (four brigades, eight separate regiments), GRU Intelligence Forces (GRU Spetsnaz) brigades and three or four elite Ground Force units as well as air and naval support. The MoD planned that, in the coming years, all of these units would be made up of professionals. On this basis, the Airborne Forces already count up to 20 battalions. There is every reason to believe that the 30,000–40,000 troops transferred to the south-eastern border of Ukraine in February 2014 were the backbone of these rapid deployment forces that realistically may have 100,000 and more troops ready for rapid deployment. The GRU Spetsnaz forces, in particular, have both expanded — with two new brigades, the 100th and the 25th — and developed. Most of the 15,000–17,000 Spetsnaz are essentially very well-trained light infantry and intervention forces. However, a growing awareness of the need for truly "tier-one" special forces able to operate in small teams and complex political environment led to the decision to create the Special Operations Command (or KSO in Russian) in 2010. Becoming operational in 2013, the KSO first saw action in the seizure of Crimea in 2014. Numbering about 500 operators with integral airlift and close air support assets, the KSO represents a genuine enhancement of Russian capabilities and one designed for precisely the kind of military political operations described for the first time in the 2014 doctrine. On the other hand, attempts to increase the proportion of the Armed Forces staffed on a professional, volunteer basis continue to lag behind plans. As of December 2014, the total such kontraktniki in the military numbered 295,000: a solid increase from 186,000 during 2013 but still well short of the 499,000 meant to be in the ranks by 2017. As of December 2015, the total of such kontraktniki in the military numbered 352,000 while their number should have reached 384,000 in 2016. It can be assumed that the number of professional soldiers is likely to increase until 2017. Thus, the term lagging behind will become obsolete.

General Yuri Borisov, Deputy Minister of Defence for Procurement (hereafter cited as General Borisov), said in late January 2015 that: "The segment of modern equipment in the Aerospace Defence Forces (or VKO in Russian), the Navy and the Strategic Missile Forces (or RVSN in Russian) is at the rate of more than 40%." Currently, only 28% of the Russian Air Force inventory consists of modern equipment while the figure stands at 26%

warfare, nuclear modernisation, dual-use information systems, precision-guided munitions, advanced conventional weapons, anti-stealth radar, indigenously stealthy air-launched cruise missiles, the S-400 anti-aircraft/anti-ballistic missile,[36] plasma coatings to make fifth-generation aircraft invisible to radar, chemical and biogenetic weapons, direct-energy weapons, lasers, microwave radiation emitters, particle-beam generators and subatomic particles to destroy targets at the speed of light. A new plasma weapon has been developed that could ionise the atmosphere and destroy incoming missiles. Moscow is moving in the direction of high-tech combat aircraft, electronic control and information systems, weapons based on

---

for the Ground Forces and the rest of the Russian military. RIA Novosti reported in early October 2015 by citing General Borisov that: "Modern hardware now makes up 45.8% of the Aerospace Forces (or VKS in Russian)." Finally, in early February 2016, General Sergey Shoigu, Minister of Defence, said that: "Forty seven percent of the country's arms and equipment inventory is now considered 'modern'." The most modern area is its nuclear deterrent which between the three elements of its nuclear triad are reported to be 55% modernised. The Aerospace Forces are at 52% with the Navy sitting at 39% and the Ground Forces at 35% at the close of 2015. A further increase in modern equipment requires substantial funds that, despite the current economic crisis, President Vladimir Putin and his administration are ready to shoulder. Therefore, the pronounced target for the Armed Forces to have 70% of modern equipment by 2020 is no longer a far-fetched scenario but a fact that the West at large need to acknowledge, carefully monitor and think through as to what it can do about it." The author's assertion may be dismissed out of hand by the expert community, but the facts presented above reinforce the author's assertion. Furthermore, the subsequent section, entitled Defence Spending, reinforces the author's view that the reshaping of the Russian military and equipping it with modern weapons is on the right track.

[36]The S-400 Triumf (Russian: С-400 Триумф) is an anti-aircraft weapon system developed in the 1990s by Russia's Almaz Central Design Bureau as an upgrade of the S-300 family. It has been in service with the Russian Armed Forces since 2007. The S-400 uses four missiles to fill its performance envelope: the very long-range 40N6 (400 km), the long-range 48N6 (250 km), the medium-range 9M96E2 (120 km) and the short-range 9M96E (40 km). On March 1, 2016, acting commander of the 14th Air Force and Air Defence Army major-general Vladimir Korytkov said that six S-400 units had been activated pursuant to his order in the anti-aircraft missile regiment of the Novosibirsk air defence formation in Russia's Novosibirsk region. TASS also reported that as of the end of 2015, a total of 11 Russian missile regiments were armed with S-400, and by the end of 2016, their number was expected to increase to 16. "S-400 Triumph missile systems put on combat duty in Siberia". TASS.

new physical principles, tactical nuclear weapons to be used in conventional conflicts to achieve strategic impact and reconnaissance fire (or strike) system that can make a strategic difference in large theatre wars. Topol-M ICBMs (intercontinental ballistic missiles) are replacing older land-based missiles for use as first- and second-strike weapons,[37] and Moscow has threatened to transform them into MIRVs (multiple independently targeted re-entry vehicles) if the United States goes forward with its national missile defence programme.[38]

New smart conventional weapons coming online include the Shkval torpedo missile[39], the M-55 reconnaissance plane,[40] the Kh-31

---

[37]The RT-2PM2 «Topol-M» (Russian: РТ-2ПМ2 «Тополь-М) is one of the most recent intercontinental ballistic missiles to be deployed by Russia and the first to be developed after the dissolution of the Soviet Union. It was developed from the RT-2PM Topol mobile intercontinental ballistic missile. By the end of 2010, the Russian Strategic Missile Troops operated 70 Topol-M missile systems including 52 silo-based and 18 mobile systems. A further eight missiles were to join the Forces by 2011–2012.

A new missile loosely based on Topol-M and equipped with multiple re-entry vehicles (MIRV) is called RS-24 Yars. In January 2009, Russian sources hinted that the production of the mobile Topol-M missile would be shut down in 2009 and that the new MIRVed RS-24 version would replace it.

[38]*Ibid.*

[39]The VA-111 Shkval (from Russian: шквал — squall) torpedo and its descendants are supercavitating torpedoes originally developed by the Soviet Union. They are capable of speeds in excess of 200 knots (370 km/h). See Kyle Mizokami, "Russia has a super torpedo that kills submarines at 200 miles per hour (and America can't match it)", *The National Interest*, January 1, 2017, http://nationalinterest.org/blog/the-buzz/russia-has-super-torpedo-kills-submarines-200-miles-per-hour-18917. "Imagine the sudden revelation of a weapon that can suddenly go six times faster than its predecessors. The shock of such a breakthrough system would turn an entire field of warfare on its head, as potential adversaries scrambled to deploy countermeasures to a new weapon they are defenseless against. While a lull in great power competition delayed the impact of this new technology, the so-called 'supercavitating torpedo' may be about to take the world by storm."

[40]The Myasishchev M-55 (NATO reporting name: Mystic-B) is a high-altitude geophysical research aircraft developed by OKB Myasishchev in the Soviet Union, similar in mission to the Lockheed ER-2, but with a twin-boom fuselage and tail surface design. It is a twin-engine development of the Myasishchev M-17 Stratosphera with a higher maximum take-off weight.

supersonic anti-ship missile,[41] Kh55 strategic cruise missile[42] and Iskander anti-aircraft missile,[43] and unmanned aerial vehicles, all embodying

---

[41] Dave Majumdar, "The U.S. Navy's AEGIS missile defense vs. Russia's supersonic Kh-31 cruise missile: Who wins?" *The National Interest*, December 7, 2016, http://nationalinterest.org/blog/the-buzz/the-us-navys-aegis-missile-defense-vs-russias-supersonic-kh-18662.   "The Russian Navy will be deploying Sukhoi Su-30SM Flanker-H fighters to its Baltic Fleet in 2017."

The powerful multirole fighters will be equipped with the Kh-31 supersonic sea-skimming anti-ship cruise missiles — which would significantly boost Russian maritime anti-access/area denial capabilities in the region. In addition to the jets headed, to the Baltic Fleet, Moscow will be deploying the fighters to its Severomorsk-3 facility, where the aircraft will be able to provide air cover for Russian naval operations in the Barents Sea. The Russian Navy's Su-30SM are being equipped with an anti-ship variant of the Mach 3.5-capable Kh-31 that has a range of roughly 120 miles. The Kremlin-owned *Izvestia* news outlet brags that even a single such weapon would be able to destroy a U.S. Navy ship. "Even one missile is guaranteed to send a Ticonderoga-class missile cruiser — currently in service with the U.S. Navy — to the bottom," *Izvestia* columnist Alex Ramm writes.

While the Kh-31 (X-31 in Cyrillic) is a fearsome weapon, Aegis cruisers and destroyers are equipped with a formidable array of defences to protect both themselves and the vessels they are escorting. It is not clear how the SPY-1 radar and the Aegis combat system in combination with Raytheon Standard SM-2 and SM-6 missiles would perform against the Kh-31 — assuming the Su-30SM got close enough to launch such a weapon at a U.S. Navy warship. An Aegis-equipped warship is also armed with Raytheon RIM-162 Evolved SeaSparrow missiles, RIM-116 Rolling Airframe Missiles (RAM) and Phalanx point defence systems.

The Kh-55 (Russian: X-55) is a Soviet/Russian subsonic air-launched cruise missile, designed by MKB Raduga. It has a range of up to 2,500 km (1,350 nmi) and can carry nuclear warheads. Kh-55 is launched exclusively from bomber aircraft and has spawned a number of conventionally armed variants mainly for tactical use, such as the Kh-65SE and Kh-SD, but only the Kh-101 and Kh-555 appear to have made it into service.

Andrei Akulov, "Russian Iskander-M Missile System: Credible Deterrent", *Strategic Culture*, September 19, 2016, http://www.strategic-culture.org/news/2016/09/19/russian-iskander-m-missile-system-credible-deterrent.html. "The Iskander-M is a mobile short-range ballistic missile system designed to be used in theatre level conflicts with an official range of up to 500 km (minimum-50 km) to comply with the limits of the INF Treaty. Highly mobile and stealth, it can hardly be detected even with the help of space reconnaissance assets. The accuracy, range and ability to penetrate defenses allow it to function as an alternative to precision bombing for air forces that cannot expect to launch bombing or cruise missile fire missions reliably in the face of superior enemy fighters and air defenses. The missile cruises at hypersonic speed of 2100–2600 m/s (Mach 6–7). The high velocity of the missile allows it to penetrate antimissile defenses. The Iskander has several conventional warhead options weighing between 480 and 700 kg, depending on type. These include a high explosives (HE) variant, sub-munition dispenser variant, fuel-air explosive variant, a HE penetrator variant or a nuclear payload (50 thousand tons of TNT to make it a truly versatile weapon)."

[42] *Ibid.*

[43] *Ibid.*

large amounts of information, some upgradable to reconnaissance strike missions. The genstab (Russian General Staff) is promoting anti-satellite technologies for space wars.[44] Genstab analysts say that Russia will still have 3,000 "non-strategic" warheads[45] and should be able to field 1,000 tactical nuclear weapons by 2020 (within the Strategic Offensive Arms Reduction Treaty) [SORT]. Some even argue that Moscow has achieved nuclear superiority with its recent deployment of the hypersonic warhead "Object 4202".[46]

Russia moreover is revamping its tank armies, replacing the fourth-generation T-90 main battle tank with a far superior T-14 Armata. It plans to deploy 2,300 of these tanks before 2020.[47] In 2012, President Vladimir Putin announced a plan to build 51 modern ships and 24

---

[44] Weston Williams, "Russia launches anti-satellite weapon: A new warfront in space?", *Christian Science Monitor*, December 22, 2016, http://www.csmonitor.com/USA/Military/2016/1222/Russia-launches-anti-satellite-weapon-A-new-warfront-in-space. "It was the fifth time the weapon, a PL-19 Nudol missile, had been tested. Some military analysts have expressed concern over the test, saying that it was a provocative demonstration of Moscow's might on a relatively new military frontier: outer space. But they suggest that it's more about Russian posturing than an imminent threat."

[45] Amy F. Woolf, "Nonstrategic Nuclear Weapons", *Congressional Research Service*, February 21, 2017, https://fas.org/sgp/crs/nuke/RL32572.pdf. "Estimates vary, but experts believe Russia still has between 1,000 and 6,000 warheads for nonstrategic nuclear weapons in its arsenal".

[46] Scott Ritter, "The U.S.-Russia nuclear arms race is over, and Russia has won," *Newsweek*, April 12, 2017, http://www.newsweek.com/us-russia-nuclear-arms-race-over-and-russia-has-won-581704. "'Object 4202' was a new kind of weapon, a hypersonic warhead capable of speeds 15 times the speed of sound, and capable of evading any anti-missile system the United States has today, or may develop and deploy for decades to come. While the October 26 test used an older RS-26 intercontinental ballistic missile (ICBM) as the launch vehicle, 'Object 4202' will ultimately be carried on a newer ICBM, the RS-28. The RS-28 is itself a wonder of modern technology, capable of flying in excess of five times the speed of sound, altering its trajectory to confuse anti-missile radars, and delivering 15 independently targetable nuclear warheads (each one 10 times as powerful as the bombs the United States dropped on Japan at the end of World War II) or three 'Object 4202' hypersonic warheads, which destroy their targets through kinetic energy (i.e., through impact). A nuclear warhead-armed RS-28 would take about 30 minutes to reach the United States from a silo in central Russia; its warheads would be capable of destroying an area about the size of Texas."

[47] The T-14 Armata (Russian: T-14 «Армата») is mainly a Russian battle tank based on the Armata Universal Combat Platform. It is the first series-produced next-generation tank. See Giles (2017).

submarines by 2020. Of the 24 submarines, 16 will be nuclear-powered. On January 10, 2013, the Russian Navy accepted its first new Borei-class SSBN (Yury Dolgorukiy) for service. A second Borei (Aleksandr Nevskiy) was undergoing sea trials and entered service on December 21, 2013, and the Kremlin commissioned a third Borei-class boat (Vladimir Monomakh) in late 2014. The more advanced Borei II was launched in 2017 (Gady, 2017).

The US Defense Department revealed in January 2018 that Russia tested an unmanned undersea vehicle capable of delivering a nuclear weapon. The Status-6 is designed to be launched from at least two different classes of nuclear submarines, including the Oscar-class, which can carry four Status-6 drones at a time. The drone has a range of 6,200 miles, a top speed in excess of 56 knots and can descend to depths of 3,280 feet below sea level (Insinna, 2018).

Experts relying on unclassified official Western and Kremlin sources broadly acknowledge that Russia's full-spectrum defence modernisation has succeeded (Giles, 2017),[48] allowing it to challenge NATO along its eastern frontier and contested buffer states,[49] even though Russian

---

[48]For the time being, despite focus in the West on the 'hybrid' and 'nonlinear' aspects of state competition, the conclusion in Russia appears to be that the importance of high-intensity warfare remains undiminished and that strategic deterrence with nuclear weapons and updated air and missile assets, supported by strong and capable land forces, will continue to play a fundamental role in securing state interests". Cf. Gerasimov (2017); see also Major General Rogovoy (2014) and Gertz (2015).

[49]Aleksandr Khramchikhin, "Rethinking the danger of escalation: The Russia-NATO military balance", *Carnegie Endowment for International Peace*, January 25, 2018, http://carnegieendowment.org/2018/01/25/rethinking-danger-of-escalation-russia-nato-military-balance-pub-75346?mkt_tok=eyJpIjoiTnpBMU5qTTJaakUzWlRWbSIsInQiOiJ-iYWIzOCswK3hBajNDQ3lTTWdBWkxtemhiSDJ0aXJzK0Q5bVZ5bDhlRHRTRFA4bE-wwN0JrRm1LSUV5NWV0SnM5NWFuY0ZiYkZnZEZjbBBhNG50SEZ5XC9od0VJ-RUh3YkVTRWNMa3hkQ3hNQWI2YmxBTnJVYmEyNlpzT0VGQ3k3UWkifQ%3D%3D. "The August 2008 war between Russia and Georgia revealed that NATO had lost its will to fight. Despite the pro-Western policies of then president Mikheil Saakashvili and his push for Georgia to join NATO, the latter offered no assistance to Georgia during the war with Russia. Moreover, after the war, NATO introduced an unspoken but strictly enforced embargo on supplying any military hardware to Georgia. NATO's inaction during the 2008 Georgian–Russian conflict and the 2014 Ukrainian crisis sent a signal to both the Baltic and Polish elites and publics that their NATO membership would be unlikely to

save them in the event of Russian aggression and that their fellow NATO countries would not help them. 'Old' NATO countries, not least the United States, could ill afford to ignore such sentiments, and since 2014, they have felt compelled to send a political signal by deploying at least some military forces to Eastern Europe. Despite the deterioration of relations between Russia and the West, NATO countries have not adopted any new defence programs beyond programs that were already under way, none of which have been expanded. Programs crafted under the rubric of strengthening the defences of Eastern Europe cannot be taken seriously as they amount to mere manipulation of existing military forces that are simply redeployed from rearward areas to the theatre of operations. There are no plans to put any new military units in place. Any claim of a NATO revival is taking place only in rhetorical terms. Western elites seem eager to punish Russia for its perceived bad behavior; that is, its willingness to violate the West's monopoly on trampling international law. But this punishment is hardly sufficient to change the mentality of Western societies".

Richard Sokolsky, "The new NATO-Russia military balance: Implications for European security", Carnegie Endowment for Peace, March 13, 2017. "Twenty-five years after the end of the Cold War, the military balance between NATO and Russia, after years of inattention, has again become the focus of intense concern and even alarm in some Western quarters. From NATO's vantage point, Russia poses a serious military threat to its eastern flank — and to Euro-Atlantic security more broadly — for three reasons. First, a military reform and modernisation program launched in 2008, combined with significant increases in defense spending over the past several years, has improved the capabilities of Russia's armed forces. Second, in the past decade, Russia has demonstrated an unprecedented willingness to use force as an instrument of its foreign policy, as well as an improved capacity to project military power beyond its immediate post-Soviet periphery. Third, the Kremlin has been conducting a far more aggressive, anti-Western foreign policy, significantly ratcheting up provocative military manoeuvres near NATO members' borders with Russia, intimating nuclear threats, and deploying nuclear-capable missiles in the Russian exclave of Kaliningrad. As a result, there is a growing perception in the West that Russia has reemerged as a revanchist, neo-imperialist, expansionist, and hostile power bent on dismantling the post–Cold War European security system and dividing the continent into spheres of influence." Keir Giles, "Assessing Russia's Reorganized and Rearmed Military", Task Force on US Policy Towards Russia, Ukraine and Eurasia, Carnegie Endowment of International Peace and Chicago council on Global Affairs, May 3, 2017. http://carnegieendowment.org/specialprojects/taskforce onuspolicytowardrussiaukraineandeurasia/all/1546?lang=en& pageOn=1. Keir Giles, "Russia Hit Multiple Targets with Zapad-2017", *Carnegie Endowment for International Peace*, January 25, 2018. "The real value of Zapad-2017 lies in understanding how Russia is considering responding to perceptions of threat and vulnerability. Critically,

and NATO weapon and troop counts have diminished considerably from Soviet-era levels.[50]

---

this includes recognising the vulnerability of its relationship with Belarus, which remains one of the many potential triggers for offensive action by Russia. If at any point swift and substantial political change in Minsk with a possible reorientation to the West appeared possible, this would undoubtedly be construed by Russia as just as immediate a security challenge as Ukraine in 2014, necessitating just as rapid and forceful a response. In the event of more generalised conflict with Russia, the nature of the response practiced in Zapad should give further cause for concern to the West. The early stages of the exercise saw a demonstration of Russia's habit of using heavy firepower in counterinsurgency. Doing so against small groups is a consistent Russian approach, and in war has been accompanied by what seems to Western eyes an arrant disregard for collateral damage or civilian casualties. This approach caused shock and revulsion when used in Syria in 2015–2016, but it has also been used against Russia's own population, as when twenty years earlier, Russian forces, having surrounded a group of Chechen terrorists in a southern Russian village, used artillery to destroy the village together with its civilian inhabitants.

The fictitious scenario of Zapad, like the real campaigns in Chechnya, Georgia, Ukraine, and Syria, was a reminder that Russia has its own views on the law of armed conflict, on the value of civilian life, and on what constitutes proportionality overall. The Russian approach is sometimes explained as the end justifying the means, especially if the end is bringing the fighting to as swift a conclusion as possible. This means that in the event of a future conflict in Europe, the actions of Russia's armed forces should not be expected to be any less repugnant to Western values than previous Russian or indeed Soviet practice".

[50]Richard Sokolsky, "The new NATO-Russia military balance: Implications for European security", Carnegie Endownment for Peace, March 13, 2017. "Twenty-five years after the end of the Cold War, the military balance between NATO and Russia, after years of inattention, has again become the focus of intense concern and even alarm in some Western quarters. From NATO's vantage point, Russia poses a serious military threat to its eastern flank — and to Euro-Atlantic security more broadly — for three reasons. First, a military reform and modernisation program launched in 2008, combined with significant increases in defense spending over the past several years, has improved the capabilities of Russia's armed forces. Second, in the past decade, Russia has demonstrated an unprecedented willingness to use force as an instrument of its foreign policy, as well as an improved capacity to project military power beyond its immediate post-Soviet periphery. Third, the Kremlin has been conducting a far more aggressive, anti-Western foreign policy, significantly ratcheting up provocative military manoeuvres near NATO members' borders with Russia,

The Rand Corporation concurs.[51] The real danger is probably far greater. During the Cold War, the CIA seriously underestimated Soviet capabilities (Rosefielde, 1987, 2005a, 2017), and Vitaly Shlykov former co-Chairman of the Russian Defense Council, has insisted that little has changed.[52]

---

intimating nuclear threats, and deploying nuclear-capable missiles in the Russian exclave of Kaliningrad. As a result, there is a growing perception in the West that Russia has reemerged as a revanchist, neo-imperialist, expansionist, and hostile power bent on dismantling the post–Cold War European security system and dividing the continent into spheres of influence."

[51] Scott Boston and Dara Massicot, The Russian Way of Warfare A Primer, Rand Corporation, https://www.rand.org/pubs/perspectives/PE231.html. "Russia has recently carried out substantial reforms to its military forces, increasing capability in several key areas. Russia's military has improved to the extent that it is now a reliable instrument of national power that can be used in a limited context to achieve vital national interests. Russian strategists, concerned about the capability of an advanced military adversary to carry out a large-scale conventional aerospace campaign against the Russian heartland, focus on preserving Russian influence in buffer states along its borders and on reinforcing a series of defensive bulwarks. Russian operations will show a high degree of coordination across a wide range of military units, using deception and simultaneity to achieve objectives quickly and minimize periods of vulnerability to an adversary's most dangerous capabilities. Russian tactics will continue to heavily emphasize gaining and maintaining fire superiority over an adversary; leveraging improved ISR capabilities and a wide range of fires platforms; and using speed, surprise, and integrated combined arms in maneuver forces to disrupt and overwhelm enemies once encountered."

[52] In a direct response to the proceedings of the conference entitled the CIA's Analysis of the Soviet Union 1947–1991, held at Princeton University on March 9 and 10, 2001, Shlykov declared that the entire American intelligence community, including Team B, miscounted weapons, underestimated programmes, underappraised costs and misgauged the sustained mobilisation capacity of the Soviet system. Data on Soviet weapons production remain secret and scattered, but declassified published statistics show that the United States more often underestimated, rather than overestimated the size of the Soviet Union's military arsenal. For example, the Americans believed that the Soviet Union deployed 30,000 nuclear weapons and had 500–600 tons of enriched uranium. But in reality, the figure was 45,000 weapons and 1,200 tons, according to Viktor Mikhailov, former Russian Minister of Atomic Energy. The Americans were also mistaken about Soviet tank inventories. They thought that the USSR had a little more

Russia's New Market-Powered VPK

The success of Russia's arms modernisation programme during 2010–2015 is attributable in large part to a quantum jump in Russia's military industrial system and economy achieved after the 2008 global financial crisis. The Kremlin embedded competitive markets inside the VPK, military industrial complex. The literature provides a clear, if incomplete, picture of what has transpired. First, after Yeltsin's experiment with privatisation in the latter half of the 1990s, the VPK and closely associated "strategic enterprises" such as Transneft, Gazprom, Rosneftegaz and Alrosa were renationalised in 2004. Initially, state ownership included some private shareholding participation, but now 100% state proprietorship is more frequently the norm (Sprenger, 2008). However, unlike Soviet arrangements, state ownership does not bar VPK enterprises or public private partnerships (PPP) from competing among each other (Liu and Rosefielde, 2017). Military industrial firms (including holding companies) operate on a for-profit basis. They compete for state orders and export sales (contracts) and can outsource. Shareholders and/or managers are incentivised to profit-seek and incompletely profit-maximise rather than comply with MOD commands and/or rent-seek. Although, they have fewer degrees of freedom than private Western defence corporations like Boeing, VPK enterprises are self-motivated to efficiently produce in accordance with Herbert Simon's bounded rationality framework and William Baumol's satisficing concept (Baumol, 1959). Competitive profit maximisation bolstered the VPK initiative when the MOD stopped prioritising military R&D after 2008. Weapon producers could have pretended to increase output, continued rent-seeking and lived passively off state funds. This may well have been the most likely outcome, but Putin beat the odds by imposing strict discipline and containing rent-seeking, buttressed by competitive reforms and sufficient material incentives. People neither deny that rent-seeking persists nor the latent threat that kleptocracy poses to Russia's military industrial revival (Dawisha, 2014). The system

---

than 50,000 tanks, at a time when it had 64,000 or even 68,000 according to another source (see Rosefielde, 2005a, pp. 52–53).

could relapse into indolence when Putin retires, but Russia's new market-powered VPK means that sustainable Russian military modernisation is also a distinct possibility (Cooper, 2013, 2016a, 2017, 2018; Malmlöf, 2019). Military spending is set to continue increasing through 2020 (Zhavoronkov, 2017).

Russia's New Market-Powered Civilian Economy

Improvements in Russia's military industrial production potential parallel the development of the Putin-era civilian sector. Russia today is a mixed-market economy. The mixture includes markets, state institutions, virtual economy (Gaddy and Ickes, 1998, 2002; Gaddy, 2008; Treisman, 2000), Muscovite rent-granting,[53] kleptocracy (Dawisha, 2014) and Kremlin

---

[53] Anders Åslund, "Russia's neo-feudal capitalism", *Project Syndicate*, April 27, 2017, https://www.project-syndicate.org/commentary/russia-neofeudal-capitalism-putin-by-anders-aslund-2017-04. "Vladimir Putin's Russia is looking more and more like the sclerotic and stagnant Soviet Union of the Leonid Brezhnev era. But in one area, Putin's regime remains an innovator: corruption. Indeed, in this, the 18th year of Putin's rule, a new form of crony capitalism has been taking hold. Over the last decade, Putin has overseen a major renationalisation of the Russian economy. The state sector expanded from 35% of GDP in 2005 to 70% in 2015. It would seem that, in Lenin's words, the state had regained control of the 'commanding heights' of the economy. And yet, it would also seem that state-owned firms like the energy giants Gazprom and Rosneft operate like modern businesses. After all, they have corporate-governance rules and policies, supervisory and management boards, and annual shareholders' meetings. They undergo independent international audits, publish annual reports, and maintain boards with independent directors. But appearances can deceive. Major state-owned companies' rules and policies are mere formalities. They are not even really run by the state. Instead, they are controlled by a small group of cronies — former KGB officers, ministers, and senior officials in the president's administration — who act as Putin's personal representatives ... The operations of the so-called state corporations are particularly problematic. Legally, these firms, which include Vnesheconombank (VEB) and Russian Technologies (Rostec), are independent nongovernmental organisations. But they are established through the donation of state funds or property: when six such corporations were created in 2007, some $80 billion of assets and $36 billion of fresh state funds were transferred to them. This puts them under Putin's direct control. State capitalism is usually associated with publicly directed strategies for investment and technological development. And, indeed, Russia's state

resource mobilisation campaigning. The system permits freehold and leasehold property and private contracting partially enforced by the rule of law. The invisible hand (competition) plays an important role for small and medium-sized enterprise, but big business is anti-competitive, not unlike the United States (Clark, 1940, 1961).

State institutions provide public services and regulate, but mostly in the interest of Putin, the power services and oligarchs rather than for the public good. These insiders run the government for their own benefit. They enrich themselves with unearned income that economists call rents and corrupt asset transfers (hence the term kleptocrats). The system is inherently unjust from a classical economic perspective because income depends on connections and insider power rather than competitive value-added (Bergson, 1938; Rosefielde and Pfouts, 2013).

Nonetheless, the allocation of resources, choice of technologies, enterprise management and finance can be efficient in unjust economic systems, given the prevailing distribution of income and wealth (Bergson, 1954; Kantorovich, 1965). It behoves Putin, the power services and oligarchs to make Russia's mixed economy efficient and productive for their own benefit, a goal accomplished by encouraging competitive profit-seeking, labour mobility and full employment to the extent that they are compatible with insider enrichment.

Putin, the power services and oligarchs do not have to act like the ruthless capitalists caricaturised by Karl Marx in *Das Kapital*. They need not drive wages to the subsistence level and have chosen not to do so, leaving enough on the table to increase general well-being and promote regime loyalty.[54]

---

corporations are supposedly focused on advancing the public interest or creating public goods. In reality, managers do whatever they want, such as favouring friends through discretionary procurement or selling assets at submarket prices." Cf. Aslund (1995, 2001, 2007a, 2007b) and Shleifer and Vishny (2000).

[54] Benis Aris, "Over 80% of Russians are still satisfied with Putin's work", *Intellines News*, April 28, 2017. http://www.intellinews.com/over-80-of-russians-are-still-satisfied-with-putin-s-work-120382/?source=russia "Eight out of ten Russians (82%) are still happy with President Vladimir Putin performance, according to independent pollster of the Levada Center's monthly popularity poll.

The improvement is visible to the naked eye (see Chapters 1 and 2) and confirmed by World Bank assessments.[55] Living conditions today are manifestly better than they were during the Soviet era and Yeltsin's *katakhod* (catastrophic transition). Russia is no longer an "economy of shortage" (Birman, 1983; Rosefielde, 1988).

Private cars congest an expanding network of highways; retail stores brim with desirable consumer goods, and service standards have risen. Andrei Shleifer and Daniel Treisman contend that Russia has become a "normal" middle-income country (Shleifer and Treisman, 2004; Rosefielde, 2005b), and the World Bank considers the Federation to be a high-tier member of the developing nations club (World Bank Group, 2015). The change partly reflects the squalor of the Soviet and Yeltsin-era consumer sector, but Russia's evolving mixed managed market arrangements also deserve credit, even though the exact magnitude

---

That is despite more Russians expressing disappointment with Putin, saying that he has failed to improve living standards since the annexation of Crimea, the number of whom has more than doubled, reaching 32%, according to a separate poll from Levada.

The Russian leader's popularity has fallen only slightly for the year 2017 from a high of 86% set in November 2016 after Russia launched its military campaign in Syria.

Another 18% said they were unhappy with Putin in the latest poll, up one percentage point from a month earlier, but remarkably that means for the first time the number of respondents that answered 'don't know' fell to zero for the first time. Love him, hate him, everyone now has a clear opinion on Putin."

[55] World Bank, *Country Partnership Strategy (CPS) for the Russian Federation*, Report No.65115-RU, November 2011. Another version of the same document is entitled: Russian Federation — Country Partnership Strategy for the period 2012—2016 (English). "Russia is a middle income country (MIC) that strives to move to a high income status. In the period since 2005, the per capita GDP of Russia doubled to approximately US$10,500 in 2010, and the country moved to an upper MIC status. The current country context was formed in the course of a decade of turbulent adjustment following the transition from a centrally planned to a market economy and another decade of rapid economic growth driven largely by natural resources, interrupted by the 2008–2009 global financial and economic crisis. As a result of a strong fiscal and monetary counter-cyclical package, the country emerged from the global recession with lower-than expected unemployment and poverty and has returned to moderate growth rates. To escape the 'middle income trap', Russia's government pursues economic policy and institutional development that aim to modernize, diversify, and increase the competitiveness of the economy and improve the well-being of its citizens," p. 2.

of the improvement is not precisely measurable (Rosefielde, 2003, 2005, 2017c). Russia's new market-powered civilian economy is far from perfect, but it is managed market powered and, other things being equal, capable of supporting sufficient sustained economic growth to mollify popular discontent.[56]

Sustainable Growth

The deficiencies of Russia's new market-powered civilian sector and market-facilitated VPK do not preclude sustained economic growth. The only source of long-run economic growth in an otherwise steady-state system is technological progress; that is, productivity improvements in capital and labour skills responsive to consumer demand (Solow, 1956, 1957; Swan, 1956). Gains from exogenous technological progress and technological transfers can be generated by advances in science

---

[56]Chris Miller, "The Surprising Success of Putinomics behind Putin's Formula for Holding onto Power", *Foreign Affairs*, February 7, 2018, "Consumer Lifestyles in Russia", January 2016. "The recent economic downturn dampened consumer confidence and household spending declined by 10% between 2014 and 2015. The impact of the recession on consumers has been exacerbated by recent sanctions which have driven food prices higher and resulted in many coveted imported items no longer being stocked on store shelves." World Bank Group, Russia Economic Report: Dawn of a New Economic Era? Edition Number 33, April 2015, pp. iv and 31. "The past decade witnessed a dramatic drop in poverty as large numbers of Russians were able to enter the middle class. Poverty plunged from about 40 percent of the population in 2001 to about 10 percent in 2010, and in 10 years the middle class doubled from 30 percent of the total population to over 60 percent. Russia became a middle-income society where growth was driven by consumer demand. By 2010, the middle class controlled 74 percent of total household income and 86 percent of total household consumption. When it came to private consumption, in fact, the middle class became the only game in town. Positive and sustained economic growth for most of the period translated into notable growth in per capita consumption from US$9/day in 2001 to almost US$17/day in 2010 (2005 PPP). There was a significant decline in poverty, and to a lesser extent vulnerability. Upward economic mobility was the result of both increases in average incomes and changes in the distribution of income. Using an established decomposition technique (Dattand Ravallion, 1992) to examine the impact on matching balance sheet pressures have not yet fully emerged."

(exogenous technological progress)[57] or through government programmes and policies (endogenous technological progress) (Howitt and Aghion, 1998; Howitt, 2000; Romer, 1990; Lucas, 1988).

Russia's new market-powered civilian sector and market-facilitated VPK enhance growth prospects compared with the "structurally militarised" Soviet benchmark by making endogenous technological progress more responsive to consumer demand.[58] Putin's system is also more open to technology transfer. The combination of these forces should allow the Kremlin to take better advantage of Russia's comparative economic backwardness, facilitating moderate economic growth for the next several decades, even though the economic system is relatively anti-competitive (Rosefielde, 2010, 2012a, 2012b, 2014; Rosefielde and Hedlund, 2008).[59]

---

[57]Abram Bergson believed that the technological potential of the Soviet command economy was deficient and inferred that growth would eventually become subpar. Russia's mixed economy qualifies this presumption. See Bergson (1968, 1971, 1973, 1978).

[58]Vitaly Shlykov (former co-chair of Russia's Defense Council) coined the term structural militarisation to suggest that excessive defence spending is an institutionalised aspect of the Soviet and Russian economic system. Insofar as his assessment remains valid, the Kremlin may be predisposed to invest inordinately large sums in VPK R&D, which could augment the sustainable rate of Russia's armament and aggregate economic growth. This possibility is a form of the more general phenomenon of endogenous economic growth some Western macroeconomists contend can be achieved through government programmes and policies (Shlykov, 2001, 2003, 2005, 2006a, 2006b, 2008).

[59]The Muscovite rent-granting aspect of Russia's contemporary mixed economic system seriously degrades its efficiency and if unchecked would prevent the Kremlin from assembling a credible military defence. Cf. Dawisha (2014). The statistical and econometric support for the proposition is inconclusive. On the one hand, Russia has failed to catch up with and overtake Western living standards during the last 100 years. On the other hand, CIA data indicate that the post-war Soviet economy grew faster than America's until the mid-1980s even after taking account of hidden inflation. Russian growth in the new millennium has outperformed the West too, just as it should have done *ceteris paribus* given its relative economic backwardness. On balance, the historical record doesn't support the often voiced claim that inferior long-term GDP growth prospects pose a significant barrier to sustained Kremlin military competition with the West. Moscow's economy was inferior during the Soviet period when Russia was an impoverished superpower judged from the perspective of consumer sovereignty, but this didn't prevent the Kremlin from achieving military superpower status (Maddison, 2001; Rosefielde, 2017; Abramovitz, 1986).

Economic Sanctions

This assessment should have a sobering effect on American policymakers, but may not because the intelligence community firmly believes that economic sanctions,[60] like those imposed by the Jackson–Vanik amendment, can tutor Russia to mend its ways (Pregelj, 2005). The salubrious powers of economic sanctions have long been an article of faith in the West. Policymakers clung to the belief in the 1970s, even though some CIA experts contended that the Soviet military machine-building sector could support the growth of double-digit weapons indefinitely (Rosefielde, 1987, pp. 35, 38, note 15).

The scholarly literature indicates that economic sanctions are mostly ineffectual,[61] and despite ever- mounting punitive measures taken against

---

[60]The term "economic sanctions" refers to peacetime punitive measures, short of "economic war." Policymakers impose economic sanctions to chasten adversaries by denying them access to factors of production, products, technology, and finance. Export subsidy stratagems (beggar-thy-neighbour policies) can be utilised to similar effect, but are usually excluded from the concept because rivals can easily deflect them with quotas. High-intensity economic sanctions combatants employ during peace and wartime are commonly called economic warfare (blockades, blacklisting, preclusive purchases), even though the prohibitions have the same character as lower intensity punitive measures. There is a large literature on economic warfare that stresses its reciprocal character and inconclusiveness. See, for example, Frances Cappola, "U.S. sanctions on Russia are financial warfare," *Forbes*, July 18, 2014. Percy W. Bidwell, "Our economic warfare," *Foreign Affairs*, April 1942. https://www.foreignaffairs.com/articles/united-states/1942-04-01/our-economic-warfare. The use of countervalue conventional and nuclear strikes against C3 (command, communications, and control), transport and industrial targets is more effective than economic sanctions in compelling adversaries to yield, but hardly guarantees success.

[61] For a good summary of the literature on the effectiveness of sanctions, see Mark Kramer, "Exclusive: Sanctions and Regime Survival," *Ponars Eurasia*, March 11, 2015. http://www.ponarseurasia.org/article/sanctions-and-regime-survival. "In a study of 136 countries from 1947 to 1999, Nikolay Marinov sought to determine whether 'economic sanctions hurt the survival of government leaders in office [2]. After comparing the longevity of leaders in countries that were targeted by sanctions with the longevity of leaders in countries that were not targeted, he concluded that sanctions do in fact 'destabilize the leaders they target.'" "Escribà-Folch and Wright find that although economic sanctions do, on average, contribute to the destabilisation and removal of personalistic dictators, sanctions do not have any appreciable effect on the longevity of single-party regimes and military

Moscow in the wake of Russia's annexation of Crimea annexation in 2014,[62] Putin has never retreated. The belief that Russia's challenge will

---

juntas." "A different take on this question comes in a study coauthored by William Kaempfer, Anton Lowenberg, and William Mertenis that relies on a model derived from public-choice theory [4]. The three authors claim that 'damaging economic sanctions can have the counterproductive effect of encouraging the ruling regime and its supporters while at the same time undermining the political influence of the opposition.'" "One of the implications of this approach is that sanctions cannot be effective in precipitating the downfall of the regime unless 'there exists within the target country a reasonably well-organised opposition group whose political effectiveness potentially could be enhanced as a consequence of sanctions.'" "Even in this case, however, the sanctions might still have debilitating effects on the opposition." "In the case of the Soviet regime and the sanctions imposed by the Carter administration in 1980 after the Soviet invasion of Afghanistan, we know for sure from declassified CPSU Politburo transcripts that Soviet leaders hated the sanctions and resented their effects. The sanctions did not, however, produce any near-term change in Soviet policy in Afghanistan." "Hence, assessing the longer-term effects of the 1980 sanctions is inherently difficult. The sanctions may have had a small deterrent effect on subsequent Soviet foreign policy decisions (e.g., during the crisis in Poland), but they did not change fundamental Soviet goals. Gorbachev's adoption of a vastly different approach to foreign policy is not directly traceable to the impact of past sanctions (though indirectly they may have played a small role)."

"In the case of the Russian Federation today, the U.S. and EU sanctions have not produced any discernible change in Russian policy *vis-à-vis* Crimea and eastern Ukraine, and Putin's regime has given no indication that it will back down even if the sanctions are tightened. Will the sanctions help to bring about a change of regime? With Putin's popularity ratings at 85 percent and few if any signs of a debilitating split in the ruling elite, this goal, too seems elusive, at least for now. Although one cannot fully rule out a longer-term impact on the stability of the regime, that seems a distant prospect at best." Allen (2008, 916–917), Marinov (2005), Escribà-Folch and Wright (2010), which builds on Lektzian and Souva (2007), Kaempfer *et al.* (2004); see also Kaempfer and Lowenberg (1988).

[62] Jen Psaki, "United States Expands Export Restrictions on Russia," US State Department, April 28, 2014. www.state.gov/r/pa/prs/ps/2014/04/225241.htm. "Today, in response to Russia's continued actions in southern and eastern Ukraine, the United States is implementing additional restrictive measures on defense exports to Russia. Accordingly, the Department of State is expanding its export restrictions on technologies and services regulated under the U.S. Munitions List (USML). Effective immediately, the Department's Directorate of Defense Trade Controls (DDTC) will deny pending applications for export or re-export of any high technology defense articles or services regulated under the U.S. Munitions List to Russia or occupied Crimea that contribute to Russia's military

be resolved by sanctions, or be dissolved by common bonds between Russia and the West, has been proven repeatedly to be the triumph of hope over experience, impervious to disproof.

Guns and Butter

The sum and substance of the foregoing analysis is that Russia does not have an economic Achilles's Heel that prevents it from vigorously defending its spheres of influence. It has the industrial capacity and will to tilt the military correlation of forces in its favour in contemporary zones of East–West conflict without impoverishing the nation,[63] given the prevailing and foreseeable levels of NATO defence spending (Rosefielde, 2017). A quarter century ago, the Soviet Union's economy of shortage could produce guns, but not butter. This is no longer true for Russia. Putin's mixed insider-managed market and Muscovite rent-granting system have changed the game (Ellman, 2015). The Kremlin can have both guns and butter.[64] It is not seriously constrained by the budgetary restrictions

---

capabilities. In addition, the Department is taking actions to revoke any existing export licenses which meet these conditions. All other pending applications and existing licenses will receive a case-by-case evaluation to determine their contribution to Russia's military capabilities. The United States will continue to adjust its export licensing policies toward Russia, as warranted by Russia's actions in Ukraine. We urge Russia to honour the commitments it made in Geneva on April 17 to deescalate the situation in Ukraine." Susanne Oxenstierna and Per Olsson, *The Economic Sanctions against Russia: Impact and Prospects of success*, FOI-R-4097-SE, September, 2015. "The main conclusion of the report is that the targeted economic sanctions of the EU and the US have contributed to imposing a cost on the Russian economy in combination with other factors, but have so far not persuaded Russia to change its behaviour towards Ukraine." Oxenstierna and Olsson provide a complete listing of EU sanctions in their Appendix 2. Gorshkov (2017).

[63] The term correlation of forces, borrowed from physics, is a multi-factor version of the balance of power concept widely employed by Soviet and Russian security analysts. Lider (1980) and Lynch (1989).

[64] This does not mean that Russia like the West is economic and social problem free. For example, Russia is beset with demographic problems. Its population recently has declined, which means that labour force growth won't provide a fillip to economic growth. See Paul Goble, "10 Percent Decline in Number of Births in Russia over Last Year Frightens Economists — OpEd", *Eurasia Review*, May 1, 2017, http://www.eurasiareview.

implied by official Russian statistics[65] and the Stockholm International Peace Research Institute's (SIPRI) derivative estimates (Christie, 2017; Cooper, 2018).[66] Russia can cross swords with America without

---

com/30042017-10-percent-decline-in-number-of-births-in-russia-over-last-year-frightens-economists-oped/. "The number of children born in Russia during the first quarter of 2017 was 412,000, down from 458,000 in the same period a year earlier for a decline of 10 percent. And although mortality fell by one percent, the number of deaths exceeded the number of births by 76,000 or 19 percent". "During the first quarter, there were 84 divorces for every 100 marriages, a pattern that almost guarantees that 'in 2017, a loss of population will again be renewed in Russia'."

[65] Advocates of small Western defence spending have relied on budgetary data compiled by the Stockholm International Peace Research Institute to make it appear that the Soviet Union and now Russia cannot financially sustain a credible threat against the West. Its confidence in the accuracy of Soviet defence budgetary statistics was destroyed in 1989 by Gorbachev's admission that the official data excluded weapons! Vitaly Shlykov insists that the published data have little bearing on the Kremlin's ability to procure and maintain its arsenal. Nonetheless, SIPRI persists with its disinformation. Purchasing power parities are massaged to understate the dollar value of Russia's arsenal. The subject is too tangled to elaborate here. For insight into the problem, see Rosefielde (1987).

[66] Table 3: Military expenditure (excluding debt repayment) as a share of GDP (million rubles)

Year	GDP	GDP change, %	Total milex	As % GDP	'National Defence'	As % GDP
2020B	110,237,000	102.3	3,886,433[1]	3.46	2,808,300	2.55
2019B	103,228,000	102.2	3,866,242[1]	3.75	2,798,497	2.71
2018B	97,462,000	102.1	3,815,732[1]	3.92	2,771,785	2.88
2017	92,081,900	101.5	3,704,422[a]	4.02	2,665,997	2.90
2016	85,917,800	99.8	3,830,548[b]	4.45	2,983,348	3.47
2015	83,387,200	97.5	4,026,284	4.83	3,181,366	3.82
2014	79,199,700	100.7	3,224,274	4.07	2,479,074	3.13
2013	73,133,900	101.8	2,787,420	3.81	2,103,579	2.96
2012	68,164,900	103.7	2,504,600	3.67	1,812,386	2.71
2011	60,283,500	104.3	2,029,000	3.37	1,515,955	2.51

Notes: a. With debt repayment 3 891 222 m.r., 4.23% GDP. b. With debt repayment 4 623 761 m.r., 5.38% GDP; 1. Approximate.

Sources: GDP: http://www.gks.ru/wps/wcm/connect/rosstat_main/rosstat/ru/statistics/accounts/, accessed 2 February 2018 (with 2017 provisional data, third revision of 2016 GDP and final revision of 2011–2015).

condemning itself to being an impoverished superpower (Rowen and Wolf, 1990).[67]

Conclusion

Assessments of the Soviet and Russian military threats have always been complicated because they involve espionage and counterintelligence, partly obscured by special interest and partisan advocacy (peace activists, the Western military industrial complex and lobbyists for domestic social priorities). Those inclined to believe that the Kremlin's intentions are benign can find evidence to support their convictions in official Russian civilian and defence statistics and SIPRI's perfunctory adjustments. This is and has always been the KGB's and VPK's intent.[68] Those mindful of the Soviet's successful effort to disinform and manipulate the West with its custom-crafted defence budgetary data give more credence to the DIA's satellite-based weapons procurement and military activity statistics.[69] It is important to appreciate that the budgetary and hard power military indicators more often than not conflict and that the CIA and DIA are prohibited from debating the contradictions in public. Both agencies are required to negotiate a common position about the magnitude of the threat Russia poses to American national security, giving the President's and Congress's

---

Total military expenditure and 'national defence': 2016–2020 budget, as Tables 1 and 2, 2011–2015 author's calculations based on annual laws on federal budget implementation.

[67] Gertrude Schroeder (Greenslade) and Imogene Edwards insisted that Soviet consumer goods were growing rapidly throughout the postwar era. The dispute turns on plausible, but elusive, claims about hidden inflation that are no longer germane. See Schroeder and Edwards (1981, Table 14, p. 25). Schroeder's husband Rush Greenslade was the director of the CIA's SOVA shop. Khanin (1988) and Rosefielde (1980, 1991).

[68] Vitaly Shlykov, Co-Chairman of the Russian Defense Council repeatedly stressed that VPK and Goskomstat defence data bore little relation to reality. These statistics were concocted to lead the West by the nose as circumstances required. He considered it hilarious that so many Western specialists fell for the deception.

[69] The Institute for International Strategic Studies provides useful data on military effort in its *Annual Military Balance*. http://www.iiss.org/en/publications/military%20balance/issues/the-military-balance-2018-545f. Janes and a host of professional military journals provide copious information. These data are edited for a multiplicity of reasons.

broad policy latitude without having to adjudicate the conflicting evidence. Until Russiagate,[70] Washington had chosen to do little to counter the Kremlin's impressive military build-up, relying on strategic patience to handle Russia's burgeoning threat. There is now some bipartisan chatter about improving American hard power, but little evident willingness to divert spending from social programmes to enhance national security (Harrison, 2016).[71]

We know more today about Russia than Churchill did in 1939 but conceal it from public scrutiny. Russia should no longer be *a riddle wrapped in a mystery inside an enigma* because the DIA has satellite photo-reconnaissance intelligence and there has always been a key to unlocking the mystery. To paraphrase Churchill, "That key is Russian national interest. It cannot be in accordance with the interest of the safety of Russia that NATO and the EU have planted themselves upon the shores of the Black and Baltic Seas, or that NATO and the EU should overrun the Balkan States and subjugate the Slavonic people of south eastern Europe. That would be contrary to the historic life-interests of Russia".

Russia is a "guns and butter" superpower and it is imprudent to pretend otherwise.[72]

---

[70]The United States Intelligence Community concluded with high confidence that the Russian government engaged in electoral interference during the 2016 U.S. presidential election. A January 2017 assessment by the Office of the Director of National Intelligence (ODNI) stated that Russian leadership favoured presidential candidate Donald Trump over Hillary Clinton and that Russian president Vladimir Putin personally ordered an "influence campaign" to harm Clinton's electoral chances and "undermine public faith in the US democratic process." This finding, true or false, refocused Washington's attention on Russia.

[71]The Budget Control Act of 2011 (BCA) was signed into law 5 years ago on August 2, 2011. It is a resurrection of a much older law, known as Gramm-Rudman-Hollings, originally enacted in 1985. The BCA reinstates budget caps for a 10-year period ending in FY 2021 with separate caps for the defence and nondefence parts of the discretionary budget. For defence, the budget caps represent a reduction of roughly $1 trillion over 10 years compared to what the president had proposed in his FY 2012 budget request earlier in 2011.

[72]For a long-term perspective, see Golts (2019).

References

Abramovitz, M. (1986). Catching up, forging ahead, and falling behind, *The Journal of Economic History*, 46(2), 385–406.

Allen, R. (2003). A reassessment of the Soviet industrial revolution. Paper presented at the Abram Bergson Memorial Conference, Harvard University, Davis Center, November 23–24, 2003.

Allen, S. H. (2008). The domestic political costs of economic sanctions, *Journal of Conflict Resolution*, 52(6), 916–944.

Aslund, A. (1995). *How Russia Became a Market Economy*, Brookings Institution Press, Washington, DC.

Aslund, A. (2001). *Building Capitalism: The Transformation of the Former Soviet Bloc*, Cambridge University Press, New York.

Aslund, A. (2007a). *How Capitalism Was Built: The Transformation of Central and Eastern Europe, Russia, and Central Asia*, Cambridge University Press, New York.

Aslund, A. (2007b). *Russia's Capitalist Revolution: Why Market Reform Succeeded and Democracy Failed*, Peterson Institute for International Economics, Washington, DC.

Baumol, W. (1959). *Business Behavior, Value and Growth* (rev. ed.), Macmillan, New York.

Becker, A. (1969). *Soviet National Income 1958–1964*, University of California Press, Berkeley, CA.

Becker, A. (1970). The meaning and measure of Soviet military expenditure. In *Soviet Economy in a Time of Change*, Joint Economic Committee of Congress, Washington, DC, Vol. 1, pp. 252–268.

Becker, A. (1977a). *Military Expenditure Limitation for Arms Control: Problems and Prospects,* Ballinger, Cambridge, MA.

Becker, A. (1977b). Soviet proposals for international reduction of military budgets, *RAND*, P-5837.

Bergson, A. (1938). A reformulation of certain aspects of welfare economics, *Quarterly Journal of Economics,* 52(1), 310–334.

Bergson, A. (1944). *The Structure of Soviet Wages*, Harvard UP, Cambridge.

Bergson, A. (1950a). Soviet national income and product in 1937, Part I, *Quarterly Journal of Economics*, 64(2), 208–241.

Bergson, A. (1950b). Soviet national income and product in 1937, Part II, *Quarterly Journal of Economics*, 64(3), 408–441.

Bergson, A. (1951). On inequality of income in the U.S.S.R., *American Slavic and East European Statistician*, 3, 95–99.

Bergson, A. (1953a). Reliability and usability of Soviet statistics: A summary appraisal, *American Statistician*, 7(3), 13–16.

Bergson, A. (1953b). *Soviet National Income and Product in 1937*, Columbia University Press, New York, NY.

Bergson, A. (1953c). *Soviet Economic Growth: Conditions and Perspectives*, Row, Peterson, Evanston, IL.

Bergson, A. (1954). The concept of social welfare, *Quarterly Journal of Economics*, 68(2), 233–252.

Bergson, A. (1961). *The Real National Income of Soviet Russia since 1928*, Harvard University Press, Cambridge, MA.

Bergson, A. (1963). National Income, in: Bergson, A., and Kuznets, S. (eds.), *Economic Trends in the Soviet Union*, Harvard University Press, Cambridge, MA.

Bergson, A. (1968). *Planning and Productivity under Soviet Socialism*, Columbia University Press, New York.

Bergson, A. (1971). Development under two systems: Comparative productivity growth since 1950, *World Politics*, 23(4), 579–617.

Bergson, A. (1972a). Comparative national income in the USSR and the United States, in: Daly, J. D. (ed.), *International Comparisons of Prices and Output, Studies in Income and Wealth*, Volume 37, National Bureau of Economic Research, New York, 145–185.

Bergson, A. (1972b). Soviet national income statistics, in: Treml, V. and Hardt, J. (eds.), *Soviet Economic Statistics*, Duke University Press, Durham, NC, 148–152.

Bergson, A. (1972c). Productivity under two systems: USSR versus the West, in: Tinbergen, J., Bergson, A., Machlup, F., and Morgenstern, O. (eds.), *Optimal Social Welfare and Productivity: Comparative View*, Barnes and Noble, New York.

Bergson, A. (1972d). Soviet economic perspectives: Toward a new growth model, *Problems of Communism*, 32(2), 1–10.

Bergson, A. (1974). *Soviet Postwar Economic Development*, Almqvist & Wiksell, Stockholm.

Bergson, A. (1975). Index numbers and the computation of factor productivity, *Review of Income and Wealth*, 4(3), 259–278.

Bergson, A. (1978a). *Productivity and the Social System — The USSR and the West*, Harvard University Press, Cambridge, MA.

Bergson, A. (1978b). The Soviet economic slowdown, *Challenge Magazine*, 20(6), 22–33.

Bergson, A. (1979). Notes on the production function in Soviet post-war industrial growth, *Journal of Comparative Economics*, 3(2), 116–126.

Bergson, A. (1983). Technological progress, in: *The Soviet Economy toward the Year 2000*, George Allen & Unwin, London, 34–78.

Bergson, A. (1987). Comparative productivity: The USSR, Eastern Europe and the West, *American Economic Review*, 77(3), 342–357.

Bergson, A. (1989). *Planning and Performance in Socialist Economies*, Unwin and Hyman.

Bergson, A. (1991, Fall), The USSR before the fall: How poor and why?, *Journal of Economic Perspectives*, 5, 29–44.

Bergson, A. (1994). The communist efficiency gap: Alternative measures, *Comparative Economic Studies*, XXXVI(1), 1–12.

Bergson, A. (1995). Neoclassical norms and the valuation of national product in the Soviet Union and its post-communist successor states [Comment], *Journal of Comparative Economics*, 21(3), 390–393.

Bergson, A. and Heymann, H. Jr. (1954). *Soviet National Income and Product, 1940–1948*, Columbia University Press, New York.

Bergson, A. and Levine, H. (1983). *The Soviet Economy toward the Year 2000*, George Allen & Unwin, London.

Berkowitz, D., Berliner, J., Gregory, P., Linz, S. and Millar, J. (1993, Summer). An evaluation of the CIA's analysis of Soviet economic performance, 1970–1990, *Comparative Economic Studies*, 35(2), 33–48.

Birman, I. (1983). *Ekonomika Nedostach* (The Shortage Economy), Chalidize Publishing, New York.

Christie, E. H. (2017). Does Russia have the fiscal capacity to achieve its military modernisation goals?, *The RUSI Journal*, 162(5), 4–15. doi:10.1080/030718 47.2017.1406697.

CIA (2018). *The World Factbook*. Available at: https://www.cia.gov/library/publications/the-world-factbook/geos/kn.html.

Clark, J. M. (1940). Toward a concept of workable competition, *The American Economic Review* 30(2), Part 1 (June), 241–256.

Clark, J. M. (1961). *Competition as a Dynamic Process*, Brookings Institution, Washington, DC.

Cooper, J. (2013). From USSR to Russia: Fate of the military economy, in: Hare, P., and Turley, G. (eds.), *Handbook of the Economics and Political Economy of Transition*, Routledge, New York, pp. 98–107.

Cooper, J. (2016a). If war comes tomorrow: How Russia prepares for possible armed aggression. Whitehall Reports.

Cooper, J. (2016b). The military dimension of a more militant Russia, *Russian Journal of Economics* 2(2), 129–145.

Cooper, J. (2017). Prospects for military spending in Russia in 2017 and beyond. CREES Working Paper series.

Cooper, J. (2018). Military spending in Russia in 2017 and planned spending to 2020: A research note, February 3, 2018, unpublished manuscript.

Corson, W. R., Trento, S. B., and Trento, J. J. (1989). *Widows*, Crown Publishers, New York.

Dawisha, K. (2014). *Putin's Kleptocracy Who Owns Russia?*, Simon & Schuster, New York.

Donadio, R. (2007, April 22). The iron archives. *New York Times*. Available at: http://www.nytimes.com/2007/04/22/books/review/Donadio.t.html?auth=login-smartlock.

Eberstadt, N. (2018). The method in North Korea's madness [Commentary]. Available at: https://www.commentarymagazine.com/articles/method-north-koreas-madness/.

Ellman, M. (2015). Russia's current economic system: From delusion to glasnost, *Comparative Economic Studies*, 57, 693–710.

Escribà-Folch, A. and Wright, J. (2010). Dealing with tyranny: International sanctions and the survival of authoritarian rulers, *International Studies Quarterly*, 54(2), 334–359.

Firth, N. and Noren, J. (1998). *Soviet Defense Spending: A History of CIA Estimates, 1950–1990*, Texas A&M University Press, College Station, TX.

Gady, F. S. (2017). Russia to launch its most powerful ballistic missile sub in November. *Diplomat*. Available at: https://thediplomat.com/2017/10/russia-to-launch-its-most-powerful-ballistic-missile-sub-in-november/.

Gaddy, C. G. (2008). *Russia's Virtual Economy*, Brookings, Washington, DC.

Gaddy, C. G., and Ickes, B. W. (1998). Russia's virtual economy, *Foreign Affairs*, 77(5), 53–67.

Gaddy, C. G., and Ickes, B. W. (2002). *Russia's Virtual Economy*, Brookings Institution Press, Washington, DC. Vol. 77, No. 5, September/October.

Gerasimov, V. (2017). The world on the verge of war [in Russian], Voyenno-promyshlennyy kuryer, March 15, 2017, http://vpk-news.ru/articles/35591.

Gerschenkron, A. (1962a). A dollar index of output, 1927/28 to 1937, *Review of Economics and Statistics*, May, 1955 [reprinted in Gerschenkron, A., *Economic Backwardness in Historical Perspective*, Harvard UP, Cambridge, pp. 235–253].

Gerschenkron, A. (1962b). Notes on the rate of Soviet industrial growth (Notes sur le taux de croissance actuel de l'industrie sovietique), October–December

1953 [reprinted in Gerschenkron, A., *Economic Backwardness in Historical Perspective*, Harvard UP, Cambridge, pp. 254–269].

Gertz, B. CIA: Leak of nuclear-armed drone sub was intentional timed with stepped-up Moscow opposition to U.S. missile defenses, *Washington Free Bacon*, November 19, 2015, http://freebeacon.com/national-security/cia-leak-of-nuclear-armed-drone-sub-was-intentional/.

Giles, K. (2017). Assessing Russia's reorganized and rearmed military. Carnegie Foundation for Peace, http://carnegieendowment.org/2017/05/03/assessing-russia-s-reorganized-and-rearmed-military-pub-69853?mkt_tok=eyJpIjo iT0dZMFlUWXpZalEzTWpKaSIsInQiOiJOdkVISXZcLzA4UkhwNE ZGaFROd0ZWSlllRjNVazBkVXM5dU12S05QZFlSWlhMZHZFV FRHQWtHTDJrWXdKM3FqaU5NYW9jcGVuZXVRRT0tQUnZC MW1UemhyZXY1NXl2REdieXJFam1zSDdjMGtnN0lCRFI3ZWxnbVlvZ 0tLMjhxRkUifQ%3D%3D.

Golts, A. (2019). *Military Reform and Militarism in Russia*, The Jamestown Foundation, Washington, DC.

Gorshkov, V. (2017). Sanctions, in: Rosefielde, S., Kuboniwa, M., Mizobata, S., and Haba, K. (eds.), *The Unwinding of the Globalist Dream: EU, Russia, China*, World Scientific Publishers, Singapore.

Harrison, T. (2016). What has the Budget Control Act of 2011 meant for defense?, *CSIS*, August 1, 2016. https://www.csis.org/analysis/what-has-budget-control-act-2011-meant-defense.

Havrylyshyn, O. (2017). *The Political Economy of Independent Ukraine Slow Starts, False Starts, and a Last Chance?*, Palgrave Macmillan, New York.

Holesovsky, V. (1961). Karl Marx and Soviet national income theory, *American Economic Review*, 51(3), 325–344.

Holzman, F. (1975). *Financial Checks on Soviet Defense Expenditures*, Lexington Books, Lexington, MA.

Holzman, F. (1980). Are the Soviets really outspending the U.S. on defense? *International Security*, 4(4), 86–104.

Howitt, P. (2000). Endogenous growth and cross-country income differences. *American Economic Review*, 90, 829–846.

Howitt, P. and Aghion, P. (1998). Capital accumulation and innovation as complementary factors in long-run growth. *Journal of Economic Growth*, 3, 111–130.

Insinna, V. (2018). Russia's nuclear underwater drone is real and in the Nuclear Posture Review. *Defense News*, January 12, 2018.

Izyumov, A., Kosals, L. and Ryvkina, R. (2001a). Privatisation of the Russian defense industry: Ownership and control issues. *Post-Communist Economies,* 12(4), 485–496.

Izyumov, A., Kosals, L. and Ryvkina, R. (2001b). Defense industrial transformation in Russia: Evidence from a longitudinal survey. *Post-Communist Economies,* 12(2), 215–227.

Kaempfer, W. and Lowenberg, A. (1988). The theory of international economic Sanctions: A public choice approach, *American Economic Review*, 78(4), 786–793.

Kaempfer, W., Lowenberg, A. and Mertens, W. (2004). International economic sanctions against a dictator, *Economics and Politics*, 16(1), 29–51.

Kahn, M. (2012). Russia will assuredly be defeated: Anglo-American government assessments of Soviet war potential before Operation Barbarossa, *The Journal of Slavic Military Studies*, 25(2), 220–240.

Kahn, M. (2017). *The Western Allies and Soviet Potential in World War II: Economy, Society and Military Power,* Routledge, London.

Kantorovich, L. V. (1965). *The Best Use of Economic Resources*, Harvard UP, Cambridge.

Khanin, G. (1988). Ekonomicheskii Rost: Alternativnaia Otsenka [Economic Growth: Alternative Estimates], *Kommunist,* 17, 83–90.

Lee, W. T. (1977). *The Estimation of Soviet Defense Expenditures, 1955–1975,* Praeger, New York.

Lee, W. T. (1990). Trends in Soviet military outlays and economic priorities 1970–88, United States Senate Committee on Foreign Relations, Republican Staff Memorandum, July 30, 1990.

Lee, W. T. (1995). *CIA Estimates of Soviet Military Expenditures: Errors and Waste,* American Enterprise Institute, Washington, DC.

Lektzian, D. and Souva, M. (2007). An institutional theory of sanctions onset and success, *Journal of Conflict Resolution*, 51(6), 848–871.

Lider, J. (1980). The correlation of world forces: The Soviet concept, *Journal of Peace Research*, 17(2), 151–171.

Liu, Y. and Rosefielde, S. (2017). Public private partnerships: Antidote for secular stagnation? In: Rosefielde, S., Kuboniwa, M., Mizobata, S., and Haba, K. (eds.), *The Unwinding of the Globalist Dream: EU, Russia, China,* World Scientific Publishers, Singapore.

Lucas, R. (1988). On the mechanics of economic development, *Journal of Monetary Economics,* 22, 3–42.

Lynch, A. (1989). *The Soviet Study of International Relations*, Cambridge University Press, Cambridge.

Maddison, A. (2001). *The World Economy: A Millennial Perspective*, Development Centre Studies, OECD, Paris.

Malmlöf, T. (2019). *The Russian Machine Tool Industry: Prospects for a Turnaround?* FOI, Stockholm, FOI-R-4635-SE.

Marinov, N. (2005). Do economic sanctions destabilize country leaders?, *American Journal of Political Science*, 49(3), 564–576.

Martin, D. (1980). *Wilderness of Mirrors*, HarperCollins, New York.

Moorsteen, R. (1962). On measuring productive potential and relative efficiency, *Quarterly Journal of Economics,* LXXV(3), 451067.

Moorsteen, R. and Powell, R. (1966). *The Soviet Capital Stock 1928–1962*, Richard D. Irwin, Homewood, IL.

Murphy, D. (2006). *What Stalin Knew: The Enigma of Barbarossa* (Steury, D., rev. ed.), Yale University Press, New Haven.

Nove, A. (1972). *An Economic History of the USSR*, Pelican, London.

Pregelj, V. N. (2005). The Jackson-Vanik amendment: A survey, *CRS Report for Congress*, Order Code 98-545. Available at: https://fas.org/sgp/crs/row/98-545.pdf.

Rogovoy, A. V. (2014). *A Russian view of Land Power*, Conflict Studies Research Center, Cambridge, UK. Available at: http://amzn.to/2mJCS8l.

Romer, M. P. (1990). Endogenous technological change, *Journal of Political Economy,* 98, S71–S102.

Rosefielde, S. (1975a). Sovietology and index number theory, *Economia Internazionale* XXVIII(1–2), 3–15.

Rosefielde, S. (1975b). *The Transformation of the 1966 Soviet Input-Output Table from Producers to Adjusted Factor Cost Values,* G.E. TEMPO, Washington.

Rosefielde, S. (1980). A comment on David Howard's estimate of hidden inflation in the Soviet retail sales sector, *Soviet Studies*, XXXII(3), 423–427.

Rosefielde, S. (1981). Knowledge and socialism, in: Rosefielde, S. (ed.), *Economic Welfare and the Economics of Soviet Socialism*, Cambridge UP, London, pp. 5–24.

Rosefielde, S. (1986). The underestimation of Soviet weapons prices: Learning curve bias, *Osteuropa Wirtschaft,* 31, 53–63.

Rosefielde, S. (1987). *False Science: Underestimating the Soviet Arms Buildup*, Transaction Press, New Brunswick, NJ.

Rosefielde, S. (1988). The Soviet economy in crisis: Birman's cumulative disequilibrium hypothesis, *Soviet Studies,* 40(2), 222–244.

Rosefielde, S. (1991). The illusion of material progress: The analytics of Soviet economic growth revisited, *Soviet Studies,* 43(4), 597–611.

Rosefielde, S. (1998). Comparative production potential in the USSR and the west: Pre-transition assessments, in: Rosefielde, S. (ed.), *Efficiency and Russia's Economic Recovery Potential to the Year 2000 and Beyond,* Ashgate, Aldershot, London, pp. 101–135.

Rosefielde, S. (2003). The riddle of postwar Russian economic growth: Statistics lied and were misconstrued, *Europe-Asia Studies,* 55(3), 469–481.

Rosefielde, S. (2005a). *Russia in the 21st Century: The Prodigal Superpower,* Cambridge University Press, Cambridge.

Rosefielde, S. (2005b). Russia: An abnormal country, *European Journal of Comparative Economics,* 2(1), 3–16.

Rosefielde, S. (2005c). Tea leaves and productivity: Bergsonian norms for gauging the Soviet future, *Comparative Economic Studies,* 47(2), 259–273.

Rosefielde, S. (2007). *Russian Economy from Lenin to Putin,* Wiley, New York.

Rosefielde, S. (2010). *Russia's Aborted Transition: 7000 Days and Counting,* Institutional'naya ekonomika razvitie.

Rosefielde, S. (2012a). Postcrisis Russia: Counting on miracles in uncertain times, in: Pallin, C. V. and Nygren, B. (eds.), *Russian Defense Prospects,* Routledge, New York, pp. 134–150.

Rosefielde, S. (2012b). *The Impossibility of Russian Economic Reform: Waiting for Godot,* US Army War College, Carlisle Barracks.

Rosefielde, S. (2014). *Russian Military, Political and Economic Reform: Can the Kremlin Placate Washington?,* U.S. Army War College, Carlisle Barracks.

Rosefielde, S. (2017). *The Kremlin Strikes Back: Russia and the West after Crimea's Annexation,* Cambridge University Press, Cambridge.

Rosefielde, S. and Hedlund, S. (2008). *Russia since 1980: Wrestling with Westernization,* Cambridge UP, Cambridge.

Rosefielde, S. and Kleiner, G. (1998). Sources of Russian enterprise inefficiency and underproductivity in neoclassical perspective, *Voprosy Ekonomiki* (Problems of Economics).

Rosefielde, S. and Leightner, J. (2017). *China's Market Communism,* Routledge, London.

Rosefielde, S. and Lovell, K. (1977). The impact of adjusted factor cost valuation on the CES interpretation of postwar Soviet economic growth, *Economica,* 44, 381–392.

Rosefielde, S. and Mills, Q. (2021). *Rethinking American National Security*, Oxford University Press, New York.

Rosefielde, S. and Pfouts, R. W. (1988). Economic optimization and technical efficiency in Soviet enterprises jointly regulated by plans and incentives, *European Economic Review*, 32(6), 1285–1299.

Rosefielde, S. and Pfouts, R. W. (1995). Neoclassical norms and the valuation of national product the Soviet Union and its post-communist successor states, *Journal of Comparative Economics*, 21(3), 375–380.

Rosefielde, S. and Pfouts, R. W. (2014). *Inclusive Economic Analysis*, World Scientific Publishers, Singapore.

Rowen, H. and Wolf, C., Jr. (eds.). (1990). *The Impoverished Superpower: Perestroika and the Soviet Military Burden*, ICS Press, Palo Alto.

Samuelson, L. (1996). *Soviet Defence Industry Planning: Tukhachevskii and Military-Industrial Mobilisation, 1926–1937*, Stockholm Institute of East European Economies, Stockholm.

Samuelson, L. (2000). The red army and economic planning, 1925–1940, in: Barber, J., and Harrison, M. (eds.), *The Soviet Defence-Industry Complex from Stalin to Khrushchev*, Palgrave Macmillan, London, pp. 47–69.

Schroeder, G. and Denton, E. (1970). An index of consumption in the USSR, in: *USSR: Measures of Economic Growth and Development*, Joint Economic Committee of Congress, Washington, DC, December 8, pp. 317–401.

Schroeder, G. and Edwards, I. (1981). *Consumption in the USSR: An International Comparison*, Joint Economic Committee of Congress, Washington, DC.

Schroeder, G. and Severin, B. (1976). Soviet consumption and income policies in perspective, in: *Soviet Economy in a New Perspective*, Joint Economic Committee of Congress, Washington, DC, pp. 644–645.

Shaikh, A. M. (1998). The empirical strength of the labour theory of value, in: Bellofiore, R. (ed.), *Conference Proceedings of Marxian Economics: A Centenary Appraisal*, Macmillan, London.

Shleifer, A. (2005). *A Normal Country: Russia after Communism*, Harvard University Press, Cambridge, MA.

Shleifer, A. and Treisman, D. (2004). A normal country, *Foreign Affairs*, 83(2), 20–39.

Shleifer, A. and Vishny, R. (2000). *The Grabbing Hand: Government Pathologies and Their Cures*, MIT Press.

Shlykov, V. (2001). Chto pogubilo sovetskii soiuz? Amerikanskaia razvedka ili sovetskiskh voennykh raskhodakh (What destroyed the Soviet Union? American intelligence estimates of Soviet military expenditures), *Voenny Vestnik*, 8.

Shlykov, V. (2003). Russian defence industrial complex after 9-11. Paper presented at the Russian Security Policy and the War on Terrorism Conference, U.S. Naval Postgraduate School, Monterey, CA.

Shlykov, V. (2005). Globalizatsiia voennoi promyshlennosti-imperativ XXI veka, *Otechestvennye zapiski* 5, 98–115.

Shlykov, V. (2006a). Nazad v budushchee, ili Ekonomicheskve uroki kholodnoi voiny, *Rossiia v Global'noe Politike,* 4(2), 26–40.

Shlykov, V. (2006b). Nevidimaia mobilizatsii, *Forbes,* 3, 1–5.

Shlykov, V. (2008). The military reform and its implications for the modernization of the Russian armed forces, in: Leijonhielm, J., and Westerlund, F. (eds.), *Russian Power Structures*, FOI, Swedish Defense Research Agency, Stockholm, 50–60.

Solow, R. (1956). A contribution to the theory of economic growth, *Quarterly Journal of Economics*, 70, 65–94.

Solow, R. (1957). Technical change and the aggregate production function, *Review of Economics and Statistics* 39, 312–320.

Sprenger, C. (2008). State-owned enterprises in Russia, *Presentation at the OECD Roundtable on Corporate Governance of SOEs*, Moscow. Available at: https://www.oecd.org/corporate/ca/corporategovernanceprinciples/42576825.pdf.

Steury, D. P. (1998). Too much is not enough: Joseph Stalin, British Intelligence and strategic surprise in 1941, *Studies in Intelligence* 42(2).

Swan, T. (1956). Economic growth and capital accumulation, *Economic Record,* 32, 334–361.

Treisman, D. (2000). Inter-enterprise arrears and barter in the Russian economy, *Post-Soviet Affairs* 16(3), 225–256.

Treml, V. and Hardt, J. (eds.). (1972). *Soviet Economic Statistics*, Duke University Press, Durham, NC.

Turley, G. and Luke, P. (2010). *Transition Economics: Two Decades On*, Routledge, London.

Wegner, B. (1993). Hitlers Besuch in Finnland 1942 (Dokumentation), *Vierteljahrshefte für Zeitgeschichte,* 43(1), 131–32.

Wiles, P. and Efrat, M. (1985). *The Economics of Soviet Arms*, Suntory-Toyota International Centre for Economics and Related Disciplines, London.

World Bank Group (2015). *Russia Economic Report: Dawn of a New Economic Era?* Edition Number 33, pp. iv and 31. Available at: https://www.worldbank.org/content/dam/Worldbank/document/eca/russia/rer33-eng.pdf.

Zhavoronkov, S. (2017). Two lean years: Russia's budget for 2018–2020. Russia file. Available at: https://www.wilsoncenter.org/blog-post/two-lean-years-russias-budget-for-2018-2020.

Chapter 8

Military Potential Revisited

Masaaki Kuboniwa

Introduction

The exposure of Russian economic growth to changes in international oil prices is well recognised. However, it now appears that the economic impact on Russia's economy from a decline in world oil prices from over $120 a barrel in 2011 to below $40 in 2015 was partly offset by a manufacturing stimulus. The growth impetus largely came from increased output of military goods, a sector where Russia enjoys fairly high competitiveness in the global arms market.[1] This point was discussed in Kuboniwa (2016). The short analysis in this chapter stems from insights provided by updating the previous discussion based on the final version of official data on disaggregated sectoral value-added for 2011–2016. Furthermore, it suggests some changes in data for 2017–2018 due to classification shift.

What the New GDP Data Tell Us about the Value-Added of Russian Military Goods

On April 4, 2016, Russia's Federal State Statistics Service (Rosstat) posted on their website a new series of overall current GDP at market

---

[1] Cooper (2016) provides an outline of Russia's military development from 1991 to 2015. Unfortunately, his analysis could not take advantage of the new evidence on the contribution of military goods in the national accounts.

prices, as well as sectoral value-added at basic prices. Rosstat made large upward revisions of current GDP and sectoral value-added for the period 2011–2015. Looking at the disaggregated version of sectoral value-added, we are struck by Rosstat's reclassification of two disaggregated sectors. Russian sector classification code, introduced in 2003, followed an international code (NACE version 1.1) as for the 2011–2016 data. Two of Russian disaggregated sectors prior to April 4, 2016 consisted of the following:

A1: Other transport equipment (Code 35) and
A2: Other manufacturing (Codes 37 + 23.3 + 24.61 + 29.6).

More specifically,

Code 35: Manufacture of other transport equipment, including the following:

35.1 Building and repairing of ships and boats;
35.2 Manufacture of railway and tramway locomotives and rolling stock;
35.3 Manufacture of aircraft and spacecraft;
35.4 Manufacture of motorcycles and bicycles; and
35.5 Manufacture of other transport equipment and not elsewhere classified items.

Code 23.3: Processing of nuclear fuel;
Code 24.61: Manufacture of explosives (gunpowder, etc.);
Code 29.6: Manufacture of weapons and ammunition; and
Code 37: Recycling.

Concerning the data for 2011–2016, from April 4, 2016 onward, these were reclassified into two new sectors:

- **B1**: Codes 35 + 23.3 + 24.61 + 29.6 and
- **B2**: Code 37.

Obviously, goods under Codes 23.3, 24.61 and 29.6 are military manufacturing goods. Goods under Code 35 can also be considered military goods, even though about 20% of the goods of Code 35 are for civilian or mixed uses. Thus, the new classification clearly aggregates military goods into a single sector (B1), while non-military recycling is classified into another sector (B2). This may imply that Russian authorities recognise the important role and position of the military goods in the national accounts and economic growth and seek to make clear the existence of their globally competitive military goods sector and the wide range of products offered.

In any case, the military goods sector (B1) essentially covers all goods produced by the giant Russian military conglomerates, including Almaz-Antey (anti-aircraft defence systems, missiles, etc.), United Aircraft Corp3 (Sukhoi, MiG, etc.), Russian helicopters, Uralvagonzavod6 (battle tanks, etc.), RTI (military hardware and information and security systems), as well as many other smaller defence manufacturers.

Table 1 presents data on the military goods (sector B1) based on Rosstat's final version of breakdown of Russian GDP.

We see the share of value-added of the military goods sector at basic prices in overall GDP increased from 0.8 % in 2011 to 1.1 % in 2014 and

Table 1: Value-added of Russian military goods (B1).

	2011	2012	2013	2014	2015	2016
Military goods industry (B1)						
Current value-added (billion rubles)	485.8	644.5	706.9	836.7	1,161.8	1,244.2
% real change	—	14.7	5.2	7.8	15.1	22.4
Share in GDP %	0.8	0.9	1.0	1.1	1.4	1.4
Share in manufacturing value-added %	7.0	8.0	8.5	9.1	11.0	11.9
Contribution to GDP growth rate %	—	0.12	0.05	0.07	0.16	0.31
Contribution to manufacturing value-added	—	1.0	0.4	0.7	1.4	2.5
Current GDP (bln rubles)	60,283	68,164	73,134	79,058	83,094	86,014
% real change	4.3	3.7	1.8	0.7	−2.3	0.3
Current manufacturing value-added (billion rubles)	6,979	8,043	8,279	9,211	10,547	10,475
% real change	6.3	4.6	0.7	0.8	−2.0	3.0

Notes: Value-added is in basic prices, excluding net taxes on products, while GDP is in market prices.
Sources: Author's calculations based on Rosstat (www.gks.ru) as of April 2, 2019.

to 1.4% in 2015 and 2016 (a share much larger than automobiles). The share of military goods in overall manufacturing value-added at basic prices amounted to 7% in 2011, rising to 9% in 2014, 11% in 2015 and 12% in 2016. Military goods value-added in real terms grew at a rate between 5% and 15% a year during 2012–2015, then jumped to 22% in 2016. It should be noted that Rosstat frequently made substantial revisions for the military goods growth rate. On July 21, 2017, Rosstat made an upward revision from −4.8% to 5.4% for 2015. Finally, Rosstat revised this figure up to 15.1% as of April 2, 2019.

Figure 1 presents the contribution of military goods manufacturing value-added to overall GDP growth. Figure 2 shows the contribution of military goods manufacturing value-added to the overall growth of manufacturing value-added.

Figure 1 shows that the contribution of military goods to GDP growth rose from 3% in 2012 to 10% in 2014. In 2015, a counteractive contribution of military goods to the GDP contraction was seen. The share of contribution of military goods to GDP growth, 95% dominated most of the overall GDP growth in 2016. Figure 2 indicates the substantial contribution of the military goods industry to overall manufacturing. In 2014, military goods production accounted entirely for the 88% contribution to

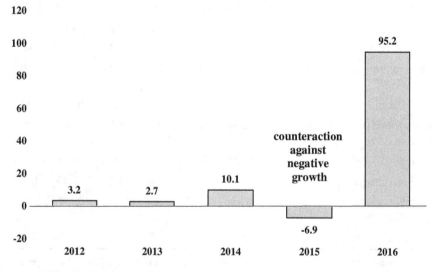

Figure 1:   Share of military goods contribution in GDP growth rate (%).

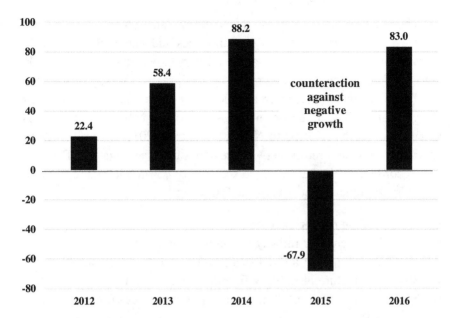

Figure 2: Share of military goods contribution in growth rate of manufacturing value added (%).

growth of manufacturing value-added. The large counteractive contribution of military goods production to the contraction in manufacturing in 2015 was witnessed. In 2016, military goods production accounted entirely for the 83% contribution to growth of manufacturing value-added. In other words, the expansion in military goods manufacturing was sufficient to keep GDP growth positive up to 2016.

Military goods production is an exceptional export-oriented manufacturing industry in Russia's case. Not only are their few manufactured Russian products in the global market but unlike oil products, which also go to Europe, military goods are generally exported to emerging or developing economies in Asia (India, China, etc.), the Middle East, Latin America and Africa. Russian defence manufacturers have enjoyed bumper export sales of military goods despite US sanctions and lower oil prices. Russian military goods exports in current US dollars increased from $10.7 billion (0.53 % of GDP) in 2011 to $13.2 billion (0.65 % of GDP) in 2014 and to $14.5 billion (1.1 % in GDP) in 2015 (Kuboniwa, 2016).

These observations suggest that the Russian military industry has managed to grow in the face of low oil prices and sanctions. Faced with stagnant oil prices, Mr. Putin may see military expansion as a sustainable means of supporting economic recovery and a robust military presence.

The analysis here has entirely relied on the final version of Rosstat's disaggregated GDP based on the classification of NACE rev 1.1. As is known, Rosstat has shifted to NACE rev 2 from 2017 onwards without providing consistent retrospective time series of disaggregated GDP.

According to NACE rev 2, the sector C of "30 Manufacture of other transport equipment" consists of the following:

- 30.1 Building of ships and boats,
- 30.2 Manufacture of railway locomotives and rolling,
- 30.3 Manufacture of air and spacecraft and related machinery,
- 30.4 Manufacture of military-fighting vehicles, and
- 30.5 Manufacture of transport equipment nec (not elsewhere classified).

This corresponds to sector 35 in NACE rev 1.1. This sector explicitly includes military-fighting vehicles. However, in the sector C, Code 23.3: Processing of nuclear fuel, Code 24.61: Manufacture of explosives (e.g. gunpowder) and Code 29.6: Manufacture of weapons and ammunition are excluded. Therefore, sector C (NACE rev 2) can be considered as a subset of sector B1 (NACE rev 1.1). Table 2 compares sector C and sector B1. The shares of sector C in GDP and manufacturing value-added are much smaller than those of sector B1. Growth rate of sector C in 2016 is similar to that of sector B1, whereas growth rate of sector C in 2015 is totally

Table 2: Value-added of B1 and C.

	NACE v 1.1 B1		NACE v 2 C			
	2015	2016	2015	2016	2017	2018
GDP share %	1.4	1.4	1.0	0.9	0.8	0.7
Manufacturing share %	11.0	11.9	7.7	7.8	6.6	6.0
Growth rate %	15.1	22.4	−6.2	22.8	−10.0	−3.1

Sources: Author's calculations based on Rosstat (www.gks.ru) as of April 2, 2019.

different from that of sector B1. Although growth rates of sector C were negative for 2017–2018, it may be debatable whether these negative rates reflect the military goods industry in a well-defined manner. Due to the discontinuous data, the impact of the military goods industry on growth remains unsolved.

Outstanding Issues

A quick assessment of the new Rosstat data on Russia's military goods sector and their impacts on growth of GDP and manufacturing suggest that the recent military expansion was sufficient to offset the downturn in Russian growth in 2012–2016 caused by falling oil prices and sanctions.

Whatever the case, Mr. Putin's aspiration to a structural export reform that increases the export share of machinery and equipment to over 20% by 2020 has yet to be adequately implemented by the defence industry (Ministry of Economic Development and Trade of the Russian Federation, 2007). Unlike the world's oil and gas giants, or consumer product manufacturers like Toyota and Apple, Russia's defence industry only has a small number of potential customers, and demand relies extensively on geopolitical tensions. Thus, even with a military expansion, Putin has yet to establish a sustainable platform for restructuring Russia's export structure. Putin needs to further develop radical reforms to resolve the 'Russian disease' suggested in Kuboniwa (2012).

References

Cooper, J. (2016). The military dimension of a more militant Russia, *Russian Journal of Economics* 2, 129–145.

Kuboniwa, M. (2012). Diagnosing the "Russian disease": Growth and structure of the Russian economy, *Comparative Economic Studies* 54(1), 121–148.

Kuboniwa, M. (2016). Military industrial potential, in Rosefielde, S., *et al.* (eds.), *The Unwinding of the Globalist Dream — EU, Russia and China*, World Scientific Publisher, pp. 154–170.

Ministry of Economic Development and Trade of the Russian Federation (2007). *The Concept of Long-Term Socio-economic Development of the Russian Federation to 2020*, Moscow, http://economy.gov.ru/minec/activity/sections/strategicplanning/concept/.

Chapter 9

Can Russia Sustain Its Defence Buildup?

Stephen Blank

Virtually every political scientist on Russia and the USSR has noted that an excessive defence burden was a major if not the principal cause for the collapse of the Soviet economy. Moreover, the vast majority of those analysts who predicted an upheaval after Putin pointed to the overall stagnation of the Russian economy — which appears to be an indisputable fact since there has been almost no growth since 2008 to speak of — as the likely culprit of that denouement if it reoccurs.[1] In the light of President Putin's most recent annual address to the Russian Duma, an address that bristled with nuclear threats and at the same time with extraordinarily ambitious economic promises, it is tempting to see the latter as virtually unattainable (which is probably true) and the former as signs of the excessive military burden on the economy that will ultimately cause it to crash.[2]

This would especially be the case, given the fact that the Russian economy is quite visibly undergoing another period of stagnation and suffers from well-known and highly visible structural afflictions. But stagnation, as we all know, can last a long time as happened in the USSR. It is unclear if the current defence burden of the Russian Federation is

---

[1] For two recent confirmations of the stagnation verdict, see Connolly (2018) and Miller (2018).

[2] See "Presidential address to the federal assembly", http://en.kremlin.ru/events/president/news/56957, accessed on 1 March 2018.

unbearable even if a protracted stagnation occurs, as is clearly the case (Christie, 2017). Indeed, the World Bank as well as the Russian government have assessed that the economy is heading into a period of growth with the World Bank — a far more disinterested observer — assessing a period of slow growth through 2019 (The World Bank, 2017). In other words, professional economists are rather increasingly sceptical about the burden of defence spending on the economy than are political observers. Consequently, they are considerably more likely to believe that Russia can, absent major crises or external shocks, support the current defence buildup (Christie, 2017, pp. 4–15). Moreover, the evidence as of April 2018 actually points to increases over the originally intended budgetary outlays for defence of 2017, largely due to the rise in oil prices to a price of just over $70/bbl, since the government budget plans stipulated a $40–55/bbl price. Given the rise of prices beyond that level, the opportunity for increased defence spending in 2018 has duly presented itself to the authorities. And an examination of budget documents shows that since October 2017 till April 2018, the opportunity anticipated in 2018 had been seized upon to increase the defence spending.[3] Therefore, we cannot and should not assume *a priori* that the elevated defence burden carried by the Russian Federation in the last decade necessarily or in and of itself presages the collapse of the economy. As long as energy prices rise, they create a floor for defence and a great deal of other spending. While Russia remains "armed to the teeth but poor" and former Finance Minister Alexei Kudrin argues that Russia would need a Chinese economy to support all the programmes Putin discussed, these prognoses for growth suggest that Putin's Russia could have not only guns but somewhat more butter as well for all things considered equal (Goble, 2018). For these reasons, as our title suggests, we must examine this question of Russia's defence burden and its impact upon the economy carefully, especially as several writers, myself included, have argued that long-term military decline is inevitable and that Russia is undermining the foundations of its own economic power by its wretched performance in regard to science, technology and education (Blank, 2016; Goble, 2017; Baev, 2017; Balzer, 2017). We cannot overlook the unforgiving demographic trends that will also affect

---

[3]These sources were made available to the author by Michael Kofman.

defence policies by substantially lowering the pool of available manpower in the future (Berman, 2017; Eberstadt, 2017).

There is no doubt that Putin and his team grasp that the Soviet defence burden was excessive and that the arms race with the US in the Cold War helped sink the USSR. Putin has frequently made it clear that he and his government will not follow that course but instead have chosen an "asymmetric" or indirect one. In 2014, in his annual address to the Federal Assembly, Putin reiterated that, "We have no intention to become involved in a costly arms race, but at the same time we will reliably and dependably guarantee our country's defence in the new conditions. There are absolutely no doubts about this. This will be done. Russia has both the capability and the innovative solutions for this."[4] Echoing such sentiments, Putin's adviser for military policy, General Alexander Burutin, wrote that, "A crucial element in our plans for the development of new armaments must be an orientation towards an asymmetric response to the development and entering into service of the expensive new systems of the developed foreign countries."[5] Commenting on Burutin's advocacy, the Norwegian scholar Tor Bukkvoll remarked that in Russian thinking asymmetric technologies should have a disruptive effect on new Western technologies, be developed in areas where Russian defence industry has particular advantages and be much cheaper to develop and produce than Western technologies. And these discussions also emphasise acquisition of anti-access and area denial (A2AD) systems and technologies.[6]

This call for new weapons and weapons based on "new physical principles" on the basis of an asymmetric strategy is a constant refrain in Russian discourse, namely, that Russia will not be drawn into the arms race that the West allegedly seeks to foist upon it but will defend itself asymmetrically with regard to both strategy and procurements. Putin has frequently charged NATO and the US with trying to force Russia into an unsustainable arms race and also argues that under his leadership Russia will not only pursue an asymmetric strategy but also produce more than

---

[4] "Presidential Address to the Federal Assembly," December 4, 2014, http://en.kremlin.ru/events/president/news/47173.

[5] Quoted in Bukkvoll (2011).

[6] *Ibid.*, pp. 690–691.

enough capability to defend its vital interests. Furthermore, he has repeatedly insisted that Russia should focus on new types of weapons.[7]

To be sure, having relentlessly hyped an ever-more impending threat assessment, Putin and his team have demanded in the last decade an enormous and impressive defence buildup. Much like Stalin in the 1930s, Putin argued in 2013 that "the changing geopolitical situation requires rapid and considered action. Russia's Armed Forces must reach a fundamentally new capability level within the next 3–5 years."[8] On March 20, 2013 Prime Minister Medvedev seconded this demand.[9] Medvedev argued that,

> The creation of large integrated structure [in the Russian defense-industrial complex] is one of [Russia's] top priority missions." — This approach has withstood the test of time, the consolidation of forces along the lines of the great variety of sectors in the military-industrial complex is necessary Medvedev indicated the restructuring of Russia's defense-industrial complex must happen "within timeframes that are compressed to the maximum extent necessary.[10]

Stalin or Brezhnev could not have said it better. Indeed, Medvedev called upon the defence industry not just to be a locomotive of economic and technological growth for the entire economy but also to grow at an annual rate of 10% in 2013–2015 and for productivity to grow at around 20% annually.[11] According to Deputy Prime Minister Dmitry Rogozin, speaking at the same venue, Russia will train around 2,000,000 technical and

---

[7] "Putin: Russia not going to join new arms race but will develop modern nuclear arms," *Interfax*, July 26, 2012, available at http://search.proquest.com/professional/login. "Meeting of the military-industrial commission", www.en.kremlin.ru, June 28, 2016; "Meeting of Russian Federation Ambassadors and Permanent Envoys", www.en.kremlin. ru, June 30, 2016; "Putin says, Russia will build new weapons but avoid arms race", *Yahoo! News*, www.yahoo.com, January 20, 2015.

[8] Расширенное Заседание Коллегии Министерства Обороны.

[9] Dmitry Medvedev attends a conference on the development of the defence sector, http:// government.ru/eng/docs/23401/, March 20, 2013.

[10] "Russia reporting on defense industries for March 20, 2013", Open Source Center, *OSC Summary*, in English, March 20, 2013, *FBIS SOV*, March 20, 2013.

[11] *Ibid.*

engineering workers for the defence-industrial complex by 2020 with a special education programme and massive state subsidies to help reach these goals.[12] Similarly, to take one example, Bloomberg reported in 2015 that Russia's federal budget had lurched towards a war economy with a large spike in the so-called "black budget" authorised by Putin but not announced publicly. Indeed, during the 2010–2015 period, military expenditures have increased by a factor of 20 since 1999 when Putin became president. Defence and security spending account for just over a third of the Russian federal budget expenses (Berman, 2017, p. 41; Biryukov, 2015).

Two conclusions flow from this. One is that nuclear weapons are at the core of this so-called asymmetry in order to forestall the application of NATO's conventional superiority. Second, this allegedly asymmetric strategy will continue well into the future. This call for "asymmetry" has come early and stayed late. Deputy Prime Minister and Defense Minister Sergei Ivanov said 2006, "Our responses should be grounded in the intellectual superiority; they will be asymmetric and less costly."[13] More recently, in May 2016, complaining about the US's placement of missile defences in Romania, Putin told the leadership of the Defense Ministry,

As we have discussed already, we are not going to be drawn into this race. We will go our own way. We will work very carefully, without exceeding the planned spending on the rearmament of the army and navy, plans we have had for years, but we will adjust them in order to curb the threat to Russia's security.[14]

Thus, and second, the impetus towards asymmetry *vis-à-vis* the West is a principled long-term Russian military strategy that clearly is a strategy for waging high-tech conventional war with substantial and potentially usable nuclear weapons on standby and always on display. Here, we must distinguish between operations like Crimea that are untypical military

---

[12] *Ibid.*

[13] "Minutes of Russian Security Council meeting", June 20, 2006, www.president.kremlin. ru/appears/2006/06/2001708_type633type63381type82364_107461.shtml.

[14] "Meeting on defense industry development", May 13, 2016, http://en.kremlin.ru/events/president/news/51911.

operations but that do typify what might be called the "whole of government" Russian national security strategy using specially tasked or designated forces, information warfare [IW] (as defined by Russia (Forss *et al.*,
2012)) media, intelligence penetration, subversion of political parties
abroad, the use of organised crime and Russian businesses (not just
energy) as conduits of this corruption and subversion strategy, the incite-
ment of ethnic tensions, etc. We saw these forces in Crimea and we can
see them in Moscow's global Cold War offensives against the West that
also employ military deployments and threats (Rogin, 2016).

In other words, to judge from his rhetoric, Putin and his subordinates
are sensitive to the danger of excessive military spending even though
they still harbour Stalinist notions about the defence sector being the locomotive of progress and will not emulate the unfortunate Soviet example.
Certainly, it appears that Putin has a visceral opposition to inflationary
trends associated with large budget deficits and will not easily let the
inflationary pressures, which always lurked in the Soviet economy and
eventually swallowed it, engulf his economy (Miller, 2018). Indeed, it
does seem clear that the new defence plan that runs from 2018 to 2027
displays a retraction or at least a contraction in the growth of defence
spending (Boulegue, 2017). Indeed, Putin suggested as much in his end-
of-year meeting with the Defense Ministry Board in 2017.[15] Western
assessments show this too (Jones and Caffrey, 2018).

Thus, from the standpoint of early 2020 February, 2018, it appears that
Putin has instituted genuine changes in the defence industrial sector to
alleviate some or even many of the defects that undid that sector in Soviet
rule even as he has preserved the patrimonial Muscovite economy that is
characterised by heavy state domination, pervasive rent-seeking and rent-
granting, reliance on a cash-crop (energy) boom-or-bust economic trends
and an inbuilt tendency towards stagnation that precludes catching up and
overtaking Russia's neighbours not to mention its great power competitors.
It also appears that structural stagnation, coupled with stagnating energy
prices — even if they reach $70–80 per barrel; this is a far cry from the
boom years of the first decade of this century — and the severe impact of

---

[15]"Expanded meeting of the Defense Ministry Board, Balashika, Moscow region",
December 22, 2017, www.kremlin.ru/ervents/president/news/56472.

sanctions will also continue to affect the entire economy. In the absence of economic reforms that are quite unlikely to materialise in Putin's next term, the economy as whole is likely to stagnate and the defence industrial sector is likely to continue to come under great pressure, i.e. remain or become more sub-optimal. Yet, this will not likely prevent the fulfilment of most of the 2018–2027 plan. In other words, all things being equal (and they are never so in the political world) barring a major political shock to the system or a global economic crisis, Russia can probably sustain most of its defence plans on its current economic basis for another decade. But by 2030 or so, its inbuilt structural economic–political-strategic crisis will therefore have become steadily more acute. So while it can continue on its current trajectory it does so at the risk of accelerating and intensifying all the current economic–political and international trends that will create a powder keg under the Russian government within a decade or so.

Examining These Conclusions

There is no doubt that the transition from the decaying Soviet defence-industrial sector to the present Russian one was traumatic, prolonged longer than it probably needed to be, and thus more severe. Nevertheless, the result is a defence sector that today can reliably serve the needs of the Russian military for the most part. This will continue into the foreseeable future. So while it is unlikely that the current plan to 2020 or that going out to 2027 will be fully realised, Russia will retain more than enough existing and developing capability, *ceteris paribus*, to ensure possession of a formidable military machine with diverse capabilities for many different forms of combat. For example, in the nuclear sphere, an examination of Russian nuclear procurements indicates that based on those procurements Moscow intends to reach a state where it can threaten nuclear strikes tailored to the occasion to retain escalation dominance, intimidate potential adversaries and be able to wage what it thinks are limited conventional or limited nuclear wars as well as larger scale contingencies with impunity (Blank, 2019). Moreover, it expects to do so sooner rather than later.

Its success in improving the quantity and quality of its weapons and military systems in the last decade beyond the nuclear domain is also not open to question. So even though this is a politically driven economy, where state officials and generals rather than consumers determine production goals, recent history as well as much of Soviet history shows that the state can largely achieve its military goals through this mechanism, albeit at costs we would clearly not wish to bear (Rosefielde, 2018).

Furthermore, the reform of the Russian defence-industrial sector (VPK) appears to have been deliberately planned as a long-term process that entailed a comprehensive reform not only of the sector but also of the state administration necessary to support the overall transformation of the economy as a whole and the state to support that long-term process (Rosefielde, 2018; Haas, 2011; Glantz, 2011; Isakova, 2004, 2006; Pallin, 2006; Trifonov, 2005). As a result of these processes, we see the ongoing surge in Russian defence production in the recent times (Rosefielde, 2018).

> The surge in Russian weapons cannot be explained by reviving up idled production lines for fourth generation equipment. It reflects modernisation of weapon characteristics, updating old production lines, building new modern production facilities and switching from managerial regimes rewarding executives for mass production rather than military R&D. However, unlike Soviet arrangements, state ownership doesn't bar VPK enterprises or public private partnerships (PPP) from competing among each other. Military industrial firms (including holding companies) are permitted to operate on a for-profit basis. They compete for state orders and export sales (contracts) and can outsource. Shareholders and/or manages are variously incentivised to profit-seek and incompletely profit-maximise rather than comply with MOD commands and/ or rent-seek. They have fewer degrees of freedom than private Western defense corporation like Boeing, but are self-motivated to efficiently produce in accordance with Herbert Simon's bounded rationality framework and William Baumol's satisficing concept. This bolstered VPK initiative when the MOD stopped prioritising military R&D. Putin beat the odds by imposing firm discipline and containing rent seeking, buttressed with competitive reforms and sufficient material incentives.

Moreover, Putin, in this case reverting to Soviet precedents, has managed to generate a stream of procurements that has visibly surprised Western governments and defence planners. It should be clear, therefore that the figure that Russia spends about $60 Billion annually on defence, a figure that has been accepted as canonical by Western analysts and is based on a market exchange rate methodology, misreads the Russian system. In fact, based on purchasing power parity (PPP) Michael Kofman and Richard Connolly have found that Russia spends the equivalent of and obtains the results of about $150–180 billion annually, a figure that allows it to sustain the enormous procurement stream we are now seeing and have seen for several years. Moreover, this system appears to be more durable than foreign observers imagine even if the longer term prognoses, given continuing stagnation, are not optimistic (Connolly and Kofman, 2019).

This assessment suggests that the growth in defence spending since the 1990s and 2000s has been slower than imagined in the West because it started at a higher level than did other powers. Second, Russia's growing autarky, a product of both state policy and sanctions, actually makes measurement by PPP more logical for the defence sector and facilitates this neo-Soviet approach. But third,

> Furthermore, the Russian state has made sure that the defense sector is on a diet in terms of the profits it is allowed to make from state defense orders. While this led to a debt bubble within the Russian defense industry, it also suggests that the state is able to get more output from the defense sector relative to other sectors of the economy. Although the level of Russian defense spending is higher than many previously thought, it is also true that it is declining as a share of GDP. The Russian government has chosen to let defense expenditure plateau for two reasons: first, because a large amount of equipment was successfully procured between 2011 and 2016, resulting in significant modernisation of a previously ageing force; and second, to avoid the sort of runaway defense spending that contributed to the Soviet Union's economic ruin. But this slowdown in the growth of defense spending should not be confused with slashing defense spending to levels that might drastically reduce Russia's military capability. There is no evidence that such steep reductions are taking place. Instead, Russia is charting a middle course, not killing itself with unsustainable Soviet-style spending on defense, but equally avoiding painful reductions in order to meet the reformists' demands (Connolly and Kofman, 2019).

These policies, which went largely unnoticed in the Western literature, provided the basis for the surge we have seen in the last 5–7 years and will also provide the foundation for the targets for the current and 2018–2027 defence programmes.

Indeed, not only are the current and future defence programmes ambitious even if they are being relatively slightly moderated, Moscow also has comparably ambitious plans for the overall development of the VPK. In 2016, the government approved a new programme for the development of this sector (also called OPK-Defense-industrial sector — Oboronno-Promyshlennyi Kompleks). This programme incorporates some earlier federally targeted programmes and is largely classified, as we would expect. But what we can discern from published data suggests the scope of the transformation Moscow wants to see. From the published sub-programme, we see the government calling for an increase in this sector's output by 75% in 2020 compared to 2014, labour productivity is supposed to increase by 137.5% and the average monthly wages by 77%. By 2020, civilian output of the defence industry was forecast to grow 28% over 2015 totals by 2020. Since the defence industry, as in Soviet times, continues to be a major part of civilian industrial production, this figure hints at a return to some Soviet ways of thinking and doing business. Overall responsibility for the programme is vested in the Ministry of Industry and Trade and total funding through 2020 would be 1.067 billion rubles, i.e. over 200 billion rubles annually.[16]

These attributes of the programme underscore the ambitious targets for renovation of the defence industry. While this programme was being formulated, announced, and in the early stages of its implementation, Russia was also formulating the state armaments programme (SAP) or defence programme for 2018–2027. Although the SAP naturally was the object of a lot of bureaucratic contention, by 2016 Putin was making clear that at some point in the next decade if not earlier defence spending would peak and then decline due to the economic crises of 2014–2016: collapsing energy prices, the devaluation of the ruble, and Western

---

[16] Julian Cooper, "Prospects for Military Spending in Russia in 2017 and beyond," unpublished paper made available to the author.

sanctions on top of the structural impediments to growth.[17] This commitment to take a step back in defence spending at the end of this decade or the beginning of the next one remains embedded in policy, as we shall see. But even though Russian officials believe Russia is now (2019–20) coming out of recession, its economic prospects are hardly rosy. Moreover, starting in 2016, high-ranking officials, possibly perceiving a deteriorating international situation that has only become worse since 2016, started advocating even more mobilisation of the state and economy towards a wartime footing.[18] Thus, the new SAP or defence plan for 2018–2027 carries within it an unresolved ambivalence, if not contradiction. Reduced defence spending denotes the leadership's satisfaction that the basic international situation and Russian defence capabilities do not warrant alarm. For example, given the rising costs of foreign imports and components and the impact of sanctions, the new SAP apparently cutback on new projects like the SU-57 fifth-generation fighter jet. Procurement objectives have been cut from 60 to about 12. The PAK-DA programme was pushed back in favour of restarting production of the TU-160. New armoured vehicles and the T-14 tank are only being purchased in small numbers. Cutbacks in components from Ukraine have also forced delays in the production of Admiral Grigorovich and Admiral Gorshkov classes of frigates. Instead, Russia aims to upgrade versions of systems like the Su-35s, TU-160s, and T-72 tanks for the time being. Such adjustments would not be as likely if the regime believed itself in imminent peril (Bisaccio, 2018).

The increasing evidence or demands for mobilisation, on the other hand, point exactly to the opposite conclusion.

So it would seem that despite grasping some of the glaring shortcomings of the Soviet model, Putin *et al.* have fallen into the same trap. That is not surprising inasmuch as the current regime resembles every preceding Russian regime as falling within the traditional patrimonial Muscovite service state framework (Pipes, 1975; Blank, 2007; Balzer, 2005; Shlapentokh and Woods, 1996, 2007; Stavrakis, 1993, 1997; Huskey,

---

[17] *Ibid.*
[18] *Ibid.*

1995; Rosefielde and Hedlund, 2009).[19] As Steven Rosefielde (2010) has written,

> Russia does not and cannot efficiently operate according to the neoclassical economic principles (democratic free enterprise) claimed by many to assure its eventual entry into *West-utopia*, a Shangri-La where everyone completely and competitively maximises his and her utility in the private, public (democracy) and civic (civil empowerment) domains. The institutions which thwart Russian Pareto optimality are — autocracy, primacy of autocratic freehold ownership, edict over constitution, the supremacy of autocracy over private rights (hence servility), and primacy of command and administratively supervised rent-granting governance over free enterprise, democracy an, civil liberty, — From the neoinstitutionalist perspective, Russian governance (including the state, politics, economics, and civil society) boils down to autocratic rent-granting, rent-seeking, rent-creating, rent controlling, and rent-management rather than individually empowered, complete and competitive utility seeking.

Given this structural framework that will not change in Putin's expected next term, 2018–2024, the government can either hope for a major spike in global energy prices or some other kind of miracle, cut defence spending substantially while reallocating funds to science, technology, infrastructure, education and health, i.e. human capital, "go for broke" with high rises in defence spending, or strive to increase the efficiency of the VPK (or OPK) while moderately trimming defence spending. It appears that it has opted for the latter of these alternatives, which intrinsically embodies the ambivalence or contradictions mentioned above between mobilisations and reduced spending. Indeed, that is the only way it can try to muddle through this ambivalence or contradiction.

Indeed, the regime has long been striving to achieve mobilisation as regards its defence capability. Recent exercises like Kavkaz-2016 and Zapad-2017 pointed to the concept of operations that correlates nuclear

---

[19] Bremmer (2010), Hellie (2005), Baker and Glasser (2005), Rosefielde (2004), Poe (2003), Hedlund (2005), Pain (2005), Kotkin (2004) are only a few of the authors who now see the vitality of the Tsarist metaphor as a means of explaining Putin's Russia. Center for Strategic and International Studies (2004, passim).

drills and exercises with the mobilisation of civilian administrative authorities and institutions as in Zapad-2017 and Kavkaz-2016 (Saradzhyan,
2016; Blank, 2019; Schneider, 2018; Howe, 2018).[20]

Recent papers by Ray Finch and Aleksandr' Golts make clear that the
government has launched a comprehensive programme of mobilisation of
the state and society for the purposes of portraying Russia as a besieged
fortress, militarising the economy in the direction of Soviet-type resource
allocation policies, creating a new National Guard and, since the conference, Putin's call for a new KGB-like organisation and profound upgrading of Russian domestic military forces (Goble, 2017; Birshtein, 2017).
Moreover, as Golts points out and as subsequent military commentary has
noted, the creation once again of divisions and even armies out of the
brigades created in the reform of 2008–2012 suggests a renewed consideration of the likelihood of large-scale conventional, if not nuclear, war as
a real contingency, if not priority (Kofman, 2016).

However, what analysts have missed is that this mobilisation programme is in fact a long-standing one. In the Russian tradition, defence
reform cannot take place until the state structure is itself subjected to a
comparably comprehensive reform. And this was true for Putin's Russia.
Defence reform only began in 2008 once it became clear how bad the military's condition was in the wake of its war with Georgia. But it had been
preceded by something few foreign analysts had noted but that was vital,
namely the administrative reform of the state after 2000 (Haas, 2011;
Glantz, 2011; Isakova, 2004, 2006; Pallin, 2006; Trifonov, 2005). In that
context and in tandem with the defence reform that began in 2008, Putin
and then President Dmitry Medvedev postulated the need for further
reform of the state structure to make it ready for mobilisation for strategic
purposes already in the national security strategy of 2009 and the defence
doctrine of 2010 (Blank, 2010; Dmitiriev *et al.*, 2015). Since then and particularly after 2014, this mobilisation process of the state has accelerated

---

[20]"Russian missile system, submarine engage simulated targets at Kavkaz-2016 drills",
http://www.globalsecurity.org/wmd/library/news/russia/2016/russia-160909-sputnik04.htm,
September 9, 2016; "Russian general calls for preemptive nuclear strike doctrine against
NATO", https://themoscowtimes.com/articles/russian-general-calls-for-preemptive-nuclear-
strike-doctrine-against-nato-39016, September 3, 2014.

to the now visible point seen by Western observers. Indeed, in the Kavkaz-2016 exercises, Russia not only has once again (having done so before) mobilised the civil administration but even mobilised banks to pay soldiers in the field and hospitals to establish field hospitals during those exercises, a true sign of a commitment to mobilising the entire state structure on behalf of a large war where the survival of the state is obviously at some risk (Monaghan, 2014, 2016; Brewster, 2016).

Arguably therefore, this drive towards a permanent mobilisation framework goes back to the 2009 national security strategy and even earlier. But before that strategy could be published, this enormous preparatory work had to be done. That document explicitly mandated that the government organs, i.e.

> The Russian Federation Government and the federal executive authorities concerned are to draw up a system of strategic planning documents: the Russian Federation Long-Term Socio-Economic Development Blueprint, Russian Federation socioeconomic development programs for the short term, development strategies (programs) for individual sectors of the economy, development strategies (programs) for the federal districts, socioeconomic development strategies and integrated programs for the Russian Federation components, interstate programs that the Russian Federation is involved in implementing, federal (departmental) targeted programs, the state defense order, the blueprints, doctrines, and fundamentals (primary directions) of state policy in the national security sphere and in separate areas of the state's domestic and foreign policy with the participation of the Russian Federation components' state authorities based upon the Russian Federation Constitution and Russian Federation federal laws and other normative legal acts.[21]

In addition, the newspaper, *Gazeta*, on April 29, 2009 reported that the Security Council under the direction of Nikolai Patrushev must report annually on the course of the implementation of the strategy, but every ministry and department must also now prepare strategy documents,

---

[21] *Natsional'naya Strategiya Bezopasnosti Rossii, do 2020 Goda* (Security Council of the Russian Federation, Moscow, Russia, May 12, 2009), available from *www.scrf.gov.ru*, in English. It is available from the Open Source Center Foreign Broadcast Information Service, Central Eurasia (henceforth *FBIS SOV*), May 15, 2009, in a translation from the Security Council website available from *www.scrf. gov.ru* (henceforth NSS).

presumably along the same lines. Furthermore, as stated by Novikova *et al.* (2009),

> At the operational conference of the Security Council at the end of last week the government was instructed to prepare a full list of such documents within three months. Ahead of the 24 March conference the ministries and departments had already presented a list of 135 different strategies, concepts, and principles in the most diverse spheres — from the banking sector to the agro-industrial complex — which should be developed in the future within the framework of the country's overall strategic planning.

This approach that demands ever-more stringent state mobilisation, a negative threat assessment and commitment to high defence spending is naturally associated with the *Silovye Struktury* (power structures) who appear to have the upper hand in policymaking and will strongly resist any effort to circumscribe either their access to resources (whether or not for corrupt purposes) or a shift in the ideological posture of the regime (Miller, 2018; Fortescue, 2017). These forces clearly constitute a major roadblock to less intense defence policies and relaxation of state controls, not to mention broader economic–political reform. And for now, they appear to have the upper hand since Putin in late 2017 called for enhancing mobilisation readiness after Zapad-2017. Specifically, Putin stated that,

> The ability of our economy to increase military production and services at a given time is one of the most important aspects of military security. To this end, all strategic and simply large-scale enterprise should be ready, regardless of ownership — "First, we checked our mobilisation readiness and ability to use local resources to meet the troops' requirements. Reservists were called up for this exercise, and we also tested the ability of civilian companies to transfer their vehicles and equipment to the armed forces and provide technical protection to transport communications.... We also assessed the provision of transport and logistics services, as well as food and medicines to the army. We need to review once again the defense companies' ability to quickly increase output.[22]

---

[22]Putin calls for enhancing mobilization readiness after Zapad-2017 exercise, http://tass.com/defense/976879, November 22, 2017; Alex Lantier, Kremlin instructs Russian

Since then, Putin has supervised a comprehensive programme of decrees and regulations, as well as exercises outlining the process and details by which the economy and entire state administration will be mobilised for war, should it be necessary (Cooper, 2016, pp. 15–52; Monaghan, 2016).

As Alex Lantier, writing on the World Socialist Website observed, "In such a war, the military would take over the economy, slash production for civilian needs, and re-direct whatever industrial capacity survived mass air and missile raids towards the war effort" (Lantier, 2017). Thus, a renewed system of mobilisation preparation is integral to military policy (Cooper, 2016, p. 37). And given the rhetoric that has come out of Moscow as well as the signs pointed to by Finch and Golts, we may say with Julian Cooper that Russia probably is currently in a kind of pre-mobilisation period for budgetary allocations that have not reflected mobilisation but rather the preparations of the capacities and capabilities needed to implement it (Cooper, 2016, p. 50).

Obviously, this presages a return to Soviet models and, in line with the overall glorification of autarky and economic substitution, points backward to the Stalinist or neo-Stalinist past. And in view of the current threat assessments that remain unrelievedly gloomy and filled with foreboding, the pressure for high levels of defence spending remains quite difficult to dislodge from its political primacy.

On the other hand, Putin had already committed to reducing defence spending by 2016 and the parlous state of the economy demanded such a move. So rather than "floor the accelerator", the regime slightly eased the pressure of defence spending. Examination of what is known about the new state budget for 2018–2019 and the SAP for 2018–2027 tends to confirm that observation. Indeed, Putin's end-of-year address to the armed forces in 2017 explicitly rejected the idea of being a global gendarme.[23] Thus, the budget for 2018 is reportedly balanced without cuts for the

---

industry to prepare for war mobilization, https://www.wsws.org/en/articles/2017/11/24/krem-n24.html, November 24, 2017.

[23] Expanded Meeting of the Defense Ministry Board, Balashika, Moscow Region, December 22, 2017.

already stressed social welfare sector.[24] Allegedly defence spending in 2018 will total $46 billion and the level of defence expenditures is 2.85% of GDP while the SAP for 2018–2027 is 20,000 billion rubles (approximately $343 billion).[25]

Yet, there is more here than was officially revealed. The new budget and SAP occurring at a time of strong demands for mobilisation, import substitution, and modernisation entail a substantial cut in R&D that can only compound Russia's existing backwardness and inhibit prospects for future growth in both the defence and civilian sectors (Boulegue, 2017). While oil prices are now about $60–70/barrel, a substantial cushion for a budget officially presumes a price of $40/barrel that only provides cash response to the structural problems that pervade the economy if not the VPK. And the increased defence spending that we now see confirms the existence of that cushion even under ongoing conditions of stagnation. Moreover, in fact the defence and domestic security sectors (from which thousands of men and enormous resources could also be mobilised as intended by the government in the event of a crisis) actually comprise $84.6 billion or 6.59% of GDP as of 2017. While the budget cut $10 billion for 2018 according to official figures from $56 to $46 billion, this total is still quite high and shows an excessively "securitised" budget and economy. In fact, in 2016–2017 Russia arguably hit the ceiling of what it can afford for these two sectors that properly comprise defence spending. Thus, the only way to a void politically unpalatable large-scale personnel cuts in the current climate if Moscow intends to retain the defence sector as getting one-third of the annual budget is to induce the defence industry to work better and more efficiently (Fortescue, 2017; Luzhin, 2017).

Yet, there is plenty of reason to suggest that even with the higher than expected energy prices and slightly less defence spending for now, these new steps will not generate the growth needed by Russia or allow the defence sector to catch up and overtake the West. Already some weapons systems have been not only stretched out but also even cancelled, e.g. the

---

[24] Russian Defense Ministry pleased with "Balanced" rearmament budget, *BBC Monitoring,* November 23, 2017.

[25] *Ibid.*; 'Russia to shell out $46 Bln on defense spending in 2018', *Tass,* December 22, 2018.

programme to put nuclear weapons on the rails, the so-called Boevoi Zheleznodorozhnyi Raketnyi Kompleks (BZHRK) appears to have been cancelled (Sharkov, 2017). Naval shipbuilding continues to be unable to cope with the demands by the state for new ships and for the Arctic Fleet (McDermott, 2018).[26] In other cases, rising costs, the depreciation of the ruble and presumably the difficulties in obtaining foreign capital and technology have slowed the development of several weapons ranging from armoured personnel carriers to the Sarmat nuclear missile. These weapons will evidently not be available in the amounts planned by 2020 until sometime afterwards (Christie, 2017, p. 10).[27]

Similarly, we can see that even if defence spending (as we have defined it here) falls slightly and social welfare spending remains high, it is easy to envision a scenario where investment will be restricted to "securitized areas and that private industry will again fail to pick up the slack and if budget deficits are funded by domestic borrowing (which is highly likely as long as sanctions continue) then the prospects for productive investment over time will be severely curtailed" (Fortescue, 2017, p. 15). Other structural factors will add to the continuing stagnation. Import substitution will shield Russia from competitive pressures and encourage more rent-seeking. Moreover, the continuing strong pressure for mobilisation, which in policy terms apparently amounts to more pressure on the VPK to do more with less, will probably not succeed as intended and may backfire. Business, like its Soviet predecessors, is constantly interceding for lower targets and less pressure and rising prices and import substitution that creates inbuilt inflationary pressures which will add to the tensions between what is expected and what is actually delivered.

In addition, as Julian Cooper (2016, p. 43) observes,

> In the defense industry in particular, the mobilisation system must still be associated with a considerable amount of unused capacity, higher costs, secrecy, and it can be assumed, not infrequent inspections by external agencies to ensure that capacities are being maintained and reserve stocks being held by enterprises are not being misused. Given

---

[26]Russian shipyards on the rocks over funding, *BBC Monitoring*, December 20, 2017.

[27]Cooper, J. Prospects for military spending in Russia in 2017 and beyond, p. 15.

the secrecy surrounding all aspects of mobilisation preparation it is probably not surprising that it is an area in which financial abuses are not uncommon.

Indeed, the VPK has long been associated with a high degree of corruption (Shlykov, 2004a, p. 160, 2004b; Kosals, 2004).[28]

As it is, the economy has had to take on a fairly substantial degree of risk that Putin probably would have preferred to avoid. Thus, Russia's reserve fund has ceased to exist as it has had to cover for almost 4 years of incessant crisis.[29] But here again the rise of energy prices creates or generates an inflow of foreign capital that is being used to undergird the economy so it is not in imminent danger of collapse. This is the case even though there is good reason to suspect that state organisations are fudging their figures to make the economic crisis look less severe than it actually is.[30] The Russian government is also taking steps to concentrate its control over the economy even further, a practice that is rife with potential dangers from the lack of transparency that will be added to an already bad situation. The Ministry of Finance has converted Promsvyazbank into a specialised defence lender to shield defence firms from foreign sanctions on borrowing abroad. Minfin has produced legislation that would override other banks' opposition and force them to subsidise the new bank with some of their own capital as well as defence loans. The amount involved is estimated at some 80 billion rubles ($1.41 billion) and is clearly a golden opportunity for more rent-seeking. But it will also curtail even more the freedom that other banks still retain.[31] Beyond this measure, the government has compiled a list of 126 companies, most of them state-owned,

---

[28] Moscow, *Ekho Moskvy in Russian*, June 4, 2004, *FBIS SOV*; Moscow, *ITAR-TASS*, April 14, 2005, *FBIS SOV*; Moscow, *Center TV in Russian*, September 30, 2003, October 1, 2003, *FBIS SOV*; Moscow, *Moskovskaya Pravda, in Russian*, April 17, 2003, *FBIS SOV*; Moscow, Interview with OAO Gipromez General director Vitaly Rogozhin, *Rossiyskaya Gazeta* (in Russian), July 13, 2005, *FBIS SOV*.

[29] Russia's reserve fund ceases to exist, *BNE News*, January 9, 2018, www.intellinews.com.

[30] Rosstat fudges the numbers, halting real income decline, *Bear Market Brief*, February 20, 2018, www.fpri.org.

[31] In creating defence lender, MinFin wants cash from other banks, *ibid.*

"whose purchases and other business activities may be made classified" to protect them from sanctions. In November 2017, several key companies were requested to approve changes to their procurement policies and classify the business deals and identities of their counterparties. Moreover, their purchases will be transferred from what is now a transparent system to Sberbank's closed military procurement database.[32]

In other words, the ongoing failure to institute reforms and to wean the economy off of its addiction to hydrocarbons while retaining steep defence spending imposes severe costs and constraints upon the economy (Fortescue, 2017; Oxenstierna, 2016). Certainly, finding the resources with which to pay for the new SAP will be difficult. *Jane's Defence Weekly*, for example, argues that to fully fund the SAP, annual funding must increase by 7% annually through 2027 while government budget projections for 2019 and 2020 show increases in defence spending of only 3.2% for that period (Jones and Caffrey, 2018). These constraints also have structural political ramifications as is well known. Among these costs are those associated with the lack of investment in non-defence sectors and the degradation over time of the "human capital" and infrastructure sectors that provide the basis for further autonomous growth. Nevertheless, constraints, challenges and problems are hardly new features of Russian or other state economies, and as Christie suggests, there are ways to raise taxes if foreign bailouts or energy price hikes are not available (Christie, 2017, pp. 4–15).

Thus, the regime has not wholly embraced the Soviet trap, although prominent elements of that economy are "baked into the cake". The cuts imposed on defence spending reflect the government's awareness that it had reached the limit of defence spending. Indeed, those cuts reflect not just awareness that Russia had reached the limits of its capability to afford its defence buildup but clearly the preferences of key policymakers, first of all Putin.

> Russia could gradually move towards a slightly higher tax burden and slightly higher total public spending, thereby generating additional resources for defense spending. Instead, the current direction of Russian

---

[32] Russia building sanctions proof black box, *ibid.*, December 8, 2017.

fiscal policy for the 2017–19 period is towards austerity and consolidation, both for defense spending and for total spending. In sum, *the current downward adjustment to defense spending is not occurring because of an unavoidable adjustment in fiscal policy, but rather due to more demanding and self-imposed constraints.* These choices are an illustration of what economists refer to as "revealed preferences." In this case, it appear that while military modernisation goals are important, Russian authorities are also strongly averse to increases in the tax burden (Author's emphasis).[33]

Conclusions

Those revealed preferences appear to go beyond strong defence spending to include a high aversion to increasing public debt and increases in the tax burden and an effort (albeit unsuccessful) to avoid depletion of the reserve fund.[34] In other words, the burden of defence spending, especially given the current domestic and foreign structural constraints upon Moscow, is substantial but not determinative in the short run. The reforms imposed by Putin upon the VPK, notwithstanding the pervasive corruption, rent-seeking, excessive securitisation of the economy at home, and foreign sanctions, do not preclude Russia from probably being able to sustain most of the SAP through 2027. Higher than expected energy prices and the ability to evade or circumvent sanctions by closer ties to countries in the Middle East and China also contribute to this outcome. But the fact that Russia is emerging from recession and will enjoy very modest but real growth also point to this conclusion.

In the longer term, it seems clear that the demographic, structural and long-term impact of these slowly growing constraints will have a boa constrictor-like effect on the economy and the political system. But that is in the long term, and as Keynes said, in the long term we will all be dead. Inasmuch as the political leadership's model is "get rich" and its time horizons visibly short term, that elite may be banking on somehow riding out the storm or simply believe that *après nous le deluge.*

---

[33] *Ibid.*, p. 8.
[34] *Ibid.*, p. 10.

Either way, the conclusion here is far from the comforting one that a crash is inevitable due to the excessive burden of defence spending upon this particularly challenged economy burdened as it is by structural domestic and foreign constraints. This is not the Soviet economy and Putin is not Gorbachev. Clearly, he grasps the dangers of the course he has imposed and is trying to impose limits upon it. This author does not believe that in the long-term Russia can evade the logic of its current and future constraints but in Russian history, economic constraint is the norm not the exception. Ultimately, this is a political economy and it stands or falls upon the willingness and the ability of the state to assert its power. While a long-term economic crisis is virtually inevitable, nobody has yet seen even the remotest attenuation of this elite's will to retain power and ability to do so. When that factor sails into view, we will then know that the long term that we envisage here has become the short term if not the present. But in the meantime we should not indulge in chimeras that the Russian military challenge will fall of its own accord. Complacency is not a strategy or a policy and hoping that Russia will follow our complacent beliefs regarding economics when it has never done so is certainly neither a strategy nor a policy. Here, as elsewhere, hope is neither a policy nor a strategy.

References

Baev, P. K. (2017). Military force: A driver aggravating Russia's decline, in Wimbush, S. E., and Portale, E. M. (eds.), *Russia in Decline*, Jamestown Foundation, Washington, DC. pp. 181–189.

Baker, P. and Glasser, S. (2005). *Kremlin Rising: Vladimir Putin's Russia and the End of Revolution,* Scribner's, New York, p. 417.

Balzer, H. (2005). Confronting the global economy after communism: Russia and China compared, Paper presented to the Annual Convention of the International Studies Association, Honolulu, Hawaii, March 1–5, 2005.

Balzer, H. D. (2017). Russia's knowledge economy: Decline views from inside, in Wimbush, S. E., and Portale, E. M. (eds.), *Russia in Decline*, Jamestown Foundation, Washington, DC. pp. 113–161.

Berman, I. I. (2017). Russia's fraught demographic future, in Wimbush, S. E., and Portale, E. M. (eds.), *Russia in Decline*, Jamestown Foundation, Washington, DC. pp. 35–53.

Birshtein, V. (2017). Russia prepares to fight itself, www.vbirshtein.com, June 4, 2017.

Biryukov, A. (2015). The secret money behind Vladimir Putin's war machine, *Bloomberg*, June 2, 2015.

Bisaccio, D. (2018). Russian president signs new state armaments program, www.blog.forecastinternational.com.

Blank, S. (2007). *Rosoboroneksport: Its Place in Russian Defense and Arms Sales Policy*, Strategic Studies Institute, US Army War College, Carlisle Barracks, PA.

Blank, S. (2010). No need to threaten us, we are frightened of ourselves: Russia's blueprint for a police state, in Blank, S. J., and Weitz, R. (eds.), *The Russian Military Today and Tomorrow: Essays in Memory of Mary Fitzgerald*, Strategic Studies Institute, US Army War College, Carlisle Barracks, PA, pp. 19–150.

Blank, S. (2016). Can Russia sustain its military capability? Available at The Jamestown Foundation, Russia in Decline Project, http://www.jamestown. org/programs/edm/single/?tx_ttnews%5Btt_news%5D=45759&tx_ttnews% 5BbackPid%5D=835&cHash=221fdfac1ce7e515ed039e8d8b28fb60#. V97DhbWA360.

Blank, S. (2019). Reflections on Russia's nuclear strategy. In Roger E. Kanet (ed.), *Routledge Handbook of Russian Security*. Routledge, London and New York, pp. 154–168.

Boulegue, M. (2017). Russia's new armament programme offers a glimpse at military priorities, www.chathamhouse.org.

Bremmer, I. (2010). *The End of the Free Market: Who Wins the War between States and Corporations?* Portfolio Books, New York.

Bukkvoll, T. (2011). Iron cannot fight — The role of technology in current Russian military theory, *Journal of Strategic Studies*, XXXIV(5), 690.

Christie, E. H. (2017). Does Russia have the fiscal capacity to achieve its military modernization goals? *The RUSI Journal*, CLXII(5), 4–15.

Connolly, R. (2018). Stagnation and change in the Russian economy, *Russian Analytical Digest*, 21, pp. 5–9.

Connolly, R. and Kofman, M. (2019). Why Russian Military Expenditure Is Much Higher Than Commonly Understood (As Is China's), *War On the Rocks*, December 16, https://warontherocks.com/2019/12/why-russian-military-expenditure-is-much-higher-than-commonly-understood-as-is-chinas/.

Cooper, J. (2016). *If War Comes Tomorrow: How Russia Prepares for Possible Armed Aggression*, Whitehall Report, pp. 4–16, www.rusi.or.uk.

Eberstadt, N. (2017). Demography and human resources: Unforgiving constraints for a Russia in decline, in Wimbush, S. E., and Portale, E. M. (eds.), *Russia in Decline*, Jamestown Foundation, Washington, DC. pp. 54–110.

Dmitiriev, M., *et al.* (2015). *Putin's Russia: How It Rose, How It Is Maintained, and How It Might End*, American Enterprise Institute, Washington, DC, www.aei.org.

Forss, S., Kiiannlinna, L., Inkinnen, P. and Hult, H. (2012). *The Development of Russian Military Policy and Finland*, National Defense University, Department of Strategic and Defense Studies, Helsinki, pp. 8–9.

Fortescue, S. (2017). Can Russia afford to be a great power? Lowy Institute Occasional Paper, p. 15.

Goble, P. A. (2017). Foreword, in Wimbush, S. E., and Portale, E. M. (eds.), *Russia in Decline*, Jamestown Foundation, Washington, DC. pp. 190–212.

Goble, P. (2017). Putin gives national guard powers even NKVD didn't have — The question now is why? Gorevoy says, http://www.windowoneurasia2. blogspot.com/2017/06/putin-givesnational-guard-powers-even-nkvd-didn't have, June 5, 2017.

Goble, P. A. (2018). Putin's speech highlights his fundamental problem: Russia is 'armed to the teeth but poor', http://windowoneurasia2.blogspot.com/2018/03/ putins-speech-highlights-his.html, accessed 2 March 2018.

Glantz, D. M. (2011). Foreword, in McDermott, R. M. *The Reform of Russia's Conventional Armed Forces: Problems, Challenges, and Policy Implementation*, Jamestown Foundation, Washington, DC.

Haas, M. D. (2011). Russia's military reforms: Victory after twenty years of failure, *Clingendael Paper No. 5*, Netherlands Institute of International Affairs, Clingendael, 2011, p. 17.

Hedlund, S. (2005). *Russian Path Dependence*, Routledge, London.

Hellie, R. (2005). The structure of Russian imperial history, *History and Theory*, 44, 88–112.

Howe, J. (2018). Future Russian strategic nuclear and non-nuclear forces: 2022, in Blank, S. J. (ed.), *The Russian Military in Contemporary Perspective*, Strategic Studies Institute, Carlisle Barracks, PA.

Huskey, E. (1995). The state-legal administration and the politics of redundancy, *Post-Soviet Studies*, XI(2), 115–143.

Isakova, I. (2004). *Russian Governance in the Twenty-first Century: Geo-strategy, Geopolitics and Governance*, Frank Cass Publishers, London.

Isakova, I. (2006). *Russian Defense Reform: Current Trends*, Strategic Studies Institute, US Army War College, Carlisle Barracks, PA.

Jones, B. and Caffrey, C. (2018). Putin signs New State Armaments Programme, *Jane's Defence Weekly*, February 28, 2018, http://www.janes.com/article/78235/ putin-signs-new-state-armaments-programme.

Kofman, M. (2016). New Russian divisions and other units shifting to Ukraine's borders — Second look with updates, https://russianmilitaryanalysis. wordpress.com/2016/08/22/russian-units-on-ukraines-borders-second-look-with-updates/.

Kosals, L. (2004). Criminal influence/criminal control over the Russian military-industrial complex in the context of global security, NATO Defense College Research Paper, No. 1, March, 2004, pp. 6–8.

Kotkin, S. (2004). It's Gogol again, Paper presented as part of the project *The Energy Dimension in Russian Global Strategy*, James A. Baker III Institute for Public Policy, Rice University, Houston.

Luzhin, P. (2017). Russia's defense capabilities in 2018, www.intersectionproject. eu.

McDermott, R. (2018). Questions plague Russia's naval modernization, *Eurasia Daily Monitor*, February 13, 2018.

Miller, C. (2018). Putin isn't a genius. He's Leonid Brezhnev, www.foreignpolicy. com, (accessed 12 February 2018).

Monaghan, A. (2016). *Russian State Mobilization: Moving the Country on to a War Footing*, Eurasia Program Research Paper, Chatham House, Russia.

Pain, E. (2005). Will Russia transform into a nationalist empire, *Russia in Global Affairs*, III(2), 71–80.

Novikova, A., Telmanov, D. and Pavlikova, O. (2009). The national security strategy of the Russian federation is ready, *Gazeta Online* (in Russian), April 29, 2009, *FBIS SOV*.

Oxenstierna, S. (2016). Russia's defense spending and the economic decline, *Journal of Eurasian Studies*, VII, 68.

Pallin, C. V. (2006). *Defense Decision Making and Russian Military Reform: The Oblomov Approach*, Swedish Defense Research Establishment (FOI), Stockholm, pp. 174–179.

Pipes, R. (1975). *Russia under the Old Regime*, Scribner's, New York.

Poe, M. T. (2003). *The Russian Moment in World History*, Princeton University Press, Princeton, NJ.

Rogin, R. (2016). Obama can't ignore Russia, or its increasingly horrendous behavior, *Washington Post*, July 4, 2016, www.washingtonpost.com.

Rosefielde, S. (2004). *Russia in the 21st Century: The Prodigal Superpower*, Cambridge University Press, Cambridge.

Rosefielde, S. (2010). Postcrisis Russia: Counting on miracles in uncertain times, Paper presented to the Conference on Russian Military Development, Stockholm, October 4–5, 2010, pp. 9–10.

Rosefielde, S. (2018). Russia's military industrial resurgence: Evidence and potential, in Blank, S. J. (ed.), *The Russian Military in Contemporary Perspective*, Strategic Studies Institute, Carlisle Barracks, PA.

Rosefielde, S. and Hedlund, S. (2009). *Russia since 1980: Wrestling with Westernization*, Cambridge University Press, New York and Cambridge.

Saradzhyan, S. (2016). Yes, Russia's military is training for a 'mega war.' That's what militaries do, http://nationalinterest.org/feature/yes-russias-military-training-mega-war-what-militaries-do-17529?page=show.

Schneider, M. B. (2018). Russian nuclear weapons policy and programs, the European security crisis, and the threat to NATO, in Blank, S. J. (ed.), *The Russian Military in Contemporary Perspective*, Strategic Studies Institute, Carlisle Barracks, PA.

Sharkov, D. (2017). Russia's nuclear 'death train': Is the Kremlin scrapping the Soviet-inspired railway weapon? http://www.newsweek.com/russias-nuclear-death-train-kremlin-scrapping-soviet-inspired-railway-weapon-741034.

Shlapentokh, V. (1996). Early feudalism — The best parallel for contemporary Russia, *Euro-Asia Studies*, XLVIII(2), 391–411.

Shlapentokh, V. and Woods, J. (2007). *Contemporary Russia as a Feudal Society: A New Perspective on the Post-Soviet Era*, Palgrave Macmillan, New York.

Shlykov, V. (2004a). The economics of defense in Russia and the legacy of structural militarization, in Miller, S. E., and Trenin, D. (eds.), *The Russian Military: Power and Purpose*, MIT Press, Cambridge, MA, pp. 160–182.

Shlykov, V. (2004b). The anti-oligarchy campaign and its implications for Russia's security, *European Security*, XVII(2), 11–128.

Stavrakis, P. (1993). State-building in post-Soviet Russia: The Chicago Boys and the decline of administrative capacity, Occasional Papers of the Kennan Institute for Advanced Russian Studies, No. 254.

Stavrakis, P. (1997). The Russian state in the twenty-first century, Paper presented to the VIII Annual Strategy Conference of the U.S. Army War College, Carlisle Barracks, PA, April 22–24, 1997.

The World Bank (2017). Russia economic report: From recession to recovery, https://openknowledge.worldbank.org/bitstream/handle/10986/27522/116237-WP-P161778-PUBLIC-RERengforweb.pdf?sequence=1&isAllowed=y.

Trifonov, D. (2005). Russian defence reform: Reversing decline, *Jane's Defence Weekly*, June 8, 2005, www.4janes.com/subscribe/jdw/doc.

Chapter 10

The Fighting Power of Russia's Armed Forces

Petteri Lalu

Introduction

After the collapse of the Soviet Union, the Russian Federation (RF) hoped that the Commonwealth of Independent States would defend the newly independent states of the former USSR. Russia's Armed Forces became the legal successor of the Soviet Armed Forces on May 7, 1992. All military formations inside the boundaries of the Russian Soviet Federative Socialist Republic (RSFSR) operated under the Russian Federation's command (June 1991).

Withdrawal of Russian troops from Eastern Europe and nuclear weapons from other former Soviet states and relocation of both was a huge endeavour for Russian military, an operation performed while the Ministry of Defence was dealing with conflicts on its southern flank in Transnistria, South Ossetia and Abkhazia. During the periods 1994–1995 and 1999–2009, Russia's Armed Forces fought two wars in Chechnya against the separatist regime.

Military reform has been a primary concern for the Russian Federation after the initial period of adjustment. The Military reform of 2008 launched soon after the 5-day war against Georgia has been pivotal. It has given the military a "new shape" (новый облик) and achieved many of its goals. Russia's military today is competent and capable of fulfilling its missions.

This chapter concentrates on the capabilities of Russia's Armed Forces now and in the near future viewed through the prisms of doctrine, leadership, organisation and warfighting potential.

Doctrine

Mission and tasks

Russian law on defence defines it as a system of political, economic, military, social, legal and other measures for the armed protection, integrity of the federation and the inviolability of its territory (Об обороне, 1996). All authorities and the populous are obliged to defend the nation. Armed Forces, including the troops of Ministry of Internal Affairs, are putatively defensive.

The Armed Forces may also perform tasks in accordance with federal law and Russia's international treaties. In 2009, the Armed Forces were permitted to deploy abroad in the following situations:

(1) to repel attacks on Russia's Armed Forces, other troops or entities deployed outside the Russian Federation;
(2) to repel or prevent armed aggression against states appealing for assistance;
(3) to protect citizens of the Russian Federation outside of the territory of the Russian Federation from armed aggression;
(4) to fight against piracy and to provide safety for shipping (Изменение, 2009).

The law formally governs the conduct of Russian forces abroad. This includes the Georgia 2008 crisis and the decision-making process during the Ukrainian 2014 crisis.

Russia's military agenda in peace and war is governed by the rule of law (Военная доктрина, 2014; Mil.ru, 2018, III, 32).[1] Russian Ministry of Defence lists the following tasks on its website (Mil.ru, 2018):

---

[1] List of task is shortened.

(1) containment of military and military–political security threats, or infringements of the Russian Federation's interests;

(2) protection of economic and political interests of the Russian Federation;

(3) the armed forces may be employed in peacetime to fulfil the following:

- obligations to alliances or treaties;
- combat terrorists, pirates, extremists and separatists (including prevention);
- for peacekeeping and peace enforcement operations;
- to comply with officially declared emergencies;
- protection of Russia's borders (airspace and underwater environment);
- implement UN sanctions;
- prevent environmental disasters and other emergencies and to participate in post-emergency repair operations.

(4) Military force can be employed to ensure the nation's security in the following cases:

- armed conflict;
- local war;
- regional war;
- large-scale war.

Armed conflict is a limited confrontation between states (international armed conflict) or opposing sides within the territory of the single state (internal armed conflict). Armed conflict can result from escalation of an armed incident, a border conflict or other limited clashes. Armed conflict does not always imply state of war.

In **local war**, military and political goals are limited. Hostilities mainly affect the warring parties (territorial, economic, political and other). A local war can be waged by groups of troops (forces) deployed in the conflict area, supplemented by reinforcements and partial strategic deployments.

Regional war involves two or more states (groups of states) in the region, waged by national or coalition armed forces using conventional and nuclear weapons. In the course of hostilities, the parties pursue important military–political goals. Regional wars apply to adjacent waters, airspace and outer space. Full deployment of armed forces and the economy is required to conduct a regional war. Nuclear states or their allies may threaten to employ nuclear weapons.

Large-scale war is a confrontation between coalitions of states comprising a significant share of the global community. It can be caused by contagion. In a large-scale war, the parties will pursue ambitious military–political goals, requiring full mobilisation of resources.

Military threat posture

One of the main functions of the Russian military doctrine is the evaluation of the sources, level and scale of military threats and devising counterstrategies. Russia published its first military doctrine in 1993, updated in 2000, 2010 and 2014. The military threats foreseen reflect the Russian foreign policy and the military scientific communities' perceptions.

Russian military experts use two terms to assess hostile possibilities: *military danger* and *military threat*. Military danger (военная опасность) is determined by interstate or domestic relations, When the term military danger is used, its source is unknown or the source and intentions are ambiguous. A military threat (военная угроза) is an interstate or domestic situation that is apt to culminate in military conflict. Threats have distinct origins (Военная доктрина, 2014, I, 8.б–в).[2]

Russian estimates of the military dangers and threats have gradually changed over the years. The 1993 military doctrine considered the threat of external aggression against Russia to be low. Current doctrine takes the position that large-scale war against Russia is improbable — but contends that military dangers have intensified. The expansion of military alliances

---

[2]Russian military thought emphasises that the *real opportunity* demands high readiness of any aggressor (state, separatist or terrorist organization) to use military force (for armed violence).

is considered dangerous. NATO from the Kremlin's perspective is particularly worrisome.

The President of the Russian Academy of Military Science, Professor Makhmut Gareev, has divided military threat scenarios into three groups (Гареев, 2014, 9–10): The threats of the first group are external actions aimed at destabilising state stability. For example, Gareev cited Libya and Syria and later the "colour revolution" of the "Euro-Maidan" type in Ukraine 2013–2014.

The threats of the second group include the challenges to the strategic balance. Gareev claims that the nuclear strategy of the United States aims to prevent Russia from launching a nuclear second-strike during the opening days of war. He claims that the United States is developing the Prompt Global Strike and Global Missile Defence capabilities for this purpose. The Russians call America's pre-emptive strategy, which relies on naval weapons, the *Massed Missile-Air Strike* (массированный ракетно-авиационный удар, МРАУ) (Полегаев and Алферов, 2015, 3–10). Their concerns are based on lessons learned from America's successful air campaigns in the Gulf War, operation Desert Fox and Kosovo War (Колтюков, 2009, passim; AktZad, 2003, pp. 25–36).

It can be counterargued that America does not seek to undermine the strategic balance or that the United States cannot nullify Russia's nuclear counterthreat because the Kremlin's nuclear forces are too large, dispersed and hardened.

Whatever the truth may be, the Kremlin takes NATO's threat seriously and is devising countermeasures. In the first phase of the Strategic Exercise Zapad 2017, Russian Air Defence reportedly successfully repelled cruise missiles and other air attacks (Mil.ru, 2018).

The threats of the third group consist of rapid technological developments in information technology, unmanned aircraft and autonomous systems. Russian military writing exaggerates these threats. The Kremlin intends to introduce new systems to countervail America's nuclear modernisation based on advanced principles.

President Vladimir Putin reflected the attitude in a recent speech, stressing the importance of artificial intelligence (AI). He contended that "Whoever becomes the leader in this sphere (AI) will become the ruler of the world" (Путин, 2017).

Nuclear and non-nuclear deterrence (containment)

Present-day Russian Military Doctrine stresses that Russia military policy aims to contain and to prevent military conflicts by maintaining its forces in permanent readiness, in a co-ordinated system of political, diplomatic, ideological, informational and economic support. The fundamental principles of strategic containment are deterrence (устрашения), localisation (ограничения) and coercion (принуждения). They complement each other, forming a unified system of strategic deterrence.

Military containment is partitioned into nuclear and conventional categories of strategic offence and defence. *Strategic containment forces* include the following: (a) strategic offensive forces, which consist of land-based intercontinental ballistic missiles (Strategic Missile Troops), strategic bombers and submarine-launched ICBMs. Non-strategic nuclear forces, which are general military formations or units (e.g. army, brigade, fleet), possess tactical nuclear weapons systems and strategic non-nuclear forces. (b) Strategic defence forces include missile launch systems, orbital control systems, missile and space defence systems and air defence (Хряпин *et al.*, 2015, pp. 18–19).

Russian Military Doctrine predicts that nuclear arms will remain the most important factor in preventing nuclear and conventional military conflicts (large-scale and regional wars) (Военная доктрина 2014, II, 16, III, 18–21). Strategic containment systems are divisible into two categories: deterrence based on conventional and nuclear means (Хряпин *et al.*, 2015, p. 19).

Russian Military Doctrine of 1993 states that the Kremlin will not use nuclear weapons against a non-nuclear weapon states, unless they attack Russia in alliance or in co-ordination with a nuclear state. MD 2000 asserts that nuclear weapons serve as deterrents to conventional attacks that imperil the Kremlin.

Military Doctrine 2010 and the current 2014 updated doctrine state that "The Russian Federation reserves the right to use nuclear weapons in response to the armed aggression against it, and/or its allies with nuclear or other weapons of mass destruction. They may also be employed if aggression with conventional weapons against the Russian Federation endangers the existence of the state" (Военная доктрина 2010, III, 22, and 2014, III, 27).

Russian theorists believe that conventional deterrence provides flexible methods for managing rapidly changing situations. *Global containment* is believed to depend on strategic nuclear forces that can threaten aggressors' military-economic potential. *Regional containment* depends on tactical nuclear weapons and non-nuclear strategic conventional weapon systems employed in any war against Russia and its allies (Хряпин *et al.*, 2015, p. 19).

Russian military theorists Sergey Chekinov and Sergey Bogdanov justify the use of asymmetric means as a response to the United States' overwhelming conventional military power (Чекинов and Богданов, 2010, pp. 46–53). "Massed Missile-Air Strikes" are most likely to employ out-of-theatre stand-off weapons. Asymmetric threats against America and Europe may countervail a "Massed Missile-Air Strike" (Полегаев and Алферов, 2015, pp. 3–10) because the threats and counterthreats would be offsetting. The asymmetric option supplements Russia's own stand-off capabilities.

Destroying American and European vital economic infrastructure: power plants, energy supply, traffic nodes and pollution control facilities (dams, nuclear reactors, chemical industry and toxic storage facilities) are examples of feasible asymmetric countermeasures employable by special forces (Чекинов and Богданов, 2010, pp. 46–53).

Russian asymmetric warfighting doctrine disregards Article 56 of the amended 1977 Geneva Convention 1949 banning attacks against vital economic infrastructure: "works or installations containing dangerous forces, namely dams, dykes and nuclear electrical generation shall not be targetable".[3]

Permanent readiness concept

Russia's Armed Forces faced significant problems with troop mobilisation at the beginning of both Chechen wars (1994 and 1999). The deployment of troops to the areas of operation was often significantly delayed and

---

[3]Geneva Conventions, 1949, 1977, Article 56, *Protection of Victims of International Armed Conflicts (Protocol I)*. Russia as the successor of the Soviet Union is a party of Protocol I. America is not a party of PI or PII.

troops were undermanned and poorly equipped (Новичков *et al.*, 1995, passim). After the active phase of Second Chechen War in 2003, Russian Minister of Defence, Sergey Ivanov expressed his dissatisfaction to the Russian Academy of Military Science asserting that " … a battalion was assembled here and a company from there and sent to Chechnya" (Иванов, 2003, p. 4).

According to the 2003 reform programme, often labelled Ivanov's doctrine, armed forces should control military conflicts and peacekeeping operations. Every military district should have the capability to conduct military operations with JOINT formations in local wars[4] and armed conflicts assisted with forces from other military districts (AktZad, 2003, pp. 41–47; Иванов, 2003).

These demands require significant readiness upgrading of Russia's Armed Forces (Иванов, 2003). This was a consequence of the 2008 reform (Макаров, 2010, 24).

There are four grades of readiness in Russia's Armed Forces: permanent (постоянная готовность), elevated (повышенная г.), high threat (военная опасность) and full (полная г.). Troops are supposed to be in states of permanent or elevated readiness. *In permanent readiness,* military units are fully manned, equipped for combat operations on short notice. The notice time varies by military branch. It is only a few minutes for the combat crews of Strategic Missile Troops and Aerospace Forces. Ground Force notice time varies from 1 hour to 24 hours (Макаров, 2010, p. 25).

These readiness requirements are unrealistic. Staffs are not normally at full strength. Some staff members are on vacation, training or missions (Маскин, 2010, pp. 26–30). The conscript system further complicates matters. Most Armed Forces personnel are conscripts, despite attempts to create a contract service system (Barabanov, 2014, p. 105). Drafting for a 1-year term is biannual and conscripts cannot engage in combat until they have completed a couple of months of training. This means that the Ground Forces spend most of their time training conscripts instead of concentrating

---

[4] JOINT formations are in Russian межвидовые группировки войск (сил). lit. Formations of inter-branch troops (forces).

on readiness. Only one or two battalions per brigade (or regiments per division) actually achieve permanent readiness (Барабанов, 2014).

Traditional Russian Doctrinal Views and Principles

Task of military science and military art — laws and principles

Russia has traditionally favoured a scientific approach to war, military and warfighting. After the Napoleonic wars, Russian Emperor Alexander I invited a Swiss general of Napoleon's army, Antoine-Henri Jomini (1779–1869), to establish the Russian General Staff Academy for senior military education and military scientific research. Carl von Clausewitz's *Vom Kriege* (*On War*) provided the core theory (Медемъ, 1836, pp. 138, 162; Rose, 1995, pp. 32–38), even though Jomini was the Academy's founder. Clausewitz became famous in Anglo-Saxon circles after the Franco-Prussian War 1870–1871.

Russian military science today is founded on a "system of knowledge governing the laws, the military-strategic character of war, means of preventing war, war preparedness, and combat methods" (VES, 2007, p. 135).

Combat (*armed struggle*) in contemporary Russian dialectic military thought is co-determined by immutable physical laws and evolving *principles* like "revolutions in military affairs". Laws of force hold invariably, but military commanders have the freedom of action in applying principles (Резниченко, 1966, pp. 74–76).[5]

The means and forms of armed combat, according to the first law, depend on armament, equipment and people. According to the second law, each battle or operation generates an advantage to the party with a greater ability to attack opponents and repel counterstrikes. Fighting power depends on readiness (Савкин, 1972, pp. 131, 146; Михневичъ, 1911).[6]

---

[5] Expression is unchanged in later editions.

[6] Savkin is published also in English: Savkin, V. Y. E. (2002). *The Basic Principles of Operational Art and Tactics (A Soviet View)*, University Press of the Pacific, Honolulu. Nikolay Mikhnevich, a professor of Imperial General Staff Academy, represented the early versions of these laws calling them still principles. He continued his service in the Red Army and his military thought is visible at least in post-second war Soviet and Russian military thought. Mikhnevich referred Napoleon, Clausewitz and Suvorov consequently.

In the Russian military thought, the laws of armed struggle are immutable, but their application is situational. Principles are discretionary and contextual (Резниченко, 1966, pp. 74–76; Воробьёв, 2002, pp. 81–83).

Russian military principles today are rooted in post-war Soviet field manuals and tactical handbooks. Before the Great Patriotic War 1941–1945, Russian theorists were chary of fixed principles of armed struggle (Vigor, 1978, p. 74). Rigid principles were scorned as relics of bourgeois thinking, but they now have been largely resurrected. The following principles dominated thinking military attitudes during the first decade of the new millennium (Воробьёв and Киселёв, 2011; BU, 2010, pp. 12–23; Воробьёв, 2002, pp. 81–291).

Concentration is one of the oldest principles of warfare. It is an aspect of the second law of combat.

Mobility allows forces to seize the day. It corresponds with Suvorov's "pressure of continuous attack" concept.

The principle of *cooperation* is synergistic. It strengthens the effectiveness of armament, equipment and personnel from different units.

Bold *manoeuvre* includes the movement of troops, equipment or firepower. It allows forces to seize initiative, to destroy opponent's battle plans and to win.

Surprise is another classic military principle. History shows that surprise attacks often devastate foes, while casualties are relatively light.

Protection — it is important to prevent high casualties from enemy fire. Protection is a part of the Russian concept of the *comprehensive support for military operations* (VES, 2007, p. 89)[7] and includes reconnaissance, logistics, guarding, etc. Its purpose is to enhance prospects for victory with minimal casualties.

Competent *leadership leverages capabilities.*

Teachings of Suvorov and Lenin

Alexander Suvorov (1729–1800), "the father" of Russia's military, is said to have won 60 battles without ever sustaining a defeat. As a member of a noble military family, he had a long career starting as a private at the age

---

[7]Боевое обеспечение also всесторонне́е обеспечение боя / боевых действий.

of 12 and culminating with the highest rank of Generalissimus, the General of Generals. His teachings remain pertinent, especially his legendary book Наука побеждать (*The Science of Victory*),[8] which succinctly distils the tactical art of war into three principles, or military skills.

The first is *recognition* (гласомер, lit. eye estimation), the ability to swiftly grasp essentials without being befuddled by details. Later Clausewitz used the term *coup d'œil* for the same purpose in *Vom Kriege* (On War) (von Clausewitz, 1976, p. 102). Swift recognition allows competent military leaders to choose the right place to camp, to effectively pursue the enemies, determine best point of attack and anticipate enemy countermanoeuvres.

The second principle is *speed* (быстрота). Suvorov was famous for pacing his troops so that they could advance rapidly and surprise the enemy when required.

The third skill (натиск) is the *pressure of continuous attack* (Lalu, 2014, pp. 29–30). The tenacity of Russian troops fighting doggedly wave-after-wave epitomises the method.

Surorov embodied the daring spirit of Russian military leaders. They drive brave Russian soldiers to risk their lives and careers first with the enemy and then with their commanders. Empress Catherine II said about Suvorov: "Winners are not court martialed — all of them are "heroes" (Суворов, 2001, pp. 551–552; Но ... победителя не судят, и все — «герои»). This comment refers to an occasion where Suvorov lost a risky attack, but later achieved a great victory. Superiors can be disregarded, but only if gamblers win the next battle.

Lenin had strong opinions on the *Nature of War*. He accepted Clausewitz's idea that "war was a continuation of politics with other means",[9] stressing the importance of violence (Ленин, 1969, p. 316). It is

---

[8] Suvorov's book is not available in English. Many of his quotations are mentioned in *The Art of Victory* (1965) by Philip Longworth and *Train Hard, Fight Easy: The Legacy of A. V. Suvorov and His 'Art of Victory'* by Bruce W. Menning.

[9] "Der Krieg ist eine bloße Fortsetzung der Politik *mit* anderen Mitteln." Clausewitz does not mention violence by other means alone. A careful reader should also note that Clausewitz used the word *mit* anderen Mitteln, which should be translated *with* other means, not *by* other means as it is translated on common English translation as *On War* translated by Howard and Paret (Princeton University Press, 1976, 87); Holmes (2014).

the Soviet and present Russian custom to cite Clausewitz, with Lenin's qualifications. The Clausewitzian perception of the nature of war is the starting point for Marxist theoretical thinking on the subject. This heritage still dominates Russian military thought in the areas of security and war. Dialectical thought portrays struggle as a battle to the death between opposing sides where concessions are perilous. One must kill or be killed. The attitude persists today in Russia's management of its relations with the west after Crimea's annexation, in the continuing East Ukrainian conflict and Syrian operations where war is regarded as a successful tool for achieving political ends (Lalu, 2016).

Correlation of forces

One very typical characteristic of Russian military thinking is the careful calculation of the correlation of forces (COF), which according to the Russian military encyclopaedia "results from comparing (matching) quantities and qualities of forces and means.... The estimation of COF permits informed operational decisions" (VES, 2007, p. 681, соотношение сил и средств; Thomas, 2016, pp. 92–93). Russian military histories often stress the importance of the correlation of forces for planning decisive battles (Колтюков, 2006, passim).

Soviet-era methodological handbooks view mathematical methods as effective tools for assessing combat power, defining combat possibilities, favourable military options and developing scientific armed force development. However, the numerical results generated by mathematical methods are too unreliable for practical military purposes (Шавров and Галкин, 1977, pp. 372–397). Russian military publications report the results of mathematical modelling in accordance with the second law of war fighting, but officers are expected to use their judgement in weighing COF statistics.

Forecasting

Russian military theorists believe that the broad contours of armed engagement are foreseeable and can be forecast (предвидение).

Forecasting is an integral part of military planning and decision-making. According to the Russian military encyclopaedia, planners should estimate foreseeable advances in military theory and practice, as well as changes in the strategic, operational or tactical environment (VES, 2007, p. 571, предвидение; Thomas, 2016, pp. 52–58, 92–93).

Forecasting is partly art, and partly science. The art depends on intuition, common sense and military experience. The science is based on the laws of armed struggle, scientific methods and computation (extrapolation, expert estimation, war gaming, command and staff exercises, etc.). Dialectical and Clausewitzian thinking strongly support Russian military forecasting.

Soviet military theorists adopted American operations research methods in the early 1950s. They improved them in 1960s and early 1970s, especially in the area of air defence theory by applying futuristic, mathematical and composite techniques. One of the most notable writings (Concept, Algorithm, Decision 1972) predicted that the "automation of routine aspects of decision making would prove to be less important than automated creative work. Creativity is particularly vital because it precedes technology, just as art precedes craftsmanship" (Druzhinin and Kontorov, 1975, p. 295). Soviet theories for the most part typically were far ahead of operational practice in the 1970s (Defense Intelligence Agency, 2017, pp. 87–90). Today computers are widely available, and networking technologies connect data collections, analysts and planners in ways that facilitate cybernetic collective decision-making. These capabilities are now in use in the Russian command and control system (see Leadership and Organization section in this chapter.).

Svechin's tactics, operations and strategy

Alexandr Svechin (1874–1938) wrote the classic primer on the Russian art of war. His *Strategija* (1927) set forth the fundamentals of tactics, operational art and strategy (VES, 2007, p. 139). He asserted that although the art of war is unitary, it is useful to analyse tactics, operational art and strategy separately. "Tactics addresses short term battlefield war-fighting." Operational art deals with the same problems (Свечин, 1927, pp. 14–17),[10] but from a longer perspective taking account of tactical creativity in protracted engagements (Свечин, 1927, p. 14). The purpose of strategy is to define the character of future war, the form of operations, scale, tension and ends. Strategy allows military authorities "to dictate the main lines of operational art ..." guided by politics (Свечин, 1927, pp. 15–16).

In Russian military thought, the unity of the art of war should never be compartmentalised. Politics does not "die" when war breaks out. Strategists need the full picture.

Present views on repelling massed missile-air strikes

Russian military theorists fear a pre-emptive NATO surprise first strike that obliterates the Kremlin's retaliatory option and are concerned that a regional war could start with surprise aerospace attack against vital military and civil targets.

Russia's Defence Minister, Sergey Shoigu in a televised broadcast to The National Defence Control Centre warned that if NATO prepares an attack, Soviet's computers will detect it with 90% confidence, and our peacetime forces will be promptly dispersed (Давыдов, 2016).

Highly publicised snap readiness drills are intended to dissuade the West from launching a surprise first strike (РИА Новости, 2013a).[11]

These snap readiness drills put troops on alert and train them how to rapidly leave their garrison, transit to staging areas, protect transport against diversion or air attacks and concentrate troops in the new operations hundreds or even thousands of kilometres away. The combat readiness of the troops is assessed in live-fire exercises. Strategic Missile

---

[10]Svechin's strategy is also published in English by East View Publications (1992). Svechin was the first to define the concept of operational art.

[11]This snap readiness drill of Russian Eastern Military District included formations and units from the Central Military District, Pacific Fleet, Long-Range Aviation and Military Transport Aviation and totalled 160,000 soldiers, of whom 1,000 were mobilised from the reserve. Before this drill, Russian armed forces were informed to have conducted similar but smaller exercises in the Western Military District.

Forces also practice dispersing and protecting mobile ground-based missile-launching systems (РИА Новости, 2013b, 2013c; Владыкин, 2013).

Russia's first response to a massed aerospace attack will be a prompt missile counterstrike, probably carried out with conventional precision-guided medium-range ballistic missiles (Iskander-M) and cruise missiles from ground, maritime and aerial platforms (Iskander-K, Kalibr, H-101 and H-555) (Полегаев and Алферов, 2015; Гареев 2010, p. 14).

After evasive action, troops located near the borders will defend against enemy attack from all directions. The main task of the Russian Armed forces will be to localise and de-escalate the conflict. Both nuclear and conventional deterrence means will be employed for this purpose. Long- and medium-range precision-guided weapon systems might also be used for area denial to prevent enemy reinforcements and disrupt logistic supply chains (Полегаев and Алферов, 2015).

According to the Russian theorists, there are three ways to deter and/or contain an enemy attack with modern weapon systems. First, the Kremlin must create systems that allow it to defeat superior forces with acceptable casualties by counterstriking in distant theatres. Second, it must create highly effective air and space defence system against enemy massive missile and air strikes, preventing heavy losses to the Russian infrastructure and armed forces. Third, it must devise asymmetric options that daunt foes and expedite their capitulation (Полегаев and Алферов, 2015).

Gerasimov's doctrine?

Russia's annexation of Crimea is often said to have been presaged in a February 2013 speech given by General Valery Gerasimov (in office 2012–), Russia's Chief of the General Staff (Герасимов, 2013a). The speech is sometimes described as the Gerasimov doctrine (Герасимов, 2013b; Thomas, 2017), which is an overstatement. Actually, Gerasimov discussed general trends, forms and methods of internal conflict. His key point was that conflicts are best resolved diplomatically, buttressed by force. Non-military methods in his view often are the most effective. This attitude appears to reflect the conviction of Russia's General Staff.

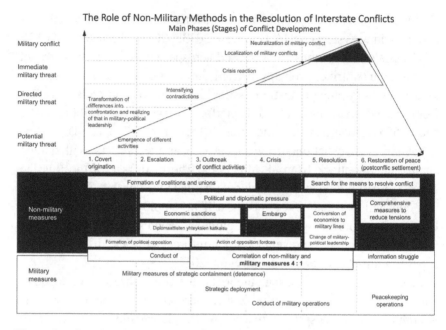

Figure 1:   Gerasimov's views on interstate conflict resolution (Герасимов, 2013b, p. 25).

Gerasimov's views on conflict resolution are illustrated in Figure 1.

His speech also contained other interesting points. Information war tends to escalate in stages. Wars are no longer declared,[12] and battles may commence before strategic deployments have been completed.[13] Gerasimov also observed that warfighting has changed. It is more likely now to entail remote exchanges rather than involve pitched, large, close-contact battles, and he claimed that information technology is flattening strategic, operational and tactical levels of war. Gerasimov's speech

---

[12] Actually, most of the western commentators did not notice that Gerasimov used here citation from Georgi Isserson's study on German invasion of Poland in 1939. Isserson's portrait is seen in the AVN version of Gerasimov's speech. See Иссерсон (1940, p. 30): "Wars are no longer declared. They just start with the armed forces deployed beforehand."

[13] Actually, this is a Russian observation from the military actions taken by the US and UK forces in 1990s, precisely in the Operation of Desert Fox 1998; see Колтюков (2009, pp. 61–71).

foreshadowed General Surovikin's comprehensive analysis of future military operations.

Surovikin's proposals

Colonel General Sergey Surovikin (commander of Russia's Aerospace Forces) and his co-author Colonel Yuri Kuleshov (Air Force Academy) developed a set of tasks for Russia's armed forces in *Voyennaya mysl'*. First, and foremost, they recommend that Russia maintain information superiority over its adversaries. The traditional tasks of Russia's armed forces like border defence and seizing territory are at the bottom of the list (Суровикин and Кулешов, 2017).[14]

Surovikin and Kuleshov also endorsed blockading maritime passages, creating no-fly zones and asymmetric tactics. The latter includes shock-and-awe operations, disrupting sea transport and inflicting environmental disasters on foes. The combination of these methods is comprehensive (комплексная борьба с противником). It integrates strategy of comprehensive civil–military actions with combined arms warfighting (Суровикин and Кулешов, 2017).

Surovikin and Kuleshov's approach is compatible with "hybrid warfare", even though Russia has denied these tactics. The Kremlin's broad approach to military forms of conflict resolution call into question Colonel General Gerasimov's contention that Moscow really believes non-military solutions are four times more effective than military coercion.

Leadership and Organisation[15]

Command and control

Russian military defines the main principles of command and control as follows:

---

[14] Actually, Surovikin proposed this task-list for the Russian Armed Forces already in January 2014; see Суровикин (2014, p. 41). At the time of publication, Surovikin was the commander of Russia's Eastern Military District.

[15] www.mil.ru, структура.

1. **Single authority** and **personal accountability**.
2. **Centralisation**: Management at all levels is subordinate to a single unitary authority, but subordinates are expected to take initiatives when appropriate.
3. **Resolute** decision-making.
4. **Flexibility** in fluid situations.
5. **Thoroughness and creativity** (VES, 2007, p. 748; *Управление войсками (силами)*).

Effective command and control requires redundancy, geographical dispersion, reliability and security (encryption) (Yarynich, 2003, p. 154; see also Defense Intelligence Agency, 2017, p. 26).

President

The President of the Russian Federation is the supreme commander of Armed Forces and other military troops. The President of the RF makes all decisions regarding the employment of nuclear weapons. The Federation Council approves special uses of Russia's Armed Forces outside the territory of the Russian Federation (Об обороне, 1996, Статья 4–5; Военная доктрина, 2014, III, 27).

Ministry of defence

The ministry of defence implements the President's directives and coordinates military activities.

The ministry of defence is part of the Armed Forces (Mil.ru, 2018; VES, 2007, 186; *Генеральный штаб вс рф*).

General staff

The main task of the General Staff (GS) of Russian Armed Forces is strategic defence planning and state security. It oversees the Armed Forces and the military organisation of Russia as a whole. The GS coordinates all Federal executive bodies in the interests of ensuring the country's defence and security. Its power was broadened by the presidential decree in 2013 to reflect the changing character of the armed struggle. The GS is now tasked to develop *The Defence Plan of the Russian Federation*. This document, drafted together with the other executive organisations, constructs the outline for the comprehensive defence of the whole society, covering the time, direction, place, forces, means and resources for the wartime *State Military Organisation* as illustrated in Figure 2 (Герасимов, 2014, p. 17).

The National Defence Control Centre (NDCC) is a part of the General Staff. It was founded in 2014. Its "purpose is to control the centralised combat of the Russian armed forces, to enable the day-to-day management of the Russian Air Force and the Navy, collection, generalisation and analysis of information on global and domestic strategic trends in times of peace and war". The Control Centre has a key role in the management and coordination of Russian military and civilian defence. It has three subdivisions: *The Control Centre of Strategic Nuclear Forces* oversees the C2 of Nuclear weapons. The *Command and Control Centre* monitors global

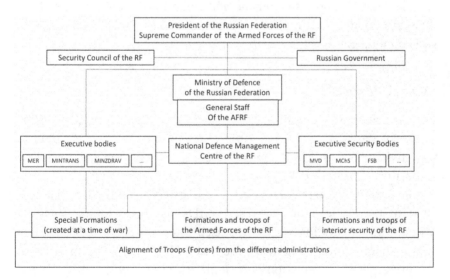

Figure 2: Management System of the Russian State Military Organization (Герасимов, 2014, p. 17).

Notes: MER, Ministry of Economic Development of the Russian Federation; MINTRANS, Ministry of Transport of the Russian Federation; MINZDRAV, Ministry of Healthcare of the Russian Federation; MVD, Ministry of the Interior of the Russian Federation; MChS, Ministry of Civil Defence, Emergencies and Disaster Relief of the Russian Federation; FSB, Federal Security Service.

relations to anticipate the development of threats to Russia and its allies in order to guarantee the operational control of Russian Armed Force and other military organisations. The *Day-to-day Actions Management Centre* manages the state of military organisation and coordinates the actions of Federal Executive bodies, which are not under the command and control of MOD (Mil.ru, 2018).

The Russian National Defence *Control Centre* (NDCC) is a sophisticated information infrastructure. Sergey Shoigu, the Minister of Defence, boasted that its supercomputers are the most powerful in the world. The information system of NDCC is based on the Astra Linux Operating System. It allows Russian designers to fine-tune the source codes according to their needs, without the assistance of foreign software companies. The Russian MOD announced at the end of 2017 that it would adopt Astra Linux on all its computers (Рамм and Круглов, 2018). NDCC controls subordinate regional and territorial defence command centres (Владыкин 2014; Мясников 2014).

The NDCC supports command and control and its algorithms affect Russian military thought. The NDCC underscores Russia's comprehensive commitment to national defence.

Military districts

The system of Russian military districts (MDs) was created in 1860s as part of the Minister of War Dmitry Milyutin's reforms. The empire was divided into 15 MDs linking the centre with the local civilian authorities (Mil.ru, 2018). MDs are Land Force commands. During the Soviet period, the number of military districts varied. After the collapse of the Soviet Union, Russia's MDs decreased to six. Russia's Military administration was reorganised into four MDs in 2010. MDs are the main *military administrative units*. They operate on the territorial principle in conjunction with *joint strategic commands* (OSK).[16]

---

[16]Объединённое стратегическое командование (ОСК) — Joint strategic command. Most of the Western sources (FOI, 2016; MilBal, 2017; Main, 2017) use the term Operational Strategic Command — present Russian term differs as *объединённое* means *joint*.

The OSK, American-style unified combat commands, have operational command over all conventional formations and troops of the Russian Armed Forces and under some circumstances other military organisations, with the exception of Airborne and Transport Aviation formations (РИА Новости, 2010). The new Joint Strategic Command "North" was created in December 2014. This command covers the large territories and waters of Russian North-west and most of Russia's Arctic islands (РИА Новости, 2014). Russian military districts are shown in Figure 3.

The new Joint Strategic Command (OSK) role of military districts highlights the Kremlin's commitment to Russian military principles of command and control. The subordination of all conventional Armed Force formations and units to the commander of MD exemplifies the concept of single authority, personal accountability, centralisation, operability and organisation. The relationship of other military organisations to MD is less consistent (Main, 2017; Миранович and Поч и нюк, 2012).

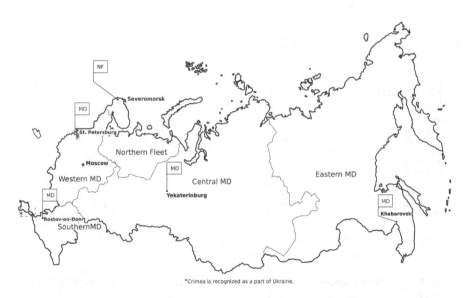

*Crimea is recognized as a part of Ukraine.

Figure 3: Russian military districts and the location of their headquarters (FOI, 2016).

It is likely that subordination of other military forces to a MD will be extend in wartime.

Service and separate troop branches

Russia's Armed Forces are divided into three service branches: Ground Forces, Aerospace Forces and Navy. It also has two separate troop branches: Strategic Missile and Airborne Forces and Special Operations Forces. The total manpower of the Russian Armed Forces is estimated as 900,000 soldiers (MilBal, 2018, p. 192). The organisation of the Russian Armed Forces is displayed in Figure 4.

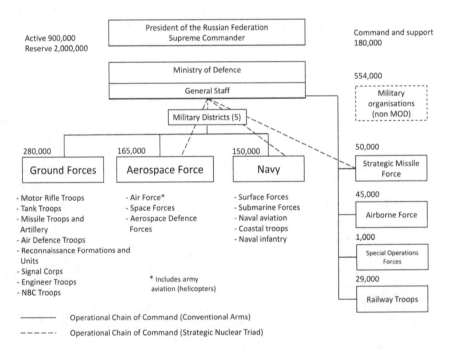

Figure 4:   The organisation of the Russian Armed Forces (Mil.ru, 2018; MilBal, 2018, p. 192).

Ground forces

The Ground Forces (Сухопутные войска, СВ) is the largest and most diversified Russian military organisation. The Ground Forces is the oldest branch of the military. It comprised 80% of the battle force of the Red Army during World War II. Today, Russian Ground Forces' formations account for one-third of the Russian military personnel. Offensively, its formations are capable of destroying enemy forces, conquering territories and carrying out strikes into the depth of enemy's rear. Defensively, Russia's Ground Forces can repel enemy offensives and airborne and landing operations. No other branch of military can hold and control territories.

The mission of the Russian Ground Forces is to repel enemy aggression in the continental theatres of military operations and to protect the territorial integrity and national interests of the Russian Federation. It is entrusted with the following tasks:

In peacetime Ground Forces maintain their combat potential and improve their combat and mobilisation readiness to repel local attacks. Weapons and equipment stockpiles are part of this readiness. Ground Forces participate in peace support operations and provide assistance in times of emergency. *In periods of military threat*, the main tasks of Ground Force are improving combat and mobilisation readiness, strengthening their combat capabilities and gathering intelligence information. Training will be increased and national borderlines secured by the formations and troops preparing their first defensive operations. *In wartime,* the most important battle tasks of the Ground Forces include fulfilling the plan for strategic deployment, localising military conflicts and repulsing aggressors if necessary — through the total mobilisation of reserve formations and military units. Ground Forces' air defence units participate in the repulsing aerospace attacks. The combined arms armies of Ground Forces contribute to joint operations. Ground Forces play an important role in territorial defence together with the other domestic security organisations (Mil.ru, 2018).

The distribution of Russian Ground Forces formations is displayed in Figure 5.

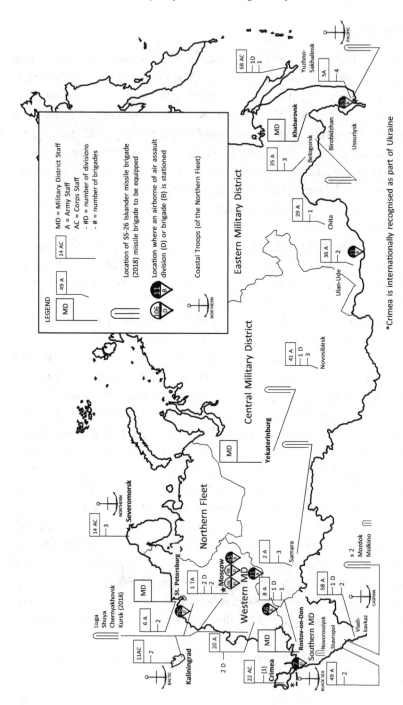

Figure 5:   Distribution of Russian Ground Force formations in 2018 (FOI, 2016; BMPD, 2018; MilKavkaz, 2018; MilBal, 2018).

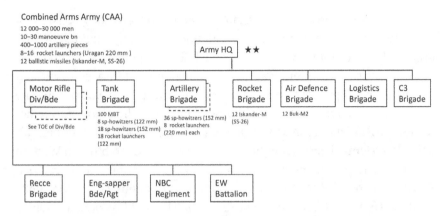

Figure 6:   Table of organisation and equipment of Russian Ground Forces' combined arms army (FOI, 2016, p. 28; MilKavkaz, 2018; Grau and Bartles, 2016, p. 30).

Units and formations

Russian Ground Forces are combined arms armies (CAA), brigades and divisions. Each military district has 2–4 CAAs, consisting of several (1–2) divisions and (1–4) brigades, artillery and missile brigades as well as communications, air defence and logistics brigades depicted in Figure 6. One of the goals of the military reform of 2008–2009 was to restructure army organisations away from "heavy" divisions to brigades. However, in the spring of 2013, Russian Ground Forces re-established two divisions, 4th Guards Tank Division and 2nd Guards Motor Rifle Brigade. One tank division and four mechanised divisions were re-established in 2016 (РИА НовостИ, 2018; Mil.ru, 2018).

According to the supreme commander of the Russian Ground Forces, both division and brigade organisations will be retained in the future. During 2012–2017, Russia created seven combined arms divisions.[17] They have greater striking force and more firepower, making them suitable for a variety of tasks (Mil.ru, 2018).

---

[17]Western MD: 4th Guards Tank Division, 2nd Guards Mechanized Division, 3rd Motor Rifle Division, 144. Motor Rifle Division; Southern MD: 150th Motor Rifle Division, 42nd Motor Rifle Division; Central MD: 90th Guards Tank Division.

The fighting power of Russian divisions and brigades consists of manoeuvre units, i.e. regiments or battalions. Typically, one motor rifle division has four infantry regiments and 1–2 tank regiments. It should be noted that Russian Ground Forces have remarkable artillery support making them less dependent on air support. The artillery, rocket and missile units of CAA supplement Russia's Ground Forces artillery power. Another feature of Russian organisations is the presence of layered land-base air defence systems. These strengths reduce Russia's vulnerability to Western air force-massed precision strikes, close air support and air superiority. A new feature of Russian Ground Force organisations is its UAV units (FOI, 2016, pp. 28–30; MilKavkaz, 2018). The table of organisation of equipment (TOEs) of Motor Rifle Division and Motor Rifle Brigade are shown in Figures 7 and 8.

The actual battle and firepower of Russian Ground Forces is overstated in the TOE tables. The combined arms army TOE is by nature flexible, new divisions and even brigades are still reorganising and it will take years before their infrastructure and manning reach the strength of TOE tables. However, the larger structural challenge is that the

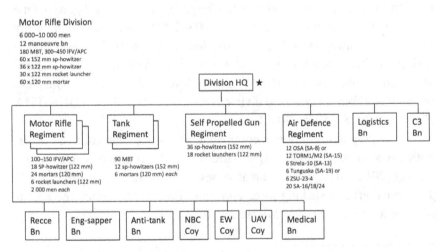

Figure 7:   TOE of Motor Rifle Division (FOI, 2016, pp. 28–30; MilKavkaz, 2018).

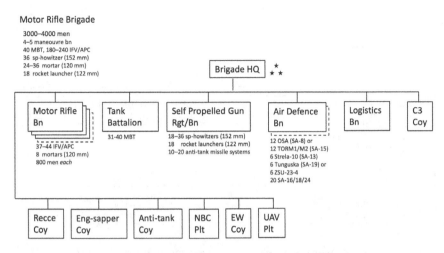

Figure 8: TOE of Motor Rifle Brigade (variant) (FOI, 2016, pp. 28–30; MilKavkaz, 2018; Указ_Президента, 2017, p. 184; Худолеев, 2015, p. 43; Sutyagin and Bronk, 2017, pp. 28–30; Grau and Bartles, 2016, pp. 31, 210–211, 224).

manning of the Russian Armed Forces relies on conscript service. Russian divisions and brigades play an important peacetime role as training centres for conscripts with a 1-year period of service. Since the conscripts are called twice a year, in the fall and spring, the army formations and troops never reach their full personnel strength of trained soldiers. Only soldiers who have been trained for at least several months may be assigned for combat tasks. Due to undermanning, the Russian armed forces have had to use Battalion Tactical Groups (BTG) instead of full-fledged brigades and divisions. BTG operations may vary depending on troop availability. Russian Ground Forces Commander-in-Chief Colonel General Oleg Salyukov claimed in 2015 that each tactical formation has 1–2 BTGs fully manned with contracted soldiers, and according to the plans, each military district will have an additional full brigade in readiness in 2021 (Худолеев, 2015; Sutyagin and Bronk, 2017, pp. 22–23; Герасимов, 2018). To achieve this goal, Russia's military increased the number of contract service personnel. An estimate of the TOE of BTG is presented in Figure 9.

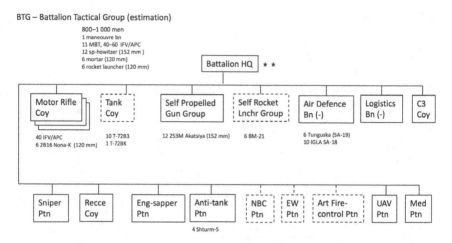

Figure 9:   Battalion Tactical Group (Fiore, 2017; Герасимов, 2018).

Airborne forces

Along with the Strategic Missile Forces, the Airborne Forces is an independent branch of the Russian Armed Forces. The highly mobile air assault or paratrooper units of Airborne Forces are designed to flank the adversary by air and to attack its rear, disrupting the command and control of troops and destroying precision weapon systems. They can impede the manoeuvre and deployment of enemy reserves, breaking its logistics and communications. Landing operations may also be used to protect flanks and for counterlanding purposes. The Russian Airborne Forces are considered as the General Staff of the Russian Armed Forces' spearhead. Traditionally, they have been used to rapidly deploy force in the military conflicts or for crisis management (FOI, 2016, p. 36; VES, 2007, pp. 150–151).

Divisions of the Russian Airborne Forces have a unified structure and are fully deployed in the TOC illustrated in Figure 10. The distribution of the Russian Airborne troops is shown in Figure 5. In air assault divisions, one of the battalions of each regiment is deployable by parachutes together with their heavy equipment (Денисов and Ленин, 2007).

The Ilyushin Il-76, the workhorse of the Russian Military Transport Aviation (VTA) used for parachute droppings, is capable of dropping four heavy equipment units (infantry fighting vehicles, trucks of guns) or three units with 20 soldiers (Airwar.ru, 2018). About half of VTA's 80 Il-76,

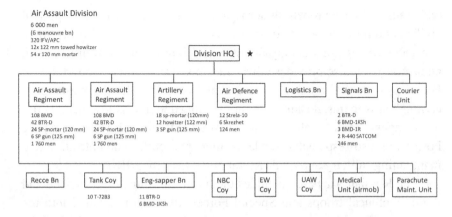

Figure 10:   Air Assault Division (MilKavkaz, 2018).

around 40 planes, could occasionally be dedicated to landing operations. One or perhaps two battalion landing operations per division could be carried out during a campaign.

Russia has 45,000 airborne troops, over 60% are contracted (professional). By 2021, the number of airborne troops is planned to be increased to 60,000, all contracted (MilKavkaz, 2018; MilBal, 2018, p. 199; FOI, 2016, p. 36).

Although the last Russian parachute landing operations in the combat were carried out in 1942 and 1943 without noteworthy success (Гончаров, 2003),[18] Russia seems confident about the readiness, professionalism and air mobility of its Airborne Forces.

Aerospace forces

Air and space defence were centralised in 2015 into one organisation of the *Aerospace Forces of Russia* (VKS). Its main branches are the Air Force, the Space Forces and the Aerospace Defence Forces. VKS has a

---

[18] Parachute landings were part of the operation of Vyazma 1942 and the Battle of Dnieper 1943. Both landings encountered major problems (organization, scattering of landed troops and air strike in the departure airfield). Due to these known problems and risks, airborne troops were used mainly as light infantry during the Great Patriotic War. In the Manchurian operation (1945), Soviet airborne troops were airlifted to the Manchurian and Korean airports without parachute dropping.

wide range of tasks: repelling aerospace threats and protecting important civilian and military targets from enemy aerospace strikes. The Air Force is capable of engaging enemy facilities and forces with conventional and nuclear arms. It also provides other branches with aviation support. Space Forces provide the supreme command and control with information concerning ballistic missile launches and warning about missile attack. Its fire units engage enemy ballistic missile warheads around Moscow. Space Forces are also responsible for launching spacecraft and controlling and maintaining military and dual-use satellites (Mil.ru, 2018).

The Russian Air Force includes the Aviation, Antiaircraft Missile and Radio-Technical troops and Special Forces. Aviation is divided into the long-range, frontline, military transport and army aviation. One of the goals of military reform of the 2008 was to ensure aviation support for ground force operations. Today, each military district including the Nordic Fleet has an Air Force and Air Defence Army (BMPD, 2018; MilBal, 2017).

Russian air defence relies heavily on anti-aircraft missile systems, which are in continuous readiness to repel aerospace attacks.[19] During the Soviet era, air defence was deployed in deep echelons along the borders. After the Soviet collapse when possibilities for the deep echeloning vanished, Russia tried to fill the gap with modern anti-aircraft missile systems. The newest S-400 (SA-21 Growler) system has been deployed around Moscow and other important cities and along Russia's borders (Mil.ru, 2018; FOI, 2016; MilBal, 2018; BMPD, 2018).

Traditionally, the Moscow area air defence was nicknamed "Golden Ring", which refers to the circle of ancient cities surrounding Moscow. It employed special air and missile defence formations. The 1st Air and Space Defence Army (ASDA) has been responsible for Moscow's air defence since the formation of VKS in 2015. Its subunits, two air defence divisions, are equipped with S-400 (SA-21 Growler) and Pantsir-S1 (SA-22 Greyhound) missile systems and third-generation S-300 (SA-10 Grumble) missile systems of the various types. The 4th Air Defence Division (ADD) covers the capital in the North-western sector

---

[19]This function is stressed in terminology: when an anti-aircraft unit receives new weapon systems, it is put in "combat-alert duty" (боевое дежурство).

and the 5th ADD covers the South-eastern sector. S-400 is an effective very long-range air defence system (maximum radius 400 kilometres and height 35 kilometres). According to Jane, the (40N6) missile with a range of 400 kilometres was not yet in operation in 2018 (Jane's, 2018). Pantsir-S1 systems are usually deployed in the vicinity of S-400 systems to give close aerial protection. At the end of 2017, the Moscow area was defended with eight air defence missile regiments. Five were equipped with S-400 systems. Altogether, there are 10 battalions — 80 missile launchers and in theory 320 are launch-ready. The anti-ballistic missile defence of 1st ASDA is carried out by A-135 (SH-08, BM-3) systems. A total of 68 silo-based missiles have been deployed around Moscow since 1995 (Mil.ru, 2018; FOI, 2016; MilBal, 2018; BMPD, 2018).

The distribution of the Russian Air Force and Air Defence Units is shown in Figure 11.

Air operations were limited during the military conflict with Ukraine. Russia and Ukraine have reliable ground-based air defences. Russia has refrained from suppressing Ukraine's air defences to camouflage its support for separatists.

Personnel of the Russian Aerospace Forces spend their time maintaining their aircraft and training. Russia tested this investment in its Syrian campaign September 2015. The intensity of the air operations has remained at a high level for over for 2 years, even though Russia has twice announced the completion of its campaign. The Russian Air Force also has been able to increase the intensity of the combat sorties quickly in response to the political and military needs. Russian resupply of munitions is adequate, and pilots from several aviation units are capable of carrying out combat sorties (MilBal, 2017, pp. 109–120; Барабанов *et al.*, 2016, p. 187).[20]

Russia's Air Force has gained experience using the ISTAR-cycle, essential for effective air-to-ground operations. Satellites, UAVs, special operation forces and tactical air controllers guiding aircraft and their munitions onto targets have performed well. Russia has used their air asset flexibly. In addition to the 30–44 combat aircraft deployed in the

---

[20]The number of combat sorties has been 30–100 per day with an average of 30.

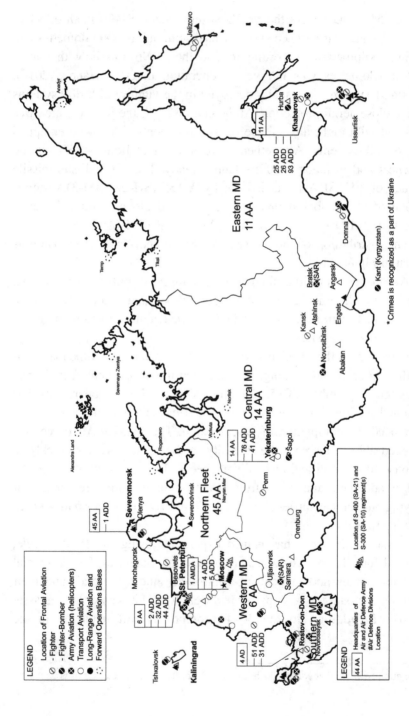

Figure 11: Russian air force and air defence units (MilBal, 2018; FOI, 2016; BMPD, 2018; MilKavkaz, 2018; Барабанов *et al.*, 2016).

Khmeymim Air Base (Барабанов *et al.*, 2016, pp. 106–120),[21] the aircraft of Long-Range Aviation (Tu-95, Tu-160) were used for precision strikes using air-launched cruise missiles or cost-effective unguided bombs (Tu-22M3) (Барабанов *et al.*, 2016, pp. 106–120; Герасимов, 2017). Su-34 fighter-bomber, which has the ability to loiter above the battle area, provides reliable laser-guided fire support using KAB-500S precision bombs (MilBal, 2017, p. 188).

Russian professional soldiers from high-ranking generals commanding military districts, armies and divisions; pilots; and the personnel of UAV units have had combat tours in Syria, giving them experience using modern air power (Mil.ru, 2018).[22]

Navy

The Navy (Военно-Морской Флот, ВМФ) provides armed defence for Russia's global interests. It conducts military operations in the sea and ocean theatres. Russia's Navy is capable of delivering nuclear strikes against enemy ground targets; destroying fleet groups at ports and at sea; disrupting enemy ocean and sea communications; protecting its maritime transport; assisting Land Force operations and naval landings; participating in the repulsing enemy amphibious assault forces; and performing other tasks (Mil.ru, 2018).

The Russian Navy includes surface forces, submarine forces, maritime aviation and coastal troops. The main tasks of surface forces are to ensure that submarines are able to leave combat areas and return to their bases; to transport and cover landing forces; to lay sea mines and carry out mine countermeasures; and to protect Russia's sea communications (Mil.ru, 2018).

---

[21] The initial inventory deployed by Hmeymim included 12 Su-34M, 12 Su-25SM, 4 Su-34, 4 Su-30SM, Il-20M1, 12 Mi-24P and 5 Mi-8AMTSh. The inventory was later reinforced by 4 Su-34 and 4 Su-35S and some Mi-28 and Ka-52. The number fluctuates as needed.

[22] Army Gen Gerasimov mentioned that all of the current commanders of MDs have been deployed in the Syrian campaign.

Russian Submarine Forces consist of nuclear missile submarines serving strategic purposes as a part of the Russian Nuclear Triad, nuclear multipurpose submarines and diesel–electric submarines. Their main tasks are destroying important enemy ground targets; submarines, aircraft carriers and other surface ships; attacking convoys; repelling landing forces; carrying out maritime reconnaissance and providing target acquisition for Russian strike forces; destroying off-shore oil and gas production systems; landing reconnaissance or special operations forces on hostile coasts and laying sea mines. The website of Russian MoD stresses the uniqueness of Russia's submarine forces. They are capable of covert actions in any oceanic aquatory, delivering nuclear strikes on important enemy military targets and conducting operations against enemy submarines and surface vessels (Mil.ru, 2018).

The task of the *Russian Naval Aviation* is to search and destroy enemy combat forces including fleets, landing detachments and transport convoys in the sea and in bases; protecting Russia's fleet against air strikes; destroying enemy aircraft and cruise missiles; conducting maritime reconnaissance and providing target acquisition for Russian strike forces. Naval Aviation can also be used for electronic warfare, combating enemy air transportation and SAR. Functionally, Naval Aviation consists of maritime missile carriers and anti-ship, fighter, reconnaissance and many other auxiliary aircraft based on airfields and aircraft carriers (Mil.ru, 2018).

Russian *Coastal Troops* protect the fleet and other troops, people and important coastal assets from enemy fleet and landing force attacks and cooperate with ground forces in littoral engagements. Coastal Troops include *Coastal Missile and Artillery Troops* and *Naval Infantry Troops* (MilBal, 2018).

The Russian Navy has four major fleets (Northern, Pacific, Black Sea and Baltic) and the Caspian Sea Flotilla. Fleets are under the operational command and control of the respective military district (OSK), but they receive orders from the Navy Staff (St. Petersburg). Russia's limited sea-based operations reflect its limited basing possibilities. Each Navy has only two major ports — only the Pacific Fleet has wide access, but the Russian Far East is distant from central Russia (MilBal, 2018; Defense Intelligence Agency, 2017, pp. 67–68).

The distribution of Russia's fleets and vessel is displayed in Figure 12.

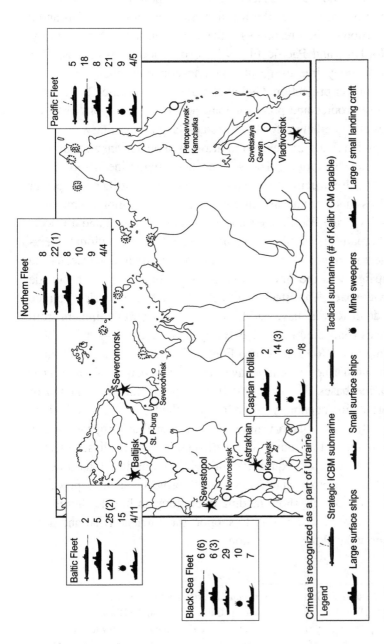

Figure 12:   Russian fleets and their vessel distribution in 2018.

Notes: The dislocation of fleet headquarters is marked with a star and additional bases with a roundel. The Artic presence of the Navy is shown as dotted roundels: (1) Novaya Zemlya, (2) Alexandra Land, (3) Severnaya Zemlya, (4) Kotelny Island, (5) Tiksi, (6) Wrangel Island, (7) Mys Schmidta and (8) Anadyr (MilBal, 2018; MilKavkaz, 2018). According to the Minister of Defence, Caspian Flotilla will be moved to the port of Dagestan (Mil.ru, 2018, 2 April 2018).

Note: Crimea is recognised as a part of Ukraine.

The Northern and Pacific Fleets are the most powerful. Their nuclear ICBM submarines are part of the Russian Strategic Nuclear Triad and a significant portion of their resources is devoted to ensuring their usability. Only the Northern and Pacific Fleets have free access to oceans. This allows them to deny free usage of seas and constrain enemy maritime transport and power projection. Global climate change, which has opened the northern sea routes and ports for long periods of transport, provides opportunities and challenges for the Russian Navy and military.

Other Russian fleets are devoted to littoral sea operations and supporting Land Forces operations. The surface and submarine assets of all Russian fleets can participate in long-range precision strikes and power projection. Russia's latest naval cruise missile system, Kalibr, is employed on all fleets (excl. the Pacific Fleet), as shown in Figure 12 and all fleets (excl. the Caspian Sea Flotilla) have participated in international operations to protect merchant shipping against piracy in the Indian Ocean. The Syrian campaign was the first notable Russian force projection outside the post-Soviet space. The Black Sea fleet, and the two other fleets on the European side of Russia, have had to purchase transport equipment from foreign sources (Барабанов *et al.*, 2016, pp. 122–132.).

According to the Russian Armed Forces TV channel, Russia's Akula-class attack submarines recently have carried out patrol missions near CONUS marine bases (Пешков, 2018). One particular phenomenon of the power projection capability of the Russian Navy (and Russian logistic system as well) is the inland waterway system of the European part of Russia, which allows the transfer of small vessels, such as diesel–electric submarines and corvettes equipped with Kalibr missiles (Давыденко, 2010).[23] Although the Russian Navy cannot project adequate power to support and carry out off-shore landing operations on hostile shores, the Kremlin has revived its capability to support the Nuclear Triad and deny potential enemy naval force projection.

---

[23] *The Unified Deep Water System of European Russia* is a system of inland waterways in Russia linking the White Sea, the Baltic Sea, the Caspian Sea and the Black Sea. Waterway is available except during icy winter conditions for the ships having depth with a maximum draft of 4 metres and beam of 17 metres. Buyan-M-class corvettes (draft 2.6 m and beam 11 m) are then deployable through the system.

Long-range precision weaponry

The Soviets recognised the importance of precision-guided conventional weapons in the 1980s (Золотарёв, 2000, pp. 476–478; Полегаев and Алферов, 2015).

The current Russian military doctrine stresses precision weapon systems. The deployment of strategic non-nuclear precision-guided system by potential foes is considered a military danger. According to the Russian military thought, long-range precision weaponry could be used for efficient and flexible strategic containment of military dangers *in lieu* of nuclear attacks (Военная доктрина, 2014, II 12г; III 21м; III 26; IV 46; Шойгу, 2017).

The Russian Military Encyclopaedia defines precision weapons (высокоточное оружие, ВТО) as "guided weapons with conventional warheads capable of destroying targets with a single munition by hitting the splash zone with a probability of at least 50%" (VES, 2007, pp. 174–175). Modern Russian precision weapons systems are divisible into ballistic and cruise missile systems and free-falling air bombs with guidance systems.

One of the most potent Russian precision-guided weapon system is the new short-range ballistic missile 9K720 Iskander (SS-26 Stone), which will replace the obsolete OTR-21 Tochka system by 2020. Iskander consists of a road mobile transporter erector launch system (TEL), armed with either ballistic (Iskander-M) or cruise missiles (Iskander-K). The ballistic and hypersonic missile is said to use a quasi-ballistic flight path (height 50 kilometres) and perform evasive manoeuvres in the terminal phase of its trajectory. The maximum range of Iskander-M is 500 kilometres. The cruise missile version Iskander-K uses the R-500 subsonic missile, with a flightpath of 6–7 metres in height and having a range of 500 kilometres. The United States contends that R-500 (SSC-8) violates the INF treaty (NPR, 2018, p. 10).[24]

---

[24]The characteristics of Iskander-M missile allow the extension of range over 500 km. Also, Iskander-K cruise missile's characteristics lead to the assumption that its range could be extended over the INF limits. See Forss (2012, 12–16). The US declared its intention to withdraw from the INF treaty on 20 October 2018, which was followed by an announcement by the US to suspend its compliance with the treaty on 2 February 2019. After the announcement, there is a 6-month period for full withdrawal. On the same day, Russia responded by announcing its withdrawal. Both parties have announced armament development programmes beyond the INF limitations.

Missiles could be loaded with various types of warheads including high explosive fragmentation, penetration, fuel-air explosion, EMP generator and nuclear, weighing 480–800 kilograms. The Iskander system has flexible targeting options, and its diverse guidance and homing options provide a CEP of 5–7 metres (McDermott and Bukvoll, 2017; Forss, 2012, pp. 8–12).

The undisputed advantage of the Iskander missile system is the mobility of the launch platform and the short warning time. The flight time of the ballistic Iskander-M at range is round 6 minutes, and the flat trajectory allows the flight under the radar (Forss, 2012, pp. 12–13). The system has demonstrated very good tactical and strategic manoeuvrability. The SS-26 was deployed to Kaliningrad in January 2018 (*Reuters*, 2018).[25] The Iskander system was deployed to Murmansk region in Russian North-west nearby Norwegian and Finnish borders in the Zapad 2017 exercise (Nilsen, 2018).[26] However, the Iskander missile battery has 12 TELs. The battery salvo is 12 × 500–800 kilograms, only equivalent to a modern fighter-bomber.

Russia's new sea-launched Kalibr and air-launched cruise missiles have received less attention, at least in Europe. Kalibr cruise missiles are usually deployed to naval platforms, in surface vessels (vertical launch systems) and on submarines (launched through torpedo tubes). They can also be launched from ground and air platforms, and some sources claim that they can be launched in a sea container. The first combat launch of Kalibr during the Russian campaign in Syria revealed a maximum range of 1,500 kilometres. Over the sea, the missile follows a low (20 metres) sea-skimming flight path. Over the terrain, the flight path height is 50–150 metres. The inertial guidance system is occasionally updated with satellite navigational data (GLONASS, GPS). The reported CEP of Kalibr is 5 metres. Warheads of 400–500 kilograms include both conventional and nuclear options (Риа Новости, 2016; Militaryrussia.ru, 2016; McDermott and Bukvoll, 2017, pp. 13–14, 23).[27]

---

[25] Deployment in Kaliningrad is permanent.

[26] Deployment in Murmansk area was temporary for exercise purposes.

[27] Maximum range of the nuclear warhead is reported as 2,600 km. Most of the technical characteristics of Kalibr missile are estimations. Also, Tu-22M3 was used for launching Kalibr, although this air frame has been used earlier in combat.

The Air Force is the primary user of cruise missiles. The Navy also employed them in the Syrian campaign in autumn 2015. Russia's current air-launched cruise missile systems are Kh-101 and Kh-555. Kh-101 and its nuclear variant Kh-102 use inertial navigation, updated in mid-course terrain reference, probably with satellite navigation. Russian sources reported that Kh-101 are re-targetable after launch. Kh-101/102 flies in subsonic speed on the flight path at a high midcourse altitude of 12,000 metres and low terminal phase of 30–70 metres. Warheads are high explosives that weigh 400 kilograms or have a 250-KT-yield nuclear payload. The maximum range of Kh-101/102 is 4,500 kilometres. Kh-555 is a new version of Kh-55 (having only nuclear warheads) cruise missile family. It has a longer range of 3,500 kilometres. Kh-555's conventional high-explosive (HE) or submunition warhead of 400 kilograms is capable of hitting targets with a CEP of 25 m (Jane's, 2017a, 2017b; Валагин, 2016).

Although Russia successfully employed long-range precision weapons in its Syrian campaign, only a few missiles were launched, perhaps because inventories were low (MilBal, 2017, p. 188).

Electronic warfare

After the collapse of the Soviet Union, the Russian military has seen electronic warfare (EW) as an important element of armed struggle. By the Russian definition, EW is called *radioelectronic struggle* (REB, радиоэлектронная борьба), which is a set of objectives, tasks, locations and time-coordinated measures to detect, destroy or suppress the adversary's radioelectronic devices and systems. REB also includes the countermeasures against the adversary's electronic warfare. The main objectives of REB are to disorganise the command and control the adversary's troops, to reduce the effectiveness their weapons, equipment and radioelectronic systems and to protect Russia's command and control systems (VES, 2007, p. 601).

Electronic warfare assets are widespread in the Russian military organisation. In the Russian Ground Forces, tactical EW units are attached in combined arms army, division, brigade and even battalion tactical group levels, which indicates that REB is always present in land operations. Most of the Russian EW units are organised in the Ground Forces. The operational and strategic level of EW consists of five REB brigades, two of which are located in the Western Military District. The organisation of REB units is modular and adjustable according to the requirements of the combat mission. Their typical TOE includes platoons or squads that are equipped with automated jamming stations for different frequencies (HF, VHF, cellular and satellite communications, radio-controlled fuses and GPS satellite navigation). Modern automated jamming stations are also capable of gathering intelligence (McDermott, 2017, pp. 5–7; see Pictures 6–9 of that article).[28]

REB was given a significant boost from the United States' operations in the Gulf War in 1991. While adapting the theory of network-centric warfare (NCW), Russian military sees synergy in mixing REB and NCW. Possible future aspects are the integration of REB assets with C2 systems and identification of friend-or-foe systems (IFF), improvements in radioelectronic components to overcome interference caused by Russia's own REB and creation of REB systems based on new technologies (McDermott, 2017, pp. 5–7).[29]

Some Russian theorists see REB as a force multiplier, which by relatively low production and personnel and almost zero ammunition costs could create a pivotal asymmetric option to fight against peer adversaries relying on high-technology weapon and command and control systems. This may elevate REB from the traditional combat support role to new combat arm (McDermott, 2017, p. 9).

One of REB's main areas of application has been air defence. To repel aerospace missile strikes, Russia has developed jamming systems against airborne radars and communications and satellite navigation. Some claim that foreign systems were jammed during the Russian military exercises. Russian electronic warfare capabilities have also been reported as being effective in ground-domain warfare, especially in Ukraine.

Public writing on Russian REB sometimes exaggerate Russian miracle weapons like the incident where the Aegis-class Donald Cook missile destroyer was engaged by a Russian Su-24M fighter-bomber on Black Sea in 2014. According to media reports, the ship's electronic systems were shut down by Su-24's electronic warfare suit *Khibiny*. This claim was first presented by the Russian parody website and then by some Russian state-owned propagandistic channels, and it spread to certain western media

---

[28] 15th REB Brigade, Tula: 16th REB Brigade, Kursk, 19th Rassvet, 18th Nizhneudinsk, 17th Mateevka.

[29] *Ibid.*

reports like Fox and Sun.[30] Both Russian and western experts have denied the possibility of shut down of all ship's electronic systems.[31]

Strategic nuclear triad and non-strategic nuclear containment

Russia's military policy treats nuclear arms as a key in deterring conflict escalation. Russian nuclear arms serve strategic and non-strategic purposes. Non-strategic nuclear weapons are part of the JOINT armed ground, air and maritime battlefield forces.[32] The Russian Strategic Nuclear Triad consists of the Strategic Missile Forces, the naval element of nuclear-powered ballistic missile submarines in the Northern and Pacific Fleets and the Long-Range Aviation wing of Aerospace Forces.

The Strategic Missile Forces (RVSN) is an independent branch of the Russian Armed Forces, subordinated to the Russian General Staff Strategic Nuclear Triad command. RVSN has three missile divisions, deployed across Russia's heartland. Their main mission is nuclear strike readiness. The navy's nuclear-powered ballistic missile submarines complement the strike capability of Strategic Missile Forces. Submerged submarines are very difficult to discover, making them a dependable counterstrike asset. The third component of Nuclear Triad, the Long-Range Aviation, has two main bases with strategic bombers capable of launching long-range cruise missiles. Their readiness is maintained by the frequent test launches of intercontinental ballistic missiles.

The Russian Federation and the United States announced the completion of the New START reductions on February 5, 2018. Both signatories are limited to 1,550 deployed strategic warheads, 700 deployed launchers and a total of 800 deployed and non-deployed launchers (Podvig, 2018; New START, 2011). The current deployment of the Russian Strategic Nuclear Triad is displayed in Figure 13.

---

[30] See https://www.nytimes.com/interactive/2017/06/07/world/europe/anatomy-of-fake-news-russian-propaganda.html, accessed on 29 May 2018. See also https://www.is.fi/ulkomaat/art-2000001223784.html, accessed on 29 May 2018.

[31] See https://vpk-news.ru/articles/27272, accessed on 29 May 2018.

[32] Russians use "non-strategic" instead of tactical nuclear weapons. This emphasises the Russian military theory of three levels of warfare. Nuclear weapons having enormous destructive power could not be considered as "tactical" weapons.

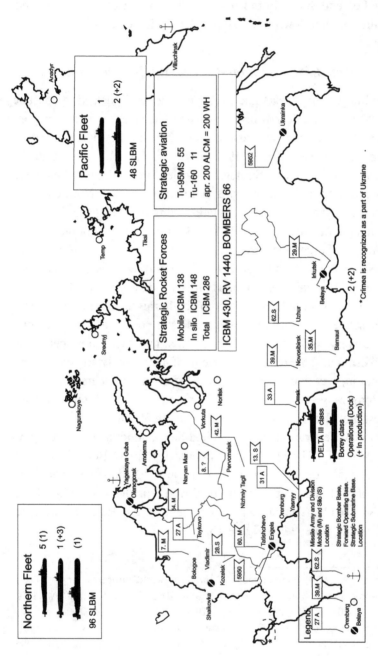

Figure 13:   The deployment and current numbers of the Russian Strategic Nuclear Triad components in 2018 (Podvig, 2018; MilKavkaz, 2018, compare MilBal, 2018, pp. 192–193).[33]

---

[33]The Military Balance claims 313 ICBM, 6 nuclear-capable Tu-160 and 60 nuclear-capable Tu-95.

Contemporary Russian military policy stresses the importance of preserving the Kremlin's strategic nuclear strike capabilities. The Russians claim that the United States' withdrawal from ABM treaty in 2002 and the Prompt Global Strike concept necessitated devising countermeasures that prevent America from destroying its counterforces by developing better anti-ballistic missile defences and adopting manoeuvrable transporter erector launchers to avoid aerospace attack. In his speech to the Russian Federal Assembly on March 1, 2018, President Putin asserted that Russia's goal is to defeat US and NATO missile defence systems. "After the unilateral withdrawal of the US from the ABM treaty, we worked hard on future technology and weapons. This allowed us to make a rapid, big step in the creation of new models of strategic weapons" (Путин, 2018).

These new weapons include the ICBM R-28 Sarmat, which is years behind the development schedule; the Avangard nuclear hypersonic boost-glide weapon system; nuclear-powered cruise missiles; and nuclear-powered torpedo Status-6. Most of these weapon systems may become operational in the 2020s (Kofman, 2018a).

While it is improbable that any present or future Western missile defence system will be able to intercept a Russian ICBM attack, Putin has put the West on notice that Moscow intends to enhance its strategic nuclear might.

Special operation forces (SSO)

During the Military reform of 2008, Russia's Armed Forces created a Special Operation Command (KSO) under the authority of the Chief of the Russian General Staff tasked to safeguard Russian citizens by evacuating them from crisis areas and carrying out counterpiracy operations. Their troops combat terrorists and enemy military–political operatives. They are trained to target precision weapon systems and sabotage infrastructure in support of military operations (MilKavkaz, 2018).

The SSO troops under the direct command of the KSO have two components, "Senezh" and "Kuba". They have six missions: (1) paratroopers operating in the enemy's rear, (2) mountain and (3) maritime special operations (based in Crimea), (4) providing personal protection for the high military leadership, (5) assault operations against enemy command and control facilities and (6) combat search and rescue operations.

Russian Army, Navy and Airborne Troops additionally have their own special operations units. The best known are the Spetsnaz units. Each military district has 1–3 Spetsnaz Brigades and the 45th Special Operations Airborne Regiment is the SSO component of the Airborne Forces. Marine Brigades also have special operations units. The main mission of the Spetsnaz units is deep reconnaissance, subject to the authority of military district commanders (MilKavkaz, 2018; MilBal, 2018, pp. 193–200; Nikolsky, 2014, p. 124).

Russian Special Operation Forces gained a lot of attention after their successful operations in Crimea. The "little green men" (polite people) are assumed to be SSO special forces (Nikolsky, 2014, pp. 124, 129–130). Russian Special Operation Forces have been used for close air support target acquisition and CSAR missions (Барабанов *et al.*, 2016, pp. 113–114; Гаврилов, 2016).

Special Operation Forces are a valuable asset in low-intensity conflicts and the opening phase of war.

Paramilitary formations and privatisation of armed forces

Paramilitary organisations refer to government-led armed formations outside the Ministry of Defence. Their main functions are guarding borders and ensuring internal security. Russian paramilitary troops mainly serve local purposes, but their equipment and capabilities are suitable for homeland defence (FOI, 2016, pp. 56–57).

The total strength of Russian paramilitary forces is estimated to be as high as 554,000 soldiers.[34] This constitutes an important addition to homeland defence and crisis management forces.

The *Federal Border Guard Service* is Russia's traditional paramilitary institution. Since 2003, border guards are subject to Federal Security

---

[34]This number is in addition to the ones mentioned in this chapter: the troops of Federal Security Service (FSO), rescue military units of Ministry of Emergency Situations (MChS) and the Special Troops of Federal Security Service (FSB); see FOI (2016, pp. 56–58) and MilBal (2018, p. 205).

Service (FSB). They control passenger traffic internally and at Russian borders. The Federal Border Guard service is estimated to have 160,000 soldiers (MilBal, 2018, p. 205).

The *National Guard of the Russian Federation* (NG) was established by a presidential decree in April 2016. It includes the former internal troops of the Russian Ministry of Internal Affairs, Special Police Forces (SOBR) against organised crime, and Special Police Units (OMON). The NG is subordinated to the president of the Russian Federation. The mission of NG is to preserve social order together with other organisations of internal security (police) and ensure public safety. During states of emergency, the NG is responsible for fighting terrorism, extremism, participating in territorial defence and safeguarding important state assets. One of NG's functions is providing for fee-paid security services for Russian enterprises and private citizens (Указ, 2016; Росгвардия, 2018; Вневедомственная_ охрана, 2018). Presumably, only those who pay will be protected.

The NG has approximately 170,000 troops deployed in seven districts. Its divisions, regiments and battalions are located in cities and towns across Russia. It possesses light infantry weapons, armoured personnel carriers, mortars and field guns and transport helicopters, even though many NG troops are only assigned to non-military police duties. *Special Police Units* (OMON) are present in every Russian town with a population exceeding 500,000. Their main tasks, since their establishment in 1988, have been riot control and maintaining and restoring social order in group gatherings. During the Chechen wars, OMON units were used as light infantry in pacification operations (MilKavkaz, 2018; Росгвардия, 2018).

The troops of both National Guard and Border Guard Service supplement the activities of the armed forces at home and abroad. Their units participate in Russian military exercises and operations. Having lighter armament than Armed Forces troops, they are suitable for the protection of important installations, communications and counterdiversion operations in the rear.

Russian private military companies

Using mercenaries in war is an age-old phenomenon and the reason is obvious: a fighter recruited for a campaign is often cheaper than standing army recruits. Although their monthly salary is higher than a soldier of regular or reserve army, mercenaries do not strain the military budget during the peacetime and do receive retirement benefits. Society considers them expendable. Clausewitz, Machiavelli and Frederick the Great believed that mercenaries were untrustworthy and poorly motivated (Carmola, 2010, pp. 11–14).

During the peak of the Iraqi War, the United States military employed 190,000 contractors. This dependency reflects *the civilisation of Armed Forces* and is related to the C4ISR (Command, Control, Communications, Computers, Intelligence, Surveillance, and Reconnaissance) network-centric need for civilian-based professionals in the battlefield (Kinsey and Hugh, 2012, pp. 1–4).

In Russia, private military companies (PMCs) until recently were prohibited by the Russian criminal code. Only at the end of 2016 were mercenaries permitted to serve outside the Russian border and participate in counterterrorism or peacekeeping operations. The law does not define the activities of PMCs, but allows their recruitment (УК РФ, 1996, ст. 359; Федеральный закон, 2016; Муртазин, 2016). Russia has been reported of using PMCs in Eastern Ukraine and Syrian conflict. Their relationship with the Russian government is unclear, but they serve the Kremlin's purposes. This loose relationship is hazardous for PMC contractors. On February 7, 2018, a significant number of employees of the Russian PMC Wagner were reported to have suffered casualties from the US air assault supporting Kurdi fighters. While US and other Western militaries avoided direct clashes with Russian troops in Syria, in this incident the US had been told that there were no Russian Ministry of Defence troops in the battle area (van Auken, 2018; Varfolomeeva, 2018; Kofman 2018b; Interfax, 2018). It is likely that PMCs will become a permanent fixture in the Kremlin's irregular military operations, using the latest commercial off-the-shelf equipment.

Operational capabilities

An estimate of Russian Armed Forces operational capabilities in the Western and Southern Military Districts is based on formations and troops illustrated in Figure 5. Russia's top priority is the European theatre. The operational capability of the Russian Armed Forces can be gauged in terms of the time needed for deploying battalion tactical groups, their fire support and logistic units and the air force battle support. Russia as a continental power prioritises its ground and air support forces. For simplicity, naval forces are excluded here from consideration. Table 1 provides estimates of Russia's deployment capabilities in its Western and Southern Military Districts for battalion tactical groups 4, 14 and 30 days following an alert.

Table 1: The ability of the Russian armed forces to bring troops in the strategic directions of the Western and Southern Military Districts.[35]

AC or Army	Peacetime dislocation		Deployable battalion tactical groups			Combatants 4–30 days (in BTGs)
	Divisions	*Brigades*	*4 days*	*10–15 days*	*20–30 days*	
North-western direction		5	7	8	11	8,000–18,000
14 AC, Northern Fleet		3	5	5	6	
6 A, Western MD		2	2	3	5	
Western direction	4	4	12	17	29	12,000–43,000
11 AC, BF/Western MD		2	2	4	5	
1 TA, Western MD	2	2	6	9	16	
20 A, Western MD	2		4	4	10	
South-western direction	2	5	15	19	26	15,000–40,000
8 A, Southern MD	1		5	7	9	
58 A, Southern MD	1	2	5	7	9	
49 A, Southern MD		2	2	2	5	
22 AC, Southern MD		1	3	3	3	
A/B troops and augments	5	9	11	23	40	*15,000–60,000*
Airborne	4	3	11	15	30	
Augments/Central MD	1	6		8	10	
Total	**11**	**24**	**46**	**67**	**109**	45,000–165,000

[35] Swedish FOI has made more detailed calculations assessing the availability of all armed forces in Russia, their estimated Force Composition in the initial phase of action is 50,000 men in Ground Forces divisions and brigades; see FOI (2016, p. 85).

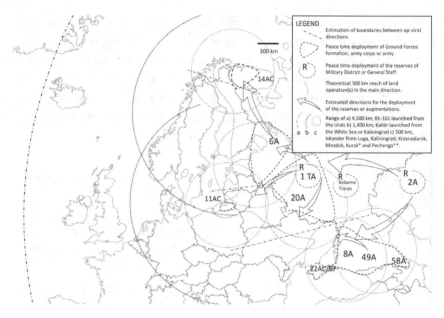

Figure 14: Estimated usage of Russian Ground Force formations and the theoretical ranges of Russian precision-guided weapons in the North-western, Western and South-western European directions.

Notes: *Planned Iskander system deployment during 2018. **Russian Armed Forces deployed an Iskander system on Pechenga Valley during the Zapad 2017 exercise (Nilsen, 2018).

According to the estimates presented in Table 1, Russia's Armed Forces in the designated districts can deploy 46 battalion tactical groups with 4 days' notice. This figure increases to 67 and 109, respectively, given 10–15 and 20–30 days' notice (Золотарёв, 2000, pp. 449–450; Lalu, 2014, p. 291).[36] Partial mobilisation of Russian military reserves is included in the latter statistics. Securing borders is the primary goal for local and regional wars on short warning. The 6th, 20th and 8th Combined Arms Armies and Army Corps of Russian Fleets are assigned to this task (see Figure 14).

The military district reserves such as 1st Tank Army or the Airborne troops under the command of the Russian General Staff and Special Operations Forces are employed in the offensive, counteroffensive or

---

[36]Days of notice are according the Soviet mobilisation demands in 1980s.

force projection tasks in the opening phase of the war. Artillery units provide combat and logistic support. Air and precision-guided assets suffer from attrition during prolonged campaigns.

Swedish researchers of Totalförsvarets forskningsinstitut (FOI) estimated the operational depth of a Russian joint inter-service combat operation (JISCO) at 300 kilometres from the Russian borders (FOI, 2016, p. 23, see also the Maps 3.1–3.4), obtaining a figure similar to the one supported by Vladimir Triandafillov in late 1920s. Triandafillov concluded that the maximum depth would be 250 kilometres in 4 weeks, taking account of impediments caused by damaged railroads and transport (Триандафиллов, 1936, pp. 197–198, 217). According to the FOI, the Russian gauge railway network facilitates the extension of combat into Finland, the former Soviet states and partially into Poland and Slovakia. Russia's military has a number of specialised railway troops for repairing damaged rail lines (FOI, 2016, p. 80; Триандафиллов, 1936, pp. 197–198).

These estimates of course do not imply that Russian Armed Forces could carry out successful offensive operations at distances of 250 kilometres in all of its neighbouring territories simultaneously — significant concentration of forces in the chosen direction of operations is always needed.

Russia's political and military leadership believe that recent military reforms allow them to use military means in a Clausewitzian fashion to continue politics with other means, mindful of Russia's strategic, technological and military discrepancies. Cruise missile attacks in Syria in 2017 and 2018 by the United States and its partners underscore the need for caution.

Russia is capable of challenging the West's cohesion (Shlapak and Johnson, 2016). Close neighbours are the most vulnerable. They have the right and must be prepared to defend their independence within the limits imposed by UN Charter Article 51, either individually or collectively.

References

Airwar.ru. (2018). Уголок неба: Большая авиационная энциклопедия, *Airwar. ru*, *http://*airwar.ru.

AktZad. (2003). *Актуальные задачи развития вооруженных сил российской федерации.*

Barabanov, M. (2014). Changing the force and moving forward after Georgia, in Colby, H., and Pukhov, R. (eds.), *Brothers Armed: Military Aspects of Crisis in Ukraine*, East View Press, Minneapolis, pp. 74–90.

BMPD. (2018). BMPD, https://bmpd.livejournal.com (accessed 24 February 2018).

BU. (2010). *Боевой устав по подготовке к ведению общевойскового боя, часть 2, батальон, рота*, Военное издательство: Москва.

Carmola, K. (2010). *Private Security Contractors and New Wars : Risk, Law, and Ethics*, Routledge, London, New York.

Суворов, А.В. (2001). Нечислом, а уменьем: Военнаясистема А.В. Суворова, Военный Университет.

Defense Intelligence Agency. (2017). *Russia Military Power*, https://www.dia.mil/portals/27/documents/news/military%20power%20publications/russia%20military%20power%20report%202017.pdf (accessed 18 February 2018).

Druzhinin, V. V. and Kontorov, D. S. (1975). Concept, Algorithm, Decision: decision making and automation (a Soviet view), Government Printing Office, Washington.

Fiore, N. J. (2017). Defeating the Russian Battalion Tactical Group, *Armor: Mounted Maneuver Journal*, CXXVIII(2), 9–17, *http://www.benning.army.mil/armor/eARMOR/content/issues/2017/Spring/2Fiore17.pdf.*

FOI. (2016). *Russian Military Capability in a Ten-Year Perspective — 2016*, Persson, G. (ed.), FOI, Stockholm.

Forss, S. (2012). The Russian operational-tactical Iskander missile system, Maanpuolustuskorkeakoulu, Strategian laitos, http://urn.fi/URN:NBN:fi-fe201210029314 (accessed 12 April 2019).

Grau, L. and Bartles, C. (2016). *The Russian Way of War, Force Structure, Tactics, and Modernization of the Russian Ground Forces*, Foreign Military Studies Office, Fort Leavenworth, https://community.apan.org/wg/tradoc-g2/fmso/m/fmso-books/199251.

Holmes, J. R. (2014). Everything you know about Clausewitz is wrong. *The Diplomat*, http://thediplomat.com/2014/11/everything-you-know-about-clausewitz-is-wrong/ (accessed 1 July 2017).

Interfax. (2018). Песков не исключил присутствия в Сирии граждан не из Вооруженных сил РФ — Москва, Interfax.ru, http://www.interfax.ru/world/599909.

Jane's. (2017a). Kh-101, Kh-102, *Jane's Air-Launched Weapons.*

Jane's. (2017b). Kh-55 (Kh-555/RKV-500/Kh-65), *Jane's Strategic Weapon Systems* 55, 1–6.

Jane's. (2018). *S-400 Land Warfare Platforms: Artillery & Air Defence* (9 February 2018).

Kinsey, C. and Hugh, M. (2012). *Contractors and War: The Transformation of United States' Expeditionary Operations*, Stanford University Press.

Kofman, M. (2018a). Russia military analysis: A blog on the Russian military, https://russianmilitaryanalysis.wordpress.com (accessed 18 March 2018).

Kofman, M. (2018b). U.S. strikes and Russian PMC casualties in Syria — Fact vs fiction, https://russianmilitaryanalysis.wordpress.com/2018/02/14/u-s-strikes-and-russian-pmc-casualties-in-syria-fact-vs-fiction/,casualties-in-syria-fact-vs-fiction/ (accessed 18 March 2018).

Lalu, P. (2014). *Syvää vai pelkästään tiheää : neuvostoliittolaisen ja venäläisen sotataidollisen ajattelun lähtökohdat, kehittyminen, soveltaminen käytäntöön ja nykytilanne. Näkökulmana 1920- ja 1930-luvun syvän taistelun ja operaation opit*, Maanpuolustuskorkeakoulu, Tampere, http://urn.fi/URN: ISBN:978-951-25-2551-5.

Lalu, P. (2016). *On war and perception of war in Russian thinking*, Finnish Defence Research Agency, https://puolustusvoimat.fi/documents/1951253/2208221/PVTUTKL_160525_DOS_J_tutkimuskatsaus_on_war_and_perception_of_war_in_Russian_thinking.pdf/2d81a143-9e98-4194-92aa-86157e84b291.

Main, S. J. (2017). Operational strategic command — the Western Military District (MD), *The British Army Review* 168, 36–47.

McDermott, R. and Bukvoll, T. (2017). *Russia in the precision-strike regime: Military theory, procurement and operational impact*, Norwegian Defence Research Establishment (FFI), FFI-RAPPORT, https://www.ffi.no/no/Rapporter/17-00979.pdf.

Mil.ru. (2018). Министерство обороны Российской Федерации (Минобороны России), www.mil.ru.

MilBal. (2017). Chapter five: Russia and Eurasia, *Military Balance* 117(1), 183–236.

MilBal. (2018). Chapter five: Russia and Eurasia, *Military Balance* 117(1), 183–236.

Militaryrussia.ru. (2016). Ракета 9 М 729 - SSC-X-8, http://militaryrussia.ru/blog/topic-849.html (accessed 22 March 2018).

MilKavkaz. (2018). MilKavkaz, http://milkavkaz.com/index.php (accessed 9 February 2018).

New START. (2011). Treaty between the United States of America and the Russian Federation on measures for the further reduction and limitation of strategic offensive arms, https://www.state.gov/documents/organization/140035.pdf.

Nikolsky, A. (2014). Little, green and polite: The creation of Russian special operation forces, in Colby, H., and Pukhov, R., *Brothers Armed: Military Aspects of the Crisis in Ukraine*, East View Press, USA, pp. 124–131.

Nilsen, T. (2018). Russian bombers simulated an attack against this radar on Norway's Barents Sea coast, https://thebarentsobserver.com/en/security/2018/03/russian-bombers-simulated-attack-against-radar-norways-barents-sea-coast (accessed 20 March 2018).

NPR. (2018). *Nuclear Posture Review*.

Podvig, P. (2018). Russian strategic nuclear forces, http://russianforces.org (accessed 11 March 2018).

Reuters. (2018). Russia deploys Iskander nuclear-capable missiles to Kaliningrad, https://www.reuters.com/article/us-russia-nato-missiles/russia-deploys-iskander-nuclear-capable-missiles-to-kaliningrad-ria-idUSKBN1FP21Y.

Rose, O. (1995). *Carl von Clausewitz: Wirkungsgeschichte seines Werkes in Rußland und der Sowjetunion 1836–1991*, Oldenbourg, München.

Shlapak, D. A. and Johnson, M. W. (2016). Reinforcing deterrence on NATO's eastern flank: Wargaming the defence of the Baltics: 16, https://www.rand.org/content/dam/rand/pubs/research_reports/RR1200/RR1253/RAND_RR1253.pdf.

Sutyagin, I. and Bronk, J. (2017). Russia's new ground forces: Capabilities, limitations and implications for international security, Royal United Service Institute, https://rusi.org/event/whitehall-paper-launch-russias-new-ground-forces-capabilities-limitations-and-implications.

Thomas, T. L. (2016). *Russia Military Strategy : Impacting 21st Century Reform and Geopolitics*, Foreign Military Studies Office, Leavenworth, https://community.apan.org/wg/tradoc-g2/fmso/m/fmso-books/195605 (accessed 17 December 2016).

Thomas, T. L. (2017). The evolving nature of Russia's way of war, *Military Review* (July–August), 34–42.

van Auken, B. (2018). Russians reported killed in US strikes in Syria, Globalresearc.ca.

Varfolomeeva, A. (2018). Updated: More than 200 Russians may have been killed in coalition strikes against 'pro-regime' forces in Syria, *The Defense Post,* https://thedefensepost.com/2018/02/10/russians-killed-coalition-strikes-deir-ezzor-syria/.

VES. (2007). *Военный энциклопедический словарь*, Военное издательство: Москва.

Vigor, P. H. (1978). The Soviet view of Fuller and Liddel Hart, *The Journal of the Royal United Service Institution* 123 (1), 74–77.

von Clausewitz, C. (1976). *On War*, Princeton University Press, New Jersey.

von Clausewitz, C. (1976). On War: Edited and Translated by Michael Howard and Peter Paret, Princeton University Press, New Jersey.

Yarynich, V. (2003). *C3: Nuclear Command, Control Cooperation*, Center for Defense Information, Washington.

Барабанов, Михаил. (2014). Испытание «нового облика» Украинский конфликт и военная реформа в России*Комментарии Центра АСТ*, http://www.globalaffairs.ru/number/Ispytanie-novogo-oblika-17097 (accessed 1 June 2015).

Барабанов, МС., Васильев, АД., Денисенцев, СА., Лавров, АВ., Ломов, НА., Лямин, ЮЮ., Никольский, АВ., Пухов, РН., and Шеповаленко, МЮ. (2016). *Сирийский рубеж*, АСТ-Центр: Москва. Ed. М..Ю. Шеповаленко.

Валагин, Антон. (2016). В России рассказали об особенностях ракет Х -101*Российская Газета*, https://rg.ru/2016/11/18/v-rossii-rasskazali-ob-osobennostiah-raket-h-101.html (accessed 22 March 2016).

Владыкин, Олег. (2013). 'Тополя' выходят на маршрут патрулирования*Независимое военное обозрение*, http://nvo.ng.ru/nvo-events/2013-07-19/2_topol.html (accessed 20 July 2013).

Владыкин, Олег. (2014). Центр круговой обороны страны – Москва*Независимое военное обозрение*, http://nvo.ng.ru/realty/2014-12-05/1_oborona.html.

Вневедомственная_охрана. (2018). Вневедомственная охрана Санкт-Петербурга и Ленинградской области *Вневедомственная охрана Санкт-Петербурга и Ленинградской области*, http://www.uvo.spb.ru (accessed 10 February 2018).

Военная доктрина. (2010). *Военная доктрина Российской Федерации*, http://news.kremlin.ru/ref_notes/461.

Военная доктрина. (2014). *Военная доктрина Российской Федерации*, http://news.kremlin.ru/media/events/files/41d527556bec8deb3530.pdf.

Воробьёв, ИН. (2002). *Тактика – искусство боя*, Общевойсковая академия Вооруженных Сил Российской Федерации, Кафедра тактики: Москва.

Воробьёв, ИН. and Киселёв, ВА. (2011). От современной тактики к тактике сетецентрических действий, *Военная мысль* (8).

Гаврилов, Юрий. (2016). Сирия: русский гром — *Российская Газета*, https://rg.ru/2016/03/23/aleksandr-dvornikov-dejstviia-rf-v-korne-perelomili-situaciiu-v-sirii.html (accessed 17 April 2018).

Гареев, МА. (2010). Россия в войнах XIX-XX веков. Уроки и выводы. Причины неудач красной армии в 1941–1942 гг, *Вестник Академии военных наук*, 33, 4–14.

Гареев, МА. (2014). Доклад президента Академии военных наук, *Вестник Академии военных наук*.

Герасимов, Валерий (2013a). Новые вызовы требуют переосмысления форм и способов ведения боевых действий — Москва*Военно-промышленный курьер*, http://vpk-news.ru/sites/default/files/pdf/VPK_08_476.pdf.

Герасимов, Валерий (2013b). Основные тенденции развития форм и способов применения Вооруженных Сил, актуальные задачи военной науки по их совершенствованию, *Вестник Академии военных наук,* 42(1), 24–29.

Герасимов, Валерий. (2014). Роль Генерального Штаба в организации обороны страны в соответствии с новым положением о генеральном штабе, утвержденным президентом Российской Федерации, *Вестник Академии Военных наук*, 1(46), 14–22.

Герасимов, Валерий. (2017). Выступление начальника Генерального штаба Вооруженных Сил Российской Федерации — первого заместителя Министра обороны Российской Федерации генерала армии Валерия Герасимова на открытом заседании Коллегии Минобороны России 7 ноября, https://function.mil.ru/news_page/person/more.htm?id=12149743@egNews, (accessed 27 February 2018).

Герасимов, Валерий. (2018). Тезисы выступления начальника Генерального штаба Вооруженных Сил Российской Федерации на брифинге, посвященном подготовке маневров войск (сил) «Восток-2018», https://structure.mil.ru/mission/practice/all/more.htm?id=12194449@egNews.

Гончаров, Библиотека В. (2003). Советские ВДВ в ВОВ — Москва*Воздушные десанты Второй мировой войны*.

Давыденко, А. А. (2010). Единая глубоководная система Европейской части России, *Mysharared.ru*, http://www.myshared.ru/slide/668738/.

Давыдов, Денис. (2016). Национальный центр управления обороной, Россия 24: Россия https://www.youtube.com/watch?v=oaDUfnah2DY.

Денисов, Виталий, and Ленин, Александр. (2007). Высоты крылатой пехоты — Москва*Красная звезда*, http://old.redstar.ru/2007/01/31_01/2_02.html (accessed 18 February 2018).

Золотарёв, В. А. (2000). *История военной стратегии России*, Кучково поле полиграфресурсы: Москва.

Иванов, СБ. (2003). Выступление министра обороны РФ С.Б. Иванова на годовом отчетном собрании академии военных наук Российской Федерации 18.1.2003, *Вестник Академии военных наук* (2).

Изменение. (2009). *О внесении изменений в Федеральный закон 'Об обороне' N 252-03, 9.11.2009.*

Иссерсон, ГС. (1940). *Новые формы борьбы*, Воениздат: Москва, http://militera.lib.ru/science/isserson/index.html (accessed 11 March 2017).

Колтюков, А. А. (2006). *История военного искусства*, Воениздат: Москва.

Колтюков, А. А. (2009). *Военное искусство локальных войнах и вооруженных конфликтах*, Воениздат: Москва.

Ленин, Владимир. (1969). Социализм и война, отношение РСДРП к войне, Издательство политической литературы: Москва, *Полное собрание сочинений, том 26*, 311–350, http://www.uaio.ru/vil/26.htm (accessed 5 November 2016).

Макаров, Николай. (2010). Характер вооруженной борьбы будущего, актуальные проблемы строительства и боевого применения вооруженных сил рф в современных условиях, *Вестник Академии военных наук* 31 (2).

Маскин, В. М. (2010). К вопросу о содержании соединений и воинских частей в категории постоянной готовности, *Военная мысль* (1), 26–30, http://dlib.eastview.com/browse/doc/21481872 (accessed 28 May 2015).

Медемъ, Николай. (1836). *Обозрѣніе извѣстнейшихъ правилъ и системъ стратегій* Санкт-Петербургъ.

Миранович, Геннадий, and Починюк, Олег. (2012). Северо-западный рубеж, *Красная звезда*, http://archive.redstar.ru/index.php/siriya/item/980-severo-zapadnyiy-rubezh.

Михневичъ, НП. (1911). *Стратегія, книга 1*, Изд. Березовскій, комиссионеръ военно-учебныхъ заведеній: С.-Петербургъ.

Муртазин, Ирек. (2016). «Воюем за Родину, но могут посадить» — Москва*Новая Газета*, https://www.novayagazeta.ru/articles/2016/12/15/70910-voyuem-za-rodinu-no-mogut-posadit.

Мясников, Виктор. (2014). Национальный центр управления обороной готов к действию — *Независимое военное обозрение*, http://nvo.ng.ru/realty/2014-11-07/1_action.html (12 November 2014).

Новичков, НН., Снеговский, ВЯ., Соколов, АГ, and Шварев, ВЮ. (1995). *Российские вооруженные силы в чеченском конфликте : анализ, итоги, выводы.*, Холвег–Инфоглоб–Тривола: Париж — Москва Statewide Agricultural Land Use Baseline 2015.

Об обороне. (1996). *Федеральный закон 'Об обороне' Россииской федерации*, http://mil.ru/elections/documents/more.htm?id=10928924@egNPA.

Пешков, Александр. (2018). Подводники рассказали, как российские АПЛ дошли до берегов США, *Телеканал Звезда,* https://tvzvezda.ru/news/forces/content/201803151801-z5tx.htm.

Полегаев, В. И. and Алферов, В. В. (2015). О неядерном сдерживании, его роли и месте в системе стратегического сдерживания, *Военная мысль* 7, 3–10.

Путин, Владимир. (2017). Путин : лидер в сфере искусственного интеллекта станет властелином мира*Риа-Новости,* https://ria.ru/technology/20170901/1501566046.html (accessed 1 September 2017).

Путин, Владимир. (2018). Послание Президента Федеральному Собранию, http://kremlin.ru/events/president/news/56957 (accessed 11 March 2018).

Рамм, Александр, and Круглов, Алексей (2018). Военные сказали Windows «прощай» — Москва*Известия.* https://iz.ru/688478/aleksandr-kruglov-aleksei-ramm/voennye-skazali-windows-proshchai.

Резниченко, ВГ. (1966). *Тактика, Военное издательство министерства обороны СССР, Москва, 1966,* Военное издательство министерства обороны СССР: Москва. Ed. В. Г. Резниченко.

РИА Новости. (2010). Новая система управления армии, https://ria.ru/analytics/20100715/255118238.html (accessed 21 April 2018).

РИА Новости. (2013a). Путин поручил начать внезапную проверку войск ВВО, https://ria.ru/defense_safety/20130712/949333629.html (accessed 20 April 2018).

РИА Новости. (2013b). Начальник Генштаба РФ поднял по тревоге авиабазы ЗВО, http://ria.ru/defense_safety/20130610/942551134.html (accessed 15 July 2013).

РИА Новости. (2013c). Начата самая масштабная после 1991 г внезапная проверка боеготовности, http://ria.ru/defense_safety/20130713/949419202.html (accessed 20 July 2013).

РИА Новости. (2014). ОСК начало исполнять задачи в Арктике*РИА Новости* https://ria.ru/defense_safety/20141201/1035928938.html (accessed 21.4.2018).

РИА Новости. (2016). Характеристики и вооружение ракетных кораблей проекта 'Буян-М'*Риа-Новости,* https://ria.ru/infografika/20160314/1389589685.html (accessed 6 March 2018).

РИА Новости. (2018). Две новые дивизии ЗВО и ЮВО полностью обустроят в мае 2017 года*РИА Новости,* https://ria.ru/defense_safety/20161111/1481182101.html.

Росгвардия. (2018). Росгвардия: Федеральная служба войск национальной гвардии Российской Федерации*Росгвардия,* http://rosgvard.ru/ru (accessed 9 February 2018).

Савкин, В. Е. (1972). *Основные принципы оперативного искусства и тактики*, Воениздат: Москва.

Свечин, А. А. (1927). *Стратегия*, Военный вестник: Москва.

Суровикин, С. В. (2014). Формы применения и организация управления межвидовой группировкой войск (сил) на театре военных действий, *Вестник Академии Военных наук* 46(1), 40–42.

Суровикин, С. В. and Кулешов, ЮВ (2017). Особенности организации управления межвидовой группировкой войск (сил) в интересах комплексной борьбы с противником, *Военная мысль*, 8, 5–18.

Триандафиллов, В. (1936). *Характер операций современных армий* Москва, http://militera.lib.ru/science/triandafillov1/index (5 January 2011).

УК РФ. (1996). *Уголовный кодекс Российской Федерации от 13.06.1996 N 63-ФЗ (ред. от* 19.02.2018).

Указ Президента. (2017). *Указ Президента РФ от 16.09.1999 N 1237 (ред. от 27.12.2017) 'Вопросы прохождения военной службы'*, http://www.consultant.ru/document/cons_doc_LAW_24400/995732e44838ee1c2f32f81eb9a91c8e2ca2cf8a/.

Указ президента. (2016). *Указ Президента Российской Федерации от 05.04.2016 г. № 157, Вопросы Федеральной службы войск национальной гвардии Российской Федерации* Россия, http://kremlin.ru/acts/bank/40689.

Федеральный закон. (2016). *Федеральный закон от 28.12.2016 № 512-ФЗ «О внесении изменений в Федеральный закон 'О воинской обязанности и военной службе'*.

Хряпин, АЛ., Калинкин, ДА. and Матвичук, В. В. (2015). Стратегическое сдерживание в условиях создания США глобальной системы ПРО и средств глобального удара, *Военная мысль* 1, 18–22.

Худолеев, Биктор. (2015). Войска с великой историей — Москва*Красная звезда*, http://www.redstar.ru/index.php/component/k2/item/25942-vojska-s-velikoj-istoriej.

Чекинов, Сергей, and Богданов, Сергей (2010). Влияние асимметричных действий на современную военную безопасность России, *Вестник Академии военных наук* 30, 46–53.

Шавров, ИЕ. and Галкин, МИ. (1977). *Методология военно-научного познания*, Военное издательство министерства обороны СССР: Москва.

Шойгу, Сергей. (2017). «Калибр» заменит атомную бомбу – *Военно-промышленный курьер*, https://www.vpk-news.ru/articles/34694.

Chapter 11

On War and Peace: Russian Security Policy and Military-Strategic Thinking

Gudrun Persson

NATO's eastward expansion is perceived by many in Russia not only as a move that is profoundly unfair in the military and political sense, but also as a move aimed against Russia as a civilisation.

— Andrei Kokoshin, 1997

"Nobody really wanted to talk to us about the core of the problem, and nobody wanted to listen to us. So listen now."[1] President Vladimir Putin spoke clearly in his Address to the Federal Assembly on March 1, 2018, as he continued to show videos of various new weapon systems, some of which actually exist and others yet to be developed.

And 3 years earlier, when he spoke at the UN General Assembly in 2015 on the eve of Russia's military operation in Syria, he talked about the Middle East and asked: "I'm urged to ask those who created this situation: do you at least realize now what you've done?"[2]

These are just two examples when the Russian president had expressed grievances against the West in general and the USA in particular for not

---

[1] Presidential Address to the Federal Assembly, 1 March 2018. Available at: http:// en.kremlin.ru/events/president/news/56957 (accessed 22 May 2018).
[2] 70th session of the UN General Assembly, 28 September 2015. Available at: http:// en.kremlin.ru/events/president/news/50385 (accessed 22 May 2018).

being listened to. There are many such allusions in his official speeches during the past 10–15 years, not to forget his speech in 2007 at the Munich Security Conference.[3]

Against the backdrop of Russia's military modernisation (Renz, 2018; Persson, 2016) and increased assertiveness in international affairs, including the illegal annexation of Crimea and military aggression in Donetsk and Luhansk in eastern Ukraine, it is relevant to examine Russia's threat perception and to analyse the current military thinking on contemporary military conflicts and future wars. In doing so, this chapter will address the following questions: What does the threat assessment look like from Moscow's perspective? What is the view of current and future military conflicts, and what are the consequences of this development?

This is important for several reasons. It is revealing when assessing military capability not least in the longer time perspective. Military capability can be assessed on three different levels: the conceptual level (in other words, doctrines and military thinking), the structural level (that is, the organisation) and the personnel level (which refers to education, motivation and the social situation). This chapter focuses on the conceptual level. It is also vital to study these developments in depth to avoid surprises in the future.

The chapter will start with a brief overview of Russian security policy, the major actors and strategic documents. Then, the Russian threat assessment will be outlined, such as it is described in the strategic documents, doctrines and key policy speeches. Thirdly, the view of contemporary military conflicts and future wars will be analysed. Finally, the implications of this development will be touched upon.

The chapter is based on open sources, both Russian primary sources and secondary literature. In spite of the fact that the old Soviet military strategy has not yet been replaced by a new Russian one, there is a lively debate among military thinkers about current changes in the art of war, what future wars might look like and what lessons are to be learned. The main platforms for these discussions are the General Staff, the Academy of Military Science and the military media. Important sources for this

---

[3] Speech and the following discussion at the Munich conference on security policy, 10 February, 2007. Available at: http://en.kremlin.ru/events/president/transcripts/24034 (accessed 22 May 2018).

debate are *Voennaia mysl*, the monthly journal of the General Staff; *Vestnik*, the journal of the Academy of Military Science; *Nezavisimoe voennoe obozrenie*; *Voenno-promyshlennyi kurer*; and the daily newspaper of the Ministry of Defence, *Krasnaia zvezda*.

Russian Security Policy and National Security

The legal basis for "national security" is the Constitution and the federal laws "On Security" and "On Defence".[4] The explicit use of the concepts of security policy and national security is relatively new in Russia.[5] During the Soviet period, the national element of security was subordinate to that of the social class and the international component (Kokoshin, 1998). It was only at the very end of the existence of the Soviet Union that the term "national security" began to be used at the political level. During the past 25 years, it has become an accepted term, and a number of laws and doctrines define and lay out the strategy for Russia's security policy. The Security Council's homepage lists 36 documents dealing with the national security of Russia.[6]

The Russian definition of "national security" is broad. The National Security Strategy, signed on December 31, 2015, encompasses nine different areas: (1) national defence, (2) security of the state and society, (3) higher living standards for Russian citizens, (4) economic growth, (5) science, technology and education, (6) healthcare, (7) culture (including history), (8) ecology and (9) strategic stability and strategic partnership.[7]

The law "On Security" (§4:1) defines security policy as part of both domestic and foreign policy. It involves a whole range of

---

[4] Konstitutsiia Rossiiskoi Federatsii 1993; http://constitution.kremlin.ru/ (accessed 22 May 2018); Federal Law No. 390, "O bezopasnosti", 28 December 2010, http://kremlin.ru/acts/bank/32417 (accessed 22 May 2018); Federal Law No. 61, "Ob oborone", 31 May 1996, http://kremlin.ru/acts/bank/9446 (accessed 22 May 2018).

[5] *Voennaia Entsiklopediia v vosmi tomakh* (Moscow: Voennoe Izdatelstvo, 1997–2004), Vol. 1, 399.

[6] Security Council of the Russian Federation, http://www.scrf.gov.ru/ (accessed 22 May 2018).

[7] Strategiia natsionalnoi bezopasnosti Rossiiskoi Federatsii, 31 December 2015, http://www.scrf.gov.ru/security/docs/document133/ (accessed 22 May 2018).

measures: political, organisational, socio-economic, military, judicial, informational, special and others. Consequently, national security from a Russian perspective entails much more than "just" defence and foreign policy.

Among the trends in Russian security policy identified when Putin returned to the presidency in 2012 were increased anti-Americanism, patriotism and authoritarianism at home (Persson, 2013). Russia's goal is to increase its authority in the world, not least through building a strong military, i.e. a more assertive position in world affairs. The Russian political leadership increasingly viewed the EU with apprehension and as closely associated with NATO. Furthermore, Europe was considered weak and decadent, as it had failed to play a dominant role in the world. Russia had chosen its own path — not in order to be isolated but rather a position of "strategic solitude". The key words here are patriotism, traditional values, military strength and Russia's national interests in international relations. It involves emphasis on cooperation within multilateral organisations such as G20, BRICS, CSTO and bilateral relations with a number of states. Indicative here are the relations between Russia and China, other states in Asia and the Middle East.

This development can be summarised with the words by Isaiah Berlin, who wrote already in 1946: "[Russia] is ready to take a part in international relations, but she prefers other countries to abstain from taking an interest in her affairs: that is to say, to insulate herself from the rest of the world without remaining isolated from it" (Berlin, 1946).

Interestingly, Vladislav Surkov, picked up the trend in 2018 and wrote in an ideological essay about Russia's "geopolitical solitude" (Surkov, 2018). In his interpretation, Russia is just at the beginning of adopting an isolationist policy. "Russia without doubt will engage in trade, attract investments, exchange know-how, and fight wars … compete and cooperate, cause fear, hatred, curiosity, sympathy, and admiration. But without false goals and self-denial," he wrote.

Decision-making

Security policy decision-making, including military security, is according to the constitutional jurisdiction of the president. And with Vladimir Putin as president, this is also the case in practice. It is the president, not the prime minister, who coordinates and controls the ministries, services and agencies that have functions related to security policy. If anything, decision-making has become even more centralised since 2013. The president is chair of the Security Council, and he appoints its secretary and members as well as decides on the size of its apparatus, its tasks and its remit through the regulations, which are fixed by presidential decree. With time, just about every sphere of Russian policymaking has become a matter of national security (Trenin, 2016) and a topic for the inner circle of the Security Council, which consists of only its 11 permanent members and the chairman (the president).

When it comes to preparing the doctrinal documents, a fairly large number of ministries and agencies are involved. This process is coordinated by the Security Council, which makes it, together with the president, a key player.

It should be noted that decision-making in the national security sector is not necessarily different from Russian policymaking as a whole. Nikolai Petrov notes that Russian decision-making at the federal level suffers from several ailments. There are no formal formats to represent the interests of the major elites, which limits the opportunities to find a compromise. Decisions are based on bilateral rather than multilateral communication (Petrov, 2013). In addition, the weakness of the political parties and the Duma and the strong state control over the media make feedback in the system very weak. According to Petrov, it takes a long time for a signal to reach the top and then come back.

The doctrines

The National Security Strategy of the Russian Federation is considered to be the most important document of all the official doctrines, which is made clear in the federal laws "On Security", Article 4:3, and "On Strategic Planning in the Russian Federation". The ambition is that all other doctrines should be in line with the Strategy. The revised Strategy was signed by the president on December 31, 2015. The law on Strategic Planning stipulates that the National Security Strategy is to be updated once in every 6 years.

The Military Doctrine is the only doctrine mentioned in the Constitution, which stipulates that the president approves the Military Doctrine.[8]

Furthermore, it should be noted that there are secret parts of the doctrines as well as completely secret plans. The Defence Plan (Plan oborony) signed by the president at the end of January 2012 is such a plan. An updated version up to 2020 was signed in November 2015.[9] This document allegedly involves 49 different ministries.

An assumption here is that official doctrines and key policy speeches reflect real intentions. Whether these intentions can be fulfilled obviously depends on a large number of factors such as economic and domestic developments and international relations. However, the past 25 years have shown that Russia has been consistent in achieving its intentions when the opportunities have come. The creation of a Eurasian Customs Union is a case in point. Its origins can be traced back to 1995 (Dragneva and Wolczuk, 2012). The use of Russia's energy resources as an instrument of foreign policy is another example (Oxenstierna and Hedenskog, 2012).

At the same time, these documents serve a bureaucratic function of achieving consensus among state institutions and therefore can have a lowest common denominator aspect to them. In Russia, they have been described as "what is left on the battlefield after the fight". Whether the declared threat perception is based on real facts or imaginary facts that are deemed necessary for purposes of domestic politics is a fair question (Pynnöniemi, 2018). What is clear, however, is that the threats — as formulated in doctrines and key public speeches — convey important information about the attitudes of the current political leadership, even if they do not reveal how the regime will deal with them at the policy level (Shlapentokh, 2009).

The more assertive security policy is a "Russia-first" policy, and this development can be traced back to the mid-1990s. For instance, in 1997, Peter Truscott noted: "Russia First, which played a dominant role in the Duma elections of 1995 and the presidential election of 1996 is here to

---

[8] Konstitutsiia Rossiiskoi Federatsii 1993, §83.
[9] Putin vvel v deistvie plan oborony RF 2016–2020 gody, *Interfax*, 17 November 2015, http://www.interfax.ru/russia/479673 (accessed 22 May 2018).

stay.... Any presidential candidate will need to adopt a Russia First strategy to win the next election, as Russia continues to evolve its Eurasian identity into the next millennium" (Truscott, 1997; for more on this development, see also Clunan, 2009).

Consequently, it is clear that the military threat perception in the Military Doctrine and the National Security Strategy has been remarkably consistent over the years, whereas the policy implementation of stated objectives has been remarkably flexible.

Threats to National Security — A View from Moscow

Russia developed its main doctrines and strategies throughout the 1990s. The Russian threat assessment in the Military Doctrines has been consistent, since the first draft of the 1993 Military Doctrine.[10] In 1997, a concept of national security was published as well as an updated foreign policy concept.[11] Although the Military Doctrine in the initial year took a more hard-line approach to Russian national security focusing on external military threats than the other documents, by the year 2000 the anti-Western view had become persistent in the political debate (Light, 2003).

One, if not the main, persistent threat is "NATO eastward expansion", which is called "unacceptable" in the National Security Concept already in 1997. The Military Doctrine in 2000 talks about the threat from "the expansion of military blocks and allies at the expense of Russia's military security."[12] Although NATO is not mentioned explicitly, it is obviously NATO that is intended. The National Security Strategy in 2009 described the NATO security plans as extending "military infrastructure at the borders of Russia" as "unacceptable."

---

[10]The 1993 Military Doctrine was never published in full, its main points was summarised in 'Osnovnye polozheniia voennoi doktriny Rossiiskoi Federatsii', *Izvestiia*, 18 November 1993, 1 and 4.

[11]Ukaz Prezidenta RF ot 17 dekabria 1997 N 1300 'Ob utverzhdenii Kontseptsii national-noi bezopasnosti Rossiiskoi Federatsii'; 'Kontseptsiia vneshnei politiki Rossiiskoi Federatsii utverzhdena Ukazom Prezidenta RF ot 17 dekabria 1997 No 1300.'

[12]Ukaz Prezidenta RF ot 21.04.2000g. No 706, 'Ob utverzhdenii voennoi doktriny RF', §5.

Another persistent threat is the "unipolar world" based on domination by developed Western countries under the leadership of the United States. A military threat in the national security concept 2000 is described as "NATO's transition to the practice of using military force outside its zone of responsibility and without UN Security Council Sanction".[13] Russia has since then emphasised the need to work for a multi-polar world. The multi-polar world, first promoted by Foreign Minister Evgenii Primakov in the 1990s, is a world dominated by the interaction between different poles, where no single power should be allowed to threaten the status quo and act unilaterally without risking reciprocal action. For instance, after NATO's intervention in Kosovo, Russia allowed itself to act according to the "Kosovo precedent" both in Georgia in 2008 and in Crimea in 2014.[14] The military elites saw Kosovo as a template of NATO's future operations (Blank, 2000). The "unipolar world of the United States" was criticised by the Chief of the General Staff, Valerii Gerasimov, at a meeting with the Academy of Military Science in 2018.[15]

Furthermore, under Putin, multi-polarity has been given a civilisational aspect that contradicts Western ideas of moral universalism (Lo, 2015). The Concept of Foreign Policy 2016 envisages growing competition. It says: "This competition involves not only human, research and technological capabilities, but has been increasingly gaining a civilisational dimension in the form of duelling values."[16] As examples, Russia once defined its ruling model as a "sovereign democracy", as opposed to the Western liberal democracy model (Konnander, 2008).

In addition, a sense of being ignored in international affairs is present in the documents. The 2000 national security concept says: "Efforts to ignore the interests of Russia in solving major international problems could break international security and stability." And the Military Doctrine

---

[13] Kontseptsiia natsionalnoi bezopasnosti, 2000, 7.

[14] Poslanie Prezidenta Rossiiskoi Federatsii, 18 March 2014, http://www.kremlin.ru/acts/bank/39444 (accessed 22 May 2018).

[15] Voennaia nauka smotrit v budushchee, *Krasnaia zvezda*, 26 March 2018.

[16] Foreign Policy Concept of the Russian Federation (approved by President of the Russian Federation Vladimir Putin on November 30, 2016), §5. Available at: http://www.mid.ru/en/foreign_policy/official_documents/-/asset_publisher/CptICkB6BZ29/content/id/2542248 (accessed 22 May 2018).

2000 notes that a military threat is "the effort to ignore (violate) Russian national interests in solving international security problems."

The threats in the 2000 documents were formulated against a background of fundamental disagreements between the US and Russia on several issues such as missile defence, the policy towards the Balkans and Iraq and the unipolar world. But, as we have seen, traces of these threats were consistent throughout the 1990s. It is worth noting that Andrei Kokoshin, one of Russia's leading strategic thinkers and secretary in the Security Council for a brief time in 1998 and not famous for a hawkish standpoint, pointed to the view in 1997 that the NATO expansion was seen as a threat to Russian civilisation (Kokoshin, 1997).

A close reading of the National Security Strategy, the Military Doctrine, the Foreign Policy Concept and a number of key speeches, not least the president's Annual Addresses to the Federal Assembly, reveal the following consistent perceived external threat assessment such as NATO eastward expansion; missile defence; regional and local wars on Russia's borders and international terrorism and radicalism.

The internal threat assessment can be summarised in the following points:

- violations of the unity and the territorial integrity of the Russian Federation;
- attempts to change the constitutional structure of the Russian Federation by force;
- economic instability as a result of the financial crisis and the changing energy market;
- foreign intelligence services, foreign organisations and terrorism.

"Besieged Fortress"

After the annexation of Crimea, the domestic and external threats are increasingly seen as linked to each other. All the major security documents were updated after the annexation: the Military Doctrine (2014), the National Security Strategy (2015), the Foreign Policy Concept (2016) and the Information Security Doctrine (2016). They reflect the view that the world is dangerous and that threats are coming from all directions. The current threats to Russia's military security in a recent university textbook cover 10 pages.[17] The Chief of the General Staff, Gerasimov, has repeatedly noted the blurred limit between war and peace, and between offensive and defensive operations (Gerasimov, 2013, 2017b).[18]

The National Security Strategy notes that the role of violence in international relations is not diminishing.[19] The term "colour revolution" was introduced in the National Security Strategy in 2015. This has intensified the search for enemies from within and without.

Another threat concerns the "besieged fortress Russia" theme, where NATO is seen as encircling the Russian Federation. The strategy is the most hostile towards the West since the first concept was published in 1997. Not only NATO but also the European Union is said to undermine Russian national security. The US and EU are pointed out as responsible for the developments in Ukraine by having supported an "anti-constitutional coup" that led to "deep divisions in Ukrainian society and the occurrence of an armed conflict". In addition, the strategy declares that the "deep socio-economic crisis in Ukraine is turning in the long term into a hardening of instability in Europe" and that this is taking place right on the border with Russia.[20]

The Russian political and military leadership has been dissatisfied with the current security order in the world for a long time. Vladimir Putin made this explicitly clear in his speech at the Security Conference in Munich 2007, where he spoke of Russia's need for a new world order.[21] In the Military Doctrine 2014, it is stated that "the current architecture (system) for international security does not provide equal security for all states."[22] This is the same wording as in the Military Doctrine 2010. To make this point even more explicit, the National Security Strategy points

---

[17] All the current strategic documents can be found at the Russian Security Council webpage: http://www.scrf.gov.ru/security/docs/ (accessed 22 May 2018).

[18] 'Voennaia nauka', 26 March 2018.

[19] Strategiia natsionalnoi bezopasnosti, 2015, §14.

[20] Strategiia natsionalnoi bezopasnosti, 2015, §17.

[21] President of Russia, 'Speech and the Following Discussion at the Munich Conference on Security Policy,' 10 February 2007, http://en.kremlin.ru/events/president/transcripts/24034 (accessed 22 May 2018).

[22] *Voennaia doktrina Rossiiskoi Federatsii*, §10, 25 December, 2014, http://www.scrf.gov. ru/security/military/document129/ (accessed 22 May 2018).

out that "the regional security system in the Euro-Atlantic region, built on NATO and the EU as a foundation, is untenable."[23]

In practice, this means a world order where a few great powers divide the world into different spheres of interest. The room for small states to act independently in such a world order is very limited. This is a world order that echoes the agreements of the 1815 Congress of Vienna and the 1945 Yalta Conference, and Putin has pointed several times at these agreements as examples to follow.[24] In fact, it goes even further back in time, to the Westphalian world order of the mid-17th century. Foreign Minister Sergei Lavrov recently emphasised the importance of this treaty and highlighted its significance in today's world (Lavrov, 2016).

This Russian perception of the world can be interpreted in ultra-realist, "Neo-Hobbesian" terms (after the British philosopher Thomas Hobbes 1588–1679) (Lo, 2015, 40–41). According to this view, Russia perceives the world today as an alien and often hostile place, in which the strong prosper and the weak are beaten. For all the talk about "win–win" solutions, which is often present in the West's approach to international relations, the world has always been divided into winners and losers. This has led to a strong Russian zero-sum mentality and approach to international affairs.

Present in the threat perception is also an awareness of a technological gap where Russia is lagging behind the West. In order to try to catch-up, two major armament programmes have been launched. The State Armament Programme up to 2020 aimed at replacing the stock of thousands of Soviet-era armoured vehicles, tanks, guns and howitzers with new pieces in the hundreds. An inherited key target in the current State Armament Programme up to 2027 from the previous armament programme is that 70% of the arms and equipment of the Armed Forces should be modern in 2021 (Malmlöf, 2018; see also Cooper, 2018). One residual task is to complete the transition from deliveries of modernised

---

[23] Strategiia natsionalnoi bezopasnosti, 2015, §16.

[24] Meeting of the Valdai International Discussion Club, 19 September 2013, http://en.kremlin.ru/events/president/news/19243, and Meeting of the Valdai International Discussion Club, 22 October 2015, http://en.kremlin.ru/events/president/news/50548 (both accessed 22 May 2018).

or updated versions of late Soviet designs to serial production of the new Russian-made designs that were developed under the 2011–2020 programme.

However, the current threat perception not only reflects concern about potential threats posed by a technologically superior enemy but also sees a direct threat to the protection of the mainland areas of Russia (Moscow and St. Petersburg) and the second-strike capability of the nuclear forces.

Regarding the Prompt Global Strike concept, the current Military Doctrine describes it as a military danger.[25] The potential militarisation of space is seen as a direct threat to the protection of the mainland areas of Russia.

Furthermore, a persistent threat since Kosovo is the use of military means to achieve regime change. The Military Doctrine notes as military dangers "the use of military force in the territories of states adjacent to the Russian Federation and its allies, in violation of the Charter of the United Nations (UN) and other norms of international law"; and "the presence (occurrence) of foci and escalated conflicts on the territory of the states bordering the Russian Federation and its allies." Add to this that a fundamental domestic military danger is said to be "information operations to influence — above all — the younger part of the population in order to undermine historical, spiritual, and patriotic traditions within the defence of the Fatherland."[26] This paragraph is also repeated in the Information Security Doctrine.[27]

It is important to remember that the view that the West was a threat to Russia was formulated long before the current talk about the threat of "colour revolutions" became prominent in the Russian threat assessment.

Military Thinking on Current and Future War

The development of the threat perception is closely intertwined with the military thinking on current and future war. This debate and the

---

[25] *Voennaia doktrina*, 2014, §12.

[26] *Voennaia doktrina*, 2014, §13.

[27] Doktrina informatsionnoi bezopasnosti RF, 5 December 2016, http://www.scrf.gov.ru/security/information/document5/ (accessed 22 May 2018), §21.

development of doctrines do not occur in a vacuum. Therefore, it is important to analyse the Russian view of current and future war, at both the strategic level in the doctrines and the military theoretical debate.

Regarding much of the debate in the West, there have been some confusions regarding Russian military thinking after 2014. The Western reaction has to a large degree been characterised by a lack of insight into the developments in Russian military thinking in later years. In the West, the label "hybrid war" quickly came to be used for Russia's behaviour in Ukraine, as if its actions were a new kind of warfare (Rácz, 2015). There have been endless writings about a "Gerasimov doctrine", although there is no such doctrine (Galeotti, 2018). In fact, a closer study of Russian military doctrinal thinking shows that there was at this point no developed doctrinal thinking on "hybrid war" (Persson, 2015). When Russian military theorists write about hybrid war, it is mentioned as a foreign, Western, capability (Giles, 2016).

What seemed to surprise many Western observers was Russia's ability to combine military and non-military means, i.e. special troops, information operations, deception and diplomatic, economic and political means. The Russian term for this is "non-linear" (*nelineinaia*) or "asymmetrical" (*asimmetrichnaia*) warfare. In fact, the annexation of Crimea and the military aggression in Donbas, Ukraine, included substantial elements of conventional warfare, albeit in a new context (Norberg *et al.*, 2014; Kofman *et al.*, 2017).

The complexity of today's armed conflicts have not been lost on Russia, and the debate on lessons learnt and future war is more lively than many outsiders realise.

Over the past 25 years, Russian military thinking has been influenced largely by (1) the technological development and (2) the political, economic and social changes in Russia and in the outside world. The military theoretical debate has reflected these fundamental changes: the dissolution of the Soviet Union, the reduced Russian territory (particularly in the Western parts) and globalisation. The search for a national identity, in later years becoming a policy of patriotism, has its equivalent in the military strategic debate, and thus the search for a new Russian military strategy. The international developments have also affected Russian military thinking, which constantly discusses the impact of Desert Storm 1991,

Serbia 1999, Afghanistan 2001, Iraq 2003 and Libya 2011. Russia's own experiences from the wars in Georgia 2008, Ukraine and Syria in recent years are persistently discussed. Interestingly, the Syria operation was preceded by a close study of the Soviet experience from the Soviet operation in Cuba 1962, according to Gerasimov.[28]

There is a distinction to be made between "doctrine" and "military thinking." The doctrine establishes the official position, whereas the debate between military strategic thinkers might sometimes be fierce. However, some theories from this debate may find their way into the doctrines. It can be assumed that open debate does not give the entire picture, but that it at least reflects some of the most urgent current issues.

Russian military thinking has impressive traditions both from Tsarist times and the Soviet period with names such as Dmitrii Miliutin, Mikhail Dragomirov, Genrikh Leer, Aleksandr Svechin, Mikhail Tukhachevskii, Georgii Isserson and Nikolai Ogarkov to mention but a few (Persson, 2010; Bukkvoll, 2011). Throughout, a debate has been described between two main schools of thought — one that emphasises the need for modern technology and the other that stresses the qualities of the soldier (Fuller, 1992). The traditionalists are warning against exaggerating the importance of high technology to win future wars. They see themselves as defenders of Clausewitz and Svechin (Konyshev and Sergunin, 2014; Popov, 2018). This is something of an oversimplification, to be sure, and in fact the different schools often go hand-in-hand and overlap each other.

In the mid-19th century, the issues in focus were (1) the appearance of conscript armies and trained reserves, (2) the growing importance of officer education and the rise of general staffs and (3) the technological development, including the military application of the steam railway, the electromagnetic telegraph and the rifling of muskets and cannons (Persson, 2010, pp. 11–23). Currently, the debate evolves around questions like (1) the relations between military and non-military means, (2) the importance of non-nuclear deterrence in relation to nuclear deterrence and (3) the role of "soft power" in contemporary warfare.

---

[28] 'Nachalnik Genshtaba Vooruzhennykh sil Rossii general armii Valerii Gerasimov', *Komsomolskaia pravda*, 26 December 2017, https://www.kompravda.eu/daily/26775/3808693/ (accessed 22 May 2018).

The Russian Armed Forces are prepared for four kinds of military conflicts, according to the Military Doctrine.[29] A military conflict is described as a type of solution for interstate or intrastate tensions through the use of military force. A military conflict encompasses all kinds of armed confrontation, including large-scale, regional or local war and armed conflicts.

An armed conflict, according to the Doctrine, is an armed clash of limited scale between states or opposing sides within the territory of a single state. Three different kinds of war are listed: local, regional and large-scale wars. A local war is said to have limited military–political objectives and involves mainly the states that are opposing each other. A regional war involves several states in a region and is conducted with national armed forces or with a coalition of armed forces. Each party is striving for important military–political objectives. A large-scale war is one between coalitions of states or between the great powers of the world. It could be a result of an escalating armed conflict or a local or regional war. A large-scale war requires mobilisation of the country's total material and moral or spiritual resources.

According to the Russian view, contemporary military conflicts are unpredictable and the time to prepare for military actions has diminished.[30] The reason for this development is the increased role of non-military means. Contemporary military conflicts are characterised as the "integrated use of military force, and by political, economic, informational or other means of a non-military character through a wide use of the population's protest potential or of special operations troops". The Doctrine points to the use of various means of weapons such as hypersonic weapons, electronic warfare, and UAVs. In addition, the Military Doctrine mentions the use of "irregular armed forces and private military companies" in military operations as well as "indirect and asymmetrical methods". As these methods are part of the Russian Military Doctrine, it hardly needs mentioning that Russia can apply them in its military operations.

---

[29] *Voennaia doktrina*, 2014, §8.
[30] *Voennaia doktrina*, 2014, §15.

Non-nuclear and Nuclear Deterrence

Strategic deterrence, with an emphasis on nuclear deterrence, is still a pillar in Russian security policy. At the same time, the concept of non-nuclear has become more important in Russian military thinking. The Military Doctrine in 2014 introduced "non-nuclear deterrence."[31] It is described as "comprehensive foreign policy, military and military-technological measure, aimed at countering aggression towards the Russian Federation with non-nuclear means". High-precision weapons are a major priority in Russian military modernisation (McDermott and Bukkvoll, 2017).

The role of nuclear weapons in Russian security policy is traditionally defined in the Military Doctrine, in nuclear deterrence policy documents and in key speeches and declarations by the political leadership. The Military Doctrine 2014 has the same wording as was previously used to explain Russia's policy with respect to the use of nuclear weapons. Paragraph 27 states: "The Russian Federation reserves the right to utilize nuclear weapons in response to the utilisation of nuclear and other types of weapons of mass destruction against it and (or) its allies, and also in the event of aggression against the Russian Federation involving the use of conventional weapons when the very existence of the state is under threat. The decision to utilize nuclear weapons is made by the president of the Russian Federation." However, the state in today's Russia is closely associated with the political system built around President Vladimir Putin. This raises the question of whether the current political leadership makes a distinction between regime survival and the state.

According to the National Security Strategy "strategic deterrence and the prevention of military conflicts are achieved by upholding nuclear deterrence at a sufficiently high level."[32]

Consequently, at the doctrinal level there has been no public change in the Russian nuclear position.

However, in July 2017 the Russian president signed the document Foundations for Russia's Naval Activity for the Period up to 2030, which

---

[31] *Voennaia doktrina*, 2014, §8.

[32] Strategiia natsionalnoi bezopasnosti, 2015, §36

is a form of a long-term naval strategy. This document states that if an armed conflict escalates, "a demonstration of preparedness and readiness to use non-strategic nuclear weapons, would be a strong deterrent factor."[33] In the previous version of this document from 2012 Foundations for Russia's Naval Activity for the Period up to 2020, Russia also mentioned the escalate to de-escalate concept. It envisaged "a limited use of weapons, including precision weapons, in order to de-escalate sources of tension and resolve the conflict situation on conditions favourable to Russia" (quoted in Zysk, 2017).

In addition to the latest public declarations, a debate is going on in military newspapers and journals regarding the use of nuclear weapons to de-escalate a conflict. Nuclear de-escalation means the use of non-strategic nuclear weapons when a local war is escalating into a regional war. The use of nuclear weapons should, according to this line of thought, frighten the adversary and lead to a de-escalation of the conflict. In the military debate over the past few years, these ideas have become more frequent. Konstantin Sivkov, a known hard-liner at the Academy for Geopolitical Problems, argued in March 2014 (before the revision of the Military Doctrine had been completed) that a preventive strike with non-strategic nuclear weapons against an enemy would be not only possible but also right (Sivkov, 2014). He and others argued for a change in the official Doctrine that would explicitly regulate Russia's possible use of a preventive nuclear strike. In addition, the collapse of the Intermediate-Range Nuclear Forces (INF) Treaty in 2019 will have a significant impact on European security. The Head of the National Nuclear Risk Reduction Center at the Defence Ministry, Sergei Ryzhkov, recently accused the US of destroying the INF Treaty (Ryzhkov, 2018).

It would be too easy to write off this line of thought as something coming from individual self-proclaimed experts — or to trivialise it by claiming that it is the task of every military staff to make plans for any conceivable event. It is more sinister than that. The advocates of a

---

[33] Ukaz Presidenta Rossijskoj Fededratsii ot 20.07.2017 g. No 327, Ob utverzhdenii Osnov gosudarstvennoi politiki RF v oblasti voenno-morskoi deiatelnosti na period do 2030 g., http://publication.pravo.gov.ru/Document/View/0001201707200015 (accessed 22 May 2018).

pre-emptive nuclear strike are challenging another school of thought that has been emphasising the importance of a non-nuclear strategic deterrence for Russia.

Andrei Kokoshin, one of Russia's leading strategic thinkers, has been arguing for years that Russia should look beyond nuclear weapons to other modern, high-precision weapon systems (Kokoshin, 2011). Gerasimov in 2018 even declared that deterrence in the future must mainly rely on the non-nuclear sphere, and he mentioned high-precision and hypersonic weapons.[34] He also put emphasis on the need to develop further electronic warfare capabilities, unmanned aerial complexes and systems for command and control.

To summarise, apparently unity has not been found yet in the Russian military elites regarding the issue of non-nuclear deterrence. All this raises the question of how far the concept of strategic deterrence in Russian military thinking has moved beyond the Cold War concept of deterrence by denial (Erickson, 1982).

"The Blitzkrieg of the 21st Century"

Another topic worth exploring is the debate in recent years on "the Blitzkrieg of the 21st century". The notion of Blitzkrieg is particularly tied to the studies of the Iraqi War of 2003. This war, including the example of Kosovo, has had a profound impact on Russian military thought.

Just how great the impact of the Iraqi War of 2003 has been on Russian military thought becomes evident in an essay in a recent and thorough study, The War of the Future, called *The Blitzkrieg of the 21st Century* (Popov and Khamzatov, 2016). In the essay, Popov and Khamzatov analyse the operations in Iraq. Was it the last of conventional wars or really a new type of war? They do not answer categorically, but claim that the impact of this war is fundamental when thinking about the future. They argue that the result was chaos and the creation of ISIS and conclude that "the real processes of fragmenting states", after the Cold War, might imply that "the world is entering an epoch of long and slow moving military conflicts in the interests of a few geopolitical forces and

---

[34] 'Voennaia nauka', 26 March 2018.

global elites. The seizure of territories and material riches of states only becomes an effect of such a strategy."

In addition, it is worth noting that Gerasimov also has been thinking about the Blitzkrieg. In an article on the lessons from the Syrian operation published in 2016, he uses the term "21st Century Blitzkrieg" (Gerasimov, 2016). His version of the new "Blitzkrieg" focuses on the combination of "colour revolutions" and Prompt Global Strike. This is hardly surprising. The official Russian view has been clear from the outset — these weapons threaten strategic stability. The weapons, even if they are armed with conventional warheads, could threaten critical Russian assets and Russia's nuclear deterrent, according to Gerasimov. He wrote

> As you know, the United States has already developed and implemented the concept of prompt global strike. The US military is calculated to achieve the ability to, in a few hours, deploy troops and defeat enemy targets at any point of the globe. It envisages the introduction of a promising form of warfare — of global integrated operations. It proposes the establishment as soon as possible in any region of mixed groups of forces capable of joint action to defeat the enemy in a variety of operating environments. According to the developers, this should be a kind of blitzkrieg of the twenty-first century.

He added "In the era of globalisation, the weakening of state borders and development of means of communication are the most important factors changing the form of resolution of interstate conflicts. In today's conflicts, the focus of the methods used to combat is shifting towards the integrated application of political, economic, informational, and other non-military measures, implemented with the support of the military force. The so-called hybrid methods." (Gerasimov, 2016).

In a public statement by the Russian Military-Historical Society in January 2015, the concept of a Blitzkrieg takes a more ideological stand. It was signed by Makhmut Gareev, Vladimir Medinskii, Minister of Culture and Dmitrii Rogozin, then Deputy Prime Minister responsible for the defence industry, among others.[35] The signatories claimed that

---

[35] Zaiavlenie Rossiiskogo Voenno-istoricheskogo obshchestva, 13 January 2015, http://rvio.histrf.ru/activities/news/item-1378 (accessed 22 May 2018).

"a Blitzkrieg has started against Russia." Their understanding of a modern Blitzkrieg has a distinct ideological character, and they describe it as a "war of the minds."

Non-military means are now seen as at least as effective as the power of the gun in achieving political and strategic objectives. Gerasimov noted that the rules of war have changed dramatically and that non-military means are four times more frequent than military means (Gerasimov, 2013). In his view, the lessons from North Africa and the Middle East have demonstrated that "fully functional states can be transformed in a short period of time into an area of an embittered, armed conflict, become the victim of foreign intervention, and end up as a chaotic swamp of humanitarian catastrophe and civil war". This line of thinking obviously concerns acts against an incumbent regime, i.e. Iraq and Libya (Allison, 2013). Russia did not oppose military intervention in Mali in support of the government versus the separatist Tuareg militias.

With regard to the tasks of defence policy, it is noteworthy that the Military Doctrine states that one of its responsibilities is to "support the mobilisation preparedness of the economy",[36] i.e. to put the economy on a war footing. Furthermore, defence policy should "increase the effectiveness within military patriotic education for the citizens of the Russian Federation, and their military service". Add to this the Doctrine's view of an endangered youth due to information operations mentioned above. All this shows that Russia is taking steps to revive the national mobilisation system (Cooper, 2016).

Before examining the implications of this, it is vital to address the Russian view of soft power and colour revolutions. This is central for understanding how the Russian view of modern conflicts has evolved.

Soft Power, Controlled Chaos and Colour Revolutions

The concepts "colour revolutions", "controlled chaos" and "colour revolutions" are all seen as tools in the hands of the West and are being used to attack Russia. In fact, the Russian interpretation of "soft power" is quite different from the conventional view of increasing a country's power of

---

[36] *Voennaia doktrina*, 2014, §21.

attraction (Nye, 2004). A factor in international politics, according to the Concept of Foreign Policy 2013, is the use of soft power.[37] The 2016 Foreign Policy Concept describes it as: "In addition to traditional methods of diplomacy, 'soft power' has become an integral part of efforts to achieve foreign policy objectives."[38]

On the one hand, soft power can be used as a complement to classic diplomacy. On the other hand, there is a risk of soft power being used as a tool to intrude into the domestic affairs of states, through "among other things to finance humanitarian projects and projects relating to human rights abroad". Vladimir Putin defines it as "instruments and methods to achieve foreign policy objectives without the use of weapons — information and other levers of influence." (Putin, 2012) And in 2018, Aleksandr Fomin, Vice Minister of Defence stated that "…it is clear that behind the term 'soft power' hide activities such as meddling in domestic affairs by organizing colour revolutions which in turn leads to a violation of the balance of power with catastrophic consequences for regions and the entire world."[39] This reflects a militarised view where soft power is seen as an instrument of statecraft.

In the military theoretical debate, soft power is seen as one weapon among others. Makhmut Gareev, an influential military theorist and a veteran of the World War II, links the annexation of Crimea with soft power and strategic deterrence (Gareev, 2017). It is, according to him, necessary to learn from Crimea in order to "perfect our soft power, political and diplomatic means, and information tools, and thus increase effectiveness in the system for strategic deterrence."

It is noteworthy that soft power, in this line of thinking, is put at the same level as strategic deterrence — a level usually associated with nuclear weapons and high-precision, long-range conventional weapons.

---

[37] Kontseptsiia vneshnei politiki Rossiiskoi Federatsii, 12 February 2013. Available at: http://www.kremlin.ru/events/president/news/17520.

[38] Foreign Policy Concept, 2016, §9.

[39] 'Podvedenie itogov MCIS 2018 general-polkovnikom Aleksandrom Fominym', (video) https://www.youtube.com/watch?v=ZLB7Zxq1pQo (accessed 21 May 2018).

Another term used in the Russian military theoretical debate is "controlled chaos" (*upravliaemyi khaos*). Putin used the term "controlled chaos" used in his pre-election article on defence in 2012. It means that Russia was under attack from the West, which by various methods — political as well as economic — was destabilising and undermining Russia's neighbours, and ultimately Russia itself. It is sometimes used in connection with a discussion of soft power. Gareev equates the two (Gareev, 2013). Since the Russian annexation of Crimea and the aggression in Donetsk and Luhansk, several articles in military theoretical journals are devoted to controlled chaos and to colour revolutions. Aleksandr Bartosh, corresponding member of the Academy of military sciences, traces the concept of "controlled chaos" to the US and claims that it was this "technology" that led to the dissolution of the Soviet Union (Bartosh, 2014).

It is worth noting that thoughts on the threat of colour revolutions were present in the Russian military strategic thinking long before any actual colour revolutions occurred (Persson, 2015, p. 57). However, the idea of the threat became much more developed after the Orange revolution in Ukraine in 2004–2005.

The Military Doctrine points to a development of "political forces and civic movements financed and controlled from abroad"[40] being used in contemporary conflicts. The most important difference from the previous Doctrine is that a protesting population is seen as a part of contemporary conflicts. Political and other organisations are seen as a part of the war. Some of this reflects the official rhetoric of the Russian political leadership on Ukraine, where Russia is said to be exposed to this kind of warfare by the West.

The term "colour revolution" was included into the National Security Strategy for the first time in 2015. It is described as a threat to Russia's state security.[41] It is also indicative that the General Staff is paying close attention to "colour revolutions" and that in recent years is thinking about developing a concept to work out a concept of to counter-act "hybrid" wars against Russia and her allies (Gerasimov, 2017). Furthermore, since 2017 a new course has been introduced at the General Staff Academy,

---

[40] *Voennaia doktrina*, 2014, §15.
[41] Strategiia natsionalnoi bezopasnosti, 2015, §43.

Army and Society. One of the purposes of the course according to Defence Minister Sergey Shoigu is to study counter-measures for "colour revolutions."[42] Among the subjects studied are information war, information security and cultural policy, not least on counter-acting the "falsification of history."[43]

According to Sergei Chvarkov, Professor of military science, and Aleksandr Likhonosov, Associate Professor at the General Staff Academy, a concept to counter "soft power" and "controlled chaos" might include five different strategic approaches (Chvarkov and Likhonosov, 2017). They write about the need to introduce a strategy, for instance, to make the general public aware of foreign and domestic threats to Russia's security, a strategy for the creation of separate internet networks for different ministries, mass media and confessions. They also call for a strategy to support the "social optimism of the population". This is to be achieved by the work by ministries and power structures to create a "national idea, national values, and a national ideology...".

There is clearly an underlying longing for an ideology in many of the current writings. General Aleksandr Vladimirov, for instance, notes that Russia needs to rally the country around the "nationally vital resources": the faith (Russian Orthodox Church), the people (Russian, russkii), the state (Russia), the idea (Russian culture) and the language (Russian) (Vladimirov, 2013). This echoes the past — though not as eloquently formulated as the catchphrase from tsarist times, "Autocracy, Orthodoxy, Nationality".

At the same time, the Constitution of the Russian Federation states: "No ideology shall be proclaimed as State ideology or as obligatory."[44] However, there is concern for the younger generation's patriotic education. It has been codified into not only the Military Doctrine and the Information Security Doctrine as we have seen but importantly into the

---

[42] 'Minoborony RF nachalo kurs lektsii "Armiia i obsjchestvo"', *TASS*, 12 January 2017, http://tass.ru/armiya-i-opk/3934635 (accessed 22 May 2018).

[43] See for instance 'Rezhisser Karen Shakhnazarov provel', *Novosti*, Voennaia akademiia, Ministerstvo oborony RF, http://vagsh.mil.ru/More/Novosti/item/82427.

[44] Konstitutsiia Rossiiskoi Federatsii 1993, §13: 2, http://constitution.kremlin.ru/.

National Security Strategy as well.[45] This also includes the official writing of Russia's history.

Patriotism and the Role of History

In developing new military strategic doctrines and concepts, the role of Russian history has a special function (see also Persson, 2018). This goes to the very core of the search for a national identity and the country's self-image. An important part of the "patriotic" efforts touches on both history and the military.

The use of history as a political tool is not a new phenomenon in Russia, nor is it a phenomenon unique to Russia. But given the authoritarian trajectory of Russia's political system, the consequences of this policy are substantial.

Russia is seen as being under attack from a hostile West, and the Russian Armed Forces are to defend Russia's historical and spiritual traditions. This view ties in nicely with the many governmental programmes on military-patriotic education and patriotic education. These state-run efforts clearly target the younger generation in Russia. The issue of what exactly the Russian spiritual and moral traditions consist of has been a subject of discussion in Russia, addressed not least by Putin himself. At the Valdai Club meeting in 2013, he devoted his speech to elaborating on his thinking on the Russian national identity.[46] The National Security Strategy 2015 codifies the Russian spiritual and moral values as the following: "Traditional Russian spiritual and moral values include the priority of the spiritual over the material, protection of human life and of human rights and freedoms, the family, creative labour, service to the homeland, the norms of morals and morality, humanism, charity, fairness, mutual assistance, collectivism, the historical unity of the peoples of Russia, and the continuity of our Motherland's history."[47]

---

[45] Strategiia natsionalnoi bezopasnosti, 2015, §§ 70, 76, 82.

[46] 'Meeting of the Valdai International Discussion Club, 19 September 2013, http://en.kremlin.ru/events/president/news/19243 (accessed 22 May 2018).

[47] Strategiia natsionalnoi bezopasnosti, 2015, §78.

The Military Doctrine — a document where the main objectives for the Russian Armed Forces are described — also involves defending Russia's history.[48]

In addition, a number of concrete steps have been taken in order to strengthen the military-patriotic traditions in Russia. The historical names of the Preobrazhenskii and Semenovskii Regiments have been added to modern military units. The first official Russian monument for the "heroes" of World War I has been erected, and a special unit has been created within the armed forces to combat "falsification of history".

This development is particularly evident in the way Victory Day, 9 May, is being used to create a sense of unity. Not only has the military parade on the Red Square in Moscow become bigger and bigger but also civilians are marching to remember their loved ones. Introduced in 2015 was the concept of the "Immortal Regiment" as a part of Victory Day. It was initially a local initiative that was taken over by the government and made into a national celebration.

Russia is trying to come to terms with its tsarist and Soviet past. The imperial Cadet Corps has been reintroduced, and the Suvorov schools for military training and the Cossack movement are being supported. The legacy of the Soviet military organisation DOSAAF (Volunteer Society for Cooperation with the Army, Aviation, and Fleet) is cherished. After briefly changing its name, DOSAAF reinstated its Soviet name in 2003.[49]

The number of military-patriotic organisations is constantly growing. In May 2016, the "Youth Army" (Iunarmiia) was created by the Ministry of Defence. Since its creation, it has attracted over 227,000 youths, according to its website. According to Defence Minister Sergey Shoigu, there are around 5,000 voluntary patriotic organisations "for those who love our history, those who believe in a great future for the country...", he said when the Youth Army was created. Furthermore, since 2015, the Ministry of Defence organises "Olympic games" in military history. It also has a unit specifically tasked with "preventing falsification of Russian history", which was created in 2013.

---

[48] *Voennaia doktrina*, 2014, §13.
[49] DOSAAF Rossii, http://www.dosaaf.ru/about/history/ (accessed 22 May 2018).

Other important organisations to promote a history that focuses on national pride and unity in Russia are the Historical Society led by Sergei Naryshkin, Director of the Foreign Intelligence Service, and the Russian Military-Historical Society, led by the Culture Minister, Vladimir Medinskii.

This development indicates a growing role of defence in the struggle with the West over values.

Conclusions

The current trends in Russian military thinking evolve around the major schools of strategic thought in Russia. Simply put, one line emphasises the imperial tradition, where territories are seen as an important instrument for the Great Power Russia and serve as a buffer zone in order to secure Russia proper. This policy is associated with, for instance, Tsar Nicholas I.

The other school argues that "to make Russia great", it should focus on the advance of its own resources, develop the economy and devote resources to its own population such as education, infrastructure and healthcare. At the international level, Russia should show its strength at the negotiating table rather than the battlefield. This school of thought is associated with Tsar Alexander II's Foreign Minister, Aleksandr Gorchakov (1798–1883), who coined the famous phrase: "Russia is not sulking, she is composing herself."

At present, the first line of thought currently has the upper hand, and Russia keeps demanding that a new international security order is needed.

These lines of thoughts often co-exist and are not mutually exclusive. The result is a security policy that oscillates between two poles. On the one hand, there is a more assertive line — anti-American and anti-European standpoint. The key words here are patriotism, traditional values, military strength and Russia's interests in the Eurasian space.

On the other hand, the other line focuses on cooperation with as many countries and international organisations as possible in various geographical directions. Key words here are multi-polarity, dialogue and norms of international law.

Currently, at the European level, Russia is trying to divide and rule. The political scientist Dimitry Suslov notes: "Russia is pursuing a ... strategy that erodes the West's anti-Russian unity, intensifies dialogue with both individual European countries and non-Western players the world over, and positions Russia as a responsible great power" (Suslov, 2018).

Russian military strategic theorists are devoting much thought not only to military force but also to all kinds of other — non-military means. The Military Doctrine is increasingly evolving to include everything from the country's history to nuclear weapons. There is no general unity among Russian military strategic thinkers about what future war will look like, but new concepts and doctrines are being developed. It is by studying and analysing these processes that future surprises can be avoided.

Will Russia succeed in finding the right balance between the declared goals and its resources, between lessons from history and adapting to future demands and between domestic and foreign threats? Any assessment of success or failure will, as Fuller points out, have to examine the interrelationship among policy objectives, strategy and the military system (Fuller, 1992, p. 453). This chapter has tried to shed some light on parts of these factors. Ten years of military modernisation have given results. The present Russian political leadership has a clear vision of its objectives and has taken steps towards establishing them, feeding into the tradition of Russia's great powers. The current political leadership likes the quote ascribed to Alexander III: "Russia has only two allies: its army and its fleet." Russia has shown that it is prepared to use military force to change borders in Europe. It continues to invest in its Armed Forces and has a considerable fighting force. At the international arena, Russia has become a power to be reckoned with — not least in the Middle East.

In the long-term perspective, as always, there are several challenges. Russia is still far away from achieving military parity with the West that it wishes. In the late 19th century, two errors resulted in a mismatch between Russia's strategy and policy: on the one hand, an excessive sense of military inferiority, and on the other hand, a reluctance to accept any diminution in Russia's international standing and prestige, which led to an avoidable overextension (Fuller, 1992, 462–463), rather than to recognise this Russia overstretched with disastrous consequences. This is a poignant lesson from the past.

References

Allison, R. (2013). *Russia, the West & Military Intervention,* Oxford University Press, Oxford.

Bartosh, A. A. (2014). Model upravliaemogo chaosa v sfere voennoi bezopasnosti [A model for controlled chaos in the sphere of military security], *Vestnik Akademii Voennych Nauk* 1(46), 69–77.

Berlin, I. (1946). Why the Soviet Union chooses to insulate itself. The Isaiah Berlin Virtual Library, http://berlin.wolf.ox.ac.uk/lists/nachlass/whysovunfull.pdf (accessed 22 May 2018).

Blank, S. (2000). *Threats to Russian Security: The View from Moscow*, The Strategic Studies Institute, Carlisle, PA.

Bukkvoll, T. (2011). Iron cannot fight — The role of technology in current Russian military theory, *Journal of Strategic Studies* 34(5), 681–706.

Chvarkov, S. V. and Likhonosov, A. G. (2017). Novyi mnogovektornyi kharakter ugroz bezopasnosti Rossii, vozroschii udelnyi ves "miagkoi sily" i nevoennykh sposobov protivoborotstva na mezhdunarodnoi arene [The new multivector character of threats to the security of Russia, and the growing weight of "soft power" in non-military ways of confrontation at the international arena], *Vestnik Akademii Voennykh Nauk* 2(59), 27–30.

Clunan, A. L. (2009). *The Social Construction of Russia's Resurgence: Aspirations, Identity, and Security Interests*, Johns Hopkins University Press, Baltimore.

Cooper, J. (2016). If war comes tomorrow — How Russia prepares for possible armed aggression, *Whitehall Reports*, 5 August, RUSI, London.

Cooper, J. (2018). The Russian State Armament Programme, 2018–2027, *Russian Studies 01/18*, NATO Defense College.

Dragneva, R., and Wolczuk, K. (2012). Russia, the Eurasian Customs Union and the EU: Cooperation, Stagnation or Rivalry? *Russia and Eurasia REP BP 01/2012*, Chatham House, London.

Erickson, J. (1982). The Soviet view of deterrence: A general survey, *Survival* 24(6), 242–251.

Fuller, W. C. Jr. (1992). *Strategy and Power in Russia 1600–1914,* Free Press, New York, 303–305, 514.

Galeotti, M. (2018). I'm sorry for creating the "Gerasimov Doctrine", *Foreign Policy*, 5 March 2018. http://foreignpolicy.com/2018/03/05/im-sorry-for-creating-the-gerasimov-doctrine/ (accessed 22 May 2018).

Gareev, M. (2013). Na 'miagkuiu silu' naidutsia zhestkie otvety [Hard answers to "soft power" will be found], *Voenno-promyshlennyi kure*r 47, 4 December.

Gareev, M. (2017). Velikaia pobeda i sobytiia na Ukraine [The great victory and the events in Ukraine], *Vestnik Akademii Voennykh Nauk* 2(47), 4–10.

Gerasimov, V. (2013). Tsennost nauki i predvidenii: "Novye vyzovy trebuiut pereosmyslit formy i sposoby vedeniia boevykh deistvii", *Voenno-promyshlennyi kurer*, No. 8, 27 February 2013.

Gerasimov, V. (2016). Po opytu Sirii [Lessons from Syria] *Voenno-promyshlennyi kurer*, No 9, 9 March.

Gerasimov, V. (2017a). Sovremennye voiny i aktualnye voprosy oborony strany [Contemporary wars and current questions on the defence of the country], *Vestnik Akademii voennykh nauk* 2(59), 13.

Gerasimov, V. (2017b). Mir na graniakh voiny [The world on the border of war], *Voenno-promyshlennyi kurer*, No. 10, 15 March 2017.

Giles, K. (2016). *Russia's "New" Tools for Confronting the West Continuity and Innovation in Moscow's Exercise of Power*, Research Paper, March 2016, Chatham House, London.

Kofman, M., *et al.* (2017). *Lessons from Russia's Operations in Crimea and Eastern Ukraine*, RAND Corporation, Santa Monica.

Kokoshin, A. (1997). Reflections on Russia's past, present, and future, *Paper, Strengthening Democratic Institutions Project,* Belfer Center, June 1997, p. 34.

Kokoshin, A. A. (1998). *Soviet Strategic Thought, 1917–91*, The MIT Press, Cambridge, MA, p. 194.

Kokoshin, A. (2011). Ensuring strategic stability in the past and present: Theoretical and applied questions, http://belfercenter.ksg.harvard.edu/files/ Ensuring%20Strategic%20Stability%20by%20A.%20Kokoshin.pdf (accessed 22 May 2018).

Konnander, V. (2008). *Ryssland. En suverän demokrati?* [Russia. A Sovereign Democracy], FOI, Stockholm.

Konyshev, V. N. and Sergunin, A. A. (2014). *Sovremennaia Voennaia Strategiia* [Contemporary Military Strategy], Aspekt Press, Moskva, pp. 85–105.

Lavrov, S. (2016). Russia's foreign policy in a historical perspective, *Russia in Global Affairs* 2.

Light, M. (2003). In search of an identity: Russian foreign policy and the end of ideology, *Journal of Communist Studies and Transition Politics* 19(3), 42–59.

Lo, B. (2015). *Russia and the New World Disorder*, Chatham House, London, p. 43.

Malmlöf, T. (2018). Russia's New Armament Programme — Leaner and Meaner. *Memo 6365*, FOI, Stockholm.

McDermott, R. N. and Bukkvoll, T. (2017). Russia in the Precision-Strike regime — Military theory, procurement and operational impact, *FFI Rapport*, Oslo. 17/00979.

Norberg, J., Franke, U. and Westerlund, F. (2014). The Crimea operation: Implications for future Russian military interventions, in: Granholm, N., *et al.* (eds.), *A Rude Awakening: Ramifications of Russian Aggression towards Ukraine*, FOI, Stockholm, pp. 41–49.

Nye, J. (2004). *Soft Power: The Means to Success in World Politics*, Public Affairs, New York.

Oxenstierna, S., and Hedenskog, J. (2012). Energistrategin, in: Pallin C. V. (ed.), *Rysk militär förmåga i ett tioårsperspektiv — 2011* [Russian Military Capability in a Ten-Year Perspective], FOI, Stockholm, pp. 125–146.

Persson, G. (2010). *Learning from Foreign Wars. Russian Military Thinking 1859–1873*, Helion, Solihull.

Persson, G. (2013). Security policy and military strategic thinking, in: Hedenskog, J., and Pallin, C. V. (eds.), *Russian Military Capability in a Ten-Year Perspective*, FOI, Stockholm, pp. 71–88.

Persson, G. (2015). Mellan krig och fred — militärstrategiskt tänkande i Ryssland, [Between War and Peace — military strategic thought in Russia.] in: Dalsjö, R., *et al.* (eds.), *Örnen, Björnen och Draken: Militärt tänkande i tre stormakter* [The Eagle, The Bear and the Dragon: Military thinking in three great powers], FOI, Stockholm, pp. 46–64.

Persson G. (ed.). (2016). *Russian Military Capability in a Ten-Year Perspective*, FOI, Stockholm.

Persson, G. (2018). Russia and the Baltic Sea — A background, in: Dahl, A. S. (ed.), *Strategic Challenges in the Baltic Sea Region: Russia, Deterrence and Reassurance*, Georgetown University Press, Washington, DC.

Petrov, N. (2013). 'Russia 2025', Lecture at the Stockholm School of Economics. https://www.hhs.se/contentassets/b1581b6b2bce47aa94f412922c082695/02.2012.pdf (accessed 22 May 2018).

Popov, I., and Khamzatov, M. (2016). *Voina Budushchego: Kontseptualnye Osnovy i Prakticheskie Vyvody, Ocherki Strategicheskoi Mysli* [The War of the Future: A Conceptual Framework and Practical Conclusions Essays on Strategic Thought], Kuchkovo pole, Moskva, 510–536.

Popov, I. (2018). *Voennaia mysl Rossii* [Military Thought in Russia]. Available at: http://futurewarfare.narod.ru/theoryRF.html (accessed 22 May 2018).

Putin, V. (2012). *Byt silnymi: garantii natsionalnoi bezopasnosti dlia Rossii* [Being strong: National security guarantees for Russia], *Rossiiskaia gazeta*. http://rg.ru/2012/02/20/putin-armiya.html (accessed 22 May 2018).

Pynnöniemi, K. (2018). Russia's national security strategy: Analysis of conceptual evolution, *The Journal of Slavic Military Studies* 31(2), 240–256.

Rácz, R. (2015). *Russia's Hybrid War in Ukraine — Breaking the Enemy's Ability to Resist*, FIIA Report 43, The Finnish Institute of International Affairs, Helsinki.

Renz, B. (2018). *Russia's Military Revival*, Polity Press, Cambridge.

Ryzhkov, S. (2018). Kto "kopaet" dogovor?, *Krasnaia zvezda*, 21 May 2018. Available at: http://redstar.ru/kto-kopaet-pod-dogovor/ (accessed 22 May 2018).

Shlapentokh, V. (2009). Perceptions of foreign threats to the regime: From Lenin to Putin, *Communist and Post-Communist Studies* 42, 305–324.

Sivkov, K. (2014). Pravo na udar' [The Right to Strike] *Voenno-promyshlennyi kurer*, No. 8, 5 March, 2014.

Surkov, V. (2018). *Odinochestvo polukrovki* [The Loneliness of the Half-Breed], *Rossiia v globalnom politike*. http://www.globalaffairs.ru/global-processes/ Odinochestvo-polukrovki-14-19477 (accessed 22 May 2018).

Suslov, D. (2018). Militarizing the confrontation: Risks of the new US nuclear posture review. Valdai Discussion Club. http://valdaiclub.com/a/highlights/ militarizing-the-confrontation-risks/ (accessed 22 May 2018).

Trenin, D. (2016). *A Five-Year Outlook for Russian Foreign Policy: Demands, Drivers and Influences*. Task Force White Paper, Carnegie, Moscow. http:// carnegie.ru/publications/?fa=63075 (accessed 22 May 2018).

Truscott, P. (1997). *Russia First: Breaking with the West*, I.B. Tauris, London.

Vladimirov, A. I. (2013). *Osnovy Obshchei Teorii Voiny, Chast I, Osnovy Teorii Voiny* [The principles for a general theory of war], *Chast I, Osnovy teorii vojny* [Part 1, the principles for a theory of war], Universitet Sinergiia, Moscow, pp. 477–494.

Zysk, K. (2017). Nonstrategic nuclear weapons in Russia's evolving military doctrine, *Bulletin of the Atomic Scientists*, 73(5), 322–327.

Part III
Russian Politics

Chapter 12

Russian International Relations: Russia's Great Power Revival and Engagement with the Global Community

Lance Alred and Madina Rubly

We now clearly see the defectiveness of the monopoly in world finance and the policy of economic selfishness. To solve the current problem, Russia will take part in changing the global financial structure so that it will be able to guarantee stability and prosperity in the world and to ensure progress. The world is seeing the emergence of a qualitatively different geopolitical situation, with the emergence of new centres of economic growth and political influence. We will witness and take part in the transformation of global and regional security and development of architectures adapted to new realities of the 21st century, when stability and prosperity are becoming inseparable notions.

— Vladimir Putin (2007)[1]

Introduction

Russia views itself as a Eurasian power with global security interests in Europe, Asia, Arctic, Middle East and Latin America. In Europe, it considers the Visegrad group (Czech Republic, Hungary, Poland and

---

[1] SCO Summit Address.

Slovakia), other members of the defunct Warsaw Pact (Bulgaria and Romania) and the Balkan states of Serbia, Montenegro and Slovenia to be part of the Kremlin's sphere of influence. In Asia, its primary geopolitical strategies involve Central Asia, China, Japan and the two Koreas, with additional interests in India, Pakistan, Bangladesh, Afghanistan, Vietnam, Thailand and Singapore. Russia is engaged in Iran, Turkey, Syria, Iraq, Israel and Egypt; against the global jihadi in the Middle East; and with Cuba, Venezuela, Brazil, Columbia and Mexico in Latin America.

Russia's stated goals are to protect the nation and ensure stable socio-economic development, increase living standards and promote global peace and fight for social justice. Russia often clashes with the United States over a host of sphere of influence issues across the globe, but neither side harbours illusions about conquering sovereign territories. Instead, they spar over nuclear deterrence and meddle in each other's internal affairs using various devices like economic sanctions and cyber-warfare, avoiding open-armed conflict. America and its European allies jointly use NATO, European Union and United Nations organisations to further their globalisation agenda at Russia's expense, but shun offensive hard-power limiting engagements for deterrence and soft power.

Moscow's management of foreign relations historically has varied with circumstances. It was conciliatory during the 1990s after the Soviet Union dissolved, leaving Russia's economy in shambles, but became more assertive in the new millennium under Vladimir Putin's leadership. The turning point in 2008 reflected the conjuncture of several forces including the completion of the first phase of the Kremlin's 2001 military modernisation programme, the Russo–Georgian War of 2008, China's emergence as a major economic power, petroleum-fuelled economic prosperity and the global financial crisis of 2008, which economically and politically weakened the West.

For the moment, the Kremlin has adopted an aggressive posture on issues like Crimea, the Sea of Azov and ballistic missile deployments in Central Europe, tempered with appeals for cooperation with the West, while endeavouring to court Asia in the East. It has created a Eurasian Economic Union (EEU) in 2014, collaborates with China on numerous projects including the Belt and Road Initiative (BRI), is negotiating with Japan over the partial return of the Northern Islands and is offering its good services in the North Korean nuclear dispute. Moscow is perpetually fishing in troubled Middle Eastern waters and is becoming increasingly active in Latin America. Russia is a nimble player in the modern global Great Game.

Russia and the West

Ukraine and Crimea

The situation created by Russia in Ukraine and Crimea is complex. The US believes it is supporting an ally in Eastern Europe and protecting it against Russian expansion. Russia argues that the US is meddling in the domestic affairs of a sovereign state. The imbroglio has been catastrophic for Ukraine and the Ukrainian people, besetting them with war, civil strife and a socio-economic quagmire. American involvement in Ukrainian affairs is problematic because Russia is well versed in exploiting American foreign policy.

To counter American efforts, Russia's operations in Ukraine [and Syria] have exposed a dynamic new tool set that gives them far reach and flexibility. The military calls this new set "New Generation Warfare". Russia diversified its military and non-military strategies. Moscow's tactics now include asymmetric, unconventional, hybrid, nonlinear, ambiguous, unrestricted and next-generation warfare tactics. These tactics are hard to detect and define. They can exacerbate threats without crossing NATO's Article 5 (8) threshold, requiring the identification of an armed attack against members.

The Russians achieved geopolitical gains and were able to avoid many conventional fights by skilfully mixing military and non-military tactics. Russia's special military forces "Spetsnaz" engage civilian armed and unarmed separatist and irregular forces. Some of the separatists belong to local militias in the Eastern Ukrainian Donbas Region, while others are local civilian supporters of the military force.

In their book, *The Eight Phases of the Next-Generation War*, Col. S.G. Chekinov and Lt. Gen. S.A. Bogdanov state that the Kremlin has adopted a multidimensional approach to war, which includes waging war against economic and political systems using Spetsnaz and civilian support.

The Georgia War of 2008 and the annexation of Crimea adhere to common strategic patterns such as destabilising conflicts that halt democratic consolidation, the presence of Russian population to justify intervention and strategic geopolitical location that have implications for other areas of the former USSR.

Russia achieved geopolitical gains and was able to avoid many conventional fights again by utilising a sophisticated combination of military and non-military tactics. Aggression against Ukraine involved cyberattacks, information operations, psychological pressure, media manipulation, economic threats, proxy actions, sophisticated propaganda, exploitation of ethnic strife and courting agents of influence in foreign countries through influence buying and framing issues in an attractive way to sympathetic audiences. In combination, these tactics can significantly weaken a state and prime it for invasion or insurrection. Over the last few years, Russia has continued to perfect the Soviet "reflexive control" concept that applies measures to lead an adversary to "reflexively" and unknowingly pursue actions sought by the Russian government. In 2008, for instance, Russia may have induced Georgian forces to launch an offensive against Russian proxies in South Ossetia, providing the Russian government with the desired justification to invade Georgia (Weitz, 2014a).

The US Army defines Irregular Forces as "armed individuals or groups who are not members of the regular forces, police or other internal security forces".[1] Deploying Special Operation Forces (SOF) and mobilising local militia and resistance forces benefit Russia in multiple ways. Irregular forces allow Russia to gather reconnaissance and important intelligence as well as lay groundwork for potential intervention while testing local and foreign responses before the actual intervention takes place.

In Crimea and Eastern Ukraine, Russian Spetsnaz supports the infamous "little green men" (undeclared Russian military personnel operating without insignia or official affiliation). The "little green men" are represented by retired Russian military personnel, active duty Russian soldiers "on vacation" and other Russian "volunteers" who join local irregular units, self-declared "Cossack" fighters and other regional militants including criminal gangs. They stage incidents against Russian interests to justify direct Russian military intervention.

The Kremlin employed people outside the government in order to allow government officials to deny direct responsibility for the disorders in a different state. Many observers noticed that Russia also employed private military and security companies, criminal organisations along with the Special Forces. These organisations could be used to link up with internal opposition groups within the targeted country in an effort to create dissent.

Members of the Russian paramilitary infiltrate the civil society institutions and security forces of target states to freely trade arms and deliver weapons to pro-Russian fighters under the guise of rendering help to distressed populations in the territories eligible for humanitarian aids, thereby providing both "bullets and bandages".

The Russian hybrid military strategy greatly benefited from the Spetsnaz, which involves civilian separatist irregular forces, including Ukrainian armed and unarmed separatists. Some of the separatists belong to local militia in the Eastern Ukrainian Donbas Region while others are local civilian supporters of the military force. According to Bret Perry of *The Wall Street Journal*, Russian Spetsnaz units were originally intended to covertly advance and develop their own agent networks to conduct special reconnaissance missions. Today, Spetsnaz is connected to GRU (Russian DIA) and serves as a subset of the Russian Special Operation Forces (SOF) command as combat support units. According to the Russian military doctrine, the mission of the Special Operation Forces incorporates the following: "to subvert the political, economic, cultural, military potential and morale of a probable or actual enemy".

Irregular forces can quickly and covertly execute missions to disrupt local governance, paving the way for additional Russian support from local civilians as well as future operations using a conventional military force. Ultimately, irregular forces help Russia to further the overarching goal of hybrid warfare by manipulating social, cultural, religious, economic and political environments within a targeted state. The use of irregular forces allowed Russia to continue to disrupt and undermine Ukraine's authority in the Donbas region without the use of conventional military intervention. Additionally, the covert use of SOF enabled Russia to deny involvement in Eastern Ukraine and cite the separatist actions as self-determined.

In Crimea, irregular forces predominantly consisted of Russian Spetsnaz units of the SOF. The SOF was deployed covertly and quickly focused on capturing key Ukrainian government and military buildings, setting the stage for an eventual turnover to Russian conventional forces. The irregular forces were used to conduct unconventional warfare and destroy civilian infrastructure in addition to government and military targets.

Since Spetsnaz forces wore no national or unit insignia, they were able to operate without providing any sign of the Kremlin's involvement. The use of SOF gave Russia plausible deniability in intervening in Ukraine. The presence of the Russian Black Sea Fleet naval base in Sevastopol as well the historical ties between Russia and population of Crimea contributed to a fast, non-violent takeover in Crimea.

The use of irregular forces in Eastern Ukraine was different than in Crimea. The SOF units were more involved and included civilian separatists and militias. The SOF provided the pro-Russian separatists, who constitute the second half of irregular forces in Eastern Ukraine, with efficient technical weapons system training and strategic advice. The pro-Russian separatists were militarily competent and were used as Russia's primary force in the region. The overarching goal of the separatists was to gain control in Donbas and then expand into other regions of Ukraine.

Energy — The cornerstone of the new great game

Events in Ukraine serve as a reminder of the role Russian energy plays in European geopolitics. Energy has helped to create the conditions for political and economic turmoil in Ukraine and helped to shape potential risks and responses across the region.

After the 2009 Russia–Ukraine gas war, there was a huge downstream crisis throughout Europe. Since Europeans obtained much of their oil and gas through pipelines that cross Ukrainian territory, gas was shut off to Europe for about 12 days. European Council and European Commission adopted a comprehensive strategy to enhance the EU energy security. They put in place massive changes in their own domestic policies and regulatory policies across the EU. A core objective was to reduce the EU dependence on Russia's energy resources, enhance bargaining leverage and reduce vulnerability to external supply disruptions.

In the past, any country that bought gas from Gazprom had to get Gazprom's permission to export gas. Today it is impossible for one country to own gas, a transit system, and the distribution system. As a result, no one can have a monopoly all the way through the system, in accordance with the Destination Clause. The EU invested in a regasification terminal and internal infrastructure to move and trade gas. This enabled western European countries to renegotiate their contracts with Gazprom and lower the price. The EU sought to extend these principles of the European gas market to Ukraine to enable Kiev to trade gas. The EU made a proposal to Russia, which included the payment of the debt, but the Russian officials walked out of this negotiation. Many analysts believe Moscow did not accept the proposal because the deal required both parties to be in a mutually binding contract. Whereas in the past, Russia had a contract for a sale of gas and offered unilateral discounts.

European dependence on Russian energy supplies can restrain energy sanction on Moscow. To enhance the EU's long-term energy security, the strategy emphasises diversifying external energy supplies, modernising energy infrastructure, raising the interconnectivity of installed electricity capacity, constructing infrastructure to permit fast redirection of energy flows within the EU to alleviate spot shortages, promoting energy conservation and coordinating national energy policies with non-EU negotiating partners (Weitz, 2014b).

However, no plausible alternative hydrocarbon supplier to Europe has the size, infrastructure and proximity advantages of Russia. Russia's position as a major energy player in Europe is well anchored in the existing network of oil and gas pipelines and long-term contracts. Since these contracts were negotiated years ago when oil and gas prices were higher, Europeans must pay higher prices than Asians, who have benefited from the region's spot market for gas purchases. Russia will also remain a major supplier of civil nuclear technology, uranium fuel, and even coal to Europeans.

Russian diplomats fostered independent relations with European leaders to prevent the EU from developing a unified energy policy. Declining North Sea production and other trends suggest that the EU's domestic oil and gas production will continue to fall.

The dearth of transparency and solidarity allows Russia to exploit EU division. For example, Russia has succeeded in inducing European companies to construct the Nord Stream pipeline that will bypass Ukraine and Poland to reach Germany through the Baltic. Other Western companies are helping Russia build its energy export infrastructure to Asia, and Ankara is supporting a "Turkish Stream" project that will deliver enormous volumes of gas from Russia through the Black Sea to Turkey and beyond.

Washington's European allies face the challenge that global energy demand continues to increase, while the EU domestic energy production is falling. EU countries rely on external supplies for more than half of their energy needs at a cost of over 1 billion euros a day. Russia is by a considerable measure the largest single supplier of oil and gas to the EU.

As gas production in Norway continues to decline, Russia's share of the EU market is likely to increase. While the EU is trying to compensate for this decline by importing costly LNG, especially cheaper US coal, many Central and Eastern European countries still rely on Russia for all their natural gas.

US–Russia energy relations remain limited. Russia did not allow the US energy corporations to purchase significant stakes in Russian energy companies. Washington is concerned that Russia will exploit its energy leverage in Europe at the expense of the US, which will weaken the US strategic partnership with Europe. The Russia–China strategic partnership could exploit the energy trade to destabilise the European economy. If this happens, the EU leading countries such as Germany or France would find it politically and strategically difficult to back the US on issues outside of the alliance, such as in Asia. The US encourages the EU to diversify their energy sources, especially by supporting the development of new pipelines connecting Europe with other Eurasian energy suppliers and a common energy policy toward Russia.

The Baltic States

The Baltic States (Estonia, Latvia and Lithuania) are a focal point of contention between the United States and the European Union and Russia. A quarter of Latvians and Estonians are Russians providing a secure foundation for the Kremlin's influence in the region. The US fears that Russia is going to "invade" the Baltic States in a move like its invasion of Ukraine and annexation of Crimea. The situation is complex. Although, Estonia, Latvia and Lithuania are NATO members, they are members of the International Congress of Industrialists and Entrepreneurs (ICIE), which is the modern version of COMECON (former Soviet-era economic trade union) (Golitsyn, 1995).

The Baltic States also work together with Russia in the Council of the Baltic Sea States (CBSS), an organisation concerned with environmentally sustainable economic development and solvency of the northern European region.[2] Since the founding of this organisation in 1992, Russia's involvement is a pivotal aspect of its "North West Russia Strategy".[3] Russia works closely with the CBSS in the spheres of energy security, the environment and sustainable development through the Baltic Sea Region Energy Cooperation (BASREC) council.[4]

The visegrad group

The Visegrad group countries (the Czech Republic, Hungary, Poland and Slovakia), a subgroup of EU members, have not developed a common policy towards Russia due to their divergent views on the security environment and national interests.

Hungary

The relations between Russia and Hungary have been growing stronger over the last decade. Moscow is Budapest's third biggest trade partner. During the Cold War, Hungary was one of the strongest allies of the Soviet Union. In the 1980s, the Hungarian government developed strong ties

---

[2] See http://www.cbss.org/council/. "The CBSS members are Denmark, Estonia, Finland, Germany, Iceland, Latvia, Lithuania, Norway, Poland, Russia & Sweden, as well as a representative of the European Union, it supports a global perspective on regional problems. These include politically and practically translating the UN Sustainable Development Goals, the Paris Climate Agreement, the Sendai Framework on Disaster Risk Reduction, the Palermo Protocol and the UN Convention on the Rights of the Child, into regional actions on the ground."

[3] See http://www.cbss.org/strategies/.

[4] See http://www.cbss.org/sustainable-prosperous-region/basrec/.

with West Germany and Austria to support its economic reform. It joined the European Union in 2003 and flourished until the global financial crisis of 2008, but hard times in the ensuing decade prodded Budapest to expand exports to Russia and Ukraine. Political relations with Russia also improved amid souring relations with the EU occasioned by the EU refugee crisis of 2015 and the resulting rise of Hungarian nationalism. The EU Parliament accused Hungary of "flouting of the EU's democratic norms" and imposed disciplinary action against Budapest, a rebuke mocked by the Hungarian Foreign Minister as "nothing less than the petty revenge of pro-immigration politicians". Hungary as an EU member voted against financial aid for Ukraine and consistently opposed EU sanctions on Russia for its aggression in Ukraine. It is becoming increasingly estranged from the EU and is pivoting diplomatically towards Moscow in an effort to hedge its bets.

Poland

Poland and Russia share a long and complex history. Relations between Poland and Russia remain ambivalent. Many Law and Justice Party voters admire Putin's leadership, and the party is opposed to EU Commission quotas on refugees, calling the EU an "imaginary community".[5] Nonetheless, enduring historical animosities are limiting Poland's pivot towards Russia.

Slovakia and the Czech Republic

Slovakia and the Czech Republic, unlike Poland, do not share centuries of animosity with Russia. Both maintained good relations with Gorbachev, Yeltsin and condemned Putin for the annexation of Crimea. While some politicians in both counties see Russia as a threat, the Czech President, Milos Zeman, supports Putin. Slovakia was one of the countries that did

---

[5] See https://foreignpolicy.com/2018/10/05/polands-new-populism-pis/.

not expel Russian diplomats in response to the poisoning of Sergei and Yulia Skripal in the UK.[6]

Eastern Europe

Bulgaria

In Bulgaria, new political developments under the leadership of President Rumen Radev demonstrate improving relations with Russia. Prime Minister Boyko Borisov and his conservative GERB party (Citizens for European Development of Bulgaria), who have been in power for almost a decade, are also turning towards Russia and away from the EU. The political elite regret that Bulgaria, under Western pressure, cooled its relationship with Russia. Bulgarian leadership argues that solidarity with the EU yielded insignificant benefits to Sofia. Bulgaria opposed Romania's initiative to permanently deploy NATO's fleet in the Black Sea, postponed the purchase of fighter jets from a NATO partner and did not expel Russian diplomats following the poisoning of the Skirpals in Salisbury. Bulgaria is considering exiting NATO, which it deemed indispensable just a while ago.[7]

Romania

Despite Russia's attempts to re-establish constructive relations with Romania across various fields, diplomatic relations remain modest.[8] Romania supports the US commitment to the Transatlantic security. It provides assistance to NATO especially in the Black Sea. The US–Romanian strategic partnership signed in 1994 in Washington remains the cornerstone of the Romanian strategy. Romanian and American troops

---

[6] See https://www.theguardian.com/world/2018/aug/20/russian-presence-divides-czechs-50-years-after-prague-spring.

[7] See https://carnegie.ru/commentary/76440.

[8] See https://www.nineoclock.ro/2018/02/09/ambassador-kuzmin-about-romania-russia-relation-still-modest-result-in-political-and-diplomatic-sphere-russian-diplomat-expresses-hope-that-bilateral-relationship-will-improve-given-that-romania-w/.

participate in military missions in the Balkans, Afghanistan and Iraq. Approximately 46,000 Romanian military personnel participated in these operations, of whom 34 were killed and 226 were wounded.[9]

Balkans

Serbia

In 1948, Tito, the communist leader of Yugoslavia, broke the country's relations with the USSR. In the 1990s, due to economic strains, Russia was unable to defend Yugoslavia from Western intervention during its civil war. Russia supported Serbia in recognising the independence of Kosovo. Relations thereafter warmed. Russia and the West compete for influence in Serbia, which seeks to maintain strategic relations with both the EU and Russia. Russia's gift of a half a dozen MiG-29 jets to Serbia is an example of Moscow's cost-effective campaign aimed at gaining influence in Belgrade. Such strategy has proved to be effective and Moscow is reaping increasing returns.[10] Russia established an emergency relief centre to assist the Serbs during floods and fires. Russia extends its information campaigns into Serbia and proliferates disinformation in the Serbian language. Moreover, Russia continuously emphasises its shared Orthodox and Slavic heritage.

Montenegro

Having become independent from Serbia in 2006, Montenegro is the youngest state and newest member of NATO. Montenegro has continuously provided forces for NATO operations in Afghanistan even before its independence and before it became a member of NATO. After Montenegro

---

[9] See https://www.moldova.org/en/russia-ukraine-moldova-romania-end-2018-challenges-united-states/.

[10] See https://www.washingtonpost.com/world/europe/russias-low-cost-influence-strategy-finds-success-in-serbia--with-the-help-of-fighter-jets-media-conspiracies-and-a-biker-gang/2018/10/03/49dbf48e-8f47-11e8-ae59-01880eac5f1d_story.html?noredirect=on&utm_term=.fd50cec3b84c.

joined NATO, Russia curtailed imports from Montenegro wine and issues travelling advisories for Russian tourists and citizens. Putin's spokesperson even has threatened retaliatory actions.[11]

Slovenia

Slovenia seeks to maintain strong energy ties with Russia and supports lifting of the sanctions imposed on Russia after annexation of Crimea. Russia is Slovenia's leading trading partner and investor.[12]

US–NATO–EU–Russian Relations

From 1991 to 2014, NATO downsized and reorganised to meet global challenges that emerged in the 1990s, and the Global War on Terror (GWOT) after 9/11. In 2014, efforts to expand NATO were undertaken in response to Russia's annexation of Crimea. This was preceded by Russia's invasion of the Republic of Georgia in summer 2008, which saw the effective annexation of South Ossetia and Abkhazia, the latter being an important port on the Black Sea at Russia's far south-western edge. The foreseeable, but unforeseen, move on Crimea by Russia in early 2014 and then eastern Ukraine, cemented Russia's control of the northern, north-eastern, and eastern reaches of the Black Sea and the entire Sea of Azov to the north, as well as the narrow Kerch Strait, which separates them. To prevent further Russian annexations in the post-Soviet space, the US and NATO continue to expand conventional forces in the Baltic States and Eastern Europe. This regional effort, which has taken place directly inside Putin's "near abroad", (a term used by the Russian Federation to refer to the 14 Soviet successor states other than Russia) has elevated tensions between America and Russia significantly.[13] In addition to utilising

---

[11] See https://foreignpolicy.com/2018/07/27/a-russian-attack-on-montenegro-could-mean-the-end-of-nato-putin-trump-helsinki/.

[12] See http://www.aalep.eu/russian-influence-slovenia.

[13] Dr. Ivan Ivanov, personal and email interviews, September 13–21, 2018.

political-military tools, the United States imposed sanctions as a primary means to correct Russia's mis-"behaviour".[14]

The EU has supported the economic sanctions that America has imposed on Moscow; however, it is tempted to increase natural resource trade with the Kremlin through the Nord Stream pipeline linking Germany with the Baltic Sea. Nord Stream 2 is especially controversial. It can be seen as an example of how Russia seeks peaceful partnerships through economic and diplomatic relations in accordance with its foreign policy doctrine of 2016; or it can be interpreted as a demonstration of Russia's strategy to undermine America's national security interests and influence in Europe while ensuring its own national security objectives.

The United States also perceives Russia's pipeline politics with the EU to be an effort to curtail NATO's effectiveness by creating a division between America and its European partners. Through this strategic manoeuvre, Russia can more effectively advance its energy security objectives in Europe. The leading Russian company operating in Europe is Gazprom, formerly the Soviet Ministry of the Gas Industry. Gazprom is, essentially, a mechanism to strengthen Russian influence in European energy markets. It manipulates the flow of gas (and prices) to European nations for a variety of political reasons including supporting Russia in disputes with America.[15]

---

[14] See http://altaempresa.ru/ekonomicheskie-sanktsii-v-2016-godu-prognoz-i-realnost/.

[15] See https://www.bakerinstitute.org/media/files/files/ac785a2b/BI-Brief-071817-CES_Russia1.pdf pp. 3–4 (accessed July 25, 2018). "Russia tolerates massive debts on the part of certain customers (such as Naftogaz of Ukraine for years), then suddenly imposes stringent payment requirements and raises prices when geopolitical tensions increase between the Russian government and the consumer government. Gazprom's inconsistent oscillation between forbearance and sharp, severe price and/or supply changes that closely correspond to geopolitical events disturbs consumers and reduces their confidence in Russia as a reliable energy supplier. If Gazprom (and ultimately the Kremlin) truly prioritised commercial concerns over political ones, we would expect to see more frequent and consistent use of legal processes to enforce agreements and settle disputes (i.e. court and arbitration cases) and fewer questionably timed price increases and supply curtailments."

American military forces in Europe and ballistic missile deployments in Central Europe/INF treaty

Since the end of the Cold War, emerging problems started to take shape across different regions, particularly in the Middle East and Northeast Asia with nuclear-armed North Korea.

Extended deterrence is protection provided to the US allies in the form of the US nuclear umbrella. Its purpose is to protect allies from attack. Extended deterrence is designed to prevent a potential aggression by adversaries and to provide security assurances to allies through policies and technical measures tailored to the regional specifics. The US deploys nuclear weapons in some allied states. The extended deterrence is surrounded by controversies related to retaliation, accidents and other issues.

After the collapse of the USSR, NATO issued its Strategic Concepts in 1991, 1999 and 2010, in which it reviewed its purpose and strategy for the security of its members.

NATO forces include strategic forces committed to the alliance by the US and the UK and the US nuclear weapons deployed in Europe. These American-deployed forward weapons could be delivered under NATO command by members' aircraft such as bombers.

The process of reduction of the US nuclear weapons deployed in Europe started in the late 1970s. It sped up with the Presidential Nuclear Initiatives of 1991. The US decided to cut its nuclear weapons deployed in Europe in 2008 by 97%. NATO decided to retain them.

Moscow's nuclear threats to NATO's members, annexation of Crimea, the Ukrainian war, Putin's promise to "snap back hard" against the post-Cold War order in Europe, the Arab Spring and changes in the security environment validated NATO's decision.

Russia has begun deploying new nuclear and non-nuclear capabilities against NATO, a process slated to expand after the termination of the INF agreement. Moscow is capable of contesting NATO in cyber and space domains (Roberts, 2015).

These new challenges drove the US to strengthen its alliances and capabilities for supporting its international commitments. It strengthened regional deterrence architectures not only in Northeast Asia but also in Europe and the Middle East to counter the Iranian nuclear threat.

The US deployed defences against regional ballistic missiles. Defences against intercontinental-range missiles were deployed during the George W. Bush administration. However, those deployments have a number of performance problems. They are effective only against early generation of technically unsophisticated missiles of Pyongyang, but cannot protect against modern forces of Chinese and Russian missiles. To improve security capabilities and adjust them to changing environment, the Obama administration addressed the deficiency by deploying additional ground-based Interceptors in silos and tailored to regional requirements.

In the past, the US deterrence included the deployment of tactical and intermediate-range weapons as well as non-strategic weapons. In the 1980s, the US eliminated the intermediate-range systems through the Treaty on Intermediate-range Nuclear forces (INF). The INF Treaty prohibited Russia and the US from designing, deploying or testing cruise or ballistic missiles with ranges between 500 and 5,500 kilometres. In the 1980s and 1990s, it eliminated all tactical weapons (Roberts, 2015).

Persistent violation of the INF Treaty, exercises and operational activities of Russia's nuclear forces vitiated the treaty's effectiveness. Russia's nuclear weapons have been upgraded from an isolated and independent deterrence force to the centre of Russia's military strategy (Johnson, 2016). The Kremlin has integrated its nuclear arsenal across the entire military structure, and now nuclear weapons are deployed much closer to their targets than ever before.

Nuclear threats play a central role in Russia's politics. The Kremlin allocates priority financing for modernisation of its nuclear forces even during the times of economic crisis. Nuclear weapons have been used as a political tool for over half of a century by Russian leaders, and it is unlikely that Moscow will agree to further reduce its nuclear arsenal.

From the Kremlin's perspective, the US missile defence system in Eastern Europe, which now stretches throughout Romania and Poland, isolates Russia and restricts Moscow's participation in the European security theatre. In response, the Kremlin is determined to become a global nuclear power, use aggressive policies and threaten the West. When the US asserts that the missile defence system is directed against Iran, Moscow argues that Tehran's ballistic missiles are technically incapable of reaching the US and that the proximity of the US defence system to

Russia destabilises the global balance of power. As a result, the Kremlin is deploying its new missile system Iskander in Kaliningrad, the western part of Russia.[16]

The US–Russia disarmament negotiations remain at a low level because there is no consensus on how to proceed. US Secretary of State Mike Pompeo's recent visit to Sochi, Russia, underscored the deadlock. Neither the US nor Russia expressed interest in saving the INF. The demise of INF is the latest evidence that arms control structure carefully built by Washington and Moscow is falling apart. The fall of INF follows the earlier collapse of the other treaties to limit defensive missile and conventional forces in Europe. Since the adoption of the New START agreement in 2010, the US and Russia adopted contrary strategic arms control strategies. The Obama administration attempted to limit the number of strategic delivery vehicles, reduce "non-deployed" strategic nuclear warheads and include nuclear tactical weapons into the agreement, whereas Russia sought to restrict ballistic missile defences (BMD), limit various non-nuclear forces and engage other countries besides Russia and the US in arms control agreements.

The Russian government has proposed a 5-year extension to the New START Treaty that expires in 2021. The Trump administration indicated that the US would wait until next year before deciding whether to pursue extension or seek more comprehensive arrangements to include limits on some other countries, such as China, and weapons systems.

Russia and the Collective Security Treaty Organisation

A foundational platform of Russia's engagement with the international community is the concept of collective security. This security system consists of many layers that often intersect and overlap with other processes, vectors, objectives and strategies across all imaginable spheres of domestic and international programmes. The Collective Security Treaty Organization (CSTO) is a key component of this system designed to protect the nation,

---

[16] See https://www.rt.com/news/362062-missiles-iskander-kaliningrad-nato/, https://missile threat.csis.org/russia-deploys-iskander-missiles-kaliningrad/ https://www.rt.com/news/ 378251-russia-icbm-combat-ready/.

increase living standards and promote global peace and social justice. The structure, mission and role of the CSTO demonstrate that the CIS is a potent organisation. The CSTO is a Moscow-led multilateral military organisation. It is the most significant regional multilateral defence structure in the post-Soviet space. The CSTO has enabled Russia to re-establish its superior political-military position across the former Soviet Union through strategic bilateral and multilateral energy and defence agreements.

In 1991, the defence industries of the former Soviet states collapsed. The newly independent states found themselves vulnerable to growing national security threats. Most of the Commonwealth of Independent States (CIS) members, except Moldova and Turkmenistan, signed a Collective Security Treaty on May 15, 1992 (also known as Tashkent Treaty), committing them to assist each other against external aggression. Through this treaty, Moscow promoted its influence across the post-Soviet space, while other members sought to secure Moscow's assistance in managing military assets inherited from the Soviet period. During that time, Russia developed strong bilateral defence ties with all members.

Ten years later, in 2002, Russia convinced the Collective Security Treaty (CST) members to sign a Charter for a new regional military structure, the Collective Security Treaty Organization (CSTO), which aimed at deepening defence cooperation in areas such as joint weapons manufacturing; integrated air defence; multinational military training; and collective peacekeeping, counterterrorism and counternarcotics activities.

During the past two decades, the CSTO's membership — currently consisting of Armenia, Belarus, Kazakhstan, Kyrgyzstan, Tajikistan and Russia — has been very stable. Uzbekistan has twice been a formal member for a couple of years, but it has never been a very active one. Members sought to turn the CSTO into a more institutionalised defence cooperation with permanent structures, regular exercises and global missions like NATO. However, it took them several years to strengthen the organisation's authority and capabilities (Weitz, 2018).

After the end of the Soviet Union, there were obvious security concerns, as the Soviet system of security was fragmented into 15 independent republics. This issue was addressed in Article 6 of the foundation of the CIS, designed to keep the armed forces of member states united under one strategic command with its headquarters in Moscow. The article additionally sought to ensure the security and control of nuclear arms and other weapons of mass destruction (WMDs) scattered throughout the former Soviet space. The CST also addressed evolving threats related to illegal migration, transnational crime, terrorism, drug trafficking, and weapons trafficking as well as 5th columns plotting to overthrow governments. Understanding how global threats and challenges constantly evolve, the heads of state of the CIS forming the Interparliamentary Assembly of the CIS agreed that the treaty should be periodically revised to effectively deal with changes in global conditions and proliferation of crises and conflicts within the CIS and globally.[17]

In the May 2002 meeting of the Interparliamentary Assembly of the CIS (IPA), it was decided to transform the CST to deal with the Global War on Terrorism (GWOT) including trafficking of drugs, weapons and humans.[18]

As stated in Article 3 of the Charter, the CSTO was established to promote "international and regional security and stability, and to ensure the collective defense of the independence, territorial integrity and sovereignty of the member States" and preserve "security on [a] collective basis". Article 2 states, "In case [of] a threat to security, territorial integrity and sovereignty of one or several Member States, or a threat to international peace and security, Member States will immediately put into action the mechanism of joined consultations with the aim to coordinate their positions and take measures to eliminate the emerged threat." This tenet is reinforced in Article 4, which affirms the responsibilities of the member states.[19]

The CSTO sought to increase cooperation with NATO through counterterrorism and counterdrug trafficking initiatives. In 2004, the CSTO Secretary General submitted an official proposal to the NATO Secretary General, Jaap de Hoop Scheffer, to establish formal contacts between the

---

[17] *Ibid.*

[18] See http://www.paodkb.ru/about/.

[19] Collective Security Treaty Organization, available from http://www.odkb.gov.ru/start/index_aengl.htm.

two organisations.[20] Two years later, Russian Defense Minister Sergei Ivanov stated that the CSTO and NATO should combine efforts to fight terrorism and reconstruct Afghanistan.[21] The fact that Russia strives to promote its interests through the CSTO as well as other considerations led NATO to refuse cooperation with the CSTO. Nevertheless, the Russian-led organization gained international recognition. For example, the CSTO built connections with the UNSC, and in 2004, the UN granted the CSTO an observer status. In 2009, the CSTO became an official supporter of the UN peacekeeping missions (Upadhyay, 2012). In 2012, the CSTO and the UN Department of Peacekeeping Operations signed a memorandum on cooperation to prevent and resolve conflicts.[22] The CSTO's ties with the Organization for Security and Cooperation in Europe (OSCE) include meetings between senior officials of both organisations and reciprocal invitations to major events (Nikitin, 2007). The CSTO has also developed extensive ties with the Anti-Terrorism Center and other security organs of the CIS, an organisation that includes former Soviet republics that are not CSTO members (notably Uzbekistan). In October 2007, the SCO signed an agreement with the CSTO to expand cooperation on internal security issues such as crime and drug trafficking (Nanay, 2007).

The geographic location of the CSTO's Central Asian members makes them vulnerable to numerous threats, notably from South Asia, the Middle East region and Afghanistan — the world's largest producer of opium smuggled across Central Asia and Russia to Europe. Regional criminal groups use narcotics revenues to buy weapons and bribe security services (Williams and Felbab-Brown, 2012). Many CSTO leaders blame NATO, which assumed responsibility for Afghanistan's security in 2003, for ineffective methods to counter the spread of opiates in the region.[23] In particular, they have decried NATO's unwillingness to undertake the

---

[20] CSTO, NATO should unite anti-drug efforts, *RIA Novosti*, December 16, 2004.

[21] Ivanov for NATO-CSTO interaction in fighting terrorism, *RIA Novosti*, February 5, 2006, available from http://en.rian.ru/russia/20060205/43344211.html.

[22] Russia-led Security Bloc, UN Sign Cooperation Memorandum, *RIA Novosti Sputnik News*, September 29, 2012, available from www.sputniknews.com/world/20120929/176292970.html.

[23] US government reviews have also faulted past NATO stabilisation efforts in Afghanistan: John F. Sopko, Special Inspector General for Afghanistan Reconstruction, Stabilization:

aerial spraying of herbicides over Afghanistan's opium poppy fields, an option consistently opposed by Afghan government and NATO commanders. More recently, CSTO leaders have expressed anxiety over NATO's withdrawal from the region (Weitz, 2018).

The situation across the southern frontiers of the CSTO worries the organisation's leadership. The emergence of ISIS along the southern borders of Russian allies led Moscow to send troops to tighten security on Tajikistan and Kyrgyzstan's borders. Terrorist infiltration through the porous frontier is a constant concern because Tajikistan, a CSTO member, shares a border of approximately 1,300 kilometres with Afghanistan. Kyrgyzstan has also experienced internal violence related to transnational terrorism and narcotics trafficking. Uzbekistan has been more stable, despite its recent presidential succession, while Turkmenistan's isolation makes it difficult to gauge its vulnerability to internal instability.[24] Even Kazakhstan, perhaps the most stable of the Central Asian countries, has experienced some terrorist incidents in recent years. Moreover, the number of Islamist groups active in the former Soviet republics keeps growing.

Capabilities

The CSTO has several types of military forces, including large combined regional forces available upon national mobilisation, rapid reaction forces and smaller special purpose forces for peacekeeping, drug interdiction and other low-intensity missions. The CSTO was originally designed to mobilise multinational coalitions in wartime under joint command. Such multinational framework is divided into three subdivisions according to their geographic locations: the East European group includes Russia and Belarus, the Caucasian group involves Russia and Armenia and the Southern group is made up of Kazakhstan, Kyrgyzstan, Russia and

---

Lessons from the US Experience in Afghanistan, May 2018, available from https://www.sigar.mil/pdf/lessonslearned/SIGAR-18-48-LL.pdf.

[24]Country reports on terrorism 2014, Bureau of Counterterrorism, US Department of State, June 2015, Chapter 2, http://www.state.gov/j/ct/rls/crt/2014/239408.*htm*.

Tajikistan.[25] In theory, the CSTO members fall under the protection of Russia's nuclear umbrella, though the precise extent of any extended deterrent guarantee remains unclear (Trenin, 2005). In 2009, the CSTO established a Kollektivniye Sily Operativnogo Reagirovaniya (Collective Rapid Reaction Force, CRRF, abbreviated as KSOR in Russian) (Upadhyay, 2012), which has approximately 25,000 troops, of which roughly half would be provided by the Russian military (Bodner, 2017). Each CSTO member state makes substantial contributions to the CRRF. The CRRF's troops are kept in a higher state of readiness than other CSTO forces; if deployed, it would fall under the multinational command and engage in regular exercises. In addition to the CRRF, the CSTO maintains the Central Asian Regional Collective Rapid Deployment Force (KSBR TsAR). The CSTO plans to establish a collective Crisis Reaction Center (CRC), which would work closely with Russia's Ministry of Defence (Daly, 2015), and already has an anti-terrorism centre in Bishkek, Kyrgyzstan, which contains a database of regional terrorist organisations and individuals (Mihalka, 2006).

Exercises

The CSTO has been quantitatively and qualitatively increasing its military exercises since the 2014 Ukrainian conflict. These drills aim at improving the CSTO's interoperability and rapid reaction capabilities for a variety of missions, including collective defence, counternarcotics, counterinsurgency, reconnaissance and logistics (McDermott, 2015). The most notable drills are annual drills: "Interactive Operations Center", "Unbreakable Brotherhood" and "Clear Sky."

Russia is the dominant CSTO member. Russia has the largest population, economy, and military of the member countries. Russia accounts for 95% of the aggregate military spending of the CSTO countries (Keaney, 2017). The Russian defence industry provides the CSTO members with military equipment. Russia exploits its influence in the UN and the SCO to promote the CSTO (Kropatcheva, 2016).

---

[25] Plugatarev (2006); and CSTO to Create Central Asia Military Group, *Interfax*, February 7, 2006.

Moscow seeks enhance its power projection capabilities, legitimise its policies and reshape regional policies closer to Moscow's liking. Moscow exploits the CSTO to balance and limit NATO's military activities in the former Soviet space (Mowchan, 2009).[26] The CSTO increases Russia's international influence by allowing Moscow to act as the head of an alliance of states or on their behalf or in defence of their interests (Mrvaljevic, 2015). Acting as a leader of a bloc shows that other states support Russia, which legitimises Moscow's actions. The CSTO states have supported Russia on important issues, such as Moscow's position on Syria, as well as criticising US missile defence plans.

Another benefit for Moscow is that the CSTO helps legitimise Russia's military presence in other member countries. For example, Russian officials can justify their military facilities in Armenia, Tajikistan and the Kyrgyz Republic as contributing to CSTO multinational missions (Pannier, 2004). (The CSTO as the institution does not have its own military bases; they all belong to the member governments.[27]) According to the CSTO Charter, a member can host a foreign military base by a non-member country only after it receives Russian authorisation.

Current structure and the "long-arm" of Moscow

The key to understanding the global influence of the CSTO is clearly delineated in its organisational structure and objectives of each component including its parliamentary dimension as an actual component of the Interparliamentary Assembly (IPA) of the CIS. Utilising a parliamentary method through this international organisation similar to the Soviet period, it is easier to "harmonize national legislation, develop model laws to solve the CSTO statutory tasks, and organize interaction on international and regional security."[28]

---

[26] Re-examining the Collective Security Treaty Organization, *Stratfor Global Intelligence*, August 6, 2012, available from www.stratfor.com/analysis/re-examining-collective-security-treaty-organization.

[27] Russia not to set up more military bases in Central Asia, ITAR-TASS, November 11, 2005.

[28] See http://www.paodkb.ru/about/.

From a structural and legislative perspective, the CSTO is a subsidiary committee of the IPA of the CIS, which involves all members of the CIS, not just CSTO participants.[29] Although Russia presents a presidential construct to the global community similar to the US with a president in charge of the nation with a three-branch system including executive, judicial and legislative, the parliamentary, collective construct inherent to the Soviet Union is maintained through the CIS which oversees organisations across the CIS. The legal basis for this involves all members of the CIS through the agreement between the Secretariat of the CSTO with the Secretariat of the Coordination Council of General Prokuratura of the CIS.[30]

The document that merges the CIS with the CSTO via the CIS Border Security Services is the Agreement between the Secretariat of the Parliamentary Assembly of the CSTO with the CIS Coordination Council of Commanders of the Border Security Services.[31]

Perhaps the most significant document concerns the order that merges the CIS Anti-Terrorism Center with the Secretariat of the IPA of the CSTO. This centre involves the intelligence and security services, military force and police force to work together as one collective.[32]

The main takeaway here is the continuity and evolution of Russian-led regional collective security. Russian leaders clearly consider collective security vital to the national interest.

Russia and Asia

China

Russia and China are the most significant powers seeking to change global economic and security structures established by the US after World

---

[29] See http://www.paodkb.ru/stryctyra/parlamentskaya-assambleya-odkb.php.

[30] See http://www.paodkb.ru/upload/iblock/aa3/soglashenie-pa-odkb-_-ksgp-sng.pdf, accessed on February 11, 2019.

[31] See http://www.paodkb.ru/upload/iblock/fdc/soglashenie-pa-odkb-_-ks-skpv.pdf, accessed on February 11, 2019.

[32] See http://www.paodkb.ru/upload/iblock/bdf/memorandum-pa-odkb_atts-sng.pdf, accessed on February 11, 2019.

War II. Neither is content with the existing US-led global order based on liberal internationalist principles, norms and institutions. They frequently denounce US-led military alliances as anachronistic legacies of the Cold War and reflections of an outdated "bloc" mentality of containing Moscow and Beijing.[33] Russian and Chinese representatives insist that they do not view one another as military threats and avoid publicly expressing concern about the other's activities. In their joint statements, Russian and Chinese officials present a shared vision on global affairs, profess their commitment to enhanced bilateral security cooperation[34] and mutual support, express solidarity against transnational terrorism and other menaces, affirm trust and understanding and advocate non-aggression, antiterrorism and international law. They both resent what they perceive as America's penchant for interfering in their internal affairs as well as in their spheres-of-influence, especially by siding with other countries in their disputes with Russia and China. For Moscow, the US relations with Georgia, Ukraine and Central Asia are key sources of concern. For Beijing, the US intervention in China's disputes with Japan and ASEAN countries as well as support for Taiwan's *de facto* separation from the PRC are major sore spots.

Russia and China have historically been rivals, not partners. The relationship has most often been marked by bloody wars and mutual denunciations. The language barrier, mutual ignorance and reciprocal contempt made the development of the relations difficult. There were conflicts between Cossacks and the Manchus over the territories along the Amur River basin in the 17th century. In the late 19th century, Russia had surpassed China in military and economic development. Russia exploited the Second Opium War in 1858 to annex the north bank of the Amur River and the coast down to the Korean border through two unequal treaties. During the 1800s and early 1900s, the rising Russia gained control over

---

[33] See, for example, Admiral Sun Jianguo, Deputy Chief, Joint Staff Department, Central Military Commission, China, "IISS Shangri-La Dialogue 2016 Fourth Plenary Session," June 5, 2016, published on August 17, 2016, http://www.iiss.org/en/events/shangri%20 la%20dialogue/archive/shangri-la-dialogue-2016-4a4b/plenary4-6c15/jianguo-6391.

[34] Putin and Xi make joint statement following talks, June 8, 2018, http://tass.com/ world/1008712.

the Far Eastern regions called "Outer Manchuria" after two "unequal treaties" (from 1858 and 1860, respectively) between St. Petersburg and Beijing. Russia's vital Pacific Ocean naval base, Vladivostok ("Ruler of the East") is situated in the *Primorsky Krai* (Richard Weitz, 2018).

In the 20th century, Maoist China initially became a communist ally of the Soviet Union, only to turn into a rivalry later. Stalin exploited the Chinese Communist Party and used it as a political instrument. Border disputes caused frictions during the Cold War, when Mao Zedong opposed anti-Stalinist politics of Nikita Khrushchev. Despite signing a non-aggression pact in 1950, ideological and cultural differences drove the two countries apart.

China tried to raise issues related to the unequal treaties and border issues, but the Soviets refused to discuss them. This led to militarisation of the borders and armed clashes in the 1970s. In the 1980s, Russia and China started building friendly relationships, but Russia has also sought to strengthen its defences against Chinese expansion. Since the breakup of the Soviet Union, Moscow has tried to rebuild old linkages with the former Soviet republics with surrogate arrangements like the Commonwealth of Independent States (CIS), the Collective Security Treaty Organization (CSTO), a Customs Union and a Eurasian Economic Union (EEU), supplemented by a plethora of bilateral arrangements. Russian officials deny that they use these bilateral and multilateral arrangements to counter China's economic presence in Central Asia, stressing the benefits of cooperation. Nonetheless, CSTO (Russia, Armenia, Belarus, Kazakhstan, Kyrgyzstan and Tajikistan) is a crucial tool for Russia's military management of the Kremlin's relations with China. It serves as a bulwark against Chinese expansion. This relationship has become significantly stronger over the last 30 years.

Belt and road initiative/one belt one road

Russia however also has been mindful of the benefits of cooperation, agreeing to harmonise trade and security relations in Central Asia with China. The People's Republic of China (PRC) is playing a critical role in modernising regional infrastructure by providing substantial loans to build new east–west transport links — energy pipelines, rail networks, bridges and highways — that expand direct land links between the PRC and Europe. Under its flagship project, the One Belt One Road initiative (OBOR),[35] China seeks to develop commercial networks throughout Asia and to Europe. China has funded physical infrastructure projects in Central Asia that the Russian government cannot afford and Western companies shun. Some Russians fear that China will transform Central Asia into a regional economic appendage, while other believe that Russians will gain jobs, investments and capital from the traffic through these land routes. Russian policymakers also believe that China's commitment to OBOR makes it more accommodating to Moscow.

Russia and the Shanghai Cooperation Organization

Russia and China also have substantially extended their cooperation in the security domain and developed a number of arms control and confidence-building measures, broadened national security agreements and standardised their regional security consultations and military exchanges, within both bilateral and multilateral frameworks under the Shanghai Cooperation Organization (SCO). Their shared goals include preventing bilateral conflicts, maintaining border security, promoting arms transfers and influencing third parties such as the United States. Most importantly, the two countries have declared that they do not view each other as military threats. In September 2001, they signed the Sino-Russian Treaty of Good-Neighborliness and Friendly Cooperation, a solid foundation for security cooperation.

One of the main functions of the SCO is the unification of nations from the former communist sphere of influence. The goal is to replace American hegemony in all spheres from financial-economic to humanitarian, sociological, cultural and political-military by creating an alternative global construct. The process began during the Soviet period and gained momentum with the dissolution of the USSR and its subsequent reorganisation into the CIS.

Based on the idea of "Socialism with Chinese Specifics", the theoretical concept known as the "Shanghai spirit" is at the core of the political

---

[35] See https://mgimo.ru/upload/iblock/8b8/111-avtor-logo-CHINA2-01.pdf.

activities and goals of the SCO. Russia and China consider the Shanghai spirit the foundation of a new model of international security. The Shanghai spirit consists of "mutual trust, mutual benefit, equality, mutual consultations, respect for diversity of cultures, and striving towards collective development in all spheres of life and society".[36]

The 2016 SCO summit agenda focused on celebrating its 15th anniversary, accepting Pakistan and India as members, broaching the possibility of Iran becoming an official member in the near future. Various other agreements were also reached from economics and access, transport and control of natural resources to tourism and athletics, the Syrian war, the Ukraine crisis, Afghanistan, and increased interaction with organisations such as ASEAN +3.[37]

According to the SCO General Secretary Rashid Alimov (Tajik Ambassador to China) on March 26, 2018, "Eurasia is rapidly becoming the main driving force of world politics and economy — its most important component is the Shanghai Cooperation Organization, which occupies more than 60% of the territory of Eurasia with more than 40% of the world's population, and the member states of the 'Big Eurasian Eight' collectively produce almost a quarter of the world's GDP."[38]

Moscow and Beijing have promoted information sharing against cyberterrorism and espionage threats from the West, as well deny Internet resources to civil liberties groups and other opponents of their regimes, under the guise of defending against terrorists and other extremist groups within the framework of the SCO.

North Korea

During the past two decades, Russia, China, the United States, South Korea/the Republic of Korea (ROK) and Japan have striven to prevent North Korea/the Democratic People's Republic of Korea (DPRK) from developing nuclear weapons. Russia and China share concerns regarding the Korean Peninsula, which border both countries and have pursued

---

[36] See http://russian.china.org.cn/exclusive/txt/2012-11/09/content_27054579.htm.
[37] *Ibid.*
[38] See http://rus.sectsco.org/news/20180326/400827.html.

often-parallel policies towards the DPRK. The US, Russia and China have cooperated within the UN Security Council to impose mandatory sanctions on the DPRK. The Kremlin has threatened to embargo military and energy resources and employ military force (Richard Weitz, 2018).

Russia seems more open to Korean reunification than China. Moscow is trying to persuade Pyongyang to stop nuclear proliferation with promises of economic assistance and security assurances. Russia has some influence over North Korea because it is a key importer and provides essentials such as fuel.[39] The Kremlin allows over 20,000 North Korean contractors to earn remittances in Russia and overlooks numerous illegal business deals and transactions within Russia's jurisdiction. Russia maintains ground and air transportation links with Pyongyang. The Air Koryo's fleet consists of Russian-produced aircraft, which are dependent on Moscow for services and spare parts. Moscow supports modest international sanctions on Pyongyang to avert more severe ones and utilises public diplomacy and UN vetoes to constrain the ROK–US response to DPRK provocations. Russia strives to strengthen its position in the Asian security environment and insists that it is a player on all Korean security issues promoting harmonious relations with both Koreas. Putin has strengthened bilateral ties with North Korea thereby increasing Moscow's influence with China, South Korea and the United States. The Kremlin denies that it sells weapons to North Korea.[40] Foreign Minister Sergey Lavrov contends that Moscow's goal is to achieve the denuclearisation of the entire Korean Peninsula — "not [just] to ensure that North Korea has no nuclear weapons but to ensure that there are no such weapons on the peninsula at all and the United States should not bring nuclear arsenal elements there."[41] Russia opposes regime change in North Korea fearing that the collapse of the DPRK would precipitate economic and humanitarian

---

[39] See http://www.washingtontimes.com/news/2017/feb/7/north-korea-puts-russia-atop-friendly-countries-li/.

[40] Russian official slams allegations of passing rocket technology to N Korea, *Sputnik*, February 8, 2016, http://sputniknews.com/world/20160208/1034384289/rogozin-allegations-rocket-technology-russia-pyongyang.html.

[41] Russian FM: Five-party nuclear talks 'not a good idea', Yonhap, January 27, 2016, http://english.yonhapnews.co.kr/national/2016/01/27/78/0301000000AEN2016012700060003
15F.html.

disaster, including a refugee crisis and military conflict on Russia's doorstep. It also fears Washington's geopolitical gains from having a powerful reunified Korea as an ally (Rozman, 2015). Moscow is concerned that the spread of nuclear weapons may degrade its nuclear deterrent and worries Russia because North Korea's nuclear test site is located near Vladivostok, Russia's largest city in the Far East.

South Korea

The longstanding US–ROK alliance has deep roots. The US played a significant role in the development and history of the Republic of Korea (ROK). After the Second World War, the US liberated the southern part of the Korean Peninsula from Japanese annexation (1910) and created a condition for an independent ROK in 1948. A year later, after American troops left South Korea, in tandem with Soviet troop withdrawals from North Korea, the DPRK exploited the security vacuum and invaded the South. During the 1950–1953 Korean War, 36,516 Americans were killed. The continuous presence of the US troops in the ROK has been the main factor preventing another attack from the North. The 1950–1953 Korean War ended with an armistice, not a peace treaty, between the governments of North Korea and People's Republic of China (PRC) on one side and the US-led United Nations Command on the other. South Korea supported US efforts to contain Soviet and Chinese communism during the Cold War. During the Vietnam War, the ROK deployed more than 50,000 troops to support the US-allied South Vietnamese government against a Soviet–Chinese-backed Hanoi.

In the 1980s, the ROK added a new vector to its foreign policy — "Northern Policy" (*pukpang chongch'aek*) — designed to develop relations with the Communist bloc countries aligned with North Korea to engage in direct dialogue with Pyongyang (Savada and Shaw, 1990). The Northern Policy and the ROK's rising economy enabled it to expand its global presence in the 1990s across more than 130 countries in sports, trade and diplomacy. South Korea's economic and diplomatic ties with the former Soviet states grew stronger at the end of the Cold War. The Soviet collapse deprived Pyongyang of its diplomatic anchor and forced North

Korea to explore new diplomatic options with South Korea, the United States and Europe (Weitz, 2015).

In June 2018, the ROK's President Moon Jae-in visited Russia. In his speech at the Russian Duma, Moon called for trilateral cooperation between the ROK, North Korea and Russia on the preservation of security in Northeast Asia. Moon's visit to Russia opened opportunities for Moscow to develop economic ties through implementation of joint projects such as the construction of LNG pipeline links and railways across the Korean Peninsula. Moon and Putin released a joint statement emphasising their commitment to the denuclearisation of the Korean Peninsula.[42]

Cooperation with the ROK may further Russia's aspirations in the Asia-Pacific region. For example, it may facilitate Russian economic objectives in Vietnam, Thailand and the Philippines. Moscow is aware of Japan's reluctance to condemn Russia for poisoning of Sergei and Yulia Skripal, and the trade dispute between the US and Russia. Even though Japan imposes sanctions on Russia, Moscow may believe that Russia could persuade Japan to be more accommodating by improving in the Kremlin's relations with the ROK.

Russia–India

Russia and India have maintained strong cooperative relations across shared geopolitical, security and economic interests. The rise of Chinese economic power, the growing role of the US defence equipment in India's national security and India's growing GDP however have reduced Moscow's importance to New Delhi. On the economic front, Rosneft's purchase of a 49% stake in India's largest private oil refiner, Essar Oil, represents one of the biggest foreign investment in India's history (Frolovskiy, 2018). Indian firms also bought shares in Russian domestic energy projects (Jha, 2016). However, the idea of building pipelines that would connect India and Russia through Afghanistan, Iran or Pakistan remains unrealised due to high costs and geopolitical issues.

---

[42] See https://thediplomat.com/2018/07/are-warming-russia-south-korea-relations-a-game-changer/.

Russian–Indian diplomatic ties remain important as the leaders of these two nations meet regularly at bilateral and multilateral meetings such as at the BRICS (Brazil–Russia–India–China–South Africa), the Shanghai Cooperation Organization (SCO) and the UN Security Council (UNSC). India supported Western sanctions imposed on Moscow for the Soviet military occupation of Afghanistan in the 1980s, occupation of Georgian territory since 2008, annexation of Crimea in March 2014 and interference in the eastern Ukraine and other countries (Chacko, 2014). Just like Russia, India favours a multipolar world system as it seeks its accession to an important global position (Chaudhury, 2016). However, New Delhi is concerned that the US–Russia tensions may force Moscow to cooperate with Beijing more closely (Madan, 2014).

Russian–Indian defence and security cooperation remains substantial and is facilitated by frequent consultations on mutual security challenges and regular military exercises. Russia and India have held regular "INDRA" naval manoeuvres since 2003. The fleets of the two nations rehearse maritime law enforcement, sharing intelligence, surface warfare, anti-air and anti-submarine defence and countering piracy, terrorism, and narcotics trafficking in various locations in the Indian and Pacific Oceans.[43] The two national militaries also hold joint Aviandra air force drills.[44] These exercises promote mutual interoperability, generate arms sales and strengthen other defence ties (Richard Weitz, 2019).

India has become the leading importer of foreign military technology (Panda, 2013). Despite India's increased arms trade with the US and Israel, Russia's arms sales to India remain significant (Mastny, 2010). India has acquired more weaponry from Russian/Soviet suppliers than from any other country. An enormous amount of the Soviet weapons possessed by India provide Russian defence companies with opportunities to sell spare parts and services to existing systems, in addition to providing

---

[43] India-Russia bilateral maritime exercise kicks off, *The Times of India*, December 15, 2016, http://timesofindia.indiatimes.com/city/visakhapatnam/India-Russia-bilateral-maritime-exercise-kicks-off/articleshow/55987598.cms.

[44] Russia, India to Continue Joint Air Force Drills in November — Moscow, *RIA Novosti*, August 29, 2014, http://en.ria.ru/military_news/20140829/192465494/Russia-India-to-Continue-Joint-Air-Force-Drills-in-November--.html.

upgrades to old weapons and weapon systems. Thus, Indian military platforms, consisting mostly of the Soviet or Russian planes, tanks and warships, depend substantially on Russian firms for maintenance and upgrading. Approximately half of the major surface combatants and combat submarines in service with the Indian Navy were constructed in Russia or the Soviet Union (Gorenburg, 2011). Russia has leased nuclear-powered attack submarines (SSN) to India to allow the Indian Navy to gain experience with maritime nuclear propulsion.

The Indian government requires any foreign arms transfer to be accompanied with the transfer of technology (Kramnik, 2008). In order to meet this demand, Moscow strove to transform the bilateral buyer–seller relationship into a partnership founded on joint research, development and production of weapons systems for both countries as well as for global sales. In addition, Russian arms production is cost-effective compared to their Western equivalents.

The US announcement that countries engaged with Russia's defence and intelligence sectors face secondary US sanctions poses a threat to the US–India relations. A 2017 law imposed by Congress requires the president to penalise countries that conduct a "significant transaction" with Russia's defence sector.[45]

Despite the US reminding India about the sanctions under the Countering America's Adversaries Through Sanctions Act (CAATSA), in mid-July 2018, former Defence Minister Nirmala Sitharaman said that India and Russia are close to concluding the S-400 deal and that India would go forward with the deal, adding that the new US law isn't binding on India. The sale of the S-400 from Russia would result in the deployment of the three regiments of the S-400s in western India near Pakistan and two regiments in the east near China (Gady, 2018).

India received a warning from the US about buying weapons from Russia on August 30, 2018 (Trivedi and Pande, 2018). But after lobbying from Defense Secretary James Mattis, Congress granted the US president and the secretary of state the option of approving waivers, such as when an ally nation is transitioning from Russian legacy gear to Western arms.

---

[45]See https://thediplomat.com/2018/07/the-us-india-partnership-and-its-discontents-managing-trump-era-turbulence/.

At this point, it is unclear whether the US will grant a waiver to India or not.[46] The US admitted India to a tier-one strategic partner (Farley, 2018), granting New Delhi an access to a spectrum of military technologies by relaxing requirements for individual licenses. President Trump needs to make the waiver decision, which most members of Congress would support.

The deterioration of Russian–US ties has raised concerns among the US officials about potential Russian access to advanced US defence technologies provided to India, which remains highly dependent on the Russian strategic technologies.

Russia and the Middle East

Russian relations in the Middle East

During the Cold War, the Middle East became a critical zone of strategic competition between Russia and the US. Russia has been increasingly influential throughout the Middle East since 2000. In 2003, Putin announced that Russia would cooperate with the Islamic world, particularly in conflicts involving the US. Russia together with Iran opposed the invasion of Iraq. After 2012, Moscow conducted reconnaissance, tested the ground for deeper involvement and strengthened relations with regional leaders. Russia positioned itself as an opportunistic power by abstaining from involvement in domestic regional affairs. Later, involvement in the Syrian conflict increased Moscow's confidence in its ability to shape regional dynamics.

The western sanctions imposed on Russia after its aggression in Ukraine targeted Russia's energy sector — the key proxy of Russia's influence. In response, Moscow turned to the fast-growing energy consumer China. However, slow progress in dealing with the Chinese re-directed Russia's attention back to the Middle East, which during the Cold War was a critical zone of strategic competition between Russia and the US.

After the collapse of the USSR, Russia's interest in the region faded because it strove to become a part of the West at the same time that the

---

[46] See https://www.voanews.com/a/india-not-guaranteed-us-sanctions-waiver-for-russian-missiles-official-says/4549808.html.

Kremlin sought to recover Russia from the 1990s turmoil. Israel, however, was an exception because it was considered a Western state in the region.

The 9/11 attacks and improved relations between Russia and the US impeded Russia's cooperation with Iran. However, the US invasion of Iraq boosted relations between Russia and Iran as they both opposed it. Reduction of tensions between the US and Russia in 2009 forced Moscow to adopt a harder line towards Tehran for its nuclear programme.

To broaden ties throughout the region, in 2003, Putin declared that Russia will cooperate with the Arab world and visited Egypt, Algeria, Jordan, Iran and some other regional countries. In 2007, Putin visited Saudi Arabia, UAE and Qatar in order to assert Russia's new role and influence in the region.

New approaches to the Middle East appeared in updated versions of the 2014 Russia's Military Doctrine and the 2013 Foreign Policy Concept of the Russian Federation. The documents stressed the importance of protecting Russia's interests abroad and increased its role in global security. The 2016 Foreign Policy Concept specifically mentioned the Middle East and foreign interference there as a reason for instability and extremism that directly affect Russia. This statement justified Russia's intervention in Syria. The document emphasised the President's intention to counter instability before it reached Russia's borders.

The Kremlin has changed its policy towards the Middle East. It has stopped treating the region as a tool to dealing with the West and started focusing on mutual benefits. Putin included the Middle East in Russia's sphere of influence and called the US and the EU "new crusaders".

Russia has conducted reconnaissance, tested the ground for deeper involvement and strengthened relations with the regional leaders, positioning itself as an opportunistic power by abstaining from involvement in domestic regional affairs. This helped Russia to strengthen its relations with Iran and develop a basis for political relations with Egypt.

After strengthening its existing relations with Syria, Egypt and Israel, Russia expanded its outreach to other countries including those with which it encountered difficulties developing dialogues such as Qatar. Within a framework of the Russia–GCC Strategic Dialogue and the Arab–Russia Cooperation Forum, Moscow was able to engage with many leaders of dominant regional countries. Through its dialogue with Israel, Moscow secured Israel's neutral position on the Russian aggression in Ukraine. Further out, in order to prevent the Middle Eastern states from thinking of Russia as an enemy of Islam, Moscow encouraged political groups from the Organisation of Islamic Cooperation (OIC) and League of Arab States (LAS) to support radical Islamists in Caucasus and central Asia. Finally, Russia sought to demonstrate that it is an important player in the regional affairs.

Aspirations to restore Russia's position as a world power and growing tensions with the West after the Ukrainian crisis drove Russia to interfere in the Syrian war. Moscow sought to signal to the US that it can cause problems if its views are ignored.[47]

Russia sought to establish a permanent military presence in Syria to acquire air and naval supremacy in the Black Sea and the Eastern Mediterranean. The USSR operated the Soviet 5th Squadron in the Mediterranean despite Moscow having no permanent bases in the region. In 2013, the Russian President decided to revive a naval presence there and established the Mediterranean Task Force (MTF) within the Black Sea Fleet. The establishment of permanent bases in Syria allows Russia to overcome the difficulties related to refuel and restocking food and water. In 2013, Vladimir Putin said that Russia may use these warships for operations in the Atlantic and the Indian Ocean, if such a need emerges.

Russia has essentially developed what some analysts call an anti-access, area-denial (A2/AD) strategy in the Mediterranean. Along with the deployment of the S-400 air-defence system to Syria, in November 2015 (and to Crimea, in August 2016), the Russian naval group in the Eastern Mediterranean is equipped with Kalibr cruise missiles and P-800 Onyx anti-ship missiles, which create an added advantage against a potential enemy. Russia's presence in the Mediterranean challenges NATO's

---

[47]Official website of the President of Russia (2012), 'Vstrecha s Prezidentom Irana Makhmudom Akhmadinezhadom' [Meeting with Iranian President Mahmud Ahmadinejad], 7 June 2012, http://www.kremlin.ru/news/15590 (accessed on February 17, 2015). Interviews with experts on Russian domestic policy in St Petersburg, Moscow, London and Washington DC, in November 2014, and between January and July 2015. For more details, see Kozhanov (2015, 2018) and Ministry of Foreign Affairs of the Russian Federation (2015).

freedom of action there as well as parts of the Middle East. This was demonstrated by the *de facto* no-fly zone that Russian air-defence systems established over parts of Syria, Turkey as well as the Eastern Mediterranean.

Syrian conflict

In 2013, Russia gained positive influence in the region after it prevented the Western military operation against the Assad regime. The reluctance of the US and the UK governments to get approval to intervene after the use of chemical weapons in Damascus provided Russia with critical time to provide assistance. The Obama administration strived to reduce the US involvement in the region and particularly in the Syrian civil war helped Russia to raise its stance in the region as well.

As the Syrian conflict unfolded, Russia became concerned over the growing number of Russian-speaking jihadists from the post-Soviet space, who fought against Assad. In addition to its desire to prevent the West from overthrowing Assad, Russia feared that the fall of the Assad regime would promote jihadist movements, which could spread to Russia. To protect its position in the region, Russia made a decision to send troops to Syria. Moscow's actions in Syria, Egypt and Iran signalled Russia's growing international power (Evstratov, 2012).[48]

Syria's "Arab Spring"

The Arab Spring helped Russia to strengthen its relations with the Middle East. The Arab uprisings began in January 2011 with the Tunisian revolution, and then reached Syria by March, when peaceful protests erupted into a serious internal conflict. The torture of students, who drew anti-government graffiti, drove residents of Dara to the streets to protest violence. The unrest spread around the country. People demanded reforms, political freedom, the ousting of Assad and equal rights for Kurds. In April, the government invoked the 1963 emergency law, which enabled it to suspend constitutional rights. The government shut down water and

---

[48]Interviews with US experts on Russia in San Francisco and Washington DC, January 22–28, 2016. Kozhanov (2018).

electricity, confiscated food and began a series of crackdowns by deploying tanks and opening fire on demonstrators. The fact that the Assad's and the elite belong to Alawite sect, a minority in Sunni country, complicated the conflict.[49]

Through its description of "colour revolutions", Moscow accuses the West of interfering in other states' affairs and destabilising the world order by engineering revolutions to impose American-style democracy on other countries. The Arab Spring affected Russia's interests in many ways. Russia's arms exports declined due to the fall of the Gaddafi regime, the railway corporation RZD that planned to work with the Gaddafi government lost its potential profits, more opportunities were lost in the energy sector as Russia was planning to develop Libya's resources in exchange for cancelling Libya's debt ($4.5 billion) to the USSSR. In Syria, Russian investment had increased because the Kremlin had agreed to forgive Syria's debt ($14 billion) to the USSR, allowing Russian business to participate in the development of Syria's resources. The fall of Gaddafi and the potential fall of Assad threatened Russia. The Arab Spring interfered in Russia' development of closer relations with the regional powers.

The Syrian conflict sparked Islamic radicalism across the post-Soviet space. It helped Russian jihadists unite, to reach out to international terrorist organisations and become a part of global terrorist network. In 2016, the number of the Russian fighters in Syria and Iraq has significantly increased. These fighters were represented in the Al-Qaeda-affiliated Hayat Tahrir al-Sham and ISIS.

Moscow feared that Russian-speaking jihadists would use their experiences and connections to fight the Kremlin. Meanwhile, economic stagnation intensified by the Western sanctions imposed after aggression in Ukraine and annexation of Crimea forced Russia to seek closer cooperation with the Middle East — an attractive market for Russia's machinery and military equipment, oil and gas, petrochemical, and metallurgical and agricultural products. Russia has expanded its cooperation with the region across airspace and nuclear fields.

---

[49] Arab Spring: A Research Study & Study Guide, Cornell University Library, http://guides.library.cornell.edu/c.php?g=31688&p=200753.

The region's disappointment with the West drove the regional states to cooperate with Russia as a tool to dealing with the West.

Significant changes in the Russian relations with the West could affect Russian policy towards the Middle East. However, changes are unlikely in the short term. Russia sees itself as a Eurasian power with an ability to balance between Middle Eastern powers. Moscow will continue to exploit the regional condition against the US and seize profitable opportunities for Russia. Developments in Syria and ties with Iran and Egypt strengthen Moscow's confidence. The potential areas of interests between the West and Russia include countering WMDs in the region and energy cooperation.

Russia and Iran

During the Soviet period, relations between the Kremlin and Iran centred on arms sales. After the Iranian Revolution of 1979, Tehran was isolated from the West and Russia was the only country that provided Iran with arms through the 2000s.

The Syrian war improved relations between Russia and Iran. The two countries supported the Assad regime and contributed military assets to the conflict. In 2015, Russia participated in the Joint Comprehensive Plan of Action seeking removal of international sanctions against Iran. The changes strengthened energy cooperation between the two petroleum competitors. Russia is providing Iran with much-needed investment, perhaps in part to undermine Saudi Arabia's influence and make Moscow the oil superpower (Baulch, 2017).

Iraq

Russian energy companies participated in the development of Iraqi oil reserves following the toppling of Saddam Hussein. In 2009, Lukoil became a shareholder of one of the largest oil fields in the world. Gazpromneft also won the contract to develop the Badra field. Moreover, Gazpromneft holds a participating interest in several developments in Kurdistan.

Rosneft acquired the controlling stake of another Russian oil company, Bashneft, with rights to operate inside Iraq. Rosneft agreed to take control of Kurdistan's main oil pipeline during the political crisis in September 2017. Kurdistan plans to repay the loan with future oil sales. Iraqi oil is important for Russia as it could strengthen Russia's economic and political presence in Iraq and Kurdistan.

There's no conclusive indication whether Russia's energy diplomacy with Iraqi Kurdistan will yield the expected strategic dividends, though it's also too early to discount the possibility.

Turkey

In Turkey, President Recep Tayyip Erdoğan and his Justice and Development Party (AKP) used the attempted coup in July 2016 to justify a crackdown on suspected plotters as well as other members of the population. Western powers opposed Erdoğan's actions, but Putin called Erdoğan to tell him that Moscow supports his campaign to remove the dissent. Putin hosted his Turkish counterpart in St. Petersburg less than a month after the failed coup and provided Erdoğan "moral support" and "solidarity". All this happened right after Erdoğan's apology to Russia for the November 2015 downing of a Russian Su-24 jet over Syria.

The Turkish Stream project is an example of convergence of Russian and Turkish strategic interests. Russia needs Turkey in order to gain important energy access to the Balkans, while Turkey needs Russia in order to do the same through its transit role in facilitating this project.

Over the past few months, the agreement between Russia and Turkey on avoiding ground offensive in demilitarised zone in rebel-held areas of the northwest of Syria has been consistently violated. A number of attacks on Turkish troops, a Turkish observation post and other events point at the tensions between Russia and Turkey. "Moscow has run out of patience with Ankara and its inability to rein in Hayat Tahrir al-Sham (Organization for the Liberation of the Levant) and secure the full implementation of the demilitarised zone, while the Turkish side has grown frustrated that Russian promises to push the Kurdish YPG International (People's Protection Units International) out of Tel Rifaat have remained unfulfilled" (Macaron, 2019).

Israel

Russia's intervention in Syria has strengthened Moscow's ties with Israel. Russia seeks to protect Iran and Israel strives to avoid confrontation with the Kremlin by strengthening military communications with Russia's military.[50] Russian elite appreciates Israel's military economic technological progress and is aware of its connections to the US. Israel has curried the Russian favour by refusing to impose economic sanctions against Russia for its annexation of Crimea.

Russia intensified its diplomacy with Israel and Palestine in 2016. In 2017, Russia hosted all major Palestinian political organisations, including Fatah, Hamas, the PLO and the Palestinian Islamic Jihad, for direct talks.

With the US recognition of Jerusalem as the capital of Israel, Washington and its allies cannot lead the Israeli–Palestinian talks. This presented a unique opportunity for Moscow to position itself as a mediator. Russian diplomats engaged both parties following President Trump's announcement (Barmin, 2018).

Egypt

Egypt has gone through a wave of authoritarianism, with President Abdel Fattah El Sisi cracking down on dissent. Moscow supports Sisi's fight against extremism in the Sinai as well as his crackdown on dissent. Egypt has become a key partner for Russia in the Middle East. The two countries signed a protocol on military cooperation in March 2015 and ramped up joint military exercises. Just as in Syria, counterterrorism cooperation has become a key element of the bilateral relationship.

Egypt and Turkey demonstrate that Vladimir Putin seeks to strengthen authoritarian permanence across the region. Putin's support for autocratic regimes will be welcomed by other powers in the region.

---

[50] Stephen Blank, Russia and Israel: Friends with benefits, https://thehill.com/opinion/international/388217-russia-and-israel-friends-with-benefits.

In terms of energy, by obtaining influence over Egyptian gas supplied to the EU, Moscow seeks to undermine Western diversification of energy supply strategies developed to bring gas from Central Asia.

Russia is pursuing closer military cooperation with Cairo, a partner with which Moscow had a strong partnership under Gamal Abd'el Nasir and more recently with President Abdel Fatah El Sisi. Military-technical cooperation between the two countries is on the rise and now extends to annual joint naval drills and military exercises as Russia looks for additional access to Egypt's military infrastructure. It has intensified its use of Egyptian facilities at the border with Libya, including the port of Marsa Matrouh and the base at Sidi Barrani.

Saudi Arabia

The relationship between Russia and Saudi Arabia, the two former adversaries, has warmed. Initially, driven by the collapse of energy prices in 2014, the relationship between the world's largest energy producers was based on stabilising the oil market that affects both economies. Lately, cooperation between energy powers has been acquiring strategic overtones. Both countries understand that in order to protect their petroleum export-dependent economies they need to cooperate to maintain stable oil prices. Cooperation in oil markets revealed new opportunities across other areas of interests such as economic, military and diplomatic spheres. For example, last October, King Salaman travelled to Moscow for the first time and agreed to form a $1 billion joint energy investment fund with President Putin. King Salaman also agreed to purchase Russia's S-400 air defence system for Saudi Arabia, which previously has relied on Western military equipment. Saudi Arabia's investments help Russia mitigate the effects of American sanctions. As for Saudi Arabia, it is seeking to improve its position in Syria by improving relations with Russia. Last November, Russian Foreign Minister Sergei Lavrov reaffirmed Russia's commitment to cooperate with Saudi Arabia. Improved relations between Russia and Saudi Arabia include some potential conflict of interest with Russia's strategic approach to the Middle East. Saudi Arabia wants to isolate Iran and neutralise its relations with Russia, Iraq, Yemen and other countries (Rahman, 2018).

Libya

Moscow's energy cooperation with Libya, Algeria and Egypt represent one of the core elements of its global energy strategy. Russia seeks to establish its superpower status across the region by exploiting its relations with Libyan leaders to shape energy supplies to the EU. As in Syria, Russia strives to position itself as an important player capable of resolving regional conflicts under the pretext of the fight against terrorism (Mammadov, 2018).

Moscow suffered economic losses from the overthrow of Gaddafi. It wants to secure its construction, arms sales, railway and other projects. Moreover, during the early 2000s, Gaddafi granted Russia access to the port of Benghazi. Moscow may now wish to revive and perhaps expand this type of relationship.

The US–Russia relations play an important role in Russia's position on the 2011 Libyan's crisis. Russia stopped arms exports to the Gaddafi regime; however, it did not veto the UN Security Council Resolution of 1973.

Algeria

Russia is increasingly looking at ports in Algeria, Tunisia and Morocco. Moscow has significantly improved its diplomatic engagement with each of these actors since the collapse of the USSR. Algeria has been Moscow's most committed partner since the 1960s. In 2001, during the visit of Algerian President Abdelaziz Bouteflika to Russia, the two countries signed a declaration of strategic partnership. Moscow continues to export its weapons to the country: 91% of Algerian arms are purchased from Russia. In 2006, the two governments signed Algeria's largest post-Cold War arms deal, which amounted to $7.5 billion. Moscow's ambition to play a role in the resolution of the Libyan crisis, combined with threats from terrorist groups that find refuge in Mali, Niger and Chad, drove Russia to expand its security cooperation with the country. In 2010, Moscow asked Algeria for access to the Mers el-Kebir naval base, near Oran. The two countries signed an agreement on counterterrorist cooperation in 2016 and have already held two rounds of consultations on stepping up joint countering violent extremism strategy in North Africa as well as set up regular exchanges of intelligence on extremist groups (Mammadov, 2018).

The October 2017 visit of Prime Minister Dmitry Medvedev to Algeria is also remarkable in that it demonstrated that the Maghreb is again on Moscow's radar. Besides regular arms deals talks, the two sides reportedly discussed an agreement on a potential purchase of Russian S-400 missile systems, which Moscow only exports to select clients. If implemented, such an arms sale would symbolise a new strategic era in Russian–Algerian relations. Russia seeks presence in the Maghreb's energy sector because Algeria, the second largest gas exporter to Europe, creates uncertainties to Russia's strategies in the EU.

Russia and the Arctic

The Arctic region is a significant aspect of the New Great Game yet receives little attention in Western media in comparison to the Middle East and China. The competition for natural resources, transportation routes and for communications infrastructure in the Arctic is well underway. Since 1821,[51] Russia has been successful at exploring and utilising various channels and routes to achieve national interests and security objectives.[52] Russia's engagement strategy in this region is outlined in its Concept of Foreign Policy Doctrine of 2016 under items 75 and 76.[53]

---

[51] See http://csef.ru/ru/politica-i-geopolitica/501/geopoliticheskie-interesy-rossii-v-arktike-5931, accessed on 28 January 2019.

[52] *Ibid.*

[53] See http://www.mid.ru/en/foreign_policy/official_documents/-/asset_publisher/CptICk B6BZ29/content/id/2542248. Item 75: "The Russian Federation is open to building relations with Canada based on respect for mutual interests and the experience amassed in the course of cooperation, including in the Arctic". Item 76: "Russia pursues a policy aimed at preserving peace, stability and constructive international cooperation in the Arctic. The Russian Federation believes that the existing international legal framework is sufficient to successfully settle any regional issues through negotiation, including the issue of defining the outer limits of the continental shelf in the Arctic Ocean. Russia considers that the Arctic States bear special responsibility for the sustainable development of the region and in this connection advocates enhanced cooperation in the Arctic Council, the coastal Arctic Five and the Barents Euro-Arctic Council. Russia will be firm in countering any attempts to introduce elements of political or military confrontation in the Arctic, and, in general,

Russian jockeying in the Arctic region can be viewed as part of an overarching strategy to develop its economic security strategy in the world's oceans and seas. It allows the Kremlin to increase its naval presence in the Atlantic and Pacific Oceans and in the Barents Sea and Bering Sea.

Russia and Latin America

Russian policy towards Latin America is opportunistic. The Kremlin has recently intensified its activities in Latin America for economic and geopolitical reasons. It seeks to contain the US, avoid international isolation, counter the effects of Western sanctions, promote energy and trade partnerships and increase weapons' sales in conjunction with military cooperation. Moscow is constructing military bases and pursuing energy partnerships in accordance with the Russian Concept of Foreign Policy signed in 2013 and again in 2016. The concepts emphasise "the expansion of political cooperation, promotion of trade and economic, investment, innovation, cultural and humanitarian cooperation, joint search for answers to new challenges and threats, consolidation of Russian companies in the dynamically developing sectors of industry, energy, communications and transport in the region".[54]

Latin America greatly benefits from closer relations with Russia. Moscow helps Latin American states to develop their natural resources, militaries and tools to counterbalance the US. Areas of cooperation include nuclear energy, oil and gas, IT and telecommunications, military-technical, large-scale infrastructure projects and agriculture.

The most troubling aspect of Russian ties with Bolivia, Venezuela, Ecuador and Nicaragua is military. Russia is not only constructing missile bases but also assisting Bolivian president Evo Morales build a nuclear research facility. The government of Nicaragua has allowed Russia to

---

politicize international cooperation in the region. Using the Northern Sea Route as Russia's national transport route in the Arctic, as well as for transit shipments between Europe and Asia is significant for the region development."

[54] See http://csef.ru/ru/politica-i-geopolitica/326/geopoliticheskie-interesy-rossii-v-latinskoj-amerike-4835.

establish a Global Navigation Satellite System (GLONASS) facility in Managua (Ellis, 2017).[55,56,57] The President of Suriname, Desi Bouterse, plans to sign a military cooperation agreement with Russia. El Salvador's president will likely ally with Russia, as he did during the El Salvador Civil War, unless the US fully sponsors the Alliance for Prosperity (AFP) aid programme for the region and maintains temporary status for hundreds of thousands of Salvadorian migrants, who send their remittances to El Salvador. It is possible that Russia will re-establish its signal intelligence collection facility at Lourdes, Cuba. In Venezuela, which is on the verge of bankruptcy, Russia will likely extend its credits to the Maduro regime, deepen its engagement in regional oil production and expand its air and naval bases.

Russia's activities in Latin America raise concerns about its interference with regional elections. In Mexico, Russia Today (RT) and Sputnik had been transmitting programmes that support Andres Manuel Lopez Obrador, a potential ally of Moscow, for over a year prior to the election day of July 1, 2018. By capitalising on tensions between the Trump administration and some Latin American countries, Russia is successfully disseminating anti-American propaganda to Latin American audiences in Spanish 24/7. President Trump's censure of NAFTA and crack down on immigration from Latin America has significantly reduced Washington's influence in the region. The number of Mexicans who view the US in negative terms has doubled over the last 2 years (Weiss, 2018). In Brazil, Moscow will try to align with Bolsonaro, a new nationalist leader, by exploiting his conservative views. Bolsonaro's rise may revive important arms deals, including the Pantsir S-1 air defence system. At the same time, Russia is concerned about its investments in Venezuela as Bolsonaro

---

[55] https://www.csis.org/analysis/russian-engagement-latin-america-update.

[56] See http://www.sldinfo.com/preparing-for-2018-implementing-the-trump-administration-national-security-strategy/.

[57] The mysterious Russian Satellite Station in Nicaragua, June 30, 2017, https://havana-times.org/?p=126001. President of Russia (July 23, 2014), Law Ratifying Russia-Nicaragua agreement on space cooperation, http://eng.kremlin.ru/acts/22735.

could potentially counter the influx of Venezuelan refugees with military forces and align with the US.[58]

Ultimately, Russia's interests, goals and diplomacy in Latin America have significantly changed since 2013. Targeted strategies enable Russia to strengthen its position across Latin America, counterbalance Western sanctions through economic activities and constantly pressure the US with new security challenges.[59,60]

Western Vulnerabilities

Putin's Russia is fishing in the world's troubled waters. The particulars of each case are important, but there are a few critical overarching issues as follows:

(1) *The geopolitical commitment of NATO member nations:* A total of 17 out of 29 NATO participants are also members of the Russian-led organisations (CIS and/or ICIE). Due to the close ties to Russia, these NATO members also have various agreements and/or reliance on Russia in key economic and energy security sectors, in addition to political-military partnerships.

(2) *Sustainability of the West's military dominance*: Russia and its allies consider unconventional warfare superior (especially non-contact tactics such as disinformation, information warfare, cyberwarfare, utilization of 5th columns, etc.) to conventional warfare. Are they deceiving themselves?

(3) Is pan-Slavism resurgent, and if so can the Kremlin harness its geopolitical potential?

(4) The revived religious-based doctrine entails a foreign policy objective to unite enemies of the West based on religion. Of course, one result of unification may be rifts/divisions within the Slavic Church. Today, given that Islam is the second most popular religion in Russia, there

---

[58] See http://tass.com/world/1028276.

[59] See http://publications.armywarcollege.edu/pubs/2345.pdf.

[60] *Ibid.*

is a united front of the Muslim world with Eastern Christianity, including spiritual values of each against Western immorality and liberal values and schools of thought. A political by-product of this strategy is the proliferation of Russian "neo-imperialism". It is also important to note that this consideration entails modification of Russian ideological doctrines based on modernised nationalism, ultra-nationalism and xenophobia.[61]

(5) Sino-Russian energy cooperation.

(6) Fluid geopolitical landscape and changes in the composition of the European Parliament.

(7) Growing populism.

(8) Effects of growing tensions between major powers.

(9) Danger of miscommunication and miscalculation between states heightened by the absence of a rule-based international order.

Conclusion

Although Russia, China and others contend that the world is evolving peacefully into a new multipolar order, the reality is closer to Cold War: a bipolar engagement between NATO and America, and the SCO/CSTO/CIS/ICIE. Russian military power is rising rapidly in conventional, nuclear and asymmetric warfighting, while the allegiance of some members in both camps is being tested (EU, Turkey, Belarus).

Western leaders are aware of most fundamentals, but there is no consensus about the seriousness of these threats or strategies for managing them. They are content to modestly increase defence spending, dabble with economic sanctions, admonish rivals, chant the mantra of globalization and muddle through, just like their Cold War-era predecessors. They could be right, but this time the outcome could be different because Russia has become a workably competitive market economy, allied with an ascendant China. It would be wise to plan accordingly while taking into consideration that regardless of Russia's motives to promote peace and social justice on a global scale, its actions pose security and political problems to Western interests.

---

[61] See http://svop.ru/wp-content/uploads/2014/02/00strategy21_intro.pdf, accessed on 1 August 2018.

References

Barmin, Y. (2018). Russia in the Middle East Until 2024: From hard power to sustainable influence. Available at: https://jamestown.org/program/russia-middle-east-2024-hard-power-sustainable-influence/?mc_cid=3c5e07d4a6&mc_eid=4c17b7b126 (accessed 8 March 2018).

Baulch, W. (2017). The future of Russia-Iran relations. Available at: https://www.foreignbrief.com/former-soviet-union/future-russia-iran-relations/.

Bodner, M. (2014). With Ukraine revitalizing NATO, Russia dusts off its own security alliance. *The Moscow Times*, 23 October 2014. Available from: www.themoscowtimes.com/business/article/with-ukraine-revitalizing-nato-russia-dusts-off-its-own-security-alliance/509986.html.

Chacko, P. (2014). Why India doesn't support Western sanctions on Russia. East Asia Forum. Available at: http://www.eastasiaforum.org/2014/05/06/why-india-doesnt-support-western-sanctions-on-russia/.

Chaudhury, N. R. (2016). Russia, India have key roles in emerging world order: Analysts. RIR. Available at: in.rbth.com/russian_india_experts/2016/11/07/russia-india-have-key-roles-in-emerging-world-order-analysts_645527.

Daly, J. C. K. (2015). Russia taps SCO and CSTO to counter Islamic state. Silk Road Reporters. Available from: http://www.silkroadreporters.com/2015/09/24/russia-taps-sco-and-csto-to-counter-islamic-state.

Ellis, E. (2017). Russian engagement in Latin America: An update. Available at: https://www.csis.org/analysis/russian-engagement-latin-america-update.

Evstratov, A. (2012). Soyuz SShA i Al-Kayedy Prevrashchayet Siriyu vo Vtoroy Afganistan [USA and Al-Qaeda Are Turning Syria into Another Afghanistan]. *Iran.RU*. Available at: http://www.iran.ru/news/analytics/83243/Soyuz_SShA_i_Al_Kaidy_prevrashchaet_Siriyu_vo_vtoroy_Afganistan (accessed 28 March 2016).

Farley, R. (2018). The question of the decade: How closely will the US and India align?, https://thediplomat.com/2018/08/the-question-of-the-decade-how-closely-will-the-us-and-india-align/ (accessed August 30, 2018).

Frolovskiy, D. (2018). The coming India-Russia split. *The Diplomat*. Available at: https://thediplomat.com/2018/01/the-coming-india-russia-split/.

Gady, F.-S. (2018). India-Russia missile air defense deal still delayed. *The Diplomat*. Available at: https://thediplomat.com/2018/01/india-russia-missile-air-defense-deal-still-delayed/.

Golitsyn, A. (1995). *The Perestroika Deception*. Edward Harle Limited. London, United Kingdom and New York, NY.

Gorenburg, D. (2011). India-Russia defense integration is likely to endure. Russia Military Reform. Available at: http://russiamil.wordpress.com/2011/01/07/ india-russia-defense-integration-is-likely-to-endure/.

Jha, S. (2016). Billions in defense and energy deals underpin closer India-Russia ties. *World Politics Review*. Available at: http://www.worldpoliticsreview. com/articles/20353/billions-in-defense-and-energy-deals-underpin-closer- india-russia-ties

Johnson, D. (2016). Nuclear Weapons in Russia's approach to conflict. Fondation pour la Recherche Strategique. https://www.frstrategie.org/publications/ recherches-documents/nuclear-weapons-in-russia-s-approach-to-conflict- 2016-06.

Keaney, J. (2017). CSTO: A military pact to defend Russian influence. American Security Project. Available from: https://www.americansecurityproject.org/ csto-a-military-pact-to-defend-russian-influence/.

Kozhanov, N. (2015). Chaos in the Arab world suits Russia's domestic propa- ganda, *The World Today*, 71(4). https://tribunecontentagency.com/article/ chaos-in-the-arab-world-suits-russia039s-domestic-propaganda/.

Kozhanov, N. (2018). *Russian Policy across the Middle East: Motivations and Methods*, Chatham House. https://www.chathamhouse.org/publication/twt/ chaos-arab-world-suits-russia-s-domestic-propaganda

Kramnik, I. (2008). Russian aviation industry keeps its grip on the Indian market. *RIA Novosti*. Available at: http://russiamil.wordpress.com/2011/01/07/india- russia-defense-integration-is-likely-to-endure/.

Kropatcheva, E. (2016). Russia and the collective security treaty organisation: Multilateral policy or unilateral ambitions? *Europe-Asia Studies* 68(9), 1526–1552. Available from: http://dx.doi.org/10.1080/09668136.2016. 1238878.

Macaron, J. (2019). Are Russia and Turkey making deals or parting ways in Syria? Available at: https://www.aljazeera.com/indepth/opinion/russia-tur- key-making-deals-parting-ways-syria-190515163715038.html.

Madan, T. (2014). Mr. Putin goes to India: Five reasons the Russian president will be welcomed there. *Brookings*. Available at: http://www.brookings.edu/ blogs/up-front/posts/2014/12/09-5-reasons-putin-will-be-welcomed-in- india-madan.

Mammadov, R. (2018). Russia in the Middle East: Energy forever? Available at: https://jamestown.org/program/russia-middle-east-energy-forever/?mc_ cid=3c5e07d4a6&mc_eid=4c17b7b126.

Mastny, V. (2010). The Soviet Union's partnership with India, *Journal of Cold War Studies* 12(3), 50–90.

McDermott, R. (2015). Russia hosts CSTO exercises in western military district. The Jamestown Foundation. Available from: http://www.jamestown.org/ programs/edm/single/?tx_ttnews[tt_news]=44317&tx_ttnews[backPid]= 786&no_cache=1#.ViKjZ2uheUl.

Mihalka, M. (2006). Counterinsurgency, counterterrorism, state-building and security cooperation in Central Asia, *China and Eurasia Forum Quarterly* 4(2), 146–147. Available from: old.silkroadstudies.org/new/docs/CEF/ Quarterly/May_2006/Mihalka.pdf.

Ministry of Foreign Affairs of the Russian Federation (2015). Intervyu Ministra Inostrannikh Del Rossiyskoy Federatcii S. V. Lavrova v Pryamom Efire Radiostantsiy "Sputnik", "Ekho Moskvy", "Govorit Moskva" [Russian Foreign Minister Sergey Lavrov's Live Interview with Sputnik, Ekho Moskvy and Govorit Moskva Radio Stations], http://archive.mid.ru//brp.

Mowchan, J. A. (2009). The militarization of the collective security treaty organization. Center for Strategic Leadership, US Army War College. Available from: www.operationspaix.net/DATA/DOCUMENT/5078~v~The_Militarization_ of_the_Collective_Security_Treaty_Organization.pdf.

Mrvaljevic, S. (2015). Collective security treaty organization: Russia's answer to NATO? International Association for Political Science Students. Available from: www.iapss.org/2015/02/04/collective-security-treaty-organization-russias-answer-to-nato/.

Nanay, J. (2007). SCO gaining importance. *The National Interest*. Available from: http://nationalinterest.org/commentary/inside-track-sco-gaining-importance-1743.

Nikitin, A. (2007). Post-soviet military-political integration: The collective security treaty organization and its relations with the EU and NATO, *China and Eurasia Forum Quarterly* 5(1), 39. Available from: www.isn.ethz.ch/Digital-Library/Publications/Detail/?lang=en&id=31677.

Panda, A. (2013). India pushes Russia for greater inclusion in fifth generation fighter aircraft development. *The Diplomat*. Available at: http://thediplomat. com/2013/11/india-pushes-russia-for-greater-inclusion-in-fifth-generation-fighter-aircraft-development.

Pannier, B. (2004). Central Asia: Russia comes on strong (Part 2). RFE/RL. Available from: www.rferl.org/featuresarticle/2004/11/ffdd150c-4daa-4577-9d8a-893ff8613e82.html.

Rahman, O. H. (2018). Bottom of form Saudi Arabia hedges its bets through closer relations with Russia. Available at: https://www.worldpoliticsreview. com/trend-lines/24211/saudi-arabia-hedges-its-bets-through-closer-relations-with-russia (accessed 16 February 2018).

Roberts, B. (2015). *The Case for US Nuclear Weapons in the 21ˢᵗ Century*, Stanford University Press.

Rozman, G. (2015). North Korea's place in Sino-Russian relations and identities. *The Asian Forum*. Available at: http://www.theasanforum.org/north-koreas-place-in-sino-russian-relations-and-identities/.

Savada, A. M. and Shaw, W. (eds.) (1990). *South Korea: A Country Study*. GPO for the Library of Congress, Washington. Available at: http://countrystudies.us/south-korea/.

Trenin, D. (2005). *Russia's Nuclear Policy in the 21ˢᵗ Century Environment*. IFRI Security Studies Department, Paris, p. 15. Available at: https://www.ifri.org/en/publications/enotes/proliferation-papers/russias-nuclear-policy-21st-century-environment.

Trivedi, A. and Pande, A. (2018). India is getting cold feet about Trump's America. Available at: http://www.southasiaathudson.org/blog/2018/9/1/india-is-getting-cold-feet-about-trumps-america (accessed September 1, 2018).

Upadhyay, D. (2012). NATO versus CSTO: The clash between competing military alliances. Global Research: Russia & India Report. Available at: www.globalresearch.ca/nato-versus-csto-the-clash-between-competing-military-alliances/28612.

Weiss, A. S. (2018). Are Mexico's elections Russia's next target? Available at: https://carnegieendowment.org/2018/02/28/are-mexico-s-elections-russia-s-next-target-pub-75680.

Weitz, R. (2014a). Countering Russia's hybrid threats. International Center for Defence and Security. Available at: https://icds.ee/countering-russias-hybrid-threats/.

Weitz, R. (2014b). EU seeks energy security solutions to Russia gas challenge. The Hudson Institute. Available at: https://www.hudson.org/research/10372-eu-seeks-energy-security-solutions-to-russian-gas-challenge.

Weitz, R. (2015). Russian policy toward North Korea: Steadfast and changing, *International Journal of Korean Unification Studies* 24(3), 1–29.

Weitz, R. (2018). *Assessing the Collective Security Treaty Organization: Capabilities and Vulnerabilities*, United States Army War College Press. Available at: https://publications.armywarcollege.edu/pubs/3661.pdf.

Williams, P. and Felbab-Brown, V. (2012). Drug trafficking, violence, and instability. Strategic Studies Institute, US Army War College, p. 44. Available from: www.strategicstudiesinstitute.army.mil/pdffiles/pub1101.pdf.

Chapter 13

Western Sanctions against Russia: How Do They Work?

Susanne Oxenstierna

The West's economic sanctions imposed against Russia in the wake of the Kremlin's annexation of Crimea in 2014 have now been in place for almost 6 years. The objective of the sanctions is to pressure Russia to change its policies. Economic sanctions are widely used instruments in international policies for signalling to countries that their behaviour violates international norms. Are they effective?

This chapter analyses how the EU and US sanctions imposed on Russia in 2014–2018 have affected the Russian economy and its policies towards Ukraine. The analysis is qualitative focusing on probable ways that sanctions may have affected the Russian economy and Russia's policies towards Ukraine.

The first section of the chapter presents the analytical framework for assessing sanction effects. The second section provides an overview of the EU and US sanctions. The third section discusses how sanctions may have affected the Russian economy. The fourth section analyses potential political effects. A conclusion summarises the results.

Analytical Framework

Before developing an analytical framework, some key terms need to be defined as follows:

- *Sender* — the party that imposes the sanctions. The sender can be a single country, a multilateral uncoordinated group of countries or a transnational union like the EU, an international organisation or a combination of the three entities.
- *Target* — the sanctioned state.
- *Economic sanctions* — government-sponsored punitive economic measures by one or several senders designed to change in the target's behaviour.
- *Targeted sanctions* — focused on specific individuals or sectors, as opposed to broad or comprehensive sanctions. All the economic sanctions against Russia have been targeted sanctions.
- *Sanction success* — an outcome where economic sanctions have made a significant contribution to a change in the policy behaviour of the target in line with the objectives of the sender.
- *Sanction costs* — costs incurred by the target caused by the sanctions.
- *Sanction costs for the sender* — costs that the sender suffers when imposing sanctions.

A basic theoretical model

The objective of economic sanctions is usually to change the political behaviour of the target country in some specific area, e.g. persuading Russia to de-annex Crimea. The sender uses economic sanctions to create costs that coerce the target into changing its policy. The impact depends as much on political judgements as on the magnitude of the economic costs. It is often difficult to disentangle the impact of sanctions from other economic factors like oil price shocks and Russia's economic system.

Figure 1 shows a simplified version of a model developed by Blanchard and Ripsman (2013, pp. 16–36).

It depicts a sanctions regime with a sender and a target. The arrows reflect how economic sanctions filtered through different kinds of international and domestic factors may strengthen or weaken the impact of sanctions on the target. The model hypothesises that economic sanctions

Figure 1: Theoretical model for analysing the effects of sanctions.
Source: Oxenstierna and Olsson (2015, p. 23).

are filtered by different factors, which increase or decrease the pressure for political change. The combination of the sanctions and co-factors determine the impact of economic sanctions (Oxenstierna and Olsson, 2015, pp. 23–24).

Factors affecting the success of economic sanctions

Empirical studies of economic sanctions have focused on identifying factors that most strongly effect the probability of sanction success.[1] They build on two main data sets, the most widely cited, the "HSE0[2] data set", was created and updated by Hufbauer *et al.* (2007). It covers sanction cases from the period 1915–2000, the majority of which were imposed by the US. Bapat *et al.* (2013) used the "TIES — Threat and imposition of economic sanctions data set" constructed by Morgan *et al.* (2009). TIES contains threatened and imposed sanctions during the period 1971–2000.

Table 1 summarises the findings regarding the expected impact of factors on the target's political behaviour, in other words, each factor's expected contribution to sanction success. An expected *positive impact* is coded (+), and a *negative impact* is coded (–). If the expected impact

---

[1] See Oxenstierna and Olsson (2015) for a fuller literature review.
[2] HSEO is the acronym of the surnames of the researchers who developed the data set — Hufbauer, Schott, Elliott and Oegg (Hufbauer *et al.,* 2007).

Table 1: Selected factors' impact on sanction success according to different studies.

	Bapat *et al.* (2013)	Major (2012)	Drezner (2011)	Hufbauer *et al.* (2007)	Kaempfer and Lowenberg (2007)
Costs for the target	+			+	
Trade dependency	+	+	+/−		+/−
Duration of sanctions				−	
Cost for sender	+/−			+/−	
Multiple senders	−	−		−	
International institutions	+				+
Third-party countries				−	
Authoritarian regime	.	−			
Importance of conflict*	−				

Notes: *This variable has limited statistical significance.
Sources: Oxenstierna and Olsson (2015, p. 86).

has been found to be *inconclusive*, it is coded (+/−).The factors found in the literature may be organised according to whether they increase the effects of sanctions, decrease the effects or have an undetermined sign.[3]

Higher the *sanction costs*, the greater the political effect. High *trade dependence* between the sender and target may not have the desired effect if sanctions are costly to both parties. However, in the most recent studies (Bapat *et al.*, 2013; Major, 2012), trade dependence has a positive sign. Hufbauer *et al.* (2007) found that the duration of sanctions has a negative sign because the target tends to adapt to the sanction regime. However, it takes time for the full sanction costs to accrue in some cases. When this occurs, duration may have a positive effect.[4] *Cost for the sender* has an indeterminate sign because, on the

---

[3] See Oxenstierna and Olsson (2015, pp. 24–33, 86) for literature overview and more data.
[4] For instance, it took a long time for the sanctions against Libya 1969–2003 to hit the oil industry sufficiently hard to have an effect (Oxenstierna and Olsson, 2015, p. 29).

one hand, the sender may be hesitant to impose and uphold sanctions; on the other hand, the fact that the sender experiences costs makes the sanctions credible.

The factor *multiple senders* in Table 1 refers to sanctions of many uncoordinated senders. Three studies found that this factor has a negative impact. When a number of uncoordinated senders impose their own sanctions, they may be contradictory, diluting their impact. If sanctions are supported by an *international organisation* like the UN, they have high legitimacy and a better chance of succeeding. According to Hufbauer *et al.* (2007), the factor *alternative trade partners* has a negative effect. When the target can easily trade with other countries that do not sanction goods and services and replace trade partners that impose sanctions, the target suffers lower costs, which is negative for sanction success. Major (2012) finds a negative sign for *authoritarian regimes*, and this is explained by the fact that authoritarian regimes are more resilient since they control resource allocation and have the power to protect loyal elites from sanction effects.[5] Finally, the *importance of the conflict* affects the probability of sanction success negatively according to Bapat *et al.* (2013). If the conflict is vital for both parties, the target may be disinclined to change its policy, diminishing chances of sanction success (Oxenstierna and Olsson, 2015, pp. 24–27).

Sanctions Imposed on Russia

Russia annexed Crimea on March 18, 2014. The international community broadly condemned the annexation. On March 27, 2014, the General Assembly of the UN adopted Resolution 68/262 on Ukraine's territorial integrity (UN, 2014). The resolution stressed that the March 16, 2014 Crimean referendum was invalid. The General Assembly urged the international community not to acknowledge Crimea's annexation.

---

[5]The sanctions against Iraq during the period 1990–2003 caused a human catastrophe, but Saddam Hussein could still keep his inner circle and military establishment sufficiently satisfied (Oxenstierna and Olsson, 2015, p. 20).

EU sanctions

The EU has imposed three different sanctions regimes in connection with Russia's annexation of Crimea and support for Ukrainian secessionists. These regimes target different subjects and are linked to specific actions by individuals, legal entities and the Russian government.

(a) Individuals and legal entities involved in actions undermining or threatening Ukraine's territorial integrity, sovereignty and independence may be listed, and their assets in the EU area may be frozen. *This regime is linked to the annexation of Crimea and Russia's actions in eastern Ukraine.*

(b) Restrictions were imposed and later a total ban on the import into the EU of goods originating in Crimea or Sevastopol was made. *This regime is linked to Russia's illegal annexation of Crimea and Sevastopol.*

(c) Economic sanctions were made against Russia restricting the use of EU financial markets and prohibiting the export of armaments and dual-use goods and of equipment and services to the oil industry. *This regime is linked to Russia's actions in eastern Ukraine.*

The EU began sanctioning Russia in March 2014. It targeted individuals and entities undermining the sovereignty of Ukraine, regime (a) In June, sanctions were extended to regime (b) banning imports from Crimea and Sevastopol and proscribing financial, technical and insurance assistance in connection with such imports (Council Regulation 692/2014).

These sanctions were extended in July to include sectoral investments and export bans (Council Regulation 825/2014).

The EU decided to introduce economic sanctions, regime (c), after the escalation of military action in eastern Ukraine and the downing of Malaysian Airlines flight MH-17 on July 17, 2014 over a separatist-controlled area. The sanctions restricted Russian state-owned banks from seeking financing on European capital markets and trading with certain sectors (Council Regulation 833/2014). They prohibited investment or trade in Russian state securities with a state share of over 50% and a maturity of over 90 days. Five state-owned Russian banks — Sberbank, VTB, VEB, Vneshekonombank and Rosselkhozbank — and financial institutions and their subsidiaries were targeted. In addition, the EU imposed an embargo on the export and import of arms from Russia and related services. The export embargo includes dual-use products and advanced technologies used by the oil industry. The latter sanctions mainly affect advanced technologies for exploration on the Arctic shelf and thus Russia's opportunities for future oil incomes. The arms embargo and the other trade restrictions are only valid for new contracts.

These economic sanctions were reinforced and broadened in September 2014 (Council Regulation 960/2014). According to the revised regulation, the duration of credits was cut to 30 days for listed state-owned banks and the restrictions were extended to three state-owned defence companies — Oboronprom, United Aircraft Corporation and Uralvagonzavod and three state energy companies — Rosneft, Transneft and Gazprom Neft. Listed companies were denied new loans with a maturity greater than 30 days. Trade credits were permitted for loans outside prohibited areas, but not elsewhere including financing for oil exploration equipment needed on the Arctic shelf. Restrictions on the export of dual-use goods to the Russian military sector were extended to other companies with both military and civilian production.

All EU sanctions against Russia are *aligned to the complete implementation of the Minsk agreements. While this condition is not fulfilled, all sanctions* stay in force and are prolonged subsequently by the European Council, usually for 6–12 months at a time. Presently, the economic sanctions targeting specific sectors of Russia's economy are in place until January 31, 2019 (European Council, 2018a). Additions to the list of individuals and companies subject to restrictive measures are made continuously. For instance, in July 2018, the Council added six entities to the list because of *their involvement in the construction of the Kerch Bridge* connecting Russia to the illegally annexed Crimean peninsula. In August 2018, a total of 155 persons and 44 entities were subject to asset freezes and visa bans (European Council, 2018b).

The US sanctions against Russia

The basis for the US sanctions is four Presidential Executive Orders. The first, Executive Order 13660, was signed by President Barack Obama on March 6, 2014 and the second and third — 13661 and 13662 — in March 2014. The final Executive Order 13665 was enacted on 9 December . These executive orders increased the severity of American economic sanctions. In August 2017, the US added a requirement that the sanctions could not be lifted without Congressional authorisation — and their potential scope was significantly increased by giving the American president discretion to sanction any company involved in the construction of Russia's hydrocarbon export pipelines. President Trump extended all the executive orders linked to sanctions against Russia for 1 year on March 2, 2018 (Executive Order, 2018).

The aims of the US sanctions are to increase Russia's political isolation as well as the economic costs to Russia, especially in areas of importance to President Vladimir Putin and those close to him (Nelson, 2015, p. 5). In December 2014, President Obama signed the Ukraine Freedom Support Act authorising additional sanctions if and when required (Nelson, 2015, p. 5).

US sanctions include the following:

- Asset freezes for specific individuals. The assets of individuals close to Vladimir Putin have been frozen. US individuals and entities are barred from conducting financial transactions with them.
- Asset freezes for specific entities, particularly state-owned banks and energy companies and arms producers.
- Restrictions on financial transactions with Russian firms in finance, energy and defence.
- Restrictions on exports of oil-related technology.
- Restrictions on exports of dual-use technology.

In April 2014, in response to Russia's continued actions in southern and eastern Ukraine, the Department of State expanded its export restrictions on technologies and services regulated under the US Munitions List. Pending applications for export or re-export to Russia or occupied Crimea of any high-technology defence articles or services regulated under the US Munitions List that contribute to Russia's military capabilities were denied. In addition, the Department was given permission to revoke any existing export licences meeting these conditions (Oxenstierna and Olsson, 2015, pp. 18–19).

In July 2014, the US Treasury imposed several economic sanctions. Two major Russian financial institutions, Gazprombank and VEB, were included. Two Russian energy firms, Novatek and Rosneft, were sanctioned, and their access to US capital markets was limited. The list of sanctioned financial institutions was extended by adding Bank of Moscow, Rosselkhozbank and VTB Bank. In addition, the Treasury listed eight Russian arms firms: Almaz-Antey, Federal State Unitary Enterprise State Research and Production Enterprise Bazalt, JSC Concern Sozvezdie, JSC MIC NPO Mashinostroeniya, Kalashnikov Concern, KBP Instrument Design Bureau, Radio-Electronic Technologies and Uralvagonzavod. All these companies produce a variety of objects that include small arms, mortar shells and tanks. Assets in the US of these entities were frozen and transactions involving these companies were prohibited. United Shipbuilding Corporation was later added to the list. It designs and constructs ships for the Russian Navy (Oxenstierna and Olsson, 2015, pp. 18–19).

In December 2014, the US Treasury included Russia's largest bank — Sberbank — in the list of sanctioned financial institutions. The maturity of Russian debt involved in transactions with US individuals or entities was reduced from 90 to 30 days for all the six banks on the list. In addition, the Treasury blocked the assets of five more Russian state-owned defence technology firms — Dolgoprudny Research Production Enterprise, Mytishchinski Mashinostroitelny Zavod, Kalinin Machine Plant JSC, Almaz-Antey GSKB and JSC NIIP (Oxenstierna and Olsson, 2015, pp. 18–19).

Sanctions were imposed prohibiting the export of goods, services (including financial services) and technology in support of exploration or production for deepwater, Arctic offshore and shale projects with a potential for producing oil. An additional five Russian energy companies — Gazprom, Gazprom Neft, Lukoil, Surgutneftegas and Rosneft — involved in these types of projects were listed. The Treasury imposed sanctions that prohibit transactions in or for the provision of financing for other dealings in new debt of greater than 90 days maturity issued by Gazprom Neft and Transneft (Oxenstierna and Olsson, 2015, pp. 18–19).

Like the EU, the US has introduced restrictive measures against individuals close to Putin. In July 2018, almost 700 Russian individuals and companies were under US sanctions. This includes sanctions imposed for Russia's interference in the 2016 presidential election (Blomberg, 2018).

Key features of the EU and US sanctions

The EU and US sanctions against Russia have many common characteristics. They have cooperated and synchronised their actions throughout the sanction process. There is no "multiple senders" syndrome. UN Resolution 68/262 gave sanctions legitimacy allowing many countries, including Norway and Canada, to follow America's and the EU's example. The EU has managed to keep its 28 member states steadfast, despite high costs borne by some, and pressure from Russia. The European Commission has successfully reconciled different members' needs and views. The fact that sanctions have been sustained despite Kremlin countermeasures is a political win for the West.

The Western sanctions reflect a good knowledge of the recent sanctions' literature on how to design sanctions. Sanctions have been designed to impose costs on the political leadership; they aim at *policy change*, not *regime change* as Russia claims. Sanctions are "targeted" for maximum impact on the regime, doing minimal harm to the population. They focus narrowly on core sectors and key companies, shunning indiscriminate embargoes that would cause unnecessary damage with potentially counterproductive consequences. This prudent approach has bolstered the sanctions sustainability.

The Russian Economy

Russia's economy situation in 2014 was weak prior to the West's imposition of sanctions. The 2008 global financial crisis caused GDP to contract by 7.8% in 2009. Oil prices were still high around 100/bbl in 2013, but economic growth languished at 1.3% due to unaddressed structural problems. The Russian economy had become increasingly state controlled benefitting kleptocrats loyal to Putin.[6] Governance and the quality of regulation were low and corruption was widespread.

In 2014, sanctions were imposed and in 2015 the oil price fell by 50%. These shocks reduced growth to 0.7% in 2014, followed by a sharp contraction of −3.7% in 2015. Capital flight more than doubled in 2014 to $152 billion from $61 billion in 2013 (IMF, 2015). The ruble depreciated more than 50% against the dollar during 2015, when the Bank of Russia (CBR) abandoned its policy of supporting the ruble and introduced a flexible exchange rate. This move has saved Russia's foreign reserves.

The effects of sanctions on the Russian economy

Table 2 details the factors that have strengthened or dampened the effects of sanctions and of falling oil prices on the economy and the federal budget.

The financial sanctions have impacted the Russian economy. Decreased capital inflows directly and indirectly hurt Russian companies. Russian financial markets are underdeveloped and banks and big companies were addicted to raising investment capital and financing debt on international capital markets. Russian state banks and sanctioned companies in the energy and defence sector after the imposition of sanctions were no longer able to raise loans with long durations on EU and US capital markets. This exerted strong pressure on government reserves. As early as August 2014, Rosneft, the large state oil giant (that has been endowed with the confiscated assets of Yukos), applied for state support of over $40 billion to refinance its debt (Kragh, 2014, p. 60). Financial sanctions triggered a sharp rise in capital flight from Russia (see preceding discussion). Putin mitigated the panic by announcing a tax amnesty for repatriated capital stashed abroad in his annual statement to the Federation Council on December 4, 2014 (Poslanie, 2014). In February 2018, the amnesty was extended to 2019 (RAPSI, 2018).

---

[6]Putin's political resource allocation is captured in Clifford Gaddy and Barry Ickes's model of "rent addiction" in which sunset industries loyal to the political leadership are kept primarily to extract rents (Gaddy and Ickes, 2015).

Table 2: Factors affecting sanction success in the Russian case.

Strengthening the effects of sanctions	Weakening the effects of sanctions
International	
Low oil price, depreciation of the ruble, deterioration of ToT, capital flight	Third-party countries (BRICS, CIS, Turkey, Latin America) may potentially replace part of the trade with the EU
Domestic	
Rent addiction and a politicised economic system where control over rent distribution is crucial for staying in power. Preference for rent-addicted sector lowers efficiency	The authoritarian political system that is less sensitive to falling living standards of the population than a democracy and can protect supporting elites from economic hardship
Weak institutions	An effective propaganda machine that controls public opinion and manipulates perceptions about the sanctions among the Russian population
Fiscal deficit, decreasing domestic reserves	
Maintained high priority for defence spending	Manifestations that Russia is a superpower, West is the enemy to encourage national cohesion and *rally-round-the-flag* policies
Import substitution (including food embargo) and more administrative control over resource allocation that increases in efficiency and produces inferior goods	

Source: Oxenstierna and Olsson (2015, SO).

Russia has sought closer economic relations with third-party countries, e.g. Turkey, Serbia, the Eurasian Union (EAEU), China and Latin America. Its relationship with China (Shanghai Cooperation Organization) is deepening, but not yet enough to displace the EU as a trade partner and financial centre. Russia has depleted its budgetary reserves (but not hard currency holdings) to mitigate the impact of sanctions. It has supported the industrial sector out of the federal budget and financed deficits from the federal budget Reserve Fund (which was depleted in 2017). Moscow has promoted "import substitution" as a vehicle for strengthening the domestic industry and national economic self-sufficiency. Russia's retaliatory embargo on certain food imports (Ukaz 1496, 2014) supports this national self-sufficiency, but has had a negative impact on consumer good choice and prices in the short run.

The import and export bans targeting trade with Crimea have made it more expensive for Russia to absorb Crimea and revitalise its economy. The oil sector, Russia's main export earner, has been adversely affected by sanctions. Oil companies or their subsidiaries cannot borrow funds on Western markets for more than 30 days. Gas production and delivery are not directly restricted by the EU sanctions, but the US targets Gazprom. The inconsistency reflects the EU's dependence on Russian gas. Oil is a homogeneous good available on the world market at a market price. Substitutes for Russian petroleum are readily available for most senders except landlocked countries. They have had problems, prompting some countries to search for new solutions. For instance, the Baltic countries now have a LNG terminal in Klaipeda, Lithuania. The terminal can supply half of the Baltic's gas requirements. Norway and the US provide the rest (*Reuters*, 2017).

Russia's defence industry does not depend heavily on imports from the West. However, electronics is a tight spot. Western assessments suggest that as much as 90% of electronic components of Russian armaments are Western, and experts estimate that it would take at least 6 years for Russia to become self-sufficient (Malmlöf, 2016, p. 17). Russia's rockets and space equipment rely heavily on imported components. Around 65–79% of their value-added originates abroad (Faltsman, 2015, p. 119). Another area of high import dependence is unmanned vehicles, and 90% of Russian civilian aircraft value-added is imported (Faltsman, 2015, p. 119).

The Western ban on exports of advanced oil exploration equipment and dual-use goods to Russia negatively affects Russia's technological progress and growth in the medium- and long run. Technological transfer allows reverse engineering to master advanced technologies. The order for French Mistral-class amphibious assault ships was intended to spur technological transfer to the Russian navy, but in August 2015, it was cancelled due to the sanctions. Sanctions foreclose this growth node and slow down technological development.

Russia's severed defence industrial cooperation with Ukraine is another negative. Ukraine accounted for 87% of Russia's major conventional arms imports between 2009 and 2013 (Malmlöf, 2016, p. 2). Machine construction for the defence industry will be a particularly tough spot (Faltsman, 2015).

Estimates of the effect on Russian GDP

Several scholars have estimated the effect of the sanctions on economic growth. Russian officials tried to ignore them, but the Russian Minister of Finance Anatoliy Siluanov acknowledged in 2014 that the annual cost of sanctions to the Russian economy could be $40 billion (2% of GDP). This is small compared to the loss of $90–100 billion (4–5% of GDP) attributed to the lower oil prices, but still very significant (*Reuters,* 2014). Putin also acknowledged that the sanctions contributed to Russia's current problem in a direct-line conversation with the nation on April 16, 2015, although he contended that they were not Russia's biggest problem (Aalto and Forsberg, 2016, p. 223). Some days later, Prime Minister Dmitry Medvedev disclosed that the estimated bill for annexing Crimea was $106 billion (*CNN,* 2015). In November 2016, Vladimir Putin acknowledged in an interview with the German daily *Bild* that denied access to international financial markets is "severely harming Russia", although the harm is not as severe as the decline of energy prices (*Independent,* 2016).

The IMF estimated in 2015 that US and EU Ukraine-related sanctions together with Russia's retaliatory ban on agricultural imports reduced output in the short term by 1–1.5%. In the medium term, the loss was estimated at 9% (Nelson, 2017, p. 8). Gurvich and Prilepskiy (2015) estimated that sanctions reduced GDP by 2.4% 2014–2017.[7] They took account of both direct and indirect effects such as higher uncertainty and country risk caused by sanctions.

The combined direct and indirect effects of sanctions may also harm the balance of payments by reducing the foreign borrowings of

---

[7] In an updated later version of this research, Gurvich and Prilepskiy (forthcoming) adjust this estimate to −1.9%, which is mainly due to reallocation of resources from non-tradeable to tradeable sectors that has occurred because of the depreciation of roble.

non-sanctioned entities, inflows of direct and portfolio investment and outflow of Russian capital.

Russian policy responses

Russia retaliated against Western economic sanctions on August 7, 2014 with countersanctions on some imported foods from the EU, the US, Australia, Canada and Norway. The list of embargoed products from these countries includes meat in all forms, fish, dairy products, fruit and vegetables. These countersanctions had economic impact in some EU countries, but food producers and others in the supply chain could quite easily circumvent these sanctions and eventually re-orientate to other export markets.

The countersanctions are protectionist measures and part of Russia's import substitution policy which aims at making Russia self-sufficient. The policy protects inefficient domestic producers and allows them to develop without foreign competition. Russian consumers have had to bear the costs in the forms of diminished variety and substantially higher food prices.

Effects on the Political Level

After sanctions were adopted, Russia has continued its aggressive posture towards Ukraine and the West. The Kremlin has employed a variety of hybrid paramilitary operations in Donetsk and Donbas and interfered in democratic EU and American elections. Putin has pushed his propaganda against Ukraine and the West at home, blaming the West for all of Russia's domestic problems including falling living standards. The strategy has been effective. Putin was re-elected for another 6 years in power on March 18, 2018.

Politics vis-à-vis Ukraine

The sanctions have not altered and are unlikely to modify Russia's strategic objectives in Ukraine over the mid-term. Russia has for many years sought to strengthen its sphere of influence over Ukraine by discouraging closer relations with the EU and NATO. Sanctions have not dampened its ambitions, compelling the Kremlin to de-annex Crimea or terminate hostilities in Donetsk and Donbas, which are main conditions that Russia must fulfil for sanctions to be lifted. However, on the ground in Ukraine, they may have contributed to freezing the military conflict along the post-Minsk demarcation line[8] and prevented the conquest of Mariupol. It can also be claimed that sanctions prevented the legitimisation of Donesk People's Republic (DNR) and Luhansk People's Republic (LNR). At the last moment, Russia refrained from "recognizing" (instead of the word "respecting" was used) the results of the November 2014 elections in DNR and LNR (Secrieru, 2015, pp. 41–42). Sanctions, moreover, may have contributed to lifting Russia's opposition to the deployment and expansion of the Organization for Security and Co-operation in Europe (OSCE) Special Monitoring Mission (SMM) (Secrieru, 2015, pp. 41–42).

Sanctions prohibiting trade with Crimea have made their connection to Russia's mainland more costly and contractors working on the Kerch Bridge are now targeted. Crimea and Sevastopol are only second to North Caucasus in subsidies from the Russian federal budget. At the same time, Ukraine profits from substantial financial and technical aid from the West (Oxenstierna and Hedenskog, 2017).

Conclusion

This chapter has discussed how the EU and US sanctions imposed on Russia in 2014 and onwards may have affected the Russian economy and its policies towards Ukraine. The impact has been significant but not decisive. The main sanction effect was reduced capital inflows attributable to restrictions placed on Russia's state banks and large corporations curbing their ability to raise investment funds and refinance their debt on international capital markets. Western sanctions are directly targeted to assets controlled by the political leadership. GDP has been adversely affected by sanctions but the sharp drop in the oil price has had a larger negative effect on growth.

---

[8]The Minsk tripartite agreement on a ceasefire in the two Eastern regions of Ukraine was reached on September 5, 2014, the so-called "Minsk II" protocol.

Russia has sought to mitigate the effect of sanctions by forging closer economic relations with third-party countries, e.g. Turkey, EAEU, and China, but the pivot towards Asia has not yet yielded dramatic budgetary benefits forcing the Kremlin to rely on domestic reserves to mitigate the damage caused by sanctions. Moscow has supported the industrial sector from the federal budget but depleted its budgetary reserves. Foreign reserves have not suffered after the CBR introduced a flexible exchange rate, but the value of the ruble plummeted. Import substitution is a protectionist measure that is supposed to strengthen the domestic industry and bolster national economic self-sufficiency. Russian retaliation in the form of an embargo on certain food imports was part of this policy, but it has been costly. Russian consumers have been forced to substitute dis-preferred products for those they desire and have had to pay more for them.

Sanctions have hurt, but Putin has been adamant. In 2015, sanctions seem to have contributed to containing Russia's further aggression in Ukraine, but there is no solution to the situation of Crimea or the non-government controlled areas in Donbass. Negotiations on the implementation of the Minsk II agreement appear to have stalled. The literature foresees that the longer sanctions are in force, the less effective they will become because the economic actors in the sanctioned state adjust and find new ways of doing business. With Russia being resilient and the West insisting that Ukraine's territory and independence should be fully restored, this conflict will take long to solve and economic sanctions alone will not do the job. Political and diplomatic measures need to be intensified. Russia's aggression towards Ukraine is not an isolated situation in global foreign policies. Over time, international developments may change the prerequisites for finding a solution. Until then, sanctions are here to stay.

References

Aalto, P. and Forsberg, T. (2016). The structure of Russia's geo-economy under economic sanctions, *Asia Europe Journal* 14(2), 221–223.

Bapat, N., Heinrich, T., Kobayashi, Y., and Morgan, C. (2013). Determinants of sanctions effectiveness: Sensitivity analysis using new data, *International Interactions: Empirical and Theoretical Research in International Relations* 39(1), 79–98.

Blanchard, J.-M. and Ripsman, N. (2013). *Economic Statecraft and Foreign Policy: Sanctions, Incentives, and Target State Calculations*, Routledge, London and New York.

Blomberg (2018). All about US sanctions aimed at Putin's Russia. Available at: https://www.bloomberg.com/news/articles/2018-07-11/ (accessed 7 August 2018).

Council Regulation 692/2014 Concerning restrictions on the import into the Union of goods originating in Crimea or Sevastopol, in response to the illegal annexation of Crimea and Sevastopol, 23 June, http://eur-lex.europa.eu/legal content/EN/TXT/PDF/?uri=CELEX:32014R0692&from=SV (accessed 2 April 2018t.

Council Regulation 825/2014 Amending Regulation (EU) No 692/2014 concerning restrictions on the import into the Union of goods originating in Crimea or Sevastopol, in response to the illegal annexation of Crimea and Sevastopol, 30 July, http://eur-lex .europa.eu/legal- content/EN/TXT/PDF/?uri=CELEX: 32014R0825&from=SV (accessed 2 April 2018).

Council Regulation 833/2014 Concerning restrictive measures in view of Russia's actions destabilising the situation in Ukraine, 31 July, http://eur-lex.europa.eu/legalcontent/EN/TXT/PDF/?uri=CELEX:32014R0833&from=EN (accessed 2 April 2018).

Council Regulation 960/2014 Amending Regulation (EU) No 833/2014 concerning restrictive measures in view of Russia's actions destabilising the situation in Ukraine. 8 September, http://eur-lex.europa.eu/legalcontent/EN/TXT/PDF/?uri=CELEX:320l 4R0960&from=EN (accessed 2 April 2018).

CNN (2015). Russia is paying a hefty price for supporting the break-up of Ukraine — $106 billion, to be precise.

Drezner, D. (2011). Sanctions sometimes smart: Targeted sanctions in theory and practice, *International Studies Review* 13, 96–108.

European Council (2018a). Russia: EU prolongs sanctions by six months. http://www.consilium.europa.eu/en/press/press-releases/2018/07/05/russia-eu-prolongs-economic-sanctions-by-six-months/ (accessed 6 August2018).

European Council (2018b). Ukraine: EU adds six entities involved in the construction of the Kerch Bridge connecting the illegally annexed Crimea to Russia to sanctions list. Available at: http://www.consilium.europa.eu/en/press/press-releases/2018/07/31/ (accessed 6 August 2018).

Executive Order (2018). On the President's continuation of the national emergency with respect to Ukraine.

Executive Order 13660 (2014). Blocking property of certain persons contributing to the situation in Ukraine. Available at: http://www.gpo.gov/fdsys/pkg/FR-2014-03-10/pdf/2014-05323.pdf (accessed 2 April 2018).

Executive Order 13661 (2014). Blocking property of additional persons contributing to the situation in Ukraine. Available at: http://www.gpo.gov/fdsys/pkg/FR-2014-03-19/pdf/2014-06141.pdf (accessed 2 April 2018).

Executive Order 13662 (2014). Blocking property and additional persons contributing to the situation in Ukraine. Available at: http://www.treasury.gov/resource-center/sanctions/Programs/Documents/ukraineeo3.pdf (accessed 2 April 2018).

Executive Order 13685 (2014). Blocking property of certain persons and prohibiting certain transactions with respect to the Crimea region of Ukraine. Available at: https://www.treasury.gov/resource-center/sanctions/Programs/Documents/ukraineeo4.pdf (accessed 9 March 2018).

Faltsman, V. (2015). Importozameshchenie v TEK i OPK, *Voprosy ekonomiki* 1, 116–124.

Gaddy, C. G. and Ickes, B. W. (2015). Putin's rent management system and the future of addiction in Russia, in Oxenstierna, S. (ed.), *The Challenges of Russia's Politicized Economic System,* Routledge, Abingdon & New York, pp. 11–32.

Gurvich, E. and Prilepskiy, I. (2016). The impact of financial sanctions on the Russian economy, *Russian Journal of Economics* 1, 1–27.

Gurvich, E. and Prilepskiy, I. (2018). Western sanctions and Russian responses: Effects after three years, in Torbjorn, B., and Oxenstierna, S. (eds.), *The Russian Economy under Putin,* Routledge, Abington & New York, pp. 30–47.

Hufbauer, G., Schott, J., Elliott, K. and Oegg, B. (2007). *Economic Sanctions Reconsidered* (3rd edition), Peterson Institute for International Economics, Washington, DC.

IMF (2015). Update (January). Available at: http://www.imf.org/external/ns/cs.aspx?id=29 (accessed 9 March 2015).

Independent (2016). *Western Sanctions Severely Harming Russia: Putin,* AFP, Berlin. Available at: http://www.theindependentbd.com/home/printnews/30049 (accessed 8 March 2018).

Kaempfer, W. and Lowenberg, A. (2007). The political economy of economic sanctions, in Sandler, T. and Hartley, K. (eds.), *Handbook of Defense Economics: Defense in a Globalized World,* Volume 2, pp. 868–911.

Kragh, M. (2014). Ryssland efter Krim — en ekonomisk konsekvensanalys, *Ekonomisk debatt* 42(8), 51–62.

Major, S. (2012). Timing is everything: economic sanctions, regime type, and domestic instability, *International Interactions: Empirical and Theoretical Research in International Relations* 38(1), 79–110.

Malmlöf, T. (2016). A case study of Russo-Ukrainian defense industrial cooperation: Russian dilemmas, *Journal of Slavic Military Studies* 29(1), 1–22.

Morgan, C., Bapat, N. and Krustev, V. (2009). The threat and imposition of economic sanctions 1971–2000, *Conflict Management and Peace Science* 26(1), 92–110.

Nelson, R. M. (2015). U.S. sanctions on Russia: Economic implications, *CRS Report* 7-5700, Congressional Research Service.

Nelson, R. (2017). U.S. sanctions and Russia's economy, *CRS Report* 7-5700, Congressional Research Service, Washington, D.C.

Oxenstierna, S., and Olsson, P. (2015). *The Economic Sanctions against Russia. Impact and Prospects of Success,* FOI-R-4097-SE

Oxenstierna, S. and Hedenskog, J. (2017). *Ukraine's economic reforms. Prospects of sustainability,* FOI-R-4472-SE.

Poslanie (2014). *Poslanie Prezidenta RF ot 04.12.2014 (Opolozhenii v strane i osnovnykh napravleniyakh vnutrennei i vneshnei politi gosudarstva).* Available at: http://kremlin.ru/acts/bank/39443 (accessed 4 April 2018).

RAPSI (2018). President Putin extends capital amnesty for one year. Available at: http://www.rapsinews.com/legislation_news/20180219/281992144.html (accessed 7 August 2018).

Reuters (2014). Russia puts losses from sanctions, cheaper oil at up to 140 billion per year. Available at: https://www.reuters.com/article/us-russia-siluanov/russia-puts-losses-from-sanctions-cheaper-oil-at-up-to-140-billion-per-year-idUSKCN0J80GC (accessed 7 August 2018).

Reuters (2017). Lithuania receives first LNG from the United States.

Secrieru, S. (2015). Have sanctions changed Russia's behaviour in Ukraine, in: *On Target? EU Sanctions as Security Policy Tools,* Issue Report 25, 39–47.

Ukaz 1496 (2014). Ukaz Prezidenta RF No 1496, O priminenenii otdelnykh spetsialnykh ekonomicheskikh mer v tselyakh obespecheniya bezopasnosti Rossiskoi Federatsii. Available at: http://www.garant.ru/hotlaw/federal/558039 (accessed 2 March 2015).

UN (2014). Resolution 68/262 *Territorial Integrity of Ukraine.*

Chapter 14

Russia's Arctic Policy: Between Confrontation in Europe and Irrelevance in Asia

Pavel Baev

Introduction

Russia's Arctic policy has two primary goals. First, the Kremlin seeks to develop the Arctic in an environmentally friendly way for commercial use cooperatively with other nations. Second, it wants to make the Arctic a bastion of Russian military power. These objectives are not mutually exclusive, but are difficult to reconcile in an era of rising tensions between Russia and the West.[1] The Kremlin's approach has been to spend lavishly on Arctic defence and allow commercial prospects to languish rather than knuckle under to Western economic sanctions. It can and should fine-tune both policies, but shows no inclination to do so.

Policymakers cling to the hope that the lure of natural resources will lead to commercial success in the Arctic, but the vagaries of the market are frustrating their expectations. The security benefits of militarising the Arctic have proven chimerical because the threat is exaggerated. Economic costs have greatly outweighed the military advantage of controlling resources and lines of sea communications (Pezard *et al.*, 2017). These

---

[1] One useful evaluation of Russia's policy is by Conley (2015).

miscalculations are likely to persist because they reflect President Vladimir Putin's judgement about Russia's position in the Arctic, encouraged by a cabal of courtiers, including Defence Minister Sergey Shoigu and Secretary of the Security Council Nikolai Patrushev.

The Kremlin and the West would both be better off if Moscow were less opportunistic in exploiting short-term European political vulnerabilities and took a more objective view of NATO's military threat. Russia and the West have more to gain from cultivating mutually beneficial long-term cooperation in the Arctic than indulging in adversarial games, and an arms race in the Arctic is superfluous if Russia's leaders properly calibrate the Arctic's military importance, especially in the Barents Region (Klimenko, 2016). Moreover, the Kremlin can integrate the China card more effectively into its foreign relations if it improves relations with the West.

This chapter investigates the shifting tides of Russia's Arctic policy with the West and its ramifications for relations with China and other Asian powers in the High North. It starts with the analysis of the economic interests and trends, focusing on the prospects for developing Arctic oil and gas resources and expanding maritime traffic on the Northern Sea Route. It proceeds by analysing Russia's Arctic military activities, spotlighting conventional power projection and the modernisation of the Kremlin's nuclear forces. Finally, the Arctic's possible futures are parsed, taking account of Putin's preferences.

Natural Resources

Moscow seeks sovereignty over the vast open spaces in the High North and its potentially abundant natural resources in particular (Staalsen, 2017a).[2] Russian perceptions of the importance of the Arctic are shaped by the assumption that rich natural resource deposits lie hidden in this vast and inhospitable region. Its Foreign Policy Concept depicts the struggle for these resources as a vital national goal and a key driver of escalating global tensions,[3] but its assessment is unsupported by hard Russian data

---

[2]On this obsession with sovereignty, see Baev (2013).

[3]This document approved in late 2016 is available (in English) on the Russian Foreign Ministry   website   (http://www.mid.ru/en/foreign_policy/official_documents/-/

on the dimensions of the "treasure chest". The only reference point for its speculations is the long-outdated appraisal of the US Geological Survey from 2008 (Bird *et al.*, 2008), completed before the "shale revolution" and the fast growth of renewable sources of energy that has diminished demand for the hard-to-get offshore Arctic resources.

Russian state-owned energy giants *Gazprom* and *Rosneft* are awakening to the declining attractiveness of high-cost offshore projects in the Arctic Sea. They are in no rush to proceed with grandiose projects. The first wake-up call for *Gazprom* was the collapse of the *Shtokman* project in the ice-free Barents Sea back in 2012, prompted by the failure of *Statoil* and *Total* to provide critical support as estimated losses mounted.[4] *Gazprom* tried to rebound by completing the *Prirazlomnaya* project in the Pechora Sea in 2013, despite protests from *Greenpeace* (Bourne, 2016). The discovery of a significant oil field by *Rosneft* and *ExxonMobil* in the Kara Sea in summer 2014 was a triumph, but one overshadowed by American economic sanctions imposed on February 2018 that compelled *ExxonMobil* to withdraw (Soldatkin, 2014).[5]

Russia can also expand exploration onshore, but even these projects are becoming too expensive. Generous subsidies to the privately owned *Novatek* firm were not enough to guarantee even minimal profitability of the Yamal LNG project. Bankruptcy was only averted through a last-minute deal with Chinese CNPC and the Silk Road Fund in mid-2016 (Krutihin, 2018). China's motivation in rescuing *Novatek* had little to do with the demand for LNG and much to do with granting a favour to Gennady Timchenko, an oligarch from Putin's inner circle, and Putin himself, who were both desperately dependent upon to China's offer (Gabuev, 2016). Although, China clearly disclosed its geostrategic Arctic ambitions in a White Paper on the Arctic published in January 2018, the Kremlin chose to look the other way (Lanteigne and Shi, 2018).

---

asset_publisher/CptICkB6BZ29/content/id/2542248). One useful comment is by Frolov (2016).

[4]For a typical Russian denial of this economic reality, see Milov (2012).

[5]Rough estimates by Russian experts point to the higher oil price of $US 115 per barrel as the benchmark for cost-efficiency of the Arctic off-shore projects; see Bashkatova (2017).

Arctic Passage

The Kremlin has long dreamed of creating an Arctic Passage linking the East with the West.[6] Soviet experience operating this domestic supply route and the experiments with traversing this shortest connection between Europe and Asia in the early 2010s by small cargo convoys made the dream appear feasible (Pastusiak, 2016). However, most shipping companies have recently concluded that navigation on the Northern Sea Route (*Sevmorput*), even in the summer months is too unpredictable, and the volume of transit traffic remains pitifully low with no realistic prospect for improvement in the next decade.

Moscow is undaunted. It hopes that *Sevmorput* will become a profitable destination for the Yamal LNG project. Infrastructure was rapidly built during 2016–2017, with most of the equipment and materials delivered by sea, and the export of LNG by the ice-class tankers set to flow Eastward in summer time and Westward in winter (Staalsen, 2017b).

This breakthrough signifies *Sevmorput*'s importance for delivering LNG to the Asian markets, but Moscow's concerns about China's Arctic intentions remain. The rules for navigation on the *Sevmorput* are becoming increasingly restrictive, and now limit the transportation of hydrocarbons to ships under the Russian flag.[7] The rules are so stringent that even *Novatek*, which operates a large fleet of LNG tankers, finds its interests affected (Vedeneeva and Barsukov, 2018). Several lobbies are engaged in bureaucratic squabbles over *Sevmorput*'s administrative control. *Rosatom*, the state-owned nuclear complex appears to have gained the upper hand by the start of 2018 (Mushanov, 2018). The conflict of business interests is set to continue because *Rosatom*, which owns a fleet of nuclear icebreakers, is poorly positioned to manage the complex logistics of *Sevmorput* (Yushkov, 2018).

These squabbles overlap with ambitions for asserting Russia's sovereignty over the Arctic waters, viewed against the backdrop of China's slow-moving plans for building its own transport avenue in the

---

[6]Good examination of this proposition can be found in Chapter 8 of Laruelle (2014).

[7]See "The State Duma banned transportation of hydrocarbons in the Sevmorput in ships under foreign flags", *Vedomosti* (in Russian), December 20, 2017 (https://www.vedomosti. ru/business/news/2017/12/20/745972-neft-sevmorputi).

High North (Schrader, 2018). One way to assert this sovereignty is to expand Russia's legitimate control over the continental shelf, even if this "ownership" cannot possibly effect maritime traffic. Russia was the first state to submit a claim for some 1.2 million square kilometres between the Lomonosov and Mendeleev underwater ridges in 2001 to the UN Commission on the Limits of the Continental Shelf (UN CLCS), but the submission was deemed inadequate. It took the Kremlin 13 years to collect the supplementary scientific evidence. It resubmitted its claim in August 2015, but the CLCS has yet to render a verdict, which cannot in any case be definitive (Balan, 2017). The Commission can only start the process of sorting out conflicting Russian, Danish and pending Canadian counterclaims.[8] The Kremlin finds this protracted process vexing and may choose to take unilateral measures, which it can blame on the UN CLCS's inaction.

Russia's economic interests in the Arctic are distorted by politics. The development of most offshore schemes has been postponed, and onshore projects require budget-busting subsidies and tax breaks.

Western investors find themselves hampered by sanctions and are discouraged by the massive corruption stemming from infighting around the Arctic enterprises, prodding Russia to look Eastward, even though this will inevitably make the Kremlin too dependent on China for comfort.

Militarisation of the Arctic

The re-militarisation of Russia's Arctic started soon after Artur Chilingarov's famous flag-planting expedition to the North Pole in August 2007. The 2020 Armament Program issued in 2011 increased the momentum, a priority sustained despite Crimea's annexation in 2014 and mounting confrontation with the West. The Arctic's claim on the defence budget has increased (Flake, 2017). This priority diminished slightly in 2017, and the 2027 Armament Program approved in the early 2018 has removed some Arctic-related programmes, especially naval forces (Barrie

---

[8] See "Russia expects Canada to submit its Arctic shelf expansion bid", *Arctic.ru*, 21 March 2018 (https://arctic.ru/international/20180321/730420.html).

and Boyd, 2018). Nonetheless, past commitments to nuclear modernisation and power projection assure that Arctic defence spending will remain high.

Nuclear arsenal is a foundation for conventional power

The Kola Peninsula became the main basing area for the Soviet fleet of nuclear submarines during the early 1960s, and in the 1990s, Russia faced huge difficulties in sorting out the heritage of this most nuclearised area in the world with the invaluable help of the US Nunn–Lugar Cooperative Threat Reduction Program (Woolf, 2003). Many of the problems with decommissioned reactors and nuclear waste remain unresolved, but Russia opted to discontinue cooperation with USA on these matters in 2015. The main priority for Moscow has been the introduction of the *Borei*-class strategic nuclear submarines, designed in the mid-1980s (Project 955) and armed with solid-propelled *Bulava* intercontinental missiles. The first sub in the series (*Yuri Dolgoruky*) entered the Northern Fleet in 2013 after 17 years of construction and trials. Two more subs (*Aleksandr Nevsky* and *Vladimir Monomakh*) joined the Pacific Fleet recently, and five more are in various stages of construction.[9] The upgraded *Borei*-B design proved exorbitantly expensive. The Kremlin therefore chose to procure six more *Borei*-A subs instead in the 2027 Armament Program (Nilsen, 2018c).

Various other strategic assets are deployed on the Kola bases, including attack submarines, the largest storage of non-strategic nuclear warheads (Olenegorsk-2) and a new early warning radar (Olenegorsk-1).[10] Some programmes are experiencing delays. Only the *Severodvinsk Yasen*-class attack submarine has entered the Northern Fleet after 22 years of construction. The nuclear-propelled underwater "drone" touted by Putin in his 2018 address to the parliament is essentially hypothetical (Mosher, 2018). The old Soviet nuclear test site on the Novaya Zemlya is now used for simulations and testing of prototypes, including nuclear-propelled cruise missiles (Macias, 2018). Kola nuclear projects are being expanded,

---

[9] All *Bulava* tests, including the four-missile salvo on May 23, 2018, were conducted from the White and the Barents seas; see Khodarenok (2018).

[10] On the non-strategic weapons, see Podvig and Serrat (2017).

while older subs and other nuclear reactors are gradually taken out of service (Nilsen, 2017).

Russian strategy requires better protection for these crucial assets, but the Northern Fleet is unable to establish anything resembling a Soviet-style "strategic bastion" in the Barents Sea. The plan instead calls for the deployment of various air defence systems (including the S-400 surface-to-air missiles) that would create a zone of Russian air superiority extending into the Western part of the Barents Region.[11] The newly created Arctic Command (on the basis of the Northern Fleet HQ) is supposed to integrate air and naval capabilities guaranteeing effective protection of strategic deterrence forces, but its more ambitious task is to build a grouping capable of projecting power in offensive and amphibious operations. The newly created Arctic brigade (Alakurtti near the border with Finland) as well as the strengthened marine brigade (which acquired combat experience in Donbass and Syria) are supposed to be the central elements of this capability.[12] The Northern Fleet now has new capabilities for missile strikes onshore in the form of the *Kalibr* (SS-N-27 *Sizzler*) cruise missile, which can be deployed on small naval platforms and was combat-tested in Syria (Sokov, 2017). Another key task is destroying the US missile defence capabilities. The Vardø radar was targeted in simulated air strikes (Nilsen, 2018b).

Overall, the grouping of forces on the Kola Peninsula is versatile, well trained and supplied, and capable of performing a wide variety of operations. It remains sidelined, nevertheless, in the emerging confrontation between Russia and the West, despite sitting on NATO's border.

Militarisation of the Eastern seaboard serves no purpose

The restoration of the old Soviet base on the Kotelny Island (the New Siberian archipelago) in summer 2013 marked the start of a fresh effort

---

[11]The A2/AD concept is still foreign for the Russian military, but the proposition for establishing dominance in the air is well established. On modernisation of the air component of the Arctic Command, see Maurin (2017).

[12]Russian media gives extensive coverage to the training of these units; see, for instance, Petrov and Zakvasin (2017).

at building a chain of modern bases along the *Sevmorput* (Staalsen, 2013). Odd as it may seem, the Northern Fleet had never prepared for missions East of the Barents Sea (except for submarine operations) and until recently had only a single ice-class ship in its combat order. Its flagship *Petr Velikiy* had to be accompanied by no less than four ice-breakers, and the first naval icebreaker *Ilya Muromets* (Project 21180) was commissioned only in late 2017 (Sharkov, 2017). Construction of bases was hampered by supply problems, the usual embezzlement and even labour strikes; nonetheless, Defence Minister Sergey Shoigu announced the completion of the military construction plan in the High North in 2017.[13]

This achievement still leaves open the question about the purpose of these bases. Their capacity to control maritime traffic along the *Sevmorput* is limited because there are no patrol crafts or aircrafts permanently based in the area. Construction of the first *Ivan Papanin* series (Project 23550) patrol craft only began during spring 2017 in the St. Petersburg shipyard, and the second is postponed, with no further contracts signed (Klimov, 2019). Moscow often touts the usefulness of these bases for search-and-rescue, but the new Cape Schmidt base failed to help a convoy trapped by floating ice in early 2017 (Staalsen, 2017c). There is much concern in the USA about the so-called "icebreaker gap", but this is an illusion. Construction of the new-generation nuclear icebreaker *Arktika* has encountered recurrent setbacks, while the new series of armed nuclear icebreakers *Lider* (Project 10510) exists only as a technical design (Bolshakova and Kostinsky, 2018).

Civilian agencies could have managed navigation along the *Sevmorput* better, but the requisite infrastructure is underfunded. Even the job of removing mountains of garbage left by the Soviet projects in the Arctic is entrusted to the Northern Fleet, which reports some success, but is not equipped for this mission (Nilsen, 2018a). Beijing opposed the deployment of an additional Arctic brigade on the Yamal Peninsula and Moscow appears to have relented.

---

[13] See "Shoigu reported on construction of military bases in the Arctic", *RIA-Novosti* (in Russian), 25 December 2017 (https://ria.ru/defense_safety/20171225/1511695359.html). On the investigation of embezzlement, see Muradov (2018).

Overall, while upgrades for ports and other infrastructure in the Russian Arctic are necessary, the new chain of bases is a strategic luxury that Moscow can ill-afford.

Putin Takes the Arctic Personally

It was Chilingarov's expedition (funded by Western sponsors) that revealed the international significance of the Arctic frontier to Putin. He has gradually developed a personal interest in various matters pertaining to the High North thereafter. The lure of fabulous wealth initially peaked Putin's interest. Visiting a research station in Yakutia in 2010, he casually mentioned to surprised environmentalists that, "According to rough estimates, the reserves discovered to date are worth approximately $5 trillion, including oil, natural gas, coal, gold and diamonds."[14] Gradually, the Arctic's appeal to Russia's unsentimental leader became more mundane. He authorised a programme to remove garbage from the old Soviet settlements.

Putin's interest in the Arctic waxes and wanes. He paid scant attention to the Arctic matters during 2014–2016. Then in spring 2017 after a visit to the Franz Josef Land, he delivered a speech at the conference on "Arctic: Territory of Dialogue" against "geopolitical games of military alliances" (Egorov, 2017). Nonetheless, despite the mood swings, Putin is unwavering in his belief that the Arctic, including the symbolically important Northern Pole, belongs to Russia. This "patriotic" assertiveness resonates in Russia and Putin exploits it to the maximum.

Putin is aware that the romantic vision of pristine North lands and frozen seas is a mirage, at odds with the reality of the pollution-ravaged Norilsk industrial cluster,[15] but he does not let this interfere with his security priorities. He treats *Greenpeace's* action against *Gazprom's* Prirazlomnaya platform as a security challenge, despite the verdicts of international courts (Sterling, 2017). Putin also seeks to tap public angst

---

[14] See the transcript of Prime Minister Vladimir Putin's conversation with Russian and German researchers (official English translation), August 23, 2010. Available at http://archive.premier.gov.ru/eng/events/news/11882/.

[15] These images are captured in Fiore (2017).

by disparaging efforts for transnational supervision over the Arctic "global commons".[16] Kremlin Arctic lobbies capitalise on this patriotic fervour in their quest for state funds (Medvedev, 2016).

One issue of particular concern for Putin is the threat presented by US strategic submarines that are allegedly "concentrated" in the Barents Sea off the coast of Norway. Putin estimated in 2013 that missiles from these submarines could reach Moscow in 16–17 minutes; he reduced that estimate to 15–16 minutes in 2014, and further to 15 minutes in 2017.[17] However, Putin is mum about whether the Northern Fleet is capable of counteracting this threat allegedly lurking close to its bases on the Kola Peninsula. Russia likewise has neither published any data on the number of US strategic submarines in area, the duration of their stationing, patrol schedules and surface ship protection, nor is there any responsible discussion of the US ballistic missile defence system, and why the Kremlin has been unable yet to take effective countermeasures.[18] The Arctic comes into this picture as the frontier along which the key assets of the presumed US missile defence system would be deployed, so their neutralisation is a major task for the Russian Arctic Command.

Putin's Arctic chauvinism is skilfully exploited by an Arctic lobby, close to Nikolai Patrushev, the Secretary of Security Council and Putin's long-time loyalist (he succeeded Putin as the Director of the FSB in 1999). Defence Minister Sergey Shoigu and Dmitry Rogozin, newly appointed Director of *Roskosmos* space agency (he was the head of the Arctic Commission until the government reshuffle in May 2018), are major lobby members.[19] Sergei Kiriyenko, first Deputy Chief of Presidential

---

[16]On one such exchange, see Raibman (2013).

[17]See "Putin: Transferring the Arctic to international control is complete stupidity", *Interfax* (in Russian), 3 October 2013 (http://www.interfax.ru/russia/332580); "Putin stated that Russia will pay more attention to strengthening its positions in the Arctic", *TASS* (in Russian), 29 August 2014 (http://tass.ru/politika/1408542); "Putin: Russia will monitor the activity of US Navy in the Arctic", *RIA-Novosti* (in Russian), 15 June 2017 (https://ria.ru/defense_safety/20170615/1496565509.html).

[18]One competent Russian view is that by Arbatov (2018).

[19]Patrushev spelled the plan for building Russia's military strength in the Arctic in the April 2013 interview; see "Nikolai Patrushev: Arctic's potential attracts many parties", *Argumenty & Facty* (in Russian), April 10, 2013 (http://www.aif.ru/society/42323).

Administration, is a lobbyist for *Rosatom*'s interests (he was the director of this corporation in 2005–2016) seeking to take control over the *Sevmorput* (Dzaguto, 2018).

These power players both promote Arctic ventures and fight fiercely for their piece of the action. Putin serves both as a mediator among contending lobbies and as an advocate for the greater Arctic venture.

Reluctant Shifts and Risky Experiments

Russia's Arctic policy may seem to be relatively stable, impervious to mounting tension between Russia and the West, but the Kremlin — as of the start of the 2020s — finds itself at difficult crossroads, where the traditional combination of cooperation and militarisation is becoming increasingly unsustainable.

The resources Moscow can invest in either of commercial or military tracks are constrained by Russia's subpar rate of economic growth, while the funds required to complete the existing projects keep mounting. It is possible to reduce the military build-up and pivot towards cooperative undertakings, but Western economic sanctions make this unattractive. Likewise, the Kremlin is loath to work with Western NGOs (Chater, 2017). China offers a cooperative alternative, but Chinese companies demand more privileges and subsidies than seem warranted (Shagina, 2018). Moreover, granting privileged access to Russia's presumed riches in the High North to China doesn't sit well with Russian public opinion, and Putin is far from comfortable with the one-sided dependency on the good will of increasingly ambitious Chinese leaders (Thompson, 2017).

Russia's leadership may try to harvest political dividends from upgrading and expanding the military infrastructure and assets in the High North theatre. Domestic stability could be the main driver of such experiments. The huge success of Moscow's annexation of Crimea in terms of mobilising "patriotic" feelings offers an appealing paradigm. The Kola Peninsula is indeed one of the few places where Russia is militarily dominant, but the Kremlin is unable to convert this position of strength into a tangible political gain. Mere demonstrations of the power-projecting capabilities tend to be counterproductive with Russia's Nordic neighbours, but

Moscow could occupy Svalbard. Norway's sovereignty over this archipelago is limited by the Spitsbergen Treaty (1920), so that it cannot deploy military forces there and has little control over Russian settlements.[20] Moscow may opt to test the limits of NATO solidarity with a carefully camouflaged special forces operation against this indefensible target. A possible trigger for such exercise in projecting military power could be an accident involving a Russian submarine.

Russia's military leadership may also find it expedient to resume nuclear tests as a show of the nation's prowess. The nuclear test site on the Novaya Zemlya is the most convenient location for such low-yield explosion.[21]

In sum, Russia's military modernisation drive in the Arctic and great power engagement with the West are likely to be losing propositions for the Kremlin because spending could be better reallocated to other national security projects, and Moscow's aggressiveness is a barrier to environmental and commercial cooperation with its neighbours. Putin does not appear prepared to cut the Gordian knot. He is reluctant to rationalise Arctic defence spending or bow to Western sanctions. The Kremlin could do both, but seems intent on doing neither.

References

Arbatov, A. (2018). Real and imaginary threats to strategic stability, *Russian Council* (in Russian), April 28, 2018. Available at: http://russiancouncil.ru/ analytics-and-comments/comments/ugrozy-strategicheskoy-stabilnosti-mnimye-i-realnye/?sphrase_id=12995625.

Baev, P. K. (2013). Russia's Arctic ambitions and anxieties, *Current History*, 112(756), 265–270.

Balan, D. (2017). Russia engages in a long dispute about the ownership over the Arctic shelf. RIA Federal News Agency, 13 November 2017 (in Russian). Available at: https://riafan.ru/996291-rossiyu-ozhidaet-dolgoletnii-spor-o-prinadlezhnosti-shelfa-v-arktike.

---

[20]Norwegian concerns are revealed in Stormark (2017).

[21]According to Russian official sources, explosions simulating the nuclear impacts are continuing on this test site; see "Russia will strengthen its military presence on the Arctic islands", *INTERFAX* (in Russian), February 14, 2018 (http://www.interfax.ru/russia/599894).

Barrie, D. and Boyd, H. (2018). Russia's State Armament Program 2027: A more measured course on procurement. IISS, Military Balance Blog. Available at: https://www.iiss.org/en/militarybalanceblog/blogsections/2018-f256/february-1c17/russia-state-armament-programme-d453.

Bashkatova, A. (2017). The Arctic brings net loss. *Nezavisimaya Gazeta*, March 30, 2017 (in Russian). Available at: http://www.ng.ru/economics/2017-03-30/1_6961_arktic.html.

Bird, K. J., *et al.* (2008). *Circum-Arctic Resource Appraisal: Estimates of Undiscovered Oil and Gas North of the Arctic Circle*. Fact Sheet 2008-3049, US Geological Survey. Denver, CO. Available at: https://pubs.usgs.gov/fs/2008/3049/.

Bolshakova, E. and Kostrinsky, G. (2018). Arktika tilts to the left, *Kommersant* (in Russian), February 19, 2018. Available at: https://www.kommersant.ru/doc/3553777.

Bourne, J. K. (2016). In the Arctic's cold rush, there are no easy profits. *National Geographic*. Available at: https://www.nationalgeographic.com/magazine/2016/03/new-arctic-thawing-rapidly-circle-work-oil/.

Chater, A. (2017). Valuable lessons about Russia from the bear's role in the Arctic, *Arctic Deeply*, August 7, 2017, News Deeply. Available at: https://www.newsdeeply.com/arctic/articles/2017/08/07/valuable-lessons-about-russia-from-the-bears-role-in-the-arctic.

Conley, H. A. (2015). *The New Ice Curtain: Russia's Strategic Reach to the Arctic,* CSIS Report, Washington, DC, August 27, 2015. Available at: https://www.csis.org/analysis/new-ice-curtain.

Dzaguto, V. (2018). New government in the old ice-hummocks. *Kommersant* (in Russian), May 29, 2018. Available at: https://www.kommersant.ru/doc/3642798.

Egorov, I. (2017). The Arctic without ultimatums and threats. *Rossiyskaya Gazeta* (in Russian), August 30, 2017. Available at: https://www.rg.ru/2017/08/30/patrushev-berezhnoe-otnoshenie-k-bogatstvam-arktiki-glavnyj-prioritet.html.

Fiore, V. (2017). A toxic closed-off city on the edge of the world, *The Atlantic*, November 8, 2017. Available at: https://www.theatlantic.com/video/index/545228/my-deadly-beautiful-city-norilsk/.

Flake, L. E. (2017). Contextualizing and disarming Russia's Arctic security posture, *Journal of Slavic Military Studies*, 30(1), 17–29.

Frolov, V. (2016). Russia's new foreign policy — A show of force and power projection, *Moscow Times*, 6 December 2016. Available at: https://themoscowtimes.com/articles/russias-new-foreign-policy-based-on-force-and-power-projection-56431.

Gabuev, A. (2016). Friends with benefits? Russian-Chinese relations after the Ukraine crisis. Briefing paper, Carnegie Moscow Center. Available at: http://carnegie.ru/2016/06/29/friends-with-benefits-russian-chinese-relations-after-ukraine-crisis-pub-63953.

Khodarenok, M. (2018). Defense Ministry would not tell about setbacks with Bulava. *Gazeta.ru* (in Russian), May 23, 2018. Available at: https://www.gazeta.ru/army/2018/05/23/11761255.shtml.

Klimenko, E. (2016). Russia's Arctic security policy: Still quiet in the High North?, *SIPRI Policy Paper* 45, February 2016. (https://www.sipri.org/publications/2016/sipri-policy-papers/russias-arctic-security-policy-still-quiet-high-north).

Klimov, M. (2019). Universal ship Ivan Papanin, Voenno-Promyshlenny Kurier (in Russian), October 29, 2019. Available at: https://www.vpk-news.ru/articles/53303.

Krutihin, M. (2018). Masters of the Arctic: Why Putin and Total believe in Novatek of Mihelson and Timchenko, *Forbes.ru* (in Russian). Available at: http://www.forbes.ru/milliardery/362219-hozyaeva-arktiki-pochemu-putin-i-total-poverili-v-novatek-mihelsona-i-timchenko.

Lanteigne, M. and Shi, M. (2018). China stakes its claim to the Arctic. *The Diplomat*, January 29. Available at: https://thediplomat.com/2018/01/china-stakes-its-claim-to-the-arctic/.

Laruelle, M. (2014). *Russia's Arctic Strategies and the Future of the Far North,* M.E. Sharpe, Armonk, New York.

Macias, A. (2018). Putin claimed a new nuclear-powered missile had unlimited range — but it flew only 22 miles in its most successful test yet. *CNBC*, May 21, 2018. Available at: https://www.cnbc.com/2018/05/21/russian-missile-with-unlimited-range-crashed-after-only-22-miles.html.

Maurin, F. (2017). Military aviation in the Arctic: Status and prospects, *Nezavisimoe voennoe obozrenie* (in Russian), 18 August 2017, http://nvo.ng.ru/armament/2017-08-18/6_961_arctic.html.

Milov, V. (2012). It is wrong to abandon Shtokman, *Forbes.ru* (in Russian), August 31, 2012. Available at: http://www.forbes.ru/sobytiya-column/kompanii/108894-brosat-razrabotku-shtokmana-nelzya.

Mosher, D. (2018). Putin's nuclear 'doomsday machine' could trigger 300-foot tsunamis, *Business Insider*, April 24, 2018. Available at: http://www.businessinsider.com/russia-doomsday-weapon-submarine-nuke-2018-4?r=UK&IR=T.

Muradov, M. (2018). The Arctic case doesn't fit the criminal code, *Kommersant* (in Russian), March 21, 2018. Available at: https://www.kommersant.ru/doc/3579133.

Mushanov, I. (2018). Snow kings: Rosatom and Kovalchuk brothers overtake Gazprom in the battle for Sevmorput money. *Versiya* (in Russian), January 29, 2018. Available at: https://versia.ru/rosatom-i-kovalchuki-obxodyat-gazprom-v-bitve-vokrug-deneg-sevmorputi.

Nilsen, T. (2017). Satellite images show expansion of nuclear weapon sites on Kola. *Barents Observer,* May 8. Available at: https://thebarentsobserver.com/en/content/satellite-images-show-expansion-nuclear-weapons-sites-kola.

Nilsen, T. (2018a). Navy cleans off 5,000 waste-drums from Arctic island. *Barents Observer*, May 14. Available at: https://thebarentsobserver.com/en/arctic/2018/05/navy-cleans-5000-waste-drums-arctic-island.

Nilsen, T. (2018b). Russian bombers simulated an attack against this radar on Norway's Barents Sea coast. *Barents Observer*, May 5. Available at: https://thebarentsobserver.com/en/security/2018/03/russian-bombers-simulated-attack-against-radar-norways-barents-sea-coast.

Nilsen, T. (2018c). TASS: Russia drops plan to redesign Borei sub, will build six more of existing. *Barents Observer,* Available at: https://thebarentsobserver.com/en/security/2018/05/tass-russia-drops-plan-redesign-borei-sub-will-built-six-more-existing.

Pastusiak, T. (2016). *The Northern Sea Route as a Shipping Lane: Expectations and Reality*, Springer, Berlin.

Petrov, S. and Zakvasin, A. (2017). The Northern frontier: The development of the Arctic grouping of Russian forces, *RT* (in Russian), 1 December 2017. Available at: https://russian.rt.com/russia/article/455340-strategicheskoe-komandovanie-sever.

Pezard, S., *et al.* (2017). *Maintaining Arctic Cooperation with Russia: Planning for Regional Change in the Far North*, RAND Research Report. Available at: https://www.rand.org/pubs/research_reports/RR1731.html.

Podvig, P. and Serrat, J. (2017). *Lock Them Up: Zero-Deployed Non-Strategic Weapons in Europe*, UNIDIR, Geneva.

Raibman, N. (2013). HSE professor responded to Putin's criticism, *Vedomosti* (in Russian), 4 October 2013. Available at: https://www.vedomosti.ru/politics/articles/2013/10/04/professor-vshe-razyasnil-svoe-antinarodnoe-predlozhenie-ob.

Schrader, M. (2018). Is China changing the game in trans-polar shipping? *China Brief*, April 24. Available at: https://jamestown.org/program/is-china-changing-the-game-in-trans-polar-shipping/.

Shagina, M. (2018). Is the Yamal LNG project overhyped? Oil Price. Available at: https://oilprice.com/Energy/Energy-General/Is-The-Yamal-LNG-Project-Overhyped.html.

Sharkov, D. (2017). New 6,000 ton icebreaker joins Russian Navy to bolster Putin's Arctic ambitions. *Newsweek*, November 30, 2017. Available at: http://www.newsweek.com/new-6000-tonne-icebreaker-joins-russian-navy-bolster-arctic-ambitions-726763.

Sokov, N. (2017). Russia's new conventional capability: Implications for Eurasia and beyond. PONARS Eurasia Memo 472. Available at: http://www.ponarseurasia.org/memo/russias-new-conventional-capability-implications-eurasia-and-beyond.

Soldatkin, V. (2014). Rosneft discovers offshore Arctic oil jointly with Exxon. *Reuters*, September 27. Available at: https://www.reuters.com/article/rosneft-arctic-discovery/rosneft-says-discovers-offshore-arctic-oil-jointly-with-exxon-idUSL6N0RS04Z20140927.

Staalsen, A. (2013). In remotest Russian Arctic, a new Navy base. *Barents Observer,* September 17. Available at: http://barentsobserver.com/en/security/2013/09/remotest-russian-arctic-new-navy-base-17-09.

Staalsen, A. (2017a). Methane explodes under Yamal tundra, creates another sinkhole, *Barents Observer*, July 3, 2017. Available at: https://thebarentsobserver.com/en/arctic/2017/07/methane-explodes-under-yamal-tundra-creates-another-sinkhole.

Staalsen, A. (2017b). New era starts on Northern Sea Route. *Barents Observer,* December 8. Available at: https://thebarentsobserver.com/en/arctic/2017/12/new-era-starts-northern-sea-route.

Staalsen, A. (2017c). 100 sailors trapped in ice near Arctic outpost. *Barents Observer*, February 7. Available at: https://thebarentsobserver.com/en/arctic/2017/02/100-sailors-trapped-ice-near-arctic-outpost.

Sterling, T. (2017). Arbitration panel tells Russia to pay Dutch $6 million over Greenpeace boat seizure. *Reuters*, July 18. Available at: https://www.reuters.com/article/us-netherlands-russia-arbitration/arbitration-panel-tells-russia-to-pay-dutch-6-million-over-greenpeace-boat-seizure-idUSKBN1A31J0.

Stormark, K. (2017). Russiald trente på invasjon av Svalbard [Russia prepares for an invasion of Svalbard], *AldriMer.no*, October 18, 2017. Available at: https://www.aldrimer.no/russland-trente-pa-invasjon-av-svalbard/.

Thompson, J. (2017). An uneasy alliance: The limits of the China-Russia Arctic partnership. *Arctic Deeply*, June 21, 2017. Available at: https://www.newsdeeply.com/arctic/community/2017/06/21/an-uneasy-alliance-the-limits-of-the-china-russia-arctic-partnership.

Vedeneeva, A. and Barsukov, Y. (2018). Sevmorput comes to the Kremlin. *Kommersant* (in Russian), May 3, 2018. Available at: https://www.kommersant.ru/doc/3619227.

Woolf, A. F. (2003). *The Nunn-Lugar Cooperative Threat Reduction Programs,* Novinka Books, NY.

Yushkov, I. (2018). The battle of alliances: Who will win the struggle for Arctic authority? *Forbes.ru* (in Russian), May 28, 2018. Available at: http://www.forbes.ru/biznes/pmef-2018361579-bitva-alyansov-kto-vyigraet-borbu-za-arkticheskie-polnomochiya.

Chapter 15

Russia's "Turn to the East", 2012–2018

Andrei P. Tsygankov

The return of Vladimir Putin as Russia's President in March 2012 signalled a critically important change in foreign policy. Russia revived the assertive course in relations with the West and — following the interventions in Ukraine and Syria — moved in the direction of a new foreign policy. In response to the new crisis in relations with the West generated by Russia's role in Ukraine, the Kremlin sought to demonstrate its power and relevance by strengthening its relations with China and the non-Western countries. In Russia's assessment, the failure of the United States to successfully complete its military operations in Afghanistan and Iraq, stabilise the Middle East, impose its rules on Russia and China and maintain a viable international economic order indicates that the world was departing from its politically unipolar state of the 1990s. Economically, the world witnessed the emergence of a coalition of non-Western powers seeking to diversify global commercial and monetary transactions. The rising economies of China, India, Brazil and others have challenged the dominant position of the West by establishing institutional venues including annual meetings of BRICS (Brazil, Russia, India, China and

South Africa) and SCO (Shanghai Cooperation Organization), pooling financial resources and producing around 30% of the world's GDP.[1]

Instead of relying on the protection and welfare of Western hegemony, nations increasingly sought refuge in reformulating their interests to better protect their societies and readjust to their regional environments. China and the Asia-Pacific region were increasingly emerging as new centres of the world's gravity.

The Idea of Cooperation with the Non-West

Russia's newly discovered non-Western identity assumed the need to develop relations with the non-West. In 2014, Putin defended preservation of a "new balance of economic, civilizational and military forces" in global politics.[2] Consistent with such a worldview, Putin worked on strengthening Russia's relations with China, Iran and India and exploiting non-Western institutional vehicles, such as BRICS (Brazil, Russia, India, China and South Africa) and SCO (Shanghai Cooperation Organization). In the summer of 2015, Russia hosted summits of both organisations in the city of Ufa. The BRICS members pledged $100 billion as a reserve currency pool and additional resources for development projects (Golubkova, 2015), while the SCO began the process of admitting India and Pakistan as members. The positions of Russia and non-Western nations on various international issues were increasingly close. BRICS countries did not publicly condemn Russia's incorporation of Crimea, did not join Western sanctions and did not support the campaign to isolate Russia politically. According to the Russian Foreign Ministry, a "top priority" for Russia's presidency in BRICS is to transform the assembly into "a full-scale mechanism of strategic interaction on key issues of global policy and economics" (Nikolsky, 2015). Other agenda items

---

[1] "BRICS pomeryayetsya siloi s MVF," Editorial, *Nezavisimaya Gazeta*, April 2, 2015, http://www.ng.ru/editorial/2015-04-02/2_red.html.

[2] Putin further insisted on the preservation of a "new balance of economic, civilizational and military forces" and instructed the government to pay more attention to the development of patriotic and military education. See his Annual Address to the Federal Assembly, Moscow, the Kremlin, December 12, 2012, www.kremlin.ru.

include plans to strengthen strategic stability and international information security, reinforce the non-proliferation regime and combat international terrorism (Nikolsky, 2015).

In comparison with the West, non-Western nations largely shared Russia's values and priorities. China, India, Brazil and the Middle Eastern nations have never been critical of human rights violations or the domestic political system in Russia. On the Middle East and Syria, Russia frequently acted jointly with China by vetoing Syria's resolutions introduced in the UNSC by the Western nations. Moscow and Beijing were concerned that such resolutions would pave the way for a military intervention and regime change in Syria, as happened in Libya. By building on non-Western resentment towards US hegemony and military interventions, Putin strengthened his global reputation as an advocate for sovereignty, national unity and cultural values. While meeting with Barack Obama during the G-20 summit in St. Petersburg, Putin obtained support of most non-Western leaders present for his position on Assad and the Middle East. In addition, the Kremlin was able to take advantage of the Snowden affair. By granting Snowden asylum, Moscow again positioned itself as a defender of national sovereignty and protector against global interferences from a hegemonic power.

Strengthening "Greater Eurasia" in Partnership with China

Relations with China, Russia's largest neighbour, obtained a strategic dimension, as the two nations demonstrated an increased convergence in global priorities and solutions to existing issues in world politics. Although Beijing did not recognise Russia's annexation of Crimea, the two nations had complementary interests in the areas of commerce and regional security. Their energy-related ties continued to progress. In May 2014, Putin travelled to Beijing to sign a $400-billion agreement to export almost 40 billion cubic metres (bcm) of gas annually to China, thereby further diversifying Russia's trade away from Europe. In November 2014, Russia signed another massive gas deal by pledging to supply an additional 30 bcm starting in 2019 (Nikolsky, 2014).

Other important agreements were signed in Moscow in May 2015 on the eve of a military parade on the Red Square marking the end of World

War II. The parade also featured China's President Xi Jinping and Putin presiding over the ceremony in the front row while observing the marching of Russian, Chinese and Indian soldiers. Western leaders were invited but chose not to attend due to disagreement with the Kremlin over Ukraine (Soldatkin and Heritage, 2015).

Russia's main priority, however, remained that of Eurasia's regionalism. Moscow's vision of "Greater Eurasia" included China and Europe but excluded the United States. At the International Economic Forum in St. Petersburg in June 2016, Putin articulated the perspective of creating various economic agreements between the Eurasian Economic Union (EAEU), China, member states of the SCO and ASEAN as well as the EU (Kaczmarski and Rodkiewicz, 2016). The Kremlin anticipated several policies to consolidate Russia's place in Eurasia as that of a great power such as strengthening relations within the EAEU, developing ties with neighbours through the CSTO and bilaterally, and proposing wider projects with China, European countries, Turkey and Iran. As some speculated, Russia hopes to serve as a tipping-point state avoiding excessive commitments and determining the balance of power among the world's largest actors such as China, the United States and the EU (Khanna, 2008).

China was especially active in promoting its vision for the development of Eurasia and offering itself as a key partner in developing the region. Increasingly, Beijing acted on its economic ambitions by inviting former Soviet states to join a larger China-centred trade and transportation initiative known as the Silk Road Economic Belt (Tavrovsky, 2013). In this scheme, the Eurasian Union would become an integrated part of an economic and transportation project advanced by China. On May 8, 2015, the vision was solidified with the endorsement by leaders of Russia and China. During President Xi Jinping's visit to Moscow, the two nations signed an agreement on cooperation between the Eurasian Union and the Silk Road.[3] Among the objectives were the establishment of the network of land and sea routes to connect the western regions of China with the

---

[3] "Rossiya i Kitai podpisali dogovor o 'Shelkovom puti'," *BBC*, May 8, 2015, http://www.bbc.com/russian/rolling_news/2015/05/150508_rn_china_putin_jingping_silk_route.

main markets of Central Asia and Europe via the territories of Kazakhstan and Russia.[4]

The new vision and practice of the Russia-initiated Eurasian Union and China-advocated Silk Road's convergence encouraged those who viewed the two nations' cooperation in terms of being a value alternative to the European Union (Lukin, 2014). The fact that the United States and the European Union have worked to keep Ukraine away from the Russia-dominant Eurasian Union may have contributed to the Kremlin's motivation to develop Russia's ideology as a part of non-West. The West's sanctions against the Russian economy in response to the Kremlin's annexation of Crimea and support for eastern fighters in the Ukrainian civil war[5] served to strengthen Russia's reorientation away from Western nations and towards China (Trenin, 2015). Such foreign pressures also emboldened those defending the objective of Russia's development in isolation from Europe (Glazyev, 2014). Although China's system of values is distinct from that of Russia, the two systems may be compatible, especially relative to the West's system (Rozman, 2014). Therefore, the cultural pillar may strengthen the rapidly progressing economic and political partnership between the two nations.

China was also an essential partner in bringing jobs and investments to Russia's non-European regions, especially Siberia and the Far East, although the Russia–China contacts were not always harmonious and not free of tensions. For instance, Moscow has long advocated that Russia and China use their own currencies for conducting all bilateral economic transactions. As of the end of 2018, Beijing opposed the transition to national payment system out of fear that such transition may complicate its trade negotiations with the United States (Korostikov, 2018). To offset a potentially excessive dependence on one partner, the

---

[4]For detailed proposals by Russian experts of Russia-China cooperation in Eurasia, see The Valdai Club's Report "Toward the Great Ocean—3: Creating Central Eurasia (Moscow, June 2015), http://valdaiclub.com/publication/77920.html.

[5]For research on Ukrainian conflict as a civil war, see, for example, Kudelia (2018). Other authors view the conflict as combining dimensions of civil war with those of international struggle for power (Sakwa, 2015; Hahn, 2018). Few others attribute the conflict to international factors that incorporate Russia's interference and Russia–West struggle for power in Europe. For a review of various approaches, see Kuzio and D'Anieri (2018, chapter 1).

Kremlin continued earlier developed policies of building relations with non-Chinese countries and strengthening regional integration in Asia. In 2014, Moscow wrote off $10 billion of North Korean debt on the condition of building a gas pipeline and rail link into the south (Weafer, 2014). Russia also increased diplomatic contacts with Japan in order to eventually solve the territorial issue and open a new page of economic relations with the East Asian power. In the fall of 2013, Putin visited Japan to make progress on the issue and sign a number of investment and trade agreements. Moscow also increased its level of participation in regional arrangements and forums such as the APEC summits in June 2012 and November 2014. In May 2015, Russia and other members of the Eurasian Union signed a free trade agreement with Vietnam, pledging reduction of tariffs from 10% to 1% (Yedovina, 2015).

Russia's stagnating economy made it difficult to make progress in strengthening ties within the EAEU. GDP growth was negative during 2015–2016 and grew by less than 2% in 2017. Trade among members of the union also declined, reflecting its poor performance. Intraregional trade, which stood at $65 billion in 2012 and 2013, shrank by some 40% to $42.5 billion in 2016 (Molchanov, 2018). The situation improved in 2016–2017. As the Russian economic slowdown bottomed out and was reversed, trade and investments within the EAEU began to recover. According to the Eurasian Development Bank, after three consecutive years of decline, investments increased by 16% in 2016, reflecting Russia's contribution of over 78% of the stock in the Union member states (Nuttell, 2017).

Despite the economic slowdown, the Kremlin managed to strengthen its bilateral relations with those neighbouring countries interested in such relations. Following the change of power in Uzbekistan in 2016, Russia improved ties with the country's new leader, Shavkat Mirzioyev. In 2017, the newly elected leader of Kyrgyzstan made his first foreign trip to Russia to proclaim continuity of strategic relations between the two countries. In October 2017, Putin also visited Turkmenistan, concluding important economic agreements in the country. In all these cases, Russia sought to position itself as a security provider and a means to reduce China's influence in the region (Krickovic and Breatersky, 2016). Turkmenistan, in particular, was supplying China with natural gas, but sought to transport some of its ample reserves through Russian pipelines to Europe.

Russia and China also reached an understanding on Central Asia. As described by analysts of their relations, "Moscow and Beijing found ways to divide their influences, with China dominating the energy realm and Russia the security realm" (Kaczmarski, 2016). Russia's power in Central Asia was primarily, though not exclusively, based on military capabilities. The Kremlin worked on consolidating its military presence in the former Soviet region since the mid-2000s and possesses important military and geopolitical advantages. On the other hand, the power of China in the region was largely economic and based on its ability to finance important regional projects and offset various threats to Central Asian economies. While Russia has the ambition to preserve economic influence in the region, it is increasingly unable to compete with Beijing and has learned to accept China's lead in exchange for Beijing's recognition of Russia's military and political dominance in the former Soviet region. In the meantime, Chinese military attention is directed less at Central Asia than the regions of East Asia and the Asia Pacific. In the Central Asian region, Beijing deployed no troops and expressed no desire to lease any military facilities (Kaczmarski, 2016, p. 12). Therefore, from a military standpoint, Russia remains the regionally dominant power. This is acceptable to Beijing, which focuses on fighting local threats of terrorism and separatism.

The Russia–China coordination should not be viewed as a consolidation of stagnation in Central Asia. Uzbekistan's current reform agenda is a case in point. Since the election of Shavkat Mirziyoyev as the country's President, Uzbekistan has moved in the direction of controlled economic change, media freedom, and international openness (Schatz, 2018). Against the common expectations of Western analysts, "it was precisely Western disengagement that opened the door for change," with Russia and China both favouring it (Schatz, 2018).

Overall, the Russia–China division of power and its success in Central Asia was a model for potential solutions to other problems in Asia such as North Korean nuclear ambition, economic development, greater regional security and future Korean unification. Increasingly, these solutions were being found without the involvement of the United States and at the expense of US global interests. In all prominent political and security issues in Asia, Moscow acting jointly with Beijing was able to advance Russia's objectives of preserving great-power status and delivering stability on Russian, not American, terms. The Kremlin fostered negotiations with North Korea, developed special relations in Central Asia and pushed resolution of Afghanistan and counterterrorism towards the SCO framework. It also made progress in attracting Asian investors despite US insistence that Asian nations maintain sanctions on Russia. As American presence in the region shrinks, the room for US–Russia rivalry in the region also declines.

As a result of Russia's stagnating economy and relations within the EAEU, Moscow's overall ties with Asia remained heavily centred on China, while Moscow's attempts to diversify these relations by strengthening ties with Japan and others did not bring an impressive result. The pivot to China resulted in growing trade and military ties. Bilateral trade in 2017 increased by 25% relative to the previous year, though it was yet to reach the level of 2013 (Solovyeva, 2017). Revitalisation of the EEU too increasingly meant working in partnership with China in conjunction with its Silk Road Economic Belt.

Rebuilding Influence in the Middle East

In order to compensate for its internal economic weakness and realign with quickly changing international political economic trends, Russia has sought to actively participate in transregional projects. In addition to developing ties with China and preserving energy relations with European countries, the Kremlin worked to build relations with Iran, Turkey and other countries in the Middle East. The fact that Russia and China had similar perspectives on international crises, including those in the Middle East and East Asia, assisted the Kremlin with developing influence in the regions. Both Russia and China supported Assad in his fight with militant opposition and terrorism, although Beijing refrained from providing military assistance and tended to abstain, rather than veto, the United States-sponsored resolutions on Syria in the United Nations Security Council. Russia and China's position on handling North Korea's nuclear ambitions too aligned and was markedly different from the tough, threatening tone assumed by the United States.

In 2014, following Western attempts to impose sanctions on Russia over its annexation of Crimea and position on Ukraine's crisis, Moscow and Tehran increased their level of economic relations. In particular, they discussed an energy deal worth $10 billion that would involve a barter trade of oil in exchange for building electricity stations in Iran (Novikova, 2014). As the United States intensified its diplomacy to assure Iran's compliance with the nuclear non-proliferation treaty, the Kremlin was supportive, but had its own priorities in mind. Among them were the strengthening of bilateral commercial and political ties with Tehran and its membership in non-Western institutions such as the SCO. In April 2015, to further revitalise relations with Iran, Putin removed the ban for delivering the S-300 (advanced military system for air defence).

Outside Iran, Russia focused on regional stability by encouraging negotiations between Syria's Assad and moderate elements of the opposition. Here too, Russia worked jointly with its non-Western partners. The BRICS summits supported negotiations in Syria such as those that started in Geneva in February 2014. In addition, with continued destabilisation of Syria and Iraq by Islamic radicals, the focus by Russia and other powers was on shifting to countering the region-wide threats posed by the self-proclaimed Islamic State (IS). By early 2015, the IS emerged to be the leading force with capacity to topple Assad and secure important territorial gains in Iraq. In particular, the IS militants conquered western Iraq and eastern Syria, claiming to control territory with six and half million residents (Laub and Masters, 2015). In June 2014, they took control of Mosul, Iraq's second largest city, and in May 2015, they seized the ancient and UNESCO-protected town of Palmyra in Syria. To contain and defeat the IS, Russia consulted both Western and non-Western nations, especially Iran. Moscow continued to strengthen economic and political relations with Tehran, in part for the purpose of jointly assisting stabilisation in Syria and Iraq. Increasingly, Moscow was also reviving strong ties with Egypt (Suponina, 2015) and Israel, and — disagreements on Syria and Iran notwithstanding — sought to strengthen relations with Saudi Arabia (Kerr and Hille, 2015).

Another important partner of Russia in the Middle East was Turkey. Although the two nations supported different sides in the Syrian conflict, they were both critical of the Western role in the region and shared a desire to stabilise it by local powers. The relations between Russia and Turkey were also made easier by shared values of a civilisational identity and a strong modernising state able to overcome pressures from domestic and foreign influences (Bilgin and Bilgiç, 2011). In addition to similarity of values, their interests were compatible. In particular, Moscow and Istanbul continued cooperation on energy issues. As Russia sought to circumvent Ukraine in developing an alternative transportation route to European markets, Turkey wanted to position itself as a major energy hub. In January 2015, Putin travelled to Istanbul to propose the building of a gas pipeline through Turkish territory to Europe's borders. The European Union objected to the development in part because of the need to build the required infrastructure (Aris, 2015). Previously, due to disagreements with Ukraine, Russia cut gas supplies for European customers to pressure Kiev into paying the negotiated fees.

Due to military successes and engagement in negotiations with all relevant actors in the Middle East, the Kremlin strengthened its ties even with leading critics of Assad such as Saudi Arabia, Turkey and Egypt. Following the conclusion of the most active stage of civil war in Syria and the United States' decision to withdraw from the nuclear agreement with Iran in May 2018, Russia has continued efforts to preserve a fragile stability in the region. It contributed to multiple rounds of negotiations within the framework of the Astana peace process. Launched in January 2017 by Russia, Iran, Syria and Turkey, the process was focused on ceasing hostilities, creating "de-escalation zones" in Syria and facilitating political transition in the country. In October 2017, the Saudi King Salman visited Russia to build on an earlier agreement limiting oil production, to sign economic and military agreements and to signal a new political understanding of the region's realities not based on Assad's departure (Barmin, 2017). Since then, Moscow continued to its energy production with the most important oil-producing state (Kennedy *et al.*, 2018). Putin also travelled to Tehran to discuss jointly with Azerbaijan, among other projects, the idea of developing an economic corridor to the Arabian Sea and Indian Ocean. If developed, the project could save costs for transporting goods from the Middle East, India and other South Asian countries. In a longer perspective, the project could become the necessary complement to Russia's limited participation in China's Silk Road (Труевцев, 2017). Although Turkey remained a difficult partner for the Kremlin, Russia continued to develop relations and negotiate possible construction of additional natural gas pipelines through Turkish territory to European markets. The Kremlin also continued to foster military and energy ties with Egypt.

Assessment

Following the ongoing state of international instability, the Kremlin continued with its policy of asserting Russia's status of an independent great power, while seeking partners for its course among both Western and non-Western politicians. Russia worked to strengthen its reputation as a global security provider and advocated building new global economic and political institutions alternative to those centred on the West. The Kremlin strengthened Russia's national security by strengthening ties with China, fighting terrorism in the Middle East and developing and testing new weapons systems. Russia also made progress in strengthening its autonomy and reputation as a great power, particularly through demonstrating its importance in ending the military conflict in Syria. Furthermore, the Kremlin continued to make progress in building ties with Asian, Middle Eastern and Latin American partners outside the West.

Still, the foreign policy of Russia had limitations. First, it rested on weak economic foundations, overestimating the country's capacity to challenge the West-centred international order. In response to the collapse of energy prices in 2015, Western economic sanctions and the absence of domestic reforms, the economy was underperforming. Instead of becoming part of a vibrant non-Western alternative system, Russia was stagnating and experiencing difficulties. Russian living standards had been declining, while the state continued to generously fund its military and limit investments in education and health. Second, while being based on assumption of a global transition of power from the West to the non-West, Russia's strategy often lacked specifics regarding transition towards a new international system. In terms of relations with non-Western nations, these specifics concerned participation in developing alternative geoeconomic projects with China, Turkey, Iran and other countries. Against the Kremlin's wishes, China, India and others non-Western countries were not as proactive in building foundations of alternative international system and remained interested in building economic and political relations with the United States and other Western countries.

Conclusion

Moscow's annexation of Crimea and the Russia-gate furore have terminated Russia's status as a NATO "partner for peace," recast the Kremlin as an arch villain and imperilled the EU's and America's globalist strategy. Both sides acknowledge the tidal shift and blame each other. The tide could turn, but there are no signs that a return to the "partner for peace" framework is imminent.

The prospect of a protracted new Cold War does not seem to perturb the West enough to do much about it. Even though economic sanctions have been applied and strengthened with no visible effect on the Kremlin's behaviour, Western policymakers have steadfastly refused to consider diverting funds from domestic spending towards defence on the blithe supposition that Russia is an inferior power. They surmise that "strategic patience" will suffice and that the Kremlin will simply give up its unsustainable ambitions as it did in 1991 because of its defective economy, the prospect of social unrest and insider squabbles.

Western leaders were right about strategic patience the first time, and may be right again. However, the research assembled in this book shows clearly that Russia is not the Soviet Union. The Kremlin is capable of providing Russians with guns and butter. If it learns how to improve its market efficiency, while Western economies sputter, Moscow may succeed this time in sustainably expanding its empire.

References

Aris, B. (2015). The Riga summit of disappointment, *Business New Europe*, May 21, 2015.

Barmin, Y. (2017). What's Behind the Saudi King's Historic Visit to Russia, *Moscow Times*, October 4, 2015.

Bilgin, P. and Bilgiç, A. (2011). Turkey's 'new' foreign policy toward Eurasia, *Eurasian Geography and Economics* 52, 2.

Glazyev, S. (2014). Moment istiny: Rossiya i sanktsiyi Zapada. Moscow, The Izborsky Club, 26 June. Available at: http://www.dynacon.ru/content/articles/3397 (accessed 15 July 2014).

Golubkova, K. (2015). New BRICS Bank to look at local, international borrowing, *Reuters*, July 9.

Hahn, G. M. (2018). *Ukraine over the Edge: Russia, the West and the New Cold War*, McFarlane.

Kaczmarski, M. (2016). The asymmetric partnership? Russia's turn to China, *International Politics* 53(3), 415–434.

Kaczmarski, M. and Rodkiewicz, W. (2016). Russia's greater Eurasia and China's New Silk Road: Adaptation instead of competition, OSW COMMENTARY. Available at: https://www.osw.waw.pl/en/publikacje/osw-commentary/2016-07-21/russias-greater-eurasia-and-chinas-new-silk-road-adaptation.

Kennedy, W., Mazneva, E. and Mahdi, W. (2018). Russia-Saudi plans for super-OPEC could reshape global oil order, *Bloomberg*.

Kerr, S. and Hille, K. (2015). Saudi defence minister to meet Vladimir Putin for talks on Syria, *Financial Times*, June 17 2015.

Khanna, P. (2008). *The Second World: Empires and Influence in the New Global Order,* Random House, New York.

Korostikov, M. (2018). Kitai ne Risknul Svyazyvatsya s Rublem, *Kommersant*, December 27, 2018.

Krickovic, A. and Breatersky, M. (2016). Benevolent hegemon, neighborhood bully, or regional security provider? Russia's efforts to promote regional integration after the 2013–2014 Ukraine crisis, *Eurasian Geography and Economics* 57(2), 180–202.

Kudelia, S. (2018). Ways to end the Donbas conflict, *PONARS Eurasia*, September 24, 2018.

Kuzio, T. and D'Anieri, P. (2018). *The Sources of Russia's Great Power Politics: Ukraine and the Challenge to the European Order*, E-International Relations.

Laub, Z. and Masters, J. (2015). The Islamic State, Council on Foreign Relations. Available at: http://www.cfr.org/iraq/islamic-state/p14811.

Lukin, A. (2014). What the Kremlin is thinking: Putin's vision for Eurasia, *Foreign Affairs*.

Molchanov, M. (2018). The Eurasian Union, in: Tsygankov, A. P. (ed.), *The Routledge Handbook of Russian Foreign Policy*, Routledge, Abingdon, 410–420.

Nikolsky, A. (2014). *Russia-China Gas Deal Requires Moscow's Reconciliation with US, EU*, Sputnik.

Nikolsky, A. (2015). *Russia Charts New Course for BRICS Nations as Presidency Begins*, TASS.

Novikova, Y. (2014). Moskva i Tegeran soprotivlyayutsya sanktsiyam, *Nezavisimaya Gazeta*, April 30, 2014.

Nuttell, C. (2017). Investment revives within Eurasian Economic Union after 3-year decline. Intellnews, October 17, 2017. Available at: http://www. intellinews.com/investment-revives-within-eurasian-economic-union-after-3-year-decline-130661/.

Rozman, G. (2014). *The Sino-Russian Challenge to the World Order: National Identities, Bilateral Relations, and East versus West in the 2010s,* Stanford University Press, Stanford.

Sakwa, R. (2015). *Frontline Ukraine: Crisis in Borderlands,* I.B. Touris, London.

Schatz, E. (2018). How western disengagement enabled Uzbekistan's "spring" and how to keep it going, *Ponars, Policy Memo 531.*

Soldatkin, V. and Heritage, T. (2015). Russia and China deepen ties with new economic deals, *Reuters.*

Solovyeva, O. (2017). Tovarooborot s Kitayem vyros na chetvert', *Nezavisimaya Gazeta*, August 9, 2017.

Suponina, Y. (2015). Kak Yegipet opyat' stal luchshim drugom Rossiyi na Blizhnem Vostoke, *Nezavisimaya Gazeta,* June 10, 2015.

Tavrovsky, Y. (2013). Pekin sobirayet gory i morya [Beijing collects mountains and seas], *Nezavisimiaya Gazeta*. Available at: http://www.ng.ru/ideas/2013-11-15/5_china.html.

Труевцев, К. (2017). *Rossiya-Azerbaijan-Iran*, Valdai Club, November 2.

Trenin, D. (2015). *From Greater Europe to Greater Asia? The Sino-Russian Entente,* The Carnegie Endowment for International Peace, Washington, DC.

Yedovina, T. (2015). Kevraez prisoyedinili vyetnamsky rynok, *Kommersant*, May 30, 2015. Available at: http://www.kommersant.ru/doc/2738346.

Weafer, C. (2014). Russia needs to pivot east and west, *Moscow Times,* May 8, 2014.

Index

CPSIA information can be obtained
at www.ICGtesting.com
Printed in the USA
LVHW050924220820
663884LV00005B/6

9 789811 212673